Classical Approaches to the Study of Religion

Religion and Reason 4

Method and Theory
in the Study and Interpretation of Religion

MOUTON·THE HAGUE·PARIS

Classical Approaches to
the Study of Religion

Aims, Methods and Theories of Research

2: Bibliography

by

JACQUES WAARDENBURG

University of Utrecht

MOUTON·THE HAGUE·PARIS

Library of Congress Catalog Card Number: 70–152082

Jacket-design by Jurriaan Schrofer

© 1974, Mouton & Co.

Printed in Hungary

Preface

Although several bibliographies exist in the field of the study of religion there is none, as far as we know, that classifies publications made by and about a number of scholars of the past who carried out literary, historical, anthropological, sociological or psychological research on religion. If any need for such an historical, be it selective, bibliography exists at all, we hope that the present volume may contribute to satisfying it.

Originally this bibliography was conceived to contain only listings concerning the 41 scholars represented in the Anthology contained in Volume One of *Classical Approaches to the Study of Religion*, and it would then have been part of that volume. As the work proceeded, however, it became clear that the interest and value of such a bibliography would be much greater if publications were also included of and about the other 127 scholars who are treated in the Introduction of that volume, "View of a Hundred Years' Study of Religion". This would raise the number of listings to 168 and it was decided to publish this as Volume Two, together with an Introductory Bibliography with references to existing bibliographies and to some general works on the history and methodology of the study of religion until the post-war period. As such, although meant to be a companion volume to the Anthology and its Introduction, this Bibliography can very well be used as an independent reference work.

As mentioned before, this Bibliography remains limited to the period which we would be inclined to call that of the "classical" approaches to the study of religion. Consequently, all publications with regard to present-day discussions on method and theory in the study and interpretation of religion have been left out and will require a separate listing and treatment.

The book consists of two parts: An *Introductory Bibliography* and a *General Bibliography*.

The *Introductory Bibliography* contains a selected number of publications dealing with the study of religion prior to the mid-twentieth century. These publications are of a somewhat general nature: Bibliographies, histories of the various disciplines within the field of the study of religion, and readers bringing together fragments from specialized studies made in these disciplines. We have included here also some publications on methodology which date from the period before 1950, apart from those publications mentioned under the heading "Method and Theory" in the listings of publications by the 41 scholars represented in the Anthology. Books and articles which may be considered a part of the increasing discussions on method and theory since World War II were excluded. We also left aside works of a more philosophical nature, be it more for practical reasons than for reasons of principle. Although such works are indeed of primary importance for a correct understanding of the intellectual and social background of the existing approaches to the religious phenomenon, to include them would lead beyond the practical possibilities of this volume.

The *General Bibliography* contains publications of and on those scholars to whom reference has been made in the *Introduction* to the Anthology. These scholars, who have been put in alphabetical order, fall into two categories.

In the *first* place there are 127 scholars who may be considered characteristic representatives of the main approaches to the subject of religion. Their names were printed in italics in the Introduction. The listings are given by author under three headings. First, indications are given where the complete bibliography of the scholar, if existing, can be found *(Bibliography)*. Second, some major studies by others on the work of these scholars are mentioned *(Biography and Appreciation)*. Third, a selection of their publications is listed including those which are of interest to questions of method and theory, but excluding those which do not deal with the scholarly study of religion. If an English translation is known to exist, its title was added to the original one. These publications have been arranged chronologically *(Main Publications)*.

In the *second* place there are the 41 scholars who figure in the *Anthology* and who deserve a special place. Their names were printed in small capitals in the Introduction and provided with an asteriks in the Bibliography. Their listings are given in a more elaborate way than those of the other 127 scholars. They are given again by author, but here a differentiation is made. First, indications are given to where the complete bibliography of the scholar can be found *(Bibliography)*. Second, an alphabetical listing according to authors is given of all relevant publications which deal with the scholar or his work. Book reviews have here been omitted as well as biographical accounts of a general nature such as given in Biographical Dictionaries and Encyclopedias. Much attention has been given to bring together evaluative studies on the work of the scholar in question, insofar as his studies on religion are concerned *(Biography and Appreciation)*. Third, the scholar's own writings are listed chronologically. A distinction, however, has been introduced here. On one hand, works of a methodological nature have been set apart, and a complete listing of such publications has been attempted *(Method and Theory)*. Relevant sections on methodology in monographs and handbooks, as written by the scholar in question have not been mentioned separately, however. On the other hand, a list has been given of all other publications which may be considered to be of scholarly interest, with their translations in other languages including English as far as they could be found *(Main Publications)*. Although the listings of these 41 scholars, given the size of the present volume, could not be exhaustive, they may be considered to be fairly complete.

In all indications we have strived after bibliographical precision. Sometimes, indeed, only a general indication could be given. In the case of some articles the volume number and the year of publication of the periodical concerned appears without the page numbers of the article in question. In the case of some books, especially for older publications, the year and place of appearance is given without the name of the publisher. Again, it was not always possible to check all existing translations of a given book or article or to find all publications which have appeared about a particular scholar. Publications written by one scholar about another are to be found under the name of the latter in the category of "Biography and Appreciation" and not under the name of the author. Scholarly and other titles of the authors have been omitted. In the case of some wide-ranging scholars like Durkheim, Max Weber or Söderblom, we had to limit the secondary literature to those publications that explicitly deal with their scholarly study of religion. It is fair, nevertheless, to say that our selection of titles has been made with flexible standards. The selection of the scholars themselves is that made in the Introduction of Volume One. It is unavoidable that in the practical use of this Bibliography, a number of names of scholars in the field of the study of religion will turn out to be lacking. The limits of our possibilities were such that we could not strive after completeness.

Although it can be used very well independently, this Bibliography has been conceived as an essential part of *Classical Approaches to the Study of Religion*. Its aim is, first of all, to provide the reader with sufficient materials for further scholarly research about 168 scholars of a recent or more remote past: Their work, their background, their motivations and aims, their tools, techniques and theories. In the second place, it should provide enough materials for further research not only on methods and theories which have been current during the last hundred years, but also on the history of the study of religion as such, including history, anthropology, sociology, and psychology insofar as they deal with religious data. In the third place, it is felt that prominent scholars of the past wrestled with perennial problems, and though the terms of reference have changed in the meantime and new materials have come to light since then, the student of today may recognize to advantage his own research problems in those of former generations.

This is intended to be a basic bibliography for the period 1850—1950, with the exclusion of scholars now alive. It has not been organized according to themes or subjects of research, since such bibliographies are regularly given in specialized publications including periodicals. For his own actual and concrete research the reader will have to refer to those publications. The need of a more comprehensive bibliography is felt, however, even apart from all historical interest, as soon as one wants to reach beyond one's own specialization. In the study of religious data one has to look at the problems encountered by those who work from a different perspective than one's own, and one has to look at other proposed solutions than one's own. In that light, a bibliography like this one may render also a service to a more interdisciplinary approach to the subject of inquiry.

Now that it is finished, it may safely be said that a work like this ought rather to have been assigned to a professional bibliographer. Unfortunately for such an enterprise as for many others, no means were available, and we had to do it ourselves, ultimately for the sheer sake of sound documentation with regard to a century of scholarship. On the practical side we want to thank Professor D. J. Hoens of the University of Utrecht who showed interest in this work and kindly provided valuable assistance for a three months' period, Mrs. M. A. G. T. van Kooij and Mr. H. Kleyer generously assisted in proofreading. Special thanks should be extended to Mouton Publishers, to Mr. A. Bornkamp for supporting the publication of an ever-growing manuscript, to Hilda Verloren van Themaat for taking care of much correspondence, and to Mr. A. J. van Vliet for working indefatigably on the text of these listings, often beyond his hours of duty. It gives the author satisfaction that this Bibliography can appear as Volume Four of the series "Religion and Reason". May a tiresome listing of past achievements be instrumental to creative efforts in the future.

Utrecht, December 31, 1972   Jacques Waardenburg

Introductory Bibliography

Publications on the Study of Religion before 1950

1. BIBLIOGRAPHIES

Adams, C. J., *A Reader's Guide to the Great Religions*. A comprehensive and critical survey of the available literature on the history, beliefs, and institutions of the world's great religions. New York, Free Press; London, Collier-Macmillan, 1965.

Barrow, John G., *A Bibliography of Bibliographies in Religion*. Ann Arbor, Mi., 1955.

Berkowitz, Morris I., and Johnson, J. Edmund, *Social Scientific Studies of Religion: A Bibliography*. Pittsburgh, University of Pittsburgh Press, 1967.

Bibliographie zur Symbolik, Ikonographie und Mythologie. Internationales Referatorgan unter Mitarbeit von ... herausgegeben von Manfred Lurker, 1968 – . Baden-Baden, Verlag Librairie Heitz, 1968 – (yearly). *See also under:* Lurker, Manfred

A Bibliography of Religious Studies. Prepared by the Joint Inquiries Committee on Religious Studies. Department of Religious Studies, Kyushu University, Tokyo, 1957.

Clemen, Carl, ed., *Religionsgeschichtliche Bibliographie*. Im Anschluss an das *Archiv für Religionswissenschaft*. Vol. I–X, 1914–1923.

Diehl, Katharine Smith, *Religions, Mythologies, Folklores: an Annotated Bibliography*. New Brunswick, N. J., The Scarecrow Press, 1956.

Hanayama, Shinsho, *Bibliography on Buddhism*. Edited by the Commemoration Committee for Prof. Shinsho Hanayama's Sixty-first Birthday. Tokyo, The Hokuseido Press, 1961.

Henrichs, Norbert, *Bibliographie der Hermeneutik und ihrer Anwendungsbereiche seit Schleiermacher*. Düsseldorf, Philosophie Verlag, 1968.

International Bibliography of the History of Religions / Bibliographie Internationale de l'Histoire des Religions. Published by the International Association for the History of Religions, 1952 – . Leiden, E. J. Brill, 1954 – (yearly).

International Bibliography of Social and Cultural Anthropology. Prepared by the International Committee for Social Sciences Documentation. *Bibliographie Internationale d'Anthropologie Sociale et Culturelle*. Etablie par le Comité International pour la Documentation de Sciences Sociales. *(International Bibliography of the Social Sciences / Bibliographie Internationale des Sciences Sociales)*. See especially Section F: *Religion, Magic, and*

Witchcraft / Religion, Magie, Sorcellerie. London, Tavistock Publications; Chicago, Aldine Publishing Company, 1955—   (yearly).
Internationale Volkskundliche Bibliographie / International Folklore and Folklife Bibliography / Bibliographie Internationale des Arts et Traditions Populaires. Bibliographie fondée en 1917 par John Meier et E. Hoffmann-Krayer.
For the years 1967 and 1968: Ouvrage publié par la Société Internationale d'Ethnologie et de Folklore sous les auspices du Conseil International de la Philosophie et des Sciences Humaines et avec le concours de l'Unesco. Im Auftrag der Deutschen Gesellschaft für Volkskunde bearbeitet von Robert Wildhaber. Bonn, Rudolf Habelt Verlag, 1970.
Kiell, Norman. *See under: Psychoanalysis, Psychology and Literature. A Bibliography.*
Lurker, Manfred, *Bibliographie zur Symbolkunde.* Unter Mitarbeit von Ferdinand Herrmann, Eckhard Unger und weiteren Fachgelehrten. (Bibliotheca Bibliographica Aureliana, XII). Baden-Baden, Verlag Heitz, 1964.
    See also under: Bibliographie zur Symbolik, Ikonographie und Mythologie.
Psychoanalysis, Psychology and Literature. A Bibliography. Compiled and edited by Norman Kiell. Madison, University of Wisconsin Press, 1963.
Puech, H.-Ch., "Introduction à l'histoire des religions: Bibliographie générale," in: Jacques Vandier, *La Religion égyptienne.* (Collection "Mana", Tome 1). Paris, P.U.F., 1944, 1949², pp. XVII—LXIII.
Richardson, Ernst Cushing, *An Alphabetical Subject Index and Index Encyclopaedia to Periodical Articles on Religion, 1890—1899.* New York, Charles Scribner's Sons, 1907.
Smith Diehl, Katharina. *See under:* Diehl, Katharina Smith.

2. STUDIES

Achelis, Th., *Abrisz der vergleichenden Religionswissenschaft.* Leipzig, 1908².
Alatas, Syed Hussein, *Reflections on the Theories of Religion.* The Hague, Pasmans, 1963.
Anwander, A., *Die allgemeine Religionsgeschichte im katholischen Deutschland während der Aufklärung und Romantik* (Salzburger Abhandlungen und Texte, IV). Salzburg, 1932.
Baal, J. van, *Symbols for Communication: An Introduction to the Anthropological Study of Religion* (Studies of Developing Countries, 11). Assen, Van Gorcum, 1971. [Ch. II—VIII on the history of the discipline].
Bettis, Joseph Dabney, ed., *Phenomenology of Religion: Eight Modern Descriptions of the Essence of Religion.* New York — Evanston, Harper & Row (Harper Forum Book), 1969. [Reader].
Bianchi, Ugo, *Problemi di storia delle religioni.* Roma, Editrice Studium, 1958. *German* translation by Elisabeth Serelman: *Probleme der Religionsgeschichte.* (Die kleine Vandenhoeck-Reihe, 203/204). Göttingen, Vandenhoeck & Ruprecht, 1964.
Birnbaum, Norman and Lenzer, Gertrud, *Sociology of Religion: A Book of Readings.* Englewood Cliffs, N. J., Prentice Hall, 1969. [Reader].
Burnouf, Emile, *La science des religions.* Paris, 1872.

Buschman, Harold, *A Critical Survey of some Recent Theories of the Origin and Nature of Religion*. Unpublished Ph. D. Dissertation, University of Chicago, 1934.

Capps, Walter, *On Ways of Understanding Religion*. New York, Macmillan, 1972. [Reader].

Clemen, Carl, "Die Anwendung der Psychoanalyse auf Mythologie und Religionsgeschichte," *Archiv für Gesamte Psychologie*, LXI (1928), pp. 1—128. Also published separately.

Colpe, C., *Die religionsgeschichtliche Schule. Darstellung und Kritik ihres Bildes vom gnostischen Erlösermythos*. Göttingen, 1961.

Desroche, H., "Science des religions et théologie chrétienne," in: *Bilan de la théologie du XXe siecle*, Vol. I (Tournai—Paris, 1970), pp. 221—243.

Dilthey, Wilhelm, "Das Problem der Religion," in: *Gesammelte Schriften*, Vol. VI. Stuttgart—Göttingen, 1924, 1958³, pp. 288—305.

Dussaud, R., *Introduction à l'histoire des religions*. Paris, 1914.

Ecole Pratique des Hautes Etudes (Paris, Sorbonne), Section des Sciences Religieuses, *Problèmes et méthodes d'histoire des religions*. Mélanges publiés par la Section des Sciences Religieuses à l'occasion du centenaire de l'Ecole Pratique des Hautes Etudes. Paris, P.U.F., 1968.

Edsman, Carl-Martin, "Religionshistoriska principfrågor i ljuset av nyare litteratur," *Ny Kyrklig Tidskrift*, Vol. 21 (1952), pp. 19—44.

—, "Religionsforskningen i går och i dag," *Finsk Tidskrift*, Nr. 169/170 (1961), pp. 111-125.

—, "Theologie oder Religionswissenschaft?," *Theologische Rundschau*, N. F. 35. Jg., Heft 1 (March 1970), pp. 1—32.

Eliade, Mircea, "The History of Religions in Retrospect: 1912—1962," *The Journal of Bible and Religion*, Vol. 31 (1963), pp. 98—107. Revised and expanded under the title of "The History of Religions in Retrospect: 1912 and after," in: Mircea Eliade, *The Quest*, 1969, pp. 12—36.

—, "The Quest for the 'Origins' of Religion," *History of Religions*, Vol. 4 (1964), pp. 154—169. Revised and expanded in: Mircea Eliade, *The Quest*, 1969, pp. 37—53.

—, "Crisis and Renewal in History of Religions," *History of Religions*, Vol. 5 (1965), pp. 1—17. Revised and expanded under the title of "Crisis and Renewal," in: Mircea Eliade, *The Quest*, 1969, pp. 54—71.

—, *The Quest: History and Meaning in Religion*. Chicago and London, The University of Chicago Press, 1969. (See especially Chapters I—V).

Eliade, Mircea, and Kitagawa, J. M., eds., *The History of Religions: Essays in Methodology*. Chicago—London, The University of Chicago Press, 1959. German translation: *Grundfragen der Religionswissenschaft. Acht Studien* (Wort und Antwort. Begegnung der Religionen). Salzburg, Otto Müller Verlag, 1963.

Engels, Friedrich: *See under* Marx, Karl.

Evans-Pritchard, E. E., "Religion and the Anthropologists". The Aquinas Lecture, March 1959. Oxford, 1960. Reprinted in: E. E. Evans-Pritchard, *Essays in Social Anthropology*. London, Faber & Faber, 1962, pb. 1968, pp. 29—45.

—, *Theories of Primitive Religion*. Oxford, Clarendon Press, 1965.

Foucart, G., *La méthode comparative dans l'histoire des religions*. Paris, Alph. Picard, 1909. Revised and expanded edition under the title of *Histoire des religions et méthode comparative*. Paris, A. Picard, 1912.

Gennep, A. van, "La méthode à suivre dans l'étude des rites et des mythes", *Revue de l'Université de Bruxelles*, XVI (1910—11), pp. 505—523.
—, "Religions, mœurs et légendes," 5e série. *Mercure de France* (Paris), XIX, esp. pp. 93—125. [On the history of the discipline].
Gensichen, Hans-Werner, "Tendenzen der Religionswissenschaft," in: Helge Siemers and Hans-Richard Reuter, eds., *Theologie als Wissenschaft in der Gesellschaft. Ein Heidelberger Experiment*. Göttingen, Vandenhoeck & Ruprecht, 1970, pp. 28—40.
Gölz, Friedrich, *Der primitive Mensch und seine Religion*. Gütersloh, Gütersloher Verlagshaus Gerd Mohn, 1963. [On the history of the discipline, see especially Chapters I—V].
Goblet d'Alviella, E., *Croyances, rites, institutions*. Tome II: *Hiérologie. Questions de méthode et d'origines*. Paris, 1911.
Goldammer, Kurt, "Die Frühentwicklung der allgemeinen Religionswissenschaft und die Anfänge einer Theologie der Religionen," *Saeculum*, XVIII, 1—2 (1967), pp. 181—198.
Gruppe, O., *Geschichte der klassischen Mythologie und Religionsgeschichte während des Mittelalters im Abendlande und während der Neuzeit*. (Supplement zu W. H. Roscher, *Ausführliches Lexikon der Griechischen und Römischen Mythologie)* Leipzig, 1921.
Hahn, Herbert F., *Old Testament in Modern Research*. Philadelphia, Mahlenberg Press, 1954.
Hardy, Edmund, *Die allgemeine vergleichende Religionsgeschichte im akademischen Studium unserer Zeit. Eine akademische Antrittsrede*. Freiburg im Breisgau, 1887.
—, "Was ist Religionswissenschaft? Ein Beitrag zur Methodik der historischen Religionsforschung," *Archiv für Religionswissenschaft*, I, 1 (1898), pp. 9—42.
—, "Zur Geschichte der Religionsforschung," *Archiv für Religionswissenschaft*, IV (1901), pp. 45—66, 97—135, 193—228.
Harnack, Adolf von, *Die Aufgabe der theologischen Fakultäten und die allgemeine Religionsgeschichte*. Rektoratsrede 3. August 1901. Giessen, 1901, 1901². Reprinted in: Adolf von Harnack, *Reden und Aufsätze*, II. Band, 1. Abteilung. Giessen, 1904, pp. 159—187.
Harris, Marvin, *The Rise of Anthropological Theory: A History of Theories of Culture*. New York, Th. Y. Crowell, 1968.
Hays, H. R., *From Ape to Angel: An Informal History of Social Anthropology*. New York, Capricorn Books, 1964.
Heck, E., *Roger Beacon. Ein mittelalterlicher Versuch einer historischen und systematischen Religionswissenschaft*. Bonn, 1957.
Hering, Jean, *Phénoménologie et philosophie religieuse*. Strasbourg, 1925.
Hirschmann, Eva, *Phänomenologie der Religion. Eine historisch-systematische Untersuchung von 'Religionsphänomenologie' und 'religionsphänomenologischer Methode' in der Religionswissenschaft*. Diss. Groningen. Würzburg, 1940.
Isambert, F. A., "The early days of French sociology of religion," *Social Compass*, Vol. 16, Nr. 4 (1969), pp. 435—452.
—, "La phénoménologie religieuse," in: *Introduction aux sciences humaines des religions*. Symposium recueilli par H. Desroche et J. Séguy. Paris, Editions Cujas, 1970, pp. 217—240.
Ittel, Gerhard Wolfgang, *Urchristentum und Fremdreligionen im Urteile der religionsgeschichtlichen Schule*. Diss. Erlangen, 1956.

Jordan, L. H., *Comparative Religion: Its Genesis and Growth*. With an Introduction by Principal Fairbairn. Edinburgh, T. & T. Clark, 1905.
—, *Comparative Religion: A Survey of its Recent Literature*. First section: *1900 – 1905*, Edinburgh, Otto Schulze & Co., 1906. Second section: *1906 – 1909*, Edinburgh, Otto Schulze & Co., 1910. Second edition of both sections combined, revised and augmented, New York – London, Humphrey Milford and Oxford University Press, 1920².
—, *Comparative Religion: Its Method and Scope*. A paper read in part at the Third International Congress of the History of Religions, Oxford, September 18, 1908. Oxford, Henry Frowde, 1908.
—, *The Study of Religion in the Italian Universities*. In collaboration with Baldassare Labanca, containing a translation of the latter's "Difficoltà antiche e nuove degli studi religiosi in Italia". London, Henry Frowde, 1909.
—, "The history of religions and its introduction into the German universities," *The Expository Times*, Vol. 22 (1910 – 11), pp. 198 – 201.
—, "The study of the history of religions in the German universities," *The Expository Times*, Vol. 24 (1912 – 13), pp. 136 – 139.
—, *Comparative Religion: Its Adjuncts and Allies*. New York – London, Humphrey Milford and Oxford University Press, 1915.
—, *Comparative Religion: Its Range and Limitations*. A Lecture. Oxford, Henry Milford, 1916.
—, *The History of Religions in Italian Universities: A Half-Century's Survey, 1873 – 1918*. Chicago, The University of Chicago Press, 1919.
Kardiner, Abram, and Preble, Edward, *They studied Man*. Cleveland – New York, The World Publishing Comp. (Meridian Books), 1965.
Kitagawa, Joseph M., "The History of Religions in America," in: Mircea Eliade and Joseph M. Kitagawa, eds., *The History of Religions: Essays in Methodology*. Chicago – London, The University of Chicago Press, 1959, 1962², pp. 1 – 30.
Kitagawa, Joseph M., Eliade, Mircea, and Long, Charles H., eds., *The History of Religions: Essays on the Problem of Understanding* (Essays in Divinity, Vol. I). Chicago – London, The University of Chicago Press, 1967.
Knudten, R. D., ed., *The Sociology of Religion: An Anthology*. New York, 1967. [Reader].
Kraeling, Emil G., *The Old Testament since the Reformation*. London, Lutterworth Press, 1955.
Kraus, Hans-Joachim, *Geschichte der historisch-kritischen Erforschung des Alten Testaments*. Neukirchen, Neukirchener Verlag, 1969.
Kümmel, Werner Georg, *Das Neue Testament. Geschichte der Erforschung seiner Probleme*. (Orbis Academicus, III, 3). Freiburg – München, Karl Alber, 1958.
Lanczkowski, Günter, ed., *Selbstverständnis und Wesen der Religionswissenschaft* (Wege der Forschung, Band 263). Darmstadt, Wissenschaftliche Buchgesellschaft, 1974.
Lehmann, Edvard, "Zur Geschichte der Religionsgeschichte," in: *Lehrbuch der Religionsgeschichte*. Begründet von P. D. Chantepie de la Saussaye. Vierte Auflage herausgegeben von A. Bertholet und Ed. Lehmann. Vol. I, Tübingen, J.C.B. Mohr, 1925, pp. 1 – 22.
—, "Der Lebenslauf der Religionsgeschichte," *Actes du Vᵉ Congrès d'histoire des religions* (Lund 1929), pp. 43 – 52.
Lessa, William A., and Vogt, Evon Z., eds., *Reader in Comparative Religion. An*

Anthropological Approach. Evanston—Elmsford, Harper & Row, 1958; New York—Evanston—London, Harper & Row, 1965². [Reader].

Lowie, Robert H., *The History of Ethnological Theory*. New York, Farrar & Rinehart, 1937.
  Spanish translation by Paul Kirchhoff: *Historia de la Etnología*. Mexico City, Fondo de Cultura Económica, 1946.

Mann, Ulrich, ed., *Theologie und Religionswissenschaft. Der gegenwärtige Stand ihrer Forschungsergebnisse und Aufgaben im Hinblick auf ihr gegenseitiges Verhältnis*. Darmstadt, Wissenschaftliche Buchgesellschaft, 1973.

Margul, Tadeusz, "Krótka charakterystyka zachodnich szkòt religionznawczych," *Euhemer*, V, 1 (1961), pp. 83—105.
  —, *Sto lat nauki o religiach* (A hundred years of study of religion). Warszawa, 1964.

Martino, Ernesto de, "Fenomenologia religiosa e storicismo assoluto," *Studie Materiali di Storia delle Religioni*, 24/25 (1953—54), pp. 1—25.

Marx, Karl, and Engels, Friedrich, *On Religion*. Moscow, 1955.
  American edition with the same title, and with an Introduction by Reinhold Niebuhr. New York, Schocken Books (SB 67), 1964, 1971⁴.
  German edition: *Über Religion*. Berlin, 1958.
  Polish edition: *O religii*. Warszawa, 1962².

Meinhold, Peter, "Entwicklung der Religionswissenschaft im Mittelalter und zur Reformationszeit," in: Ulrich Mann, ed., *Theologie und Religionswissenschaft*. Darmstadt, Wissenschaftliche Buchgesellschaft, 1973, pp. 357—380.
  —, "Entwicklung der Religionswissenschaft in der Neuzeit und in der Gegenwart," in: Ulrich Mann, ed., *Idem*, 1973, pp. 381—412.

Mensching, Gustav, *Geschichte der Religionswissenschaft*. Bonn, Universitäts-Verlag, 1948.

Mercier, P., *Histoire de l'anthropologie*. Paris, P.U.F., 1966.

Merkel, Rudolf Franz, "Anfänge der Erforschung amerikanischer Religionen," *Studi e Materiali di Storia delle Religioni*, XII (1936), pp. 66 ff.
  —, "Anfänge religionsgeschichtlicher Forschung in Europa: die Erforschung primitiver Religionen," *Zeitschrift für Missionskunde und Religionswissenschaft*, 1936, pp. 42 ff.; 1937, pp. 17 ff.
  —, "Anfänge der Erforschung germanischer Religion," *Archiv für Religionswissenschaft*, 1936, pp. 18 ff.
  —, "Zur Geschichte der Erforschung chinesischer Religionen," *Studi e Materiali di Storia delle Religioni*, XV (1939), pp. 90 ff.
  —, "Anfänge der Erforschung indischer Religionen im 18. Jahrhundert," in: *Rudolf Otto-Ehrung*, Vol. II *(Aus der Welt der Religion, Forschungen und Berichte*: Religionswissenschaftliche Reihe, N. F. Heft 2). Berlin, Töpelmann, 1940, pp. 39 ff.
  —, "Beiträge zur vergleichenden Religionsgeschichte. I: Ein vergessener deutscher Religionsforscher, Chr. W. Flügge," *Archiv für Religionswissenschaft*, 1940, pp. 193 ff.
  —, "Zur Geschichte der Religionsphänomenologie," in: *In Deo Omnia Unum*. Eine Sammlung von Aufsätzen Friedrich Heiler zum 50. Geburtstage dargebracht. München, Ernst Reinhardt, 1942, pp. 38—61.
  —, "Zur Religionsforschung der Aufklärungszeit," in: *Festschrift Alfred Bertholet zum 80. Geburtstag gewidmet*. Tübingen, J. C. B. Mohr, 1950, pp. 351—364.

Meslin, Michel, *Pour une science des religions*. Paris, Ed. du Seuil, 1973.

Neill, Stephen, *The Interpretation of the New Testament 1861—1961*. The Firth Lectures, 1962. London—New York—Toronto, Oxford University Press, 1964.

Nowaczyk, M., *Zarys dziejów religioznawstwa w Polsce* (Short history of the study of religion in Poland). Warszawa, 1962. See also *Euhemer*, Vol. 10 (1966), Nr. 6.

Padovani, U. A., "La storia delle religioni in Italia," *Scuola Cattolica*, VI (1925), pp. 401—420.

Parsons, Talcott, "The theoretical development of the sociology of religion," *Journal of the History of Ideas*, 1944, pp. 176—190. Reprinted as Chapter 10 in: Talcott Parsons, *Essays in Sociological Theory: Pure and Applied*. Glencoe, Ill., The Free Press, 1949, 1954[2].

Pettazzoni, Raffaele, "La science des religions et sa méthode," *Scientia*, XIII (1913), pp. 128—136 of the "Supplément".

—, *Svolgimento e carattere della storia delle religioni*. Bari, Laterza, 1924

Pfister, Oskar, *Religionswissenschaft und Psychoanalyse*. Giessen, 1927.

Pinard de la Boullaye, H., S. J., "Quelques précisions sur la méthode comparative," *Anthropos*, V (1910), pp. 534—558.

—, "La théorie de l'expérience religieuse de Luther à William James," *Revue d'Histoire Ecclésiastique*, XVII (1921), pp. 63—83, 306—348, 547—574.

—, *L'Etude comparée des religions. Essai critique*. Vol. I: *Son histoire dans le monde occidental*. 1922, 1925[2], 1929[3]. Vol. II: *Ses méthodes*. 1925, 1929[5]. Paris, Gabriel Beauchesne.

Poniatowsky, Zygmunt, *Wstep do religioznawstwa* [Introduction to the Study of Religion]. Warszawa, 1959. Second, enlarged edition 1961[2]; third edition, revised, 1962[3].

Poulat, O. and E., "Le développement institutionnel des sciences religieuses en France," *Archives de Sociologie des Religions*, 21e Année (1965), pp. 23—36. Reprinted in: *Introduction aux sciences humaines des religions*. Symposium recueilli par H. Desroche et J. Séguy. Paris, Editions Cujas, 1970, pp. 79—98.

Puech, H. Ch., et Vignaux, P., "La science des religions," in: *Introduction aux sciences humaines des religions*. Symposium recueilli par H. Desroche et J. Séguy. Paris, Editions Cujas, 1970, pp. 9—36.

Ratschow, Carl Heinz, "Metodik der Religionswissenschaft," in: *Enzyklopädie der geistenswissenschaftlichen Arbeitsmethoden*. Hg. von Manfred Thiel. München—Wien, R. Oldenburg Verlag, 1973, 9. Lieferung, pp. 347—400.

Réville, Jean, "L'histoire des religions et les facultés de théologie. A propos d'une récente brochure de M. le professeur Ad. Harnack," *Revue d'Histoire des Religions*, XLIV (1901), pp. 423—438.

—, *Phases successives de l'histoire des religions*. Paris, E. Leroux, 1909.

Robertson, Roland, ed., *Sociology of Religion: Selected Readings* (Penguin Modern Sociology Readings). Harmondsworth—Baltimore, Penguin Books, Inc., 1969 [Reader].

Rudolph, Kurt, *Die Religionsgeschichte an der Leipziger Universität und die Entwicklung der Religionswissenschaft*. (Sitzungsberichte der Sächsischen Akademie der Wissenschaften zu Leipzig, Phil.-Hist. Klasse, Band 107, Heft 1). Berlin, Akademie Verlag, 1962.

—, "Leipzig und die Religionswissenschaft," *Numen*, IX (1962), pp. 53—68.

Schleiter, Frederick, *Religion and Culture: A Critical Survey of Methods of Ap-*

proach to Religious Phenomena. New York, Columbia University 1919.

Schmidt, Wilhelm, *Ursprung und Werden der Religion. Theorie und Tatsachen.* Handbuch der Vergleichenden Religionsgeschichte, zum Gebrauch für Vorlesungen an Universitäten, Seminaren usw. und zum Selbststudium. Münster i. Westf., Aschendorffsche Verlagsbuchhandlung, 1930. [For the history of the discipline, see especially Chapters II—XIII].
Chinese translation by Hermann Köster, Ch'en Hsiang-Ch'un, and Su Shih-i: *Pi-chao tsyng-chiao shih.* Peking, 1948.
English translation by H. J. Rose: *The Origin and Growth of Religion: Facts and Theories.* New York—London, Methuen, 1931.
French translation by A. Lemonnyer: *Origine et évolution de la religion. Les théories et les faits* (Collection "La Vie Chrétienne"). Paris, 1931.
Italian translation by Giuseppe Bugatto: *Manuale di storia comparata delle religioni. Origine e sviluppo della religione. Teorie e fatti.* (Collezione Fides, 7). Brescia, 1934, 1938² (revised and enlarged), 1943³, 1949⁴ (enlarged).
Spanish translation by Emilio Huidobro Tech de Huizobro: *Manual de historia comparada de las religiones. Origen y formaciòn de la religiòn. Teorias y hechos.* Bilbao—Madrid—Barcelona, 1932, 1941² (enlarged).

Schmitz, Carl August, ed., *Religions-Ethnologie.* (Akademische Reihe. Auswahl repräsentativer Texte). Frankfurt am Main, Akademische Verlagsgesellschaft, 1964. [Reader].

Schneider, L., *Religion, Culture, and Society: A Reader in the Sociology of Religion.* New York, 1964. [Reader].

Schröder, Christel Matthias, *Geschichte der Religionswissenschaft.* (Die Religionen der Menschheit, Vol. 35). Stuttgart, W. Kohlhammer Verlag (In preparation).

Schütz, W., *J. F. Kleuker. Seine Stellung in der Religionsgeschichte des ausgehenden 18. Jahrhunderts.* 1927.

Sharpe, Eric J., *A Hundred Years of Comparative Religion.* London, Gerald Duckworth, 1974.

Sierksma, F., *Phaenomenologie der religie en complexe psychologie.* Diss. Groningen, 1951. Commercial edition under the title of *Freud, Jung en de religie.* Assen, Van Gorcum, 1951 (With a summary in English).

Stephenson, Gunther, "Religionswissenschaft in Deutschland," *Frankfurter Hefte,* 19. Jahrgang, Heft 8, (1964), pp. 567—574.

—, "Geschichte und Religionswissenschaft im ausgehenden 18. Jahrhundert," *Numen,* Vol. XIII (1966), pp. 43—79.

Strich, F., *Die Mythologie in der deutschen Literatur von Klopstock bis Wagner,* 2 Vols. Halle, M. Niemeyer, 1910.

Szolc (Scholz), Piotr O., "Religionswissenschaft in Poland," *Numen,* XVIII (1971), pp. 45—80.

Toutain, J., "La section des Sciences Religieuses de l'Ecole Pratique des Hautes Etudes de 1886 à 1911," *Annuaire de la Section des Sciences Religieuses.* Paris, E. P. H. E., 1911, pp. 9—103.

Vernes, M., *L'histoire des religions. Son esprit, sa méthode et ses divisions. Son enseignement en France et à l'étranger.* Paris, 1887.

Vries, Jan de, *Forschungsgeschichte der Mythologie.* (Orbis Academicus, I, 7). Freiburg—München, Karl Alber, 1961.

—, *Godsdienstgeschiedenis in vogelvlucht.* (Aula Series, Nr. 56). Utrecht—Antwerpen, Spectrum, 1961.

English translation with Introduction by Kees W. Bolle: *The Study of Religion: A Historical Approach.* New York—Chicago—San Francisco—Atlanta, Harcourt, Brace and World, 1967.

Waal Malefijt, Annemarie de, *Religion and Culture: An Introduction to Anthropology of Religion.* New York, The Macmillan Company; London, Collier-Macmillan, 1968, 1969². [For the history of the discipline, see Chapters 2—4].

Waardenburg, Jacques, "Religion between Reality and Idea: A Century of Phenomenology of Religion in the Netherlands," *Numen*, XIX, 2—3 (August and December 1972), pp. 128—203.

—, "Grundsätzliches zur Religionsphänomenologie," *Neue Zeitschrift für Systematische Theologie und Religionsphilosophie*, Vol. 14, Nr. 3 (1972), pp. 315–335.

—, "Introduction: View of a Hundred Years' Study of Religion," in: Jacques Waardenburg, *Classical Approaches to the Study of Religion*, Vol. 1 (Religion and Reason, Vol. 3). The Hague—Paris, Mouton, 1973, pp. 1—76.

Wach, Joachim, *Religionswissenschaft. Prolegomena zu ihrer wissenschaftstheoretischen Grundlegung.* (Veröffentlichungen des Forschungsinstituts für Vergleichende Religionsgeschichte an der Universität Leipzig, Nr. 10). Leipzig, J. C. Hinrichs, 1924.

Wackenheim, Charles, *La faillite de la religion d'après Karl Marx.* Paris, P. U. F., 1963.

Welker, Klaus Eberhard, *Die grundsätzliche Beurteilung der Religionsgeschichte durch Schleiermacher.* Leiden–Köln, E. J. Brill, 1965.

Widengren, G., "Die religionswissenschaftliche Forschung in Skandinavien," *Zeitschrift für Religions- und Geistesgeschichte*, V (1953), pp. 193 ff.; 320 ff.

Wobbermin, Georg, *Die Methoden der religionspsychologischen Arbeit.* Appeared in: Emil Abderhalden, ed., *Handbuch der biologischen Arbeitsmethoden*, Vol. 22, 1928. First edition: Berlin—Wien, Urban und Schwarzenberg, 1921.

Yoroi, Kiyoshi, "Oranda no Shûkyo-gaku Kenkyû" [History of Religions in the Netherlands], *Journal of Religious Studies* (Japanese Association for Religious Studies, Tokyo), XLIII, 1 (December 1969), pp. 139—161.

General Bibliography

NICOLAUS ADRIANI

1. Bibliography

Lijst van geschriften van Dr. N. Adriani. Leiden, E. J. Brill, 1928.
Adriani, Annette E., "Lijst van de geschriften van Dr. N. Adriani," in: *Verzamelde geschriften van Dr. N. Adriani*, ed. by M. Adriani-Gunning, 3 vols. Haarlem, De erven F. Bohn, 1932, vol. III, pp. 396–412.

2. Biography and Appreciation

Kraemer, H., *Dr. N. Adriani, schets van leven en arbeid.* Amsterdam, H. J. Paris, 1930[1], 1935[2]. Includes also: A. E. Adriani, "Zoals wij hem zien uit zijn brieven".

3. Main Publications

1893 *Sangireesche spraakkunst.* Leiden, A. H. Adriani.
1894 *Sangireesche teksten met vertaling en aanteekeningen, uitgegeven door dr. N. Adriani.* Ed. by Het Koninklijk Instituut voor Taal-, Land- en Volkenkunde van Nederlandsch-Indië. The Hague, M. Nijhoff.
1912–1914 *De Bare'e sprekende Toradjas van Midden-Celebes. De Oost Toradjas.* By N. Adriani and Albert C. Kruyt. 3 vols. Batavia, Landsdrukkerij. New completely revised edition by A. C. Kruyt, 4 vols. (Verhandelingen der Koninklijke Nederlandsche Akademie van Wetenschappen, Afd. Letterkunde. Nieuwe Reeks, 54–56, no. 1–3). Amsterdam, Noord-Hollandsche Uitg. Mij., 1950–1951.
1928 *Bare'e — Nederlandsch Woordenboek met Nederlandsch — Bare'e register.* Leiden, E. J. Brill.
1931 *Spraakkunst der Bare'e-taal.* Bandoeng, A. C. Nix and Co.
1939 *Koelawische Taalstudiën.* By N. Adriani and dr. S. J. Esser. Bandoeng, A. C. Nix and Co.

TOR J. E. ANDRAE

1. Bibliography

"Curriculum Vitae," in *Uppsala Universitets Matrikel Höstterminen 1936*, ed.
by Th. Fries and E. von Döbeln. Uppsala, 1937, pp. 15 ff.

2. Biography and Appreciation

Hassler, O. and Murray, R., *Tor Andrae: In Memoriam*. Stockholm, 1947.
Widengren, G., *Tor Andrae*. Uppsala, 1947.

3. Main Publications

1917 *Die Person Muhammeds in Lehre und Glauben seiner Gemeinde* (Archives
d'Etudes Orientales, Vol. 16). Stockholm, Kungl. Boktrycerriet. P. A.
Norstedt, 1918[2].

1923—1925 *Der Ursprung des Islams und das Christentum* (Extracts from *Kyrk-
kohistorisk Arsskrift* (Stockholm) 1923—1925. Uppsala, Almqvist och
Wiksells, 1926.
French translation by Jules Roche: *Les origines de l'Islam et le Christianisme*. Paris, Maisonneuve, 1955.

1930 *Muhammed. Hans liv och hans tro*. Stockholm, Bokforlaget natur och
kultur. 1950[2] (rev.).
English translation (from the German edition) by Th. Menzel: *Mohammed.
The man and his faith*. New York, Barnes and Noble, 1935; 1955 (rev.);
New York, Scribner, 1936; London, Allen and Unwin, 1936; New York —
Evanston, Harper Torchbooks, 1960.
German translation: *Mohammed. Sein Leben und sein Glaube*. Göttingen,
Vandenhoeck und Ruprecht, 1932.

1930 *Modern Mystik. En blick pa teosofien och den ockulta vetenskapen*. Stockholm, Bonnier.

1932 *Die Frage der religiösen Anlage. Religionsgeschichtlich beleuchtet*. (Uppsala
Universitets Arsskrift 1942, Program 5). Uppsala, Almqvist och Wiksells.
Reprinted in: *Die letzten Dinge*. Leipzig, Hinrichs, 1940.
Swedish edition: *Det religiösa anlaget och andra religionshistoriska essayer*.
Ed. with intr. by Åke V. Ström. Uppsala, Lindblad, 1951.

1933 *Det osynligas värld*. Uppsala, Lindbad. 1934[4].
German translation by H. H. Schaeder in: *Die letzten Dinge*. Leipzig,
Hinrichs, 1940.

1940 *Den gamla prästgården. Studier och minen*. Uppsala, Lindblad. 1941[3].

1947 *I myrtenträdgården. Studier i sufisk mystik*. Stockholm, Bonnier.
German translation by Helmhart Kanus-Credé: *Islamische Mystiker*. (Urban
Bücher, 46). Stuttgart, W. Kohlhammer, 1960.

BERNHARD ANKERMANN

1. *Bibliography*

Schachtzabel, "Prof. Dr. B. Ankermann, zum 80. Geburstage. Mit Verzeichnis seiner Veröffentlichungen," in: *Baessler-Archiv* XXI, 4 (1938): Sonderbeilage.

2. *Biography and Appreciation*

Hirschberg, W., "Das Werk B. Ankermann's," *Zeitschrift für Ethnologie*, LXX (1938—1939), pp. 130—143.

3. *Main Publications*

1901 *Die Afrikanischen Musikinstrumenten.* Sonderabdruck aus dem *Ethnologische Notizblatt,* Bd. III, Hft. 1. Berlin.

1905 "Kulturkreisen und Kulturschichten in Afrika," *Zeitschrift für Ethnologie,* XXXVII, pp. 54—84.

1918 "Totenkult und Seelenglaube bei afrikanischen Völkern," *Zeitschrift für Ethnologie,* L, pp. 89—153.

1924 "Die Religion der Naturvölker," in: *Lehrbuch der Religionsgeschichte.* Begründet von P. D. Chantepie de la Saussaye. 4. Auflage von A. Bertholet und E. Lehmann. Vol. I, Tübingen, Mohr, pp. 131—192.

1929-1930 *Das Eingeborenenrecht.* Sitte und Gewohnheitsrechte der Eingeborenen der ehemaligen deutschen Kolonien in Afrika. By B. Ankermann and E. B. Th. Schulz-Ewerth. 2 Vols. Herausg. von dr. E. Schult-Ewerth und dr. L. Adam; "Ost-Afrika," von B. Ankermann. Stuttgart.

B

JOHANN JAKOB BACHOFEN*

1. Bibliography

Bessmerty, Alexander, "J. J. Bachofen-Bibliographie," in:
  a) *Der Mythus von Orient und Okzident. Eine Metaphysik der alten Welt. Aus den Werken von J. J. Bachofen.* Edited by Manfred Schröter, with an introduction by Alfred Baeumler. München, C. H. Beck, 1925, pp. 620–624.
  b) J. J. Bachofen, *Mutterrecht und Urreligion. Eine Auswahl.* Edited with an introduction by Rudolf Marx. Leipzig, Kröner, 1927, pp. 463–469.

2. Biography and Appreciation

Andler, Charles, "J. J. Bachofen. Son Œuvre et sa méthode d'après un livre récent," *Revue de l'Histoire des Religions,* 47ᵉ année, tome XCIII (1926), pp. 224–241.
Bachofen J. J., "Autobiographische Aufzeichnungen," (edited by Herm. Blocher), *Basler Jahrbuch,* 1917, pp. 295–348.
—, "Eine Selbstbiographie, zugleich ein Gedenkblatt zu seinem 100. Geburtstag. Mit Nachwort von Joseph Kohler," *Zeitschrift für Vergleichende Rechtswissenschaft,* XXXIV (1917), pp. 337–380. Reprinted as J. J. Bachofen, *Selbstbiographie und Antrittsrede über das Naturrecht.* Edited with an introduction by Alfred Baeumler. Halle/Saale, M. Niemeyer, 1927.
—, *Autobiographische Rückschau.* München, Ruprecht-Presse, 1923.
—, *Griechische Reise.* Edited by Georg Schmidt. Heidelberg, Richard Weiszbach, 1927.
—, *Briefe.* Edited by Fritz Husner. *(Gesammelte Werke,* vol. X). Basel–Stuttgart, Schwabe & Co., 1967.
Baeumler, Alfred, "Wider die Philologen unter Bachofens Verächtern," *Wissen und Leben* (Zürich), XVII, 14 (1924), pp. 841–848.
—, "Einleitung," in: *Der Mythus von Orient und Okzident. Eine Metaphysik der alten Welt. Aus den Werken von J. J. Bachofen.* Edited by Manfred Schröter. München, C. H. Beck, 1925, pp. XXIII–CCXCIV. Reissued later as: Alfred Baeumler, *Das mythische Weltalter. Bachofens romantische Deutung des Altertums.* München, C. H. Beck, 1965.
—, "Einleitung," in: J. J. Bachofen, *Selbstbiographie und Antrittsrede über*

das Naturrecht. Edited with an introduction by Alfred Baeumler. Halle/
Saale, M. Niemeyer, 1927.

—, *Bachofen und Nietzsche.* Zürich, Verlag der Neuen Schweizer Rundschau,
1929.

—, "Nachwort. Bachofen und die Religionsgeschichte," in: Alfred Baeumler,
Das mythische Weltalter. Bachofens romantische Deutung des Altertums.
München, C. H. Beck, 1965.

Bernoulli, Carl Albrecht, *Johann Jakob Bachofen und das Natursymbol. Ein
Würdigungsversuch.* Basel, W. Schwabe, 1924.

—, *Johann Jakob Bachofen als Religionsforscher.* ("Die Schweiz im deutschen
Geistesleben", Bd. 37). Leipzig, H. Haessel, 1924.

—, "Einleitung," in: Johann Jakob Bachofen, *Urreligion und antike Symbole.*
Vol. I, pp. 5–14; Vol. II. pp. 3–10; Vol. III, pp. 3–7. Edited by Carl
Albrecht Bernoulli, 3 vols. Leipzig, 1926. Also accompanying text by
C. A. Bernoulli.

—, "Schluszwort," in: *Idem*, Vol. III, pp. 270–276.

Boas, Georg, "Preface," in: *Myth, Religion and Mother Right. Selected Writings
of J. J. Bachofen.* Translated by Ralph Manheim from the German. With
a Preface by George Boas and an Introduction by Joseph Campbell
(Bollingen Series, Vol. 84). Princeton, Princeton University Press, 1967,
pp. XI–XXIV.

Burckhardt, Max, *J. J. Bachofen und die Politik.* Basel, 1943.

Campbell, Joseph, "Introduction," in: *Myth, Religion and Mother Right. Selected
Writings of J. J. Bachofen.* Translated by Ralph Manheim from the German.
With a Preface by George Boas and an Introduction by Joseph Campbell
(Bollingen Series, Vol. 84). Princeton, Princeton University Press, 1967,
pp. XXV–LVII.

Deubel, W., "Der Kampf um Johann Jakob Bachofen," *Preussische Jahrbücher*,
1926.

Fehrle, Eugen, "Johann Jakob Bachofen und das Mutterrecht," *Neue Heidelberger Jahrbücher*, 1927.

Howald, Ernst, "Wider Johann Jakob Bachofen," *Wissen und Leben* (Zürich),
XVII, 13 (1924), pp. 757–768.

Kelles-Krauz, Casimir von, "J. J. Bachofen (1861–1901). Aus den Studien über
die Quellen des Marxismus," *Die Neue Zeit* (Stuttgart), 20. Jhrg. Band I
(1902), pp. 517 ff.

Kerényi, Karl, *Bachofen und die Zukunft des Humanismus. Mit einem Intermezzo
über Nietzsche und Ariadne.* Zürich, 1945.

—, "Zu J. J. Bachofen's Portrait," *Neue Schweizerische Rundschau*, 1952, pp.
676–683.

Kohler, Joseph, "Johann Jakob Bachofen," *Zeitschrift für Vergleichende Rechtswissenschaft*, VIII (1889), pp. 148–155.

Kraemer, Rudolf, *Rilke und Bachofen.* Würzburg, 1939.

Marx, Rudolf, "Einleitung," in: J. J. Bachofen, *Mutterrecht und Urreligion.
Eine Auswahl.* Edited with an introduction by Rudolf Marx. Leipzig,
Kröner, 1927.

Muschg, Walter, *Bachofen als Schriftsteller.* Rektoratsrede gehalten am 25.
November 1949. Basel, Helbing & Lichtenhahn, 1949.

Philipp, Wolfgang, *Weibwertung oder Mutterrecht? Eine grundsätzliche Arbeit
über Rasse und Gesittung. Bachofens Geisteserbe und die Keltenfrage.*
Königsberg and Berlin, Ost-Europa Verlag, 1942.

Schmidt, Georg, *Johann Jakob Bachofens Geschichtsphilosophie*. Inaug. diss. Basel. München, C. H. Beck, 1929.

Schröter, Manfred, "Zur geistesgeschichtlichen Bedeutung J. J. Bachofens," in: J. J. Bachofen, *Oknos der Seilflechter. Ein Grabbild*. Edited with an introduction by Manfred Schröter. München, C. H. Beck, n. d. (1923).

—, "Johann Jakob Bachofen," *Münchener Neueste Nachrichten*, 1923, Nr. 167; also *Neue Zürcher Zeitung*, 1923, Nr. 802.

—, "Einleitung," in J. J. Bachofen, *Das lykische Volk und seine Bedeutung für die Entwicklung des Altertums*. Edited with introduction by Manfred Schröter. ("Die Schweiz im deutschen Geistesleben," Band 30). Leipzig, H. Haessel, 1924.

—, "Vorwort des Herausgebers," in: *Der Mythus von Orient und Okzident. Eine Metaphysik der alten Welt. Aus den Werken von J. J. Bachofen*. Edited by Manfred Schröter, with an introduction by Alfred Baeumler. München, C. H. Beck, 1925, pp. XVII–XXI.

Turel, Adrien, *Bachofen–Freud. Zur Emanzipierung des Mannes vom Reich der Mütter*. Bern, H. Huber, 1939.

Winter, Karl Ernst, "Bachofen-Renaissance," *Zeitschrift für die gesamte Staatswissenschaften*, 1928.

3. Main Publications

1840 *De Romanorum iudiciis civilibus, de legis actionibus, de formulis et de condictione*. Göttingen.

1841 *Das Naturrecht und das geschichtliche Recht in ihren Gegensätzen*. (Inaugural lecture). Basel, J. G. Neukirch.

1843 *Das nexum, die nexi und die lex Petillia*. Basel, J. G. Neukirch.

1843 *Die lex Voconia und die mit ihr zusammenhängende Rechtsinstitute*. Eine rechtshistorische Abhandlung. Basel, Schweighauser.

1847 *Das römische Pfandrecht, I*. Basel, Schweighauser.

1848 *Ausgewählte Lehren des römischen Zivilrechts*. Bonn, Adolph Marcus.

1851 Fr. Dor. Gerlach and J. J. Bachofen, *Die Geschichte der Römer, I*. Basel, Bahnmaier (C. Dettloff), 1851 ("Die Grundlagen des römischen Staatsrechts", pp. 209–372).

1857 "Über das Weiberrecht," *Verhandlungen der 16. Versammlung deutscher Philologen, Schulmänner und Orientalisten in Stuttgart, 1856*. Stuttgart, J. B. Metzler, pp. 40–63.

1857 J. J. Bachofen and Karl Stehlin, *Beiträge zur Schweizer Geschichte aus englischen Manuskripten* (Archiv für Schweizer Geschichte, Band 12). Zürich.

1858–1861 "Sul significato de'dadi e delle mani nei sepolcri degli antichi," I: "De'dadi"; II: "Delle mani", *Annali dell'Istituto di corrispondenza archeologica*, XXX (1858), pp. 141–163; and XXXIII (1861), pp. 257–275.

1859 *Versuch über die Gräbersymbolik der Alten*. Basel, Bahnmaier (C. Detloff). 1925² (with preface by Carl Albrecht Bernoulli and "Würdigung" by Ludwig Klages). Parts reissued:
a) *Oknos der Seilflechter. Ein Grabbild*. Edited and introduced by Manfred Schröter. München, C. H. Beck, n. d. (1923).
b) In: *Der Mythus von Orient und Okzident. Eine Metaphysik der Alten Welt. Aus den Werken von J. J. Bachofen*. Edited by Manfred Schröter,

with an introduction by Alfred Baeumler. München, C. H. Beck, 1925.
c) In: *Mutterrecht und Urreligion. Eine Auswahl*. Edited by Rudolf Marx.
Leipzig, Kröner, 1927.
English translation, see under 1927.
d) In: *Gesammelte Werke*, Vol. IV.

1861 *Das Mutterrecht. Eine Untersuchung über die Gynaikokratie der alten Welt
nach ihrer religiösen und rechtlichen Natur*. Stuttgart, Krais & Hofmann.
1897². Parts reissued:
a) "Sappho," *Neue Deutsche Beiträge* (München), I, 3 (1923), pp. 61–79.
b) In: *Der Mythus von Orient und Okzident* . . ., etc., 1925.
c) In: *Mutterrecht und Urreligion. Eine Auswahl*. Edited by Rudolf Marx.
Leipzig, Kröner, 1927.
Englisch translation, see under 1927.
d) In: *Gesammelte Werke*, Vols. II, III.

1862 *Das lykische Volk und seine Bedeutung für die Entwicklung des Altertums*.
Freiburg i. Br., Herder, 1862. Parts reissued:
a) *Das lykische Volk und seine Bedeutung für die Entwicklung des Altertums*.
Slightly abridged edition with introduction by Manfred Schröter ("Die
Schweiz im deutschen Geistesleben," Band 30). Leipzig, H. Haessel, 1924.
b) In: *Der Mythus von Orient und Okzident* . . . etc., 1925.

1862 "Die Grundlagen der Steuerverfassung des römischen Reiches," *Neues
Schweizer Museum* (Zürich).

1863 *Der Bär in den Religionen des Altertums*. Basel, Ch. Meyri.

1867 *Die Unsterblichkeitslehre der orphischen Theologie auf den Grabdenkmälern
des Altertums*. Nach Anleitung einer Vase aus Canosa im Besitz des Herrn
Prosper Biardot in Paris dargestellt. Basel, Felix Schneider. Parts reissued:
a) In: *Der Mythus von Orient und Okzident* . . . etc., 1925.
b) In: *Gesammelte Werke*, Vol. VII.

1867–1869 "La lupa romana su monumenti sepolcrali dell'impero," I: "I monumenti publici"; II: "Monumenti sepolcrali"; III: "Monumenti sepolcrali",
Annali dell'Istituto di correspondenza archeologica, XXXIX (1867), pp.
183–200; XL (1868), pp. 421–432; XLI (1869), pp. 288–308.

1870 *Die Sage von Tanaquil. Eine Untersuchung über den Orientalismus in Rom
und Italien*. Heidelberg, J. C. B. Mohr. Parts reissued:
a) In: *Der Mythus von Orient und Okzident* . . . etc., 1925.
b) *Mutterrecht und Urreligion. Eine Auswahl*, Edited by Rudolf Marx.
Leipzig, Kröner, 1927.
English translation, see under 1927.
c) In: *Gesammelte Werke*, Vol. VI.

1870 *Beilage zu der Schrift Die Sage von Tanaquil*. Theodor Mommsen's Kritik
der Erzählung von Cn. Marcius Coriolanus. Heidelberg, J. C. B. Mohr.

1880–1886 *Antiquarische Briefe, vornehmlich zur Kenntnis der ältesten Verwandt-
schaftsbegriffe*, 2 vols. Straszburg, Karl J. Trübner.

1890 *Römische Grablampen, nebst einigen andern Grabdenkmälern, vorzugsweise
eigener Sammlung*. Vorgelegt und mit Ausführungen zu einzelnen
Teilen der römischen Gräbersymbolik begleitet. Herausgegeben von seiner
Witwe und seinem Sohne. Introduction by A. Giraud-Teulon. Basel.
1912². Reissued in *Gesammelte Werke*, Vol. VIII.

1925 *Der Mythus von Orient und Okzident. Eine Metaphysik der alten Welt. Aus
den Werken von J. J. Bachofen*. Edited by Manfred Schröter, with an
introduction by Alfred Baeumler. München, C. H. Beck, 1925. The "Ein-

leitung" by Alfred Baeumler (pp. XXIII–CCXCIV) has been reprinted separately: Alfred Baeumler, *Das mythische Weltalter. Bachofens romantische Deutung des Altertums.* (With a "Nachwort: Bachofen und die Religionsgeschichte"). München, C. H. Beck, 1965.

1926 *Urreligion und Antike Symbole. Systematisch angeordnete Auswahl aus seinen Werken.* Edited by Carl Albrecht Bernoulli, 3 vols. Leipzig, P. Reclam. (Without references).

1927 *Mutterrecht und Urreligion. Eine Auswahl.* Edited with an introduction by Rudolf Marx. Leipzig, Kröner.
English translation by Ralph Manheim: *Myth, Religion and Mother Right. Selected writings of J. J. Bachofen.* With a Preface by George Boas and an Introduction by Joseph Campbell (Bollingen Series, Vol. 84). Princeton, Princeton University Press, 1967.

1927 *Selbstbiographie und Antrittsrede über das Naturrecht.* Edited with an introduction by Alfred Baeumler. Halle/Saale, M. Niemeyer.

1927 *Griechische Reise.* Edited by Geo Schmidt. Heidelberg.

1938 *Du règne de la mère au patriarcat.* Pages choisies par Adrien Turel. Paris, F. Alcan.

1943–1967 *Johann Jakob Bachofens Gesammelte Werke.* Mit Benützung des Nachlasses unter Mitwirkung von Max Burckhardt, . . . etc., herausgegeben von Karl Meuli, 10 vols. Basel–Stuttgart, B. Schwabe & Co., (With commentary).

JEAN BARUZI

Main Publications

1907 *Leibniz et l'organisation religieuse de la terre d'après des documents inédits.* Paris, Alcan.

1909 *Leibniz. Avec de nombreux textes inédits.* Paris, Bloud et cie.

1924 *Saint Jean de la Croix et le problème de l'experience mystique.* Paris, Alcan. 1931[2] (revised).

1926 *Philosophie générale et métaphysique.* Paris, Alcan.

1926 *Le problème moral.* Paris, Alcan.

1935 *Problèmes d'histoire des religions.* Paris, Alcan.

1951 *Création religieuse et pensée contemplative.* I: La mystique paulinienne et les données autobiographiques des Epitres; II: Angelius Silesius. Paris, Aubier.

1966 *Louis de Léon interprète du Livre de Job.* Paris, Presses Universitaires de France.

ADOLF BASTIAN

1. Bibliography

"Schriften von Prof. Dr. A. Bastian," in: *Festgabe zur Feier des 70sten Geburts-tages von Prof. Ad. Bastian*. Supplement Band IX, *Internationales Archiv für Ethnographie*. Leiden, E. J. Brill, 1896, pp. 68–85.

2. Biography and Appreciation

Achelis, T., *Adolf Bastian*. (Deutsche Denker. Heft 7). Dantzig, 1880.
—, *Adolf Bastian*. (Samml. wissensch. Vorträge. N. F., Heft 128). Hamburg, 1891.
—, "Adolf Bastian," *Vierteljahresschrift für wissenschaftliche Philosophie*, 1896, pp. 249–260.
Grünwedel, A., "Zur Erinnerung an Adolf Bastian," *Jahrb. d. Kgl. Preus. Kunstsamml.* (Berlin), 1905.
Koningsheim, P., "Adolf Bastian und die Entwicklung der ethnologischen Sozio-logie," *Kölner Vierteljahresschrift für Soziologie*, VI (1916–1917), pp. 61–76.
Preuss, K. Th., "Adolf Bastian und die heutige Völkerkunde," *Ipek (Jahrb. für Prähist. und Ethnogr. Kunst)*, 1927, pp. 82–91.
Steinen, K. von, "Gedächtnisrede auf Adolf Bastian," *Zeitschrift für Ethnologie*, XXXVII (1905), pp. 386–392.

3. Main Publications

1860 *Der Mensch in der Geschichte. Zur Begründung einer psychologischen Welt-anschauung*, 3 vols. Vol. I: Die Psychologie als Naturwissenschaft; Vol. II: Psychologie und Mythologie; Vol. III: Politische Psychologie. Leipzig, Otto Wigand.
1866–1871 *Die Völker des östlichen Asien. Studien und Reisen*. 6 vols. Vols. 1–2: Leipzig, Otto Wigand; Vols. 3–6: Jena, Hermann Costenoble.
1881 *Der Völkergedanke im Aufbau einer Wissenschaft vom Menschen,und seine Begründung auf ethnologische Sammlungen*. Berlin.
1881 *Die Vorgeschichte der Ethnologie*. Berlin.
1883 *Zur naturwissenschaftlichen Behandlungsweise der Psychologie durch und für die Völkerkunde. Einige Abhandlungen*. Berlin.
1884 *Religions-philosophische Probleme auf dem Forschungsfelde buddhistischer Psychologie und der vergleichenden Mythologie* . Berlin.
1887 *Die Welt in ihren Spiegelungen unter dem Wandel des Völkergedankens. Prolegomena zu einer Gedankenstatistik*. Berlin.
1893 *Controversen in der Ethnologie*. Berlin.
1895 *Zur Lehre vom Menschen in ethnischer Antropologie*. 2 Abt. Berlin.
1895 *Ethnische Elementargedanken in der Lehre vom Menschen*. 2 Abt. Berlin.
1901 *Die Probleme humanistischer Fragestellungen und deren Beantwortungswei-sen unter den Zeichen der Zeit*. Berlin.

1901 *Die humanistischen Studien in ihrer Behandlungsweise nach comparativ-*
genetischer Methode auf naturwissenschaftlicher Unterlage. Prolegomena zu
einer ethnischen Psychologie. Berlin.
1901 *Der Menschheitsgedanke durch Raum und Zeit. Ein Beitrag zur Anthropologie*
und Ethnologie in der "Lehre vom Menschen". Berlin.
1909–1905 *Die Lehre vom Denken. Zur Ergänzung der naturwissenschaftlichen*
Psychologie in Anwendung auf die Geisteswissenschaften, 3 vols. Berlin

FERDINAND CHRISTIAN BAUR

1. Bibliography

Hodgson, Peter C., *The Formation of Historical Theology: A Study of Ferdinand*
Christian Baur. New York, Harper & Row, 1966, pp. 285–294.

2. Biography and Appreciation

Worte der Erinnerung an Ferdinand Christian von Baur. Adresses by Decan
Georgii and others. Tübingen, 1861.
Barnikol, Ernst, "Der Briefwechsel zwischen Strauss und Baur. Ein quellenmässi-
ger Beitrag zu Strauss — Baur — Forschung," *Zeitschrift für Kirchen-
geschichte.* Vol. 73 (1962), pp. 74–125.
Berger de Beaucourt, Samuel, *F. C. Baur. Les Origines de l'école de Tubingue et*
ses Principes, 1826–1844. Thèse. Strasbourg, 1867.
Boettger, Heinrich, *Baur's historische Kritik in ihrer Consequenz. Ein Beitrag zur*
Religionsgeschichte der ersten Jahrhunderte unserer Zeitrechnung, 3 vols.
1840–41.
Dietlein, W. O., *Das Urchristenthum. Eine Beleuchtung der von der Schule des Dr.*
von Baur über das apostolische Zeitalter aufgestellten Vermuthungen. Halle,
1845.
Fraedrich, G., *Ferdinand Christian Baur, der Begründer der Tübinger Schule, als*
Theologe, Schriftsteller und Charakter. Gotha, 1909.
Hodgson, Peter C., *The Formation of Historical Theology: A Study of Ferdinand*
Christian Baur (Makers of Modern Theology). New York, Harper & Row.
1966.
Hodgson, Peter C., *Ferdinand Christian Baur on the Writing of Church History.*
Edited and translated by Peter C. Hodgson. (Library of Protestant
Thought.) New York, Oxford University Press, 1968.
Schneider, Ernst, *Ferdinand Christian Baur in seiner Bedeutung für die Theologie.*
München, 1909.
Scholder, Klaus, "Ferdinand Christian Baur als Historiker," *Evangelische*
Theologie, XXI (1961), pp. 435–458.
Thiersch, H. W. J., *Einige Worte über die Aechtheit der neutestamentlichen Schrif-
ten und ihr Erweisbarkeit aus der ältesten Kirchengeschichte gegenüber den
Hypothesen der neuesten Kritiker.* Zur Erwiederung auf die Schrift des Dr.
F. C. Baur "Der Kritiker und der Fanatiker". Erlangen, 1846.
Troeltsch, Ernst, "Adolf von Harnack und Ferdinand Christ. Baur," in: *Fest-
gabe für A. von Harnack zum 70. Geburtstage.* Tübingen, 1921.

Weizsaecker, C. von, *Ferdinand Christian Baur.* Rede zur akademischen Feier seines 100. Geburtstages. Stuttgart, 1892.

Zeller, Edvard, "Die Tübinger historische Schule," in: Edvard Zeller, *Vorträge und Abhandlungen geschichtlichen Inhalts.* 1865, pp. 267–353.

3. Main Publications

1824 *Symbolik und Mythologie, oder die Naturreligion des Altertums,* 2 vols. Stuttgart, Metzler.

1831 *Das Manichäische Religionssystem nach den Quellen neu untersucht und entwickelt.* Tübingen, Osiander. Repr. Göttingen, Vandenhoeck & Ruprecht, 1928.

1832 *Apollonius von Tyana und Christus, oder das Verhältniss des Pythagoreismus zum Christentum.* Ein Beitrag zur Religionsgeschichte der ersten Jahrhunderte nach Christus. Tübingen, Fues. Repr. Hildesheim, G. Olms, 1966.

1834 *Der Gegensatz des Katholicismus und Protestantismus nach den Principien und Hauptdogmen der beiden Lehrbegriffe. Mit besonderer Rücksicht auf Herrn Dr. Möhler's Symbolik.* Tübingen, Fues. 1836² (enlarged).

1835 *Die christliche Gnosis, oder die christliche Religionsphilosophie in ihrer geschichtlichen Entwicklung.* Tübingen, Osiander.

1835 *Die sogenannten Pastoralbriefe des Apostels Paulus aufs neue kritisch untersucht.* Stuttgart und Tübingen, Cotta.

1838 *Die christliche Lehre von der Versöhnung in ihrer geschichtlichen Entwicklung von der ältesten Zeit bis auf die neueste.* Tübingen, Osiander.

1838 *Ueber den Ursprung des Episcopats in der christlichen Kirche. Prüfung der neuestens von Hrn. Dr. Rothe aufgestellten Ansicht.* Tübingen, Fues.

1841 *Die christliche Lehre von der Dreieinigkeit und Menschwerdung Gottes in ihrer geschichtlichen Entwicklung,* 3 vols. Tübingen, Osiander.

1845 *Paulus, der Apostel Jesu Christi. Sein Leben und Wirken, seine Briefe und seine Lehre. Ein Beitrag zu einer kritischen Geschichte des Urchristenthums.* Stuttgart, Becher & Müller. Zweite Auflage besorgt von Dr. E. Zeller, 2 vols. Leipzig, Fues, 1866–1867.
English translation of the second German edition: *Paul the Apostle of Jesus Christ. His Life and Works, his Epistles and Teachings. A Contribution to a Critical History of Primitive Christianity,* 2 vols. London–Edinburgh, Williams & Norgate, 1873–1875.

1847 *Kritische Untersuchungen über die kanonischen Evangelien, ihr Verhältniss zu einander, ihren Charakter und Ursprung.* Tübingen, Fues.

1847 *Lehrbuch der christlichen Dogmengeschichte.* Stuttgart, Becher; Tübingen, Fues, 1858² (enlarged); Leipzig, Fues, 1867³.

1851 *Das Markusevangelium nach seinem Ursprung und Character. Nebst einem Anhang über das Evangelium Marcion's.* Tübingen, Fues.

1852 *Die Epochen der kirchlichen Geschichtschreibung.* Tübingen, Fues. Repr. Hildesheim, G. Olms, 1962.

1853–1863 *Geschichte der christlichen Kirche,* 5 vols. Leipzig, Fues. 1863–1877².
1. *Kirchengeschichte der drei ersten Jahrhunderte.* [*Das Christentum und die christliche Kirche der ersten drei Jahrhunderte*]. 1852; 1853²; 1863³.
English translation by Rev. Allan Menzies: *The Church History of the First Three Centuries,* 2 vols. London–Edinburgh, Williams & Norgate, 1878.

2. *Die christliche Kirche vom Anfang des vierten bis zum Ende des sechsten Jahrhunderts in den Hauptmomenten ihrer Entwicklung.* 1859; 1863².
3. *Die christliche Kirche des Mittelalters in den Hauptmomenten ihrer Entwicklung.* Herausg. von F. F. Baur. 1861; 1869².
4. *Kirchengeschichte der neueren Zeit, von der Reformation bis zum Ende des achtzehnten Jahrhunderts.* Herausg. von F. F. Baur. 1863.
5. *Kirchengeschichte des neunzehnten Jahrhunderts.* Herausg. von Ed. Zeller. 1862; 1877².

1859 *Die Tübinger Schule und ihre Stellung zur Gegenwart.* Tübingen, Fues. 1860².
1864 *Vorlesungen über Neutestamentliche Theologie.* Herausg. von F. F. Baur. Leipzig, Fues. Neue Ausgabe, mit einer Einleitung von D. Otto Pfleiderer, 2 vols. (Bibliothek theologischer Klassiker. Vol. 45, 46). Gotha, 1892.
1865–1867 *Vorlesungen über die christliche Dogmengeschichte*, 3 vols. Herausg. von F. F. Bauer. Leipzig, Fues.
1963–1966 *Ausgewählte Werke in Einzelausgaben*, 3 vols. Stuttgart — Bad Cannstatt, Frommann.

RUTH FULTON BENEDICT

Main Publications

1923 *The Concept of the Guardian Spirit in North America.* Menasha, Wis., Amer. Anthrop. Assoc., 1923. Repr. New York, Kraus Reprint Corp., 1964.
1931 *Tales of the Cochiti Indians.* Washington, U. S. Government Printing Office.
1934 *Patterns of Culture.* Boston–New York, Houghton Mifflin Company, 1934; New York, Penguin Books, 1946; New York, New Amer. Library, 1946, 1956¹³; Mentor Books, MD 89; With an introduction by Franz Boas and a new preface by Margaret Mead: New York, New. Amer. Library, 1959; 2nd ed.: Cambridge, Houghton Mifflin, 1961. London, G. Routledge, 1935, 1945, 1961.
1935 *Zuni Mythology.* New York, Columbia University Press.
1942 *Race and cultural relations: America's answer to the myth of a master race.* Analysis by Ruth Benedict . . . teaching aids by Mildred Ellis. Washington D. C., Nat. Council for the Social Studies, etc. 1949².
1942 *Race and Racism.* London, Routledge. Reprinted.
1943 *The Races of Mankind*, by Ruth Benedict and Gene Weltfish. New York, Public Affaires Committee. 1953¹⁵.
1959 *Race: Science and Politics.* (Including: *The Races of Mankind*). New York, Viking Press.
1959 *An Anthropologist at Work: Writings of Ruth Benedict.* Edited by Margaret Mead. Boston, Houghton Mifflin; London, Secker & Warburg. New York, Atherton Press, 1966.
1967 *The Chrysanthemum and the Sword: Patterns of Japanese Culture.* London, Routledge & Kegan Paul.

GASTON BERGER*

1. Bibliography

Varet, Gilbert, "Bibliographie de Gaston Berger," *Les Etudes Philosophiques,*
N. S. XVI, 4 (1961), pp. 419–434.

2. Biography and Appreciation

Bayen, Maurice, "Gaston Berger (1896–1960)," *Revue de l'Enseignement Supérieur,* 1960, Nr. 4, pp. 5–12.

Delorme, Suzanne, "In memoriam Gaston Berger (1896–1960)," *Revue de Synthèse,* 3e Série, Nr. 19–20 (Série générale: Tome LXXXI), juillet–décembre 1960, pp. 217–222.

Delpech, L. J., "Adieu á Gaston Berger," *Revue de la Méditerranée,* 1961.

—, "Gaston Berger, philosophe, homme d'action," *La Revue des Deux Mondes,* janvier 1968, pp. 117–132.

Les Etudes Philosophiques. Special iussue 'Gaston Berger', N. S., XVI, 4 (1961).
Of the contributions may be mentioned:
Duméry, Henry, "La théorique," pp. 349–362;
Lacroze, René, "Gaston Berger devant le mystère du temps," pp. 317 326;
Mesnard, Pierre, "Gaston Berger et la caractérologie," pp. 327–338;
Moreau, Joseph, "Sagesse de Gaston Berger," pp. 339–349;
Morot-Sir, Edouard, "Ascèse philosophique et amitié selon Gaston Berger," pp. 311–316;
Mucchielli, Roger, "La philosophie et la vie," pp. 363–378;
Tournier, Gilbert, "Gaston Berger et la prospective," pp. 379–388.

Ginesty, B., *Prospective spirituelle et engagement prospectif. Essai pour une lecture de Gaston Berger.* Paris, Ed. Ouvrières, 1966.

Gouhier, Henri, *Notice sur la vie et les travaux de Gaston Berger.* Institut de France, Académie des Sciences Morales et Politiques, 1962.

Guy, Alain, "El spiritualismo fenomenólogico de Gaston Berger," *Revista de Filosofía,* April–September 1960, pp. 169–183.

Prospective (Paris). Special issue 'Gaston Berger, un philosophe dans le monde moderne,' Nr. 7 (avril 1961). Of the contributions may be mentioned:
Bourbon–Busset, Jacques de, "Gaston Berger," pp. 5–8;
Delpech, Léon, "Maurice Blondel et Gaston Berger. Les courants précurseurs et la Prospective," pp. 17–28;
Morot-Sir, Edouard, "René Le Senne et Gaston Berger," pp. 9–16.

Rossi, F., *Discorso metafisico di Gaston Berger.* Parma, Casa editrice Maccari, 1970, 114 p.

3. Method and Theory

1941 *Recherches sur les conditions de la connaissance. Essai d'une théorique pure.* Paris, P. U. F.

1957 "Avant-Propos" to the section "Philosophie," *Encyclopédie Française,* Vol. XIX, "Philosophie et Religion," Paris, Larousse, pp. 1902.5–1902.8.

1957 "Avant-Propos" to the section "Religion," *Encyclopédie Française*, Vol. XIX, "Philosophie et Religion," Paris, Larousse, pp. 1932.1–1932.4.
1964 "La méthode phénoménologique," in: Gaston Berger, *Phénoménologie du temps et prospective*. Paris, P. U. F., pp. 1–67.

4. Main Publications

1939 "Husserl et Hume," *Revue Internationale de Philosophie*, I (1939), pp. 342–353.
1941 *Le Cogito chez Husserl*. Paris, Aubier.
1941 "Le progrès de la réflexion chez Bergson et chez Husserl," in: *Hommage à Bergson*. Neuchâtel, La Baconnière. 1950².
1944 "Les thèmes principaux de la phénoménologie de Husserl," *Etudes de Métaphysique et de Morale*, 1944, pp. 23–43.
1946 "The different trends of contemporary French philosophy," *Philosophy and Phenomenological Research*, VII, 1 (1946), pp. 1–11.
1950 *Traité pratique d'analyse du caractère*. Paris, P. U. F., 1955³.
1950 "Expérience et transcendance," in: Marvin Farber, ed., *L'activité philosophique en France et aux Etats Unis*. Vol. II: *La philosophie française*. Paris, P. U. F., pp. 96–112.
   English translation: "Experience and Transcendence," in the English edition of this book: *Philosophic Thought in France and the United States*. New York, University of Buffalo Press, 1950.
1950 "Quelques aspects phénoménologiques du temps," *Bulletin de la Société Française de Philosophie*, XLIV (1950), pp. 89–132.
1950 "Psychology in France," *French Bibliographical Digest*. New York, Ambassade de France, Services culturels.
1954 *Caractère et personnalité*. Paris, P. U. F. 1956².
1954 "L'originalité de la phénoménologie," *Etudes Philosophiques*, IX, 3 (1954), pp. 249–259.
1957 "La phénoménologie transcendentale," *Encyclopédie Française*, Vol. XIX, Paris, Larousse, pp. 1910.06–1910.08.
1957 "La vie mystique," *Encyclopédie Française*, Vol. XIX, Paris, Larousse, pp. 1936.10–1936.15. Reprinted in: *Prospective* (Paris), Nr. 7 (avril 1961), pp. 113–130.
1958 "Préface. L'attitude prospective," *Prospective* (Paris), I (mai 1958).
1959 "L'attitude prospective," *Encyclopédie Française*, Vol. XX, Paris, Larousse, pp. 2054.12–2054.14.
1961 "Textes de Gaston Berger," *Prospective* (Paris), Nr. 7 (avril 1961), pp. 31–152.
1962 *L'homme moderne et son éducation*. Paris, P. U. F.
1964 *Phénoménologie du temps et prospective*. Paris, P. U. F.

ALFRED BERTHOLET

1. Bibliography

Tamann-Bertholet, Verena, "Bibliographie A. Bertholet," in *Festschrift Alfred Bertholet zum 80. Geburtstag gewidmet.* Herausg. von Walter Baumgartner, Otto Eisfeldt, Karl Elliger und Leonard Rost. Tübingen, Mohr, 1950, pp. 564–578.

2. Main Publications

1896 *Die Stellung der Israeliten und der Juden zu den Fremden.* Freiberg i. B. – Leipzig, Mohr.

1902 *Buddhismus und Christentum.* (Sammlung gem. Vorträge, 28). Tübingen–Leipzig, Mohr. 1909².

1904 *Seelenwanderung.* (Religionsgeschichtliche Volksbücher III, 2). Halle a. d. S., Gebauer und Schwetschke; Tübingen, Mohr, 1909².
Englisch translation by H. I. Chaytor: *The Transmigration of Souls.* London– New York, Harper and Brothers, 1909.

1908 *Religionsgeschichtliches Lesebuch.* Ed. by Alfred Bertholet (in coll.). Tübingen, Mohr. 1926², etc.

1910 *Das Ende des jüdischen Staatswesens.* Sechs populäre Vorträge. Tübingen, Mohr.

1911 *Die jüdische Religion von der Zeit Esras bis zum Zeitalter Christi,* Zweiter Band in: *Biblische Theologie des Alten Testaments.* Hrsg. von B. Stade. Tübingen, Mohr.

1913 *Die Eigenart der alttestamentlichen Religion.* Eine akademische Antrittsrede. Tübingen, Mohr.

1918 "Über den Ursprung des Totemismus," in: *Festgabe für Julius Kaftan zu seinem 70. Geburtstag am 30. September 1918.* Tübingen, Mohr. pp. 1–14.

1919 *Kulturgeschichte Israels.* Göttingen, Vandenhoeck und Ruprecht.
English translation by A. K. Dallas: *A History of Hebrew Civilization.* New York, Brentano's, 1919; London–Calcutta–Sydney, G. G. Harrap and Comp., 1926.

1923 *Der Beitrag des Alten Testamentes zur Allgemeinen Religionsgeschichte.* (Sammlung gem. Vorträge, 106). Tübingen, Mohr.

1924 *Kultur und Religion.* Festrede. Göttingen, Dieterische Universitäts-Buchdruckerei.

1924–1925 *Lehrbuch der Religionsgeschichte,* by A. Bertholet and Ed. Lehmann. eds., 2 vols. Begründet von Chantepie de la Saussaye. Tübingen, Mohr.

1926 *Das Dynamistische im Alten Testament.* (Sammlung gem. Vorträge, 121), Tübingen, Mohr.

1927 "Das Wesen der Magie," in: *Nachrichten der k. Gesellschaft der Wissenschaften zu Göttingen, Geschäftl. Mitteilungen,* pp. 1–23.

1929 "Über Gemination von Kultriten. Ein Beitrag zur Unterscheidung von Religion und Magie," in: *Reinhold Seeberg-Festschrift 1929,* II, pp. 157–167. Leipzig, A. Deichert.

1933 *Götterspaltung und Göttervereinigung.* (Sammlung gem. Vorträge, 164). Tübingen, Mohr.

1934 *Das Geschlecht der Gottheit.* (Sammlung gem. Vorträge, 173). Tübingen, Mohr.
1938 "Über kultische Motivverschiebungen," *Sitzungsberichte der Preusz. Akad. der Wissensch., Phil.-hist. Klasse* XVIII (Berlin), pp. 164–184.
1940 "Wortanklang und Volksetymologie in ihrer Wirkung auf religiösen Glauben und Brauch," *Abhandlungen der Preusz. Akademie, Phil.-hist Klasse* (Berlin), 1940, Nr. 6.
1942 "Der Sinn des Kultischen Opfers," *Abhandlungen der Preusz. Akademie, Phil.-hist. Klasse* (Berlin). 1942, Nr. 2.
1948 "Religionsgeschichtliche Ambivalenzerscheinungen," *Theologische Zeitschrift* (Basel), IV (1948), pp. 1–16.
1949 *Die Macht der Schrift im Glauben und Aberglauben,* (Abhandlungen der Deutschen Akademie der Wissenschaften zu Berlin, Phil.-hist. Klasse, 1949, Nr. 1) Berlin, Akademie-Verlag.
1952 *Wörterbuch der Religionen.* In Verbindung mit Hans Freiherr von Campenhausen. Stuttgart, A. Kröner.
1953 *Grundformen der Erscheinungswelt der Gottesverehrung.* Eine nachgelassene Vorlesung, gehalten an der Universität Basel. Für den Druck durchgesehen von Johannen Hempel. Tübingen, Mohr.

KARL BETH

1. Bibliography

Schneider, Erwin, "Bibliographie Karl Beths," *Theologische Literaturzeitung,* 78. Jg. (1953), pp. 698–704.

2. Biography and Appreciation

Schneider, Erwin, "Das Lebenswerk Karl Beths," *Theologische Literaturzeitung,* 78. Jg. (1953), pp. 695–698.

3. Main Publications

1904 *Das Wesen des Christentums und die moderne historische Denkweise.* Leipzig.
1908 *Das Wunder.* Prinzipielle Erörterung des Problems (Biblische Zeit- und Streitfragen, Reihe IV, Heft 5). Berlin.
1913 *Die Entwicklung des Christentums zur Universalreligion.* Leipzig, Quelle und Meyer.
1914 *Religion und Magie bei den Naturvölkern. Ein religionsgeschichtlicher Beitrag zur Frage nach den Anfängen der Religion.* Leipzig–Berlin, B. G. Teubner.
      Second edition: *Religion und Magie bei den Naturvölkern. Ein religionsgeschichtlicher Beitrag zur psychologischen Grundlegung der religiösen Prinzipienlehre.* 2. umgearbeite Auflage. Leipzig–Berlin, B. G. Teubner. 1927.

1916 *Die Urreligion.* (Biblische Zeit- und Streitfragen, Reihe XI, Heft 3). Berlin. 1917².
1920 *Einführung in die vergleichende Religionsgeschichte.* Leipzig–Berlin, B. G. Teubner.

FRANZ BOAS

1. Bibliography

Edel, Bertha C., "Bibliography of Franz Boas," *American Anthropologist,* Vol. 45, No. 3, Part 2 (July—September, 1943), pp. 67—109.

2. Biography and Appreciation

American Anthropologist. Special issue *"Franz Boas 1858–1942,"* Vol. 45, No. 3, Part 2 (July—September, 1943). With contributions by Ruth Benedict, Murray B. Emenau, Melville J. Herskovits, A. L. Kroeber, J. Alden Mason, Gladys A. Reichard.
American Anthropologist. "Franz Boas and Anthropology," *American Anthropologist,* Vol. 58 (1956), pp. 63–74, 151–170.
Herskovits, Melville Jean, *Franz Boas. The science of Man in the Making.* New York, Scribner's Sons, 1953.
Kroeber, A. L., R. Benedict, and others, *Franz Boas, 1858–1942.* (Memoires of the American Anthrop. Assoc. No. 61). Menasha, Wisc., 1943.
Lowie, Robert H., "Franz Boas, 1858–1942," in: Robert H. Lowie, *Selected Papers in Anthropology* (1960), pp. 425–440.
Goldschmidt, Walter Rochs, ed., *The Anthropology of Franz Boas: essays on the centennial of his birth.* (Amer. Anthrop. Assoc.) Menasha, Wisc., 1959.
White, Leslie A., *The Ethnography and Ethnology of Franz Boas.* Austin, Texas Memorial Museum (Mus. of the Univ. of Texas), 1963.

3. Main Publications

1881 "The Central Eskimo," in: *Sixth Annual Report. Bureau of Ethnology.* Washington, D. C., Smithsonian Institution.
1900 "The Mythology of the Bella Coola Indians," in: "Publications of the Jesup North Pacific Expedition, vol. 1," in: *Memories of the American Museum of Natural History.* Vol. 2.
1906 *The Measurement of Variable Quantities.* (Archives of Philosophy, Psychology and Scientific Methods. No. 5). New York.
1911 *The Mind of Primitive Man* . . . A course of lectures. New York, Macmillan; 1938². (revised).
1911–1938 *Handbook of American Indian Languages,* by F. Boas and others. (Smithsonian Institution. Bureau of American Ethnology, Bulletin Nr. 40). Part 1 and 2: Washington, 1911, 1922; Part 3: ed. by F. Boas. New York, J. J. Augustin, 1933–1938.

1916 "The origin of totemism," *American Anthropologist*, XVIII, pp. 319–326.
1927 *Primitive Art*. Oslo.
1929 *Anthropology and Modern Life*. London, Allen and Unwin.
1930 *The Religion of the Kwakiutl Indians*. (1: Texts; 2: Translations). New York, Columbia University Press.
1935 *Kwakiutl Culture as reflected in Mythology*. New York.
1938 *General Anthropology*. Ed. by F. Boas. Boston, Heath.
1940 *Race, Language and Culture*. New York, Macmillan.

WILHELM BOUSSET

1. Biography and Appreciation

Gunkel, J. F. H., "Wilhelm Bousset. Gedächtnisrede," in: *Evangel. Freih.*, 1920 Nr. 20, pp. 141ff.

2. Main Publications

1892 *Jesu Predigt in ihrem Gegensatz zum Judentum. Ein religionsgeschichtlicher Vergleich*. Göttingen, Vandenhoeck und Ruprecht.
1894 *Textkritische Studien zum Neuen Testament*. Leipzig, J. C. Hinrichs.
1895 *Der Antichrist in der Überlieferung des Judentums, des Neuen Testaments und der alten Kirche. Ein Beitrag zur Auslegung der Apokalypse*. Göttingen, Vandenhoeck und Ruprecht.
   English translation and a prologue on the Babylonian dragon myth by A. H. Keane: *The Antichristlegend: a chapter in Christian and Jewish folklore*. London, 1896.
1903 *Volksfrömigkeit und Schriftgelehrtentum*. Antwort auf Herrn Perles' Kritik meiner "Religion des Judentums im N. T. Zeitalter". Berlin, Reuther und Reichard.
1903 *Die Religion des Judentums im neutestamentlichen Zeitalter*. Berlin, Reuther und Reichard 1903, 1906². 3. Aufl. hrsg. von Hugo Gressmann. Tübingen, Mohr, 1926.
1903 *Das Wesen der Religion dargestellt an ihrer Geschichte*. Halle a. d. S. Gebauer; Tübingen, Mohr, 1920⁴.
   English translation by F. B. Low: *What is Religion?* London, T. F. Unwin, 1907.
1905 *Jesus*. Halle a. d. Saale, Gebauer—Schwetschke; Tübingen, Mohr, 1907³, 1922⁴.
   English translation by Janet Penrose Trevelyan: *Jesus*. London, Williams and Norgate, 1906; New York, G. P. Putnam's Sons, 1906; London, New York, 1911².
1907 *Hauptprobleme der Gnosis*. Göttingen, Vandenhoeck und Ruprecht.
1912 *Religion und Geschichte*. Groningen, J. B. Wolters.
1913 *Kyrios Christos. Geschichte des Christusglaubens von den Anfängen des Christentums bis Irenaeus*. Göttingen, Vandenhoeck und Ruprecht. 1965⁵.

1915 *Jüdisch-christlicher Schulbetrieb in Alexandria und Rom.* Literarische Untersuchungen zu Philo und Clemens von Alexandria, Justin und Irenaeus. Göttingen, Vandenhoeck und Ruprecht.
1916 *Jesus der Herr.* Nachträge und Auseinandersetzungen zu Kyrios Christos. Göttingen, Vandenhoeck und Ruprecht.
1923 *Apophtegmata.* Studien zur Geschichte des Aeltesten Mönchtums.Tübingen, Mohr.

KURT BREYSIG

1. Bibliography

Knoll, Samson B., *Kurt Breysig. A Bibliographical Outline.* 1958.
"Bibliographie," in: *Geist und Gesellschaft. Festschrift Kurt Breysig*, 3 Vols. Breslau, 1927–28.

2. Biography and Appreciation

Breysig, Gertrud, *Kurt Breysig. Ein Bild des Menschen.* Heidelberg, Lothar Stiehm Verlag, 1967.
Breysig, Kurt, *Aus meinen Tagen und Träumen. Memoiren, Aufzeichnungen, Briefe, Gespräche.* Aus dem Nachlass herausgegeben von Gertrud Breysig und Michael Landmann. Berlin, 1962.
Ehrenreich, Paul M. A., "Götter und Heilbringer. Eine ethnologische Kritik," *Zeitschrift für Ethnologie*, Vol. 38 (1906), pp. 536–610.
Hering, Ernst, *Das Werden als Geschichte. Karl Breysig in seinem Werk.* Berlin, 1939.
Schilling, Friedrich, "Werkschau Kurt Breysigs," in: *Geist und Gesellschaft. Festschrift Kurt Breysig*, Vol. III, Breslau, 1928.

3. Main Publications

1900–1901 *Kulturgeschichte der Neuzeit*, Vols. 1 + 2.
1905 *Der Stufen-Bau und die Gesetze der Welt-Geschichte.* Berlin, 1927². Shortened version: *Der Stufenbau der Weltgeschichte*, 1950.
1905 *Die Entstehung des Gottesgedankens und der Heilbringer.* Berlin.
1907–1955 *Die Geschichte der Menschheit.* Berlin. Complete edition in five volumes in 1955, with a preface by Arnold J. Toynbee.
1925–1928 *Vom geschichtlichen Werden*, 3 Vols. Stuttgart. Vol. I: *Persönlichkeit und Entwicklung* (1925); Vol. II: *Die Macht des Gedankens in der Geschichte* (1926); Vol. III: *Der Weg der Menschheit* (1928).
1927 *Eindruckskunst und Ausdruckskunst.*
1931 *Der Aufbau der Persönlichkeit von Kant. Aufgezeigt an seinem Werke. Ein Versuch zur Seelenkunde des Gelehrten.* Stuttgart–Berlin, 1931.
1933 *Naturgeschichte und Menschheitsgeschichte.*
1935 *Vom Naturgeschehen zum Geistgeschehen.*

1935–1944 *Vom Sein und Erkennen geschichtlicher Dinge*, 4 Vols. Berlin. Vol. I:
Psychologie der Geschichte (1935); Vol. II: *Die Meister der entwickelnden
Geschichtsforschung* (1936); Vol. III: *Gestaltungen des Entwicklungsgedankens*
(1940); Vol. IV: *Das neue Geschichtsbild im Sinne der entwickelnden Geschichtsforschung* (1944).
1958 *Gesellschaftslehre. Geschichtslehre.* Vorwort von Gertrud Breysig. Berlin.
1964 *Gedankenblätter.* Berlin, Walter de Gruyter & Co.

CHARLES DE BROSSES

1. Bibliography

Florenne, Yves, *Le Président de Brosses*. Paris, 1964.
Pilon, Edmond, "Bibliographie de Charles de Brosses" in: *Le président de Brosses
en Italie: Lettres familières écrites d'Italie en 1739 et 1740*. Paris, Les Arts
et Le Livre, 1928.

2. Biography and Appreciation

Lettres familières écrites d'Italie en 1739 et 1740 par Charles de Brosses. 2e éd.
authentique, revue sur les manuscripts, annotée et précédée d'un Essai
sur la vie et les écrits de l'auteur par R. Colomb, Paris, 1861. 2. Vols.,
3e éd. . . . précédée d'une étude biographique par R. Colomb. Paris:
Didier et Cie., 1869. 2 Vols.; Paris, Perrin et Cie., 1904[5]. 2 Vols.

3. Main Publications

1741 *Histoire des navigations aux Terres Australes*. Paris, Durand. 1756[2].
English translation Anonymus. Paris, Durand, 1756.
Second *English* translation with additions by John Callander: *Terra Australis Cognita*. Or, Voyages to the Terra australis, or Southern hemisphere,
during the sixteenth, seventeenth, and eighteenth centuries. Printed for
the author, and sold by Hawes, Clark and Collins, London, 1766–1768,
3 vols. *A collection of voyages to the Southern hemisphere*, London, 1788.
1760 *Du culte des dieux fétiches.* Ou parallèle de l'ancienne religion de l'Egypte
avec la religion actuelle de Nigritie. Paris.

PETER H. BUCK (TE RAN GI-HIROA)

1. Biography and Appreciation

Elkin, A. P., "Obituary," *Oceania* 22 (1951/52), pp. 162–163.

2. Main Publications

1930 *The Coming of the Maori*. New Plymouth; Wellington, 1949 (Produced by the Department of Internal Affairs, New Zealand).

1936 *Reginal Diversity in the Elaboration of Sorcery in Polynesia*. (Yale University Publications in Anthropology. No. 2). New Haven (Conn.)

1938 *Vikings of the Sunrise*. New York, Stokes; New Zealand Edition: Christchurch, Whitcombe & Tombs, 1954; Chicago, 1959 (Phoenix Books No. F. 31); 1967[4].

1939 *Anthropology and Religion*. (The Terry Lectures). New Haven, Yale University Press; Honolulu.

C

JEAN-FRANÇOIS CHAMPOLLION

1. Bibliography

Ricci, Seymour de, "Essay de bibliographie de Champollion le jeune", *Sciences historiques et philologiques*, fasc. 234. (Bibliothèque de l'École des Hautes Etudes). Paris, 1922.

2. Biography and Appreciation

Brière, L. de la, *Champollion inconnu. Lettres inédites*. Paris, E. Plon, Nourrit et Cie, 1897.

Champollion-Figeac, Aimé-Louis, *Les deux Champollion*. Leur vie et leurs œuvres, etc. Grenoble, 1887.

Hartleben, H., *Champollion. Sein Leben und sein Werk*, 2 vols. Berlin, Weidmann, 1906.

Silvestre de Sacy, A. I. Baron, *Notice sur la vie et les ouvrages de M. Champollion le jeune*. Paris, 1833.

3. Main Publications

1814 *L'Egypte sous les Pharaons*. Ou recherches sur la géographie, la religion, la langue, les écritures de l'histoire de l'Egypte avant l'invasion de Cambyse, 2 vols. Paris.

1822 *Lettre à M. Dacier* . . . relative à l'alphabet des hiéroglyphes phonétiques employés par les Egyptiens pour inscrire sur leurs monuments les titres, les noms et les surnoms des souverains grecs et romains. Paris.

1823–1825 *Panthéon égyptien*. Collection des personnages mythologiques de l'ancienne Egypte, d'après les monuments; avec un texte explicatif par M. J. F. Champollion le jeune, et les figures d'après les dessins de M. L. J. J. Dubois. Livres 1–15. Paris.

1824 *Précis du système hiéroglyphique des anciens Egyptiens*. Ou recherches sur les éléments premiers de cette écriture sacrée, sur leurs diverses combinaisons, et sur les rapports de ce système avec les autres méthodes graphiques égyptiennes, 2 vols. Paris. Seconde éd., revue par l'auteur, et augmentée de la lettre à M. Dacier, 2 vols. Paris.

1835–1846 *Monuments de l'Egypte et de la Nubie*. D'après les dessins exécutés sur les lieux sous la direction de Champollion-le-jeune, et les descriptions autographes qu'il en a rédigées. Ed. by J. J. Champollion-Figeac. 4 vols. Paris.

1836 *Grammaire égyptienne.* Ou principes généraux de l'écriture sacrée égyptienne appliquée à la représentation de la langue parlée. Ed. with a preface by J. J. Champollion-Figeac. Paris.

1841 *Dictionnaire égyptienne en écriture hiéroglyphique.* Publié d'après les manuscrits autographes .... par M. Champollion-Figeac. Paris.

1844–1847 *Monuments de l'Egypte et de la Nubie.* Notices descriptives conformes aux manuscrits autographes rédigés sur les lieux par Champollion le jeune, 2 vols. Vol. 1 ed. by J. J. Champollion-Figeac; Vol. 2 ed. by Viscount O. C. C. E. de Rougé. Paris.

PIERRE DANIËL CHANTEPIE DE LA SAUSSAYE*

1. Bibliography

See H. W. Obbink, "Pierre Daniël Chantepie de la Saussaye (1848–1920)," in: *Ernst en Vrede.* Opstellen rondom de ethische theologie, aangeboden aan Prof. Dr. M. van Rhijn op 15 November 1951. The Hague, Boekencentrum, 1951, pp. 100–120.

2. Bibliography and Appreciation

Kraemer, H., "In memoriam Prof. Dr. P. D. Chantepie de la Saussaye, 9 April 1848–19 April 1920," *Minerva* (Algemeen Nederlandsch Studenten-Weekblad), Vol. 46, Nr. 23 (29 April 1920), pp. 279–280.

Kuiper, K., "Levensbericht van Pierre Daniel Chantepie de la Saussaye, 9 April 1848–20 April 1920," in: *Jaarboek der Koninklijke Akademie van Wetenschappen,* 1920–1921, pp. 103–128.

Nes, H. M. van, "Levensbericht van Pierre Daniël Chantepie de la Saussaye, 9 April 1848–20 April 1920," in: *Handelingen van de Maatschappij der Nederlandsche Letterkunde te Leiden en Levensberichten harer afgestorven medeleden,* 1920–1921, pp. 68–85.

Obbink, H. W., "Pierre Daniël Chantepie de la Saussaye (1848–1920)," in: *Ernst en Vrede.* Opstellen rondom de ethische theologie, aangeboden aan Prof. Dr. M. van Rhijn op 15 November 1951. The Hague, Boekencentrum, 1951, pp. 100–120.

Roessingh, K. H., "In memoriam Pierre Daniël Chantepie de la Saussaye," in K. H. Roessingh, *Verzamelde Werken,* edited by G. J. Heering, vol. II. Arnhem, Van Loghum Slaterus, 1926, pp. 459–471 (First published in *Onze Eeuw,* 1920).

3. Method and Theory

1871 *Methodologische bijdrage tot het onderzoek naar den oorsprong van den godsdienst* (Diss.). Utrecht.

1878 *Het belang van de studie der godsdiensten voor de kennis van het Christendom* (Inaugural Address, Amsterdam). Groningen, P. Noordhoff.
1885 "Mythologie en folklore," *De Gids*, XLIX (August 1885), pp. 213–242.
1891 "Max Müller als Gifford-Lecturer," *De Gids*, LV (May 1891), pp. 262–272. Reprinted in: P. D. Chantepie de la Saussaye, *Portretten en Kritieken*. Haarlem, F. Bohn, pp. 230–242.
1897 *Die vergleichende Religionsforschung und der religiöse Glaube*. Vortrag gehalten auf dem ersten religionswissenschaftlichen Kongress in Stockholm, 1897. Freiburg i. B., 1898. Reprinted in: P. D. Chantepie de la Saussaye, *Portretten en Kritieken*. Haarlem, F. Bohn, 1909, pp. 337–367.
1899 *De taak der Theologie* (Inaugural Address, Leiden). Haarlem, F. Bohn.
1902 "Levensbericht Cornelis Petrus Tiele," *Jaarboek der Koninklijke Akademie van Wetenschappen*, 1902, pp. 125–154. Reprinted in: P. D. Chantepie de la Saussaye, *Portretten en Kritieken*. Haarlem, F. Bohn, 1909, pp. 82–120.
1907 *Geestelijke Stromingen*, Haarlem, F. Bohn. See the following papers: "De godsdienst der wetenschap" (pp. 243–269), "Het evolutiegeloof" (pp. 270–303), "Het absolute" (pp. 304–345).
1913 "De absoluutheid des Christendoms," *Eltheto*, LXVIII (1913), pp. 1–6.

4. Main Publications

1883 *Vier schetsen uit de godsdienstgeschiedenis*. Utrecht, Breyer.
1887–1889 *Lehrbuch der Religionsgeschichte* ("Sammlung Theologischer Lehrbücher"). 2 vols. Freiburg i. Br. Chantepie de la Saussaye was the author of this first edition; he was the editor with a number of collaborators of the second and third editions of the *Lehrbuch der Religionsgeschichte*. Freiburg i. Br., 1897², 1905³.
English translation of the first German edition by Beatrice S. Colyer-Fergusson: *Manual of the Science of Religion*. London and New York, Longmans, Green & Co., 1891.
French translation: *Manuel d'Histoire des Religions*. Introduction by Henry Hubert. Paris, 1904.
1892 *Germaansche cosmogonieën*. Verslagen en Mededeelingen der Koninklijke Akademie van Wetenschappen, Afd. Letterkunde, 3ᵉ reeks, deel VIII (1892), pp. 336–364.
1900 *Geschiedenis van den godsdienst der Germanen vòòr hun overgang tot het Christendom*. Haarlem.
English translation by Bert J. Vos: *The Religion of the Teutons*. Boston and London, Given & Co., 1902 (considerably expanded).
1907 *Geestelijke Stroomingen. Verzamelde voordrachten en opstellen*. Haarlem, Bohn. 1914².
1908 *Tijd en Eeuwigheid*. Haarlem, Bohn.
1909 *Portretten en Kritieken*. Haarlem, Bohn.
1910–1912 *Het Christelijk leven*, 2 vols. Haarlem, Bohn. 1913²; the third edition, which appeared posthumously, was edited by K. H. Roessingh: 2 vols., Haarlem, Bohn, 1922–1923³.

ARTHUR EMANUEL CHRISTENSEN

1. Bibliography, Biography and Appreciation

Barr, K., and Andersen, H., "A. Christensen" (pp. 65–82) and "Fortegnelse over trykte Arbejder af Arthur Christensen" (pp. 83–101), *Oversigt over Det Kongelige Danske Videnskabernes Selskab. Forhandlingar*, (København) 1945/46, pp. 65–101.

2. Main Publications

1905 *Recherches sur les Rubā'iyāt de 'Omar Hayyām*. Heidelberg, C. Winter.

1907 *L'Empire des Sassanides, le peuple, l'état, la cour*. København, B. Lunos.

1917–1934 *Le premier homme et le premier roi dans l'histoire légendaire des Iraniens*, 2. Vols. Stockholm, P. A. Norstedt og söner.

1925 *Le règne du roi Kawādh I et le communisme mazdakite*. København, Høst og søn.

1927 *Critical studies in the Rubā'iyāt of 'Umar-i-Kkayyám*. A revised text with English translation. København.

1028 *Etudes sur le Zoroastrisme de la Perse antique*. København, Høst og søn.

1931 *Les Kayanides*. København, Høst og søn.

1936 *Les gestes des rois dans les traditions de l'Iran antique*. Paris, P. Geuthner.

1936 *L'Iran sous les Sassanides*. København, Levin og Munksgaard; Paris, P. Geuthner, 1936; København, E. Munksgaard, 1944² (revised).

1937 *Kulturskitser fra Iran*. København, Levin og Munksgaard.

1941 *Essai sur la démonologie iranienne*. København, Munksgaard.

1943 *Le premier chapitre du Vendidad et l'histoire primitive des tribus iraniennes*. København, Munksgaard.

CARL CHRISTIAN CLEMEN

Main Publications

1904 *Paulus, sein Leben und Werken*. Giessen, J. Ricker.

1904 *Die religionsgeschichtliche Methode in der Theologie*. Giessen, Ricker and Töpelmann.

1906 *Die Entstehung des Neuen Testaments*. Leipzig, Göschen. 1919; Berlin— Leipzig, W. de Gruyter, 1926² (revised).

1908 *Die Entwicklung der christlichen Religion innerhalb des Neuen Testaments*. Leipzig, Göschen; Berlin, W. de Gruyter, 1919.

1909 *Religionsgeschichtliche Erklärung des Neuen Testaments*. Giessen, Töpelmann, 1924².

English translation by Robert G. Nisbet: *Primitive Christianity and its non-Jewish sources*. Edinburgh, T. & T. Clark, 1912.

1911 *Der geschichtliche Jesus. Eine allgemeinverständliche Untersuchung der Frage: Hat Jesus gelebt, und was wolte er?* Giessen, Töpelmann.

1912 *Die Entstehung des Johannesevangeliums.* Halle a. d. S., Niemeyer.
1913 *Der Einfluss der Mysterienreligionen auf das älteste Christentum.* Giessen, Töpelmann.
1914 "Wesen und Ursprung der Magie," *Archiv für Religionspsychologie,* I (1914), pp. 108–135.
1916 *Die Reste der primitiven Religion im ältesten Christentum.* Giessen, Töpelmann.
1920 *Die griechische und lateinische Nachrichten über die persische Religion.* Giessen, Töpelmann.
1920 *Das Leben nach dem Tode im Glauben der Menschheit.* Leipzig—Berlin, Teubner.
1921 *Die nichtchristlichen Kulturreligionen in ihrem gegenwärtigen Zustand.* Leipzig, Teubner.
1923 *Die Mystiek nach Wesen, Entwicklung und Bedeutung.* Bonn, Röhrscheid.
1926–1931 *Religionsgeschichte Europas,* 2 Vols. Heidelberg, Winter.
1927 *Die Religionen der Erde, ihr Wesen und ihre Geschichte.* In Verbindung mit Franz Babinger, Leo Baeck, Heinrich Hackmann, u. a. dargestellt. Ed. by Carl Clemen. München, Bruckmann.
　　English translation by A. K. Dallas: *Religions of the World. Their Nature and their History.* London–Bombay, G. Harrap & Co.; New York–Chicago, Harcourt, Brace and Company, 1931.
1928 *Die Anwendung der Psychoanalyse auf Mythologie und Religionsgeschichte.* Leipzig, Akademische Verlagsgesellschaft.
1930 "Die Anwendung der Psychoanalyse auf die Erklärung der israelitisch-jüdischen Religion, *Archiv für die gesamte Psychologie,* vol. 77 (1930), pp. 1–14.
1930 "Der sogenannte Monotheismus der Primitiven," *Archiv für Religionswissenschaft,* vol. 27 (1930), pp. 290–334.
1932–1933 *Urgeschichtliche Religion. Die Religion der Stein-, Bronze-, und Eisenzeit,* 2 vols. Bonn, Röhrscheid.
1933 *Der Einfluss des Christentums auf andere Religionen.* Leipzig, A. Deichertse Verlagsbuchhandlung D. Werner Schol.
1934 *Grundriss der Religionsphilosophie.* Bonn, Röhrscheid.
1937 *Dunkle Stellen in der Offenbarung Johannis religionsgeschichtlich erklärt.* Bonn, Röhrscheid.
1939 *Die phönikische Religion nach Philo Byblos.* Leipzig, Hinrichs.

ROBERT HENRY CODRINGTON

Main Publications

1885 *The Melanesian Languages.* Oxford, Clarendon Press.
1891 *The Melanesians. Studies in their anthropology and folklore.* Oxford, Clarendon Press. New Haven, Human Relations Area Files Press, 1957.
1896 *A Dictionary of the language of Mota, Sugarloaf Island, Bank's Islands, with a short grammar and index.* London, Soc. for promoting Christ. Knowledge.

BENJAMIN CONSTANT Y DE REBECQUE

1. Bibliography

Rudler, G., *Bibliographie critique des œuvres de Benjamin Constant*. Paris, Colin, 1909, 114 p.

2. Biography and Appreciation

Clercq, V. de, "La Pensée religieuse de Benjamin Constant," *Vie Catholique*, 27 déc. 1930.

David, M., "Vue comparée des idées de Herder et de Benjamin Constant sur l'étude des religions," *Numen*, TTT (1956), pp. 14–27.

Deguise, Pierre, *Benjamin Constant méconnu. Le Livre de la religion avec des documents inédits.* Genève, Librarie Droz, 1966.

Maurier, René, "Benjamin Constant, historien des societés et des Religions," *Revue d'Histoire des Religions*, CII (1930).

Saltet, M., *Benjamin Constant, historien de la religion*. Paris, 1905.

3. Main Publications

1824–1831 *De la religion considerée dans sa source, ses formes et ses développements* 6 vols. Paris, Bossange Père, Pichon et Didier.

1833 *Du polythéisme romain, considerée dans ses rapports avec la philosophie grecque et la religion chrétienne.* (Ouvrage posthume de B. Constant, précédé d'une Introduction de H. J. Matter, 2 vols. Paris, Béchet Aîné.

GEORG FRIEDRICH CREUZER

1. Bibliography

In: G. F. Creuzer, *Aus dem Leben eines alten Professors.* (Deutsche Schriften, 11). Leipzig, Leske, 1848, pp. 344–358.

2. Biography and Appreciation

Briefe und Dichtungen von Fr. Creuzer und Karoline von Günderode. Herausg. von R. Rohde. Heidelberg, Winter, 1896.

Creuzer, G. F., *Aus dem Leben eines alten Professors.* (Deutsche Schriften, 11). Leipzig, Leske, 1848.

—, *Paraligomena der Lebensskizzen eines alten Professors*. Frankfurt a. M., Baer, 1858. (Autobiogr.)
—, *Die Liebe der Günderode*. Hrsg. und eingel. von Karl Preisandaur. München, R. Piper, 1912.
Howald, E., *Der Kampf um Creuzers Symbolik*. Tübingen, Mohr, 1926.

3. Main Publications

1805 *Studien*. Herausg. von Karl Daub und Fr. Creuzer. Frankfurt–Heidelbergi Mohr und Zimmer.
1810–1812 *Symbolik und Mythologie der alten Völker, besonders der Griechen*, 4 vols., Leipzig, Leske; 2d revised ed. Leipzig und Darmstadt, Heyer und Leske, 1819–1823, 6 vols.; 3d ed., idem, 1836–1843.
   French translation by J. D. Guigniaut: *Religions de l'Antiquité, considérées principalement dans leurs formes symboliques et mythologiques*. Paris, Treuttel et Würz, 1825–1841.
1817 *Opuscula mythologica, philosophica, historica et grammatica*. Lipsiae, Hahn.
1827 ,,Explication d'une inscription romaine inédite (précédée de quelque observations sur les causes et l'origine de l'esclavage chez les anciens en général et particulièrement chez les romains," in: *Mémoires de l'Académie des Inscriptions et Belles-Lettres*. Paris, 1845. (Read in August and December 1827).
1836–1848 *Deutsche Schriften, neue und verbesserte*, 11 vols. Leipzig, Leske; 1848–58 [5].
1846 *Luther (1483–1546) und Grotius (1583–1645) oder Glaube und Wissenschaft*. Heidelberg, Winter.
1854 *Friderici Creuzeri Opuscula Selecta*. Lipsiae, Hahn.

FRANZ V. M. CUMONT

1. Bibliography

,,Mélanges Franz Cumont," In: *Annuaire de l'Institut de Philologie et d'Histoire Orientales et Slaves*. Tome 4. (Université Libre de Bruxelles). Bruxelles, 1936, pp. VII–XXXI.

2. Biography and Appreciation

Dussaud, René, "Nécrologie Franz Cumont," *Syria*, Vol. 26 (1949), pp. 168–172.
Mayence, M. F., "Franz Cumont. Hommage à l'occasion de la remise de son buste à la classe," *B. Cl. L. Ac. R. Belge*, XLII (1956), pp. 363–379.
"Note e Notizie: Franz Cumont," *Studi e Materiali di Storia delle Religioni*, Vol. 21 (1947–48), pp. 163–164.
Préaux, Claire, "Nécrologie Franz Cumont," *Chronique d'Egypte*, Nr. 45–46, Vol. 23 (avril 1948), pp. 242–247.

3. Main Publications

1894–1899 *Textes et monuments figurés relatifs aux mystères de Mithra*, 2 vols.
Bruxelles.
1900 *Les Mystères de Mithra*. Extrait des *Textes et monuments figurés*..., vol. I,
pp. 223–350. Bruxelles, 1900, 1913³.
English translation by Thomas J. McCormack: *The Mysteries of Mithra*.
(Transl. from the second, revised ed.). London, Trübner and Co., 1903;
Chicago, 1910².
1906 "Les Religions orientales dans le paganisme romain," *Annales du Musée
Guimet, Bibliothèque de Vulgarisation*, Vol. 24, Paris, 1906, 1929⁴.
English authorized translation: *The Oriental Religions in Roman Paganism*.
With an introductory essay by Grant Showermen. Chicago, The Open
Court, 1911; New York, Dover, 1956.
1908 "La Cosmogonie manichéenne d'après Théodore bar Khôni," *Recherches
sur le Manichéisme*, (Bruxelles), No. 1.
1912 *Astrology and Religion among the Greeks and Romans*. London–New York,
G. P. Putnam's Sons.
1917 *Études syriennes*. Paris.
1922 *After Life in Roman Paganism*. Lectures delivered at Yale University.
New Haven, Conn., Yale University Press.
1926 *Fouilles de Doura Eurepos 1922–1923*. Avec un appendice sur la céramique
de Doura par M. et Mme. Félix Massoul. Paris.
1937 *L'Egypte des astrologues*. Bruxelles.
1942 "Recherches sur le symbolisme funéraire des Romains," *Bibliothèque
Archéologique et Historique* (Paris), Tome 35.

D

FRIEDRICH C. G. DELITZSCH*

1. Bibliography

Meissner, Bruno, "Friedrich Delitzsch," in: *Deutsches Biographisches Jahrbuch,* IV (1922). Stuttgart–Berlin–Leipzig, Deutsche Verlags-Anstalt, 1929, pp. 31–35 (Not complete).

Weissbach, F. H., "Friedrich Delitzsch," in: *Reallexikon der Assyriologie,* Vol. II. Berlin–Leipzig, Walter de Gruyter & Co, 1938, p. 198 (Not complete).

2. Biography and Appreciation

Budde, Karl F. R., *Das Alte Testament und die Ausgrabungen. Ein Beitrag zum Streit um Babel und Bibel.* Giessen, 1903.

—, *Was soll die Gemeinde aus dem Streit um Babel und Bibel lernen?* Ein Vortrag. Tübingen–Leipzig, 1903.

Delitzsch, Friedrich, *Mein Lebenslauf.* Leipzig, Reclams Universum, Jahrgang XXXVI, Heft 47 (1920).

Gunkel, J. F. Hermann, *Israel und Babylonien. Der Einflusz Babyloniens auf die israelitische Religion.* Göttingen, 1903.
English translation by E. S. B.: *Israel und Babylon. The influence of Babylon on the religion of Israel* (A reply to Delitzsch). Philadelphia, John Jos. McVey, 1904.

Harnack Adolf, *Prof. Harnack's Letter to the "Preussische Jahrbücher" on the German Emperor's Criticism of Prof. Delitzsch's Lectures on ,,Babel und Bibel''.* English translation by T. B. Saunders. London, Williams and Norgate, 1903.

Jeremias, Alfred, *Im Kampfe um Babel und Bibel.* Ein Wort zur Verständigung und Abwehr. Leipzig, J. C. Hinrichs, 1903³.

Johns, C. H. W., "Introduction," in: Friedrich Delitzsch, *Babel and Bible.* Two lectures delivered before the members of the Deutsche Orient-Gesellschaft in the presence of the German Emperor. Edited, with an Introduction, by C. H. W. Johns. New York, G. P. Putnam's Sons, and London, Williams and Norgate, 1903, pp. I–XXIX.

Kittel, Rudolf, *Die babylonischen Ausgrabungen und die biblische Urgeschichte.* Leipzig, 1903[2].

—, *Der Babel-Bibel-Streit und die Offenbarungsfrage. Ein Verzicht auf Verständigung.* Leipzig, 1903.

Klüger, H., *Friedrich Delitzsch, der Apostel der neubabylonischen Religion. Ein Mahnruf an das deutsche Volk.* Leipzig, Krügen, 1912, 180 pp.

König, Friedrich E., *Bibel und Babel. Eine kulturgeschichtliche Skizze* (mit Beurteilung von Delitzsch's zweitem Vortrag und der andern neuesten Babel und Bibel-Literatur). Berlin, 1902, 1903[10].

—, *Friedrich Delitzsch's "Die grosse Täuschung" kritisch beleuchtet.* Gütersloh, C. Bertelsmann, 1920, 1921.

—, *Wie weit hat Delitzsch Recht? Beantwortet durch kritische Beleuchtung des zweiten Teils von Delitzschs "Die grosse Täuschung".* Berlin 1921.

—, *Die moderne Babylonisierung der Bibel in ihrer neuesten Erscheinungsform. Delitzschs "Babel und Bibel" 1921 kritisch betrachtet.* Stuttgart, 1922.

Kugler, Fr. X., *Babylon und Christentum,* 1. Heft: *Delitzsch's Angriffe auf das Alte Testament.* Freiburg i. Br., 1903, IV + 68 p. (This appeared first in *Stimmen aus Maria Laach,* 1903).

Meissner, Bruno, "Delitzsch, Friedrich," in: *Deutsches Biographisches Jahrbuch,* IV (1922). Stuttgart–Berlin–Leipzig, Deutsche Verlagsanstalt, 1929, pp. 31–35.

Münz, Wilhelm, "*Es werde Licht!*". *Eine Aufklärung über Babel und Bibel.* Breslau, W. Koebner, 1903.

Plato, Immanuel, *Reflexionen über 'Babel und Bibel'. Ein Beitrag zur Geschichte der deutschen Kultur und jüdischen Religion.* Offener Brief an Herrn Friedrich Delitzsch. Hamburg, M. Lessmann, 1903.

Price, Ira M., "Friedrich Delitzsch," *Beiträge zur Assyriologie und semitischen Sprachwissenschaft,* X, 2 (1927), pp. I–XII.

Rosenthal, Ludwig A., *Babel und Bibel oder Babel gegen Bibel? Ein Wort zur Klärung.* Berlin, 1902.

Schreiber, Emilio, *Bibbia e Babele.* Appunti alle conferenze del prof. Gustavo Sacerdoti [di] Immanuel Sofer [pseud.]. Trieste, Tip. Morterra & Co., 1904.

Theisz, J., *Friedrich Delitzsch und seine 'Grosze Täuschung', oder Jaho und Jahwe.* Trier, 1921.

Thieme, Carl, *Der Offenbarungsglaube im Streit über Babel und Bibel. Ein Wort zur Orientierung.* Leipzig, 1903.

Weber, Otto, *Theologie und Assyriologie im Streite um Babel und Bibel.* Leipzig, 1904.

Wegener, Armin, *Babel und Bibel, was sie verbindet und scheidet.* Vortrag. Moscow, 1903.

Weissbach, F. H., "Delitzsch, Friedrich," in: *Reallexikon der Assyriologie,* Vol. II. Berlin–Leipzig, Walter de Gruyter & Co, 1938, p. 198.

Winckler, Hugo, *Der alte Orient und die Bibel.* Nebst einem Anhang: *Babel und Bibel — Bibel und Babel.* Leipzig, E. Pfeiffer, 1906.

Zimmern, Heinrich, *Keilinschriften und Bibel nach ihrem religionsgeschichtlichen Zusammenhang. Ein Leitfaden zur Orientierung im sog. Babel-Bibel-Streit.* Mit Einbeziehung auch der neutestamentlichen Probleme. Berlin, 1903.

—, "Friedrich Delitzsch und Carl Bezold. Ein Nachruf," *Zeitschrift der Deutschen Morgenländischen Gesellschaft,* N. F. II (Band 77, 1923), pp. 121–136 (On Friedrich Delitzsch, pp. 121–129).

N. B. On "Babel and Bible", see also the literature mentioned in: Friedrich Delitzsch, *Babel und Bibel. Ein Rückblick und Ausblick*. Stuttgart, Deutsche Verlags-Anstalt, 1904.

3. Main Publications

1873 *Studien über Indogermanisch-Semitische Wurzelverwandtschaft*. Leipzig, 1884².
1874 *Assyrische Studien*. Heft I: *Assyrische Thiernamen*. Mit vielen Excursen und einem assyrischen — und akkadischen Glossar. Leipzig.
1876 *Assyrische Lesestücke*. Nach dem Originalen theils revidirt, theils zum ersten Male herausgegeben und durch Schrifttafeln eingeleitet. Leipzig, J. C. Hinrichs, 1872². In later editions with subtitle: Mit grammatischen Tabellen und vollständigem Glossar. Einführung in die assyrische und babylonische Keilschriftlitteratur bis hinauf zu Hammurabi. Leipzig, J.C. Hinrichs, 1885³, 1900⁴, 1912⁵ (revised editions).
1881 *Wo lag das Paradies?* Eine Biblisch-Assyriologische Studie. Mit zahlreichen assyriologischen Beiträgen zur biblischen Länder- und Völkerkunde und einer Karte Babyloniens. Leipzig.
1883 *The Hebrew Language viewed in the Light of Assyrian Research*. London–Edinburgh, Williams and Norgate.
1884 *Die Sprache der Kossäer. Linguistisch-historische Funde und Fragen*. Leipzig.
1886 *Prolegomena eines neuen Hebräisch-Aramäischen Wörterbuchs zum Alten Testament*. Leipzig.
1887–1890 *Assyrisches Wörterbuch zur gesamten bisher veröffentlichten Keilschriftliteratur*. Unter Berücksichtigung zahlreicher unveröffentlichter Texte (Assyriologische Bibliothek, VII). (Three Parts appeared).
1889 *Assyrische Grammatik*. Mit Paradigmen, Übungsstücken, Glossar, und Literatur. Berlin. Second edition: Assyrische Grammatik. Mit Übungsstücken und kurzer Literatur-Übersicht, Berlin, 1906².
       English translation by R. S. Kennedy: *Assyrian Grammar*. With paradigms, exercises, glossary and bibliography. Berlin, H. Reuther; New York, B. Westermann & Co., 1889.
1891 *Geschichte Babyloniens und Assyriens* (Reiche der Alten Welt, II), by F. Mürdter. Second edition completely revised by F. Delitzsch. Calw–Stuttgart, Verlag der Vereinsbuchhandlung.
1894 *Beiträge zur Entzifferung und Erklärung der kappadokischen Keilschrifttafeln*. (Abhandlungen der Kön. Sächs. Gesellschaft der Wissenschaften, XIV, 4). Leipzig.
.... *Beiträge zur Erklärung der babylonisch-assyrischen Briefliteratur*.
1896 *Assyrisches Handwörterbuch*. Leipzig.
1897 *Das babylonische Weltschöpfungsepos*. (Abhandlungen der Kön. Sächs. Gesellschaft der Wissenschaften, XVII, 2). Leipzig.
1897 *Die Entstehung des ältesten Schriftsystems oder der Ursprung der Keilschriftzeichen*. Leipzig. 1898² (mit Nachwort).
1898 *Ex Oriente Lux!* Ein Wort zur Förderung der Deutschen Orient-Gesellschaft. Leipzig, F. Hinrich.
       English translation: "Discoveries in Mesopotamie," in: Smithsonian Institution. *Annual Report*, 1900 (Washington, 1901), pp. 535–549

1899 *Babylon.* Mit einem Plan des Ruinenfeldes. (Sendschreiben der Deutschen Orient-Gesellschaft, Nr. 1). Berlin, 1901.

1902 *Das Buch Hiob.* Neu übersetzt und erklärt. Ausgabe mit sprachlichem Kommentar. (Biblia Germanica). Leipzig.

1902 *Babel und Bibel.* Ein Vortrag. Leipzig, J. C. Hinrichs. 1903[4], etc.
English translation: *Babel and Bible. A lecture on the significance of Assyriological Research for Religion.* Chicago, The Open Court Publishing Company, 1902, 1903.

1903 *Anmerkungen zu dem Vortrag Babel und Bibel.* Leipzig.

1903 *Zweiter Vortrag über Babel und Bibel.* Mit . . . einem Vorwort "zur Klärung". Stuttgart, Deutsche Verlags-Anstalt, 1903, etc.
Two *English* translations, of the first and the second lecture together, are in existence:
F. Delitzsch, *Babel and Bible.* Two lectures delivered before the members of the Deutsche Orient-Gesellschaft in the presence of the German Emperor. Edited with an Introduction, by C. H. W. Johns, M. A. New York, G. P. Putnam's Sons; London, Williams and Norgate, 1903.
F. Delitzsch, *Babel and Bible.* Two lectures on the significance of Assyriological research for religion. Embodying the most important criticisms and the author's replies. Translated from the German by Thomas J. McCormack and W. H. Carruth. Chicago, The Open Court Publishing Company, 1903.

1903 *Im Lande des einstigen Paradieses.* Ein Vortrag. (Sendschreiben der Deutschen Orient-Gesellschaft, Nr. 3). Stuttgart, Deutsche Verlags-Anstalt.

1904 *Babel und Bibel. Ein Rückblick und Ausblick.* Stuttgart, Deutsche Verlags-Anstalt.

1905 *Babel und Bibel. Dritter (Schluss-) Vortrag.* Stuttgart, Deutsche Verlags-Anstalt.

1906 *Die babylonische Chronik nebst einem Anhang über die synchronistische Geschichte P.* (Abhandlungen der Kön. Sächs. Gesellschaft der Wissenschaften, XXV, 1). Leipzig.

1907 *Mehr Licht. Die bedeutsamsten Ergebnisse der babylonisch-assyrischen Grabungen für Geschichte, Kultur und Religion.* Ein Vortrag. Leipzig.

1908 *Zur Weiterbildung der Religion.* Zwei Vorträge. Stuttgart, Deutsche Verlags-Anstalt.
English translation by F. L. Pogson: *Whose son is Christ? Two Lectures on Progress in Religion.* Boston, American Unitarian Association; London, Philip Green, 1908.

1909 *Asurbanipal und die assyrische Kultur seiner Zeit.* Leipzig.

1910 *Handel und Wandel in Altbabylonien.* Stuttgart, Deutsche Verlags-Anstalt.

1911 *Das Land ohne Heimkehr. Die Gedanken der Babylonier-Assyrer über Tod und Jenseits.* Nebst Schlussfolgerungen. Stuttgart, Deutsche Verlags-Anstalt.

1912 *Ernste Fragen.* Eine Erwiderung. Stuttgart–Berlin, Deutsche Verlags-Anstalt.

1914 *Grundzüge der sumerischen Grammatik* (Hilfsbücher zur Kunde des alten Orients, Band V). Leipzig.

1914 *Kleine sumerische Sprachlehr für Nichtassiryologen.* Grammatik, Vokabular, Textproben. Leipzig.

1914 *Sumerisches Glossar.* Leipzig.

1914 *Sumerisch-akkadisch-hettitische Vokabularfragmente* (Abh. der **Kön.** Akademie der Wissenschaften, Phil.-hist. Klasse, 1914, 3). Berlin.
1915 *Die Welt des Islam.* Berlin–Wien.
1917 *Philologische Forderungen an die Hebräische Lexikographie.* Leipzig.
1920 *Die Lese- und Schreibfehler im Alten Testament, nebst den dem Schrifttexte einverleibten Randnoten klassifiziert.* Berlin.
1920–1921 *Die grosze Täuschung. Kritische Betrachtungen zu den alttestamentlichen Berichten über Israels Eindringen in Kanaan, die Gottesoffenbarung vom Sinai und die Wirksamkeit der Propheten.* 2 vols. Berlin–Stuttgart, Deutsche Verlags-Anstalt. In one volume: Stuttgart, Verlags-Anstalt 1921, 1922 etc.

ALBRECHT DIETERICH

1. Bibliography

Dieterich, A., *Kleine Schriften.* Leipzig–Berlin, Teubner, 1911, pp. 11–42.

2. Main Publications

1891 *Abraxas; Studien zur Religionsgeschichte des spätern Altertums.* Leipzig, Teubner.
1893 *Nekyia; Beiträge zur Erklärung der neuentdeckten Petrusapokalypse.* Leipzig, Teubner.
1897 *Pulcinella, pompejanische Wandbilder und römische Satyrspiele.* Leipzig, Teubner.
1898 *Eine Mithrasliturgie.* Leipzig, Teubner, 1903[2], 1923[3].
1911 *Kleine Schriften.* Leipzig–Berlin, Teubner.

ROLAND BURRAGE DIXON

1. Bibliography

Coon, Carleton S. and J. M. Andrews: *Studies in the Anthropology of Oceania and Asia. Presented in Memory of R. B. Dixon.* (Papers of the Peabody Museum of American Archaeology and Ethnology, vol. 20). Cambridge, Mass., Harvard Un. Press, 1943.

2. Main Publications

1902 *Maidu myths.* (Extract from *Bulletin of the Amer. Museum of Natura[l] History.* Vol. XVII, Part II, pp. 33–118). New York.
1903 *System and sequence in Maidu mythology.* (Extract from *Journal of American Folklore.* Vol. XVI, 1903.) Boston.
1905 *The Northern Maidu.* (Extract from *Bulletin of the Amer. Museum of Natural History.* Vol. XVII, Part III, pp. 119–346). New York.

1907 *The Shasta.* (Extract from *Bulletin of the Amer. Museum of Natural History.* Vol. XVII, Part V, pp. 381–498). New York.
1916 *Oceanic Mythology.* Boston, Marshall Jones company. New York, 1964.
1923 *The Racial History of Man.* New York–London, Scribner's Sons.
1928 *The Building of Cultures.* New York–London, Scribner's Sons.

EMILE DURKHEIM*

1. Bibliography

"Comprehensive Bibliography of Emile Durkheim (1858–1917)," in: Harry Alpert, *Emile Durkheim and his Sociology.* New York, Columbia University Press, and London, P. S. King & Son, Ltd., 1939, pp. 217–224.

2. Biography and Appreciation

Adams, George P., "The interpretation of religion in Royce and Durkheim," *Philosophical Review*, XXV (1916), pp. 297–304.
Alpert, Harry, "Durkheim's functional theory of ritual," *Sociology and Social Research*, XXIII (1938), pp. 103–108. Reprinted in R. A. Nisbet, *Emile Durkheim*, 1965.
—, *Emile Durkheim and his Sociology.* New York, Columbia University Press, and London, P. S. King & Son, Ltd., 1939. Reprint New York, Russell and Russell, 1961.
—, "Emile Durkheim and sociologismic psychology," *The American Journal of Sociology*, XXXXV (1939), pp. 64–70.
—, "Emile Durkheim and the theory of social interpretation," *Journal of Social Psychology*, VI, 2 (January 1941).
—, "Emile Durkheim: enemy of fixed psychological elements," *American Journal of Sociology*, LXII (May, 1958), pp. 662–664.
—, "Emile Durkheim: a perspective and appreciation," *The American Sociological Review*, XXIV (1959), pp. 462–465.
American Journal of Sociology, "A Commemorative Issue for Emile Durkheim and Georg Simmel," LXII (May, 1958).
Annales de l'Université de Paris, "Centenaire de la naissance d'Emile Durkheim" (1960, no. 1).
Apchié, M., "Quelques remarques critiques sur la sociologie d'Emile Durkheim," *Archives de Philosophie du Droit et de Sociologie Juridique*, VI (1936), pp. 182–195.
Bellah, Robert N., "Durkheim and history," *The American Sociological Review*, XXIV (1959), pp. 447–461. Reprinted in R. A. Nisbet, *Emile Durkheim*, 1965.
Belot, Gustave, "Emile Durkheim: 'L'Année sociologique'," *Revue Philosophique*, XLV (1898), pp. 649–657.
—, "Une théorie nouvelle de la religion," *Revue Philosophique*, 1913, pp. 329–379.
Benoit-Smullyan, Emile, "The sociologism of Emile Durkheim and his school," in: Harry Elmer Barnes, ed., *An Introduction to the History of Sociology*. Chicago, University of Chicago Press, 1948, pp. 499–537.

Bierstedt, Robert, *Emile Durkheim*. New York, Dell Publishing Co., 1966.
Binsbergen, W. van, "Durkheims begrippenpaar 'sacré/profane'," *Kula*, VIII (1967–68), pp. 14–21.
Bohannan, Paul, "Conscience collective and culture," in: Kurt H. Wolff, ed., *Emile Durkheim, 1858–1917*... 1960.
Bouglé, C., "Le spiritualisme d'Emile Durkheim," *Revue Bleue*, LXII (1924), pp. 550–553.
Branford, V. D., "A brief memoir," *The Sociological Review*, X (1918), pp. 77–82.
Catlin, George E. G., "Introduction to the translation," in: Emile Durkheim, *The Rules of Sociological Method*. Chicago, 1938, pp. XI–XXXVI.
Conze, E., "Zur Bibliographie der Durkheim-Schule," *Kölner Vierteljahrshefte für Soziologie*, VI (1927), pp. 279–283.
Cuvillier, A., *Où va la sociologie française? Avec une étude d'Emile Durkheim sur la sociologie formaliste*. Paris 1953.
Cuzzort, R. P., "The sacred and the profane: an introduction to Emile Durkheim," in: R. P. Cuzzort, *Humanity and Modern Sociological Thought*. London and New York, Holt, Rinehart and Winston, 1971, pp. 24–47.
Davy, Georges, "La sociologie de M. Durkheim," *Revue Philosophique*, LXXII (1911), pp. 42–71, 160–185.
—, "Emile Durkheim," *Revue de Métaphysique et de Morale*, XXVI (1919), pp. 181–198 ("L'homme"); XXVII (1920), pp. 71–112 ("L'œuvre").
—, "Emile Durkheim," *Revue Française de Sociologie*, I (1960), pp. 3–24.
Diaconide, E., "Emile Durkheim (1858–1917)," *Mensch en Maatschappij*, XX (1945), pp. 308–326.
Dohrenwend, Bruce P., "Egoism, altruism, anomie: a conceptual analysis of Durkheim's types," *American Sociological Review*, XXIV (1959), pp. 466–472.
Duncan, Hugh Dalziel, "The development of Durkheim's concept of ritual and the problem of social disrelationships," in: Kurt Wolff, ed., *Emile Durkheim, 1858–1917*... 1960, pp. 97–117.
Duvignaud, Jean Augier, *Durkheim. Sa vie, son œuvre, avec un exposé de sa philosophie*. (Philosophes). Paris, Presses Universitaires de France, 1965.
Europe, "L'œuvre sociologique d'Emile Durkheim". With contributions by Célestin Bouglé, Georges Davy, Marcel Granet, Raymond Lenoir, and René Maublanc. *Europe*, XXII (1930), pp. 281–304.
Fauconnet, Paul, "The Durkheim school in France," *Sociological Review*, XIX (1927), pp. 15–20.
Gehlke, Charles Elmer, *Emile Durkheim's Contributions to Sociological Theory*. (Studies in History, Economics and Public Law, 151). New York, Columbia University Press, 1915.
Ginsberg, Morris, "Durkheim's theory of religion," in: Morris Ginsberg, *On the Diversity of Morals*. New York, Macmillan, 1957, pp. 230–242. (Ch. XIV).
Ginsberg, R. B., *Anomie and Aspirations ; a Reinterpretation of Durkheim's Theory*. Ph. D. thesis, Columbia University, New York, 1966.
Gisbert, Pascual, "Social facts in Durkheim's system," *Anthropos*, LIV (1959), pp. 353–369.
Goddijn, H. P. M., *De sociologie van Emile Durkheim*. Amsterdam, De Bussy, 1969.

Goldenweiser, Alexander A., "The views of Andrew Lang, and J. G. Frazer and E. Durkheim on totemism," *Anthropos*, X–XI (1915–16), pp. 948–970.

—, "Religion and society. A critique of Durkheim's theory of the origin and nature of religion," *Journal of Philosophy, Psychology and Scientific Methods*, XIV (1917), pp. 113–124.
Reprinted in: A. A. Goldenweiser, *Early Civilization*. New York, 1922. Also reprinted in: A. A. Goldenweiser, *History, Psychology and Culture*. New York, Alfred A. Knopf, 1933, pp. 361–373 (Part IV, Ch. I).

Gurvitch, Georges, "La science des faits moraux et la morale théorique chez Emile Durkheim," *Archives de Philosophie du Droit et de Sociologie Juridique*, VII (1937), pp. 18–44.

Halbwachs, Maurice, "La doctrine d'Emile Durkheim," *Revue Philosophique*, LXXXV (1918), 353–411.

—, *Les origines du sentiment religieux d'après Durkheim*, Paris, Librairie Stock, 1925.
English translation by John A. Spaulding: *Sources of Religious Sentiment*, New York, Free Press of Glencoe, 1962.

Hinkle, Jr., Roscoo C., "Durkheim in American sociology," in: Kurt H. Wolff, ed., *Emile Durkheim, 1858–1917*...1960, pp. 267–295.

Høffding, H., "Les formes élémentaires de la vie religieuse," *Revue de Métaphysique et de Morale*, XXII (1914), pp. 828–848 (review article).

Honigsheim, Paul, "The influence of Durkheim and his school on the study of religion," in: Kurt H. Wolff, ed., *Emile Durkheim, 1858–1917*... 1960, pp. 233–246.

König, R., "Die Religionssoziologie bei E. Durkheim," in: *Probleme der Religionssoziologie*. Sonderheft 6 von *Kölner Zeitschrift für Soziologie und Sozialpsychologie*. Köln–Opladen, 1962, pp. 36–49.

Koseki, Toichiro, "Social factors in E. Durkheim's theory," *Japanese Sociological Review*, VI (1955), pp. 51–67.

Kruijt, J. P., "Het sociologisme van Emile Durkheim," *Mens en Maatschappij*, XXXIII (1958), pp. 3–20.

La Fontaine, A. P., *La philosophie d'E. Durkheim*. Paris, J. Vrin, 1926[4].

Lacombe, Roger, *La méthode sociologique de Durkheim. Etude critique*. Paris, Félix Alcan, 1926.

Lang, Andrew, "Dr. Durkheim on 'Social origins'," *Folk-Lore*, XV (1904), pp. 100–102.

Le Bras, Gabriel, "Note sur la sociologie religieuse dans l'*Année Sociologique*," *Archives de Sociologie des Religions*, 11e Année, No 21 (janvier–juin 1966), pp. 47–53.

Lenoir, Raymond, "Emile Durkheim et la conscience moderne," *Mercure de France*, vol. 128 (1918), pp. 577–595.

Leuba, James H., "Sociology and psychology. The conception of religion and magic and the place of psychology in sociological studies. A discussion of the views of Durkheim and of Hubert and Mauss," *American Journal of Sociology*, XIX (1913), pp. 323–342.

Lévi-Strauss, Claude, "Ce que l'ethnologie doit à Durkheim," *Annales de l'Université de Paris*, 1960, no. 1, pp. 45–50.

Lukes, Stephen, *Emile Durkheim. His life and work*. London, Allen and Unwin, 1973.

Lupu, I., *Die Grundlagen der Gesellschaft, das Recht und die Religion in der*

Durkheimschule: Ihr besonderer Widerhall in der Jenenser Jerusalemschen Soziologie. Iasi, Viata Românească, 1931.

Marica, Em. G., *Emile Durkheim. Seine Ideenentwicklung und seine Stellung in der Soziologie.* Jena, Fischer, 1932. Reprinted as Vol. VI of "Sozialwissenschaftliche Bausteine" with the title *Emile Durkheim. Soziologie und Soziologismus.* Jena, Fischer, 1932.

Marjolin, Robert, "French sociology: Comte and Durkheim," translated by Alice Price Duncan and Hugh Dalziel Duncan, *American Journal of Sociology*, XLII (1937), pp. 693–704, 901–902.

Masson-Oursel, Paul, "La sociologie de Durkheim et la psychanalyse," *Psyché. Revue internationale de psychanalyse et des sciences de l'homme*, II (1947), pp. 1439–1442.

Mauss, Marcel, "In memoriam. L'œuvre inédite de Durkheim et de ses collaborateurs," *Année Sociologique*, N. S., I (1923), pp. 7–29.

McFarland, H. N., "Theories of the social origin of religion in the tradition of Emile Durkheim," Ph. D. thesis, Columbia University, New York, 1954.

Neyer, Joseph, "Individualism and socialism in Durkheim," in: Kurt H. Wolff, ed., *Emile Durkheim, 1858–1917 . . .* 1960, pp. 32–76.

Nisbet, Robert A., *Emile Durkheim. With Selected Essays.* Englewood Cliffs, N. J., Prentice-Hall, 1965. Contains essays by Harry Alpert, Robert N. Bellah, Morris Ginsberg, Robert K. Merton, and Hanan C. Selvin.

Ouy, Achille, "La méthode sociologique de Durkheim," *Revue Internationale de Sociologie*, XXXV (1927), pp. 371–383.

—, "Les sociologies et la sociologie. Deuxième partie: Le sociologisme, Emile Durkheim," *Revue Internationale de Sociologie*, XLVII (1939), pp. 245–275.

Parodi, Dominique, "Emile Durkheim et l'école sociologique," in: Dominique Parodi, *La philosophie contemporaine en France. Essai de classification des doctrines*, Paris, Félix Alcan, 1920² (rev. ed.), pp. 113–160 (Ch. V).

Parsons, Talcott, "Durkheim's contribution to the theory of integration of social systems," in: Kurt H. Wolff, ed., *Emile Durkheim, 1858–1917 . . .* 1960, pp. 118–153.

Pécaut, F., "Emile Durkheim," *Revue Pédagogique*, N. S., LXXII (1918), pp. 1–20.

—, "Auguste Comte et Durkheim," *Revue de Métaphysique et de Morale*, XXVIII (1921), pp. 639–655.

Peyre, Henri, "Durkheim: the man, his time, and his intellectual background," in: Kurt H. Wolff, ed., *Emile Durkheim, 1858–1917 . . .* 1960, pp. 3–31.

Pickering, W. S. F., *Durkheim and Religion.* London, Routledge and Kegan Paul, 1974.

Pierce, Albert, "Durkheim and functionalism," in Kurt H. Wolff, ed., *Emile Durkheim, 1858–1917 . . .* 1960, pp. 154–169.

Poggi, G., "The place of religion in Durkheim's theory of institutions," *Archives Européennes de Sociologie*, XII, 2 (1971), pp. 229–260.

Richard, Gaston, *L'athéisme dogmatique en sociologie religieuse. (Revue d'Histoire et de Philosophie Religieuses*, 7ᵉ cahier). Strasbourg, Istra, 1923.

—, "La pathologie sociale d'E. Durkheim," *Revue Internationale de Sociologie*, XXXVIII (1930), pp. 113–126.

Salomon, Albert, "Some aspects of the legacy of Durkheim," in: Kurt H. Wolff, ed., *Emile Durkheim, 1858–1917 . . .* 1960, pp. 247–266.

Seger, Imogen, *Durkheim and his Critics on the Sociology of Religion*. New York, Columbia University, Bureau of Applied Research (Monograph Series),1957.

Simpson, George, "Emile Durkheim's social realism," *Sociology and Social Research*, XVIII (1933), pp. 3–11.

—, "An estimate of Durkheim's work," in: Emile Durkheim, *The Division of Labor in Society*. New York, Macmillan Co., 1933, pp. XXV–XLIV.

Spencer, Robert F., "Culture process and intellectual current: Durkheim and Atatürk," *American Anthropologist*, LX (1958), pp. 640–657.

Stanner, W. E., "Reflections on Durkheim and aboriginal religion," in: *Social Organization. Essays Presented to Raymond Firth*. Edited by Maurice Freedman. London, Frank Case & Co Ltd., 1967, pp. 217–240.

Sumpf, Joseph, "Durkheim et le problème de l'étude sociologique de la religion," *Archives de Sociologie des Religions*, 10ᵉ Année, No 20 (juillet-décembre 1965), pp. 63–73.

Taylor, S., "Some implications of the contribution of Emile Durkheim to religious thought, "*Philosophy and Phenomenological Research*, XXIV (1963–64), pp. 125–134.

Telezhnikov, F., "E. Durkheim o predmete i metode sociologii," *Vestnik Kommunisticheskoi Akademii*, XXX (1928), pp. 159-188.

Tosti, Gustavo, "The delusions of Durkheim's sociological objectivism,"*American Journal of Sociology*, IV (1898), pp. 171–177.

Wallis, Wilson D., "Durkheim's view of religion," *Journal of Religious Psychology*, VII (1914), pp. 252–267.

Wilson, Ethel M., "Emile Durkheim's sociological method," *Sociology and Social Research*, XVIII (1934), pp. 511–518.

Wolff, Kurt H., "The challenge of Durkheim and Simmel," *American Journal of Sociology*, LXII (May, 1958), pp. 590–596.

—, ed., *Emile Durkheim, 1858–1917. A Collection of Essays, with Translations and a Bibliography*. Columbus, Ohio State University Press, 1960. Pocket book edition with the title *Essays on Sociology and Philosophy by Emile Durkheim et al*. With appraisals of his life and thought edited by Kurt H. Wolff. Harper Torchbook, New York, Evanston, and London, Harper & Row, 1964.

3. *Method and Theory*

1894 "Les règles de la méthode sociologique," *Revue Philosophique*, XXXVII (1894), pp. 465–498; XXXVIII (1894), pp. 14–39; 168–182. Also published separately: *Les règles de la méthode sociologique*. Paris, Alcan, 1895, 1901² (revised and enlarged), 1927⁸, 1938⁹. New edition: Paris, P. U. F., 1947.
   English translation by Sarah A. Solovay and John H. Mueller, edited by George E. G. Catlin: *The Rules of Sociological Method*. Chicago, University of Chicago Press, 1938 etc.; Glencoe (Ill.) New York, Free Press, Pb. 1950, 1962, 1964, 1968.
   German translation of the 4th French edition: *Die Methode der Soziologie*. Leipzig, 1908.

1898 "Représentations individuelles et représentations collectives," *Revue de Métaphysiques et de Morale*, VI (1898), pp. 273–302. Reprinted in *Sociologie et philosophie*. Paris, Alcan, 1924.

1899 "De la définition des phénomènes religieux," *L'Année Sociologique*, II (1899), pp. 1–28.
1900 "La sociologia ed il suo dominio scientifico," *Rivista Italiana di Sociologia*, IV (1900), pp. 127–148.
1901 "De la méthode objective en sociologie,": Preface *Les règles de la méthode sociologique, revue et augmentée d'une préface nouvelle*. Paris, Alcan, 1901². Also in *Revue de Synthèse Historique*, II (1901), pp. 3–17.
1903 E. Durkheim et P. Fauconnet, "Sociologie et sciences sociales," *Revue Philosophique*, LV (1903), pp. 465–497.
    Abridged *English* translation: "Sociology and the social sciences," in: *Sociological Papers* (London), I (1905), pp. 258–280.
1909 "Science et religion" (discussion), *Bulletin de la Société d'Economie Politique*, IX (1909), séance du 19 novembre, 1908.
1909 "Examen critique des systèmes classiques sur les origines de la pensée religieuse," *Revue Philosophique*, LXVII (1909), pp. 1–28, 142–162.
1909 "Sociologie religieuse et théorie de la connaissance," *Revue de Métaphysique et de Morale*, XVII (1909), pp. 733–758.
1909 "Sociologie et sciences sociales," in: *De la méthode dans les sciences*, 1ère série, Paris, Alcan, pp. 259–285.
1913 "Le problème religieux et la dualité de la nature humaine," *Bulletin de la Société d'Economie Politique*, XIII (1913), séance du 4 février, 1913.
1914 "Le sentiment religieux à l'heure actuelle." Paris, Vrin, 1914 ("3e fascicule"). Réédité dans: *Archives de Sociologie des Religions*, Vol. 27 (1969), pp. 71–77.
1914 "Le dualisme de la nature humaine et ses conditions sociales," *Scientia*, XV (1914), pp. 206–221.
1915 "La sociologie," in: *La science française*. Paris, Ministère de l'Instruction Publique et des Beaux-arts, Vol. I, pp. 39–49. Reprinted separately, Paris, Larousse, 1915. Reprinted in *La science française*, nouvelle édition entièrement refondue, Paris, Larousse, Vol. I, 1933², pp. 27–35.
1955 *Pragmatisme et sociologie*. Cours inédit prononcé à la Sorbonne en 1913–14 et restitué d'après des notes d'étudiants par Armand Cuvillier. Paris, J. Vrin.
1960 English translations: "Sociology and its scientific field", "Sociology", "Pragmatism and sociology" (seven lectures) in Kurt H. Wolff, ed., *Emile Durkheim, 1858–1917*. Columbus (Ohio); As *Essays on Sociology and Philosophy*, Harper Torchbook, 1964, pp. 354–436.

4. Main Publications

1893 *De la division du travail social. Etude sur l'organisation des sociétés supérieures*. Paris, Alcan. 1902² (enlarged, with new preface), 1932⁶, 1960⁷ 1967⁸.
    English translation by George Simpson: *The Division of Labor in Society*. With an Introduction by Simpson. New York, Macmillan, 1933; Glencoe (Ill.)–New York, Free Press, Pb. 1949, 1965².
1897 *Le suicide. Etude de sociologie*. Paris, Alcan. New edition: 1960, 1967². *English* translation by John A. Spaulding and George Simpson: *Suicide. A Study in Sociology*. With an Introduction by Simpson. Glencoe (Ill.), Free Press, 1951, 1960; Pb. 1966; London, 1952.

1898 "La prohibition de l'inceste et ses origines," *L'Année Sociologique*, I (1896–97), 1898, pp. 1–70.
English translation with Introduction by Edward Sagarin: *Incest, the Nature and Origin of the Taboo*. Together with: Albert Ellis, "The origins and the development of the incest taboo." New York, L. Stuart, 1963.

1902 "Sur le totémisme," *L'Année Sociologique*, V (1900–01), 1902, pp. 82–123.

1903 E. Durkheim and M. Mauss, "De quelques formes primitives de classification. Contribution à l'étude des représentations collectives," *L'Année Sociologique*, VI (1901–02), 1903, pp. 1–72.
English translation and Introduction by Rodney Needham: *Primitive Classification*. Chicago, University of Chicago Press, 1963.

1905 "Sur l'organisation matrimoniale des sociétés australiennes," *L'Année Sociologique*, VIII (1903–04), 1905, pp. 118–147.

1910 "Note sur les systèmes religieux des sociétés inférieures," *L'Année Sociologique*, XI (1910), pp. 75–76.

1912 *Les formes élémentaires de la vie religieuse. Le système totémique en Australie*. Paris, Alcan, 1912, 1925², 1937³, 1960⁴, 1968⁵.
English translation by Joseph Ward Swain: *The Elementary Forms of the Religious Life: A Study in Religious Sociology*. London, Allen & Unwin; New York, Macmillan, 1915, 1926², 1954³, 1957⁴. Reprinted Glencoe, (Ill.), Free Press, and London, Allen & Unwin, 1947, 1954. Pb. New York Collier Books, 1961; New York, Free Press, 1965.

1913 E. Durkheim and M. Mauss, "Note sur la notion de civilisation," *L'Année Sociologique*, XII (1913), pp. 46–50.

1913 E. Durkheim and M. Mauss, "Note sur les systèmes religieux des sociétés inférieures," *L'Année Sociologique*, XII (1913), pp. 90–91.

1922 *Education et sociologie*. Introduction de Paul Fauconnet. Paris, Alcan. New edition: Paris, P. U. F., 1968.
English translation and Introduction by Sherwood D. Fox: *Education and Sociology*, Foreword by Talcott Parsons. Glencoe (Ill.), Free Press, 1953, 1956².

1924 *Sociologie et philosophie*. Paris, Alcan. (Contains three previous publications).
English translation by D. F. Pocock, with an Introduction by J. G. Peristiany: *Sociology and Philosophy*. London–Glencoe (Ill.), Free Press, 1953.

1925 *L'éducation morale*. Paris, Alcan. 1938² (Preface Paul Fauconnet).
English translation by Everett K. Wilson and Herman Schnurer, edited with Introduction by Everett K. Wilson: *Moral Education ; a Study in the Theory and Application of the Sociology of Education*. New York, Free Press, 1961.

1928 *Le socialisme. Sa définition, ses débuts, la doctrine Saint-Simonienne*. Edited with a Preface by Marcel Mauss. Paris, Alcan.
English translation by Charlotte Sattler, edited and with an Introduction by Alvin W. Gouldner: *Socialism and Saint-Simon*. Yellow Springs (Ohio), Antioch Press, 1958. Pb. New York, Collier Books, 1962.

1950 *Leçons de sociologie. Physique des mœurs et du droit*, Avant-propos de H. Nail Kubali; introduction de Georges Davy. (Publications de l'Université, Faculté de Droit, No. 111). Istanbul, l'Université d'Istanbul; Paris, P.U.F., 1950.

English translation by Cornelia Brookfield: *Professional Ethics and Civic Morals*. London, Routledge & Kegan Paul, 1957; Glencoe (Ill.), Free Press, 1958.

1953 *Montesquieu et Rousseau, précurseurs de la sociologie* (Translation of *Quid secundatus politicae scientiae instituendae contulerit*, Diss. Bordeaux, Gounouilhou, 1892). Paris, Marcel Rivière. New edition with introduction by Georges Davy. Paris, 1966.
English translation: *Montesquieu and Rousseau. Forerunners of Sociology*. With a Foreword by Henri Peyre, an Introduction "Durkheim, Montesquieu and Rousseau" by Georges Davy, and a Note by A. Cuvillier. Ann Arbor, 1960.

1963 *Emile Durkheim. Selections from his work*. With an Introduction and Commentaries by Georges Simpson. New York, Crowell.

1969 *Selected Works*. Introduced and edited by Robert Bierstedt. London, Weidenfeld.

1969 *De sociologie van Emile Durkheim*. Texts chosen and introduced by H. P. M. Goddijn. Amsterdam.

1969 *Journal sociologique*. Introduction et notes de Jean Duvignaud. Paris, P. U. F.

1970 *La science sociale et l'action*. Introduction et présentation de Jean-Claude Filloux. Paris, P. U. F.

.... *Emile Durkheim. Textes choisis et présentés*, par Roger Gilbert. Bruxelles n. d.

E

PAUL M. A. EHRENREICH

1. Bibliography, Biography and Appreciation

Rivet, P., "Paul Ehrenreich," *Journal de la Société des Américanistes de Paris*, N. S. XI (1914), pp. 245f.
In: *Mitra*, Vol. 1 (1914), p. 157.
In: Petermann, *Geographische Mitteilungen*, Vol. 60 (1914), pp. 342ff.
In: *Zeitschrift für Ethnologie*, Vol. 46 (1914), pp. 455ff.

2. Main Publications

1904 "Die Ethnographie Südamerikas im Beginn des XX. Jahrhunderts unter besonderer Berücksichtigung der Naturvölker," *Archiv für Anthropologie*, XXXI (1904), pp. 39–75.
1905 *Die Mythen und Legenden der südamerikanischen Urvölker und ihre Beziehungen zu denen Nordamerikas und der Alten Welt.* Berlin, Asher.
1904 "Über die Verbreitung und Wanderungen der Mythen bei den Natürvölkern Südamerikas," *Internatonal Congress of Americanists, 14th session, 1904.* Vol. 2. Stuttgart, pp. 659–680.
1906 "Götter und Heilbringer. Eine ethnologische Kritik," *Zeitschrift für Ethnologie*, XXXVIII (1906), pp. 536–610.
1910 *Die allgemeine Mythologie und ihre ethnologischen Grundlagen.* (Mythologische Bibliothek, IV, 1). Leipzig, Hinrichs.
1915 *Die Sonne im Mythos.* Aus den hinterlassenen Papieren, hrsg., bevorwortet und mit Zusätzen versehen von Ernst Siecke. Leipzig, Hinrichs.

F

GEORGE FOUCART

1. Bibliography

Annuaire du Service des Antiquités de l'Egypte, Vol. 44 (1944), pp. 5–13.

2. Main Publications

1897 *Histoire de l'ordre lotiforme. Etude d'archéologie égyptienne*. Paris.
1909 *La méthode comparative dans l'histoire des religions*. Paris, Picard. Second edition revised and expanded under the title: *Histoire des religions et méthode comparative*. Paris, Picard, 1912.
1928 *Tombes thébaines*. Avec la collaboration de Mlle Marcelle Baud et de M. Et. Drioton. (Mémoires publiées par les membres de l'Institut Français d'Archéologie Orientale du Caire, Tome 57). Le Caire.

HENRI FRANKFORT

1. Bibliography

Delougaz, Pinhas and Jacobson, Th., "Henri Frankfort," *Journal of Near Eastern Studies*. Vol. XIV (1955), pp. 1–13.

2. Main Publications

1939 *Cylinder Seals*. A documentary essay on the art and religion of the ancient Near East. London, Macmillan; Farnborough, Eng. Gregg Press, 1965[2].
1946 *The Intellectual Adventure of Ancient Man*. An essay on speculative thought in the ancient Near East. By H. and H. A. Frankfort, John A. Wilson, Thorkild Jacobsen, William A. Irwin. Chicago, University of

Chicago Press. 1967². A later edition of this book is: *Before Philosophy: the Intellectual Adventure* .... etc. (Pelican A 198). Penguin Books, 1949, 1951², etc.

1948 *Kingship and the Gods.* A study of ancient Near Eastern religion as the integration of society and nature. (Oriental Institute Essay). Chicago, University of Chicago Press. 1955², 1962³.

1948 *Ancient Egyptian Religion. An Interpretation.* New York, Columbia University Press. 1949²; New York, Harper Torchbook, 1961.

1951 *The Problem of Similarity in Ancient Near Eastern Religions.* (Frazer Lecture 1950). Oxford, Clarendon Press.

1951 *The Birth of Civilization in the Near East.* London, Williams and Norgate; Bloomington, Indiana University Press, 1951, 1954²; Garden City, N. Y., Doubleday Anchor Book (A 89), 1956.

1954 *The Art and Architecture of the Ancient Orient.* (The Pelican History of Art, Z. 7). Penguin Books, 1954, 1955², 1963³.

JAMES GEORGE FRAZER*

1. Bibliography

Theodore Besterman, *A Bibliography of Sir James George Frazer O. M.* With portraits and facsimiles, and a Note by Sir J. G. Frazer. London, Macmillan, 1934.

2. Biography and Appreciation

Campion, S., "Autumn of an anthropologist," *New Statesman and Nation,* XLI (January 13, 1951), pp. 34–36.

Downie, R. Angus, *James George Frazer. The Portrait of a Scholar.* London, 1940.

—, *Frazer and the Golden Bough.* London, Victor Gollancz, 1970.

Ehnmark, E., "Religion and magic: Frazer, Söderblom and Häagenström," *Ethnos,* XXI, 1–2 (1956), pp. 1−60.

Elkin, A. P., "James George Frazer. Obituary (1854–1941)," *Oceania,* XI (1940–41), p. 402.

Fleure, H. J., "James George Frazer, 1854–1941," *Royal Society of London, Obituary Notices of Fellows,* III, 10 (December 1941), pp. 877–914.

—, "James George Frazer," *Man,* LIV, 1 (1954), pp. 1–2.

Folk-Lore, XXI (1910), pp. 389–396, and XXII (1911), pp. 81–104, 362–374, 486–491. Contributions on J. G. Frazer, *Totemism and Exogamy,* by A. van Gennep, L. Gomme, E. S. Hartland, A. Lang, N. W. Thomas and E. Westermarck.

Goldenweiser, A., "Totemism and Exogamy," *Current Anthropological Literature,* II (1913), pp. 199–212.

—, "The views of Andrew Lang, and J. G. Frazer and E. Durkheim on totemism," *Anthropos,* X–XI (1915–16), pp. 948–970.

Hodgart, M. J. C., "In the shadow of the Golden Bough," *The Twentieth Century,* CLVII (1955), pp. 111–119.

Hyman, Stanley Edgar, *The Tangled Bank. Darwin, Marx, Frazer and Freud as Imaginative Writers*. New York, 1962.

Jaloux, Edward, "A visit to Sir James Frazer," *Living Age*, Nr. 348 (1935) pp. 135–139.

James, E. O., "James George Frazer," *Man*, XLII, 2 (1942).

Lang, A., "J. G. Frazer's 'Totemism and Exogamy," *Anthropos*, V (1910), pp. 1092–1108.

Leach, E. R., "The Golden Bough or Gilded Twig," *Daedalus*, XC (1961).

Leach, Edmund, and Jarvie, I. C., "Frazer and Malinowski. A CA discussion," with comments by E. Ardener, J. H. M. Beattie, E. Gellner and others, *Encounter*, XXV, 5 (1965), pp. 24–36. Reprinted in *Current Anthropology*, VII (1966), pp. 560–576.

Malinowski, B., "James George Frazer. A biographical appreciation," in: B. Malinowski, *A Scientific Theory of Culture and Other Essays*, Chapel Hill, The University of North Carolina Press, 1944, pp. 177–221.

Marett, R. R., "Magic or religion?", *Edinburgh Review*, 219 (1914), pp. 489–508. Reprinted in R. R. Marett, *Psychology and Folklore*, 1920.

—, "The interpretation of survivals," *Quarterly Review*, Nr. 231 (1919), pp. 445–461.

—, "James George Frazer, 1854–1941," *Proceedings of the British Academy, Obituary Notices*, Vol. XXVII (1941), pp. 377–391.

Munz, P., *When the Golden Bough Breaks*. London, Routledge & Kegan Paul, 1973.

Osler Club, "James George Frazer, 1854–1941," a commemoration at the Osler Club." *Man*, LIV, 5 (1954), pp. 9–10.

Peterson, R., *Sir J. G. Frazers Theorie vom Wesen und Ursprung der Magie*. Phil. Diss., Bonn, 1929.

Pettazzoni, R., "Giacomo Giorgio Frazer," *Studi e Materiali di Storia delle Religioni*, XVII (1941), pp. 123–125.

Radcliffe-Brown, A. R., "James George Frazer, 1 Jan. 1854–7 May 1941," *Man*, XLII (1942).

Spencer, Herbert, *Spencer's Scientific Correspondence with Sir J. G. Frazer and Others*. Edited by R. R. Marett and T. K. Penniman. Oxford, Clarendon Press, 1932.

Steiner, Franz, "Frazer and his critic Marett," *Taboo*, 1956.

Symmons-Symonolewicz, Konstantin, "On Malinowski, Frazer, and evolutionism," *Current Anthropology*, 1968, pp. 66–67. Comp. "Reply" by Edmund Leach, *The same*, p. 68.

Vickery, John B., *The Literary Impact of the Golden Bough*. Princeton, Princeton University Press, 1974.

3. Method and Theory

1889 "Questions on the manners, customs, religions, superstitions, etc. of uncivilized or semi-civilized peoples," *The Journal of the Anthropological Institute* (London), XVIII (1889), pp. 431–439.

1907 *Questions on the Customs, Beliefs, and Languages of Savages*. Cambridge, University Press, 1907.

1908 *The Scope of Social Anthropology*. A lecture delivered before the University of Liverpool, May 14th, 1908. London, Macmillan. Reprinted in *Psyche's Task* (1909) 1913², etc.

1921 "Sur l'étude des origines humaines," *La renaissance politique, littéraire, artistique*, IX, Nr. 51 (15 décembre 1921), pp. 6881–6885 (1–5). Reprinted in *The Gorgon's Head*, 1927, pp. 337–355.

1922 "The scope and method of mental anthropology," *Science Progress* (London), XVI (April, 1922), pp. 580–594. Reprinted in *Garnered Sheaves*, 1931, pp. 234–251.

4. Main Publications

1885 "The primitive ghost and his relations," *The Contemporary Review* (London), XLVIII (July, 1885), pp. 106–120.

1885 "On certain burial customs as illustrative of the primitive theory of the soul?" *The Journal of the Anthropological Institute* (London), XV (August, 1885), pp. 64–101. Reprinted in *Garnered Sheaves*, 1931, pp. 3–47, 49–50.

1885 "The Prytaneum, the Temple of Vesta, the Vestals, perpetual fires," *The Journal of Philology* (London and Cambridge), XIV (1885), pp. 145–172. Reprinted in *Garnered Sheaves*, 1931, pp. 51–76.

1887 *Totemism.* Edinburgh, Adam and Charles Black. Reprinted in *Totemism and Exogamy*, Vol. I, 1910, pp. 1–87.
French translation by A. Dirr and A. van Gennep: *Le totémisme. Etude d'ethnographie comparée.* Paris, Reinwald, Schleicher Frères, 1898.

1888 "The language of animals," *The Archaeological Review* (London), I (April–May, 1888), 81–91 and 161–181. Reprinted in *Garnered Sheaves*, 1931, pp. 93–127.

1888 "Taboo," *Encyclopaedia Britannica*, 9th ed., Vol. XXIII. Edinburgh, 1888, pp. 15–18.

1888 "Totemism," *Encyclopaedia Britannica*, 9th edition., Vol. XXIII. Edinburgh, 1888, pp. 295–297.

1890 *The Golden Bough. A Study in Comparative Religion*, 2 vols. London–New York, Macmillan.
—2nd edition: *The Golden Bough. A Study in Magic and Religion*, 3 vols. Revised and enlarged. London–New York, Macmillan, 1900.
French translation: *Le rameau d'or. Etude sur la magie et la religion*, 3 vols. Paris, Schleicher Frères. I: *Magie et religion, les tabous* (tr. by R. Stiébel), 1903. II: *Les meurtres rituels. Périls et transmigration de l'âme* (tr. by R. Stiébel and J. Toutain), 1908. III: *Les cultes agraires et silvestres* (tr. by R. Stiébel and J. Toutain), 1911.
—3rd edition: *The Golden Bough. A. Study in Magic and Religion*, 7 parts in 12 vols. Revised and enlarged. London–New York, Macmillan.
Part I: *The Magic Art and the Evolution of Kings*, 2 vols. 1911, etc.
Part II: *Taboo and the Perils of the Soul*. 1911, etc.
Part III: *The Dying God*. 1911, etc.
Part IV: *Adonis, Attis, Osiris. Studies in the History of Oriental Religion*. 1914 (Revised and enlarged of the editions of 1906 and 1907), etc.
Part V: *Spirits of the Corn and of the Wild*, 2 vols. 1912 etc.
Part VI: *The Scapegoat*. 1913.
Part VII: *Balder the Beautiful. The Fire-Festivals of Europe and the Doctrine of the External Soul*, 2 vols. 1913 etc.
Vol. XII: *Bibliography and General Index*. 1915 etc.
French translation: *Le cycle du rameau d'or. Etudes comparées d'histoire*

des religions. Paris, Geuthner, 1921, etc.; 3ᵉ éd. revue et augmentée, 12 vols. 1930, etc.

Tabou et les périls de l'âme (by Henri Peyre). 1927 *(G.B.*, Part II).

Le dieu qui meurt (by Pierre Sayn). 1931 *(G.B.*, Part III).

Adonis. Etude de religions orientales comparées (by Lady Frazer). 1921, 1934² *(G.B.*, Part IVa).

Atys et Osiris (by Henri Peyre). 1926 *(G.B.*, Part IV b, c).

Esprits des blés et des bois (by Pierre Sayn), 2 vols. 1935 *(G.B.*, Part V).

Le bouc émissaire. Etude comparée d'histoire des religions (by Pierre Sayn). 1925 *(G.B.*, Part VI).

Balder le magnifique. Etude comparée d'histoire des religions (by Pierre Sayn), 2 vols. 1931–1934 *(G.B.*, Part VII).

Bibliographie et Table des Matières. Préface de L. Lévy-Bruhl. 1930 *(G.B.*, Vol. XII).

French translation by Lady Frazer: *Le rameau d'or. Edition abrégée.* Paris, Geuthner, 1923, 1939.

German translation by Dr. Helen von Baur: *Der goldene Zweig (The Golden Bough). Das Geheimnis von Glauben und Sitten der Völker*. Leipzig, C. L. Hirschfeld Verlag, 1928.

Italian translation by Lauro de Bosis: *Il ramo d'oro. Storia del pensiero primitivo. Magia e religione* ("Le Conquista del Pensiero": Il Pensiero Filosofico. N. 1), 3 vols. Roma, Alberto Stock, 1922.

Swedish translation by Ernest Klein, with a foreword by Martin P. Nilsson: *Den gyllene grenen. Studier i magi och religion*, 2 vols. Stockholm, Bokförlaget Natur och Kultur, 1925.

1890 "Some popular superstitions of the Ancients," *Folk-Lore* (London), I (June, 1890), pp. 145–171. Reprinted in *Garnered Sheaves*, 1931, pp. 128–150.

1895 *Passages of the Bible*. Chosen for their historic beauty and interest. London, Black, 1895, 1899; 1909², 1927.

1898 *Pausanias's Description of Greece*. Translated with a commentary; 6 vols. London–New York, Macmillan 1898, 1913² (with corrections).

1899 "The origin of totemism," *The Fortnightly Review*, N.S. LXV (April–May, 1899), pp. 647–665, 835–852. Reprinted in *Totemism and Exogamy*, Vol. I, 1910, pp. 89–138.

1900 „A suggestion as to the origin of gender in language," *The Fortnightly Review*, N.S. LXVII (January, 1900), pp. 79–90. Reprinted in *Garnered Sheaves*, 1931, pp. 183–197.

1900 *Pausanias and Other Greek Sketches*. London–New York, Macmillan. Reprinted under the title of *Studies in Greek Scenery, Legend and History*. Selected from his [i.e. Frazer's] Commentary on Pausanias' 'Description of Greece'. 1917, 1919², 1931³.

French translation by Georges Roth, and with a Preface by Maurice Croiset: *Sur les traces de Pausanias*. Paris, Société d'édition "Les Belles Lettres," 1923.

1904 "Artemis and Hippolytus," *The Fortnightly Review*, N.S. LXXVI (December, 1904), pp. 982–995. Reprinted in *The Golden Bough*, 3rd ed., Part I, 1911, pp. 24–40.

1905 "The beginnings of religion and totemism among the Australian aborigenes," *The Fortnightly Review*, N.S. LXXVIII (July–September, 1905) pp. 452–466. Reprinted in *Totemism and Exogamy*, Vol. I, 1910, pp. 139–172.

1905 *Lectures on the Early History of the Kingship*. London–New York, Macmillan. Reissued in 1920 under the title of *The Magical Origin of Kings*. *French* translation by Paul Hyacinthe Loyson: *Les origines magiques de la royauté*. Paris, Geuthner, 1920.

1905 "The origin of circumcision," *The Independent Review* (London), IV (November, 1905), pp. 204–218.

1906 *Adonis, Attis, Osiris. Studies in the History of Oriental Religion*. London–New York, Macmillan. 1907² (revised and enlarged), 1914³ (revised and enlarged, as Part IV of *The Golden Bough*, 3rd edition.)
Also separately the first part: *Adonis. A study in the History of Oriental Religion*. London, Watts.

1907 "Folk-Lore in the Old Testament," in: *Anthropological Essays presented to Edward Burnett Tylor*, Oxford, 1907, pp. 101–174.

1909 *Psyche's Task. A Discourse concerning the Influence of Superstitions on the Growth of Institutions*. London, Macmillan. 1913² (including "The scope of social anthropology," 1908), 1920. Reissued under the title of *The Devil's Advocate. A Plea for Superstition*. Second revised and enlarged edition. 1927.
French translation by Georges Roth: *La tâche de Psyché. De l'influence de la superstition sur le développement des institutions*. Préface de Salomon Reinach. Paris, Armand Colin, 1914. Reissued in 1927 under the title of *L'avocat du diable*. Paris, Geuthner, 1927.

1909 "Some primitive theories of the origin of man," in: A. C. Seward, ed., *Darwin and Modern Science*, Cambridge, 1909, pp. 152–170.

1909 "Howitt and Fison," *Folk-Lore* (London), XX (June, 1909), pp. 144–180. Reprinted in *Sir Roger de Coverley and Other Literary Pieces*, 1920, pp. 210–259.

1910 *Totemism and Exogamy. A Treatise on Certain Early Forms of Superstition and Society*, 4 vols. London, Macmillan. (Includes some previously published essays and papers by Frazer).
French translation of the "Conclusion" by Jean de Pange: *Les origines de la famille et du clan*. Paris, Geuthner, 1922.

1912 *Letters of William Cowper*. Chosen and edited with a memoir and a few notes, 2 vols. London, Macmillan. Reprinted in *Sir Roger de Coverley and Other Literary Pieces*, 1920, pp. 105–193, and in *The Gorgon's Head*, 1927, pp. 205–277.

1913–1924 *The Belief in Immortality and the Worship of the Dead*. The Gifford Lectures, St. Andrews, 1911–1912. 3 vols., London, Macmillan.
1. *The Belief among the Aborigines of Australia, the Torres Straits Islands, New Guinea and Melanesia*, 1913.
2. *The Belief among the Polynesians*, 1922.
3. *The Belief among the Micronesians*, 1924.

1913 "The Serpent and the Tree of Life," in: E. C. Quiggin, ed., *Essays and Studies Presented to William Ridgeway*. Cambridge, pp. 413–426.

1916 "Ancient stories of a Great Flood," *The Journal of the Royal Anthropological Institute* (London), XLVI (1916), pp. 231–283. Also published separately.

1917 "Jacob and the Man-Drakes," *Proceedings of the British Academy, VIII, 1917–18*. London, 1921, pp. 57–79. Also published separately: London, Humphrey Milford and Oxford University Press, 1917.

1917–1918 "The killing of the Khazar kings," *Folk-Lore*, XXVIII (December

1917), pp. 382–407, and XXIX (June, 1918), pp. 162–163. Reprinted in *Garnered Sheaves*, 1931, pp. 212–233.

1918 *Folk-Lore in the Old Testament. Studies in Comparative Religion, Legend and Law.* 3 vols. London, Macmillan. 1919², 1919³. Abridged edition: 1923.

French translation of Vol. I, pp. 52–77 by Pierre Sayn: "Mythes relatifs à l'origine de la mort," *Revue Politique et Littéraire: Revue Bleue* (Paris), LXV (1927), pp. 289–292, 322–327, 365–370.

1920 *Sir Roger de Coverley and Other Literary Pieces.* London, Macmillan. (Contains previously published essays and papers by Frazer).

French translation of half of the book by L. Chouville, with a Preface by Anatole France: *Sir Roger de Coverley et autres essais littéraires.* Paris, Société d'Edition "Les Belles Lettres," 1922. Reissued in 1927 under the title of *Heures de loisir.* Paris, Geuthner, 1927.

1921 "Ernest Renan et la méthode de l'histoire des religions," *La Grande Revue* (Paris), CV (mars 1921), pp. 3–14. Reprinted in *Sir Ernest Renan*, 1923, pp. 33–68; and in *Garnered Sheaves*, 1931, pp. 266–278.

1921 *Apollodorus. The Library.* With an English translation, 2 vols. London, William Heinemann (The Loeb Classical Library); New York, G. P. Putnam's Sons.

1923 *Sur Ernest Renan.* Paris, Claude Avelein. Reprinted in *Garnered Sheaves*, 1931, pp. 261–280.

1923 *Folk-Lore in the Old Testament. Studies in Comparative Religion, Legend and Law.* Abridged edition. London–New York, Macmillan.

French translation by E. Audra, with an Introduction by René Dussaud: *Le folklore dans l'Ancien Testament.* Edition abrégée avec Notes. Paris, Geuthner, 1924.

1924 *Sir James George Frazer. Selected Passages from his Works.* Chosen by Georges Roth ("Les Classiques pour tous," No. 14). Paris, Hatier.

1924 *Leaves from the Golden Bough.* Culled by Lady Frazer. London, Macmillan.

French translation by Lady Frazer: *Le trésor légendaire de l'humanité. Feuilles détachées du Rameau d'Or.* Paris, Librairie de France, F. Sant' Andra, 1925. Geuthner, 1929².

1926 *The Worship of Nature.* Vol. I. London, Macmillan.

French translation of the first part of this book by Pierre Sayn: *Les dieux du ciel.* Paris, Librairie de France, F. Sant'Andra. Geuthner, 1929².

1927 *The Gorgon's Head and Other Literary Pieces.* With a Preface by Anatole France. London, Macmillan. (New edition of *Sir Roger de Coverley and Other Literary Pieces*, 1920, plus reprints of other publications).

1927 *Man, God and Immortality. Thoughts on Human Progress.* Passages chosen from the writings of Sir James George Frazer. Revised and edited by the author. London–New York, Macmillan.

Dutch translation by J. A. Blok: *Mensch, God en onsterfelijkheid. Gedachten over 's Menschen Evolutie.* Stukken, getrokken uit de Geschriften van Sir James George Frazer. Deventer, A. E. Kluwer, 1929.

French translation by Pierre Sayn: *L'homme, Dieu et l'immortalité.* Paris, Geuthner, 1928.

German authorized translation by Dr. H. Frank and Dr. A. Thalheimer: *Mensch, Gott und Unsterblichkeit. Gedanken über den menschlichen Fort-schritt.* Anmerkungen von Dr. H. Frank. Leipzig, C. L. Hirschfeld, 1932.

1929 *Publii Ovidii Nasonis Fastorum Libri Sex. The 'Fasti' of Ovid.* Edited with a translation and commentary by Sir James George Frazer. 5 vols. London, Macmillan. Text, translation and extracts from the commentary reprinted in *Ovid's Fasti* (The Loeb Classical Library). London, William Heinemann, and New York, G. P. Putnam's Sons, 1931; Cambridge, Mass., Harvard University Press, 1951.

1930 *Graecia Antiqua. Maps and Plans to illustrate 'Pausanias's Description of Greece'.* Compiled by Sir James George Frazer. With an explanatory text by A. W. van Buren. London, Macmillan. 1940 (Consists chiefly of the maps and plans from *Pausanias's Description of Greece*, 1898).

1930 *Myths of the Origin of Fire.* London–New York, Macmillan.
    French translation by G. M. Michel Drucker: *Mythes sur l'origine du feu* (Bibliothèque Scientifique). Paris, Payot, 1931; Pb. 1969.

1930 *The Growth of Plato's Ideal Theory.* London, Macmillan.

1931 *Garnered Sheaves. Essays, Addresses and Reviews.* London, Macmillan. (Contains reprints of previous publications).

1933 *The Fear of the Dead in Primitive Religion.* London, Macmillan.
    French translation by Mme la Marquise de Lupré, with a Preface by B. Malinowski: *La crainte des morts dans la religion primitive.* Paris, Geuthner, 1937.

1935 *Creation and Evolution in Primitive Cosmogonies and Other Pieces.* London.
    French translation by Léon Chouville, la marquise de Luppé, la comtesse Jean de Pange: *Essais et souvenirs.* Paris, Geuthner, 1936.

1936 *Aftermath. A Supplement to the Golden Bough.* London.

1937 *Totemica. A Supplement to Totemism and Exogamy.* London, Macmillan.

1938–1939 *Anthologia Anthropologica.* Edited by Robert Angus Downie, 2 vols. Vol. I: *The Native Races of Africa and Madagascar.* Vol. II: *The Native Races of Asia and Europe.* London, Humphries and Co.

1959 *The New Golden Bough.* Edited by Theodor H. Gaster. New York, Criterion Books.

SIGMUND FREUD*

1. Bibliography

See "Titelregister" of Sigmund Freud, *Gesammelte Werke, Chronologisch Geordnet,* Vol. 18 (Frankfurt a. M., Fischer Verlag, 1968), pp. 1075–1099. The titels are in alphabetical order and refer to the publications reproduced in the *Gesammelte Werke.* Comp. "Bibliographische Anmerkung" and "Inhaltsverzeichnis der gesamten Ausgabe" at the end of each volume.

See the introductory sections to each of Freud's writings in English translation being part of *The Standard Edition of the Complete Psychological Works of Sigmund Freud,* 23 vols. London, Hogarth Press and Institute of Psycho-Analysis. Vol. 24 will contain a complete bibliography.

Bentz, Hans W., *Sigmund Freud in Übersetzungen. Eine Bibliographie, 1945–1960/1961.* (Weltliteratur in Übersetzungen, Ser. 1. Vol. 2). Frankfurt a. M., 1961.

See the bibliographies in the following books on Freud:

Bally, Gustav, *Einführung in die Psychoanalyse Sigmund Freuds. Mit Original-texten Freuds*. Unter Mitarbeit von Ambros Uchtenhagen. Rowohlts Deutsche Enzyklopädie 131/132, 1961, 1965.
Fine, Reuben, *Freud. A Critical Re-evaluation of his Theories*. New York, McKay, 1962; London, 1963.
Lavaissière, J. de, *La théorie psychoanalytique de Freud*. (Archives de Philo-sophie, Vol. 8, Cahier 1). 1930.

2. Biography and Appreciation

Allers, Rudolf, *The Successful Error. A critical study of Freudian psychoanalysis*. London, 1940.
Alm, K. A. I., *Den religösa funktionen i människiosjälen. Studier till frågan om religionens innebörd och människans väsen i modern psykologi, särskilt hos Freud och Jung*. Oslo, 1936.
Andreas-Salomé, Lou, *In der Schule bei Freud. Tagebuch eines Jahres 1912/13*. Aus dem Nachlass herausgegeben von Ernst Pfeiffer. Zürich, 1958.
Andersson, Ola, *Studies in the prehistory of psychoanalysis. The etiology of psychoneuroses and some related themes in Sigmund Freud's scientific Writings and Letters, 1886–1896*. Stockholm, Svenska bokförlaget, 1962.
Aron, W., "Notes on Sigmund Freud's ancestry and Jewish contacts," *Yivo Annual of Jewish Social Science*, XI (1956–57), pp. 280–295.
Bakan, David, *Sigmund Freud and the Jewish Mystical Tradition*. Princeton (N. J.), Van Nostrand, 1958. Pb. edition New York, Schocken Books, 1965.
—, "Moses in the thought of Freud," *Commentary*, XXVI (1958), pp. 322–331.
Baron, Salo W., "Book Review of Moses and Monotheism," in: Bruce Mazlish, ed., *Psychoanalysis and History*. Englewood Cliffs, N. J., Prentice Hall, 1963, pp. 50—56.
Binswanger, Ludwig, *Erinnerungen an Sigmund Freud*. 1956.
English translation by Norbert Guterman: *Sigmund Freud. Reminiscen-ces of a Friendship*. New York, Grune & Stratton, 1957.
Bleuler, E., "Die Psychanalyse Freuds. Verteidigung und kritische Bemerkun-gen", *Jahrbuch für Psychoanalytische Forschung*, II (1910), pp. 623–730.
Blondel, Charles, *La psychanalyse*, (Cahiers de la Revue d'Histoire et de Philo-sophie Religieuses, 3). Paris, 1922, 1924².
Blum, Ernest, "Über Sigmund Freuds: Der Mann Moses und die monotheis-tische Religion," *Psyche* (Heidelberg), X (1956), pp. 367–390.
Brown, J. A. C., *Freud and the post-Freudians*. Baltimore, etc., Penguin Books, 1961 (Pelican A 522). Also London, Cassell, 1963.
Brill, A. A., *Freud's Contribution to Psychiatry*. New York, Norton, 1944; London, Chapman & Hall, 1945.
Bry, Ilse, and Rifkin, Alfred H., "Freud and the history of ideas: primary sources, 1886–1910," Academy of Psychoanalysis. *Science and Psycho-analysis* (New York), V (1962), pp. 6–36.
Campbell, Coyne H., *Induced Delusions. The Psychopathy of Freudism*. Chicago, Regent House, 1957.
Cavé, Madeleine, *L'œuvre paradoxale de Freud. Essai sur la théorie des névroses*. Paris, Payot, 1948².
Clemen, Carl, *Die Anwendung der Psychoanalyse auf Mythologie und Religions-geschichte*. Leipzig, 1928.

Clouzet, Maryse (Choisy), *Sigmund Freud. A New Appraisal.* New York, Philosophical Library, 1963. Pb. New York, Citadel Press, 1963.

Dalbiez, R., *La méthode psychanalytique et la doctrine freudienne,* 2 vols. Paris, 1936, 1949².
English translation: *Psychoanalytical Method and the Doctrine of Freud.* 1941.

Eissler, K. R., *Sigmund Freud und die Wiener Universität.* 1966.

Feldman, A. B., "Freudian Theology," *Psychoanalysis,* I, 3 (1952), 31–52 and I, 4 (1953), 37–53.

Fine, Reuben, *Freud. A critical Re-evaluation of his Theories.* New York, McKay, 1962; London, Allen & Unwin, 1963.

Freud, Martin, *Glory Reflected. Sigmund Freud, Man and Father.* London, Angus & Robertson, 1957; New York, Vanguard Press, 1958 (Title: *Sigmund Freud: Man and Father*).

Freud, Sigmund, "Selbstdarstellung," in L. R. Grote, ed., *Die Medizin der Gegenwart in Selbstdarstellungen.* Leipzig, Meiner, 1925 (Band IV). Also published separately. *(Gesammelte Werke,* Vol. XIV, pp. 33–96). See *3. Main Publications* under 1925, and under 1935: "Nachschrift 1935 zur 'Selbstdarstellung'".

—, *Aus den Anfängen der Psychoanalyse. Briefe an Wilhelm Fliess, Abhandlungen und Notizen aus den Jahren 1887–1902.* London, Imago, 1950.
English authorized translation by Eric Mosbacher and James Strachey: *The Origins of Psycho-Analysis. Letters to Wilhelm Fliess, Drafts and Notes: 1887–1902.* Edited by Marie Bonaparte, Anna Freud, Ernst Kris. Introduction by Ernst Kris. London, Imago, 1954.

—, *Psycho-Analysis and Faith. The Letters of Sigmund Freud and Oskar Pfister.* Edited by Heinrich Meng and Ernst L. Freud. Translated by Eric Mosbacher. (Int. Psycho-analytical Library, 59). London, Hogarth Press, 1963.

—, *Briefe 1873–1939.* Ausgewählt und herausgegeben von Ernst L. Freud. Frankfurt am Main, Fischer Verlag, 1960.
English translation by Tania and James Stern: *Letters of Sigmund Freud, 1873–1939.* Selected and edited by Ernst L. Freud. New York, Basic Books, 1960; London, 1961.
Spanish translation by J. M. Perez: *Epistolario 1873–1939.* Madrid, 1963.

Freud in der Gegenwart. Ein Vortragszyklus der Universitäten Frankfurt und Heidelberg zum 100. Geburtstag. Mit Beiträgen von Franz Alexander et al. (Frankfurter Beiträge zur Soziologie, Band 6). Frankfurt am Main, Europäische Verlagsanstalt, 1957.

Fromm, Erich, *Sigmund Freud's Mission. An Analysis of his Personality and Influence.* New York, Harper, 1959.

Gicklhorn, Josef and Renée, *Sigmund Freuds akademische Laufbahn im Lichte der Dokumente.* Wien, Urban & Schwarzenberg, 1960.

Glover, Edward, *Freud or Jung.* London, Allen & Unwin, 1950; New York, Meridian Book M 34, 1956.
French translation: *Freud ou Jung.* Paris, 1954.

Grollman, Earl A., *Judaism in Sigmund Freud's World.* Foreword by Nathan W. Ackerman. New York, Block, 1965, 1966².

Gross, Leonard, *God and Freud.* New York, McKay, 1959.

Guirdham, Arthur, *Christ and Freud. A Study of Religious Experience and Observance.* Preface by Lawrence Durrell. London, Allen & Unwin, 1959.

Hesnard, A. L. M., *L'œuvre de Freud et son importance pour le monde moderne*. Préface de Maurice Merleau-Ponty. (Bibliothèque Scientifique). Paris, Payot, 1960.

Hitschmann, E., "Freud's conception of love," *Int. Journal of Psychoanalysis*, XXXIII (1952,), pp. 421–428.

Hoffman, Frederick J., *Freudianism and the Literary Mind*. Baton Rouge (La.), State University Press, 1945, 1957², 1959³.

Hoop, J. H. van der, *Character and the Unconscious. A Critical Exposition of the psychology of Freud and Jung*. Translated by Elizabeth Trevelyan. London, 1923.

Jones, Ernest *Sigmund Freud. Life and Work*. 3 vols. New York, Basic Books; London, Hogarth Press, 1953–1957, 1964².
    Abridged edition, *The Life and Work of Sigmund Freud*. Edited and abridged by Lionel Trilling and Steven Marcus. With an Introduction by Lionel Trilling. New York, Basic Books, 1961.

—, *Sigmund Freud. Four Centenary Addresses*. New York, Basic Books, 1956.

—, "The psychology of religion," in: Sandor Lórand, ed., *Psychoanalysis Today*. New York, International Universities Press, 1944, pp. 315–325.

—, "The psychology of religion," in: *Essays in Applied Psychoanalysis*, Vol. II: *Essays in Folklore and Religion*. (Int. Psychoanalytical Library). London, Hogarth Press, 1951.

Jugnet, L., *Un psychiatre philosophe. Rudolf Allers ou l'Anti-Freud*. Paris, 1950.

Kardiner, A.; Karush, A.; Ovesey, L., "A Methodological Study of Freudian Theory," *Journal of Nervous and Mental Disease*, CXXIX (1959), Nos. 1–4.

Klauber, John, "Freuds Ansichten zur Religion aus der heutigen Sicht," *Psyche* (Stuttgart), XVI, 1 (1962), pp. 50–57.

Kroeber, A. L., "Totem and Taboo: an ethnological psychoanalysis," *American Anthropologist*, XXII, 1 (1920), pp. 48–55. Reprinted in: *The Nature of Culture* (1952).

—, "Totem and Taboo in retrospect," *American Journal of Sociology*, XL (1939), pp. 446–451. Reprinted in: *The Nature of Culture* (1952).

Laforgue, René, "Au delà du scientisme. I: Freud et le monothéisme; II: Psychologie du mérite et de la grâce," *Psyche* (Paris), IV (1949), pp. 2–29, 30–49.

La Piere, R., *The Freudian Ethic*. New York, Duell, Sloan & Pearce; London, Allen & Unwin, 1959.

Lauzun, Gérard, *Sigmund Freud, the Man and his Theories*. Translated from the French by Patrick Evans. London, Souvenir Press, 1963: New York, Eriksson, 1965.
    Spanish translation by Adolfo Castaño: *Siegmund Freud*, Madrid, 1962.

—, *Sigmund Freud. Présentation, choix de textes, bibliographie*. Paris, Seghers, 1962.

Lee, Roy Stuart, *Freud and Christianity*. New York, A. A. Wyn, 1949.

Ludwig, E., *Der entzauberte Freud*. 1946.

MacIntyre, Alasdair C., *The Unconscious; a Conceptual Analysis*. London, Routledge & Kegan Paul; New York, Humanities Press, 1958.

Madison, Peter, *Freud's concept of repression and defense, its theoretical and observational language*. Minneapolis, University of Minnesota Press, 1961.

Marcuse, Herbert, *Eros and Civilization. A Philosophical Inquiry into Freud*. Boston, Beacon, 1955. London, 1956.

Marcuse, L., *Sigmund Freud. Sein Bild vom Menschen*. 1956.

Masih, Y., "Metapsychology of James and Freud," *Journal of Bihar University*, I (1956), pp. 61–69.

Mead, Margaret, "An ethnologist's footnote to 'Totem and Taboo'," *Psychoanalytic Review*, XVII (1930), pp. 297–304.

Meadow, Arnold, and Vetter, Harold J., "Freudian theory and the Judaic value system," *Int. Journal of Social Psychiatry*, V (1959), pp. 197–207.

Meyerhoff, Hans, "Freud and the ambiguity of culture," in: Bruce Mazlish, ed., *Psychoanalysis and History*. Englewood Cliffs, N. J., Prentice Hall, 1963, pp. 56–69.

Mitscherlich, Alexander, ed., *Entfaltung der Psychoanalyse. Das Wirken Sigmund Freuds in die Gegenwart*. Stuttgart, Klett, 1956.

Moxon, C., "Freud's denial of religion," *British Journal of Medical Psychology*, XI (1931), 151–157.

Murphy, M. B., "Freud and Nietzsche on religion," *Insight*, III, 1 (1964), pp. 19–34.

Natenberg, Maurice, *Freudian Psycho-antics. Fact and Fraud in Psychoanalysis*. Chicago, Regent House, 1953.

—; *The Case History of Sigmund Freud. A Psycho-Biography*. Chicago, Regent House, 1955.

Nelson, Benjamin N., ed., *Freud and the 20th Century*. New York, Meridian Book M 45, 1957.

Oerlemans, A. C., *Development of Freud's Conception of Anxiety*. Amsterdam, North-Holland Publ. Co., 1949.

Perls, F. S., *Ego, Hunger and Aggression. A Revision of Freud's Theory and Method*. Durban, 1945; London, Allen & Unwin, 1947.

Pesch, Edgar, *La pensée de Freud*. Paris, 1960.

Pfister, O., "Illusion einer Zukunft," *Imago*, XIV (1928), 149–184.

Philp, Howard L., *Freud and Religious Belief*. London, Rockliff; New York, Pitman, 1956.

Plé, Albert, *Freud et la religion*. Paris, Ed. du Cerf, 1968.
German translation by E. M. Kittelmann and A. Wucherer: *Freud und die Religion. Eine kritische Bestandsaufnahme für die Diskussion der Zeit*. Wien, Cura Verlag, 1969.

Puner, Helen Walker, *Freud, his Life and his Mind. A Biography*. New York, Howell, Soskin (Grosset & Dunlap), 1947; London, 1949.
Spanish translation by Miguel Siguán: *Freud. Su vida y su muerte*. Barcelona, 1951.

Racker, Heinrich, "On Freud's position towards religion," *American Imago*, XIII, 2 (1956), 97–121.

Reik, Theodor, *Freud als Kulturkritiker*, 1930.

—, *From Thirty Years with Freud. Listening with the inner ear*. Translated by Richard Winston. New York, Farrar & Rinehart, 1940.

Ricœur, Paul, *De l'interprétation. Essai sur Freud*. Paris, Ed. du Seuil, 1965.

—, *Le conflit des interprétations. Essais d'herméneutique*. Paris, Ed. du Seuil, 1969 (Part II: "Herméneutique et psychanalyse").

Rieff, Philip, "The meaning of history and religion in Freud's thought," *Journal of Religion*, XXXI, 2 (1951), 114–131. Reprinted in: Bruce Mazlish, ed., *Psychoanalysis and History*. Englewood Cliffs, N. J., Prentice Hall, 1963, pp. 23—45.

—, *Freud. The Mind of the Moralist*. New York, Viking Press, 1959, 1960². Pb. New York, Doubleday Anchor Book, 1961; London, Gollancz, 1959.

Riemann, Fritz, ed., *Lebendige Psychoanalyse. Die Bedeutung Sigmund Freuds für das Verstehen des Menschen*. Unter Mitarbeit von Walter Seitz et al. München, Beck, 1956.

Riesman, David, "Freud: religion as neurosis," *University of Chicago Round Table*, No. 638 (1950), pp. 13–20.

Roazen, Paul, *Freud: political and social thought*. New York, Alfred A. Knopf, 1968; London, Hogarth Press, 1969.

—, *Brother Animal. The Story of Freud and Tausk*. Harmondsworth, Penguin Books, 1973.

Roback, A. A., *Freudiana*. Including unpublished letters from Freud, Havelock Ellis, Pavlov, Bernard Shaw, Romain Rolland, et alii. Cambridge (Mass.), Sci-Art Publ., 1957.

Rümke, H. C., *Karakter en aanleg in verband met het ongeloof*. Amsterdam, 1939 etc.

Sachs, Hans, *Freud, Master and Friend*. London, Imago, 1945.
  German translation by Emmy Sachs: *Freud, Meister und Freund*. London, Imago, 1950.

Schafer, R., "The Loving and beloved Superego in Freud's structural theory," *Psychoanalytic Study of the Child*, XV (1960), pp. 163–188.

Scharfenberg, Joachim, *Sigmund Freud und seine Religionskritik als Herausforderung für den christlichen Glauben*. Göttingen, Vandenhoeck & Ruprecht, 1968.

Schoenwald, Richard L., *Freud, the Man and his Mind, 1856–1956*. New York, Knopf, 1956.

Shakow, David, and Rapaport, David, *The Influence of Freud on American Psychology*. New York, International Universities Press, 1964.

Sierksma, Fokke, *Freud, Jung en de religie*. With English summary. Original title: *Phaenomenologie der religie en complexe psychologie*. Assen, Van Gorcum, 1951.

Spehlmann, Rainer, *Sigmund Freuds neurologische Schriften: eine Untersuchung zur Vorgeschichte der Psychoanalyse*. Vorwort Paul Vogel. Berlin, Springer, 1953.

Stoodley, Bartlett H., *The Concepts of Sigmund Freud*. Glencoe (Ill.), Free Press, 1959.

Tourney, G., "Freud and the Greeks. A study of the influence of classical Greek mythology and philosophy upon the development of Freudian thought," *Journal of the History of the Behavioral Sciences*, I, 1 (1965), pp. 67–85.

Tuinstra, C. L., *Het symbool in de psychoanalyse. Beschrijving en theologische kritiek*. Amsterdam, 1933.

Vennes, Gaston, *Inconscient freudien et problèmes de liberté*. Trois Rivières (Québec), 1960.

Weser, H. A., *Sigmund Freuds und Ludwig Feuerbachs Religionskritik*. 1936.

Whyte, Lancelot L., *The Unconscious before Freud*. New York, Basic Books, 1960.

Wittels, Fritz, *Sigmund Freud. Der Mann, die Lehre, die Schule*. Leipzig–Wien–Zürich, Tal, 1924.
  English translation by Eden and Cedar Paul: *Sigmund Freud, his Personality, his Teaching, and his School*. London, Allen & Unwin, 1924.

—, *Freud and his Time*. Translated by Louise Brink. New York, Liveright, 1931, 1956[2]; London, Owen, 1931.

Wortis, Joseph, *Fragments of an Analysis with Freud.* New York, Simon & Schuster; London, Vision, 1954.

Zilboorg, Gregory, *Psychoanalysis and Religion.* Ed. with intr. by Margaret Stone Zilboorg. New York, 1962.

—, *Sigmund Freud. His Exploration of the Mind of Man.* New York, Scribner, 1951.

—, *Freud, 1956.* An address delivered at the Grolier Club. New York, 1956.

—, *Freud and Religion. A Restatement of an old Controversy.* Westminster (Md.), Newman Press, 1958.
  French translation: "Freud et la religion," *Suppl. Vie Spirituelle,* XII (1959), pp. 251–294.
  Spanish translation in: *Revista de Psicología* (Bogota), V (1960), pp. 19–50.

3. General Editions of the Works of Sigmund Freud

a) German:

1906–1922 *Sammlung Kleiner Schriften zur Neurosenlehre (SKSN),* 5 vols. Leipzig–Wien, Verlag Hugo Heller.

1924–1934 *Gesammelte Schriften (GS),* 12 vols. Herausgabe besorgt unter Mitwirkung des Verfassers von Anna Freud, Otto Rank und A. J. Storfer. Leipzig–Wien–Zürich, Internationaler Psychoanalytischer Verlag.

1940–1968 *Gesammelte Werke, Chronologisch Geordnet (GW),* 18 vols. Unter Mitwirkung von Maria Bonaparte, Prinzessin Georg von Griechenland, herausgegeben von Anna Freud, E. Bibring, W. Hoffer, E. Kris, O. Isakower. Gesamtregister zusammengestellt von Lilla Veszy–Wagner. London, Imago Publ., Vol. 1–17 (1940–1950); Frankfurt am. M., Fischer Verlag, Vol. 18 (1968).

b) English:

1924–1950 *Collected Papers (CP),* 5 vols. Authorized translation under the supervision of Joan Riviere. Vol. 5 edited by James Stachey. London, Hogarth Press (International Psycho-Analytical Library, 7–10, 37).

1953 *Standard Edition of the Complete Psychological Works of Sigmund Freud (SE),* 24 vols. Translated from the German under the general editorship of James Strachey, in collaboration with Anna Freud, assisted by Alix Strachey and Alan Tyson. London, Hogarth Press and Institute of Psycho-Analysis.

c) Spanish:

1922–1934 *Obras Completas (OC),* 17 vols. Madrid.

1948 *Obras Completas,* 2 vols. Translation by Luis López Ballesteros y de Torres. Madrid, Biblioteca Nueva.

4. Main Publications

1895 *Studien über Hysterie*, by J. Breuer and S. Freud (in collaboration). Leipzig–Wien, Deuticke. 1922[4]. *(GS* 1; *GW* 1, both without the sections: "Krankengeschichte Frl. Anna O..." and "Theoretisches", written by J. B.).
English translation by A. A. Brill (without the sections by J. B.) in: *Selected Papers on Hysteria and other Psychoneuroses.* New York–Washington, Nervous and Mental Disease Publ., 1909, 1912[2], 1920[3]. Complete translation by A. A. Brill: *Studies in Hysteria.* New York–Washington, The same, 1936. New translation by John Rickman (without the sections by J. B.) *(CP* 1). New complete translation by James Strachey: *Studies on Hysteria (SE* 2).
Spanish translation: *La Histeria.* Madrid, 1925 *(OC* 10), 1967.
Other translations: Japanese 1930, Czech 1947.

1900 *Die Traumdeutung.* Leipzig–Wien, Deuticke. 1930[8], (revised). *(GS* 2–3; *GW* 2–3).
English translation by A. A. Brill: *The Interpretation of Dreams.* London, Allen, 1913; London, Allen & Unwin; New York, Macmillan, 1932[3] (revised; reprinted 1950, 1951, etc.). *(SE* 4–5).
French translation by J. Meyerson. Paris, Alcan, 1926.
Italian translation: *L'interpretazione dei sogni.* Roma, 1948, 1952[2].
Spanish translation: *La interpretación de los sueños,* 2 vols. Madrid, 1922, 1928[2]. *(OC* 6–7).
Other translations: Russian 1913, Swedish 1927, Japanese 1930, Hungarian 1934, Czech 1938.

1901 *Über den Traum,* in: *Grenzfragen des Nerven- und Seelenlebens.* Edited by Löwenfeld and Kurella. Wiesbaden, Bergmann, 1901, 1922[3]. *(GS* 3; *GW* 2–3).
English translation by M. D. Eder: *On Dreams.* With an Introduction by W. Leslie Mackenzie. London, Heinemann, 1914. New translation by James Strachey: *On Dreams (SE* 5).
French translation by Hélène Legros. Paris, Gallimard. (Les Documents Bleus), 1925.
Italian translation: *Il sogno.* Napoli, 1919 (Biblioteca psicoanalitica Italiana, 2).
Spanish translation 1923. *(OC* 2).
Other translations: Russian 1909, Dutch 1913, Hungarian 1915, Danish 1920, Polish 1923, Swedish 1924, Japanese 1929.

1901 "Zur Psychopathologie des Alltaglebens (Über Vergessen, Versprechen, Vergreifen, Aberglaube und Irrtum)," *Monatsschrift für Psychiatrie und Neurologie,* X, 1, 2 (1901). Reissued as a book: Berlin, Karger, 1904, 1919[6], Leipzig–Wien–Zürich. Int. Psy. Verlag, 1920[7], 1924[10] (exp.) London, Imago, 1947[12] *(GS* 4, *GW* 4).
English translation by A. A. Brill: *Psychopathology of Everyday Life.* London, Fischer Unwin; New York, Macmillan, 1914, 1935[16]; London, Pelican Books, 1938, 1939, etc. London, Ernest Benn, 1949; London, Collins (Comet Books), 1958. *(SE* 6), with title "The Psychopathology of Everyday Life".
French translation by S. Jankélévitch: *La psychopathologie de la vie quotidienne.* Paris, Payot, 1922.

Italian translation: *Psicopatologia della vita quotidiana.* Roma, 1948.
Spanish translation: *Psicopatología de la vida cotidiana. Olvidos, equivocaciones, torpezas, supersticiones y errores.* Prólogo de José Ortega Y Gasset. Madrid, 1922, 1967²; Barcelona, 1966. *(OC* 1)
Other translations: Russian 1910, Polish 1912, Dutch 1916, Hungarian 1923, Japanese 1930, Serbo-croatian 1937, Czech 1938, Portuguese n. d., Swedish n. d.

1905 *Drei Abhandlungen zur Sexualtheorie.* Leipzig–Wien, Deuticke, 1905, 1925⁶. *(GS* 5; *GW* 5).
English translation by A. A. Brill: *Three Contributions to the Sexual Theory.* New York–Washington (Nervous and Mental Disease Monograph Series, 7), 1910. Reprinted: *Three Contributions to the Theory of Sex* (Same Series, 7), 1916², 1918³, 1930⁴. New translation by James Strachey: *Three Essays on the Theory of Sexuality.* London, Imago, 1949; London, Hogarth Press, 1962. *(SE* 7).
French translation by B. Reverchon-Jouve: *Trois essais sur la théorie de la sexualité.* Paris, Gallimard (Les Documents Bleus, 1), 1923, 1925²; reprinted in 1962 (in series "Idées").
Italian translation by M. Levi-Bianchini. Napoli, 1921 (Biblioteca Psicoanalytica Italiana, 3). New translation by Francesco Adami: *Enciclopedia sessuale.* Roma, 1947. New translation by G. L. Douglas Scotti: *Tre saggi sulla teoria della sessualità.* Milano, 1960.
Spanish translation: Madrid, 1922. *(OC* 2).
Other translations: Hungarian 1915, Polish 1924, Czech 1926, Japanese 1931, Danish 1934.

1905 *Der Witz und seine Beziehung zum Unbewussten.* Leipzig–Wien, Deuticke, 1905, 1925⁴. *(GS* 9; *GW* 6).
English translation by A. A. Brill: *Wit and its Relation to the Unconscious.* New York, Moffat, Yard & Co., 1916, 1917²; London, Fisher Unwin, 1916; London, Kegan Paul, 1922. New translation by James Strachey: *Jokes and their Relation to the Unconscious.* London, Routledge & Kegan Paul, 1960. *(SE* 8).
French translation by Marie Bonaparte and M. Nathan. Paris, Gallimard (L'Homme, 19), n. d.
Spanish translation: *El chiste y su relaciòn con lo inconsciente.* Madrid, 1923. *(OC* 3).
Other translation: Japanese 1930.

1907 *Der Wahn und die Träume in W. Jensens 'Gradiva'.* (Schriften zur angewandten Seelenkunde, Heft 1). Wien, Heller. Später: Leipzig–Wien, Deuticke, 1912², 1924³. *(GS* 9; *GW* 7).
English translation by Helen M. Downey: *Delusion and Dream. An Interpretation in the Light of psychoanalysis of Gravida. A Novel, byWilhelm Jensen, which is here translated.* Preface G. Stanley Hall. NewYork, Moffat, Yard & Co., 1917; London, Allen & Unwin, 1921. New translation: *Delusions and Dreams in Jensen's Gravida (SE* 9).
Italian translation: Napoli, 1923 (Biblioteca Psicoanalitica Italiana, 7).
Spanish translation: Madrid, 1923. *(OC* 3).
Other translations: Russian 1912, Japanese 1929.

1907 "Zwangshandlungen und Religionsübungen," *Zeitschrift für Religionspsychologie,* I, 1 (1907). *(SKSN* 2, 1909, 1912², 1921³; *GS* 10; *GW* 7).
English translation by R. C. McWalters: *Obsessive Acts and Religious*

Practices (CP 2). New translation: *Obsessive Actions and Religious Practices
(SE* 9).
Other translation: Dutch 1914.

1908 "Die 'kulturelle' Sexualmoral und die moderne Nervosität," *Mutter-
schutz* (section "Sexualprobleme", N. F., IV (1908). *(SKSN* 2, 1909, 1912²,
1921³; *GS* 5; *GW* 7).
English translation (incomplete) by William J. Robinson: "Modern sexual
morality and modern nervousness," *American Journal of Urology,* XI
(1915). pp. 391–405. New York, Eugenics Publ., 1931 (incomplete). New
translation by E. B. M. Herford and E. Colburn Mayne *(CP* 2). New
translation: *'Civilized' Sexual Morality and Modern Nervous Illness
(SE* 9).
Spanish translation: Madrid, 1929. *(OC* 13).

1910 *Über Psychoanalyse.* Fünf Vorlesungen gehalten zur zwanzigjährigen
Gründungsfeier der Clark University in Worcester (Mass.), September
1909. Leipzig–Wien, Deuticke. 1930⁸. *(GS* 4; *GW* 8).
English translation by H. W. Chase: *Five Lectures on Psycho-Analysis.*
First in *The American Journal of Psychology,* XXI, 2–3 (1910), pp. 181–218.
Also in: "Lectures and Addresses Delivered before the Departments of
Psychology and Pedagogy in Celebration of the Twentieth Anniversary
of the Opening of Clark University in Worcester (Mass.)". Part I, pp.
1–38. New translation *(SE* 11).
French translation by L. Le Lay. Genève, 1921.
Italian translation: *Sulla psicoanalisi.* Cinque conferenze tenute nel
Settembre 1909 alla Clark University di Worcester (Mass.), in occasione
del 20 anniversario di fondazione. Napoli, 1915 (Biblioteca Psicoanalitica
Italiana).
Spanish translation: Madrid, 1923. *(OC* 2).
Other translations: Russian 1911, Polish 1911, Hungarian 1912, Dutch
1912, Danish 1920, Japanese 1933.

1910 *Eine Kindheitserinnerung des Leonardo da Vinci.* (Schriften zur ange-
wandten Seelenkunde, Heft VII). Leipzig–Wien, Deuticke. 1912², 1923³.
(GS 9; *GW* 8).
English translation by A. A. Brill: *Leonardo da Vinci: a psychosexual
study of an infantile reminiscence.* New York, Moffat, Yard & Co., 1916;
London, Kegan Paul, 1922; New York, Dodd Mead, 1932. New translation
by Alan Tyson: *Leonardo da Vinci and a Memory of his Childhood.* With
an Introduction by Brian Farrell. Harmondsworth, Penguin Books
(Pelican A 519), 1963. *(SE* 11).
French translation by Marie Bonaparte. Paris, Gallimard (Les Documents
Bleus, 32), 1927.
Spanish translation: Madrid, 1924. *(OC* 8).
Other translations: Russian 1912, Japanese 1931, Czech 1933.

1912 "Einige Bemerkungen über den Begriff des Unbewussten in der Psycho-
analyse," *Internationale Zeitschrift für ärtzliche Psychoanalyse,* I (1913).
(SKSN 4; *GS* 5; *GW* 8).
Original *English* text: "A Note on the unconscious in psycho-analysis,"
Proceedings Society for Psychical Research, Medical Supplement, Part
LXVI, Vol. XXVI. *(CP* 4; *SE* 12).

1912 "Einige Übereinstimmungen im Seelenleben der Wilden und der Neurotiker, *Imago,* I (1912), II (1913). Issued as a book: *Totem und Tabu.*

Einige Übereinstimmungen im Seelenleben der Wilden und der Neurotiker. Leipzig–Wien, Heller, 1913. *(GS* 10; *GW* 9).
English translation by A. A. Brill: *Totem and Taboo: resemblances between the psychic lives of savages and neurotics.* New York, Moffat, Yard & Co., 1918, 1919[2]; London, Routledge, 1919. New translation by James Strachey: *Totem and Taboo. Some points of agreement between the mental lives of savages and neurotics.* London, Routledge & Kegan Paul, 1950; pb. idem, 1960 *(SE* 13).
French translation by S. Jankélévitch. Paris, Payot, 1924.
Italian translation: *Totem e tabu. Di alcune concordanze nella vita psichica dei selvaggi e dei nevrotici.* Bari, 1930, 1946[2], 1953[3].
Spanish translation: *Totem y Tabú.* Madrid, 1923, 1968[2].
Other translations: Hungarian 1918, Japanese 1930, Hebrew 1939 (with preface by the author), Portugese n. d.

1913 "Das Interesse an der Psychoanalyse," *Scientia,* XIV, 31–32 (1913) pp. 240–250, 369–384. *(GS* 4; *GW* 8).
English translation by James Strachey: *The Claims of Psycho-Analysis to Scientific Interest (SE* 13).

1913 "Märchenstoffe in Träumen," *Int. Zeitschrift für ärztliche Psychoanalyse,* I, 2 (1913), pp. 147–151. *(SKSN* 4; *GS* 3; *GW* 10).
English translation by James Strachey: *The Occurence in Dreams of Material from Fairy Tales (CP* 4; *SE* 12).
Other translations: Japanese 1931 and 1932.

1914 "Zur Geschichte der psychoanalytischen Bewegung," *Jahrbuch für psychoanalytische und psychopathologische Forschungen,* VI (1914). *(SKSN* 4; *GS* 4; *GW* 10).
English translation by A. A. Brill: "The history of the psychoanalytic movement," *Psychoanalytical Review,* LLL (1916), pp. 406–454. New York, Nervous and Mental Disease Publ. 1916. New translation by Joan Riviere: *On the History of the Psychoanalytic Movement (CP* 1; *SE* 14).
Spanish translation: Madrid, 1928. *(OC* 12).
Other translations: Japanese 1931, Hungarian 1936.

1914 "Der Moses des Michelangelo," *Imago,* III, 1 (1914), pp. 15–36; Frankfurt a. Main, Insel Bücherei no. 817, 1964 *(GS* 10; *GW* 10. See also "Nachtrag" in *GS* 11; *GW* 14).
English translation by Alex Strachey: *"The Moses of Michelangelo" (CP* 4; *SE* 13).
French translation in *Revue française de psychanalyse,* I (1927).
Other translations: Japanese 1931 and 1933.

1913 "Das Unbewusste," *Int. Zeitschrift für Psychoanalyse,* 111, 4–5 (1913), pp. 189–203 and 257–269 *(SKSN* 4; *GS* 5; *GW* 10).
English translation by Cecil M. Baines: *The Unconscious (CP* 4; *SE* 14).

1916–1917 *Vorlesungen zur Einführung in die Psychoanalyse,* 3 vols. Leipzig–Wien, Heller. 1918[2] (one vol.) *(GS* 7; *GW* 11). See also *Neue Folge der Vorlesungen zur Einführung in die Psychoanalyse,* 1932.)
English translation by G. Stanley Hall: *A General Introduction to Psychoanalysis.* New York, Boni & Liveright, 1920, 1935[2]. New translation by Joan Riviere, with a preface by Ernest Jones: *Introductory Lectures on Psycho-Analysis.* London, Allen & Unwin, 1922, 1923[2], 1929[3] (revised), 1933[4], 1936[5], etc. *(SE* 15–16).
French translation by S. Jankélévitch: *Introduction à la psychanalyse.*

Paris, Payot, 1922; reprinted 1962 (Petite Bibliothèque Payot, 6).
Italian translation: *Introduzione allo studio della psicoanalisi*, 2 vols.
Napoli, 1922 (Biblioteca Psicoanalitica Italiana, 8–9).
Spanish translation: *Introducciòn al psicoanálisis*. Madrid, 1923. *(OC* 4–5).
Other translations: Dutch 1917, Russian 1922–23 (2 vols.), Japanese 1928, Norwegian 1929, Hebrew 1930, Hungarian 1932, Serbo-croatian 1933, Chinese 1934, Polish 1935, Czech 1936, Yiddish 1936–38 (2 vols.), Braille printing n.d.

1919 "Vorrede" zu '*Probleme der Religionspsychologie*' von Dr. Theodor Reik.
(Int. Psychoanalytische Bibliothek, 25). Leipzig–Wien–Zürich, Int. Ps. Verlag, 1919, 1928² (Teil I: Das Ritual, pp. VII–XII). *(GS* 11; *GW* 12).
English translation in Theodor Reik, *Ritual: Psycho-Analytical Studies*.
(Int. Psychoanalytical Library, 19). London, Hogarth Press; New York, Norton, 1931. *(CP* 5; *SE* 17).

1920 *Jenseits des Lustprinzips*. Leipzig–Wien–Zürich, Int. Ps. Verlag. 1921², 1924³. *(GS* 6; *GW* 13).
English translation by C. J. M. Hubback: *Beyond the Pleasure Principle*.
(Int. Psychoanalytical Library, 4). London–Vienna, 1922. New translation by James Strachey: *Beyond the Pleasure Principle*. (Idem). London, Hogarth Press & Institute of Psycho-Analysis, 1950, 1961. New York, Bantam Classic FC 49, 1959. *(SE* 18).
French translation by S. Jankélévitch, in: *Essais de Psychanalyse*. Paris, Payot, 1927.
Italian translation: "Al di la' del principio del piacere," in: *Nuovi saggi di psicoanalisi*. Roma, 1946.
Spanish translation: Madrid, 1922. *(OC* 9).
Other translations: Dutch 1922, Hungarian 1923, Japanese 1930 (twice).

1921 *Massenpsychologie und Ich-Analyse*. Leipzig–Wien–Zürich, Int. Ps. Verlag. 1924². *(GS* 6; *GW* 13).
English translation by James Strachey: *Group Psychology and the Analysis of the Ego*. (Int. Psychoanalytical Library, 6). London–Vienna, 1922. *(SE* 18).
French translation by S. Jankélévitch: *Psychologie collective et analyse du moi*. Paris, Payot, 1924.
Italian translation: "Psicología delle masse e analisi dell'io," in: *Nuovi saggi di psicoanalisi*. Roma, 1946.
Spanish translation: *Psicología de las masas y análisis del yo*. Madrid, 1924. *(OC*, 9).
Other translations: Dutch 1924, Japanese 1929 and 1930.

1923 *Das Ich und das Es*. Leipzig–Wien–Zürich, Int. Psychoanalytischer Verlag. *(GS* 6, *GW* 13).
English translation by Joan Riviere: *The Ego and the Id*. (Int. Psychoanalytical Library, 12). London, Woolf, Institute of Psycho-Analysis, 1927, 1950². New translation by James Strachey *(SE* 19).
French translation by S. Jankélévitch, in: *Essais de Psychanalyse*. Paris, Payot, 1927.
Italian translation: "L'Io e l'Es," in: *Nuovi saggi di psicoanalisi*. Roma, 1946.
Spanish translation: *El Yo y el Ello*. Madrid, 1924. *(OC* 9).
Other translations: Japanese 1930, Hungarian 1937, Braille printing n.d.

1923 "Eine Teufelsneurose im siebzehnten Jahrhundert," *Imago*, IX (1923). Issued as a book: Leipzig–Wien–Zürich, Int. Psychoanalytischer Verlag, 1924, 1927². *(GS* 10; *GW* 13).
English translation by Edward Glower: *A Neurosis of Demoniacal Possession in the seventeenth Century (CP* 4). New translation by James Strachey: *A seventeenth-century Demonological Neurosis (SE* 19).
French translation by Mme. Edouard Morty and Mme. Marie Bonaparte, in: *Revue Française de Psychanalyse*, I (1927). Also in: *Essais de Psychanalyse appliquée*. Paris, Gallimard, n.d.
Other translation: Japanese 1932.

1924 *Beiträge zur Psychologie des Liebeslebens*. Leipzig–Wien–Zürich, Int. Ps. Verlag. (Contains previously published essays and papers).

1924 *Psychoanalytische Studien an Werken der Dichtung und Kunst*. Leipzig–Wien–Zürich, Int. Ps. Verlag. (Contains previously published essays and papers).

1924 *Zur Technik der Psychoanalyse und zur Metapsychologie*. Leipzig–Wien–Zürich, Int. Ps. Verlag. (Contains previously published essays and papers).

1924 *Kurzer Abriss der Psychoanalyse. (GS* 11; *GW* 13).
First published in *English*, translated by A. A. Brill: "Psychoanalysis: exploring the hidden recesses of the mind," in: *These eventful Years. The twentieth century in the Making, as told by Many of its Makers.* London–New York, Encyclopaedia Britannica Publ., 1924: Vol. II, Chap. 73, pp. 511–523. New translation by James Strachey: *A Short Account of Psycho-Analysis (SE* 19).

1925 "Selbstdarstellung," in: L. R. Grote, ed., *Die Medizin der Gegenwart in Selbstdarstellungen*. Leipzig, Meiner 1925, Band IV. Leipzig–Wien–Zürich, Int. Ps. Verlag, 1934, 1936² (revised); London, Imago, 1946, etc. *(GS* 11, *GW* 14).
English translation by James Strachey: *An Autobiographical Study*, together with *The Problem of Lay-Analyses*, translated by A. Paul Maerker-Branden, with Introduction by S. Ferenczi. New York–London, Brentano, 1927. London, Woolf, Hogarth Press; New York, Norton as: *Autobiography*, 1935. *(SE* 20).
French translation by Marie Bonaparte. Paris, Gallimard, (Les Documents Bleus, 45) 1928.
Italian translation: *Mia vita ed opera*. Roma, 1948. Also in: *La mia vita e la psicanalisi*. Milano, 1956.
Spanish translation: Madrid, 1924. *(OC* 9).
Other translations: Hungarian 1925 and 1936, Japanese 1932, Czech 1936, Braille printing n.d.

1925 "Die Widerstände gegen die Psychoanalyse," *Imago*, XI (1925). *(GS* 11, *GW* 14).
First published in *French* in: *La Revue Juive*, May 1925.
English translation by James Strachey: *The Resistance to Psycho-Analysis (CP* 5; *SE* 20).
Other translation: Norwegian 1930.

1926 *Hemmung, Symptom und Angst*. Leipzig–Wien–Zürich, Int. Ps. Verlag. *(GS* 11, *GW* 14).
English translation: *Inhibition, Symptom and Anxiety*. With a Preface by S. Ferenczi. Stanford (Conn.), The Psychoanalytic Institute, 1927. New translation by H. A. Bunker: *The Problem of Anxiety*. New York,

The Psychoanalytic Quarterly Press and Norton, 1936. Third translation by Alix Strachey: *Inhibitions, Symptoms and Anxiety (SE* 20).
Italian translation: *Inibizione, sintomo e angoscia.* Torino, 1951.
Spanish translation: *Inhibición, síntoma y angustia. La neuropsicosis de defensa y otros ensayos.* Madrid, 1926. *(OC* 11).
Other translations: Russian 1926, Japanese 1931, Braille printing n.d.

1926 *Die Frage der Laienanalyse. Unterredungen mit einem Unparteiischen.* Leipzig–Wien–Zürich, Int. Psychoanalytischer Verlag. *(GS* 11, *GW* 14).
English translation by A. Paul Marker-Branden: *The Problem of Lay-Analyses,* together with *An Autobiographical Study,* translated by James Strachey, with Introduction by S. Ferenczi. New York–London, Brentano, 1927. New translation by Nancy Procter-Gregg: *The Question of Lay Analysis. An Introduction to Psycho-Analysis.* Preface by Ernest Jones. London, Imago, 1947. *(SE* 20).
French translation by Marie Bonaparte. Paris, Gallimard (Les Documents Bleus, 45) 1928.
Italian translation, in: *La mia vita e la psicanalisi.* Milano, 1956.
Spanish translation: *Análisis profano.* Madrid, 1928. *(OC* 12).
Other translation: Japanese 1932.

1926 *Psycho-Analysis. (GS* 12; *GW* 14).
First published in *English* under the title of "Psychoanalysis: Freudian School," in: *Encyclopaedia Britannica.* London, 13th edition, 1926, Vol. III, pp. 253–255; 14th edition, 1929, Vol. XVIII, pp. 672–674. *(SE* 20).

1927 "Fetischismus," *Internationale Zeitschrift für Psychoanalyse,* XIII (1927). *(GS* 11; *GW* 14).
English translation by James Strachey: "Fetishism," *The International Journal of Psycho-Analysis,* IX (1928), pp. 161–166. *(SE* 21).
Other translations: Japanese 1932, 1933.

1927 *Die Zukunft einer Illusion.* Leipzig–Wien–Zürich, Int. Ps. Verlag, 1928². *(GS* 11; *GW* 14).
English translation by W. D. Robson-Scott: *The Future of an Illusion.* (Int. Psychoanalytical Library, 15). London, Hogarth Press, Woolf, 1928; New York, Liveright, 1928. New translation by James Strachey *(SE* 21).
French translation by Marie Bonaparte. Paris, Denoël & Steele, 1932.
Spanish translation: *El porvenir de las religiones.* Madrid, 1930. *(OC* 14).
Other translations: Swedish 1928, Dutch 1929, Czech 1929, Japanese 1931 and 1932, Hungarian 1945.

1927 *Essais de Psychanalyse.* Translation by S. Jankélévitch (Au-delà du principe du plaisir; Psychologie collective et analyse du moi; Le Moi et le ça; Considérations actuelles sur la guerre et sur la mort).

1928 "Ein religiöses Erlebnis," *Imago,* XIV (1928). *(GS,* 11; *GW* 14).
English translation by James Strachey: "A religious experience," *Int. Journal of Psycho-Analysis,* X (1929), pp. 1–4. *(SE* 21).
French translation: Paris, Payot, 1927; reprinted 1963 (Petite Bibliothèque Payot).
Spanish translation: Madrid, 1930. *(OC* 14).

1928 "Dostojewski und die Vatertötung," in: Fritz Eckstein und René Fülöp-Miller, ed., *Die Urgestalt der Brüder Karamasoff.* München, Piper, 1928. *(GS* 12; *GW* 14).
English translation by D. F. Tait: "Dostoevsky and parricide," in: *The*

Realist, (London), I, 4 (1929). Reprinted in *Int. Journal of Psycho-Analysis*, XXVI (1945), pp. 1–8; also in: *Partisan Review* (New York), XII (1945); and in: Th. M. Dostoevsky, *Stavrogin's Confession*, 1947, pp. 87–114. *(SE* 21).

1930 *Das Unbehagen in der Kultur.* Leipzig–Wien–Zürich, Int. Ps. Verlag. 1931². *(GS* 12; *GW* 14).
 English translation by Joan Riviere: *Civilization and its Discontents.* (Int. Psychoanalytical Library, 17). London, Hogarth Press, Woolf, Institute of Psycho-Analysis; New York, Cape & Smith, 1930. *(SE* 21).
 Spanish translation: Santiago de Chile, Ediciones Extra, Empresa Letras, 1936.
 Other translations: Japanese 1931, 1932, Swedish 1932.

1931 *Kleine Schriften zur Sexualtheorie und zur Traumlehre.* Leipzig–Wien–Zürich, Int. Ps. Verlag. (Contains previously published essays and papers).

1931 *Schriften zur Neurosenlehre und zur psychoanalytischen Technik (1913–1926).* Leipzig–Wien–Zürich, Int. Ps. Verlag. (Contains previously published essays and papers).

1931 *Theoretische Schriften.* Leipzig–Wien–Zürich, Int. Ps. Verlag. (contains previously published essays and papers).

1931 *Vier psychoanalytische Krankengeschichten.* Leipzig–Wien–Zürich, Int. Ps. Verlag. (contains previuosly published essays and papers).

1932 *Neue Folge der Vorlesungen zur Einführung in die Psychoanalyse.* Leipzig–Wien–Zürich, Int. Ps. Verlag. *(GS* 12; *GW* 15).
 English translation by W. J. H. Spratt: *New Introductory Lectures on Psycho-Analysis.* New York, Norton; London, Hogarth Press and the Institute of Psycho-Analysis, 1933. New translation by James Strachey *(SE* 22).
 French translation by Anne Berman: *Nouvelles conférences sur la Psychanalyse.* Paris, Gallimard, 1936.
 Italian translation: *Introduzione alla psicoanalisi. Nuove lezioni.* Roma. 1934. Comp.: *Introduzione allo studio della psicoanalisi. Prima serie e nuova serie.* Roma, 1947.
 Spanish translation: *Nuevas aportaciones a la psicoanálisis. Ultimos complementos (1933) a la introducción a la psicoanálisis.* Madrid, 1934. *(OC* 17).
 Other translations: Norwegian 1934.

1935 "Nachschrift 1935 zur 'Selbstdarstellung'," *Almanach der Psychoanalyse 1936.* Leipzig–Wien–Zürich, Int. Psychoanalytischer Verlag, 1936, pp. 9–14. Reprinted together with *Selbstdarstellung:* Leipzig etc., Int. Ps. Verlag, 1936²; London, Imago, 1946. *(GW* 16).
 English translation by James Strachey: "Postscript" to *An Autobiographical Study.* (International Psychoanalytical Library). London, Hogarth Press; New York, Norton, 1935. *(SE* 20).
 Italian translation: *Mia vita ed opera.* Roma, 1948.

1937 "Die endliche und die unendliche Analyse," *Int. Zeitschrift für Psychoanalyse*, XXIII, 12 (1937), pp. 209–240. *(GW* 16).
 English translation "Analysis terminable and interminable," *Int. Journal of Psycho-Analysis*, XVIII, 14 (1937), pp. 373–405. *(CP* 5; *SE* 22).

1937 *A General Selection from the Works of Sigmund Freud.* Edited by John Rickman. (Psycho-Analytical Epitomes, 1). London, Hogarth Press, Institute of Psycho-Analysis. 1953².

1938 *The Basic Writings of Sigmund Freud*. Translated and edited by A. A. Brill. New York, The Modern Library.

1939 *Der Mann Moses und die monotheistische Religion. Drei Abhandlungen*. Amsterdam, Allert de Lange. (The first section had appeared earlier in *Imago*, XXIII, 1 (1937), pp. 5–13; the second section in *Imago*, XXIV, 4 (1937), pp. 387–419). *(GW* 16).
English translation by Katherine Jones: *Moses and Monotheism*. London, Hogarth Press and Institute of Psycho-Analysis; New York, Knopf, 1939. (The first two sections had appeared earlier in *Int. Journal of Psycho-Analysis*, XIX, 3 (1938), pp. 291–298; XX, 1 (1939), pp. 1–32. New translation by James Strachey *(SE* 23).
French translation by Anne Berman. Paris, Gallimard, 1948.
Italian translation: *Mose' e il monoteismo*. Milano, 1952.
Other translations: Hungarian 1946, Dutch 1947.

1939 *Civilization, War and Death*. Selections from three works. Edited by John Rickman. (Psycho-Analytical Epitomes, 4). London, Hogarth Press. 1953² (enlarged).

1940 "Abriss der Psychoanalyse," *Imago*, XXV, 1 (1940), pp. 7–67. Together with "Some elementary lessons in psycho-analysis." *(GW* 17).
English translation by James Strachey: *An Outline of Psycho-Analysis*. First published in: *Int. Journal of Psycho-Analysis*, XXI, 1 (1940), pp. 27–82. Revised translation as book: London, Hogarth Press and Institute of Psycho-Analysis; New York, Norton, 1949. Considerably revised version of the translation of 1949 *(SE* 23).
Italian translation: *Sommario di psicoanalisi*. Firenze, 1951, 1957³.

1941 *The Living Thoughts of Freud*. Presented by Robert Waelder. New York–Toronto, Longmans. London, Cassell, 1942.

1952 *The Major Works of Sigmund Freud*. (Great Books of the Western World, 54). Chicago, Encyclopaedia Britannica Publ.

1958 *Dictionary of Psychoanalysis*. A Compilation of selections from Freud's Works. Edited by Nandor Fodor and Frank Gaynor. Preface by Theodor Reik. New York. Greenwich (Conn.), Fawcett Publications, 1963.

1962 *Two Short Accounts of Psycho-Analysis. Five lectures on psycho-analysis and The Question of Lay Analysis*. Translated and edited by James Strachey. Pelican Book A 571.

1963 *Psychoanalyse*. Textes choisis par Dine Dreyfus. (Les Grands Textes). Paris, P. U. F.

HEINRICH FRICK*

1. Bibliography

Käthe Neumann, "Bibliographie Heinrich Frick," *Theologische Literaturzeitung*, LXXVIII, 7 (1953), pp. 440–442.

2. Biography and Appreciation

Heinrich Frick zum Gedächtnis. Commemoration Addresses, 1953, 18 p.
Röhr, Heinz, *Der Einfluss der Religionswissenschaft auf die Missionstheorie Heinrich Fricks*. Theol. Diss., Marburg, 1959, 161 p.

Schwarz, Eva, "Gedenken an Heinrich Frick," *Alma Mater Philippina*, Marburger Universitätsbund E. V., 1967–68 (Wintersemester), pp. 40–44.
Wünsch, Georg, "Heinrich Frick in Memoriam," *Theologische Literaturzeitung*, LXXVIII, 7 (1953), pp. 435–439.

3. Method and Theory

1926 "Der Katholisch-Protestantische Zwiespalt als religionsgeschichtliches Urphänomen," in: Paul Tillich, ed., *Kairos: Zur Geisteslage und Geisteswendung*. Darmstadt, Reichl, pp. 345–384.
1928 *Vergleichende Religionswissenschaft*. Berlin–Leipzig, de Gruyter.
1928 "Missions- und Religionswissenschaft als theologische Disziplinen," in: A. Titius, ed., *Deutsche Theologie, Bericht über den 1. deutschen Theologentag zu Eisenach 1927*. Göttingen, Vandenhoeck & Ruprecht, pp. 160–167.
1933 *Das Evangelium und die Religionen*. Basel, Reinhardt.
 English translation by J. Haire: *The Gospel, Christianity and Other Faiths*. London, 1938.
1943 "Regionale Religionskunde. Georeligiöse Erwägungen zum Zusammenhang zwischen Boden und Religion," *Zeitschrift für Geopolitik* (Berlin), XX, 8 (1943), pp. 281–291.
1950 "Die aktuelle Aufgabe der Religionsphänomenologie," *Theologische Literaturzeitung*, LXXV, 10 (1950), pp. 641–646.

4. Main Publications

1919 *Ghazālīs Selbstbiographie. Ein Vergleich mit Augustins Konfessionen*. Leipzig, Hinrichs.
1929–1930 "Über den Ursprung des Gottesglaubens und die Religion der Primitiven," *Theologischer Rundschau* (Tübingen), N. F., 1, 4 (1929), pp. 241–265 and II, 2 (1930), pp. 65–93.
1931 *Ideogramm, Mythologie und das Wort*. (Marburger Theologische Studien, Rudolf Otto-Festgrusz, Heft 3). Gotha, Klotz.
1935 "Der Begriff des Prophetischen in Islamkunde und Theologie," *Festschrift für Paul Kahle*. Leiden, E. J. Brill, pp. 79–94.
1938 "Rudolf Otto innerhalb der theologischen Situation," *Zeitschrift für Theologie und Kirche* (Tübingen), N. F., XIX, 1/2 (1938), pp. 3–15.
1940 "Das christliche Ja zur Natur. Ein Olympiade-Vortrag," in: Heinrich Frick, ed., *Rudolf Otto-Ehrung*. Berlin, Töpelmann, pp. 62–82.
1942 "Die dynamische Denkweise des Protestantismus," in: *In Deo Omnia Unum. Zu Friedrich Heilers 50. Geburtstag*. München, Reinhardt, pp. 216–229.
1944 "Zur Diskussion um 'das Heilige' nach Rudolf Otto," *Theologische Literaturzeitung*, LXIX, 1/2 (1944), pp. 1–10.
1944 "Christliche Grundbegriffe in ihrer Besonderheit gegenüber Fremdreligionen," *Evangelische Missionszeitschrift*, V, 1 (1944), pp. 193–205.
1952 "Der Islam zwischen Ost und West. Zur Phänomenologie einer Weltreligion," in: *Ökumenische Einheit*, III, 2 (1953), Mahāyāna. *Festgabe für Friedrich Heiler zum 30. Januar 1952 von Freunden und Schülern*.

LEO FROBENIUS

1. Bibliography

Wieschoff, Heinz, "Das Schrifttum von Leo Frobenius," in L. Frobenius, *Ein Lebenswerk aus der Zeit der Kulturwende*. Zum 60. Geburtstag. Leipzig, 1933, pp. 163–170.
Afrika Rundschau, 1938, pp. 119–121.

2. Biography and Appreciation

Petri, H., "Leo Frobenius und die historische Ethnologie," *Saeculum*, IV (1953), pp. 45–60.

3. Main Publications

1894 *Die Geheimbünde Afrikas. Ethnologische Studie*. Hamburg, Richter.
1898 *Der Ursprung der afrikanischen Kulturen*. Berlin, Bornträger.
 English translation: *The Origin of African Civilization*. Washington, Government Printing Office.
1898 *Die Weltanschauung der Naturvölker*. Weimar, Emil Felber.
1901 *Aus den Flegeljahren der Menschheit. Bilder des Lebens, Treibens und Denkens der Wilden*. (Völkerkunde in Charakterbildern). Hannover, Jänecke.
 English translation by A. H. Keane: *The Childhood of Man*. Philadelphia, Lippincott, 1909. Pb. New York, Meridian Books *(MG 23)*, 1960.
1902 *Die reifere Menschheit. Bilder des Lebens, Treibens und Denkens der Halbkulturvölker*. Hannover, Jänecke.
1904 *Das Zeitalter des Sonnengottes*. Berlin, Reimer.
1912–1913 *Und Afrika sprach*. Vol. I: *Auf den Trümmern des klassischen Atlantis*; Vol. II: *An der Schwelle des verehrungswürdigen Byzanz*; Vol. III: *Unter den unsträflichen Äthiopen*. Berlin–Charlottenburg, Vita Deutsches Verlagshaus.
 English translation by R. Blind: *The Voice of Africa*, 2 vols. London, Hutchinson, 1913.
1921 *Paideuma. Umrisse einer Kultur- und Seelenlehre*. München, Beck.
1921–1929 *Atlas Africanus*, 7 vols. Preceded by *Karten als Sinnbilder der Kulturbewegung. Einführung in den Atlas Africanus*. München, Beck, 1921–1929.
1925–1929 *Erlebte Erdteile*, 7 vols. Frankfurt a. M., Frankfurter Societäts-druckerei.
1937 *African Genesis*. New York, Stackpole Sons, 1937; London, Faber & Faber, 1938.
1937 Leo Frobenius and Douglas C. Fox, *Prehistoric Rock Pictures in Europe and Africa*. From material in the Archives of the Research Institute of the Morphology of Civilisation, Frankfort-on-Main. New York, 1937.

NUMA D. FUSTEL DE COULANGES*

1. Bibliography

Liste chronologique des œuvres de Fustel de Coulanges" in: Paul Guiraud
Fustel de Coulanges. Paris, Hachette, 1896, pp. 273–278.

2. Biography and Appreciation

Guiraud, Paul, *Fustel de Coulanges*. Paris, Hachette, 1896.
Seston, William, "Préface" to *La cité antique*. Paris, Club du meilleur livre,
1959, pp. IX–XXIV.

3. Method and Theory

1882 "De la manière d'écrire l'histoire en France et en Allemagne depuis 50 ans,"
Revue des Deux Mondes, 1ᵉʳ septembre 1872. Reprinted in: *Questions
historiques*. Paris, Hachette, 1893.
1887 "De l'analyse des textes historiques," *Revue des Questions Historiques*,
janvier 1887.
1887 "Réponse à M. Monod," *Revue des Questions Historiques*, avril 1887.
1923 *Questions historiques. De la manière d'écrire l'histoire*. Paris.

4. Main Publications

1856 *Mémoire sur l'île de Chio*. Archives des missions scientifiques et littéraires.
Paris.
1858 *Quid Vestae cultus in institutis veterum privatis publicisque valuerit*. Thèse
de doctorat. Paris.
1858 *Polybe ou la Grèce conquise par les Romains*. Thèse de doctorat. Paris.
Reprinted in: *Questions historiques*. Paris, Hachette, 1893.
1864 *La cité antique. Etude sur le culte, le droit, les institutions de la Grèce et de
Rome*. Paris, Durand. Numerous editions: Paris, Hachette, 1866², 1879⁷
(enlarged), 1881⁹, 1900¹⁷, 1924²⁸. New editions Paris, 1928 etc., 1952,⁴²
1959 (Club du meilleur livre; préface William Seston). Abridged
Edition 1947: *La cité antique*. Extraits, avec une notice biographique,
une notice littéraire et des notes explicatoires par M. Pierre Fabre. Paris,
Hachette, 1947.
English translation by Willard Small: *The Ancient City. A Study on the
Religion, Laws, and Institutions of Greece and Rome*. Boston, Lee and
Shepard etc., 1874, 1921¹². Pb. New York, Doubleday, 1956.
German authorized translation by Paul Weis: *Der antike Staat. Studie
über Kultus, Recht und Einrichtungen Griechenlands und Roms*. Berlin,
1907. New edition with introduction by Heinrich Schenkl: Graz, 1961.
1875–1889 *Histoire des institutions politiques de l'ancienne France*, 3 vols.
Paris, Hachette. Enlarged edition of 6 vols. Paris, Hachette, 1888–1891.

New edition, revised (Vols. I, II, V, VI) and edited („revue et complétée sur le manuscrit et d'après les notes de l'auteur") by Camille Jullian, 6 vols. Paris, Hachette, 1889–1912.

1874–1875 "Etude sur les origines du régime féodal," *Comptes rendus de l'Académie des Sciences Morales*, CII (1874) et CIII (1875).

1876 "Les institutions politiques au temps de Charlemagne," *Comptes rendus de l'Académie des Sciences morales*, CV et XVI (1876).

1879 "La question de droit entre César et le Sénat," *Journal des Savants*, juillet 1879. Reprinted in: *Questions Historiques*. Paris, Hachette, 1893.

1879 "Recherche sur le tirage au sort appliqué à la nomination des archontes athéniens," *Nouvelle Revue Historique du Droit*, 1879. Reprinted in: *Nouvelles Recherches sur quelques problèmes d'histoire*. Paris, Hachette, 1891.

1879 "Comment le druidisme a disparu," *Comptes rendus de l'Académie des Sciences Morales*, CXII (1879). Comp. *Revue Archéologique*, XXXIX (1880). Reprinted in: *Nouvelles Recherches sur quelques problèmes d'histoire*. Paris, Hachette, 1891.

1880 "Etude sur la propriété à Sparte," Compte rendu de l'*Académie des Sciences Morales*, CIII et CIV (1880). Reprinted in: *Nouvelles Recherches...* Paris, Hachette, 1891.

1885 *Recherches sur quelques problèmes d'histoire*. Paris, Hachette, 1885, 1923[4].

1890 *Les origines du régime féodal: le bénéfice et le patronat*. Paris, Hachette.

1891 *Nouvelles recherches sur quelques problèmes d'histoire*. Rev. et compl. par Cam. Jullian. Paris, Hachette.

1892 *Les transformations de la royauté pendant l'époque carolingienne*. Paris, Hachette.

1893 *Questions historiques*. Rev. et compl. d'après les notes de l'auteur par Cam. Jullian (Papers and Essays) Paris, Hachette. 1923[2].

1916 *Questions contemporaines* (Essays). Paris, Hachette.

1930 *Leçons à l'impératrice sur les origines de la civilisation française*. Préface par Pierre Fabre. Paris, Hachette.

G

ARNOLD VAN GENNEP*

1. Bibliography

Gennep, K. van, *Bibliographie des œuvres d'Arnold van Gennep*. Préface de
G.-H. Rivière. Introduction par K. van Gennep. Paris, A. & J. Picard &
Cie, 1964.

2. Biography and appreciation

Kimball, Solon T., "Introduction," in: Arnold van Gennep, *The Rites of Passage*.
Translated by Monika B. Vizedom and Gabrielle L. Caffee. Chicago,
University of Chicago Press; London, Routledge and Kegan Paul, 1960;
Chicago, Phoenix Book, University of Chicago Press, 1964, pp. V–XIX.
Needham, Rodney, "Introduction," in: Arnold van Gennep, *The Semi-Scholars*.
Translated from the French and edited with an Introduction by Rodney
Needham. London, Routledge and Kegan Paul, 1967, pp. IX–XX.

3. Method and Theory

1904 "La théorie générale de la magie de Hubert et Mauss," *Revue des Traditions
populaires*, XIX (1904), pp. 548–554.
1908 "Totémisme et méthode comparative," *Revue de l'Histoire des Religions*,
VIII (1908), pp. 34–76. Published separately under the title of *Tabou,
totémisme et méthode comparative*. Paris, 1908. Reprinted in *Religions,
mœurs et légendes. Essais d'ethnographie et de linguistique*, vol. II. Paris,
Mercure de France, 1909, pp. 22 ff.
1909 "La faillite de la méthode historique," in *Religions, mœurs et légendes.
Essais d'ethnographie et de linguistique*, vol. II. Paris, Mercure de France,
1909, pp. 82 ff.
1910 "Paul Ehrenreich's Methode in der Deutung der allgemeinen Mythologie,"
Hessische Blätter für Volkskunde, IX (1910), pp. 199–206.
1911 "De la méthode à suivre dans l'étude des rites et des mythes," *Revue de
l'Université de Bruxelles*, April 1911, pp. 505–523.

Dutch translation: "Over de studie van riten en mythen," *Wetenschappelijke Bladen,* III, pp. 97–110.

1913 "Contribution à l'histoire de la méthode ethnographique," *Revue de l'Histoire des Religions,* LXVII (1913), pp. 320–338; LXVIII (1913), pp. 32–61.

1919 "Nouvelles recherches sur l'histoire en France de la méthode ethnographique: Claude Guichard, Richard Simon, Claude Fleury," *Revue de l'Histoire des Religions,* LXXXII (1919), pp. 139–162. Also published separately: Paris, E. Leroux, 1919.

1920 *L'état actuel du problème totémique. Etude critique des théories sur les origines de la religion et de l'organisation sociale.* Paris, Ernest Leroux. Previously published as articles in *Revue de l'Histoire des Religions,* LXXV, pp. 295–374; LXXVI, pp. 281–347; LXXIX, pp. 14–74; LXXX, pp. 86–153, and 193–270.

1934 "Contribution à la méthodologie du folklore," *Lares,* V (March, 1934), pp. 20–34. Also published separately: Rocca S. Casciano, Stabilimento Tipografico L. Cappelli.

4. Main Publications

1903 "Notes sur le Domovoï," *Revue de l'Histoire des Religions,* XLVII (1903), pp. 206–221. Also published separately: Paris, Ernest Leroux, 1903.

1903 "De l'emploi du mot 'chamanisme'," *Revue de l'Histoire des Religions,* XLVII (1903), pp. 51–57. Also published separately: Paris, Ernest Leroux, 1903.

1904 "Le mécanisme du tabou," *Revue des Idées,* I (1904), pp. 349–356.

1904 "Notes sur les religions grecques," *Revue des Traditions populaires,* XIX (1904), pp. 227–236.

1904 *Tabou et totémisme à Madagascar. Etude descriptive et théorique* (Bibliothèque des Hautes Etudes, Sciences Religieuses, t. XVII). Paris, E. Leroux.

1905–1947 "Chroniques d'Ethnographie, Folklore, Préhistoire, Histoire de Religions, Anthropologie," regularly in *Mercure de France,* between 1905 and 1947.

1906 *Mythes et légendes d'Australie. Etude d'ethnographie et de sociologie.* Paris, E. Guilmoto.

1907 "La question d'Homère," *Revue des Idées,* IV (1907), pp. 97–124.

1907 "La situation actuelle des enquêtes ethnographiques," *Revue des Idées,* IV (1907), pp. 314–322.

1907 "Le rite du refus," *Archiv für Religionswissenschaft,* XI (1907), pp. 1–10

1908 "Y a-t-il progrès de la civilisation?" *Revue des Idées,* V (1908), pp. 510–534

1908 "La valeur historique du folklore," *Revue des Idées,* VI (1908), pp. 173–179.

German translation: "Über den historischen Wert der Volkskunde," *Internationale Wochenschrift für Wissenschaft, Kunst und Technik* (Berlin), (30 January 1909), pp. 129–136.

1908–1914 *Religions, mœurs et légendes. Essais d'ethnographie et de linguistique,* 5 vols. Paris, Mercure de France. (Collected Essays).

1909 *Les rites de passage.* Paris, Emile Nourry. Reprinted: Paris-La Haye, Mouton; New York, Johnson Reprint Corporation, 1969.

English translation by Monika B. Vizedom and Gabrielle L. Caffee: *The Rites of Passage*. With an Introduction by Solon T. Kimball. Chicago, University of Chicago Press; London, Routledge and Kegan Paul, 1960; Pb. 1964.

1909 *La question d'Homère*. Les poèmes homériques, l'archéologie et la poésie populaire. Suivi d'une bibliographie critique par A. J. Reinach (Les Hommes et les Idées). Paris, Mercure de France.

1910 "Was ist Mythus?" *Internationale Wochenschrift für Wissenschaft, Kunst und Technik* (10 September 1910), pp. 1167–1174.

1910 *La formation des légendes*. Paris, Ernest Flammarion. 1922[2].

1911 "Qu'est-ce que le totémisme," *Folklore* (London), XXII (1911), pp. 93–104.

1911 "Etudes d'ethnographie algérienne," *Revue d'Ethnographie et de Sociologie*, II (1911), 112 pp.

1911 "Mythologie et ethnographie à propos d'un livre récent," *Revue de l'Histoire des Religions*, LXIII (1911), pp. 40–52.

1911 *Les Demi-Savants*. Paris, Mercure de France.
English translation edited with an introduction by Rodney Needham: *The Semi-Scholars*. London, Routledge and Kegan Paul, 1967.

1913 *La Savoye vue par les écrivains et les artistes* ("La France pittoresque et artistique"). Paris, Louis Michaud.

1913 "Notes d'ethnographie persane," *Revue d'Ethnographie et de Sociologie*, III (1913), pp. 73–89.

1913 "Les lacunes de l'ethnographie actuelle," *Scientia*, XIV (1913), pp. 409–411. Also published separately: Bologna, N. Zanichelli; Paris, Alcan, 1913.

1914 *En Algérie*. Paris, Mercure de France.

1914 "La signification du Premier Congrès d'Ethnographie (Neuchâtel)," *Mercure de France* (16 July 1914), pp. 322–332.

1914 "Le problème de l'Islam," *Revue du Mois* (Uin.), (1914), pp. 706-726

1916 *En Savoie*. Vol. I: *Du berceau à la tombe*. Chambéry, Dardel.

1922 "Religion et nationalité," *Journal de Psychologie normale et pathologique*, XIX (15 January, 1922), pp.24–46.

1922 *Traité comparatif des nationalités*. Vol. I: *Les éléments extérieurs de la nationalité (Les symboles des nationalités)*. Paris, Payot.

1923 "A propos du totémisme prèhistorique," *Actes du Congrès International d'Histoire des Religions, Paris, octobre 1923*. Paris, Vol. 1, pp. 323–358.

1923 "Essai d'un classement des modes de la sépulture," *Actes du Congrès International d'Histoire des Religions, Paris, octobre 1923*. Paris, 1925, Vol. I, pp. 360–375.

1924 *Le Folklore. Croyances et coutumes populaires françaises*. (La Culture Moderne). Paris, Stock.

1924 "Le symbolisme ritualiste de l'Apocalypse," *Revue de l'Histoire des Religions*, LXXXIX (1924), pp. 163–182. Also published separately: Paris, E. Leroux, 1924.

1925 "Le cycle cérémonial de Carnaval et du Carême en Savoie," *Journal de Psychologie normale et pathologique*, XII (1925), pp. 421–445, 585–612, 728–767.

1926 "Le cycle de Pâques dans les coutumes populaires de la Savoie," *Revue de l'Institut de Sociologie Solvay*, VI (1926), pp. 191–230. Also published separately: Bruxelles, Imprimerie Scientifique et Littéraire, 1926.

1926 "Découverte d'une civilisation indo-sumérienne datant de 3 à 4000 avant J.-C. (Harappa)," *Mercure de France* (1 April 1926), pp. 370–477.

1927 "Essai sur le culte populaire des Saints Franciscains en Savoie," *Revue d'Histoire franciscaine*, IV (1927), pp. 113–211. Also published separately: Paris, Vrin, 1927.

1927 "Le cycle des douze jours (Noël, Premier de l'An, Rois) dans les coutumes et croyances populaires de la Savoie," *Revue de l'Institut de Sociologie Solvay*, VII (January–March, 1927), pp. 1–66. Also published separately; Bruxelles, Imprimerie Scientifique et Littéraire, 1927.

1927 "La Saint-Jean dans les croyances et dans les coutumes populaires de la Savoie," *Journal de Psychologie normale et pathologique*, XXIV (15 January, 1927), pp. 26–77.

1927 "Enquête sur le folklore," *La Psychologie et la Vie. Revue de psychologie appliquée*, I (August, 1927), pp. 16–19. Reprinted with changes in: *Revue du Folklore français*, I (1930), pp. 40–44.

1927 "Note sur la valeur documentaire folklorique des canons des conciles et des constitutions synodales," *Congrès d'Histoire du Christianisme, Jubilé Alfred Loisy, 1927*. Paris, Rieder; Amsterdam, Van Holkema, 1929, pp. 94–108.

1927–1930 "Contes et légendes de Savoie," Weekly articles in *Savoyard de Paris*, 1 January, 1927 until 2 August, 1930.

1930 "Survivances primitives dans les cérémonies agraires de la Savoie et du Dauphiné (Isère)," *Studi e materiali di storia della religion*, LVI, 1, 2 (1930), pp. 86–134. Also published separately: Roma, Optima, 1930.

1932–1933 *Le Folklore du Dauphiné (Isère). Etude descriptive et comparée de psychologie populaire.* (Les Littératures populaires de toutes les Nations, N. S., 2–3), 2 vols. Paris, G. P. Maisonneuve.

1934 *Le Folklore de la Bourgogne (Côte-d'Or) avec une discussion théorique sur le prétendu culte des sources.* (Contributions au Folklore des Provinces de France, 1). Gap, Imprimerie Louis Jean.

1934 "Le Folklore préhistorique de l'ancienne Savoie (départements de la Haute-Savoie et de la Savoie)," in: P. Saintyves, ed., *Corpus du Folklore préhistorique*, 1934, pp. 302–386.

1934 "Over het teekenen van Folkloristische Kaarten," *Mensch en Maatschappij* (Groningen), (1934), pp. 337–351.

1935 *Le Folklore de la Flandre et du Hainaut français (département du Nord).* I: *Une étude sur la répartition géographique des géants processionnels ;* II: *Une contribution à la théorie générale des patronages.* (Contributions au Folklore des Provinces de France, 2–3), 2 vols. Paris, G. P. Maisonneuve.

1935 *Mercure de France*, vol. XIX, 372 pp.; vol. XX, 288 pp.

1937 *Manuel de Folklore français contemporain.* Paris, Picard.
Vol. I, 1ʳᵉ partie: *Introduction général et première partie: du berceau à la tombe. Naissance, baptême, enfance, adolescence, fiançailles.* 1943.
Vol. I, 2ᵉ partie: *Du berceau à la tombe (fin). Mariage-Funérailles.* 1946.
Vol. I, 3ᵉ partie: *Cérémonies périodiques cycliques. 1. Carnaval–Carême-Pâques.* 1947.
Vol. I, 4ᵉ partie: *Cérémonies périodiques cycliques. 2. Cycle de mai, La Saint-Jean.* 1949.
Vol. I, 5ᵉ partie: *Cérémonies périodiques cycliques et saisonnières. 3. Les cérémonies agricoles et pastorales de l'été.* 1951.
Vol. I, 6ᵉ partie: *Les cérémonies périodiques cycliques et saisonnières. 4. Les cérémonies agricoles et pastorales de l'automne.* 1953.
Vol. I, 7ᵉ partie: *Cycle des douze jours. Tournées et chansons de quête.*

Personnification du cycle: feux, bûchers et brandons mobiles. La bûche et le tison de Noël. 1958.
Vol. III.: *Questionnaires. Provinces et Pays. Bibliographie méthodique.* 1937.
Vol. IV: *Bibliographie méthodique (fin). Index des noms d'auteurs. Index par Provinces.* 1938.
1939 "Le Folklore en France," *Revue de Paris*, XLVI (1 July, 1939), pp. 195–216.
Dutch translation: "Folklore in Frankrijk," *Wetenschappelijke Bladen*, XII, pp. 254–278.
1939 "Patronages, chapelles et oratoires de la Haute-Maurienne. Etude statistique et critique," *Revue de l'Histoire de l'Eglise de France*, XXV (1939), pp. 145–182.
1942 *Le Folklore de l'Auvergne et du Velay.* (Contributions au Folklore des Provinces de France, 5). Paris, G. P. Maisonneuve.
1950 "Projet de publication d'un lexique international d'ethnographie et de folklore," in: *C. I. A. P. Informations* (March–April, 1950).

HELMUTH VON GLASENAPP

1. Bibliography

Helmuth von Glasenapp Bibliographie. Bearbeitet von Zoltán Karolyi. Wiesbaden, Steiner Verlag, 1968. (a. Schriftenverzeichnisse; b. Würdigungen und Nachrufe; c. Vortragstätigkeit im Spiegel der Presse).

2. Biography and Appreciation

Glasenapp, H. von, *Meine Lebensreise. Länder und Dinge, die ich sah.* Wiesbaden, Brockhaus, 1964.

3. Main Publications

1915 *Die Lehre vom Karman in der Philosophie der Jainas nach den Karmagranthas dargestellt.* Leipzig, Kreysing.
English translation: *The Doctrine of Karman in Jain Philosophy.* Translated from the orig. German by G. Barry Gifford and rev. by the author. Ed. by Hiralal R(asikdas) Kapadia. (Foreword by Robert Zimmermann, S. J.). Bombay, Vijibai Jivanlal Panalal Charity Fund, 1942.
1922 *Der Hinduismus.* Religion und Gesellschaft im heutigen India. München, Kurt Wolff.
1923 *Madhva's Philosophie des Vishnu-Glaubens.* Mit einer Einleitung über Madhva und seine Schule. Ein Beitrag zur Sektengeschichte des Hinduismus. (Geistesströmungen des Ostens, 2). Bonn–Leipzig, Schröder.
1925 *Der Jainismus.* Eine indische Erlösungsreligion. Nach den Quellen dargestellt. (Kultur und Weltanschauung, 1). Berlin, Häger.

1926 *Brahma und Buddha.* Die Religionen Indiens in ihrer geschichtlichen
Entwicklung. Berlin, Deutsche Buch-Gemeinschaft. 1933[2]; 1943 (Neubearbeitung: *Die Religionen Indiens.* Stuttgart, 1943).

1928 *Heilige Stätten Indiens.* Die Wallfahrtsorte der Hindus, Jainas und Buddhisten, ihre Legenden und ihr Kultus. (Der indische Kulturkreis in Einzeldarstellungen). München, Müller.

1936 *Der Buddhismus in Indien und im Fernen Osten.* Schicksale und Lebens-
formen einer Erlösungsreligion. Berlin–Zürich, Atlantis Verlag.

1938 *Unsterblichkeit und Erlösung in den indischen Religionen.* (Schriften der
Königberger Gelehrten Gesellschaft. Geisteswissenschaftliche Klasse,
1, 1). Halle, Niemeyer.

1940 *Entwicklungsstufen des indischen Denkens.* Untersuchungen über die
Philosophie der Brahmanen und Buddhisten. (Schriften d. Königsberger
Gelehrten Gesellschaft. Geisteswissenschaftliche Klasse, 15/16,5). Halle,
Niemeyer.

1940 *Buddhistische Mysterien.* Die geheimen Lehren und Riten des Diamant-
Fahrzeugs. (Sammlung Völkerglaube). Stuttgart, Spemann.

1943 *Die Religionen Indiens.* (Kröners Taschenausgabe, 190). Stuttgart, Kröner.
1956[2].

1945 *Kant und die Religionen des Ostens.* (Jahrbuch der Albertus-Universität
Königsberg/Pr., Beiheft 5) (Der Göttinger Arbeitskreis, Veröffentlichung
Nr. 100). Kitzingen-Main, Holzner.

1946 *Die Weisheit des Buddha.* Baden-Baden, Bühler.

1948 *Der Stufenweg zum Göttlichen.* Shankaras Philosophie der All-Einheit.
Baden-Baden, Bühler.

1948 *Die indische Welt als Erscheinung und Erlebnis.* Baden-Baden, Bühler.

1949 *Die Philosophie der Inder.* Eine Einführung in ihre Geschichte
und ihre Lehren. (Kröners Taschenausgabe, 195). Stuttgart, Kröner.
1958[2].

1951–1952 *Die fünf grossen Religionen,* 2 vols. Vol. I. *Brahmanismus, Buddhismus, Chinesischer Universismus.* Vol. II. *Islam und Christentum.* Düsseldorf–Köln, Diederichs. A slightly shortened edition appeared under the
title of *Die fünf Weltreligionen.* Brahmanismus, Buddhismus, Chinesischer
Universismus, Christentum, Islam. Düsseldorf–Köln, Diederichs, 1963,
1967[2].
French translation by Pierre Jundt: *Les cinq grandes religions du monde.*
(Bibliothèque scientifique). Paris, Payot, 1954.
Greek translation by Nikephoros Brettakos: *Pankosmios historia ton
threskeion.* Athens, Supsas-Siamatas, 1959.
Swedish translation by Margareta Edgarth: *De fem världsreligionerna.*
Hinduismen, kristendomen, buddhismen, universismen och islám. Fack-
granskning av Gunnar Andersson. (Aldusbok A 132) Stockholm, Bonnier,
1965.

1953 *Das Spiel des Unendlichen.* Gott, Welt und Mensch in der Dichtung der
Hindus. In deutscher Nachbildung. (Sammlung Kloterberg, N. F.). Basel,
Schwabe.

1954 *Buddhismus und Gottesidee.* Die Buddhistischen Lehren von den überweltlichen Wesen und Mächten und ihre religionsgeschichtlichen Paral-
lelen. (Akad. d. Wiss. u. d. Literatur. Abhandlungen d. Geistes- und sozial-
wiss. Klasse, 1954, 8). Mainz, Akad. d. Wiss. u. d. Literatur; Wiesbaden,
Steiner in Komm.

1954 *Die Religionen der Menschheit, ihre Gegensätze und ihre Übereinstimmungen.* (Schriftenreihe d. Österr. UNESCO-Kommission, 7; vielmehr 6). Wien, Frick.

1956 *Der Pfad zur Erleuchtung.* Grundtexte der buddhistischen Heilslehre. In deutscher Übersetzung. (Diederichs Taschenausgaben, 4). Düsseldorf–Köln, Diederichs.

1957 *Die nichtchristlichen Religionen.* (Das Fischer Lexikon, A–Z, 1). Frankfurt a. M., Fischer Bücherei.
  English translation by Eric Potter: *Non-Christian Religions, A to Z.* Based on the Work of Helmuth von Glasenapp. Edited under the supervision of Horace L. Friess. (Universal reference library; Grosset's universal library, 4623). New York, Grosset & Dunlap.

1958–1959 *Indische Geisteswelt.* Eine Auswahl von Texten in deutscher Übersetzung. Eingeleitet und herausgegeben, 2 vols. Vol. I. *Glaube und Weisheit der Hindus.* Vol. II. *Weltliche Dichtung, Wissenschaft und Staatskunst der Hindus.* (Geist des Morgenlandes). Baden-Baden, Holle.

1959 *Buddhism and Christianity. Buddhism and the vital Problems of our Time.* 2 Essays. (The Wheel Publications, 16). Kandy, Ceylon, Buddhist Publ. Soc.

1960 *Glaube und Ritus der Hochreligionen in vergleichender Übersicht.* (Fischer Bücherei, 346). Frankfurt a. M., Fischer Bücherei.

1960 *Das Indienbild deutscher Denker.* Stuttgart, Koehler.

1967 *Buddhism and comparative Religion, and other Essays.* (The Wheel Publications, 111). Kandy, Ceylon, Buddhist Publ. Soc.

EUGÈNE F. A. COMTE GOBLET D'ALVIELLA

1. Bibliography, Biography and Appreciation

"Goblet d'Alviella," *Notices biographiques et bibliographiques.* Bruxelles, Académie Royale des Sciences, des Lettres et des Beaux Arts de Belgique, Année 1907/1909, pp. 436–457.

2. Main Publications

1884 *L'Evolution religieuse contemporaine chez les Anglais, les Américains et les Hindous.* Paris, Baillière.
  English translation by J. Moden: *The contemporary evolution of religious thought in England, America and India.* London–Edinburgh, Williams & Norgate, 1885; New York, Putnam's Sons, 1886.

1885 *Des préjugés qui entravent l'étude scientifique des religions.* Bruxelles.

1887 *Introduction à l'histoire générale des religions.* (Resumé du cours public donné à l'Université de Bruxelles en 1884–1885). Bruxelles–Gand.

1891 *La Migration des Symboles.* Paris.
  English translation: *The Migration of Symbols.* With an introduction by Sir George Birdwood. London, Constable, 1894.

1892 *L'idée de Dieu d'après l'anthropologie et l'histoire.* Bruxelles, Muquardt. *English* translation by P. H. Wicksteed: *Lectures on the origin and growth of the conception of God as illustrated by anthropology and history.* The Hibbert Lectures 1891. London, Williams & Norgate. 1897².
1894 "La loi des progrès dans les religions," *Revue de Belgique*, 1894, pp. 1 ff.
1897 *Ce que l'Inde doit à la Grèce: des influences classiques dans la civilisation de l'Inde.* Paris, Leroux.
1911 *Croyances, rites, institutions*, 3 vols. Paris.

JOHANN JOSEPH VON GÖRRES

1. Bibliography

Galland, J., *Joseph von Görres.* Freiburg i. Br., Herder, 1876, pp. 663–673.

2. Biography and Appreciation

Brandt, G. A., *Herder und Görres. 1798–1807.* Ein Beitrag zur Frage Herder und die Romantik. Berlin, 1939.
Habel, R., *Joseph Görres. Studien über den Zusammenhang von Natur, Geschichte und Mythos in seinen Schriften.* Wiesbaden, 1960.
Hirth, F., *Der junge Görres.* Baden-Baden, 1948.
Kriselius, Käthe, *Joseph Görres, die Stadien seiner geistigen Entwicklung 1776–1805.* München, 1950.
Pascher, J., *Die plastische Kraft im religiösen Gestaltungsvorgang nach Joseph von Görres.* Würzburg, Becker, 1928.
Rehr, I., *Görres in seinem Verhältnis zur Geschichte.* Eine Analyse seiner Heidelberger Abhandlung: *Wachstum der Historie*, etc. Hamburg, 1935.
Reisse, R., *Die weltanschauliche Entwicklung des jungen Joseph Görres. 1776–1806.* Breslau, Müller & Seiffert, 1926.
Saitschick, R., *Joseph Görres und die abendländische Kultur.* Freiburg, i. Br., Walter, 1953.
Schneppe, R., *Görres Geschichtsphilosophie. Frühzeit.* (Abhandlungen zur mittleren und neueren Geschichte, Heft 50). Berlin–Wilmersdorf, Rotschild, 1913.

3. Main Publications

1810 *Mythengeschichte der asiatischen Welt.* Heidelberg.
1836–1842 *Die christliche Mystik.* 4 vols. Regensburg–Landshut.
1854 *Gesammelte Schriften.* Hrsg. von M. Görres. Augsburg.
1880 *Über Grundlage, Gliederung und Zeitenfolge der Weltgeschichte.* Drei Vorträge, gehalten ... November 1829, von J. Görres. In 2. Auflage mit einem Vor- und Nachwort.... Hrsg. von Dr. M. A. Strodl. München, 1880².
1911 *Ausgewählte Werke und Briefe.* 2 vols. Hrsg., mit Einleitung und Anmerkungen versehen, von Wilhelm Schellberg. Kempten–München.

ALEXANDER A. GOLDENWEISER

Main Publications

1912 "The Origin of Totemism," *American Anthropologist*, Vol. 14 (1912), pp. 600–607.
1915 "Spirit, Mana, and the Religious Thrill," *Journal of Philosophy*, Vol. 12 (1915), pp. 632–640.
1918 "Form and content in Totemism," *American Anthropologist*, Vol. 20 (1918), pp. 280–295.
1922 *Early Civilization: An Introduction to Anthropology.* New York, Knopf.
1931 *Robots or Gods: An Essay on Craft and Mind.* New York, Knopf.
1933 *History, Psychology and Culture.* [Revisions of previously published material] New York, Knopf.
1937 *Anthropology: An Introduction to Primitive Culture.* New York, Crofts.

IGNÁCZ GOLDZIHER

1. Bibliography

Heller, B., *Bibliographie des œuvres de Ignace Goldziher.* Paris, Geuthner, 1927.
Kratchkovsky, I., "Ergänzungen und Berichtigungen," in: *Ignace Goldziher Memorial Volume.* Vol. I. Budapest, 1948, pp. 430–431.
Scheiber, A., "A supplementary bibliography of the literary work of Ignace Goldziher," in: *Ignace Goldziher Memorial.* Vol. I. Budapest, 1948, pp. 419–429. Vol. II. Jerusalem, 1958, pp. 207–214.

2. Biography and Appreciation

Somogyi, J. de, "Biographie I. Goldzihers," in: I. Goldziher, *Gesammelte Schriften.* Vol. I. Hildesheim, Olm, 1967, pp. XI–XXXI.

3. Main Publications

1876 *Der Mythos bei den Hebräern und seine geschichtliche Entwicklung.* Leipzig, Brockhaus.
English translation by R. Martineau (With additions by the author): *Mythology among the Hebrews and its Historical Development.* London, Longmans Green, 1877, 1882².
1882 *Die Zâhiriten, ihr Lehrsystem und ihre Geschichte.* Ein Beitrag zur Geschichte der islamischen Theologie. Leipzig, Schulze, 1884.
English translation and ed. by W. Behn: *The Zâhiris. Their Doctrine and their History.* A contribution to the history of Islamic theology. Leiden, Brill, 1971.
1889–1890 *Muhammedanische Studien.* 2 vols. Halle a. d. Saale, Niemeyer. Repr. 1971.

English translation by C. R. Barber and S. M. Stern: *Muslim Studies*,
2 vols. London, Allen & Unwin, 1967.
1904 "The Progress of Islamic science in the last three decades," in: *Congress
of Arts and Science, Universal Exposition*. St. Louis, 1904, Vol. II (1905),
pp. 497–517.
1910 *Vorlesungen über den Islam*. Heidelberg, Winter. 2nd. revised ed. by
Franz Babinger. Heidelberg, Winter, 1925². Reprint 1963.
1916 *Stellung der alten islamischen Orthodoxie zu den antiken Wissenschaften*.
(Abh. der Königl. Preuss. Ak. der Wiss., Phil.-hist. kls., 1915, Nr. 8).
Berlin, Kön. Akademie der Wissenschaften.
1920 *Die Richtungen der islamischen Koranauslegung*. Leiden, Brill. 1952².
1962 *Etudes islamologiques*. Traduction analytique par G. H. Bousquet. Leiden,
Brill. (First published in *Arabica*, 1961–1962).
1966 *A short history of classical Arabic*. A translation by Joseph de Somogyi
of *Az arab irodalom rövid története*. Hildesheim, G. Olm.
1967 *Gesammelte Schriften*. Ed. by Joseph de Somogyi, 5 vols. Hildesheim,
G. Olm.

FRITZ GRAEBNER

1. Bibliography, Biography and Appreciation

Leser, Paul, "Fritz Graebner. 4. März 1877 bis 13. Juli 1934," *Ethnologischer
Anzeiger* (Stuttgart), III (1932–1935), pp. 294–301. With Bibliography.

2. Main Publications

1911 *Methode der Ethnologie*. Heidelberg.
1924 *Das Weltbild der Primitiven*. Eine Untersuchung der Urformen Welt-
anschaulichen Denkens bei Naturvölkern. München.

VILHELM GRØNBECH

1. Bibliography

Holst, Paul, *Vilhelm Grønbech. En bibliografi*. København, Branner, 1948, 80 p.
Danske Skønlitteraert Forfatterleksikon, I. København, 1959.

2. Biography and Appreciation

Grønbech, V. P., *Spillemaend og andre folk, tanker under praediken af organisten
ved Sebastians Kirken*. København, 1949.
Hind, T., *Engle uden basun*. Fredensborg, Arena forfatternes forlag, 1958.
Ljungdell, R. E., *Vilhelm Grønbech, Diktare och Profet*. København, 1939.

3. Main Publications

1909–1912 *Vor Folkeaet i Oldtiden.* 4 vols. København.
  English translation by W. Worster (Revised by the author): *The Culture of the Teutons*, 3 vols. London, Oxford University Press, 1931, København, Jespersen and Pies, 1931.
  German translation by Ellen Hofmeyer: *Kultur und Religionen der Germanen*, 2 vols. Hamburg, Hanseatische Verlagsanstalt, 1937; Darmstadt, Wissenschaftliche Buchgesellschaft, 1961⁶.
1922 *Religiòse Strominger i det nittende Aarhundrede.* København, Gyldendal.
  English translation by P. M. Mitchell and W. D. Paden: *Religious Currents in the Nineteenth Century.* Lawrence, University of Kansas Press, 1964.
1927 *Nordiska Myter og Sagn. Med Kulturhistorisk Indledning.* København, Gyldendal. 1964².
1932–1934 *Mystikere i Europa og Indien.* København, Branner.
1939 *Hellenismen*, 2 vols. København, Branner.
1942 *Hellas. Kultur og Religion.* København, Gyldenhal. 1961².
1963 *Primitiv Religion, med et Kapittel om primitiv Kult af Torkil Kemp.* Reprinted København, Reitzel.

OTTO GRUPPE

1. Biography and Appreciation

(loeren, H. J., *O. F. Gruppe und die Sprachanalytische Philosophie.* Münster, 1967.

2. Main Publications

1887 *Die griechischen Culte und Mythen in ihren Beziehungen zu den orientalischen Religionen.* Leipzig.
1906 *Griechische Mythologie und Religionsgeschichte*, 2 vols. München.
1918 "Die Anfänge des Zeuskultus," *Neue Jahrbücher für das klassische Altertum, Geschichte und Deutsche Literatur und für Pädagogik*, Vol. 41.
1921 *Geschichte der klassischen Mythologie und Religionsgeschichte während der Neuzeit.* Leipzig.

J. F. HERMANN GUNKEL

1. Biography and Appreciation

Eucharistèrion. Studien zur Religion und Literatur des Alten und Neuen Testaments. Hermann Gunkel zum 60. Geburtstage, 2 vols. Hrsg. von Hans Schmidt. Göttingen, Vandenhoeck & Ruprecht, 1923.

James (The elder), Fl., *Thirty Psalmists. A study in personalities of the Psalter as seen against the background of Gunkel's type-study of the Psalms.* New York, 1938.

Klatt, W., *Hermann Gunkel. Zu seiner Theologie der Religionsgeschichte und zur Entstehung der formgeschichtlichen Methode.* Göttingen, 1969.

2. Main Publications

1895 *Schöpfung und Chaos in Urzeit und Endzeit.* Eine religionsgeschichtliche Untersuchung über Gen. 1 and Ap. Joh. 12. Göttingen, Vandenhoeck & Ruprecht.

1901 *Handkommentar zum Alten Testament.* (Genesis). Göttingen, Vandenhoeck & Ruprecht.
English translation of the Introduction by W. H. Carruth: "Die Sagen der Genesis," in: *The Legends of Genesis.* Chicago, Open Court Publishing Co., 1901; London, Treibner, 1907.

1903 *Zum religionsgeschichtlichen Verständnis des Neuen Testaments.* Göttingen, Vandenhoeck & Ruprecht, 1910².

1903 *Forschungen zur Religion und Literatur des Alten und Neuen Testaments.* Ed. by W. Bousset and H. Gunkel. Göttingen, Vandenhoeck & Ruprecht.

1903 *Israel und Babylonien. Der Einfluss Babyloniens auf die Israelitische Religion.* (With reference to F. Delitzsch's "Babel und Bibel"). Göttingen, Vandenhoeck & Ruprecht.
English translation by E. S. B.: *Israel and Babylon. The influence of Babylon on the religion of Israel.* (A reply to Delitzsch). Philadelphia, John Jos. McVey, 1904.

1905 *Das alte Testament im Licht der modernen Forschung.* (Extract from: *Beiträge zur Weiterentwicklung der christlichen Religion,* 4). München, Lehmann's Verlag, pp. 40–76.

1913 *Reden und Aufsätze.* Göttingen, Vandenhoeck & Ruprecht.

1914 *Was will die religionsgeschichtliche Bewegung?* Deutsch-Evangelischer Verlag.

1916 *Was bleibt vom Alten Testament?* Göttingen, Vandenhoeck & Ruprecht.
English translation by A. K. Dallas: *What remains of the Old Testament and other Essays.* New York, Macmillan; London, Allen & Unwin, 1928.

1917 *Die Propheten.* Göttingen, Vandenhoeck & Ruprecht.

1928 *Einleitung in die Psalmen. Die Gattungen der religiösen Lyrik Israels.* Göttingen, Vandenhoeck & Ruprecht.
English translation by Th. M. Horner: *The Psalms. A form-critical introduction.* Philadelphia, 1967.

H

HANS HAAS

1. Biography and Appreciation

Rudolph, Kurt, "Die Bedeutung von Hans Haas für die Religionswissenschaft," *Zeitschrift für Religions- und Geistesgeschichte*, XXI (1969), pp. 238–252.

2. Main Publications

1902–1904 *Geschichte des Christentums in Japan*, 2 vols. Tokyo, Rikkyo Gakuin Press. (Mitteilungen der Deutschen Gesellschaft für Natur- und Völker- kunde Ostasiens. Supplementband 5, 7). Hamburg.

1908 *Annalen des japanischen Buddhismus*. (Mitteilungen der Deut. Ges. f. Nat. u. Völk. Ostas. 11, 3). Hamburg.

1910 *Amida Buddha unsere Zuflucht*. Urkunden zum Verständnis des japanischen Sukhavati-Buddhismus. Leipzig, Hinrichs.

1920 *Das Spruchgut K'ung-tszês und Lao-tszês in gedanklicher Zusammen- ordnung*. Leipzig, Hinrichs.

1922 *Bibliographie zur Frage nach den Wechselbeziehungen zwischen Buddhismus und Christentum*. Leipzig, Hinrichs.

1924–1934 Hans Haas with H. Bonnet and others, *Bilderatlas zur Religionsge- schichte*. 20 Lieferungen (20 fascicules). Leipzig, Hinrichs.

1926 "Rechte und schlechte Apologetik in der allgemeinen Religionsgeschichte," *Zeitschrift für Missions- und Religionswissenschaft*, Vol. 41 (1926), pp. 225–239.

EDMUND G. N. HARDY

1. Bibliography

Streitberg, W., "Verzeichnis der indologischen Schriften und ausgegebenen indischen Texte," *Indogermanische Forschungen*, XVII (Beiblatt, Anzeiger) 1905, pp. 139–144.

2. Biography and Appreciation

Gottlob, A., "E. Hardys denkwürdiges Jahr," *Hochland*, Vol. 7 (1909–1910), pp. 49–63.
Rhys Davids, T. W., "E. Hardy," *Journal of the Royal Asiatic Society*, Vol. 37 (1905), pp. 213—215.
Streitberg, W., "E. Hardy," *Hochland*, Vol. 2 (1905), pp. 427–445.

3. Main Publications

1887 *Die allgemeine vergleichende Religionswissenschaft im akademischen Studium unserer Zeit*. Eine akademische Antrittsrede. Freiburg im Breisgau.
1890 *Der Buddhismus nach alteren Pâli-Werken*. Münster i. W., Aschendorff.
1893 *Die Vedisch-brahmanische Periode der Religion des alten Indiens*. Münster i. W., Aschendorff.
1898 "Was ist Religionswissenschaft? Ein Beitrag zur Methodik der historischen Religionsforschung," *Archiv für Religionswissenschaft*, I, 1 (1898), pp. 1 ff.
1901 "Zur Geschichte der Religionsforschung," *Archiv für Religionswissenschaft*, IV (1901), pp. 45ff, pp. 97ff.
1902 *Indiens Kultur in der Blütezeit des Buddhismus*. Mainz, Kirchheim.

CARL GUSTAV ADOLF VON HARNACK

1. Bibliography

Christlieb, M., *Harnack-Bibliographie*. Zum 60. Geburtstag Adolf Harnacks. Leipzig, Hinrichs, 1912.
Smend, Fr., *Adolf von Harnack. Verzeichnis seiner Schriften*. Leipzig, Hinrichs, 1927. Ergänzung: 1927–1930/31. Mit einem Nachtrag durch Axel von Harnack.

2. Biography and Appreciation

Benz, E., "Adolf von Harnack, zum 100. Geburtstag," *Jahrbuch Mainz A. W.*, 1952, pp. 207–227.
Bonaccorsi, G., *Harnack e Loisy*. Firense, Librerià editrice Fiorentina, 1904.
Colpe, C., "Bemerkungen zu Adolf von Harnacks Einschätzung der Disziplin 'Allgemeine Religionsgeschichte'," *Neue Zeitschrift für Systematische Theologie und Religionsphilosophie*, Vol. 6 (1964), pp. 51—69.
Glick, Garland W., *Adolf Harnack as Historian and Theologian*. Chicago, University of Chicago Press, 1957.
Holl, K., *Briefwechsel mit Adolf von Harnack*. Ed. by H. Karpp. Tübingen, Mohr, 1966.
Lacey, T. A., *Harnack and Loisy*. London, Longmans, 1904.
Pavek, Wilhelm, *Harnack and Troeltsch: Two Historical Theologians*. New York, Oxford University Press, 1968.

Slotemaker de Bruïne, M. C., *Adolf von Harnacks kritische dogmengeschiedenis.* The Hague, Martinus Nijhoff, 1933.
Troeltsch, Ernst, "Adolf von Harnack und Ferdinand Christian Baur," in: *Festgabe für A. von Harnack zum 70. Geburtstage.* Tübingen, 1921.
Zahn-Harnack, Agnes von, *Adolf von Harnack.* Berlin-Tempelhof, Bott, 1936, 1951[2].

3. Main Publications

1881 *Das Mönchtum, seine Ideale und seine Geschichte.* Giessen. 1895[4].
  English translation by E. E. Kellett: *Monasticism: its Ideals and History.* London, Williams & Norgate, 1901.
1882 *Die Überlieferung der griechischen Apologeten des zweiten Jahrhunderts in der alten Kirche und im Mittelalter.* Leipzig, Hinrichs.
1885–1890 *Lehrbuch der Dogmengeschichte,* 3 vols. Freiburg i. Br., Mohr, 1886–1892[2], 1894–1897[3], 1909–1910[4]; Tübingen, Mohr, 1922[6].
  English translation by N. Buchanan (Vols. 1, 2), J. Millar (Vols. 3–5) and W. Macgilchrist (Vols. 6, 7): *History of Dogma,* 7 vols. London, 1894–1899. Later reeditions.
1886 *Die Quellen der sogenannten Apostolischen Kirchenordnung.* Nebst einer Untersuchung über den Ursprung des Lectorats, und der anderen niederen Weihen. (Texte und Untersuchungen zur Geschichte der altchristlichen Literatur Bd. 2, Heft 5). Leipzig, Hinrichs.
  English translation by L. A. Wheately: *Sources of the Apostolic Canons,* with a treatise on the origin of the Readership and other lower orders. London, Black, 1895.
1889 *Grundriss der Dogmengeschichte.* Freiburg i. Br., Mohr. 1893[2].
  English translation by E. K. Mitchell: *Outlines of the History of Dogma.* New York, Funk & Wagnalls Co.; London, Hodder & Stoughton, 1893.
1892 *Das Apostolische Glaubensbekenntnis.* Berlin, Haack, 1892[2–23].
  English translation by Stewart Means: *The Apostles' Creed.* (A translation from an article in the third edition of Herzog's Realencyclopädie.). Rev. and ed. by T. B. Saunders. London, Black, 1901.
1893–1904 *Geschichte der altchristlichen Litteratur bis Eusebius,* 2 vols. Leipzig, Hinrichs.
1895[2] *Das Christentum und die Geschichte.* Leipzig, Hinrichs. 1895[2], 1904[5].
  English translation by T. B. Saunders: *Christianity and History.* London, Black, 1896, 1900[2].
1896 *Zur gegenwärtigen Lage des Protestantismus.* (Hefte zur Christlichen Welt, 25). Tübingen, Mohr.
  English translation by T. B. Saunders: *Thoughts on the present Position of Protestantism.* London, Black, 1899.
1900 *Das Wesen des Christentums.* (Sechzehn Vorlesungen ... im Wintersemester 1899–1900). Leipzig, Hinrichs.
  English translation by T. B. Saunders: *What is Christianity?* London, Williams & Norgate, 1901, 1903[3] (Revised).
1901 *Die Aufgabe der theologischen Fakultäten und die allgemeine Religionsgeschichte.* Berlin, Schade. Reprinted in: A. Harnack, *Reden und Aufsätze,* Vol. 2 (Giessen, 1904), pp. 159–187.

1902 *Die Mission und Ausbreitung des Christentums in den ersten drei Jahrhunderten,* 2 vols. Leipzig, Hinrichs. 1906², 1915³.
  English translation by J. Moffat: *The Expansion of Christianity in the
  first three centuries,* 2 vols. London, Williams & Norgate, 1904–1905.
  The Mission and Expansion of Christianity in the first three centuries,
  2 Vols. (Second, enlarged and revised ed.). London, Williams & Norgate;
  New York, Putnam's Sons, 1908. Repr. New York, Harper, 1962.
1904–1906 *Reden und Aufsätze,* 2 vols. Giessen, Ricker and Töpelmann.
  Partial *English* translation by G. M. Craik, in: *Essays on the Social Gospel,*
  by A. von Harnack und W. Herrmann. (Crown Theological Library,
  Vol. 18). London, Williams & Norgate; New York, Putnam's Sons, 1907.
1905 *Militia Christi.* Die christliche Religion und der Soldatenstand in den
  ersten drei Jahrhunderten. Tübingen.
1906–1916 *Beiträge zur Einleitung in das Neue Testament,* 7 Hefte. Leipzig,
  Hinrichs.
  English translation by J. R. Wilkinson: *New Testament Studies,* 6 vols.
  (Crown Theological Library. Vols. 20, 23, 27, 33, 36, 45). London, Williams
  & Norgate, 1907–1925.
1911 *Aus Wissenschaft und Leben.* Giessen, Töpelmann.
1911–1916 *Reden und Aufsätze. Neue Folge,* 3 vols. Giessen, Töpelmann.
1921 *Marcion: das Evangelium vom fremden Gott.* Leipzig, Hinrichs. 1924².
1927 *Die Entstehung der christlichen Theologie und des kirchlichen Dogmas.*
  Sechs Vorlesungen. Gotha.
1931 *Studien zur Geschichte des Neuen Testaments und der alten Kirche,* 3 vols.
  Berlin–Leipzig, De Gruyter.
1951 *Ausgewählte Reden und Aufsätze.* Anlässlich des 100. Geburtstages des
  Verfassers neu hrsg. von Agnes von Zahn-Harnack und Axel von Harnack.
  Berlin.

JANE ELLEN HARRISON

1. Bibliography

"Bibliography," in: Stewart, Jessie G., *Jane Ellen Harrison. A Portrait from
  Letters.* London, The Merlin Press, 1959, pp. 203–207.

2. Biography and Appreciation

Harrison, Jane, *Alpha and Omega.* (Essays). London, Sidgwick & Jackson, 1915.
  —, *Reminiscences of a Student's Life.* London, Hogarth Press, 1925.
Stewart, Jessie G., *Jane Ellen Harrison. A Portrait from Letters.* London, The
  Merlin Press, 1959.
Svyatopolk-Mirsky, Prince D. P., *Jane Ellen Harrison and Russia.* (Jane
  Harrison Memorial Lecture, Nr. 2.). Cambridge, Heffer, 1930.

3. Main Publications

1882 *Myths of the Odyssey in art and literature.* London, Rivington.
1885 *Introductory Studies in Greek Art.* London, T. Fisher Unwin, 1897[4].
1903 *Prolegomena to the study of Greek religion.* Cambridge, University Press. 1907[2], 1922[3]. Pb. New York, Meridian Books, 1955; London, Merlin Press, 1961.
1905 *The religion of ancient Greece.* London, Constable.
1912 *Themis: A Study in the Social Origins of Greek Religion.* With an excursus on the ritual forms preserved in Greek tragedy by Prof. Gilbert Murray and a chapter on the origin of the Olympic games by Mr. F. M. Cornford. Cambridge, University Press. 1927[2] (revised). Pb. New York, Harper & Row, 1957. Repr. London, The Merlin Press, 1963.
1913 *Ancient art and ritual.* London, Williams & Norgate.
1915 *Alpha and Omega.* Essays. London, Sidgwick & Jackson.
1919 *Rationalism and Religious Reaction.* London, Watts.
1921 *Epilegomena to the Study of Greek Religion.* Cambridge, University Press, Pb. New York, Meridian Books.
1924 *Mythology.* London, Harrop; Boston, Mass., Marshall Jones. 1925.
1927 *Myths of Greece and Rome.* London, Benn; Garden City, N. Y., Doubleday, 1928.
1937 *Sanctuary.* New York, Speller.

EDWIN SIDNEY HARTLAND

1. Bibliography

Folk-Lore, Vol. 37 (1926), pp. 180–192.

2. Main Publications

1890 *English Fairy and other Folk Tales.* London, Scott.
1891 *The Science of Fairy Tales. An Enquiry into Fairy Mythologies.* London, Nutt. London, Methuen, 1925[2].
1894–1896 *The Legend of Perseus. A Study of Tradition in Story, Custom, and Belief,* 3 vols. London, Nutt.
1899 *Folklore. What is it, and what is the good of it.* London, Nutt.
1900 *Mythology and Folktales: their relation and interpretation.* London, Nutt.
1909 *Primitive Paternity. The Myth of Supernatural Birth in Relation to the History of the Family.* London, Nutt.
1914 *Ritual and Belief. Studies in the History of Religion.* London, Williams & Norgate.
1921 *Primitive Society. The Beginnings of the Family and the Reckoning of Descent.* London, Methuen, 1921.

FRIEDRICH HEILER*

1. Bibliography

Heiler, Anne Marie, "Bibliographie Friedrich Heiler," in: Christel Matthias Schröder, ed., *In Deo Omnia Unum*. Eine Sammlung von Aufsätzen Friedrich Heiler zum 50. Geburtstage dargebracht. München, Ernst Reinhardt, 1942, pp. 370–399. (This bibliography contains publications from 1914 through 1941).

— in Zusammenarbeit mit Gerd Muschinski, "Bibliographie Friedrich Heiler," in: *Inter Confessiones. Beiträge zur Förderung des interkonfessionellen und interreligiösen Gesprächs*. Friedrich Heiler zum Gedächtnis aus Anlasz seines 80. Geburtstages am 30.1.1972. Herausgegeben von Anne Marie Heiler. Marburg, Elwert Verlag, 1972, pp. 154–195.

2. Biography and Appreciation

Bleeker, C. J., "In memoriam Friedrich Heiler," *Numen*, XIV, 3 (November 1967), pp. 161–162.

Boncev, Atanasij, "Professor episkop Fridrick Heiler, in piam memoriam," *Curkoven Vestuik Organ na Bulgarskata pravoslavna curkva za religioska i curkovno—obsestvena prosveta* (Sofia), 11 July 1967, pp. 14–15.

Fries, Heinrich, "Friedrich Heiler zum 75. Geburtstag," in E. Jungclaussen, ed., *Die grössere Oekumene...* (1970), pp. 9–14.

Goldammer, Kurt, "Die Frühentwicklung der Allgemeinen Religionswissenschaft und die Anfänge einer Theologie der Religionen. Friedrich Heilers Beitrag zur Methodik der Religionsgeschichte und zur Religionstheologie," *Saeculum*, XVIII, 1–2 (1967), pp. 181–198.

—, "Der Beitrag Friedrich Heilers zur Methodologie der Religionswissenschaft," *Theologische Literaturzeitung*, Vol, 92 (1967), Nr. 2, pp. 87–94.

—, "Ein Leben für die Erforschung der Religion. Friedrich Heiler und sein Beitrag zur Aufgabestellung und Methodik der Religionswissenschaft," in: *Inter Confessiones. Beiträge zur Förderung des interkonfessionellen und interreligiösen Gesprächs*. Friedrich Heiler zum Gedächtnis aus Anlasz seines 80. Geburtstages am 30.1.1972. Herausgegeben von Anne Marie Heiler. Marburg, Elwert Verlag, 1972, pp. 1–16.

Hamada, H., "In memory of Doctor Friedrich Heiler," *Journal of Religious Studies* (Tokyo), December 1967, pp. 93—99 (in Japanese).

Heiler, Anne Marie, ed., *Interconfessiones. Beiträge zur Förderung des interkonfessionellen und interreligiösen Gesprächs*. Friedrich Heiler zum Gedächtnis aus Anlasz seines 80. Geburtstages am 30. Januar 1972. Marburg, Elwert Verlag, 1972.

Jungclaussen, Emmanuel, ed., *Die gröszere Oekumene. Gespräch um Friedrich Heiler*. Regensburg, Pustet, 1970. See by this author: "Werk im Widerspruch," pp. 25–94.

Lanczkowski, Günter, "Erkenntnis und Wertung der Religionen," *Kairos*, 1966, Nr. 3/4, pp. 166–170.

Manthey, Franz, "Friedrich Heiler In Memoriam," *Rivista di Storia e Letteratura Religiosa*, 1967, Nr. 2, pp. 361–367.

Philippidis, Leonidas Jo., "Friedrich Heiler, ὁ Διαπρεπὴς Θεόλογος Θρησκειόλογος. Τακτικοῦ Καθηγητοῦ τῆς Ἱστορίας τῶν θρησκευμάτων καὶ τῆς Φιλοσοφίας τῆς Θρησκείας ἐν τῇ Θεολογικῇ Σχολῇ τοῦ Πανεπιστημίου Ἀθηνῶν 23 pp., 1962.
Ratschow, Carl Heinz, "Friedrich Heilers Bedeutung für die ökumenische Bewegung," in E. Jungclaussen, ed., *Die grössere Oekumene* . . . (1970), pp. 15—19.
Röhr, Heinz, "Friedrich Heiler zum 75. Geburtstag am 30.1.1967," *Freies Christentum*, January 1967, pp. 7–8.
Schimmel, Annemarie, "Friedrich Heiler zum 75. Geburtstag," *Numen*, October 1966, pp. 161–163.
Schmidt, Eugen, "Zum Gedenken an Friedrich Heiler," *Baha'i-Briefe. Blätter für Weltreligion und Weltbewusztsein*, July 1967, pp. 734 ff.

3. Method and Theory

1914 "Die Entwicklung der Religionspsychologie," *Das Neue Jahrhundert, Wochenschrift für religiöse Kultur*, VI (1914), pp. 318–321, 326–330, 341–342, 352–355.
1920 "Die Absolutheit des Christentums im Lichte der allgemeinen Religionsgeschichte," *Christliche Welt*, XXXIV (1920), pp. 226–230, 244–248, 258–262. Reprinted in *Das Wesen des Katholizismus*, 1920, pp. 116–137.
1931 *Die Mission des Christentums in Indien* (Marburger Theologische Studien, Heft 5). Gotha, Leopold Klotz.
Dutch translation by J. C. Helders: *De Openbaring in de Godsdiensten van Britsch-Indië en de Christusverkondiging*. Preface by H. Th. Obbink. Amsterdam, H. J. Paris, 1931.
1938 "Die Frage der 'Absolutheit' des Christentums im Lichte der vergleichenden Religionsgeschichte," *Eine Heilige Kirche*, XX (1938), pp. 306–336
1952 "Um die Zusammenarbeit der Christenheit mit den auszerchristlichen Religionsgemeinden," *Schweizerische Theologische Umschau*, XXII (1952), pp. 1–11.
1953 " 'Mut zur Liebe' — Die Zusammenarbeit der Religionen im Dienste der ganzen Christenheit," *Eine Heilige Kirche*, XXVII (1953–54), pp. 18–33.
1959 "The History of Religions as a preparation for the co-operation of religions," in: Mircea Eliade and Joseph M. Kitagawa, ed., *The History of Religions. Essays in Methodology*. Chicago, University of Chicago Press, 1959, 1962², pp. 132–160.

4. Main publications

1916 "Die buddhistischen Versenkungsstufen," in: *Aufsätze zur Kultur- und Sprachgeschichte des Orients, Ernst Kuhn zum 70. Geburtstage gewidmet*. Breslau, pp. 357–387.
1918 *Die buddhistische Versenkung. Eine religionsgeschichtliche Untersuchung*. München, Ernst Reinhardt. 1922² (revised and enlarged).
1918 *Das Gebet. Eine religionsgeschichtliche und religionspsychologische Untersuchung*. München, Ernst Reinhardt. 1923⁵ (enlarged); Reprinted with enlarged bibliography, München–Basel, Ernst Reinhardt, 1969.

English translation and edition by Samuel McComb: *Prayer. A Study in the History and Psychology of Religion.* London–New York–Toronto, Oxford University Press, 1932. Pb. Galaxy Book, New York, Oxford University Press, 1958.
French translation from the 5th German edition by Etienne Kruger and Jacques Marty: *La prière.* Paris, Payot, 1931.
Swedish translation by Gunhild Tegen: *Bönen. En religionshistorisk och religionspsykologisk undersökning.* Stockholm, Svenska Diakonistyrelses Bokförlag, 1922.

1918 *Luthers religionsgeschichtliche Bedeutung* (Address). München, Ernst Reinhardt.

1919 *Die Bedeutung der Mystik für die Weltreligionen* (Address). München Ernst Reinhardt.

1919 *Das Geheimnis des Gebets, Kanzelreden in schwedischen Kirchen.* München, Chr. Kaiser.

1920 *Das Wesen des Katholizismus.* Sechs Vorträge, gehalten im Herbst 1919 in Schweden. München, Ernst Reinhardt.
Swedish translation by Ingrid Ljungqvist: *Katolicismen.* Stockholm, Sveriges Kristliga Studentrörelses Förlag, 1920.

1921 *Katholischer und evangelischer Gottesdienst.* München, Chr. Kaiser; Second, newly prepared and enlarged edition, München, Ernst Reinhardt, 1925².
English translation by W. Montgomery, with a foreword by the Very Rev. G. K. A. Bell: *The Spirit of Worship. Its Forms and Manifestations in Christian Churches.* London, Hodder and Stoughton, 1926 (tr. from the 2nd edition).
Swedish translation: "Den kristna gudstjänstens huvudformer," in: *Kristendom och vår tid,* 1924 (tr. from the 2nd edition).

1923 *Der Katholizismus, seine Idee und seine Erscheinung.* Völlige Neubearbeitung der schwedischen Vorträge über das Wesen des Katholizismus. München, Ernst Reinhardt. 1970².

1924 *Sadhu Sundar Singh, ein Apostel des Ostens und Westens.* München, Ernst Reinhardt. 1926⁴ (revised and enlarged).
Danish translation by Ingrid Koch and Ed. Geismar, with a foreword by Eduard Geismar: *Oestens och Vestes Apnostel, Sadhu Sundar Singh.* København, J. Frimodts Forlag, 1925.
Abridged *English* translation by Olive Wyon: *The Gospel of Sadhu Sundar Singh.* London, Allen & Unwin, 1927.
Japanese translation by Tame-ichirō and Kiyoi Takemura: *Tōyō oyobi seiyō shito, sei San-da Shin-gu.* Tokayo, Shinsei-dō, 1930.
Swedish translation by Signe Bosson-Alin: *Sadhu Sundar Singh, ett österns sändebud till västerlandet.* Uppsala, Lindblads Förlag, 1925.

1925 *Apostel oder Betrüger? Dokumente zum Sadhustreit.* München, Ernst Reinhardt.

1925 *Die Mystik in den Upanishaden (Untersuchungen zur Geschichte des Buddhismus und verwandter Gebiete).* München, O. Schlosz.

1926 *Christlicher Glaube und indisches Geistesleben. Rabîndranâth Tagore, Mahâtmâ Gândhi, Brahmabandhav Upâdhyâya, Sâdhu Sundar Singh.* München, Ernst Reinhardt.

1926 "Morgenländischer und abendländischer Katholizismus," *Internationale Kirchliche Zeitschrift* (Bern), XVI (1926), pp. 1–30. Second, revised edition in *Gesammelte Aufsätze und Vorträge,* Vol. II. (1926–),1931,pp.61–97.

English translation by W. Montgomery: "Catholicity, Eastern, Roman and Evangelical," in: *The Spirit of Worship, its Forms and Manifestations in the Christian Churches.* London, Hodher & Stoughton, 1926, pp. 123–195.

1926–1931 *Gesammelte Aufsätze und Vorträge.* Vol. I: *Evangelische Katholizität;* Vol. II: *Im Ringen um die Kirche.* München, Ernst Reinhardt. (Collected essays and papers previously published).

The second volume has been translated into *Dutch* by J. K. van den Brink, with a Preface by G. van der Leeuw: *De Strijd om de Kerk.* Baarn, Bosch en Keuning, n. d.

1927 *Die Wahrheit Sundar Singhs. Neue Dokumente zum Sadhustreit.* München, Ernst Reinhardt.

1927 "Die hochkirchliche Bewegung (Catholic Movement) in der anglikanischen Kirche," *Die Hochkirche,* IX (1927), pp. 79–85, 105–115, 136–144, 169–173. Revised edition in *Gesammelte Aufsätze und Vorträge,* Vol. II, 1931, pp. 391–441.

English translation: "A Lutheran review of Anglo-Catholicism," *The Church Quarterly Review,* CCIX (1929), pp. 2–49.

1931 "Die Gottesmutter im Glauben und Beten der Jahrhunderte," *Die Hochkirche,* XIII (1931), pp. 172–209, 251 f.

Italian translation: "La madre di Dio nella fede e nella preghiera dei primi secoli," and "Il culto postefesino della madonna," in *Ricerche Religiose* (Roma), VII (1931), pp. 390–409, and VIII (1932), pp. 16–39.

1933 "Die Kontemplation in der christlichen Mystik," *Eranos-Jahrbuch* (1933), Zürich, Rhein-Verlag, pp. 245–326.

1934 "Die Madonna als religiöses Symbol," *Eranos-Jahrbuch* (1934), Zürich, Rhein-Verlag, pp. 277–317.

English translation "The Madonna as Religious Symbol" in: *The Mystic Vision.* Papers from the Eranos Yearbooks. (Bollingen Series XXX, 6). New York, 1968, pp. 348–374.

1937–1941 *Die katholische Kirche des Ostens und Westens.* Vol. I: *Urkirche und Ostkirche ;* Vol. II: *Altkirchliche Autonomie und päpstlicher Zentralismus.* München, Ernst Reinhardt. A second revised edition of *Urkirche und Ostkirche* appeared in 1971 under the title: *Die Ostkirchen ; 2. Völlig neu bearbeitete Auflage von 'Urkirche und Ostkirche'.* Aus dem Nachlasz in Zusammenarbeit mit Hans Hartog herausgegeben von Anne Marie Heiler. München–Basel, Ernst Reinhardt, 1971.

1940 "Weltabkehr und Weltrückkehr auszerchristlicher Mystiker. 1. Teil: Lao-tse's Tao-teh-king und die Bhagavadgîtâ," *Eine Heilige Kirche,* XXII (1940), pp. 181–213.

1947 *Der Vater des katholischen Modernismus, Alfred Loisy (1857–1940).* München, Erasmus Verlag & Reinhardt Verlag.

1950 *Die Stellung der Frau in den auszerchristlichen Religionen und im Christentum.* (Heim und Familie, Heft 2). Darmstadt.

1950 *Unsterblichkeitsglaube und Jenseitshoffnung in der Geschichte der Religionen.* (Glauben und Wissen, Nr. 2). Basel, Ernst Reinhardt.

1952 "Um die Zusammenarbeit der Christenheit mit den auszerchristlichen Religionsgemeinschaften," *Schweizerische Theologische Umschau* (Bern), XXII, 2 (1952), pp. 1–11.

English translation: "How can Christian and non-Christian Religions co-operate?" *Hibbert Journal,* LII (January 1954), pp. 3–14.

A revised edition of the German original appeared in *Mitteilungen des Instituts für Auslandsbeziehungen* (Bonn), V, 1/2 (1955).

1954 "Der Gottesbegriff in der Mystik," *Numen*, I, 3 (1954), pp. 161–183. *Turkish* translation by Annemarie Schimmel: "Mistisizmde tankri mefhumu," *Ilâhiyat Fakültesi Dergisi*. *Ankara Universitesi Ilâhiyat Fakültesi Tarafindan üç Ayda bir Cikarilir*, I–II (1955), pp. 58–72.

1957 "Einheit und Zusammenarbeit der Religionen," *Gemeinschaft und Politik* (Institut für Geosoziologie und Politik, Bad Godesberg), (1957, Nr. 12), pp. 1–19.

1957 "Stada kristnidómsins medal trúarbragdanna. Sérpretun úr Morgoni" ("The position of Christianity among the religions", translated into *Icelandic* by Jón Auduns), *Morgen* (Reykjavik), (1957), pp. 51–85.

1959 Friedrich Heiler, in collaboration with Kurt Goldammer, Franz Hesse, Günter Lanczkowski, Käte Neumann, Anne-Marie Schimmel, *Die Religionen der Menschheit in Vergangenheit und Gegenwart*. Stuttgart, Reclam Verlag. 1962[2].

1959 "Fortleben und Wandlungen des antiken Gottkönigtums im Christentum," in: *Sacral Kingship*. Leiden, E. J. Brill.

1960 "The History of Religions as a Way to Unity of Religions," *Proceedings of the IXth International Congress for the History of Religions, Tokyo and Kyoto, 25 VIII–9 IX 1958*. Tokyo, pp. 8–22.

1960 "The influence of Eastern Religions on the European intellectual and spiritual life," *Proceedings of the IXth International Congress* ... Tokyo, pp. 709–716.

1960 "The Idea of God in Indian and Western Mysticism," *The Indo-Asian Culture* (New Delhi), IX, 1 (July 1960), pp. 123–140.

1960 "The influence of Eastern religions on Western thought," *The Indo-Asian Culture* (New Delhi), IX, 2 (October 1960), pp. 42–60.

1960 "Buddhism in Western perspective," in: *Buddhism and Culture*. Dedicated to Dr. Daisetz Teitaro Suzuki in Commemoration of his 90th Birthday. Kyoto, pp. 46–52.

1961 "Die Lage der Weltreligionen in Ostasien," in: *Tradition und Gegenwart. Fünf Gastvorlesungen anläszlich des hundertfünfzigjährigen Bestehens der Berliner Theologischen Fakultät*. Berlin, Evangelische Verlagsanstalt, pp. 30–51.

1961 *Erscheinungsformen und Wesen der Religion*. (Die Religionen der Menschheit, I). Stuttgart, Kohlhammer.

1961 "Religion und Religionen," in: Gerhard Günther, ed., *Die groszen Religionen*. Hamburg, pp. 9–26.

1962 "Das Geistesleben Asiens in westlicher Sicht," in: *Bild und Verkündigung. Festgabe für Hanna Jursch zum 60. Geburtstag*. Berlin, Evangelische Verlagsanstalt, pp. 54–70.

1963 *Die Verständigung der Religionen in alter und neuer Zeit* (Sonderheft der Wissenschaftlichen Zeitschrift der Friedrich Schiller-Universität). Jena.

1964 "Das Christentum und die Religionen," in: Carl Schneider, ed., *Einheit des Geistes* (Jahrbuch der Evangelischen Akademie der Pfalz). Speyer.

1965 "Das Wirklichwerden Gottes in der Liebe. Eine Betrachtung über Buddha," *Baha'i–Briefe* (Blätter für Weltreligion und Weltbewusztsein), Heft 20 (April 1965), pp. 499–502.

1965 "Das Gebet in der Problematik des modernen Menschen," in: *Interpretation der Welt. Romano Guardini zum 80. Geburtstag*. Würzburg, Echter-Verlag, pp. 227–246.
1966 "Il Buddismo. Religione della Toleranza," in: *Introduzione al Buddismo*. Palermo. pp. 227–246.
1966 "Vom Naturwunder zum Geistwunder. Der Wandel des primitiven Wunderglaubens durch die Religion," in: *Festschrift für Walter Baetke zu seinem 80. Geburtstag*. Weimar, Hermann Bühlaus Nachf., pp. 151–166.
1967 "Die religiöse Einheit der Menschheit," in: Richard Schwarz, ed., *Menschliche Existenz und moderne Welt*, II. Teil, Band 3. Berlin, pp. 578–593.
1967 "Vivekananda. Der Künder der Harmonie der Religionen," in: *Religion und Religionen. Festschrift für Gustav Mensching zu seinem 65. Geburtstag*. Bonn, Ludwig Röhrscheid Verlag, pp. 35–63.
1967 "Die Weltreligionen und der Friede der Welt," *Areopag. Ein politisch-literarisches Forum* (Marburg), Heft 4 (1967), pp. 193–209.

GOTTFRIED JACOB HERMANN

1. Biography and Appreciation

Koechly, H., *Gottfried Hermann*. Heidelberg, 1874.

2. Main Publications

1819 *Über das Wesen und die Behandlung der Mythologie*. Leipzig.

ROBERT HERTZ

1. Biography and Appreciation

Evans-Pritchard, E. E., "Introduction," in: Robert Hertz, *Death and the Right Hand*. Translated by Rodney and Claudia Needham. London, Cohen and West, 1960, pp. 9—24.

2. Main Publications

1907 "Contribution à une étude sur la représentation collective de la mort," *L'Année Sociologique*. (Repr. in *Mélanges...* 1928).
   English translation by R. and C. Needham: *Death and the Right Hand* (Coll.). London, Cohen & West; Glencoe, Ill., Free Press, 1960, pp. 25–86.
1909 "La pré-éminence de la main droite. Étude sur la polarité réligieuse," *Revue Philosophique de la France et de l'Etranger*, XXXIV, 2 (1909), pp. 553–580.

English translation by R. and C. Needham in: *Death and the Right Hand*
(Coll.). London, Cohen & West; Glenoce, Ill., Free Press, 1960, pp. 87–113.
1913 *Saint Besse. Étude d'un culte alpestre.* Paris.
1913 "Saint Besse", *Revue de l'Histoire des Religions*, Tome 67, pp. 115–180.
Also published separately, Paris, 1913
1922 "R. Hertz: 'Le péché et l'expiation dans les sociétés primitives' avec
Introduction et Notice par M. Mauss," *Revue de l'Histoire des Religions*,
Tome 86, pp. 1–60
1928 *Mélanges de sociologie religieuse et folklore.* Paris, Alcan. 1970².

CHRISTIAN GOTTLIEB HEYNE

1. Biography and Appreciation

Heeren, Arnold Hermann Ludwig, *Christian Gottlieb Heyne.* Göttingen, 1813.

2. Main Publications

1778 *Sammlung antiquarischer Aufsätze.* Leipzig.
1785–1812 *Opuscula Academica.* Göttingen.
1822 *Akademische Vorlesungen über die Archäologie der Kunst des Altertums,
ins besondere der Griechen und Römer.* Braunschweig.

EDWARD WASHBURN HOPKINS

Main Publications

1881 *The Mutual Relations of the Four Castes according to the Mānavadharma-
çāstram.* Leipzig, Breitkopf & Härtel.
1895 *The Religions of India.* Boston–London, Ginn. 1898².
1901 *The Great Epic of India. Its Character and Origin.* New York, Scribner's
Sons.
1901 *India, Old and New.* New York, Scribner's Sons.
1915 *Epic mythology.* Strassburg, Trübner.
1918 "The background of totemism," *Annual Report of the Smithsonian
Institution*, 1918. Washington, 1920. pp. 573–584.
1918 *The History of Religions.* New York, Macmillan.
1923 *Origin and evolution of religion.* New Haven, Yale University Press;
London, Milford and Oxford University Press.
1924 *Ethics of India.* New Haven, Yale University Press.
1928 *Legends of India.* New Haven, Yale University Press.

ALFRED WILLIAM HOWITT

1. Biography and Appreciation

Burke, Robert O'Hara, *Burke and his Companions. The Victorian Expedition.* From its origin to the return from Carpentaria; and the death of Burke, Wills and Gray, from starvation; with Burke's and Wills' Journals, King's Narrative, Howitt's Diary. Melbourne, Herald Office, 1861.

2. Main Publications

1880 *Kamilaroi and Kurnai* (with L. Fison). New York, Macmillan.
1885 "Australian group relations," *Annual Report of the Smithsonian Institution,* 1883. Washington, 1885, pp. 797–824.
1885 *The Jeraeil, or Initiation Ceremonies of the Kurnai Tribe.* London, Harrison.
1887 *Notes on Songs and Song-makers of some Australian Tribes.* London.
1888 *Further Notes on the Australian Class Systems.* London, Harrison.
1904 *The Native Tribes of South–east Australia.* New York–London, Macmillan.

HENRI HUBERT

1. Bibliography, Biography and Appreciation

Lantier, Raymond, "Hommage à Henri Hubert," *Revue Archéologique,* XXVIII (1928), pp. 289–292. "Bibliograpy," pp. 292–307.

2. Main Publications

1897–1898 "Essai sur la nature et la fonction sociale du sacrifice," en collaboration avec M. Mauss, *L'Année sociologique,* II, pp. 29–138.
1902–1903 "Esquisse d'une théorie générale de la magie," en collaboration avec M. Mauss, *L'Année sociologique,* VII, pp. 1–46.
1904 "Introduction" à la traduction française du *Manuel de l'Histoire des Religions* de Chantepie de la Saussaye. Paris, 1904, pp. V–XLVII.
1908 "Introduction à l'analyse de quelques phénomènes religieux, en collaboration avec M. Mauss, *Revue de l'Histoire des Religions,* LVIII, pp. 163–203.
1909 *Mélanges d'Histoire des Religions,* en collaboration avec M. Mauss. (Travaux de *l'Année sociologique*). Paris, Alcan.
1914–1915 "Le culte des héros et ses conditions sociales," *Revue de l'Histoire des Religions,* LXX, pp. 1–20; LXXI, pp. 194–247.
1925 "Le Mythe d'Epona," dans *Mélanges de linguistique offerts à M. Joseph Vendryes par ses élèves et ses amis.* Paris, Champion, pp. 187–211. Republished in *Divinités gauloises, Sucellus et Nantosuelta, Epona. Dieux de l'autre monde.* Mâcon, Protat, 1925.

1934 *The Rise of the Celts.* Edited and brought up to date by Marcel Mauss, Raymond Lantier and Jean Marx. Translated from the French by M. R. Dobie. London, Kegan Paul.

FRIEDRICH VON HÜGEL

1. Bibliography

Nédoncelle, M., *La pensée religieuse de Fr. von Hügel.* 1935, pp. 209–222. *English* translation by M. Vernon: *Friedrich von Hügel.* Toronto, Longmans, 1937, pp. 195–213.

2. Biography and Appreciation

Hanbury, M., "Baron von Hügel and the Ecumenical Movement," *The Month,* N. I., XXIX (1963).
Heaney, J. J., "The Enigma of the later von Hügel," *Heytroph Journal,* VI (1965), pp. 145–159.
Petre, Maude, D. M., *Von Hügel and Tyrrel. The Story of a Friendship.* London, Dent, 1937.
Steinmann, J., *Friedrich von Hügel, sa vie, son œuvre et ses amitiés.* Paris, Montaigne, 1962.

3. Main Publications

1908 *The Mystical Element of Religion as Studied in Saint Catharine of Genoa and her Friends.* London, Dent; New York, Dutton. 1923².
1912 *Eternal Life ; A Study of Its Implications and Applications.* Edinburgh, Clark.
1921–1926 *Essays and Addresses on the Philosophy of Religion,* 2 vols. London Toronto, Dent; New York, Dutton. 1930²; 1949–1951³. Reissued 1930 and 1949–1951.
1927 *Selected Letters, 1896–1924.* Ed. with a memoir by B. Holland. London–Toronto, Dent.
1928 *Letters from Baron Friedrich von Hügel to a Niece.* Ed. by Gwendolen Greene. London–Toronto, Dent.
1928 *Readings from Friedrich von Hügel.* Selected by Algar Thorold. London–Toronto, Dent.
1930 *Some Notes on the Petrine Claims.* London, Sheed & Ward.
1931 *The Reality of God, and Religion and Agnosticism.* Ed. by E. G. Gardner. London–Toronto, Dent; New York, Dutton.
1945 *Baron von Hügel: Man of God.* An introductory Anthology, compiled with a biographical preface by P. Franklin Chambers. London, Geoffrey Bless. 1947².

J

WILLIAM JAMES*

1. Bibliography

"A list of the published writings of William James," *The Psychological Review*
(Washington), XVIII, 2 (March 1911), pp. 157–165.
Ralph Barton Perry, *Annotated Bibliography of the Writings of William James*.
New York, Longmans, Green and Co., 1920.
Journal of Philosophy, XXIV (1927), pp. 201–203.

2. Biography and Appreciation

Allen, Gay Wilson, *William James. A Biography*. New York, Viking Press
1967
Ayer, Alfred J., *The Origins of Pragmatism. Studies in the Philosophy of Charles
Sanders Peirce and William James*. London etc., 1968.
Bixler, Julius Seebye, *Religion in the Philosophy of William James*. Boston,
Marshall James Co., 1926.
Blau, Théodore, *William James. Sa théorie de la connaissance et la vérité*. Paris,
Jouve et Cie, 1933.
Boutroux, Emile, *William James*. Paris, Colin, 1911².
    English translation by Archibald and Barbara Henderson: *William
    James*. New York–London, Longmans and Green, 1912.
Compton, Charles Harrick, *William James, Philosopher and Man*. Quotations
    and references in 652 books. Foreword by Lucien Price. New York,
    Scarecrow Press, 1957.
Cornesse, Marie, *L'idée de Dieu chez William James*. Etude historique et cri-
    tique. Grenoble, Allier, 1933.
Flournoy, Théodore, *La philosophie de William James*. Paris.
    English authorized translation by E. B. Holt and W. James Jr.: *The Phi-
    losophy of William James*. New York, H. Holt, 1917.
Harberts, William, *William James' Religionsphilosophie, begründet auf persön-
    licher Erfahrung*. Erlangen, E. T. Jacob, 1913.
In commemoration of William James, 1842–1942. New York, AMS Press 1942,
    1967².

James, Alice, *The Diary of Alice James*. Edited by Leon Edel. New York, Dodd, Mead & Co., 1964.

James, Henry, *The Literary Remains of the Late Henry James*. Edited with an Introduction by William James. Boston, James R. Osgood, 1885.

—, *A Small Boy and Others*. New York, Charles Scribner's Sons, 1913.

—, *Notes of a Son and Brother*. New York, Charles Scribner's Sons, 1914.

—, *The Letters of Henry James*. Selected and edited by Percy Lubbock, 2 vols. New York, Charles Scribner's Sons, 1920.

James, William, *The Letters of William James*. Edited by (his son) Henry James, 2 vols., London, Longmans, Green and Co., and Boston, The Atlantic Monthly Press, 1920. Two vols. in one: Boston, Little, Brown, and Company, 1926.

—, *The Selected Letters*.

Leuba, J. H., "Professor Willam James' interpretation of religious experience," *International Journal of Ethics*, XV (1904), pp. 323–339.

—, "The immediate apprehension of God according to William James and William E. Hocking," *Journal of Philosophy*, XXI, 26 (Dec. 18, 1924), pp. 701–712.

Linschoten, Johannes, *Auf dem Wege zu einer phänomenologischen Psychologie ; die Psychologie von William James*. Berlin, W. de Gruyter, 1961.

Maire, Gilbert, *William James et le pragmatisme religieux*. Paris, Denoël et Steele, 1933.

Martland, T. R., Jr., *The Metaphysics of William James and John Dewey. Process and Structure in Philosophy and Religion*. New York, Philosophical Library, 1963.

Matthiesen, F. O., *The James Family*. Including selections from the writings of Henry James Sr. (1811–1882), William James, Henry James (1843–1916) and Alice James. New York, 1947, 1948.

Moore, John Morrison, *Theories of Religious Experience, with special reference to James, Otto and Bergson*. New York, Round Table Press, 1938.

Morris, Lloyd R., *William James*. New York, 1950.

Perry, Ralph Barton, *The Thought and Character of William James (1842–1910) as revealed in unpublished correspondence and notes, together with his published writings*, 2 vols. Boston, Little, Brown and Company, 1935.

—, *The Thought and Character of William James. Briefer Version*. Cambridge, Mass., Harvard University Press, 1948. Harper Torchbook, New York–Evanston, 1964.

Piane, Aristide, *William James*. Monteverde, 1943.

Pinard de la Boullaye, H., "La théorie de l'expérience religieuse de Luther à James," *Revue d'Histoire Ecclésiastique*, XVII (1921), pp. 63–83, 306–348, 547–574.

Reck, Andrew J., *Introduction to William James*. An essay and selected texts. Bloomington, Indiana University Press, 1967.

Reverdin, Henri, *La notion d'expérience d'après William James*. Genève, Georg, 1913

Roback, Abraham Aaron, *William James, his Marginalia, Personality and. Contribution*. Cambridge, Mass., Sci-art Publishers, 1942.

Royce, Josiah, *William James, and other essays on the philosophy of life*. New York, Macmillan, 1912.

Schmidt, Hermann, *Der Begriff der Erfahrungskontinuität bei William James und seine Bedeutung für den amerikanischen Pragmatismus*. Heidelberg, C. Winter, 1959.

Wild, John, *The Radical Empiricism of William James*. Garden City, N. Y., Doubleday, 1969.
Wilshire, Bruce, *William James and Phenomenology: a Study of "The Principles of Psychology"*. Bloomington, Indiana University Press, 1968.
Wisconsin University: *William James, the Man and the Thinker*. Addresses delivered at the University of Wisconsin in celebration of the Centenary of his birth, by Max C. Otto and others. Madison, University of Wisconsin Press, 1942.

3. Main Publications

1890 *The Principles of Psychology*, 2 vols. New York, H. Holt; London Macmillan. 1901², 1910³, etc. Reprint in two vols. New York, 1950.
1892 *A Text-Book of Psychology*. Briefer course [*Psychology*. Briefer course]. New York, H. Holt 1900², 1920³; London, Macmillan, 1907, 1923. Pb. edition edited by Gordon Allport, New York, Harper Torchbook, 1961. Pb. edition with a new foreword by Gardner Murphy, New York, Collier Books, 1962.
French translation by E. Baudin and G. Bertier: *Précis de psychologie*. Paris, M. Rivière, 1909, 1921⁵.
German translation by Marie Dürr: *Psychologie*. Mit Anmerkungen von E. Dürr. Leipzig, 1909.
1897 *The Will to Believe, and Other Essays in Popular Philosophy*. New York– London. Longmans, Green & Co., 1910², etc. 1919.
French translation by Louis Moulin: *La volonté de croire*. Paris, E. Flammarion, 1916.
German translation by Th. Lorenz: *Der Wille zum Glauben und andere popular-philosophische Essays*. Geleitwort Fr. Paulsen. Stuttgart, 1899.
1898 *Human Immortality. Two Supposed Objections to the Doctrine*. London, Constable & Co. and Dent & Sons; Boston, Houghton, Mifflin & Co. New edition with "Preface in Reply to His Critics." Boston, Houghton, Mifflin & Co.; London, Dent & Sons, 1899.
1899 "Preface," in E. D. Starbuck, *Psychology of Religion*. London, W. Scott, pp. V–X.
1899 *Talks to Teachers on Psychology, and to Students on Some of Life's Ideals*. New York, Henry Holt & Co. 1929²; London, Longmans, Green & Co. 1902², 1907, 1911, 1913, 1921. New edition with Introduction by Paul Woodring, New York, The Norton Library, 1958.
Separate edition of *Talk to Teachers on Psychology*. New York, 1901; and with an Introduction by John Dewey and William H. Kilpatrick, New York, H. Holt 1939.
French translation of the first part by L.-S. Pidoux: *Causeries pédagogiques*. Preface by Jules Payot. Paris, Payot, 1909, 1921⁵.
German translation of the same by Friedrich Kiesow: *Psychologie und Erziehung. Ansprachen an Lehrer*. Leipzig, 1912³.
French translation of the second part by Henri Marty: *Aux étudiants, causeries*. Preface by Emile Boutroux. Paris, Payot, 1914.
Turkish translation by Muṣṭafā Šeḵīb: *Terbiye musāhabeleri*. Istanbul, 1342/1923.

1902 *The Varieties of Religious Experience. A Study in Human Nature.* The Gifford Lectures on Natural Religion, Edinburgh, 1901–1902. New York–London, Longmans, Green & Co. 1907[14], 1908[15], 1923[44], etc. New York, The Modern Library, 1936. Pb. New York, Mentor Books, 1958.
Danish translation by E. Lehmann and C. Mönster, with introduction by H. Höffding. København, 1906.
French translation by Frank Abauzit: *L'expérience religieuse.* Preface by Emile Boutroux. Paris, 1906, 1908[2].
German translation and edition by G. Wobbermin: *Die religiöse Erfahrung in ihrer Mannigfaltigkeit. Materialien und Studien zu einer Psychologie und Pathologie des religiösen Lebens.* Leipzig, 1907, 1920[3].
Italian translation by G. C. Ferrari and M. Calderoni: *Le varie forme della coscienza religiosa, studio sulla natura umana.* Preface by R. Ardigo. Torino, Bocca, 1904.
Spanish translation by M. D. Mir, 3 vols. Barcelona, 1907–1908.
Swedish translation by I. Norberg. Stockholm, 1906.

1903 *La théorie de l'émotion.* Traduit et précédé d'une introduction par G. Dumas. Paris. (Translation of Chap. 25 of *The Principles of Psychology*, 1890).

1907 *Pragmatism. A New Name for Some Old Ways of Thinking.* New York–London, Longmans, Green & Co. 1908[2] (with subtitle: "Popular lectures on philosophy"), 1914, 1916[15]. New edition: *Pragmatism. A New Name for Some Old Ways of Thinking. Together with four related Essays selected from The Meaning of Truth.* Ed. by Ralph Barton Perry. New York—London—Toronto, Longmans, Green and Co., 1959 (Chap. 8: "Pragmatism and religion").
French translation by Emile Le Brun: *Le pragmatisme.* With an Introduction by Henri Bergson. Paris, Flammarion, 1911. Repr. Paris, Flammarion, 1968.
German translation by Wilh. Jerusalem: *Der Pragmatismus.* Leipzig, 1908.
Italian translation by Papini. Carabba, Lanciano, 1911.
Japanese translation, Tokyo, 1910.

1908 "Pluralism and religion," *Hibbert Journal*, VI (1908), pp. 721–728. Reprinted in *A Pluralistic Universe*, 1909. Chap. 8.

1909 *A Pluralistic Universe.* Hibbert Lectures at Manchester College. New York—London, Longmans, Green and Co. 1916[2].
French translation by Emile Le Brun: *Philosophie de l'expérience.* Paris, 1910.
German translation by Jul. Goldstein: *Das pluralistische Universum.* Leipzig, 1914.

1909 *The Meaning of Truth. A Sequel to Pragmatism.* New York—London, Longmans, Green and Co.
French translation by Mme L. Veil and Maxime David: *L'idée de vérité.* Paris, F. Alcan, 1913.

1910 "A pluralistic mystic," *Hibbert Journal*, VIII (1910), pp. 739–759.

1910 "A suggestion about mysticism," *Journal of Philosophy, Psychology and Scientific Methods*, VII (1910), pp. 85–92.

1911 *Some Problems of Philosophy. A Beginning of an Introduction to Philosophy.* New York—London, Longmans, Green and Co. 1940[2].
French translation by Roger Picard: *Introduction à la philosophie: essai sur quelques problèmes de métaphysique.* Paris, M. Rivière, 1914.

1911 *Memories and Studies.* Reprints edited by H. James Jr. New York—London, Longmans, Green and Co. 1912², 1917.
1912 *Essays in Radical Empiricism.* Edited by Ralph Barton Perry. New York—London, Longmans, Green and Co. 1943².
1912 *On Some of Life's Ideals.* New York, Holt.
1914 *The Energies of Man.* Reprinted.
1914(?) "The moral equivalent of war." With an introductory essay by H. M. Kallen. In Warner's Library of the World's best Literature, Vol. 13, pp. 8109k–8109z.
1917 *Selected Papers on Philosophy*, Introduction by C. M. Bakewell (Everyman's Library). London, J. M. Dent & Sons; New York, E. P. Dutton. (Chap. 12: "The positive content of religious experience"; last chap.: "A Suggestion about mysticism").
1920 *Collected Essays and Reviews.* Edited by Ralph Barton Perry. New York—London, Longmans, Green and Co.
1924 *Etudes et réflexions d'un psychiste.* Translated by E. Durandeaud. Paris, Payot.
1940 *The Philosophy of William James (1842–1910). Selected from his Chief Works.* Introduction by Horace M. Kallen. New York. 1949².
1943 *Essays on Faith and Morals.* Selected by Ralph Barton Perry. New York. 1947².
1960 *William James on Psychical Research.* Compiled and edited by Gardner Murphy and Robert O. Ballon. With an introduction and concluding remarks by Gardner Murphy. New York, Viking Press.
French translation: *William James et l'attitude pragmatiste.* Présentation, choix de textes, bibliographie par Andrew J. Reck. (Philosophes de tous les temps). Paris, Seghers, 1967.

MORRIS JASTROW

1. Bibliography

Clay, A. T. and Montgomery, J. A., *Bibliography of Morris Jastrow, Jr. 1885–1910.* Philadelphia, priv. pr., 1910.

2. Biography and Appreciation

Clay, Albert T., "In Memoriam, Morris Jastrow, Jr.," *Journal of the American Oriental Society*, Vol. 41 (1921), pp. 321–344.

3. Main Publications

1898 *The Religion of Babylonia and Assyria.* (Handbooks on the History of Religions, 2). Boston, Ginn.
German translation: *Die Religion Babyloniens und Assyriens.* (Vom Verfasser revidierte und wesentlich erweiterte Übersetzung). Giessen, Töpelmann, 1905–1912.
1901 *The Study of Religion.* London, Scott.

1911 *Aspects of Religious Belief and Practice in Babylonia and Assyria.* London, Putnam.
1914 *Hebrew and Babylonian Traditions.* The Haskell lectures delivered at Oberlin College in 1913, and since revised and enlarged. London–Leipzig, Fisher Unwin.
1914 *Babylonian–Assyrian Birth-omens and their Cultural Significance.* Ed. by Richard Wünsch and Ludwig Deubner. (Religionsgeschichtliche Versuche und Vorarbeiten, XIV, 5). Giessen, Töpelmann.
1915 *The Civilization of Babylonia and Assyria.* Its remains, history, religion, commerce, law, art, and literature. Philadelphia–London, Lippincott.
1919 *A Gentle Cynic.* Being a translation of the book of Koheleth, commonly known as Ecclesiastes, stripped of later additions; also its origin, growth and interpretation. Philadelphia–London, Lippincott.
1920 *An Old Babylonian Version of the Gilgamesh Epic.* On the basis of recently discovered texts. By Morris Jastrow and Albert T. Clay. New Haven, Yale University Press.
1920 *The Book of Job.* Its origin, growth and interpretation, together with a new translation based on a revised text. Philadelphia–London, Lippincott.

ADOLF ELLEGARD JENSEN

1. Bibliography

Seyfarth, S., and Jäger, W., "Veröffentlichungen von Ad. E. Jensen," in: *Festschrift für Adolf Ellegard Jensen*, 2 vols. München, 1964. Vol. I, pp. XI–XVI.

2. Main Publications

1933 *Beschneidung und Reifezeremonien bei Naturvölkern.* Stuttgart, Strecker & Schröder.
1933 "Kulturkreislehre als Grundlage der Kulturgeschichte," in: *Leo Frobenius. Ein Lebenswerk aus der Zeit der Kulturwende.* Leipzig, Köhler & Amelang, pp. 73–95.
1939 *Hainuwele. Volkserzählungen von der Molukken-Insel Ceram.* Gesammelt und bearbeitet von Ad. E. Jensen und H. Niggemeyer. Frankfurt a. M., Klostermann.
1944 "Das Weltbild einer frühen Kultur," *Paideuma*, III (1944), pp. 1–83.
1948 *Das religiöse Weltbild einer frühen Kultur.* Stuttgart, Schröder.
1948 *Die drei Ströme. Züge aus dem geistigen und religiösen Leben der Wemale, einem Primitiv-Volk in den Molukken.* Leipzig, Harrassowitz.
1950 "Die mythische Weltbetrachtung der alten Pflanzenvölker," *Eranos-Jahrbuch, Bd. 17, 1949.* Zürich, 1950, pp. 421–473.
1951 *Mythos und Kult bei Natürvölker. Religionswissenschaftliche Betrachtungen.* Wiesbaden, Steiner, 1960².
   English translation by Marianna Tax Cholding and Wolfgang Weissleder: *Myth and Cult among Primitive People.* Chicago–London, University of Chicago Press, 1963, 1969².

1960 "Methoden und Ziele der Ethnologie," *Völkerkunde. 12 Vorträge zur Einführung in ihre Probleme*. München, Beck.
1966 *Die getötete Gottheit. Weltbild einer frühen Kultur*. Stuttgart, Kohlhammer.

ALFRED JEREMIAS

Main Publications

1887 *Die babylonisch–assyrischen Vorstellungen vom Leben nach dem Tode*. Leipzig, Hinrichs.
1900 *Hölle und Paradies bei den Babyloniern*. Leipzig, Hinrichs.
   English translation by J. Hutchison: *The Babylonian conception of heaven and hell*. London, Nutt, 1902.
1903 *Im Kampfe um Babel und Bibel: ein Wort zur Verständigung und Abwehr*. Leipzig, Hinrichs, 1903[1, 2, 3].
1904 *Monotheistische Strömungen innerhalb der babylonischen Religion* (auf Grund eines Vortrages gehalten auf dem 2. Internationalen Kongress für Religionsgeschichte zu Basel 1904). Leipzig, Hinrichs.
1905 *Babylonisches im Neuen Testament*. Leipzig, Hinrichs.
1906 *Das Alte Testament im Lichte des alten Orients*. Leipzig, Hinrichs. 1906[2], 1916[3] (völlig neu bearb.), 1930[4].
   English translation by C. L. Beaumont: *The Old Testament in the light of the Ancient East*. London, Williams & Norgate; New York, Putnam's Sons, 1911.
1907 *Das Alter der babylonischen Astronomie*. Leipzig, Hinrichs, 1907.
1907 *Die Panbabylonisten, der alte Orient und die aegyptische Religion*. Leipzig, Hinrichs.
1913 *Handbuch der altorientalischen Geisteskultur*. Leipzig, Hinrichs. 1929[2] (völlig erneuerte Aufl.)
1918 *Allgemeine Religions-Geschichte*. München, Piper. 1924[2] (verb. Aufl.)
1927 *Die ausserbiblische Erlösererwartung*. Berlin, Hochweg.
1931 *Der Schleier von Sumer bis heute*. Leipzig, Hinrichs.

FRANK BYRON JEVONS

Main Publications

1896 *An Introduction to the History of Religion*. London, Methuen. 1902[2] (revised[2]).
1906 *Religion in Evolution*. London, Methuen.
1908 *An Introduction to the Study of Comparative Religion*. New York, Macmillan. 1916[2]. (Cambridge Manuals of Science and Literature)
1910 *Comparative Religion*. (Cambridge Manuals of Science and Literature.) Cambridge, Cambridge University Press. 1913[2].
1910 *The Idea God in Religions*. Cambridge, University Press.
1914 *Philosophy, what is it?* Cambridge, University Press.

WILLIAM JONES

1. Biography and Appreciation

Arberry, Arthur J.: *Asiatic Jones*. The Life and Influence of Sir William Jones (1746–1794), Pioneer of Indian Studies. Published for the British Council. London, Longmans, 1946.

Asiatic Society of Bengal, Calcutta. Afterwards Royal Asiatic Society of Bengal: *Sir William Jones. Bicentenary of his Birth. Commemoration Volume. 1746–1946*. By various authors. Ed. by Kālidāsa Nāga. Calcutta, 1948.

2. Main Publications

1799 *The Works of Sir William Jones*. Edited by Anna Maria Jones, with a discourse on the Life and Writings of Sir W. Jones, by Lord Teignmouth, 6 vols. London.
Another Edition, 13 vols. London, 1807.

1801 *Supplemental Volumes to the Works of Sir W. Jones*, containing the whole of the Asiatic Researches hitherto published, excepting those papers already inserted in his Works, 2 vols. London, 1801.

JAN P. B. DE JOSSELIN DE JONG

1. Bibliography, Biography and Appreciation

Baal, Jan van, "Jan Petrus Benjamin de Josselin de Jong, 13 maart 1886–15 November 1964," *Bijdragen tot de Taal-, Land- en Volkenkunde* (The Hague, Nijhoff), Vol. 121 (1965), Nr. 3, pp. 293–300.
With bibliography by Dr. Chr. Nooteboom, pp. 300–302.

2. Main Publications

1913 *De Waardeeringsonderscheiding van "levend" en "levenloos" in het Indogermaansch, vergeleken met hetzelfde verschijnsel in enkele Algonkin-talen. Ethnopsychologische Studie*. Dissertation, Leiden.

1922 *Cultuurtypen en Cultuurphasen*. Inaugural Address. The Hague.

1929 *De Oorsprong van de goddelijken bedrieger*. Mededeelingen van de Koninklijke Akademie van Wetenschappen, Amsterdam, Afd. Letterkunde, Vol. 68, Serie B, Nr. 1.

1937 *Studies in Indonesian Culture I: Oirata, a Timorese Settlement on Kisar*. Verhandelingen der Koninklijke Akademie van Wetenschappen (Amsterdam), Afd. Letterkunde, N. R. Vol. 39.

1938 "Religionen der Naturvölker Indonesiens," *Archiv für Religionswissenschaft*, XXX (1938), pp. 174–198, 360–382.

1947 *Studies in Indonesian Culture II: The Community of Erai (Wetar), Texts and Notes.* Verhandelingen der Koninklijke Akademie van Wetenschappen, (Amsterdam), Afd. Letterkunde, N. R. Vol. 1, Nr. 2.
1952 *Lévi-Strauss's Theory on Kinship and Marriage.* (Mededelingen Rijks-Museum voor Volkenkunde, Vol. 10). Leiden, Brill.
1959 "W. H. Rassers and the Anthropological Study of Religion." Introduction to: Dr. W. H. Rassers, *Panji, the Culture Hero. A Structural Study of Religion in Java.* (Koninklijk Instituut voor Taal-, Land- en Volkenkunde, Translation Series 3). The Hague.

CARL GUSTAV JUNG*

1. Bibliography

"Verzeichnis der deutschen Schriften von C. G. Jung," in: Jolande Jacobi, *Die Psychologie von C. G. Jung.* Zürich–Stuttgart, Rascher Verlag, 1967[5], pp. 267–292.
    Also in English translation: *The Psychology of C. G. Jung.* London–New Haven, 1951, pp. 213–240.
A definite bibliography will appear in the last volume of C. G. Jung, *Gesammelte Werke.* Zürich–Stuttgart, Rascher Verlag.
    English translation: C. G. Jung, *Collected Works.* London, Routledge and Kegan Paul; New York, Pantheon Books, Inc.

2. Biography and Appreciation

Adler, G., *Etudes de psychologie jungienne.* Genève, Georg, 1957.
—, ed., *Current Trends in Analytical Psychology.* London, Tavistock, 1961.
Affemann, R., *Psychologie und Bibel: eine Auseinandersetzung mit C. G. Jung.* Stuttgart, Klett, 1957.
Baudouin, Charles, *De l'instinct à l'esprit.* Paris, Desclée de Brouwer, 1950.
—, *L'œuvre de Jung et la psychologie complexe.* (Etudes et Documents). Paris, Payot, 1963.
Bennett, E. A., "Archetype and Aion," *British Medical Journal,* I (1960), p. 1484.
—, "Jung's concept of the time stream," *Journal of Analytical Psychology,* 1960
—, *C. G. Jung.* London, Barrie and Rockliff, 1961.
—, *What Jung really said.* London, Macdonald, 1966.
Bertine, Eleanor, "Jung's contribution to our time," in: E. C. Rohrbach, ed., *The Collected Papers of Eleanor Bertine.* New York, 1967.
Böhler, E., "Die Bedeutung der komplexen Psychologie C. G. Jungs für die Geisteswissenschaften und die Menschenbildung," in: C. G. Jung, *Bewusstes und Unbewusstes.* Frankfurt–Hamburg, Fischer Bücherei, 1957, pp. 7–10.
Boss, M., "Über Herkunft und Wesen des tiefenpsychologischen Archetypus-Begriffes," *Psyche* (Zeitschrift für Tiefenpsychologie), VI (1952–53), pp. 584–597.

Bruneton, J.-L., "Jung: l'homme, sa vie, son caractère," *Revue d'Allemagne,* VII (1933), pp. 673–689.
Carp, E. A. D. E., *De analytisch-psychologische behandelingsmethode volgens Jung.* Amsterdam, Meulenhoff, n. d.
Corrie, Joan, *C. G. Jungs Psychologie im Abriss.* Zürich, Rascher Verlag, 1929.
Cox, David, *Jung and St Paul.* A study of the doctrine of justification by faith and its relation to the concept of individuation. London, Longmans, Green and Co., 1959.
Daim, W., "Der Grundfehler C. G. Jungs," *Wissenschaft und Weltbild,* VI (1953), pp. 58–66.
Dry, Avis, M., *The Psychology of Jung. A Critical Interpretation.* New York– London, Methuen, 1961.
Evans, R. I., *Conversations with Carl G. Jung and Reactions from Ernest Jones.* New York, Van Nostrand, 1964.
  French translation: *Entretiens avec C. G. Jung. Avec des commentaires de Ernest Jones.* (Petite Bibliothèque, 155) Paris, Payot, 1970.
Fordham, Frieda, *An Introduction to Jung's Psychology.* London, Pelican Books, 1953; Harmondsworth, Penguin Books, 1963.
Fordham, Michael S. M., *The Objective Psyche.* London, Routledge & Kegan Paul, 1958.
—, ed., *Contact with Jung: Essays on the Influence of his Work and Personality.* London, Tavistock; Philadelphia, Lippincott, 1963.
Frei, G., "Die Methode und die Lehre C. G. Jungs," *Annalen der philosophischen Gesellschaft Innerschweiz und Ostschweiz,* 1948.
Frischknecht, Max, *Die Religion in der Psychologie C. G. Jungs.* (Religiöse Gegenwartsfragen 12). Bern, P. Haupt, 1945.
Froboese-Thiele, F., *Träume: eine Quelle religiöser Erfahrung?* Göttingen, Vandenhoeck & Ruprecht, 1957.
Glover, Edward G., *Freud or Jung.* First published in *Horizon,* XVIII (1948), pp. 225–258, 303–318; XIX (1949), pp. 209–228. Appeared as a book: London, George Allen and Unwin, 1950.
  French translation by Lucy Jones: *Freud ou Jung?* Paris, P.U.F., 1954.
Goldbrunner, Josef, *Die Tiefenpsychologie von C. G. Jung und christliche Lebens-gestaltung.* Freiburg i. Br., 1940.
—, *Individuation. Die Tiefenpsychologie von Carl Gustav Jung.* Krailing vor München, 1949.
  English translation: *Individuation. A Study of the Depth Psychology of Carl Gustav Jung.* London, 1955.
Guggenbuhl–Craig, A., ed., *The Archetype.* Proceedings of the Second International Congress for Analytical Psychology. Basel–New York, Karger, 1964.
Haendler, Otto, "C. G. Jung," *Theologische Literatur Zeitung,* 84. Jg., 8 (August 1959), pp. 561–588.
Haberlandt, H., "Diskussion um Hiob," *Wissenschaft und Weltbild,* VI (1953), pp. 52–58.
Harms, Ernest, "Carl Gustav Jung — defender of Freud and the Jews," *Psychiatric Quarterly,* XX (1946), p. 199.
Helsdingen, René Jacques van, *Beelden uit het onbewuste. Een geval van Jung.* With a preface by C. G. Jung and an introduction by E. A. D. E. Carp. Arnhem, 1957.
Hochheimer, W., *Die Psychotherapie von C. G. Jung.* Bern–Stuttgart, Huber, 1966.

Hondius, J. M., *Religie en werkelijkheid in het licht der psychologie van C. G. Jung.* Deventer, n. d.
Hoop, J. H. van der, *Character and the Unconscious. A Critical Exposition of the Psychology of Carl Gustav Jung.* London–New York, 1923.
Hostie, Raymond G.E.M., *Analytische psychologie en godsdienst.* Diss. Nijmegen. *English* translation by G. R. Lamb: *Religion and the Psychology of Jung.* London and New York, Sheed & Ward, 1957.
   German translation: *C. G. Jung und die Religion.* Freiburg, 1957.
—, *Du mythe à la religion dans la psychologie analytique de C. G. Jung.* Bruges, 1955. Reissued Paris, Desclée de Brouwer (Foi Vivante 88), 1968² (revised).
Hüllen, Jürgen Wilhelm, *Die philosophischen Relationen der Komplexen Psychologie C. G. Jungs.* Diss. Münster. 1966.
Jacobi, Jolande, *Die Psychologie von C. G. Jung.* Zürich–Stuttgart, Rascher, 1939, 1944², 1949³, 1959⁴. A fifth revised and enlarged edition appeared in 1967 with an introduction by C. G. Jung under the title of *Die Psychologie von C. G. Jung. Eine Einführung in das Gesamtwerk.* Zürich–Stuttgart, Rascher, 1967⁵.
   Dutch translation by M. Drukker: *De psychologie van C. G. Jung.* Amsterdam–Antwerpen, Contact, 1949.
   English translation by K. W. Bash: *The Psychology of C. G. Jung. An Introduction with Illustrations.* London, Routledge & Kegan Paul; 1951.
   French translation: *La psychologie de C. G. Jung.* Neuchâtel–Paris, Delachaux et Niestlé, 1950.
—, "Komplex, Archetypus und Symbol," *Schweizerische Zeitschrift für Psychologie und ihre Anwendungen,* IV (1945), pp. 276–313. Appeared as a book with a preface by C. G. Jung: *Komplex, Archetypus, Symbol in der Psychologie C. G. Jungs.* Zürich–Stuttgart, Rascher, 1957.
   English translation: *Complex, Archetype, Symbol in the Psychology of C. G. Jung.* London, Routledge & Kegan Paul, 1959.
—, *Der Weg zur Individuation.* Zürich, Rascher, 1965.
Jaffé, Aniela, *Der Mythus vom Sinn im Werk von C. G. Jung.* Pb. Zürich–Stuttgart, Rascher, 1967.
—, *Jung over parapsychologie en alchemie. Jungs laatste jaren.* Rotterdam, Lemniscaat, 1969.
Jung, C. G., *Erinnerungen, Träume, Gedanken.* Aufgezeichnet und herausgegeben von Aniela Jaffé. Zürich–Stuttgart, Rascher, 1962, etc.
   English translation by Richard and Clara Winston: *Memoires, Dreams, Reflections.* Edited by Aniela Jaffé. New York, Pantheon Books, 1963.
   French translation by Roland Cahen and Yves Le Lay, in collaboration with Salomé Burckhardt: *Ma vie. Souvenirs, rêves et pensées.* Recueillis par Aniela Jaffé. (Témoins). Paris, Gallimard, 1966.
Kaune, Fritz Jürgen, *Selbstverwirklichung. Eine Konfrontation der Psychologie C. G. Jungs mit der Ethik.* (Psychologie und Person, 13). München, 1967.
Keller, Adolf, "Analytische Psychologie und Religionsforschung," in: Julius Springer, ed., *Die kulturelle Bedeutung der komplexen Psychologie.* Berlin, 1935, pp. 271–297.
Keller, Tina, M. D., "C. G. Jung—Some Memoires and Reflections," *Inward Light,* Vol. XXXV. No. 81 (Spring 1972), pp. 6–25.
Leibbrand, W., "C. G. Jung's Versuch einer psychologischen Deutung des Trinitätsdogmas," *Zeitschrift für Religions- und Geistesgeschichte,* III (1951), pp. 122–134.

Lénard, A., "La psychologie religieuse de Jung," *Supplément de La Vie Spirituelle*, V (1951), pp. 325–334.

Lewis, Aubrey, "Jung's early work," *Journal of Analytical Psychology*, 1957.

Londero, D., *Il simbolismo religioso nel pensiero di C. G. Jung*. Roma, Ateneo Antoniano, 1959.

Makhdum, Mohammad A., *A Comparative Study of Freudian and Jungian Methods of Analysis*. Ph. D. Dissertation. University of London, 1952.

Martin, Percival W., *Experiment in Depth. A Study of the Work of Jung, Eliot and Toynbee*. London, 1956², 1958³.

Michaelis, E., "Le livre de Job interprété par C. G. Jung," *Revue de Théologie et de Philosophie*, III (1953), pp. 183–195.

Philp, Howard L., *Jung and the Problem of Evil*. London, Barrie and Rockliff; New York, McBride, 1959.

Progoff, Ira, *Jung's Psychology and its Social Meaning*. An introductory statement of C. G. Jung's psychological theories and a first interpretation of their significance for the social sciences. London, Routledge & Kegan Paul; New York, Julian Press, 1953.

Rochedieu, Edmund, *C. G. Jung et l'individu dans le monde d'aujourd'hui*. Présentation, choix de textes, biographie, bibliographie. (Philosophes de tous les temps, 63). Paris, P. Seghers, 1970.

Roth, Paul, *Anima and Animus in der Psychologie C. G. Jungs*. Winterthur, 1954.

Rudin, J., "Antwort auf Hiob," *Orientierung*, 1953, pp. 41–44.

—, "Die Tiefenpsychologie und die Freiheit des Menschen," *Orientierung*, 1954, pp. 169–173.

Rümke, H. C., "Aanteekeningen over het instinct, den archetypus, den existentiaal, over de werelden, die zij oproepen, over reductie en misvorming van het mensbeeld," in: W. J. Kooiman and J. M. van Veen, eds., *Pro Regno Pro Sanctuario* ("Festschrift" G. van der Leeuw). Nijkerk, Callenbach, 1950, pp. 451–468.

Schär, Hans, *Religion und Seele in der Psychologie C. G. Jungs*. Zürich, Rascher, 1946.
   English translation by R. C. F. Hull: *Religion and the Cure of Souls in Jung's Psychology* (The Bollingen Series 21). New York, Pantheon Books, 1950; London, 1951.

—, "C. G. Jung und die Deutung der Geschichte," *Schweizerische Theologische Umschau*, XXII (1952), pp. 91–96.

Schultz-Hencke, H., "Über die Archetypen," *Zentralblatt für Psychotherapie*, IX (1936), pp. 335–343.

Sierksma, F., *Phaenomenologie der religie en complexe psychologie*. Diss. Groningen. Commercial edition: *Freud, Jung en de religie*. Assen, Van Gorcum, 1951. (With English summary).

Serrano, Miguel, *El circulo hermético*, 1966.
   English translation by Frank MacShane: *C. G. Jung and Hermann Hesse. A Record of Two Friendships*. London, 1966; New York, Schocken Books, 1968.

Spengler, Ernst, *Das Gewissen bei Freud und Jung. Mit einer philosophisch-anthropologischen Grundlegung*. Diss. Zürich, 1964.

Thompson, Cl., *Psychoanalysis, Evolution and Development*. London, Allen and Unwin, 1952.

Thomson, James S., "Jung's interpretation of religion," *Transactions of the Royal Society of Canada*, 1953. Also published separately.

Trüb, Hans, *Heilung aus der Begegnung.* Stuttgart, Klett, 1951.

Tuinstra, C. L., *Het symbool in de psychoanalyse.* Diss. Groningen. Amsterdam, H. J. Paris, 1933.

—, "De psychologie van C. G. Jung," *Nederlands Theologisch Tijdschrift,*XV (1961–62). pp. 468–488.

Walder, Peter, *Mensch und Welt bei C. G. Jung. Die anthropologischen Grundlagen der komplexen Psychologie.* Diss. Zürich. Leiden, 1951.

White, V., *God and the Unconscious.* With a Foreword by C. G. Jung, and an Appendix by Gebhard Frei. London, Harvill Press, 1953; pb. London Collins (Fontana Books, 463 R), 1960.

Winckel, E. van de, *De l'inconscient à Dieu; ascèse chrétienne et psychologie de C. G. Jung.* Paris, Aubier, 1959.

Wingenfeld, B., *Die Archetypen der Selbstwerdung bei C. G. Jung.* Pfullendorf-Baden, Schmidt, 1955.

Wolff, Toni, "Exposé d'ensemble de la doctrine," *Revue d'Allemagne,* VII (1933), pp. 709–743.

—, "Einführung in die Grundlagen der komplexen Psychologie," in: Julius Springer, ed., *Die kulturelle Bedeutung der komplexen Psychologie.* Berlin, 1935, pp. 1–168.

—, "Der Begriff des Archetypus in der komplexen Psychologie," in: *Beiträge zur Gesellungs- und Völkerwissenschaft.* Prof. Dr. Richard Thurnwald zu seinem 80sten Geburtstag gewidmet. Berlin, 1950.

—, *Studien zu C. G. Jungs Psychologie.* Vorrede von C. G. Jung. Edited by C. A. Meier. Zürich, Rhein-Verlag, 1960.

Zacharias, Gerhard P., *Psyche und Mysterium. Die Bedeutung der Psychologie C. G. Jungs für die christliche Theologie und Liturgie.* (Studien aus dem C. G. Jung Institut, Zürich, 5.) Zürich, Rascher, 1954.

Collective works:

Springer, Julius, ed., *Die kulturelle Bedeutung der komplexen Psychologie.* Festschrift zum 60. Geburtstag C. G. Jungs. Berlin, 1935.

Studien zur analytischen Psychologie C. G. Jungs, 2 vols. Zürich, Rascher, 1955.

3. Main Publications

The *W* refers to the volume of *Gesammelte Werke/Collected Works,* into which the publication in question has been incorporated. The English titles are given only for those publications which first appeared in English, or which were translated into English, independently of the *Collected Works.*

1902 *Zur Psychologie und Pathologie sogenannter occulter Phänomene. Eine psychiatrische Studie.* Leipzig, Oswald Mutze. *(W* 1).
French translation by E. Godet and Y. Le Lay: *Phénomènes occultes.* Paris, Montaigne, 1939. Reprinted in: C. G. Jung, *L'énérgétique psychique.* Genève, Georg; Paris, Buchet-Chastel, 1956.

1906–1909 *Diagnostische Assoziationsstudien.* Beiträge zur experimentellen Psychopathologie, 2 vols. Leipzig, Barth. 1911², 1915³. *(W* 2).

1907 *Über die Psychologie der Dementia praecox. Ein Versuch.* Halle, Karl Marhold. *(W* 3).

English translation: *Psychology of Dementia Praecox.* London, Nervous and Mental Diseases Publishing Co., 1936.

1909 "Die Bedeutung des Vaters für das Schicksal des Einzelnen," *Jahrbuch für Psychoanalytische und Psychopathologische Forschungen*, I (1909). Published separately: Leipzig–Wien, Deuticke, 1909, 1927²; Zürich, Rascher, 1949³ (revised), 1962⁴ (revised). *(W* 4).

French translation by L. de Vos and O. Raevsky in: C. G. Jung, *Conflits de l'âme enfantine.* Paris, Montaigne, 1935.

1910 "Über die Konflikte der kindlichen Seele," *Jahrbuch für Psychoanalytische und Psychopathologische Forschungen*, II (1910). Published separately: Leipzig–Wien, Deuticke, 1916²; Zürich, Rascher, 1939³. Reprinted in: *Psychologie und Erziehung.* Zürich, Rascher, 1946, 1950², 1963.

French translation by L. de Vos and O. Raevsky in: C. G. Jung, *Conflits de l'âme enfantine.* Paris, Montaigne, 1935. *(W* 17).

1911–1912 *Wandlungen und Symbole der Libido.* Ein Beitrag zur Entwicklungsgeschichte des Denkens. First published in: *Jahrbuch für Psychoanalytische und Psychopathologische Forschungen*, III (1911) and IV (1912). Published separately: Leipzig–Wien, Deuticke, 1912, 1925², 1938³. A fourth, revised and enlarged edition appeared in 1952, see there). *(W* 5).

English translation of the first German edition by Beatrice M. Hinkle: *Psychology of the Unconscious.* A study of the transformation and symbolisms of the libido; a contribution to the history of the evolution of thought. New York, Dodd, Mead, 1916, 1963².

French translation of the second German edition by L. de Vos: *Métamorphoses et symboles de la libido.* Paris, Montaigne, 1931. Another French translation was made of the fourth German edition by Y. Le Lay: *Métamorphoses de l'âme et ses symboles.* Analyse des prodromes d'une schizophrénie. Genève, Georg, 1953; Genève–Paris, Buchet-Chastel, 1967.

1912 "Neue Bahnen der Psychologie," *Raschers Jahrbuch für Schweizer Art und Kunst*, III (1912). *(W* 7). For revised editions, see below under 1917, 1926(a), and 1943(a).

1913 "Versuch einer Darstellung der psychoanalytischen Theorie," *Jahrbuch für Psychoanalytische und Psychopathologische Forschungen*, V (1913). Published separately: Leipzig–Wien, Deuticke, 1913; Zürich, Rascher, 1955² (enlarged).

French translation of the first German edition by M. Schmid-Guisan: *La théorie psychoanalytique.* Paris, Montaigne, 1932. *(W* 4).

1914 *Psychotherapeutische Zeitfragen.* Ein Briefwechsel von C. G. Jung und R. Loy. Leipzig–Wien, Deuticke. *(W* 4).

1916 *Die transzendente Funktion.* Private publication. Later reprinted in: *Geist und Welt. Festschrift zu Dr. Bródys 75. Geburtstag.* Zürich, Rhein-Verlag, 1958. *(W* 8).

1917 *Die Psychologie unbewuszter Prozesse.* Schriften zur angewandten Seelenkunde. Zürich, Rascher. This is the 2nd, revised and enlarged edition of "Neue Bahnen der Psychologie" of 1912. For revised editions, see below under 1926(a) and 1943(a). *(W 7)*.

1920 *Collected Papers on Analytical Psychology.* London, Baillière, Tindall and Cox. (English translation of some previously published essays and papers).

1921 *Psychologische Typen.* Zürich, Rascher, 1950⁸. *(W 6)*.

Dutch translation by Rob Limburg: *Psychologische Typen.* The Hague, Servire, 1947.

English translation by H. Godwin Baynes: *Psychological Types, or, the Psychology of Individuation.* London, Kegan Paul, 1923. Second edition under the title of: *Psychological Types.* London, Kegan Paul, 1933, etc. *French* translation by Y. Le Lay: *Types psychologiques.* Genève, Georg, 1950; Genève, Librairie de l'Université; Paris, Buchet-Chastel, 1968[3].

1922 "Über die Beziehungen der analytischen Psychologie zum dichterischen Kunstwerk," *Wissen und Leben,* XV, Heft 19–20 (1922). Reprinted in: *Seelenprobleme der Gegenwart,* 1931, etc. *(W 15).*

1926 *Das Unbewuszte im normalen und kranken Seelenleben.* Zürich, Rascher. 1926[3], 1936[4]. This is the third, again revised and enlarged edition of "Neue Bahnen der Psychologie" of 1912, after its 2nd edition of 1917. *(W 7).*
French translation by Dr. Grandjean-Bayard: *L'inconscient dans la vie psychique normale et anormale.* Paris, Payot, 1928.

1926 *Analytische Psychologie und Erziehung.* Heidelberg, Kampmann; Zürich, Rascher, 1936[2]. Reprinted in: *Psychologie und Erziehung,* 1946, etc. *(W 17).*

1927 "Die Frau in Europa," *Europäische Revue* (Zürich), III, 7 (1927). Published separately: Zürich, Verlag der Neuen Schweizer Rundschau, 1929; Zürich, Rascher, 1932[2], 1948[3], 1959[4], pb. 1965[5]. *(W 10).*

1928 "Psychoanalyse und Seelsorge," *Sexual- und Gesellschaftsethik,* V, 1 (1928). *(W 11).*

1928 *Die Beziehungen zwischen dem Ich und dem Unbewuszten.* Darmstadt, Reichl, 1928; Zürich, Rascher, 1935[2] etc.; pb. 1963[6] (revised). *(W 7).*
English translation in: C. G. Jung, *Contributions to Analytical Psychology,* 1928. Revised in: C. G. Jung, *Two Essays on Analytical Psychology,* c. 1953.
French translation by A. Adamov: *Le moi et l'inconscient.* Paris, Gallimard, 1938. Second French translation by R. Cahen: *Dialectique du moi et de l'inconscient.* Paris, Gallimard, 1964.

1928 *Über die Energetik der Seele.* (Psychologische Abhandlungen, 2). Zürich, Rascher. A second, revised and enlarged edition appeared in 1948(b); see below under that year. *(W 8).*
French translation by R. Cahen-Salabelle in: C. G. Jung, *L'homme à la découverte de son âme.* Genève, Ed. du Mont Blanc, 1944.

1928 *Contributions to Analytical Psychology.* London, Kegan Paul, Trench, Trübner. (English translation of some previously published essays and papers).

1929 C. G. Jung and R. Wilhelm, *Das Geheimnis der goldenen Blüte.* Aus dem Chinesischen übersetzt von R. Wilhelm. Europäischer Kommentar von C. G. Jung. München, Dorn; Zürich, Rascher, 1938[2] (revised and enlarged), 1939[3], 1944[4], 1948[5], 1957[6]. *(W 13).*
Dutch translation: *Het geheim van de gouden bloem. Een Chinees levensboek.* Pb. Amsterdam, L. J. Veen, n. d.
English translation: *The Secret of the Golden Flower.* Translated and explained by Richard Wilhelm, with a European commentary by C. G. Jung. London, Kegan Paul, 1931.

1931 *Seelenprobleme der Gegenwart.* (Psychologische Abhandlungen, 3; contains thirteen previously published essays and papers). Zürich, Rascher. 1933[2], 1939[3], 1946[4], 1950[5].
English translation: *Modern Man in Search of a Soul.* London, Kegan Paul, 1933; New York, Harcourt, 1956.

French translation by Y. Le Lay: *Essais de psychologie analytique.* Paris, Delamain, 1931. Reissued under the title of *Problèmes de l'âme moderne.* Paris, Buchet-Chastel-Corrêa, 1961.

1932 *Die Beziehungen der Psychotherapie zur Seelsorge.* Zürich, Rascher. 1948². *(W* 11).

 French translation by R. Cahen in: C. G. Jung, *La guérison psychologique.* Genève, Georg; Paris, Buchet-Castel, 1953.

1932 "Sigmund Freud als kulturhistorische Erscheinung," *Charakter*, I, 1 (1932). Reprinted in: *Wirklichkeit der Seele*, 1934. *(W* 15).

 English translation: "Sigmund Freud in his historical setting," *Character and Personality*, I, 1 (1932).

1933 "Bruder Klaus," *Neue Schweizer Rundschau*, I, 4 (1933). *(W* 11).

1934 *Wirklichkeit der Seele.* Anwendungen und Fortschritte der neueren Psychologie. (Psychologische Abhandlungen, 4; contains nine previously published essays and papers by Jung, and four papers written by other authors). Zürich, Rascher. 1939², 1947³.

 English translation: *The Integration of the Personality.* London, Kegan Paul, 1940.

 French translation by R. Cahen-Salabelle: *L'homme à la découverte de son âme.* Genève, Ed. du Mont-Blanc, 1944.

1935 "Über die Archetypen des kollektiven Unbewuszten," *Eranos Jahrbuch 1934.* Zürich, Rhein-Verlag. Reprinted in: *Von den Wurzeln des Bewusztseins. Studien über den Archetypus.* Zürich, Rascher, 1954. *(W* 9/1).

1935 "Psychologischer Kommentar zum 'Bardo Thödol'," in: W. Y. Evans-Wentz, ed., *Das Tibetanische Totenbuch.* Translation and Introduction by L. Göpfert-March. Zürich, Rascher. 1960⁸. *(W* 11).

1936 "Über den Archetypus mit besonderer Berücksichtigung des Animabegriffes," *Zentralblatt für Psychotherapie und ihre Grenzgebiete*, IX, 5 (1936). Reprinted in: *Von den Wurzeln des Bewusztseins. Studien über den Archetypus.* Zürich, Rascher, 1954. *(W* 9/1).

1936 "Psychologischer Kommentar zu Hauers Seminar über den Tantra Yoga," *Bericht über das Hauer-Seminar 1935.* Private publication. *(W* 11).

1936 "The concept of the collective unconscious," *St. Bartholomew's Hospital Journal*, XLIV, 3 and 4 (1936). *(W* 9/1).

1937 "Die Erlösungsvorstellungen in der Alchemie," *Eranos Jahrbuch 1936.* Zürich, Rhein-Verlag. Reprinted in: *Psychologie und Alchemie.* Zürich, Rascher, 1944, 1952² (revised). *(W* 12).

1937 "Über die Archetypen," Vortrag in Berlin; Seminarbericht. Private publication. *(W).*

1938 *Psychology and Religion.* Terry Lectures of 1937 held at Yale University. New Haven, Yale University Press, pb. 1962.

 German original text (with additions): *Psychologie und Religion.* Zürich, Rascher, 1940; pb. 1962 (revised).

 French translation by M. Bernson and R. Cahen: *Psychologie et Religion.* Paris, Buchet-Chastel-Corrêa, 1958, 1960.

1939 "Geleitwort," in D. T. Suzuki, *Die grosze Befreiung. Einführung in den Zen-Buddhismus.* Leipzig, Curt Weller. 1947², 1958³; Zürich, Rascher, 1958⁴. *(W* 11).

1939 "Psychological Commentary," in W. Y. Evans-Wentz, *The Tibetan Book of the Great Liberation.* London. 1954².

French translation in: W. Y. Evans-Wentz, *Le livre tibétain de la grande libération.* Paris, Adger, 1960.
German translation in: W. Y. Evans-Wentz, *Das Tibetische Buch der groszen Befreiung.* München, Barth, 1955. *(W* 11).

1940 "Die verschiedenen Aspekte der Wiedergeburt," *Eranos Jahrbuch 1939.* Zürich, Rhein-Verlag. Reprinted under the title of "Über Wiedergeburt" in: *Gestaltungen des Unbewuszten.* Zürich, Rascher, 1950. *(W* 9/1).

1941 C. G. Jung and K. Kerényi, *Das göttliche Kind.* (Albae Vigiliae, 6/7). Amsterdam–Leipzig, Pantheon Akademische Verlagsanstalt. Reprinted in: *Einführung in das Wesen der Mythologie,* 1941, etc. *(W* 9/1).

1941 C. G. Jung and K. Kerényi, *Das göttliche Mädchen.* (Albae Vigiliae, 8/9). Amsterdam–Leipzig, Pantheon Akademische Verlagsanstalt. Reprinted in: *Einführung in das Wesen der Mythologie,* 1941, etc. *(W* 9/1).

1941 C. G. Jung and K. Kerényi, *Einführung in das Wesen der Mythologie. Das göttliche Kind; Das göttliche Mädchen.* Amsterdam–Leipzig, Pantheon Akademische Verlagsanstalt. Zürich, Rhein-Verlag, 1951² (revised.)
English translation by R. F. C. Hull: *Introduction to a Science of Mythology. The Myth of the Divine Child and the Mysteries of Eleusis.* London, Routledge and Kegan Paul, 1951.
French translation by H. E. del Medico: *Introduction à l'essence de la mythologie.* Paris, Payot, 1953; pb. 1968.

1942 *Paracelsica.* Zwei Vorlesungen über den Arzt und Philosophen Theophrastus. Zürich, Rascher. *(W* 13 and 15).

1942 "Das Wandlungssymbol in der Messe," *Eranos Jahrbuch 1940–1941.* Zürich, Rhein-Verlag. Reprinted in: *Von den Wurzeln des Bewusztseins. Studien über den Archetypus.* Zürich, Rascher, 1954. *(W* 11).

1942 "Zur Psychologie der Trinitätsidee," *Eranos Jahrbuch 1940–1941.* Zürich, Rhein-Verlag. Reprinted under the title of "Versuch einer psychologischen Deutung des Trinitätsdogma" in: *Symbolik des Geistes. Studien über psychische Phänomenologie.* Zürich, Rascher, 1948, 1954² *(W* 11).

1943 *Über die Psychologie des Unbewuszten.* Zürich, Rascher, 1943⁵, 1948⁶, 1960⁷, pb. 1966. This is the fifth, again revised and enlarged edition of "Neue Bahnen der Psychologie" of 1912, after its 2nd edition of 1917(b) and its 3th and 4th edition of 1926(a) and 1936. *(W* 7).
English translation by R. F. C. Hull in: C. G. Jung, *Two Essays on Analytical Psychology.* New York, Meridian Books, c. 1953.
French translation with notes by R. Cahen: *Psychologie de l'inconscient.* Genève, Georg, 1952. Genève, Librairie de l'Université; Paris, Buchet–Chastel, 1963².

1943 "Zur Psychologie östlicher Meditation," *Mitteilungen der Schweizerischen Gesellschaft der Freunde ostasiatischer Kultur,* V (1943). Reprinted in: *Symbolik des Geistes. Studien über psychische Phänomenologie.* Zürich, Rascher, 1948, 1954². *(W* 11).

1944 *Psychologie und Alchemie.* (Psychologische Abhandlungen, 5; contains three previously published essays and papers, and an epilogue). Zürich, Rascher. Revised 1952². *(W* 12).
English translation: *Psychology and Alchemy.* London, Routledge and Kegan Paul, 1953.
French translation: *Psychologie et alchimie,* Paris.

1944 "Über den indischen Heiligen." Preface and introduction to H. Zimmer, *Der Weg zum Selbst.* Edited by C. G. Jung. Zürich, Rascher. *(W* 11).

1945 *Psychologische Betrachtungen.* Edited by Jolande Jacobi (An anthology from Jung's essays and papers). Zürich, Rascher. 1949². *French* translation by Roland Cahen and Yves Le Lay: *L'âme et la vie.* Paris, Buchet–Chastel, 1965.

1946 *Psychologie und Erziehung* (Contains three previously published essays and papers). Zürich, Rascher. 1950², pb. 1963. *(W 17).* *French* translation by Y. Le Lay: *Psychologie et éducation.* Paris, Buchet-Chastel, 1963.

1946 *Aufsätze zur Zeitgeschichte.* (Contains four previously published essays and papers, and an epilogue). *English* translation by Elizabeth Welsh, Barbara Hannah and Mary Briner: *Essays on Contemporary Events.* London, Kegan Paul, 1947. *French* translation by R. Cahen-Salabelle: *Aspects du drame contemporain.* Genève, Georg, 1948.

1946 *Die Psychologie der Übertragung.* Erläutert anhand einer alchemistischen Bilderserie für Ärzte und praktische Psychologen. Zürich, Rascher. *(W 16).* *French* translation: *La psychologie du transfert.* Paris.

1947 "Der Geist der Psychologie," *Eranos Jahrbuch 1946.* Zürich, Rhein-Verlag. Reprinted under the title of "Theoretische Überlegungen zum Wesen des Psychischen" in: *Von den Wurzeln des Bewusztseins. Studien über den Archetypus.* Zürich, Rascher, 1954. Also reprinted in: *Welt der Psyche*, 1954, etc. *(W 8).*

1948 *Symbolik des Geistes. Studien über psychische Phänomenologie.* Mit einem Beitrag von Dr. Riwkah Schärf. (Psychologische Abhandlungen, 6; contains four previously published essays and papers by Jung, and one essay by R. Schärf). Zürich, Rascher. 1954².

1948 *Über psychische Energetik und das Wesen der Träume.* Zürich, Rascher. 1948², pb. 1964. This is the second, revised and enlarged edition of *Über die Energetik der Seele* of 1928. *(W 8).* *French* translation by Y. Le Lay: *L'énergétique psychique.* Genève, Georg; Paris, Buchet-Chastel, 1956.

1949 "Über das Selbst," *Eranos Jahrbuch 1948.* Zürich, Rhein-Verlag. Reprinted under the title of "Beiträge zur Symbolik des Selbst" in: *Aion. Untersuchungen zur Symbolgeschichte.* Zürich, Rascher, 1951. *(W. 9/2).*

1950 *Gestaltungen des Unbewuszten.* Mit einem Beitrag von Aniela Jaffé. (Psychologische Abhandlungen, 7; contains four previously published essays and papers by Jung, and an essay by A. Jaffé). Zürich, Rascher.

1951 *Aion. Untersuchungen zur Symbolgeschichte.* Mit einem Beitrag von Dr. Marie-Louise von Franz. (Psychologische Abhandlungen, 8). Zürich, Rascher. *(W 9/2).* *English* translation: *Aion. Researches into the Phenomenology of the Self.* London, Routledge and Kegan Paul; New York, Pantheon Books, 1959. *French* translation: *Aion.* Paris.

1951 "Foreword," in: *The I Ching or Book of Changes, the Richard Wilhelm Translation.* Rendered into English by Cary F. Baynes. London, Routledge and Kegan Paul.

1952 *Symbole der Wandlung.* Zürich, Rascher. 1952⁴. This is the fourth, revised and enlarged edition of *Wandlungen und Symbole der Libido* (1911–1912). *(W 5)* *French* translation by Y. Le Lay: *Métamorphoses de l'âme et ses symboles.* Analyse des prodromes d'une schizophrénie. Genève, Georg, 1953.

1952 *Antwort auf Hiob.* Zürich, Rascher. 1953², 1961³ (revised), pb. 1967. *(W* 11).
English translation: *Answer to Job.* Great Neck, New York, Pastoral Psychology Book Club, 1956; London, Routledge & Kegan Paul, 1958; pb. Meridian Books, Cleveland (Ohio), World Publishing Co., 1960. *French* translation by R. Cahen: *Réponse à Job.* Postface de Henry Corbin. Paris, Buchet-Chastel, 1964.

1952 "Über Synchronizität," *Eranos Jahrbuch 1951.* Zürich, Rhein Verlag.*(W* 8).

1952 C. G. Jung and W. Pauli, *Naturerklärung und Psyche.* (Studien aus dem C.G. Jung Institut, Zürich, 4; contains "Synchronizität als Prinzip akausaler Zusammenhänge" by Jung. Zürich, Rascher. *(W* 8).

1952 "Religion und Psychologie. Eine Antwort an Professor Buber," *Merkur,* IV/5 (1952).

1952 "Foreword," in R. J. Z. Werblowsky, *Lucifer and Prometheus.*

1953 "Foreword," in V. White, *God and the Unconscious.* London, Harvill Press. pb. Fontana Books, 1960.

1954 *Von den Wurzeln des Bewusztseins. Studien über den Archetypus.* (Psychologische Abhandlungen, 9; contains seven essays and papers previously published). Zürich, Rascher.
French translation of three of these essays: *Les racines de la conscience.* Paris.

1954 C. G. Jung, P. Radin and K. Kerényi, *Der göttliche Schelm. Ein indianischer Mythenzyklus.* (Contains "Zur Psychologie der Schelmenfigur" by Jung). Zürich, Rhein-Verlag. *(W* 9/1).
English translation: Paul Radin, *The Trickster. A Study in American Indian Mythology.* With Commentaries by Karl Kerényi and C. G. Jung. London, 1956.
French translation by A. Reiss: *Le fripon divin.* Genève, Georg; Paris, Buchet-Chastel, 1958.

1954 *Welt der Psyche.* Edited by Aniela Jaffé and G. P. Zacharias. (An anthology from Jung's essays and papers). Köln–Zürich, Rascher; München, Kindler Taschenbücher Nr. 2010, 1965.

1955–1956 *Mysterium Coniunctionis.* Untersuchungen über die Trennung und Zusammensetzung der seelischen Gegensätze in der Alchemie, unter Mitarbeit von Dr. Marie-Louise von Franz, 2 vols. (Psychologische Abhandlungen, 10/11), Zürich, Rascher, 1955 and 1956. *(W* 14).

1955 "Mandalas," *DU* (Schweizerische Monatsschrift), XXIII, 4 (1955). *(W* 9/1).

1955 "Seelenarzt und Gottesglaube," *Weltwoche,* Nr. 1116, Vol. XXIII (1955). *(W,* last volume).

1957 *Bewusztes und Unbewusztes. Beiträge zur Psychologie.* Edited with a Preface by E. Böhler and an Epilogue by Aniela Jaffé. (Contains four essays and papers by Jung, previously published). Frankfurt a. M.–Hamburg, Fischer Bücherei.

1957 *Gegenwart und Zukunft.* First published in *Schweizer Monatshefte,* XXXVI, 12 (March 1957). It then was published separately: Zürich, Rascher, 1957², 1958³, 1964.
English translation by R. F. C. Hull: *The Undiscovered Self.* Boston, Little, Brown, 1958.
French annotated translation by R. Cahen in collaboration with René and Françoise Baumann: *Présent et avenir.* Paris, Buchet-Chastel, 1962; Paris, Denoël–Gouthier, 1970².

1958 *Ein moderner Mythos. Von Dingen, die am Himmel gesehen werden.* Zürich, Rascher. Pb. 1964.
   English translation: *Flying Saucers: a Modern Myth of Things seen in the Skies.* London, Routledge and Kegan Paul, 1959.
   French translation by R. Cahen in collaboration with René and Françoise Baumann: *Un mythe moderne des signes du ciel,* Paris, Gallimard, 1960.
1958 *Psychology and Religion: West and East.* (Contains previously published essays and papers). London, Routledge and Kegan Paul; New York, Pantheon Books. (With additions). *(W* 11).
1958 *Psyche and Symbol.* A selection from the Writings of C. G. Jung. Edited with Introduction by Violet S. de Laszlo. Preface by C. G. Jung. Garden City, (N. Y.), Doubleday Anchor Books, 1958.
1959 *The Archetypes and the Collective Unconscious.* (Contains previously published essays and papers). London, Routledge and Kegan Paul; New York, Pantheon Books. *(W* 9/2).
1961 *Erinnerungen, Träume, Gedanken von C. G. Jung.* Aufgezeichnet und herausgegeben von Aniela Jaffé. Zürich, Rascher. 1962², 1963³, 1967⁴.
   English translation by Richard and Clara Winston: *Memories, Dreams, Reflections.* Recorded and edited by Aniela Jaffé. New York, Pantheon Books, 1963.
   French translation by Roland Cahen and Yves Le Lay, in collaboration with Salomé Burckhardt: *"Ma vie", Souvenirs, rêves et pensées.* Recueillis par Aniela Jaffé. Paris, Gallimard, 1966.
1964 C. G. Jung, in collaboration, *Man and his Symbols.* (Other contributions by M.-L. von Franz, Joseph L. Henderson, Jolande Jacobi, Aniela Jaffé. Introduction by John Freeman). London, Aldus Books.
   German edition: *Der Mensch und seine Symbole.* (With Jung's "Zugang zum Unbewuszten"). Olten, Walter Verlag, 1968.
   Dutch translation: *De mens en zijn symbolen.* (With Jung's "De benadering van het onbewuste", pp. 17–110). Rotterdam, Lemniscaat, 1966.
   French translation of the book: *L'homme et ses symboles.* Paris, Laffont, Pont Royal, 1964. French translation by Laure Deutschmeister of Jung's essay published also separately: *Essai d'exploration de l'inconscient.* Introduction by Raymond de Becker. Paris, Gouthier, 1965.
1968 *Analytical Psychology, its Theory and Practice.* (Tavistock Lectures, London, 1935). London, Routledge and Kegan Paul.

4. Gesammelte Werke/Collected Works

Editors of the German edition: Marianne Niehus-Jung, Lenn Hurwitz–Eisner, and Franz Riklin. Zürich–Stuttgart, Rascher Verlag.
Editors of the English edition: Sir Herbert Read, Michel Fordham, Gerhard Adler, William McGuire. Translated by R. F. C. Hull. London, Routledge and Kegan Paul; New York, Pantheon Books.
(The German edition runs parallel to the edition in English translation).

1. *Psychiatrische Studien,* 1966.
   Psychiatric Studies, 1957.
2. *Experimentelle Untersuchungen.*
   Experimental Researches.

3. *Psychogenese der Geisteskrankheiten*, 1968.
   The Psychogenesis of Mental Disease, 1960.
4. *Freud und die Psychoanalyse*, 1969.
   Freud and Psychoanalysis, 1961.
5. *Symbole der Wandlung.*
   Symbols of Transformation, 1956, 1967².
6. *Psychologische Typen*, 1960, 1967².
   Psychological Types.
7. *Zwei Schriften über analytischen Psychologie*, 1964.
   Two Essays on Analytical Psychology, 1953, 1966².
8. *Die Dynamik des Unbewuszten*, 1967.
   The Structure and Dynamic of the Psyche, 1960, 1969².
9/I. *Die Archetypen und das kollektive Unbewuszte.*
   The Archetypes and the Collective Unconscious, 1959, 1968².
9/II. *Aion.*
   Aion: Researches into the Phenomenology of the Self, 1959, 1968².
10. *Zivilisation im Übergang.*
   Civilization in Transition, 1964.
11. *Zur Psychologie westlicher und östlicher Religion*, 1963.
   Psychology and Religion: West and East, 1958, 1969².
12. *Psychologie und Alchemie.*
   Psychology and Alchemy, 1953, 1968².
13. *Studien über alchemistische Vorstellungen.*
   Alchemical Studies, 1968.
14. *Mysterium Coniunctionis. Untersuchungen über die Trennung und Zusammensetzung der seelischen Gegensätze in der Alchemie*, 1968.
   Mysterium Coniunctionis. An Inquiry into the Separation and Synthesis of Psychic Opposites in Alchemy, 1963, 1970².
15. *Über das Phänomen des Geistes in Kunst und Wissenschaft.*
   The Spirit in Man, Art and Literature, 1966.
16. *Praxis der Psychotherapie*, 1958.
   The Practice of Psychotherapy, 1954, 1966².
17. *Über die Entwicklung der Persönlichkeit.*
   The Development of Personality, 1954, 1964².

Final volumes:
   Verschiedene Schriften, Bibliographie und Allgemeiner Index.
   Miscellaneous Works, Bibliography and General Index.

K

IRVING KING

Main Publications

1905 *The differentiation of the religious consciousness.* London–New York, Macmillan.
1909 "The Evolution of Religion from the psychological point of view," *American Journal of Sociology*, XIV, 4 (1909), pp. 433–450.
1910 *The Development of Religion: A Study in Anthropology and Social Psychology.* London–New York, Macmillan.

JOHN HENRY KING

Main Publications

1892 *The Supernatural. Its Origin, Nature and Evolution*, 2 vols. London, Williams & Norgate; New York, Putman's Sons.
1893 *Man an organic Community: being an exposition of the Law that the human Personality in all its Phases in Evolution, both co-ordinate and discordinate, is the multiple of many Sub-personalities*, 2 vols. London, Williams & Norgate; New York, Putman's Sons.
1904 *Three hundred days in a Yankee prison.* Reprinted Kennesaw, Ga., Continental Book Co., 1959, 114 p.

CLYDE K. M. KLUCKHOHN

Main Publications

1927 *To the Foot of the Rainbow.* A Tale of twenty-five hundred miles of wandering on horseback through the Southwest enchanted land. New York–London, The Century Co. London, Nash & Grayson, 1928.

1933 *Beyond the Rainbow.* Boston, The Christopher Publ.
1938 *Navaho Classification of their Song Ceremonials.* By Clyde Kluckhohn and Leland C. Wyman. Menasha, Wis., American Anthropological Association.
1940 *An Introduction to Navaho Chant Practice, with an Account of the Behaviors observed in Four Chants.* By Clyde Kluckhohn and Leland C. Wyman. Menasha, Wis., American Anthropological Association.
1940 *A Bibliography of the Navaho Indians.* By C. Kluckhohn and Katherine Spencer. New York, Augustin.
1942 "Myths and rituals: a general theory," *Harvard Theological Review*, XXXV (1942), pp. 45–79.
1944 *Navaho Witchcraft* (Papers of the Peabody Museum of Archeology and Ethnology, XXII, 2). Boston, Beacon Press, 1967².
1945 *The Personal Document in Anthropological Science.* The Use of Personal Documents in History, Anthropology, and Sociology. 1945.
1946 *The Navaho.* By C. Kluckhohn and Dorothea C. Leighton. Cambridge, Mass., Harvard University Press. 1947².
1950 *Mirror for Man. The Relation of Anthropology to Modern Life.* London, Harrap.
1951 *Navaho means People.* By Evon Z. Vogt and C. Kluckhohn. 1951.
1962 *Culture and Behavior. Collected Essays.* Edited by Richard Kluckhohn. New York, Free Press.

HENDRIK KRAEMER*

1. Bibliography

Hucht, J. van den, *Prof. Dr. H. Kraemer 17 mei 1888–11 nov. 1965. Bibliographie.* Katwijk aan Zee, Holland, 1966 (mimeographed).
"Printed Sources: Kraemer," in: Carl F. Hallencreutz, *Kraemer towards Tambaram. A Study in Hendrik Kraemer's Missionary Approach.* Lund, C. W. K. Gleerup, 1966, pp. 313–317 (not complete).

2. Biography and Appreciation

Aagaard, Johannes, "Revelation and Religion," *Studia Theologica*, XIX, 2 (1960), pp. 148–158.
Bavinck, J. H., "Kraemer als denker en medewerker," *De Heerbaan*, No. 2, May–June, 1958, pp. 84–95.
Brisbois, Jacques, S. J., *Apostolat, religion, eschatologie dans la théologie de la mission selon H. Kraemer, J. C. Hoekendijk, A. T. van Leeuwen.* Thèse de doctorat en Théologie, Institut Catholique de Paris, mars 1972, 379 + XLIV p.
Conway, G., *An Exposition and Critical Analysis of the Theology of Missions as Proposed by Dr. H. Kraemer.* Diss. New York, 1966.
Dietrich, S. de, "Kraemer à Bossey," *De Heerbaan*, XIX, 1 (1966), pp. 45–51.
Doorn, C. L. van, "Kraemer in het veld," *De Heerbaan*, XIX, 1 (1966), pp. 29–44.

Gualtieri, Antonio Roberto, *Theological evaluations by Christians of the religious faith of non-Christians*. Ph. D. Divinity, McGill University, Montreal, 1969, XIII + 413 p.

Haitjema, Th. L., "Academische theologie en bijbels realisme," *Onder eigen Vaandel*, XVII, 1 (1942).

Hallencreutz, Carl F., *Kraemer towards Tambaram. A Study in Hendrik Kraemer's Missionary Approach* (Studia Missionalia Upsaliensia, VII), Lund, C. W. K. Gleerup, 1966.

—, "Islam-missionären Kraemer in memoriam," *Svensk Missionstidskrift*, LIV (1966), pp. 78–90.

—, *New Approaches to Men of Other Faiths*. Geneva, World Council of Churches, 1970.

Hocking, W. E., *Living Religions and a World Faith*. New York, 1940.

Hogg, A. G., *Towards Clarifying my Reactions to Dr. Kraemer's Book*. Madras, 1938.

Horton, Walter, "Tambaram: Twenty-Five Years After," in: Leroy S. Ronner, ed., *Philosophy, Religion, and the Coming World Civilization*. Essays in Honor of William Ernest Hocking. The Hague, Nijhoff, 1966, pp. 225–234.

Jansen Schoonhoven, E., "A. Th. van Leeuwen en H. Kraemer," *Nederlands Theologisch Tijdschrift*, Vol. 23 (1968–69), pp. 15–36.

—, "Inleiding," in: *Uit de nalatenschap van Dr. H. Kraemer*. Kampen, J. H. Kok, 1970, pp. 7–17.

Latuihamallo, P. D., *Church and World. A Critical Study of the Relation Church and World in the Writings of Hendrik Kraemer*. Th. D. Thesis, Union Theological Seminary, New York, March 1959, CV + 324 p.

—, "De dienst van Kraemer aan kerk en maatschappij van Indonesia," *De Heerbaan*, XIX, 1 (1966), pp. 6–17.

Leeuwen, A. Th. van, *Hendrik Kraemer. Dienaar der Wereldkerk*. Amsterdam, W. ten Have, 1959.
    German translation: *Hendrik Kraemer Pionier der Oikumene*. Basel, Basileia Verlag, 1962.

—, *In Memoriam Hendrik Kraemer*. 1965 (sermon).

Menasce, P. de, "La théologie de la mission selon M. Kraemer," *Neue Zeitschrift für Missionswissenschaft*, I (1945), pp. 241–257.

Noordmans, O., "Militia Christi," in: O. Noordmans, *Zoeklichten*. Amsterdam, 1949, pp. 108–115.

Rajotte, Gordon R., *A critical examination of the concept of Truth in religion as held by Hendrik Kraemer, with regard to the underlying philosophical assumptions and problems; and alternative approaches, especially that of Radhakrishnan*. S. T. M. Thesis, McGill University, Montreal, 1968.

Samartha, S. J., "H. Kraemer in asiatischer Sicht heute," *Evangelisches Missionsmagazin*, 1968, pp. 31–35.

Robb, J. Wesley, "Hendrik Kraemer versus William Ernest Hocking," *Journal of Bible and Religion*, Vol. 29, No. 2 (April 1961), pp. 93–101.

Ruitenberg, L. H., "Prof. Dr. H. Kraemer", *Wending*, I, 1 (1946), pp. 20–24.

Veen, H. van der, "Dr. Kraemer en het werk van de Bijbelvertaling in Indonesië," *De Heerbaan*, XIX, 1 (1966), pp. 18–28.

Verkuyl, J., "Het diepste geheim van Kraemer's leven," *De Heerbaan*, XIX (1966), pp. 3–5.

Visser 't Hooft, W. A., "Herdenking van Hendrik Kraemer (17 mei 1888–11
november 1965)," *Jaarboek der Koninklijke Nederlandse Akademie van
Wetenschappen*, 1965–1966, pp. 404–408.
Wood, C. T., "Dr. Kraemer, Dr. Grant and Père Charles," *The East and West
Review*, VII (1941), pp. 165–167.

3. *Method and Theory*

1946 "De theologische studie aan de universiteit," in: *Gedachten over de vernieuw-
ing der theologische studie*. The Hague, Boekencentrum, pp. 3–28.
1959 *De plaats van godsdienstwetenschap en godsdienstfenomenologie in de theologische faculteit*. Nijkerk, Callenbach.
1970 "De waarde van vergelijkende studie der godsdiensten," in: *Uit de nalatenschap van Dr. H. Kraemer*. Kampen, Kok, pp. 127–131.
1970 "Enige principiële en methodische opmerkingen over de studie der lette-
ren," in: *Uit de nalatenschap van Dr. H. Kraemer*. Kampen, Kok, pp.
101–114.

4. *Main Publications*

1921 *Een Javaansche Primbon uit de zestiende eeuw*. Diss. Lit., Leiden
1928–1933 *Agama Islam* (The Religion of Islam), 2 vols. Bandoeng, Christelijke
Boekhandel voor Ned. Indië.
1929 "Kritische beschouwing van begrip en toepassing der neutraliteit in
godsdienstzaken in de Overzeesche Gewesten," *Verslagen der Vergaderingen
van het Indische Genootschap*, 1929 (October), pp. 65–81.
1930 "Christianity and Secularism," *The International Review of Missions*,
XIX (1930), pp. 195–208.
1930 *Dr. N. Adriani. Schets van leven en arbeid*, Amsterdam, H. J. Paris.
1935².
1933 "The Christian Message in Relation to Other Religions,", in: *Christ and
Students of the East*. Geneva, World Student Christian Federation, pp.
83–88.
1935 "Imperialism and Self-Expression," *The Student World*, XXVIII (1935)
pp. 328–348.
1935 "Culture, Politics and Religion," in: A. McLeish, ed., *The Netherlands
Indies*. London, World Dominion Press, pp. 76–108.
1935 "Eenige grepen uit de moderne Apologie van de Islam," *Tijdschrift voor
Indische Taal-, Land- en Volkenkunde*, LXXV (1935), pp. 1–35 and 165–
217.
1937 *De wortelen van het syncretisme* (Inaugural Address). The Hague, Boekencentrum.
1937 "A survey of the Netherlands Indies," *The Moslem World*, XXVII, 1
(1937), pp. 44–55.
1938 *The Christian Message in a Non-Christian World*. With Foreword by
His Grace the Archbishop of York. London–Edinburgh, Edinburgh
House Press; New York, Westminster Press and Harper. Third edition
with Foreword by the late Archbishop of Canterbury. Grand Rapids
(Mich.), Kregel, 1956³.

German translation: *Die christliche Botschaft in einer nicht-christlichen Welt.* Zürich, Zollikon, 1940.

Swedish translation: *Kristendomens Budskap i en icke-Kristen Värld.* Stockholm, Svenska Kyrkans Diakonislyrelses Bokförlag, 1940.

1939 *Continuity or Discontinuity?* (Tambaram Madras Series, Vol. I) Oxford–London.

1947 *De Kerk in Beweging.* The Hague, Boekencentrum (selection of mostly previously published essays and papers on the Church).

1956 *The Communication of the Christian Faith.* London, Lutterworth Press; Philadelphia, Westminster Press.

Dutch translation: *Communicatie; een tijdvraag.* The Hague, Boekencentrum.

German translation: *Die Kommunikation des christlichen Glaubens.* Zürich, Zwingli Verlag.

1956 *Religion and the Christian Faith.* London, Lutterworth Press; Philadelphia, Westminster Press.

Dutch translation: *Godsdienst, godsdiensten en het Christelijk geloof.* Nijkerk, Callenbach, 1958.

French translation: *La foi chrétienne*, Neuchâtel, Delachaux—Niestlé, n. d. (1956).

German translation: *Religion und christlicher Glaube.* (Theologie der Oekumene, 8). Göttingen, 1959.

1958 *A Theology of the Laity.* London, Lutterworth Press; Philadelphia, Westminster Press.

Dutch translation: *Het vergeten ambt in de kerk.* The Hague, Boekencentrum, 1960.

French translation: *Théologie du laicat.* Genève, Labor et Fide, 1966.

1958 *From Missionfield to Independent Church.* Reports on a decisive decade in the growth of Indigenous Churches in Indonesia. The Hague, Boekencentrum; London, SCM Press. (English abridged translation of some reports written between 1926 and 1935).

1959 *Vormen van godsdienstcrisis.* (Mededelingen der Koninklijke Nederlandse Akademie van Wetenschappen, Afd. Letterkunde, Nieuwe Reeks, Deel 22, No 3). Amsterdam, Noordhollandse Uitg. Mij.

1959 "L'Islam, une religion, un mode de vie; l'Islam, une culture; points de confrontation entre l'Islam et le Christianisme," *La Revue de l'Evangélisation*, XVI, 87 (janvier–février 1960), pp. 2–38.

1959 *Waarom nu juist het Christendom?* Nijkerk, Callenbach. 1964[2].

English translation: *Why Christianity among all Religions?* London, Lutterworth Press; Philadelphia, Westminster Press, 1962.

Finnish translation: *Suomen Lähetysseura*, Helsinki, 1965.

German translation: *Weshalb gerade das Christentum?* Basel, Basileia Verlag, 1962, 1966[2].

1959 "Mission im Wandel der Völkerwelt," in: *Der Auftrag der Kirche in der modernen Welt.* Festgabe zum 70. Geburtstag von Emil Brunner. Zürich–Stuttgart, Zwingli Verlag, pp. 291–309.

Dutch translation: "De zending in de wisseling der tijden," in: *Uit de nalatenschap van Dr. H. Kraemer.* Kampen, Kok, 1970, pp. 70–82.

1960 *World Cultures and World Religions: the Coming Dialogue*, London–Southampton, Lutterworth Press/Westminster Press/The Lucknow Publishing Co.

Dutch translation: *Godsdiensten en Culturen, de komende dialoog.* The Hague, Boekencentrum, 1963.

1960 "Die grundsätzlichen Schwierigkeiten in der Begegnung von Christentum und Islam," in: W. Holsten, *Neue Begegnung von Kirche und Islam.* Stuttgart, Evang. Missions Verlag, pp. 15–27.

1960 "Die Lage der islamischen Welt und die christliche Kirche," in: W. Holsten, *Neue Begegnung,* pp. 28–36.

1960 "Islamic Culture and Missionary Adequacy," *The Muslim World.* 1960, pp. 245–251.
Dutch translation: "Islamitische cultuur en missionaire heroriëntatie," in: *Uit de nalatenschap van Dr. H. Kraemer.* Kampen, Kok, 1970, pp. 83–90.

1960 "De Oecumene der Wereldreligies," in: *Oecumene in 't Vizier.* Feestbundel voor Dr. W. A. Visser 't Hooft. Amsterdam, W. ten Have, pp. 121–130.

1961 "De Zending in Nederlands Indië," in: H. Baudet and I. J. Brugmans, *Balans van beleid. Terugblik op de laatste halve eeuw van Nederlands Indië.* Assen, van Gorcum.

1962 *Een nieuw geluid op het gebied der Koranexegese.* (Mededelingen der Koninklijke Nederlandse Akademie van Wetenschappen, Afdeling Letterkunde, Nieuwe Reeks, Deel 25, No 1). Amsterdam, Noordhollandse Uitg. Mij.

1966 "The role and responsibility of the Christian mission," in: Leroy S. Ronner, ed., *Philosophy, Religion, and the coming World Civilization.* Essays in Honor of William Ernest Hocking. The Hague, Nijhoff, pp. 235–249.

1970 *Uit de nalatenschap van Dr. H. Kraemer.* (16 essays mostly previously published). Edited by B. J. Brouwer, E. Jansen Schoonhoven, S. C. Graaf van Randwijk. Kampen, Kok.

WILLIAM BREDE KRISTENSEN*

1. Bibliography

"Lijst van geschriften van Prof. Dr. W. B. Kristensen," *Jaarboek Ex Oriente Lux* (Leiden), I, 5 (1937–38), pp. 284–286.

"List of publications of W. Brede Kristensen," in: W. Brede Kristensen, *The Meaning of Religion.* The Hague, Nijhoff, 1960, 1968², pp. 497–500.

2. Biography and Appreciation

Beek, M. A., "Le professeur W. B. Kristensen et l'Ancien Testament," in *Liber Amicorum. Essays in honour of Prof. Dr. C. J. Bleeker.* Leiden, E. J. Brill, 1969, pp. 14–26.

Bleeker, C. J., "In memoriam Professor Dr. W. Brede Kristensen," *Numen,* I, 3 (1954), pp. 235–236.

Buck, A. de, "Herdenking W. B. Kristensen," *Jaarboek der Koninklijke Akademie van Wetenschappen,* 1953–54, pp. 295–305.

Kraemer, H., "Introduction," in: W. Brede Kristensen, *The Meaning of Religion.* The Hague, Nijhoff, 1960, 1968², pp. XI–XXV.

3. Method and Theory

1901 *Om religionernes inddeling i naturreligioner og etiske religioner.* Kristiania.
1914 "Hvad religionshistorisk studium berøver os og gir os," *For Kirke og Kultur* (Oslo), XXI (1914).
1915 "Over waardering van historische gegevens," *Onze Eeuw*, XV (1915), pp. 415–440. Reprinted in *Symbool en Werkelijkheid*, 1954, pp. 66–84.
1916 "De 'Primitieven' of wij voorop?," in *Nagelaten Sporen, aangeboden aan Prof. Dr. P. D. Chantepie de la Saussaye, te Leiden, 2 Juni 1916*, pp. 100–104.
1918 " 'Diepte-psychologie'?," *De Gids*, LXXXII, 6 (1918).
1919 "De inaugureele rede van Prof. Van der Leeuw," *Theologisch Tijdschrift*, LIII (1919), pp. 260–265.
1928 "De absoluutheid van het Christendom," *Eltheto*, LXXXII, 5 (1928), pp. 129–140. Reprinted in *Symbool en Werkelijkheid*, 1954, pp. 85–95.
1931 "Symbool en werkelijkheid," *De Gids*, XCV (July 1931), pp. 76–85. Reprinted in *Symbool en Werkelijkheid*, 1954, pp. 7–14.
1934 "Schleiermacher's opvatting van godsdienstgeschiedenis," *Vox Theologica*, V (1934), pp. 97–101. Reprinted in *Symbool en werkelijkheid*, 1954, pp. 24–30.
1936 "Rede gehouden bij de aanvang der theologische colleges," *Leidsch Universiteitsblad*, 23 October 1936. Reprinted in *Symbool en werkelijkheid*, 1954, pp. 347–355.
1938 "Geschiedenis der godsdiensten," *Vox Theologica*, X, 3 (December 1938) pp. 80–85.
1946 *Tro eller overtro.* Oslo.
    Dutch translation: "Geloof of bijgeloof?," *Vox Theologica*, XVI (August 1946). Reprinted in *Symbool en werkelijkheid*, 1954, pp. 15–23.

4. Main Publications

1896 *Aegypternes forestillinger om livet efter døden i forbindelse med guderne Ra og Osiris.* Kristiania.
1896 "Om udødelighetstroen i Orientens gamle religioner," *For Kirke og Kultur* (Kristiania), III (1896), pp. 513–526 and 577.
1898 *Brahma, et stykke indisk religionshistorie.* Kristiania.
1901 "Helvedet," *Samtiden* (Kristiania), (1901), pp. 14–23.
1901 *Het verband tusschen godsdienst en de zucht tot zelfbehoud* (Inaugural Address). Leiden, E. J. Brill.
1904 "Dualistische en monistische denkbeelden in den Egyptischen godsdienst," *Theologisch Tijdschrift*, XXXVIII (1904), pp. 233–255.
1909 "De Ruach Elohim vóór de schepping," *Theologisch Tijdschrift*, XLIII (1909), pp. 398–400.
1913 "Mysteriereligion i Oldtiden," *Norsk Theologisk Tidskrift*, Ny Raekke IV (1913), pp. 294–336.
1916 "Idealen van inzicht bij de volken der oudheid," *Jaarboek der Rijksuniversiteit te Leiden.*
1922 "Over den wetenschappelijken arbeid van Herman Bavinck," *Jaarboek van de Koninklijke Akademie van Wetenschappen.*

1925 *Livet fra døden. Studier over Aegyptisk og gammel Graesk religion.* Olaus Petri Foralaesninger ved Uppsala Universitet. Oslo, Gyldendalske Bokhandel.
Dutch translation by J. Kristensen-Heldring: *Het leven uit den dood. Studiën over Egyptischen en Oud-Griekschen godsdienst.* Haarlem, De Erven Bohn, 1926, 1949².

1941 "Den antikke tragedie og Henrik Ibsens verker," *Kirke og Kultur* (1941) pp. 393–412.
Comp. *Dutch* text "De antieke tragedie en Hendrik Ibsen," in *Symbool en werkelijkheid*, 1954, pp. 49–65.

1943 "De godsdienstige beteekenis van de gesloten perioden," *Ex Oriente Lux* (Leiden), 1943.

1947 *Bijdragen tot de kennis der antieke godsdiensten* (11 papers read at the Royal Academy between 1915 and 1942). Amsterdam, Noord-Hollandsche Uitgevers Mij. Paperback edition under the title of *Godsdiensten in de oude wereld.* (Aula). Utrecht–Antwerpen, Het Spectrum.

1952 "Primitiv visdom," *Kirke og Kultur* (1952).
Dutch translation: *Primitieve wijsheid.* Leiden, 1952. Reprinted in *Symbool en werkelijkheid*, 1954, pp. 333–346.

1954 *Religionshistorisk studium.* Oslo. (There is a non-authorized stencilled text *Symbol og virkelighet i oldtidens religioner. Et sammenstrengt resumé av foredrag og forelesninger, holdt av Professor Brede Kristensen*, published by: Neunden for Frimurerisk Forskning og Oplysning, Oslo, n.d.).
Dutch translation by J. Kristensen-Heldring: *Inleiding tot de godsdienstgeschiedenis.* Arnhem, Van Loghum Slaterus, 1955.

1954 *Symbool en werkelijkheid. Een bundel godsdiensthistorische studiën.* Arnhem, Van Loghum Slaterus. Paperback edition Palladium, Zeist-Arnhem–Antwerpen, 1962. (Mostly previously published essays and Papers).

1960 *The Meaning of Religion. Lectures in the Phenomenology of Religion.* With an Introduction by Hendrik Kraemer. Translated by John B. Carman. The Hague, Martinus Nijhoff, 1960, 1968².

ALFRED LOUIS KROEBER

1. Bibliography, Biography and Appreciation

Driver, Harold E., *The Contribution of A. L. Kroeber to Culture Area Theory and Practice.* Baltimore, 1962.
Lowie, Robert H., ed., *Essays in Anthropology.* Presented to A. L. Kroeber in Celebration of his 60th Birthday, June 11, 1936. Berkeley, University of California Press, 1936. "Bibliography of A. L. Kroeber," pp. 423–428.

2. Main Publications

1904 *Types of Indian Culture in California.* Berkeley, University of California Press.

1907 *The Religion of the Indians of California.* Berkeley, University of California Press.

1907 *Indian Myths of South Central California.* Berkeley, University of California Press.
1918 *The History of Philippine Civilisation in Religious Nomenclature.* New York, American Museum of Natural History.
1919 *Peoples of the Philippines.* Vol. I: *Philippine Islands;* Vol. II: *Ethnology: Philippine Islands.* New York, American Museum Press. 1928² (revised).
1920 *Source Book in Anthropology.* Edited by A. L. Kroeber and T. T. Waterman. Berkeley, University of California Press. 1924². Revised edition: New York, Harcourt, Brace and Company, 1931.
1922 *Elements of Culture in Native California.* Berkeley, University of California Press.
1923 *Anthropology.* New York, Harcourt, Brace and World, 1948².
1925 *Handbook of the Indians of California.* Washington, Government Printing Office.
1939 *Cultural and Natural Areas of Native North America.* Berkeley, University of California Press.
1944 *Configurations of Culture Growth.* Berkeley, University of California Press.
1948 *Seven Mohave Myths.* (Anthropological Records, Vol. 11, No. 1). Berkeley–Los Angeles, University of California Press.
1952 *The Nature of Culture.* Chicago, University of Chicago Press.
1952 *Culture: A Critical Review of Concepts and Definitions.* By A. L. Kroeber and C. Kluckhohn. (Papers of the Peabody Museum of Archeology and Ethnology, XLVII, 1). Cambridge, Mass.
1953 *Anthropology Today: An Encyclopedia Inventory.* Ed. by A. L. Kroeber. Chicago, University of Chicago Press.
1957 *Style and Civilisation.* Second edition: London, Cambridge University Press; Berkeley–Los Angeles, University of California Press, 1963².

ALBERTUS CHRISTIAAN KRUYT

1. Bibliography, Biography and Appreciation

Boetzelaer van Asperen en Dubbeldam, Dr. C. W. Th. Baron van, "Albertus Christiaan Kruyt (1869–1949)," *Bijdragen tot de Taal-, Land- en Volkenkunde,* Vol. 105 (1949), pp. 143–146.
Brouwer, K. J., *A. C. Kruyt, Dienaar der Toradja's.* The Hague, Voorhoeve, 1951. Bibliography, pp. 171–185.
Kruyt, J., *Het Zendingsveld Poso.* Kampen, Kok, 1970.
Rassers, W. H., "Herdenking van Albertus Christiaan Kruyt (1869–1949)," *Jaarboek Koninklijke Nederlandse Akademie van Wetenschappen, 1948–1949.* Amsterdam, 1949, pp. 161–170.

2. Main Publications

1889 *Het koppensnellen der Toradja's van Midden-Celebes, en zijne beteekenis.* (Konklijke Nederlandsche Akademie van Wetenschappen. Verslagen en Mededeelingen. Afdeeling Letterkunde. Reeks 4. Deel 3). Amsterdam.

1906 *Het Animisme in den Indischen Archipel.* The Hague.
1912–1914 *De Bare'e-sprekende Toradjas van Midden-Celebes. De Oost-Toradjas,*
    3 vols. Batavia, Landsdrukkerij. New, completely revised edition by
    A. C. Kruyt, 4 vols. (Verhandelingen der Koninklijke Nederlandsche
    Akademie van Wetenschappen. Afd. Letterkunde. Nieuwe Reeks, Deel
    54–56, No. 1–3). Amsterdam, Noord-Hollandsche Uitg.-Mij. 1950–1951².
1933 *De oorsprong van de priestertaal in Poso.* (Mededeelingen der Koninklijke
    Nederlandsche Akademie van Wetenschappen. Afd. Letterkunde. Deel
    76, Serie B, No. 7). Amsterdam.
1937 *Het leggen van een knoop in Indonesië.* (Mededeelingen der Koninklijke
    Nederlandsche Akademie van Wettenschappen. Afd. Letterkunde. Deel
    84, Serie B, No. 4). Amsterdam.
1938 *De West-Toradja's op Midden-Celebes.* (Verhandelingen der Koninklijke
    Nederlandsche Akademie van Wetenschappen. Afd. Letterkunde. Nieuwe
    reeks. Deel 40). Amsterdam.

ABRAHAM KUENEN

1. Bibliography

Vuonon, A., *Gesammelte Abhandlungen*..., 1894, pp. 501–511.
Klugt, W. van der, "Werken van Abraham Kuenen," in "Levensbericht...,"
    1893 (see below).

2. Biography and Appreciation

Manen, W. C. van, "A. Kuenen," *Jewish Quarterly Review,* IV (1892), pp. 471–
    489.
Réville, A., *Dr. Abraham Kuenen.* (Mannen van Beteekenis in onze Dagen,
    Vol. 21). Haarlem, 1890.
Schets, J., *Prof. Kuenen's Pentateuch Critiek, historisch-critisch onderzocht.*
    Leiden, van Leeuwen, 1891.
Tiele, C. P., *A. Kuenen.* (Karakterschetsen van vermaarde Nederlanders).
    Haarlem, Tjeenk Willink, 1906.
Vlugt, W. van der, "Levensbericht van A. Kuenen, 16 Sept. 1828–10 Dec. 1891,"
    *Handelingen en Mededeelingen van de Maatschappij der Nederlandsche
    Letterkunde,* 1893, pp. 245–355. With bibliography.

3. Main Publications

1861–1865 *Historisch-kritisch Onderzoek naar het Ontstaan en de Verzameling
    van de Boeken des Ouden Verbonds,* 3 vols. Leiden. 1887² (completely
    revised).
    English translation from the Dutch and edited with notes by J. W.
    Colenso: *The Pentateuch and Book of Joshua critically examined.* Lon-
    don, 1865.

English translation with the Assistance of the author by P.H. Wicksteed: *An Historico-critical Inquiry into the Origin and Composition of the Hexateuch (Pentateuch and Book of Jushua)*. London, Macmillan, 1886, XL + 344 pp.

1869–1870 *De Godsdienst van Israel tot den Ondergang van den Joodschen Staat,* 2 vols. Haarlem.

English translation from the Dutch by A. H. May: *The Religion of Israel to the Fall of the Jewish State,* 3 vols. London, Williams & Norgate, 1873–75.

1875 *De Profeten en de Profetie onder Israel.* Historisch-dogmatische Studie, 2 vols. Leiden.

English translation by A. Milroy: *The Prophets and Prophecy in Israel.* An Historical and critical Enquiry. With an Introduction by J. Muir. London, 1877.

1882 *Volksgodsdienst en Wereldgodsdienst.* Vijf Voorlezingen. Leiden.

English translation by P. W. Wickstead: *National Religions and Universal Religions.* The Hibbert Lectures, 1882. London, Williams & Norgate, 1882.

1894 *Gesammelte Abhandlungen zur biblischen Wissenschaft.* Aus dem Höllandischen übersetzt von K. Budd. Freiburg i. B. und Leipzig, 1894. Bibliography, pp. 501–511.

FRANZ FELIX ADALBERT KUHN

Main Publications

1843 *Märkische Sagen und Märchen nebst einem Anhange von Gebräuchen und Aberglauben.* Gesammelt von A. Kuhn. Berlin.

1848 *Norddeutsche Sagen, Märchen und Gebräuche aus Meklenburg, Pommern, der Mark*... Aus dem Munde des Volkes gesammelt und herausgegeben von Adalbert Kuhn und Wilhelm Schwartz. Leipzig, 1848.

1858 *Gebräuche und Märchen aus Westfalen.* Gesammelt und herausgegeben von A. Kuhn. Vol. I: *Sagen;* Vol. II: *Gebräuche und Märchen.* Leipzig.

1859 *Die Herabkunft des Feuers und des Göttertranks.* Beitrag zur Vergleichender Mythologie der Indo-Germanen. Berlin.

JOSEPH-FRANÇOIS LAFITAU

1. Biography and Appreciation

Kaelin, Kaspar, *Indianer und Urvölker nach Joseph-François Lafitau, 1681–1746.*
Dissertation. Freiburg in der Schweiz, 1943.

2. Main Publications

1724 *Mœurs des Sauvages Amériquains comparées aux mœurs des premiers temps*, 2 vols. Paris, Saugrain l'aîné.
1727 *Histoire de Jean de Brienne, Roy de Jérusalem et empereur de Constantinople.* Paris, Moette & Simon.
1733 *Histoire des découvertes et conquestes des Portugais dans le Nouveau Monde*, 2 vols. Paris, Saugrain père.

ANDREW LANG*

1. Bibliography

Falconer, Charles M., *Specimens of a Bibliography of Andrew Lang.* Dundee, 1889.
—, *The Writings of Andrew Lang, M. A., LL. D., Arranged in the Form of a Bibliography. With Notes.* Dundee, 1894.
—, *Catalogue of a Library, chiefly the Writings of Andrew Lang.* Dundee, 1898.
Green, Roger Lancelyn, "A Short-Title Bibliography of the Works of Andrew Lang," in: Roger Lancelyn Green, *Andrew Lang. A Cricitical Biography with a Short-Title Bibliography of the Works of Andrew Lang.* Leicester, Edmund Ward, 1946, pp. 241–249.

2. Biography and Appreciation

Beerbohm, Max, *Two Glimpses of Andrew Lang*. 1928.
Brown F. S. A., Robert, *Semitic Influences in Hellenic Mythology. With special reference to the recent mythological works of the Rt. Hon. F. Max Müller and A. Lang*. London, 1898.
Cazamain, L., *Andrew Lang and the Maid of France*. Edinburgh, 1931. Reprinted in: *Concerning Andrew Lang*, 1949.
Clodd, E. and Ang, A., "Address", "Protest of a psycho-folklorist" and "Reply to the protest", *Folk-Lore*, VI (1895), pp. 54–81 and pp. 236–258.
Cocq, A. P. L. de, *Andrew Lang, a Nineteenth Century Anthropologist*. Tilburg (Holland), Zwijsen, 1968.
Concerning Andrew Lang. Being the Andrew Lang Lectures delivered before the University of St. Andrews 1927–1937. With an Introduction by A. Blyth Webster and a Preface by J. B. Salmond. Oxford, Clarendon Press, 1949. The volume contains the following essays:
Buchan, John, "Andrew Lang and the border";
Cazamain, Louis, "Andrew Lang and the maid of France";
Darwin, Bernard, "Andrew Lang and the literature of sport";
Gordon, George, "Andrew Lang";
Grierson, H. J. C., "Lang, Lockhart and Biography";
Mackie, J. D., "Andrew Lang and the House of Stuart";
Marett, R. R., "The raw material of religion";
Rait, Robert S., "Andrew Lang as historian";
Shewan, Alexander, "Andrew Lang's work for Homer";
Webster, A. Blyth, "Andrew Lang's poetry".
Falconer, Charles M., "Andrew Lang," *Athenaeum*, No. 4422 (27 July 1912), pp. 92–93.
Gennep, A. van, "Andrew Lang: folklorist and critic," *Folk-Lore*, XXIII (1912), pp. 366–369.
Goldenweiser, A. A., "Andrew Lang on method in the study of totemism," *American Anthropologist*, N. S. XIV (1912), pp. 382–391.
—, "The views of Andrew Lang, and J. G. Frazer and E. Durkheim on totemism," *Anthropos*, X–XI (1915–1916), pp. 948–970.
Gordon, George, *Andrew Lang*. Edinburgh, 1927. Reprinted in: *Concerning Andrew Lang*, 1949.
Jacobs, Joseph, "Andrew Lang as man of letters and folk-lorist," *The Journal of American Folklore*, XXVI (1913), pp. 367–372.
Marett, R. R., "Reply to A. Lang's criticism," *Folk-Lore*, XI (1900), pp. 162–182.
—, "Discussion with Lang on totemism," *Folk-Lore*, XIII (1902), pp. 396–397.
—, "The late Andrew Lang," *The Athenaeum*, No. 4423 (August 3, 1912).
—, "Andrew Lang. Born 31st March 1844, died 20th July 1912," *Man*, Nr. 85, XII (1912), pp. 153–154.
—, *The Raw Material of Religion*. Edinburgh, 1929. Reprinted in: *Concerning Andrew Lang*, 1949.
Murray, George G. A., *Andrew Lang the Poet*. London, 1948.
Rait, Robert S., *Andrew Lang as historian*. Edinburgh, 1930. Reprinted in: *Concerning Andrew Lang*, 1949.
Rivers, W. H., "Andrew Lang", *Folk-Lore*, XXIII (1912), pp. 367–371.
Rose, Herbert J., *Andrew Lang. His place in Anthropology*. Edinburgh, 1951.

Salmond, James B., *Andrew Lang and Journalism*. Edinburgh, 1951.
—, "Introduction" in: *Andrew Lang and St. Andrews. A Centenary Anthology*. St. Andrews, 1944.
Salvatorelli, Luigi, "Andrew Lang," *Lares*, I (1912), pp. 133–136.
Schmidt, Wilhelm, "Andrew Lang: folklorist and critic," *Folk-Lore*, XXIII (1912), pp. 363–375.
—, "Andrew Lang," *Anthropos*, VII (1912), pp. I–VI.

3. Method, Theory and Publications on Religion

1873 "Myth and fairy tales," *Fortnightly Review*, XIX (1873).
1884 *Custom and Myth*. London. 1885² (revised).
.... "Mythology", *Encyclopaedia Britannica*, 9th ed. Vol. XVII.
　　 French translation by Léo Parmentier: *La Mythologie*. With a preface by Ch. Michel and additions by the author. Paris, 1886.
1887 *Myth, Ritual and Religion*, 2 vols. London–New York, Longmans, Green and Co. 1899² (revised), 1901³, 1906⁴, 1913⁵.
　　 Dutch translation with annotations by L. Knappert: *Onderzoek naar de ontwikkeling van godsdienst, cultus en mythologie*. With a preface by P. D. Chantepie de la Saussaye, 2 vols. Haarlem, 1889, 1893².
　　 French translation by Léon Marillier avec la collaboration de A. Dirr: *Mythes, cultes et religion*. Paris, 1896.
1890 *Etudes traditionnistes*. Paris, J. Maisonneuve.
1897 *Modern Mythology*. London–New York–Bombay, Longmans, Green & Co.
1898 *The Making of Religion*. London–New York–Bombay, Longmans, Green & Co. 1909³.
1900 "J. G. Frazer's 'Totemism and Exogamy'," *Anthropos*, V (1900), ſp. 1101 f.
1901 *Magic and Religion*. London–New York–Bombay, Longmans, Green & Co.
1903 *Social Origins* (including an essay by J. J. Atkinson: "Primal Law"). London.
.... *Anthropological Essays*. Edited by H. Balfour.
1905 *The Secret of the Totem*. London.
1907–1908 "The origin of terms of human relationship," *Proceedings of the British Academy*, pp. 139–160. Also printed separately.
1908 *Origins of Religion*. London.
1909 "The Alcheringa and the All-Father," *Revue des Etudes Ethnographiques*, 1909.
1910 "Wilhelm Schmidt's 'L'origine de l'idée de Dieu' (1910)," *Folk-Lore*, XXI (1910), pp. 516–523.
1911 "Method in the study of totemism," *American Anthropologist*, N. S. XIV (1912), pp. 368–382.
1912 "Last words on totemism, marriage and religion," *Folk-Lore*, XXIII (1912).
1912 "The origin of belief in a God," *The Athenaeum*, Nr. 4423 (August 1912).
1913 "Mr Andrew Lang's theory on the origin of exogamy and totemism," *Folk-Lore*, XXIV (1913), pp. 155–186.
.... "Totemism," *Encyclopedia Britannica*, 11th. ed., Vol. XXVII, pp. 79–91.

4. Other Main Publications

1884 *Rhymes à la mode*. London.
1885 "The Merton Professorship," *The Academy*.
1886 *Letters to Dead Authors*. New York, C Scribner's Sons. 1893[2].
1886 *Books and Bookmen*. London–New York. 1887[2].
1887 *Almae Matres*. London.
1890 *How to Fail in Literature*. London.
1891 *Essays in Little*. London–New York.
1893 *Homer and the Epic*. London.
1894 *Cock Lane and Common Sense*. London.
1897 *The Book of Dreams and Ghosts*. London.
1900–1907 *A History of Scotland from the Roman Occupation*, 4 vols. London.
1902 *The Mystery of Mary Stuart*. London.
1903 *The Valet's Tragedy and Other Studies*. London.
1904 *Historical Mysteries*. London. 1905[2].
1905 *John Knox and the Reformation*. London–New York–Bombay, Longmans,
      Green & Co. New edition Port Washington, New York, 1967.
1905 *Adventures among Books*. London.
1906 *Sir Walter Scott*. London.
1906 *Homer and his Age*. London–New York.
1906 *Oxford. Brief historical and descriptive notes*. London. 1906[2].
. . . . *The Maid of France. Being the Story of the Life and Death of Jeanne d'Arc*.
      London, 1913[2].
      French translation by Louis Boucher and E. E. Clarke: *La pucelle de
      France. Histoire de la vie et de la mort de Jeanne d'Arc*. With an Introduc-
      tion by L. F. F. Goyau. Paris, 1911.
1910 *The World of Homer*. London.
1911 *A Short History of Scotland*. London.
1912 *Shakespeare, Bacon and the Great Unknown*. London–New York. 1913[2].
1923 *Poetical Works*. Edited by Leonora Blanche Lang, 4 vols. London.
1944 *Andrew Lang and St. Andrews. A Centenary Anthology*. Edited by J. B.
      Salmond. St. Andrews, St. Andrews University Press.

MORITZ LAZARUS

1. Bibliography

Kukula, R., *Biographisches Jahrbuch der deutschen Hochschulen* (1892) (Er-
      gänzungsheft I, 1893), p. 531.

2. Biography and Appreciation

Achelis, T., *Moritz Lazarus*. (Sammlung gemeinverständlicher wissenschaflicher
      Vorträge. N. F., Heft 333). 1900.
Berliner, E., *Prof. Dr. M. Lazarus und die öffentliche Meinung*, 1887.
Lazarus, M., *Professor Lazarus als religiöser Reformator*. Leipzig, 1887.
—, *Aus meiner Jugend. Autobiographie von M. Lazarus*. Mit Vorwort und
      Anhang herausg. von Nahida Lazarus. Frankfurt a. M., Kaufmann, 1913.

--, *Moritz Lazarus' Lebenserinnerungen*. Bearbeitet von Nahida Lazarus und Alfred Leicht. Berlin, Reimer, 1906.

Lazarus, Nahida Ruth, *Ein deutscher Professor in der Schweiz*. Nach Briefen und Dokumenten im Nachlass ihres Gatten, Berlin, Dümmler, 1910.

Leicht, A., *Lazarus, der Begründer der Völkerpsychologie*. 1904.

Sganzini, C., *Die Fortschritte der Völkerpsychologie von Lazarus bis Wundt*. (Neue Berner Abhandlungen zur Philosophie und ihrer Geschichte. Heft 2.). Bern, 1913.

3. Main Publications

1856–57 *Das Leben der Seele in Monographieen über seine Erscheinungen und Gesetzte*, 2 vols. Berlin, Dümmler. 1876–1882[2] (enlarged edition); 3 vols. 1883–97[3]. (Vol. II has also a special title page: *Geist und Sprache, eine psychologische Monographie*).

1865 *Über die Ideen in der Geschichte*. Rectoratsrede. Abdruck aus der Zeitschrift für Völkerpsychologie und Sprachwissenschaft. Berlin.

1903 *Der Prophet Jeremias*. Breslau, Schotlaender; New York, Stechert.

GABRIEL LE BRAS

1. Bibliography

Études d'Histoire du Droit Canonique, dédiées à Gabriel Le Bras. Paris, Sire, 1965, Vol. I, pp. IX–XXXIII.

2. Biography and Appreciation

Desroche, H., "Domaines et méthodes de la sociologie religieuse dans l'œuvre de G. Le Bras," *Revue d'Histoire et de Philosophie Religieuses*, XXXIV (1954), pp. 128–158.
English translation by E. L. Sheppard: "Areas and Methods of a Sociology of Religion. The Work of G. Le Bras," *Journal of Religion*, XXXV, 1 (1955), pp. 34–47.

Isambert, François A., "Développement et dépassement de l'étude de la pratique religieuse chez Gabriel Le Bras," *Cahiers Internationaux de Sociologie*, XX (janvier–juin 1956), pp. 149–169.

Shippey, F. A., "The relations of theology and the social sciences according to Gabriel Le Bras," *Archives de Sociologie des Religions*, 10e Année, No 20 (juillet–décembre 1965), pp. 79–93.

"La sociologie religieuse de Gabriel Le Bras," par Fernand Boulard, Jean Gaudemet, Jacques Maître et Emile Poulat. *L'Année Sociologique*, Troisième Série (1969), pp. 301–334.

3. Main Publications

1942–1945   *Introduction à l'Histoire de la Pratique Religieuse en France*, 2 vols.

1955 *Étude de sociologie religieuse*, 2 vols. Paris.

1955 *Prolégomènes à l'Histoire du Droit et des Institutions de l'Eglise en Occident.* (Programme, Méthode, Esprit des 20 Volumes préparés avec le Concours de 35 anciens Élèves de la Faculté de Droit de Paris, de l'Ecole pratique des Hautes Études – Sciences religieuses – et de l'Institut de Droit Canonique de l'Université de Strasbourg). Paris.

1955 "Sociologie religieuse et sciences sociales," *Actes du IVᵉ Congrès international de Sociologie religieuse)*, pp. 9–19.

1956 "Sociologie religieuse et science des religions," *Archives de Sociologie des Religions*, I, 1 (1956), pp. 3–17.

1956 "L'explication en sociologie religieuse," *Cahiers Internationaux de Sociologie*, pp. 59–76.

1957 "Etat présent de la Sociologie religieuse," *Encyclopédie française*, T. XIX. Paris, Larousse.

1958 "La Sociologie religieuse parmi les Sciences humaines," in: *Sociologie et Religions.* (Recherches et Débats, Cahier no. 25), pp. 11–25.

1959–1964 *Les Institutions Ecclésiastiques de la Chrétienté Médiévale*, 2 vols. Paris.

1960 "Problèmes de la sociologie des religions," in: *Traité de Sociologie*, publié sous la direction de G. Gurvitch, T. II. Paris, pp. 79–102.

1961 "Les problèmes actuels de la sociologie religieuse," *Cahiers de l'Association interuniversitaire de l'Est* (Strasbourg), pp. 7–13.

MAURICE LEENHARDT

1. Bibliography

"Bibliographie des principaux écrits de Maurice Leenhardt," *Journal de la Société des Océanistes*, X, 10 (décembre 1954), pp. 73–76.

2. Biography and Appreciation

Condominas, G., "Maurice Leenhardt," *France-Asie*, no. 10 (1954), pp. 571–582.

Journal de la Société des Océanistes. Special issue: Tome X, no. 10 (décembre 1954). With contributions by R. Becker, R.-H. Leenhardt, P. Métais, J. Poirier, Aurélien Sauvageot.

Lévi-Strauss, C., "Maurice Leenhardt," *Annuaire de l'École Pratique des Hautes Études, Section des Sciences Religieuses*, 1954–1955, pp. 2–22.

Le Monde Non-Chrétien. Special issue: No. 33 (1955). With contributions by G. Gurvitch, J. Guiart, G. Le Bras, L. Massignon, I. Meyerson, J. Poirier, P. Rontheir, A. Roux and A. Sauvageot.

3. *Main Publications*

1930 *Notes d'ethnologie néo-calédonienne.* (Université de Paris. Travaux et Mémoires de l'Institut d'Ethnologie, VIII). Paris, Institut d'Ethnologie.
1932 *Documents néo-calédoniens.* (Université de Paris. Travaux et Mémoires de l'Institut d'Ethnologie, IX). Paris, Institut d'Ethnologie.
1937 *Gens de Grande Terre.* Paris.
1946 *Langues et dialectes de l'Austro-Mélanésie.* (Université de Paris. Travaux et Mémoires de l'Institut d'Ethnologie, XLVI). Paris, Institut d'Etnologie.
1947 *Do Kamo. La personne et le mythe dans le monde mélanésien.* Paris.
1948 *Arts de l'Océanie.* Paris.
English translation by Michael Heron: *Arts of the Oceanic Peoples.* London, Thames & Hudson (Primitive Arts), 1950.

GERARDUS VAN DER LEEUW*

1. *Bibliography*

Heerma van Voss, M. S. H. G., "Lijst der geschriften van Prof. Dr. G. van der Leeuw betreffende het oude Voor-Azië en Egypte," *Jaarbericht Ex Oriente Lux*, XII (1951–52), pp. 126–129.
—, "Nécrologie G. van der Leeuw. Bibliographie égyptologique," *Chronique d'Egypte*, XXVII, no. 53 (janvier 1952), pp. 140—141.
Vos, W., *Dr G. van der Leeuw. Bibliographie zijner geschriften.* (On the occasion of his 25 years' professorship). With an Introduction by J. Lindeboom. Arnhem, S. Gouda Quint & D. Brouwer en Zoon, 1943.
—, "Dr G. van der Leeuw. Bibliographie zijner geschriften," in: W. J. Kooiman and J. M. van Veen, ed., *Pro Regno Pro Sanctuario.* (On the occasion of Van der Leeuw's 60th birthday). Nijkerk, Callenbach, 1950, pp. 553–638.

2. *Biography and Appreciation*

Baaren, Th. P. van, "De ethnologische basis van de faenomenologie van G. van der Leeuw," *Nederlands Theologisch Tijdschrift*, XI, 6 (juni 1957), pp. 321–353.
Bleeker, C. J., "In memoriam Prof. Dr. G. van der Leeuw," *De Groene Amsterdammer*, 25 november 1950.
—, "Gerardus van der Leeuw ('s-Gravenhage, 18 Maart 1890–Groningen, December 1950 [Utrecht, 18 November 1950]," *Jaarboek van de Maatschappij der Nederlandse Letterkunde te Leiden*, 1950–1951, pp. 145–146.
—, "De godsdiensthistoricus en phaenomenoloog," *De Nieuwe Stem*, VI, 2 (februari 1951), pp. 82–84.
Bolle, Kees W., "The History of Religions and Christian Theology," *Anglican Theological Review*, Vol. 53 (1971), pp. 251–269.
Buck, A. de, "Herdenking Gerardus van der Leeuw," *Jaarboek der Koninklijke Nederlandse Akademie van Wetenschappen*, 1951–1952, pp. 232–244.

Carman, John B., "The Theology of a Phenomenologist," *Harvard Divinity Bulletin*, XXIX, 3 (April 1965), pp. 13–42.

Eliade, Mircea, "Preface," in: Gerardus van der Leeuw, *Sacred and Profane Beauty: the Holy in Art*. Nashville–New York, Abingdon Press and Holt, Rinehart and Winston, Inc., 1963, pp. V–IX.

Faber, H., "Een theologische visie op de anthropologie," *Nieuw Theologisch Tijdschrift*, Vol. 31 (1942), pp. 230–245.

Gorski, Eugene Francis, *Cult-Culture: The Theological Anthropology of Gerardus van der Leeuw*. Unpublished Th. D. Dissertation, Catholic Institute of Paris *(Institut Catholique de Paris)*, 1971, VII + 495 p.

Hermelink, J. *Verstehen und Bezeugen. Der theologische Ertrag der 'Phänomenologie der Religion' des G. van der Leeuw*. (Beiträge zur evangelischen Theologie, Band 30). München, Chr. Kaiser Verlag, 1960.

Hirschmann, Eva, *Phänomenologie der Religion. Eine historisch-systematische Untersuchung von 'Religionsphänomenologie' und 'religionsphänomenologischer Methode' in der Religionswissenschaft* (Diss. Groningen). Würzburg, 1940 (esp. pp. 95–111, 116–122, 133–136).

—, "In Memoriam Gerardus van der Leeuw, 18 mars 1890–18 novembre 1950," *Le monde non-chrétien*, XVII (janvier–mars 1951), pp. 27–37.

Isambert, F. A., "La phénoménologie religieuse," in: H. Desroche and J. Séguy, eds., *Introduction aux sciences humaines des religions*. Paris, Cujas, 1970, pp. 217–240.

Jensen, Alfred, "Anmerkungen zur Phänomenologie der Religion," in: *Festschrift Alfred Bertholet zum 80. Geburtstag gewidmet*. Tübingen, Mohr, 1950, pp. 267–280.

Kristensen, W. B., "De inaugureele rede van Professor van der Leeuw," *Theologisch Tijdschrift*, LIII (1919), pp. 260–265.

Leenhardt, Maurice, "In Memoriam – G. van der Leeuw," *Revue d'Histoire et de Philosophie Religieuse*, XXXI (1951), pp. 497–499.

Leertouwer, L., "De mens en zijn ontwerp bij Van der Leeuw," *Vox Theologica* XXX, 2 (november 1959), pp. 40–49.

Leeuw, G. van der, "Confession scientifique." Faite à l'Université Masaryk de Brno le lundi 18 novembre 1946. *Numen*, I, 1 (1954), pp. 8–15.

De Nieuwe Stem, Special Issue, VI, 2 (februari 1951).
    With contributions by C. J. Bleeker, G. Bolkestein, A. Donker, C. A. van Peursen, H. C. Rümke, F. Sierksma, J. M. van Veen.

Noordmans, O., "In memoriam Prof. Dr. G. van der Leeuw," *Kerk en Theologie*, II (1951), pp. 1–3.

Oorschot, Henri van, *L'apport de van der Leeuw à la phénoménologie de la Religion*. Thèse de Maîtrise, Université de Montréal, Montreal, 1974.

Pettazzoni, Raffaele, "Commemorazione del socio straniero Gerardus van der Leeuw," *Rend. Acc. Lincei, Cl. Sc. Mor.*, VIII, 6 (1951), pp. 59–63.

—, "Gerardus van der Leeuw (1890–1950)," *Studi e Materiali di Storia delle Religioni*, XXIII (1951–52), pp. 209–211.

Rümke, H. C., "Aantekeningen over het instinct, den archetypus, den existentiaal, over de werelden, die zij oproepen, over reductie en misvorming van het mensbeeld," in: W. J. Kooiman and J. M. van Veen, eds., *Pro Regno Pro Sanctuario*. Nijkerk, Callenbach, 1950, pp. 451–468.

—, "Ter herinnering," *De Nieuwe Stem*, VI, 2 (februari 1951), pp. 88–96.

Sierksma, Fokke, "G. van der Leeuw, *Wegen en grenzen*. Amsterdam, H. J. Paris, 1948²," (review article) *Podium*, V, 2 (februari 1949), pp. 113–120.

— *Phaenomenologie der religie en Complexe psychologie* (Diss. Groningen); commercial edition under the title of *Freud, Jung en de religie*. Assen, van Gorcum, 1951 (esp. pp. 9–34).
—, *Prof. Dr G. van der Leeuw: dienaar van God en hoogleraar te Groningen*. Introduction by H. de Vos. Amsterdam, Het Wereldvenster, 1951.
—, "Tussen twee vuren," *Podium*, VI, 6 (november–december 1951), pp. 403–496 and 497–544 (esp. pp. 443–452).
—, "De Europeaan," *De Nieuwe Stem*, VI, 2 (februari 1951), pp. 74–78.
—, "Prof. Dr. G. van der Leeuw in tienjarig perspectief," *Het Parool*, 26 November 1960.
—, "Voor en na Van der Leeuw," *Vox Theologica*, XXXI, 1 (september 1960), pp. 21–26.
Veen, J. M. van, "Prof. Dr. van der Leeuw†," *Wending*, V, 10 (december 1950), pp. 529–532.
- "Prof. Dr. G. van der Leeuw. 18 Maart 1890–18 November 1950," *Nederlands Theologisch Tijdschrift*, V (1950–51), pp. 129–139.
—, "De theoloog," *De Nieuwe Stem*, VI, 2 (februari 1951), pp. 79–81.
—, "Prof. G. van der Leeuw, 1890–1950. Een portret," *Wending*, XXV, 9 (november 1970), pp. 534–541.

3. Method and Theory

1918 *Plaats en taak van de godsdienstgeschiedenis in de theologische wetenschap*. Groningen–The Hague, J. B. Wolters.
1926 "Über einige neuere Ergebnisse der psychologischen Forschung und ihre Anwendung auf die Geschichte, insonderheit die Religionsgeschichte," *Studi e Materiali di Storia delle Religioni*, II, 1 (1926), pp. 1–43.
1928 "Strukturpsychologie und Theologie," *Zeitschrift für Theologie und Kirche*. N. F., IX (1928), pp. 321–349.
1930 "Phänomenologie der Religion," in: *Religion in Geschichte und Gegenwart*, IV (1930), pp. 1171 ff.
1931 "Söderblom's wetenschappelijke beteekenis," *Stemmen des Tijds*, XX (1931), pp. 136–144.
1933 "Epilegomena," in: G. van der Leeuw, *Phänomenologie der Religion*. Tübingen, Mohr. See also below.
1935 *Inleiding tot de theologie*. Amsterdam, H. J. Paris, 1935, 1948² (enlarged)
1938 "Rudolf Otto und die Religionsgeschichte," *Zeitschrift für Theologie und Kirche*, XIX (1938), pp. 71–81.

4. Main Publications

1916 *Godsvoorstellingen in de oud-Aegyptische pyramidetexten*. Leiden, E. J. Brill.
1918 "Eenige opmerkingen over de onderlinge verhouding der begrippen God, macht en ziel," *Theologisch Tijdschrift* (1918), pp. 123 ff.
1918 "External soul, Schutzgeist und der ägyptische ka," *Zeitschrift für ägyptische Sprache und Altertumskunde*, LIV (1918), pp. 56 ff.
1919 *Historisch Christendom*. Utrecht, A. Oosthoek.
1920 "Das neuentdeckte Osirisheiligtum in Abydos und das sog. Natatorium der Villa Adriana," *Archiv für Religionswissenschaft*, XIX (1920), pp. 544 ff.

1920 "Process and drama," *The Constructive Quarterly*, VIII (1920), pp. 281 ff. *Dutch* text: "Proces en drama," in: *Nieuwe Theologische Studiën*, III (1920), pp. 209 ff.

1921 "Die do-ut-des-Formel in der Opfertheorie," *Archiv für Religionswissenschaft*, XX (1921), pp. 241 ff.

1924 *Inleiding tot de godsdienstgeschiedenis*. Haarlem, Bohn. Second, completely revised edition under the title of *Inleiding tot de phaenomenologie van den godsdienst*. Haarlem, Bohn, 1948. *German* translation: *Einführung in die Phänomenologie der Religion*. München, 1925. Second, completely revised edition by H. C. Piper, ed. München, 1961.

1924 *Mystiek*. Baarn, Hollandia.

1926 „Zum Mythus und zur Gestalt des Osiris," *Archiv für Orientforschung*, III (1926), pp. 9 ff.

1927 *Goden en menschen in Hellas*. Haarlem, Bohn.

1927 *Achnaton. Een religieuze en aesthetische revolutie in de veertiende eeuw voor Christus*. Amsterdam, H. J. Paris.

1928 *La structure de la mentalité primitive*. (Cahiers de la Revue d'Histoire et de Philosophie Religieuse, 15). Paris, Felix Alcan, (Publication d'abord dans la *Revue d'Histoire et de Philosophie Religieuse*, 1928).

1929 "Das Heilige und das Schöne," *Zeitschrift für Religionspsychologie*, II (1929), pp. 101 ff.

1930 "Phénoménologie de l'âme," *Bulletin de la Société d'histoire du Protestantisme*, (janvier–mars 1930).

1930 *In den hemel is eenen dans . . . Over de religieuze beteekenis van dans en optocht*. Amsterdam, H. J. Paris. *German* translation by Clercq van Weel: '*In dem Himmel ist ein Tanz . . .*' *Über die religiöse Bedeutung des Tanzes und des Festzuges*. München, 1931.

1931 "Die Struktur der Vorstellung des sogenannten Höchsten Wesens," *Archiv für Religionswissenschaft*, XXIX (1931), pp. 79 ff.

1931 "Sur le nom et la personalité des dieux dans les religions primitives," *Revue d'Histoire et de Philosophie Religieuses* (1931), pp. 241 ff.

1932 *Wegen en grenzen. Studie over de verhouding van religie en kunst*. Amsterdam, H. J. Paris. Second impression, considerably expanded, under the title of *Wegen en grenzen*. Amsterdam, H. J. Paris, 1948². Third edition, revised and edited by E. L. Smelik under the title of *Wegen en grenzen. Een studie over de verhouding van religie en kunst*. Amsterdam, H. J. Paris, 1955³). *English* translation of the German edition by David E. Green: *Sacred and Profane Beauty: the Holy in Art*. Preface by Mircea Eliade. London. Weidenfeld and Nicolson; Nashville–New York, Abingdon Press, and Holt, Rinehart & Winston, pb. 1963. *German* translation of the 3rd edition, by Frau Dr. A. Piper: *Vom Heiligen in der Kunst*. Gütersloh, Bertelsmann Verlag. 1957.

1932 "Pia fraus. Een phaenomenologisch-psychologische studie," *Mensch en Maatschappij*, VIII (1932), pp. 365 ff.

1933 *Phänomenologie der Religion*, (Neue Theologische Grundrisse). Tübingen, J. C. B. Mohr. Revised and enlarged, on the basis of the French edition (1956²). *English* translation by J. E. Turner: *Religion in Essence and Manifestation: a Study in Phenomenology*. London, Allen & Unwin, 1938. Second edition in two volumes with Appendices, incorporating the additions of the second German edition, made by Hans H. Penner: New York— Evanston, Harper Torch-books (TB 100/101), 1963.

French authorized translation by Jacques Marty on the basis of additions made by Van der Leeuw to the first German edition: *La religion dans son essence et ses manifestations: Phénoménologie de la religion.* (Bibliothèque scientifique). Paris, Payot, 1948, 1970².

Italian tranlation: *Fenomenologia della religione.* Torino, 1960.

Polish translation by Jerzy Prokopiuk: *Fenomenologia religii.* Warszawa, Książka i Wiedza, around 1975 (in preparation).

1933 *Onsterfelijkheid of opstanding?* Assen. 1936² (expanded), 1938³ (expanded), 1947⁴ (expanded).

German translation: *Unsterblichkeit oder Auferstehung.* (Theologische Existenz heute, 52). 1956.

1933 *Dogmatische brieven.* Amsterdam, H. J. Paris.

1933 "The Συμβολα in Firmicus Maternus," in: *Egyptian Religion*, Vol. I, p. 61.

1933 "Nog eens het oermonotheïsme. Methode en theologie," *Studia Catholica*, IV (1933), pp. 397–404.

1933 "Die sogenannte "epische Einleitung" der Zauberformeln," *Zeitschrift für Religionspsychologie*, VI (1933), p. 161.

1934 *Muziek en religie, in verband met de verhouding van woord en toon.* Amsterdam.

1934 "De psychologie van Kierkegaard," *Algemeen Nederlandsch Tijdschrift voor Wijsbegeerte en Psychologie*, XXVII (1934), pp. 21 ff.

1934 "The contending of Horus and Seth," in: *Egyptian Religion*, Vol. II, pp. 106 ff.

1934 "The reality of heathenism," *The Student World*, XXVII (1934), pp. 292 ff.
French translation: "L'actualité du paganisme," *Cahiers de Foi et Vie*, décembre 1934; *Le monde non chrétien*, Nr. 6 (1934), pp. 5 ff.
German translation: "Die Wirklichkeit des Heidentums," *Die Furche*, XXI (1935), pp. 230 ff.

1935 *Inleiding tot de theologie.* Amsterdam, H. J. Paris. Revised 1948².

1935 *De zin der geschiedenis* (Address). Groningen–Batavia, J. B. Wolters.

1935 "Refrigerium. Paradijsvoorstellingen in heidendom en christendom," *Handelingen van het 16ᵉ Nederlandse Philologencongres, gehouden te Groningen op 25 en 26 April 1935*, pp. 108 ff.
German translation (expanded): "Refrigerium," *Mnemosynes Bibliothecae Classicae Bataväe* (Leiden), Series III, Vol. 3 (1936), pp. 125–148.

1935 "In hoeverre kan men van een homo religiosus spreken en in hoeverre is deze eventueel psychologisch te beschrijven?" *Algemeen Nederlandsch Tijdschrift voor Wijsbegeerte en Psychologie*, XXIX (1935–36), pp. 36–45.

1937 *Bach's Matthaeuspassion.* Amsterdam, H. J. Paris. 1938², 1941³, 1947⁵.

1937 *De primitieve mensch en de religie. Anthropologische studie.* Groningen– Batavia, J. B. Wolters. 1952².
French translation: *L'homme primitif et la religion. Etude anthropologique.* (Bibliothèque de philosophie contemporaine). Paris, 1940.

1937 "Phaenomenologie der openbaring," *Vox Theologica*, VIII (1937), pp. 125 ff.

1938 *Vriendschap met God.* Amsterdam, Noord-Hollandsche Uitg. Mij. 1947².

1938 "Eenige opmerkingen betreffende den huidigen stand van onze kennis en ons inzicht aangaande Achnaton," *Jaarbericht Ex Oriente Lux*, V (1938), pp. 301 ff.

1938 "Das sogenannte Hockerbegräbnis und der ägyptische TJKNW," *Studi e Materiali di Storia delle Religioni*, XIV (1938), pp. 151 ff.

1939 *Het beeld Gods*. Amsterdam, Uitg. Mij. Holland.

1939 *Virginibus puerisque. A study on the service of children in worship*. Amsterdam, Noord-Hollandsche Uitg. Mij.

1939 G. van der Leeuw, in collaboration with K. Ph. Bernet Kempers, *Beknopte geschiedenis van het kerklied*. Groningen–Batavia, J. B. Wolters. 1948².

1939 "Phaenomenologie van den geest," *Vox Theologica*, XI (1939), p. 37 ff.

1940 *Balans van het Christendom*. Amsterdam, H. J. Paris. 1946², 1947³. *German* translation: *Die Bilanz des Christentums*. Zürich, 1947.

1940 *De verhouding van God en mensch vroeger en nu*. Amsterdam, Noord-Hollandsche Uitg. Mij. 1942².

1940 *Liturgiek*. Nijkerk, Callenbach. 1946².

1940 *De Bijbel als boek. Korte inleiding tot de Bijbel als geheel*. Amsterdam, H. J. Paris. 1954².

1940 "Altägyptischer Pantheismus." *Aus der Welt der Religion*, N. F. 1–3 (Rudolf-Otto-Ehrung), pp. 16 ff.

1940–41 G. van der Leeuw, ed., *De Godsdiensten der wereld*, 2 vols. Amsterdam, H. Meulenhoff. Author of "Inleiding" (Vol. I, pp. 1 ff.), "De religie der primitieven" (Vol. I, pp. 7 ff.), "Grieksche religie" (Vol. II, pp. 1 ff.). 1948².

1941 *Der Mensch und die Religion. Anthropologischer Versuch*. (Philosophia Universalis, 2). Basel, Verlag Haus zum Falken.

1941 *Gallicinium. De haan in de oudste hymnen der Westersche kerk*. Amsterdam, Noord-Hollandsche Uitg. Mij.

1941 "De twee wegen der theologie," *Vox Theologica*, XIII (1941), pp. 17 ff.

1941 "Structuur en object van de godsdienstgeschiedenis met betrekking tot geschiedenis en philologie," *Jaarboek Oostersch Instituut* (Leiden), pp. 65–70.

1942 *Antieke roep- en klaagliederen*. 's-Graveland.

1942 *Jan Hendrik Gerretsen*. The Hague.

1942 "Religionsgeschichte und persönliches religiöses Leben," in: *In Deo Omnia Unum. Eine Sammlung von Aufsätzen Friedrich Heiler zum 50. Geburtstage dargebracht*. München, pp. 4–24.

1942 "Adunata," *Jaarbericht Ex Oriente Lux*, VIII (1942), pp. 632 ff.

1942 "De beteekenis van het begrip mythe," *Het Gemeenebest*, IV (1942), pp. 223 ff.

1942 "Beeld van den mensch en beeld van God," *De Gids*, CVI, 3 (1942), pp. 130 ff.

1943 *Uren met Novalis*. Baarn. 1945².

1944 *De godsdienst van het oude Egypte*. The Hague, Servire, 1944.

1944 "Inzichten betreffende godsdienst en geschiedenis aan het eind der achttiende en het begin der negentiende eeuw," in: *Geschiedenis*. Een bundel studies, aangeboden aan Prof. Dr W. J. Aalders bij zijn afscheid als hoogleraar aan de Rijksuniversiteit te Groningen, 1942. Assen, pp. 122 ff.

1945 *Balans van Nederland*. Amsterdam, H. J. Paris.

1946 *Bach's Johannes Passion*. Amsterdam, H. J. Paris.

1946 *De botsing tusschen heidendom en christendom in de eerste vier eeuwen*. Amsterdam, Noord-Hollandsche Uitg. Mij.

1946 "Fenomenologieky popis církve," *Náboženská*, XVII (1946), pp. 354 ff. *French* translation: "Description phénoménologique de l'Eglise," *Le Monde non-chrétien*, Nr. 17 (janvier–mars 1951), pp. 15–26.

1947 *Nationale cultuurtaak.* The Hague, D. A. Daamen.
1947 "L'antropomorphisme comme forme de l'anthropologie," *Le Monde non-chrétien*, N. S., II (1947), pp. 170 ff.
1947 "Het Nabije Oosten," in: H. van Oyen, ed., *Philosophia. Beknopt handboek tot de geschiedenis van het wijsgerig denken.* Vol. I, Utrecht, pp. 20 ff.
1948 *Levensvormen.* Amsterdam, H. J. Paris.
1948 *Inleiding tot de phaenomenologie van den godsdienst.* (Theologia, 2). Haarlem, Bohn. (This is the second, completely revised edition of *Inleiding tot de godsdienstgeschiedenis* of 1924).
1948 *Menswording en cultuurverschuiving. Een anthropologisch probleem.* Antwerpen.
1948 "Les deux philosophies. Préambule à une phénoménologie de la philosophie," *Bibliothèque du Xe Congrès International de Philosophie*, Vol. II "Mélanges Philosophiques," pp. 94 ff.
1948 "De religie van de voorhistorische mens," *Mens en maatschappij*, XXIII (1948), pp. 239 ff.
1948 "Dans en beschaving," in: *Exuli Amico Huizinga historico Amici non historici Die VII mensis Decembris Anni MCMXLII.* Haarlem, p. 124 ff.
1948 "Der Anthropomorphismus als Problem der Anthropologie," in: G. van der Leeuw and R. Bultmann, *Gottesbild und Menschenbild.* Stuttgart. pp. 5 ff.
1949 *Sacramentstheologie.* Nijkerk, G. F. Callenbach.
    German translation by Eva Schwarz: *Sakramentales Denken. Erscheinungsformen und Wesen der auszerchristlichen und christlichen Sakramente.* Geleitwort von Dr. Wilhelm Stählin. Kassel, Joh. Standa Verlag, 1959.
1949 *Egyptische eschatologie.* Amsterdam, Noord-Hollandsche Uitg. Mij.
1949 "Nihilisme en Christelijk geloof. Een briefwisseling," *Wending*, IV (1949), p. 2 ff.
1949 "L'homme et la civilisation. Ce que peut comprendre le terme: évolution de l'homme," *Eranos Jahrbuch*, XVI (1948). Zürich, 1949, pp. 141 ff.
1949 "Lucien Lévy-Bruhl en de primitieve mentaliteit," *Nederlands Studieblad*, XI (1949), pp. 194 ff.
1949 "Poëzie als religie," *Podium*, V (1949), pp. 551 ff.
1950 "Die Bedeutung der Mythen," in: *Festschrift Alfred Bertholet.* Tübingen, Mohr, pp. 287–293.
1950 "Urzeit und Endzeit," *Eranos Jahrbuch*, XVII (1949). Zürich, 1950, pp. 329 ff.
1950 "The task of religion in the modern world," *Atti della Riuniona della Sodalitas Erasmiana.* Vol. I, Napoli, pp. 80 ff.
    Dutch text: "De betekenis van de religie in de ontwikkeling der moderne wereld," *Wending*, IV (1950), pp. 713 ff.
1950 "Tanz und Religion," in: *Du* (Schweizerische Monatschrift), 5. Mai 1950.
1950 "De phaenomenologie van den twijfel," in: *Twijfel en geloof.* Amsterdam, p. 45 ff.
1950 "Muziek en Literatuur," in: *Cultuurgeschiedenis van het Christendom*, Vol. III. Amsterdam, Elsevier, pp. 379–396. Reissued under the title of "De Kunst" in Vol. II. 1957², pp. 1176–1192.
1951 "Unsterblichkeit," *Eranos Jahrbuch*, XVIII (1950). Zürich, 1951, pp. 183 ff.
1951 "Krieg und Kampf bei Primitiven," in: *Vom christlichen Geheimnis.* Gesammelte Arbeiten zum Gedächtnis von Odo Casel O. S. B. Düsseldorf, Patmos-Verlag, pp. 337–343.

French translation: "Guerre et combat chez les primitifs," *Le Monde non-chrétien*, Nr. 19 (juillet–septembre 1951), pp. 350–358.

1951 "De crisis der universiteit," *Wending*, V, 11 (januari 1951), pp. 604–611.

1960 *De onrust der mensheid*. Edited by W. J. Kooiman. Amsterdam, W. ten Have.

ALFRED G. L. LEHMANN

Main Publications

1890 *Hypnosen og de dermed beslaegtede normale Tilstande*. København.
   German translation: *Die Hypnosen und die damit verwandten normalen Zustande*. Vorlesungen. Leipzig, 1890.

1893–1896 *Overtro og troldom fra de aeldste tider til vore dage*. København, Frimodt.
   German translation: *Aberglaube und Zauberei von den ältesten Zeiten an bis in die Gegenwart*. Deutsche autorisierte Übersetzung von Dr. Petersen. Stuttgart, Enke, 1898; 1908² (revised and increased); 1925³ (completed up to date).

FRIEDRICH RUDOLF LEHMANN

Main Publications

1922 *Mana. Der Begriff des "ausserordentlich Wirkungsvollen" bei Südseevölkern*. Leipzig, Otto Spamer.

1930 *Die polynesischen Tabusitten. Eine ethno-soziologische und religionswissenschaftliche Untersuchung*. (Veröffentlichungen des Staatlichen Forschungsinstituts für Völkerkunde, Band 10). Leipzig, 1930.

1966 "Versuche, die Bedeutung des Wortes 'Mana' im Bereich der Sprachen der polynesischen Inselwelt festzustellen," in: *Festschrift Walter Baetke dargebracht*, zu seinem 80. Geburtstag am 28. März 1964. Weimar, Hermann Böhlaus Nachfolger, 1966, pp. 215–240.

JOHANNES EDVARD LEHMANN

1. Bibliography

Festskrift udgivet af Københavns Universitet i anleding af Universitet Aarfest, November 1930, København, 1930, pp. 148ff.

2. Main Publications

1897 *Hedensk Monoteisme. Bidrag til Gudsbegrebets historie.* (Philologisk–Historisk Samfund. Studier fra Sprog- og Oldtidsforskning. Nr. 31). København.
1899–1902 *Zarathustra. En Bog om Persernes ganmle Tro,* 2 vols. København.
1904 *Mystik i Hedenskab og Kristendom.* København.
  English translation by G. M. G. Hunt: *Mysticism in Heathendom and Christendom.* London, Luzac & Co., 1910.
1911 *Der Buddhismus als indische Sekte, als Weltreligion.* Tübingen.
1912 *Textbuch zur Religionsgeschichte.* Herausg. von E. Lehmann. Leipzig, Deichert. Zweite Auflage herausg. von E. Lehmann und H. Haas. Leipzig–Erlangen, 1922² (enlarged edition).
1917 *Stället och vägen. Ett religionshistorisk perspektiv.* (Olaus Petri-Stiftelsens Serie). Stockholm, Geber, XII + 399 pp.
  Danish translation: *Stedet och vejen. Et religionshistorisk perspektiv.* København, 1918.
1925 *Lehrbuch der Religionsgeschichte.* Begründet von P. D. Chantepie de la Saussaye. Vierte Auflage herausg. von A. Bertholet und E. Lehmann. Tübingen, Mohr, 1925⁴. See especially "Zur Geschichte der Religionsgeschichte," (pp. 1–22), and "Erscheinungs- und Ideewelt der Religion" (pp. 23–130).

JOHANNES LEIPOLDT

1. Bibliography

"Bibliographie Johannes Leipoldt," *Theologische Literaturzeitung,* Vol. 75 (1950) pp. 755–758.
Theologische Literaturzeitung, Vol. 75 (1950), pp. 755–758.
Haufe, Günter, "Bibliographie Johannes Leipoldt 1960–1965," *Theologische Literaturzeitung,* Vol. 91, Nr. 8 (August 1966), pp. 635–638.

2. Main Publications

1903 *Schenute von Atripe und die Entstehung des national ägyptischen Christentums.* (O. von Gebhardt and A. Harnack: Texte und Unterusuchungeu zur Geschichte der altchristlichen Literatur. N. F. ,Band 10, Heft 1).
1905 *Didymus der Blinde von Alexandria.* (O. van Gebhardt and A.Harnack: Texte und Untersuchungen zur Geschichte der altchristlichen Literatur. N. F., Band 14, Heft 3).
1906 *Sinuthii Archimandritae vita et opera omnia.* Ed. J. Leipoldt. (Corpus Scriptorum Christianorum Orientalium. Scriptores Coptici. Ser. 2, Vol. 2, 4, 5, 16, etc.)
1907–1908 *Geschichte des neutestamentlichen Kanons,* 2 vols. Leipzig.
1913 *Vom Jesusbilde der Gegenwart.* Leipzig.
1927 *Das Gotteserlebnis Jesu im Lichte der vergleichenden Religionsgeschichte.* ('Αγγελος, Beihefte. Heft 2). Leipzig.

1931 *Dionysos.* (Ἄγγελος, Beihefte. Heft 3). Leipzig.
1933 *Antisemitismus in der alten Welt.* Leipzig.
1935 *Gegenwartsfragen in der neutestamentlichen Wissenschaft.* Leipzig.
1936 *Jesus und Paulus – Jesus oder Paulus? Ein Wort an Paulus' Gegner.* Leipzig.
1937 *Der Gottesdienst der ältesten Kirche jüdisch? griechisch? christlich?* Leipzig.
1952 *Der soziale Gedanke in der altchristlichen Kirche.* Leipzig.
1953 *Heilige Schriften. Betrachtungen zur Religionsgeschichte der antiken Mittelmeerwelt.* By J. Leipoldt and Siegfried Morenz. Leipzig.
1954 *Der koptische Text der Kirchenordnung Hyppolits.* Herausg. und übersetzt von W. Till und J. Leipoldt. (Texte und Untersuchungen zur Geschichte der altchristlichen Literatur, Vol. 58).

HEINRICH LESZMANN

Main Publications

1905 *Die Kyrossage in Europa.* Berlin.
1908 *Aufgaben und Ziele der vergleichenden Mythenforschung.* (Gesellschaft für vergleichende Mythenforschung. Mythologische Bibliothek. Band I, Heft 4). Berlin.
1922 *Der deutsche Volksmund im Lichte der Sage.* Herausg. und mit einem Geleitwort versehen von Georg Hüsing. Berlin–Leipzig. 1937².

JAMES HENRY LEUBA

1. Bibliography

Grinstein, A., *The Index of Psycho-Analytic Writings.* New York, International Universities Press, 1958, Vol. 3, pp. 1208–1209.

2. Biography and Appreciation

Wobbermin, G., "Leuba als Religionspsychologe," *Religion und Geisteskultur,* VII (1913), pp. 282–291.

3. Main Publications

1896 "Studies in the psychology of religious phenomena: the religious motive, conversion, facts and doctrines," *American Journal of Psychology,* VII, 3 (1896), pp. 309–385.
1909 *The Psychological Origin and the Nature of Religion.* Chicago, Open Court; London, Constable.

1909 "Magic and Religion," *Sociological Review* II, 1 (1909), pp. 20–35.
1912 *A Psychological Study of Religion. Its Origin, Function and Future.* New York, Macmillan.
1916 *The Belief in God and Immorality. A Psychological, Anthropological and Statistical Study.* Boston, Sherman, French & Company. Chicago, Open Court, 1921.
1919 "The Yoga System of Mental Concentration and Religious Mysticism," *Journal of Philosophy*, XVI (1919), pp. 197–207.
1921 "The Meaning of 'Religion' and the Place of Mysticism in Religious Life," *Journal of Philosophy*, XVIII (1921).
1925 *The Psychology of Religious Mysticism.* New York, Harcourt, Brace & Co.; London, Kegan Paul, Trench, Trübner.
1933 *God or Man? A Study of the Value of God to Man.* New York, Holt. London, Kegan Paul, Trench, Trübner, 1934.
1937 "The Making of a Psychologist of Religion," in: *Religion in Transition.* Vergilius Ferm, ed. London, Allen & Unwin; New York, Macmillan.

LUCIEN LÉVY-BRUHL*

1. Bibliography

Cazeneuve, Jean, "Principaux ouvrages de Lucien Lévy-Bruhl," in: Jean Cazeneuve, *Lucien Lévy-Bruhl. Sa vie, son œuvre, avec un exposé de sa philosophie.* ("Philosophes"). Paris, Presses Universitaires de France, 1963, pp. 15–16.
Rivaud, A., *Notice sur la vie et les travaux de Lucien Lévy-Bruhl.* Institut de France, Académie des Sciences Morales et Politiques. Paris, 1950.

2. Biography and Appreciation

Aldrich, C. R., *The Primitive Mind and Modern Civilization.* London, Kegan Paul, 1931.
Allier, Raoul, *Le non-civilisé et nous (Différence irréductible ou identité foncière?).* Paris, Payot, 1927.
Blondel, Charles, *La mentalité primitive.* Paris, Stock, 1926.
Bréhier, Emile, "Originalité de Lévy-Bruhl," *Revue Philosophique de la France et de l'Etranger,* oct.-déc. 1949, pp. 385–388.
Bunzel, Ruth L., "Introduction," in: Lucien Lévy-Bruhl, *How Natives Think.* New York, Washington Square Press, pb. 1966, pp. V–XVIII.
Cailliet, E., *Mysticisme et "mentalité mystique".* Etude d'un problème posé par les travaux de M. Lévy-Bruhl sur la mentalité primitive. Cahors, A. Coueslant, 1937.
Cazeneuve, Jean, "Les Zuñis dans l'œuvre de Lévy-Bruhl," *Revue Philosophique,* CXLVII (1957), pp. 530–538.
, *La mentalité archaïque.* Paris, A. Colin, 1961.
, *Lucien Lévy-Bruhl. Sa vie, son œuvre, avec un exposé de sa philosophie.* ("Philosophes"). Paris, Presses Universitaires de France, 1963.

—, "Note sur la sociologie religieuse de Lévy-Bruhl," *Archives de Sociologie des Religions*, 10ᵉ Année, No 20 (juillet–décembre 1965), pp. 75—77.

Chang-Chi Chang, *La morale et le sociologisme de Lucien Lévy-Bruhl*. (Diss. Grenoble). Lyon, Bosc frères, M. & L. Rion, 1937.

Charevskaia, B., "Confusions méthodologiques et terminologiques dans la question de mentalité des primitifs" (in Russian), *Sovietskaia Ethnografia*, 1958, Nr. 6, pp. 61–75.

Davy, Georges, "Pour le centième anniversaire de la naissance de Lucien Lévy-Bruhl," *Revue Philosophique*, CXLVII (1957), pp. 468–493.

Evans-Pritchard, E. E., "The theory of primitive mentality," *Bulletin of the Faculty of Arts, Egyptian University* (Cairo), 1934.

—, "Lucien Lévy-Bruhl," *Man*, XL (1940), Nr. 27, pp. 24–25.

Eysink, Rudolf, *Collectieve voorstellingen in het denken der natuurvolken*. (Diss. Utrecht). Utrecht, Neerlandia, 1946.

Fahrenfort, J. J., *Dynamisme en logisch denken bij natuurvolken. Bijdrage tot de psychologie der primitieven*. Groningen, 1933.

Faye, J.-P., "Lévy-Bruhl et l'inconscient collectif. Du rêve au rite," *Revue Philosophique*, CXLVII (1957), pp. 539–555.

Gilson, Etienne, "Le Descartes de Lucien Lévy-Bruhl," *Revue Philosophique*, CXLVII (1957), pp. 432–451.

Gurvitch, Georges, "Le problème de la sociologie de la connaissance," *Revue Philosophique*, CXLVII (1957), pp. 494–502.

Keller, E., "Lévy-Bruhl et le prélogisme des primitifs," in: *La sorcellerie dans les pays de mission*. Compte rendu de la XIVᵉ semaine de missiologie de Louvain. Bruxelles, 1936, pp. 125–141.

Kits van Heyningen, A., *Westersche intellectproeven en primitieve psyche*. Diss. Leiden, 1925.

Kohlbrugge, J. F. M., "Primitieve denkwijze," *Tijdschrift v. h. Kon. Ned. Aardrijkskundig Genootschap*, 2nd S., 37 (37 (1920), pp. 729–739.

—, "De mentaliteit van den primitieven mensch en van zijn kinderen," *De Indische Gids*, LVIII (1936), pp. 769–788.

Koppers, Wilhelm, "Lévy-Bruhl und das Ende des "Prälogischen Denkens" der Primitiven," *Actes du XIVᵉ Congrès International de Sociologie* (Rome, 30 août–3 sept. 1950), Vol. IV.

Laguna, Frederica de, "Lévy-Bruhl's contributions to the study of primitive mentality," *Philosophical Review*, XLIX (1940), pp. 552–556.

Larguier des Bancels, Jean, "Prélogique et civilisés," *Archives de psychologie* (Genève), mai 1926, pp. 1–12.

Leeuw, G. van der, *L'homme primitif et la religion. Etude anthropologique*. Paris, 1940. The original Dutch text was published in 1937.

Leenhardt, Maurice, "Les carnets de Lucien Lévy-Bruhl," *Cahiers Internationaux de Sociologie*, VI (1949), pp. 28–42.

—, "Préface," in: *Les carnets de Lucien Lévy-Bruhl*. Paris, Presses Universitaires de France, 1949, pp. V–XXI.

—, "Témoignage," *Revue Philosophique*, CXLVII (1957), pp. 414–415.

Lenoir, Raymond, "La mentalité primitive," *Revue de Métaphysique et de Morale*, 1922, pp. 199–224.

—, "Lucien Lévy-Bruhl, 1857–1939," *American Journal of Sociology*, XLIV (1938–39), p. 980.

Leroy, Olivier, *La Raison primitive (Essai de réfutation de la théorie du prélogisme)*. Paris, Geuthner, 1927.

Lévinas, Emmanuel, "Lévy-Bruhl et la philosophie contemporaine," *Revue Philosophique*, CXLVII (1957), pp. 556–569.

Lindworsky, J., "Vom Denken der Vormenschen," *Anthropos*, XII–XIII (1917–18), pp. 419 ff.

—, "Die Primitiven und das kausale Denken," *Intern. Woche für Religions-Ethnologie, IV. Tagung*. Paris, Geuthner, 1926.

Moelia, T. S. G., *Het primitieve denken in de moderne wetenschap*. (Diss. Leiden). Groningen, 1933.

Ouy, Achille, "La mentalité primitive chez les peuples civilisés," in: *Mélanges économiques et sociaux, offerts à Emile Witmeur*. Paris, Librairie du Receuil Sirey, 1939, pp. 264–270.

Podach, E. F., "Zum Abschluss von L. Lévy-Bruhls Theorie über die Mentalität der Primitiven," *Zeitschrift für Ethnologie*, LXXVI (1951), pp. 42–49.

Poirier, Jean, "La pensée ethnologique de Lucien Lévy-Bruhl," *Revue Philosophique*, CXLVII (1957), pp. 503–529.

Revue Philosophique de la France et de l'Etranger. "Numéro spécial à l'occasion du Centenaire de la naissance de Lucien Lévy-Bruhl," 82e Année, Tome CXLVII, No. 4 (octobre–décembre 1957), pp. 397–569. (This issue contains 20 contributions on L. Lévy-Bruhl).

Rivaud, A., *Notice sur la vie et les travaux de Lucien Lévy-Bruhl*. Institut de France, Académie des Sciences Morales et Politiques. Paris, 1950.

Schuhl, Pierre-Maxime, "Hommage à Lucien Lévy-Bruhl," *Revue Philosophique*, CXLVII (1957), pp. 398–403.

Storch, Alfred, "Das primitive mythische Denken und seine Beziehungen zur Psychopathologie," *Proceedings and Papers of the VIIIth Int. Congress of Psychology*, held at Groningen from 6–11 Sept. 1926. Groningen, 1927, pp. 209 ff.

Wallon, Henri, "La mentalité primitive et la raison," *Revue Philosophique*, CXLVII (1957), pp. 461–467.

"Note biographique sur Lévy-Bruhl," *Revue Philosophique*, CXLVII (1957), pp. 404–406.

3. Main Publications

1885 *L'idée de responsabilité*. Paris, Hachette.

1889 *L'Allemagne depuis Leibniz*. Essai sur le développement de la conscience nationale en Allemagne. Paris, Hachette.

1894 *La philosophie de Jacobi*. Paris, Alcan.

1899 *History of Modern Philosophy in France*. Chicago, The Open Court Publishing Comp.

1899 "Introduction," in: *Lettres inédites de John Stuart Mill à Auguste Comte*. Publiées avec les réponses de Comte. Paris, Alcan.

1900 *La philosophie d'Auguste Comte*. Paris, Alcan. 1913^3 (revised).
English authorized translation with introduction by Frederic Harrison: *The Philosophy of Auguste Comte*. New York, Putnam, 1903.
German translation by H. Molenaar: *Die Philosophie August Comte's*. Leipzig, Verlag Dürr'schen Buchhandlung, 1902.

1903 *La morale et la science des mœurs*. Paris, Alcan. 1910^4 (revised), 1919^6 (revised), 1953^15.
English translation by Elizabeth Lee: *Ethics and Moral Science*. London, Constable, 1905.

1910 *Les fonctions mentales dans les sociétés inférieures*. Paris, Alcan. 1912[2], 1922[5, 6, 7], 1928[8], 1951[9].
English authorized translation by Lilian A. Clare: *How Natives Think*. London, G. Allen & Unwin, 1926; New York, A. A. Knopf, 1927. Pb. edition with introduction by Ruth L. Bunzel: New York, Washington Square Press, Inc., 1966.
German translation, edited with introduction by W. Jerusalem: *Das Denken der Naturvölker*. Wien, Braumüller, 1921, 1926[3].
1915 *La conflagration européenne. Les causes économiques et politiques*. Paris, Alcan.
1916 *Jean Jaurès*. Esquisse biographique suivie de lettres inédites. Paris, Rieder.
1916 *Quelques pages sur Jean Jaurès*. Paris, Librairie de l'Humanité.
1922 *La mentalité primitive*. Paris, Alcan. 1922[2], 1925[4], 1947[14].
English authorized translation by Lilian A. Clare: *Primitive Mentality*. New York, Macmillan, 1923.
German translation: *Die geistige Welt der Primitiven*. München, 1927, 1959[2].
1923 "La mentalité primitive," *Bulletin de la Société Française de Philosophie* (Paris), (1923), pp. 23 ff.
1924 "L'idéal républicain," *Revue de Paris*, I (1924), pp. 805–822. Also published separately: Paris, Editions du progrès civique, 1924.
1925 "La mentalité primitive," *Revue d'Ethnographie*, VI (1925), pp. 233 ff.
1926 "Mentalité primitive et jeu de hasard," *Revue de Paris*, mars 1926.
1927 "La mentalité primitive," *Proceedings and Papers of the VIIIth International Congress of Psychology*, held at Groningen from 6–11 Sept. 1926. Groningen, 1927, pp. 203 ff.
1927 *L'âme primitive*. Paris, Alcan. New edition: Paris, 1963.
English authorized translation by Lilian A. Clare: *The "Soul" of the Primitive*. 1929.
German translation: *Die Seele der Primitiven*. Wien, Braumüller, 1930.
1930 "Préface," in: *Les carnets de Schwartzkoppen. La vérité sur Dreyfus*. Edited by Bernhard Schwertfeger, translated from the German by A. Koyré. Paris, Rieder (P. U. F.).
1931 *La mentalité primitive*. The Herbert Spencer Lecture delivered at Oxford, 29th May 1931. Oxford.
1931 *Le surnaturel et la nature dans la mentalité primitive*. Paris, Alcan. New edition: Paris, P. U. F., 1963.
English authorized translation by Lilian A. Clare: *Primitives and the Supernatural*. New York, E. P. Dutton, 1935; London, Allen & Unwin, 1936.
1933 "Quelques aspects de la mentalité primitive," *Nouvelle Revue Française*, XLI (Septembre 1933), pp. 321–352.
1935 *La mythologie primitive*. Paris, Alcan.
. . . . *Le monde mythique des Australiens et des Papous*.
1936 *Morceaux choisis*. Edited by Jacques Soustelle. Paris, Gallimard.
1938 *L'expérience mystique et les symboles chez les primitifs*. Paris, Alcan.
1938 "Lettre à Jacques Maritain," *Revue Thomiste*, XLIV (1938), pp. 482 ff.
1949 *Les carnets de Lucien Lévy-Bruhl*. Préface de Maurice Leenhardt. Paris, P. U. F. Part of this book was previously published under the title of "Les 'Carnets' de Lucien Lévy-Bruhl" in *Revue Philosophique de la France et de l'Etranger*, CXXXVII (1947), pp. 257–281.

RALPH LINTON

1. Biography and Bibliography

Gillin, J., "Ralph Linton, 1893–1953," *American Anthropologist*, Vol. 56 (1954), pp. 274–281.

2. Main Publications

1923 *Annual Ceremony of the Pawnee Medicine Man.* Chicago, Field Museum of Natural History.
1923 *The material Culture of the Marquesas Island.* Honolulu, Hawaii, Bishop Museum Press.
1925 *Archaeology of the Marquesas Islands.* Honolulu, Hawaii, Bishop Museum Press.
1926 *Ethnology of Polynesia and Micronesia.* Chicago, Field Museum of Natural History.
1933 *The Tanala, a Hill Tribe of Madagascar. Marshall Field Expedition to Madagascar, 1926.* Chicago.
1936 *The Study of Man. An Introduction.* New York–London, D. Appleton-Century.
1940 *Acculturation in seven American Indian Tribes.* Ed. by R. Linton. New York–London, D. Appleton-Century.
1945 *The Cultural Background of Personality.* New York–London, D. Appleton-Century (Century Psychology Series); London, Kegan Paul, Trench, Trübner, 1947. (International Library of Sociology and Social Reconstruction.

ALFRED F. LOISY

1. Bibliography, Biography and Appreciation

Bonaccorsi, G., *Harnack e Loisy.* Firense, Libreri Editrice Fiorentina, 1904.
Desjardins, P., *Catholicisme et critique. Réflexions d'un profane sur l'Affaire Loisy.* (Cahier de la Quinzaine, Série VI, 57). 1906.
Heiler, F., *Der Vater des Katholischen Modernismus: Alfred Loisy (1857–1940).* München, Erasmus & Reinhardt, 1947. With bibliography.
Lacey, T. A., *Harnack and Loisy.* London, Longmans, 1904.
Leblanc, S., *Un Clerc qui n'a pas trahi. Alfred Loisy d'après ses Mémoires.* Paris, 1931.
Lepin, M., *Les Théories de M. Loisy. Exposé et critique.* Paris, Beauchesne, 1908.
Levie, J., *Sous les yeux de l'incroyant.* (Museum Lessianum, Section théologique, 40). Paris, 1946; Bruxelles, 1946².
Loisey, A. F., *Simples réflexions sur le Décret du Saint Office "Lamentabili sane exitu"* [dated: July 3, 1907] et sur l'Encyclique "Pascendi Dominici Gregis" [dated: September 8, 1907]. Ceffonds, 1908.
Petre, Maude D. M., *Alfred Loisy. His religious significance.* Cambridge, Cambridge University Press, 1944.

2. Main Publications

1892 *Histoire critique du Texte et des Versions de la Bible.* Vol. I: Amiens. Vol. II: published in *L'Enseignement Biblique* (A periodical).

1901 *Études bibliques.* Paris, 1901[1] (160 pp.). 1903[3] (revised and enlarged, pp. 97–335; pp. 1–96, containing the Preface, were suppressed by the author).

1901 *Les Mythes babyloniens et les premiers Chapitres de la Genèse.* Paris.

1902 *Études évangéliques.* Paris,

1901 *La Religion d'Israel.* Ceffonds, près Montier en-Der, 1908[2]; (second edition revised and enlarged); Paris, 1933[3] (revised and enlarged).
English translation by Arthur Galton: *The Religion of Israel.* London–Leipzig, Fisher Unwin, 1910.

1902 *L'Evangile et l'Église.* [A reply to A. Harnack's *Das Wesen des Christentums*]. Paris; Bellevue (S.-et-O.), 1903[2] (enlarged edition).
English translation by C. Home: *The Gospel and the Church.* London, Isbister, 1903; also London, Pitman & Sons, 1903: new edition with prefatory Memoir by the Rev. G. Tyrrell.

1903 *Le quatrième Evangile.* Paris.

1909 *Leçon d'Ouverture du Cours d'Histoire des Religions au Collège de France,* 24 avril 1909. Paris.

1910 *Jésus et la Tradition évangélique.* Paris.

1911 *A Propos d'Histoire des Religions.* Paris.

1914 *Les mystères païens et le mystère chrétien.* Paris, 1930[2] (revised and corrected edition).

1917 *La Religion.* Paris.

1920 *Essai historique sur le Sacrifice.* Paris.

1922 "De la méthode en histoire des religions," *Revue d'Histoire et de Littérature Religieuses,* 1922, pp. 13—36.

1926 *Religion et Humanité.* Paris.

1930–1931 *Mémoires pour servir à l'Histoire religieuse de notre temps,* 3 vols. Paris.

1933 *La Naissance du Christianisme.* Paris.
English authorized translation by L. P. Jacks: *The Birth of the Christian Religion.* London, Allen & Unwin, 1947.

1933 *Y a-t-il deux sources de la religion et de la morale?* Paris. 1934[2] (revised and enlarged edition).

1934 *Le Mandéisme et les origines chrétiennes.* Paris.

1936 *Les Origines du Nouveau Testament.* Paris.
English authorized translation by L. P. Jacks: *The Origins of the New Testament.* London, Allen & Unwin, 1950.

1938 *Histoire et mythe à propos de Jésus Christ.* Paris.

1938 *Autres mythes à propos de la religion.* Paris.

HERMANN LOMMEL

1. Biography and Bibliography

Rau, W., and Hoffmann, H., "Verzeichnis der Schriften von Hermann Lommel," *Paideuma*, Vol. VII (1959–61), pp. 147–155.
Festgabe für Hermann Lommel. Zur vollendung seines 75. Lebensjahres am 7. Juli 1960. Wiesbaden, 1960.

2. Main Publications

1912 *Die Religion Zarathustras nach dem Awesta dargestellt.* Tübingen.
1927 *Die Yäst's Awesta.* Übersetzt und eingeleitet von H. Lommel. (Quellen der Religionsgeschichte, Vol. 15).
1935 *Die alten Arier; von Art und Adel ihrer Götter.* Frankfurt am Main.

ROBERT H. LOWIE*

1. Bibliography

"Robert H. Lowie," *Boletín Bibliográfico de Antropología Americana*, X (1948), pp. 324–337. (Bibliography through 1946).
"Bibliography of Robert H. Lowie," prepared by Robert H. Lowie, Louella Cole Lowie, and Madge D. Richardson, *American Anthropologist*, LX (1958), pp. 362–375.
"Bibliography," in: Robert H. Lowie, *Robert H. Lowie Ethnologist. A Personal Record.* Berkeley–Los Angeles, University of California Press, 1959, pp. 181–198.

2. Biography and Appreciation

Kroeber, A. L., "Robert H. Lowie (1883–1957)," *Sociologus*, N. F., VIII (1958), pp. 1–3.
Lowie, Robert H., *Robert H. Lowie Ethnologist. A Personal Record.* Berkeley–Los Angeles, University of California Press, 1959. Comp. review in *American Anthropologist*, LXII (1960), pp. 1068–1073.
—, "Autobiographical Data by Robert H. Lowie," in: Cora du Bois, ed., *Lowie's Selected Papers in Anthropology.* Berkeley–Los Angeles, University of California Press, 1960, pp. 1–13.
Radin, Paul, "Robert H. Lowie 1883–1957," *American Anthropologist*, LX (1958), pp. 358–361.
"Robert H. Lowie 1883–1957," *Man*, LXII, No. 143 (1962), pp. 86–88.

3. Method and Theory

1905 "Ludwig Feuerbach: A Pioneer of Modern Thought," *Liberal Review*, February 1905, pp. 20–31.
1911 "A New Conception of Totemism," *American Anthropologist*, XIII (1911), pp. 189–207.
1912 "On the Principle of Convergence in Ethnology," *Journal of American Folklore*, XXV (1912), pp. 24–42.
1915 "Psychology and Sociology," *American Journal of Sociology*, XXI (1915), 217–229.
1916 "Historical and Sociological Interpretations of Kinship Terminologies," in: *Holmes Anniversary Volume* (1916), pp. 293–300.
1916 "Theoretical Ethnology," *Psychological Bulletin*, XIII (1916), 397–400.
1918 "Survivals and the Historical Method," *American Journal of Sociology* (1918), pp. 529–535.
1918 "The True Authority of Science," *Dial* (May 9, 1918), pp. 432–434.
1918 "Anthropology put to Work," *Dial* (August 15, 1918), pp. 98–100.
1923 "Psychology, Anthropology, and Race," *American Anthropologist*, XXV (1923), pp. 291–303.
1927 "Theoretische Ethnologie in Amerika," *Jahrbuch für Soziologie*, III (1927), pp. 111–124.
1931 "Hugo Obermaier's Reconstruction of Sequences among Prehistoric Cultures in the Old World," in: Stuart Rice, ed., *Methods in Social Science*, pp. 266–274.
1936 "Cultural Anthropology: a Science," *American Journal of Sociology*, XXXXII (1936), pp. 301–320.
1936 "Lewis H. Morgan in Historical Perspective," in: *Essays in Anthropology Presented to Alfred Louis Kroeber*. Berkeley, University of California Press, pp. 169–181.
1937 *The History of Ethnological Theory*. New York, Farrar & Rinehart.
    Spanish translation by Paul Kirchhoff: *Historia de la Etnología*, Mexico City, Fondo de Cultura Económica, 1946.
1953 "Ethnography, Cultural and Social Anthropology," *American Anthropologist*, LV (1953), pp. 527–534.
1953 "On Historical and Ethnographic Techniques," *American Anthropologist*, LV (1953), pp. 55–280.
1953 "Contemporary Currents in American Ethnology," *Ethnological Research*, XVII, 2 (1953), pp. 61–76.
1955 "Contemporary Trends in American Cultural Anthropology," *Sociologus*, N. S., V (1955), pp. 113–121.
1956 "Reminiscences of Anthropological Currents in America Half a Century Ago," *The American Anthropologist*, LVIII (1956), 995–1016.
1960 "Empathy, or 'seeing from within'," in: Stanley Diamond, ed., *Culture in History. Essays in Honor of Paul Radin*. New York, Columbia University Press, pp. 145–159.
1960 "Theories and theorists," as Part IV of *Lowie's Selected Papers in Anthropology* (1960), pp. 291–493.
. . . . "Development of Anthropology as a Science," in: H. M. Evans, ed., *Essays in the History of Science*. Seattle, University of Washington Press.

4. Main Publications

1908 "The Test-Theme in North American Mythology," *Journal of American Folklore*, XXI (1908), pp. 97–148.

1913 "Dance Associations of the Eastern Dakota," *Anthropological Papers* (American Museum of Natural History), XI (1913), pp. 103–142.

1913 "Societies of the Crow, Hidatsa and Mandan Indians," *Ibidem*, pp. 145–358.

1915 "The Sun Dance of the Crow Indians," *Ibidem*, XV (1916), pp. 1–50.

1915 "Dances and Societies of the Plains Shoshone," *Ibidem*, XV (1916), pp. 803–835.

1915 "Exogamy and the Classificatory Systems of Relationship," *American Anthropologist*, XVII (1915), pp. 223–239.

1917 *Culture and Ethnology.* New York, Douglas C. McMurtrie.

1918 "Myths and Tradition of the Crow Indians," *Anthropological Papers*, XXV (1918), pp. 1–308.

1919 "The Sun Dance of the Shoshone, Ute, and Hidatsa," XVI (1919), pp. 387–431.

1920 *Primitive Society*, New York, Boni & Liveright. 1947².
French translation by E. Métraux: *Traité de sociologie humaine*, Paris, Payot, 1935. New edition under the title of *Traité de sociologie primitive*. Paris, Payot, 1969.
Japanese translation, *I. Kawamura*. Dailchi, 1939.
Chinese translation: n. d.

1922 "The Religion of the Crow Indians," *Anthropological Papers*, XXV (1922), pp. 309–444.

1924 *Primitive Religion.* New York, Boni & Liveright. Second, revised edition, New York, Liveright, 1948².

1927 *The Origin of the State.* New York, Harcourt, Brace & Co.

1929 *Are we civilized?* New York, Harcourt, Brace & Co.

1931 "Indian Theologians," *American Mercury* (1931), pp. 472–479.

1934 *An Introduction to Cultural Anthropology.* New York, Farrar & Rinehart. Enlarged edition 1940².
French translation by E. Métraux: *Manuel d'anthropologie culturelle*, Paris, Payot, 1936.

1934 "Religious Ideas and Practices of the Eurasiatic and North American Areas," in: *Essays presented to C. G. Seligman*, pp. 183–188.

1935 *The Crow Indians.* New York, Farrar & Rinehart.

1945 *The German People; a Social Portrait to 1914.* New York, Farrar & Rinehart.

1954 *Indians of the Plains.* New York, McGraw-Hill.

1954 *Toward Understanding Germany.* Chicago, University of Chicago Press.

1958 "Individuum und Gesellschaft in der Religion der Naturvölker", *Zeitschrift für Ethnologie*, Vol. 83, pp. 161—169.

1959 "Bemerkungen über die Rolle der Religion im Alltagsleben der Crow-Indianer," *Zeitschrift für Ethnologie*, Vol. 84, pp. 1—4.

1960 *Lowie's Selected Papers in Anthropology.* Edited by Cora du Bois. Berkeley–Los Angelos, University of California Press.

JOHN LUBBOCK (LORD AVEBURY)

1. Biography and Bibliography

Hutchinson, H. G., *Life of Lord Avebury*, 2 vols. London, 1914.
The Lifework of Lord Avebury (Sir John Lubbock) 1834–1913. Ed. by his
   daughter The Hon. Mrs. Adrian Grant Duff. London, Watts, 1924.
   Bibliography of his Works on Anthropology, by Sir Arthur Keith, pp.
   101–104.

2. Main Publications

1865 *Prehistoric Times. As illustrated by Ancient Remains and the Manners
      and Customs of Modern Savages*. London, Williams & Norgate. 1913⁷.
1870 *The Origin of Civilisation, and the Primitive Condition of Man. Mental
      and Social Conditions of Savages*. London, Longmans. 1875³; 1902⁶.
1911 *Marriage, Totemism and Religion. An Answer to Critics*. London, Long-
      mans.
.... *The Social and Religious Condition of the Lower Races of Man. An Address*.
      (s. l., s. d.).

M

JOHN FERGUSON MACLENNAN

Main Publications

1865 *Primitive Marriage*. An inquiry into the Origin of the forms of capture in marriage ceremonies. Edinburgh. (See also 1876).
1869–1870 "The worship of animals and plants," *The Forthnightly Review*, VI (1869), pp. 407–427; VII (1870) pp. 194–216.
1876 *Studies in Ancient History*. Comprising a reprint of *Primitive Marriage*. London. (See also 1896).
1885 *The Patriarchial Theory*. London.
1896 *Studies in Ancient History*. The second print. Comprising an inquiry into the origin of exogamy. Ed. by his widow (Eleonore A. MacLennan) ᴠnd A. Platt. London–New York.

BRONISŁAW KASPAR MALINOWSKI*

1. Bibliography

Underwood, Frances Wenrich, "Bibliography," in: George Peter Murdock "Bronisław Malinowski," *American Anthropologist*, XLV, 3 (July–September, 1943), pp. 445–451.

2. Biography and Appreciation

Firth, Raymond, ed., *Man and Culture. An Evaluation of the Work of Bronisław Malinowski*. London, Routledge & Kegan Paul, 1957.
—, "Introduction," in Bronisław Malinowski, *A Diary in the Strict Sense of the Word*. London, Routledge & Kegan Paul, 1967, pp. XI–XIX.
Gluckman, Max, "Malinowski's contribution to social anthropology," *African Studies*, VI (1947), pp. 41–46.
—, *Malinowski's Sociological Theories*. (Rhodes–Livingstone Papers, 16). London, 1949.

Homans, G. C., "Anxiety and ritual: the theories of Malinowski and Radcliffe–Brown," *American Anthropologist*, XLIII (1941), pp. 164–172.

Josselin de Jong, J. P. B. de, "Herdenking van Bronisław Kaspar Malinowski (7 April 1884–16 Mei 1942)," *Jaarboek der Koninklijke Nederlandse Akademie van Wetenschappen*, 1946–47.

Kaberry, Phyllis, "Bronisław Malinowski, a citizen of the world," *Social Horizons* (Australian Institute of Sociology), 1943, pp. 89–92.

—, "Introduction," in Bronisław Malinowski, *The Dynamics of Culture Change. An Inquiry into Race Relations in Africa*. Edited by Phyllis M. Kaberry. New Haven (Conn), 1945.

Kluckhohn, Clyde, "Bronisław Malinowski," *Journal of American Folklore*, LVI (1943), pp. 208–219.

Leach, Edmund and Jarvie, I. C., "Frazer and Malinowski. A CA discussion. With Comments by E. Ardener, J. H. M. Beattie, E. Gellner and others," *Encounter*, XXV, 5 (1965), pp. 24–36. Republished in *Current Anthropology*, VII (1966), pp. 560–576.

Métraux, A., "Bronisław Malinowski 1884–1942," *Journal de la Société des Océanistes*, II, 2 (1946), pp. 215–217.

Murdock, George Peter, "Bronisław Malinowski," *American Anthropologist*, XLV (1943), pp. 441–451. (Including "Bibliography," compiled by Frances Wenrich Underwood).

Panoff, Michel, *Bronisław Malinowski*. (Petite Bibliothèque Payot Nr. 195). Paris, Payot, 1972, 156 pp.

Redfield, Robert, "Introduction," in: Bronisław Malinowski, *Magic, Science and Religion, and Other Essays*. New York, pb. Doubleday Anchor, 1952, pp. 9–13.

Reiwald, Paul, "Malinowski und die Ethnologie," in: Bronisław Malinowski, *Eine wissenschaftliche Theorie der Kultur und andere Aufsätze*. Übersetzt von Fritz Levi. Mit einer Einleitung von Paul Reiwald: Malinowski und die Ethnologie. (Int. Bibliothek für Psychologie und Soziologie, 8). Zürich, 1949, pp. 7–19.

Richards, Audrey I., "Bronisław Malinowski. Born 1884. Died 1942," *Man*, XLIII, 1 (1943).

Seagle, William, "Primitive law and Professor Malinowski," *American Anthropologist*, N. S., XXXIX (1937), pp. 275–290.

Symmons, Konstantin, "The origin of Malinowski's theory of magic," *The Polish Review*, V, 4, pp. 36–44.

3. *Method and Theory*

1922 "Ethnology and the study of Society," *Economica* (London School of Economics), II (1922), pp. 208–219.

1924 "Psychoanalysis and anthropology," *Psyche*, IV (1924), pp. 293–332.

1930 "The rationalization of anthropology and administration," *Africa*, III (1930), pp. 405–429.

1937 "Anthropology as the basis of social science," in: R. B. Cattell *et alii*, ed., *Human Affairs*. New York, Macmillan, pp. 199–252.

1938 "The scientific basis of applied anthropology," in: Reale Accademia d'Italia, *VIII Convegno 'Volta', Promosso dalla Classe delle Scienze Morali e Storiche*. Roma.

1939 "The present state of studies in culture contact," *Africa*, XII (1939), pp. 27–47.
1939 "The group and the individual in functional analysis," *American Journal of Sociology*, XLIV (1939), pp. 938–964.
Spanish translation: "El grupo y el individua en analisis functional," *Revista Mexicana de Sociologia*, I (1939), pp. 111–133.
1940 "La 'transculturación' su vocablo y su concepto," *Revista Bimestre Cubana*, XLVI (1940), pp. 220–228.
1942 "The scientific approach to the study of man," in: Ruth N. Anshen, ed., *Science and Man*. New York, Harcourt Brace and Comp., pp. 207–242.
1944 *A Scientific Theory of Culture and Other Essays.* With a Preface by Huntington Cairns. Chapel Hill, University of North Carolina Press.
French translation by Pierre Clinquart: *Une théorie scientifique de la culture*. Paris, Maspéro, 1970.
German translation by Fritz Levi: *Eine wissenschaftliche Theorie der Kultur und andere Aufsätze*. Introduction by Paul Reiwald. Zürich, 1949.
1967 *A Diary in the Strict Sense of the Term*. See below under 'Main Publications'.

4. Main Publications

1911 "Totemizm i egsogamia," *Lud w Lwowie*, XVII–XIX (1911), pp. 153–171.
1913 *The Family among the Australian Aborigines*. London, University of London Press.
1914 *Wierzenia pierwotne i formy ustroju pierwotnego*. Kraków.
1915 *Primitive Religion and Social Differentiation* (in Polish). Cracow.
1915 "The natives of Mailu: preliminary results of the Robert Mond research work in British New Guinea," *Transactions of the Royal Society of South Australia*, XXXIX (1915), pp. 493–706.
1916 "Baloma: spirits of the dead in the Trobriand Islands," *Journal of the Royal Anthropological Institute of Great Britain and Ireland*, XLVI (1916), pp. 353–430.
1922 *Argonauts of the Western Pacific*. London, G. Routledge and Sons; New York, E. P. Dutton & Co.
French translation: *Les argonautes du Pacifique occidental*. Paris, Gallimard, 1963.
1923 "The problem of meaning in primitive languages," in: C. K. Ogden and I. A. Richards, *The Meaning of Meaning*, Supplement 1, London, Kegan Paul, Trench, Treubner and Co., pp. 451–510.
1923 "The psychology of sex and the foundations of kinship in primitive society," *Psyche*, IV (1923), pp. 98–128.
1924 "Mutterrechtliche Familie und Oedipus-Komplex," *Imago*, X (1924), pp. 228–276. Also published separately: Leipzig, Internationaler Psychoanalytischer Verlag, 1924.
1925 "Complex and myth in mother-right," *Psyche*, V (1925), pp. 194–216.
1925 "Magic, religion and science," in: J. Needham, ed., *Science, Religion and Reality*. New York, The Macmillan Company, pp. 19–84.
1926 "The role of myth in life," *Psyche*, VI (1926), pp. 29–39.
1926 "Myth in primitive psychology," in: W. R. Dawson, ed., *The Frazer Lectures, 1922–32*. London, Kegan Paul, pp. 66–119. Also published

separately, London, Kegan Paul; New York, Norton, 1932.
Chinese translation appeared in 1935.

1926 *Crime and Custom in Savage Society.* London, Kegan Paul; New York, Harcourt.
French translation by S. Jankélévitch: *Mœurs et coutumes des Mélanésiens.* Paris, Payot, 1933. Reissued as *Trois essais sur la vie sociale des primitifs.* (Petite Bibliothèque Payot, 109), Paris, Payot, 1968.

1927 *The Father in Primitive Psychology.* (Psyche Miniatures). London, Kegan Paul.

1927 *Sex and Repression in Savage Society.* London, Kegan Paul; New York, Harcourt Brace and Co.
French translation by S. Jankélévitch: *La sexualité et sa répression dans les sociétés primitives.* Paris, Payot, 1969.

1928 "The life of culture," in: G. Elliot Smith and others, *Culture: the Diffusion Controversy.* New York, Norton, pp. 26–46.

1929 *The Sexual Life of Savages in Northwestern Melanesia.* London, Routledge; New York, Horace Liveright.
A *Chinese* translation appeared in 1937.
French translation: *La vie sexuelle des sauvages du N.-O. de la Mélanésie.* Paris, Payot, 1930.
German translation: *Das Geschlechtsleben der Wilden in Northwest-Melanesien.* Leipzig, Grethlein & Co., 1930.

1931 "Culture," *Encyclopedia of the Social Sciences,* Vol. IV (1931), pp. 621–645.

1935 *Coral Gardens and Their Magic,* 2 vols. London, G. Allen and Unwin; New York, American Book Comp.
French translation: *Les jardins de corail.* Paris, Maspéro, 1971.

1936 *The Foundations of Faith and Morals.* (Riddell Memorial Lectures, Series 7). London, Oxford University Press.

1937 "Culture as a determinant of behavior," in: E. D. Adrian and others, *Factors Determining Human Behavior.* Cambridge, Harvard University Press, pp. 133–168.

1941 "An anthropological analysis of war," *American Journal of Sociology,* XLVI (1941), pp. 521–550.
Spanish translation: "Análisis antropologico de la guerra," in *Revista Bimestre Cubana,* XLVIII (1941), pp. 323–356, and in *Revista Mexicana de Sociologia,* III (1941), pp. 119–149.

1941–42 "Man's culture and man's behavior," *Sigma Xi Quarterly,* XXIX (1941), pp. 170–196 and XXX (1942), pp. 66–78.

1948 *Magic, Science and Religion, and Other Essays.* (Previously published essays). New York, Doubleday Anchor, pp. 9–13. 1952², 1954³, 1955³.

1944 *A Scientific Theory of Culture and Other Essays.* See above under 'Method and Theory'.

1944 *Freedom and Civilization.* New York.

1945 *The Dynamics of Culture Change. An Inquiry into Race Relations in Africa.* Edited by Phyllis M. Kaberry. New Haven (Conn.).

1962 *Sex, Culture, and Myth* (Previously published essays). New York, Harcourt.

1967 *A Diary in the Strict Sense of the Term.* Translated (from the Polish) by Norbert Guterman. Preface by Valetta Malinowska. Introduction by Raymond Firth. London, Routledge & Kegan Paul.

J. WILHELM E. MANNHARDT

1. Biography and Appreciation

Lid, N., *Wilhelm Mannhardt og hans Samlung av Norske Folkeminne*. Oslo, 1931.
Mannhardt, W., *Gedichte. Mit einer Lebensskizze des Dichters*. Danzig, Altenburg, 1881.
Müllenhoft, R. and Scherer, W., "Vorreden," in: W. Mannhardt, *Mythologische Forschungen*. Strassburg–London, Trübner, 1884, pp. V–XXX.
Sydow, C. W. von, "The Mannhardtian theories about the last sheaf and the fertility demons from a modern critical point of view," *Folk-lore*, LXXV (1937), pp. 291–309.

2. Main Publications

1858 *Germanische Mythen*. Forschungen von W. Mannhardt. Berlin.
1860 *Die Götterwelt der Deutschen und Nordischen Völker. Eine Darstellung*. Berlin.
1864 *Weihnachtsblüthen in Sitte und Sage*. Berlin.
1865–1866 *Roggenwolf und Roggenhund. Beitrag zur Germanischen Sittenkunde.* (Quellen und Forschungen zur Sprach- und Culturgeschichte der Germanischen Völker). Danzig.
1868 *Die Korndämonen*. Berlin.
1872 "Die praktischen Folgen des Aberglaubens. Mit besonderer Berücksich tigung der Provinz Preussen," *Streitfragen*, Jahrg. 7.
1875–1877 *Wald- und Feldkulte*. (Quellen und Forschungen zur Sprach- und Culturgeschichte der Germanischen Völker). Berlin. Reprinted Darmstadt, 1904–1905², ed. by W. Heuschkel.
1884 *Mythologische Forschungen aus dem Nachlasse von W. Mannhardt*. Hrsg. von H. Patzig, mit Vorreden von R. Müllenhoft und W. Scherer. Strassburg–London, Trübner.

ROBERT RANULPH MARETT*

1. Bibliography

Penniman, T. K., "A bibliography of the scientific writings of R. R. Marett," in: L. H. Dudley Buxton, ed., *Custom is King*. Essays presented to R. R. Marett on his seventieth birthday, June 13, 1936. London, Hutchinson, 1936, pp. 303–325.

2. Biography and Appreciation

Buxton, L. H. Dudley, "R. R. Marett," in: L. H. Dudley Buxton, ed., *Custom is King*. Essays presented to R. R. Marett on his seventieth birthday, June 13, 1936. London, Hutchinson, 1936, pp. 3–8.

Coghill; "R. R. Marett," in: *Robert Ranulph Marett. A Report of a Memorial Meeting of the Oxford University Anthropological Society, 4 March 1943.* London, Oxford University Press, 1943.

Marett, R. R., *A Jerseyman at Oxford*, London—New York—Bombay, 1941.

Penniman, T. K., "Robert Ranulph Marett, 13 June, 1866–18 February, 1943," *Man*, XLIV, Nr. 26 (1944), pp. 33–35.

Rose, H. J., "Robert Ranulph Marett, 1866–1943," *Proceedings of the British Academy*, 1943, pp. 357–370.

3. Method and Theory

1906 "Note on the origin and function of religion," *Sociological Papers*, III (1906), pp. 267–268.

1908 "A sociological view of comparative religion," *Sociological Review*, 1908, pp. 48–60. Reprinted in *The Threshold of Religion*, 1909, pp. 122–144.

1909 "The tabu-mana formula as a minimum definition of religion," *Archiv für Religionswissenschaft*, XII (1909), pp. 186–194.

1913 "Cultural anthropology," in: H. Chisholm, ed., *Britannica Year Book*, 1913, pp. 155–162.

1914 "Magic or religion?" (review of J. G. Frazer, *The Golden Bough*, 3rd ed.), Edinburgh Review, CCXIX (1914), pp. 489–508. Reprinted in *Psychology and Folklore*, 1920, pp. 168–195.

1914 "Folklore and psychology," *Folk-Lore*, XXV (1914), pp. 12–33. Reprinted under the title of "Psychology and Folklore" in *Psychology and Folklore*, 1920, pp. 1–26.

1916 "Origin and validity in religion," *American Journal of Theology* (Chicago), XX (1916), pp. 517–535. Reprinted in *Psychology and Folklore*, 1920, pp. 143–167.

1919 "The interpretation of survivals," (review of J. G. Frazer, *Folklore in the Old Testament*), Quarterly Review, CCXXXI, pp. 445–461. Reprinted in *Psychology and Folklore*, 1920, pp. 120–142.

1924 "Psychology and anthropology," in: William Brown, ed., *Psychology and the Sciences*. London, A. and C. Black, 1924.

1926 "Method in the science of man," *Times Literary Supplement*, August 19, 1926.

1927 "Anthropology and religion," in: Ogburn and A. A. Goldenweiser, *The Social Sciences and their Interrelations*. Boston, Houghton Mifflin, pp. 86–96.

1927 *The Diffusion of Culture.* (The Frazer Lecture in Social Anthropology, 1927). Cambridge, Cambridge University Press.

1929 *The Raw Material of Religion.* (Andrew Lang Lecture, St. Andrews). Oxford University Press.

1930 "Anthropology as a humane science: a reply," *Hibbert Journal*, XXVIII, pp. 638–648.

1932 "The diffusion of culture," in: *The Frazer Lectures, 1922–1932.* London, Macmillan, pp. 172–189.

1933 "Progress as a sociological category," *Sociological Review*, XXV (1933), pp. 3–15. Reprinted in *Head, Heart and Hands in Human Evolution*, 1935.

1934 "The growth and tendency of anthropological and ethnological studies," *Compte-rendu du Congrès International des Sciences Anthropologiques et Ethnologiques*. Londres, Institut Royal d'Anthropologie, pp. 39–53.

4. Main Publications

1900 "Pre-animistic religion," *Folk-Lore*, XI (1900), pp. 162–182. Reprinted in *The Threshold of Religion*, 1909, pp. 1–28.

1900 "Reply" (to A. Lang's criticism), *Folk-Lore*, XI (1908), pp. 319–321.

1902 "Totemism" (discussion with A. Lang), *Folk-Lore*, XIII (1902), pp. 396–397.

1902 "Origin and validity in ethics," in: H. Sturt, ed., *Personal Idealism*. London, Macmillan, pp. 221–287.

1904 "From spell to prayer," *Folk-Lore*, XV (1904), pp. 132–165. Reprinted in *The Threshold of Religion*, 1909, pp. 29–72.

1907 "Is taboo a negative magic?" in: Rivers, R. R. Marett and Thomas, ed., *Anthropological Essays presented to Edward Burnett Tylor*. Oxford, Clarendon Press, 1907, pp. 219–234. Reprinted in *The Threshold of Religion*, 1909, pp. 73–98.

1908 "The conception of mana," *Transactions of the 3rd International Congress of the History of Religions*, Vol. I. Oxford, Clarendon Press, pp. 46–57. Reprinted in *The Threshold of Religion*, 1909, pp. 99–121.

1909 *The Threshold of Religion* (Mostly previously published essays and papers). London, Methuen. 1914² (revised and enlarged).

1910 *The Birth of Humility* (Inaugural Lecture). Oxford, Clarendon Press Reprinted in *The Threshold of Religion*, 1914², pp. 169–202.

1910 "Savage Supreme Beings and the bull-roarer," *Hibbert Journal*, VIII (January 1910), pp. 394–410. Reprinted in *The Threshold of Religions* 1914², pp. 145–168.

1912 *Anthropology*. London, Williams and Norgate (Thornton Butterworth since 1931); New York, Henry Holt and Co.
Chinese translation by S. S. Lü. Shanghai, Commercial Press, 1931.
Spanish translation: *Antropología*. Barcelona and Buenos Aires, Editorial Labor, 1931.
Swedish translation by C. N. Carleson: *Antropologi*. Stockholm, Tidens Förlag, 1919.

1913 "Anthropology, social and religious," in: H. V. Weitbrecht, *A Bibliography for Missionary Students*. London and Edinburgh; Oliphant, Anderson and Ferrier, pp. 125–133.

1915 "Mana," in: *Hastings Encyclopaedia of Religion and Ethics*, Vol. VIII.

1915 "War and savagery," *Folk-Lore*, XXVI (1915), pp. 10–27. Reprinted in *Psychology and Folklore*, 1920, pp. 27–48.

1916 "Primitive values," *Folk-Lore*, XXVII (1916), pp. 12–30. Reprinted in *Psychology and Folklore*, 1920, pp. 49–71.

1916 "Progress in prehistoric times," in: F. S. Marvin, ed., *Progress and History*. London, Oxford University Press, 1916, pp. 28–48. Reprinted in *Psychology and Folklore*, 1920, pp. 223–245.

1917 "The psychology of culture contact," *Folk-Lore*, XXVIII (1917), pp. 13–35. Reprinted in *Psychology and Folklore*, 1920, pp. 72–98.

1918 "The transvaluation of culture," *Folk-Lore*, XXIX (1918), pp. 15–33. Reprinted in *Psychology and Folklore*, 1920, pp. 99–119.
1918 "The primitive medicine man," *Hibbert Journal*, XVII (1918), pp. 99–116. Reprinted in *Psychology and Folklore*, 1920, pp. 196–222.
1920 "Primitive relationships" (Review of Baldwin Spencer), *Quarterly Review*, CCXXXIV (1920), pp. 161–176.
1920 *Psychology and Folklore* (Mostly previously published essays and papers). London, Methuen.
1921 "Supernaturalism," in: *Hastings Encyclopaedia of Religion and Ethics*, Vol. XII.
1927 "Primitive crafts in peace and war," in: *Harmsworth's Universal History of the World*. London, Amalgamated Press, pp. 240–300. Reprinted in *Head, Heart and Hands in Human Evolution*, 1935.
1928 "Power and goodness in the primitive conception of the Divine," *Hibbert Journal*, XXVII (1928), pp. 63–77.
1928 *Man in the Making: an Introduction to Anthropology*. London, E. Benn; New York, Doubleday, Doran and Co.
1929 "Dynamism," in: *Encyclopaedia Britannica*, 14th ed., Vol. VII, p. 813.
1929 "Mana" in: *Encyclopaedia Britannica*, 14th ed., Vol. VII, pp. 770–771.
1931 "The beginnings of morals and culture," in: *An Outline of Modern Knowledge*. London, Gollancz, pp. 395–430.
1931 R. R. Marett and T. K. Penniman, eds., *Spencer's Last Journey*. Oxford, Clarendon Press, 1931.
1932 R. R. Marett and T. K. Penniman, eds., *Spencer's Scientific Correspondence with Sir J. G. Frazer and Others*. Oxford, Clarendon Press.
1932 *Faith, Hope and Charity in Primitive Religion*. Oxford, Clarendon Press; New York, Macmillan.
1933 *Sacraments of Simple Folk*. Oxford, Clarendon Press.
1933 "Survival and revival," *Journal of English Folk Dance and Song Society*, I, 2 (1933), pp. 73–78.
1934 "Anthropology and moral evolution," in: J. G. Crowther, ed., *Science To-day*. London, Eyre and Spottiswoode, 1934, pp. 83–102.
1934 "Ritualism a disease of religion," *Folk-Lore*, XLV (1934), pp. 310–316. Reprinted in *Head, Heart and Hands in Human Evolution*, 1935, pp. 143–149.
1935 *Head, Heart and Hands in Human Evolution*. London, Hutchinson; New York, Henry Holt and Co. (Mostly previously published essays and papers).
1936 *Tylor* (Modern Sociologists Series). London, Chapman and Hall.
1941 *A Jerseyman at Oxford*. London, New York—Bombay, 1941.

LOUIS F. J. MASSIGNON

1. Biography and Bibliography

Basetti-Sani, G., *Louis Massignon orientalista cristiano*. Milano, Vita e Pensiero, 1971.
Cahier Louis Massignon. Paris, Ed. l'Herne, 1970.

Mémorial Massignon. Le Caire–Dar el-Salam, 1963.

Morillon, J., *Massignon*. Paris, 1964.

Moubarac, Y., *L'œuvre de Louis Massignon*. (Pentalogie islamo-chrétienne, Tome
  I). Avec "Bibliographie" de L. Massignon (pp. 7–89) et sur L. Massignon
  (pp. 90–107), et avec "Etude" (pp. 167–202). Beyrouth, Editions du
  Cénacle Libanais, 1972–73.

Waardenburg, J.-J., "Massignon: Notes for further research," *The Moslim
  World*, LVI, 3 (July 1966), pp. 157–172.

—, "L. Massignon's study of religion and Islam. An essay à propos of his
  Opera Minora," *Oriens*, XXI–XXII (1968–1969), pp. 136–158.

—, "Regard de phénoménologie religieuse," in *Cahier Louis Massignon*,
  1970, pp. 148–157.

—, "Bibliographie sommaire de L. Massignon," in his: *L'Islam dans le miroir
  de l'Occident*. Comment quelques orientalistes occidentaux se sont penchés
  sur l'Islam et se sont formé une image de cette religion. (I. Goldziher,
  C. Snouck Hurgronje, C. H. Becker, D. B. Macdonald, L. Massignon).
  Paris–La Haye, Mouton. 1970³ (revised), pp. 351–358.

2. Main Publications

1922 *La Passion d'al-Hosayn-ibn-Mansour al'Hallâj, martyr mystique de l'Islam
  exécuté à Bagdad le 26 mars 922*. Étude d'histoire religieuse, 2 vols. Paris,
  Geuthner. Second edition, considerably enlarged, in preparation (Paris,
  Gallimard, around 1975).
  English translation of this second edition, by Herbert Mason, in preparation (Princeton, Princeton University Press, – Bollingen Series –, around
  1975).

1922 *Essai sur les origines du lexique technique de la mystique musulmane*. Paris,
  Geuthner. Paris, Vrin, 1954² (enlarged).

1962 *Parole donnée*. Introduction de Vincent Monteil. (Dossiers des "Lettres
  Nouvelles"). Paris, Julliard; Paris, Union Générale d'Editions, 1970².

1963 *Opera Minora*. Textes recueillis, classés et présentés par Y. Moubarac,
  3 vols. Beyrouth, Dar al-Maaref, 1963; Paris, Presses Universitaires
  de France, 1969.

MARCEL MAUSS*

1. Bibliography

Notice sur les titres et travaux de M. Marcel Mauss. Paris, Imprimerie des Presses
  Universitaires de France, 1930 [Not reliable].

Josef Gugler, "Bibliographie de Marcel Mauss," *L'homme. Revue française:
  d'anthropologie*, IV, 1 (1964), pp. 105–111 [Without bookreviews].

Maria Theresa Gardella, "Bibliographie des œuvres de Marcel Mauss,"*e* in
  Marcel Mauss, *Œuvres*, Vol. III, pp. 641–694. Paris, Editions de Minuit
  (Edited by Victor Karady), 1969.

2. *Biography and Appreciation*

Cazeneuve, Jean, *Mauss*. (Collection "Les Précis des Classes Supérieures: Philoso-
  phes"). Paris, Presses Universitaires de France, 1968.
—, *Sociologie de Marcel Mauss*. (Collection "Les Précis de l'Enseignement
  Supérieur: Le Sociologue"). Paris, Presses Universitaires de France, 1968.
Evans-Pritchard, E. E., "Introduction," in: Marcel Mauss, *The Gift: Forms and
  Functions of Exchange in Archaic Societies*. Translated by Ian Cunnison.
  London, Cohen and West, and Glencoe, Ill., Free Press, 1954. Pocket
  edition New York, Norton, 1967.
Gurvitch, Georges, "Marcel Mauss (1873–1950)," *Revue de Métaphysique et de
  Morale*, 1950, p. 223.
Karady, Victor, "Présentation de l'édition," in: Marcel Mauss, *Œuvres*, Vol. I,
  Les fonctions sociales du sacré. Paris, Editions de Minuit, 1968, pp. I–LIII.
Leacock, Seth, "The Ethnological Theory of Marcel Mauss," *American
  Anthropologist*, 1934, pp. 58–73.
Leenhardt, Maurice, "Marcel Mauss, 1872–1950," *Annuaire de l'Ecole Pratique
  des Hautes Etudes*, 1950, pp. 19–23.
Lévi-Strauss, Claude, "Introduction à l'œuvre de Marcel Mauss," in: Marcel
  Mauss, *Sociologie et Anthropologie*, Paris, Presses Universitaires de France,
  1950, 1966³, 1968⁴, pp. IX–LII.
—, "L'œuvre de Marcel Mauss," *Cahiers Internationaux de Sociologie*,
  VIII (1950), pp. 72–112.
Lévy-Bruhl, Henri, "In memoriam Marcel Mauss," *L'Année Sociologique*, 1951,
  pp. 1–4.
Merleau-Ponty, Maurice, "De Mauss à Claude Lévi-Strauss," in: Maurice Merleau-
  Ponty, *Signes*. Paris, Gallimard, 1960, pp. 143–157. Reprinted in: Maurice
  Merleau-Ponty, *Eloge de la philosophie et autres essais*. Pb. Paris, Gallimard,
  1968, pp. 145–169.
Needham, Rodney, "Preface," in: Emile Durkheim and Marcel Mauss, *Primitive
  Classification*. Chicago, University of Chicago Press, 1963.
Poirier, Jean, "Marcel Mauss et l'élaboration de la science ethnologique," *Critica
  Storia* (Florence), No 5–6 (30 November 1966), pp. 677–703.

3. *Method and Theory*

1901 M. Mauss and Paul Fauconnet, "Sociologie," in: *La Grande Encyclopédie*,
  Vol. XXX (1901), pp. 165–176.
  German translation in preparation.
1902 "L'enseignement de l'histoire des religions des peuples non civilisés a l'Ecole
  des Hautes Etudes. Leçon d'ouverture," *Revue de l'Histoire des Religions*,
  XXXXV (1902), pp. 36–55.
1908 Henri Hubert and Marcel Mauss, "Introduction à l'analyse de quelques
  phénomènes religieux," *Revue de l'Histoire des Religions*, LVIII (1908),
  pp. 163–203. Reprinted in: H. Hubert and M. Mauss, *Mélanges d'histoire
  des religions*. Paris, Alcan, 1909, 1929².
1909 "L'art et le mythe d'après M. Wundt," *Revue Philosophique*, LXVI
  (1909), pp. 47–79.
1913 "L'ethnographie en France et à l'étranger," *La Revue de Paris*, XX (1913),
  pp. 537–560, 815–837.

1924 "Rapports réels et pratiques de la psychologie et de la sociologie," *Journal de Psychologie*, XXI (1924), pp. 892–922.
1925 "In memoriam. L'œuvre inédite de Durkheim et de ses collaborateurs," *L'Année Sociologique*, N. S., I (1923–1924), pp. 7–29.
1927 "Divisions et proportions des divisions de la sociologie," *L'Année Sociologique*, N. S., II (1924–1925), pp. 98–176.
1928 "L'œuvre sociologique et anthropologique de Frazer," *Europe*, XVII (1928), pp. 716–724.
1934 "Fragment d'un plan de sociologie générale descriptive. Classification et méthode d'observation des phénomènes généraux de la vie sociale dans les sociétés de types archaïques (phénomènes spécifiques de la vie intérieure de la société)," *Annales Sociologiques*, série A, fasc. 1 (1934), pp. 1–56.

4. Main Publications

1899 Henri Hubert and Marcel Mauss, "Essai sur la nature et la fonction du sacrifice," *L'Année Sociologique*, II (1897–1898), pp. 29–138. Reprinted in: H. Hubert et M. Mauss, *Mélanges d'histoire des religions*. Paris, Alcan, 1909, 1929².
Summary *English* translation by Arthur Julius Nelson: "The nature and significance of the ceremony of sacrifice, according to Hubert and Mauss," *The Open Court* (Chicago), XXXX (1926), pp. 33–45, 93–108 and 169–179. Complete *English* translation by W. D. Halls: *Sacrifice: its Nature and Function*. With an Introduction by E. E. Evans-Pritchard. Chicago, University of Chicago Press, 1964. As *Essay on the Nature and Function, of Sacrifice*, with a Foreword by E. E. Evans-Pritchard. London, Cohen & West, 1964).
1903 Emile Durkheim and Marcel Mauss, "De quelques formes primitives de classification. Contribution à l'étude des représentations collectives," *L'Année Sociologique*, VI (1901–1902), pp. 1–72.
English translation and Introduction by Rodney Needham, *Primitive Classification*. Chicago, University of Chicago Press, 1963.
1904 Henri Hubert and Marcel Mauss, "Esquisse d'une théorie générale de la magie," *L'Année Sociologique*, VII (1902–1903), pp. 1–146.
English translation in preparation.
1904 "L'origine des pouvoirs magiques dans les sociétés australiennes," *Rapports Annuels de l'Ecole Pratique des Hautes Etudes*, Section des Sciences Religieuses, pp. 1–55. Reprinted in: H. Hubert and M. Mauss, *Mélanges d'histoire des religions*. Paris, Alcan, 1909, 1929².
1006 Henri Beuchat and Marcel Mauss, "Essai sur les variations saisonnières des sociétés eskimos. Etude de morphologie sociale," *L'Année Sociologique*, IX (1904–1905), pp. 39–132.
English and *German* translations in preparation.
1909 Henri Hubert and Marcel Mauss, *Mélanges d'histoire des religions*. Paris, Alcan. 1929². (This volume contains some studies by Marcel Mauss and Henri Hubert which were published previously).
1909 *La Prière. I: Les Origines*. No commercial edition.
1924 "Appréciation sociologique du Bolchévisme," *Revue de Métaphysique et de Morale*, XXXI (1924), pp. 103–132.

1925 "Essai sur le don. Forme et raison de l'échange dans les sociétés archaïques," *L'Année Sociologique*, N. S., I (1923–1924), pp. 30–186.
English translation by Ian Cunnison: *The Gift. Forms and Functions of Exchange in Archaic Societies*. With an Introduction by E. E. Evans-Pritchard. London, Cohen & West, and Glencoe (Ill.), Free Press, 1954; New York, Norton, 1967.
German translation in preparation.

1926 "Effet physique chez l'individu de l'idée de mort suggérée par la collectivité (Australie, Nouvelle-Zélande)," *Journal de Psychologie*, XXIII (1926), pp. 653–669.
English translation in preparation.

1926 "Critique interne de la 'Légende d'Abraham'," *Mélanges offerts à M. Israël Lévi . . ., Revue des Etudes Juives*, LXXXII (1926), pp. 35–44.

1930 "Les civilisations. Eléments et formes," *Centre International de Synthèse. Première Semaine Internationale de Synthèse* (1929). Deuxième fasc. *Civilisation. Le mot et l'idée*. Paris, La Renaissance du Livre, pp. 81–108, 129, 139 ff.

1935 "Les techniques du corps," *Journal de Psychologie*, XXXII (1935), pp. 271–293.
English and *German* translations in preparation.

1938 "Une catégorie de l'esprit humain: la notion de personne, celle de 'moi', un plan de travail," (Huxley Memorial Lecture 1938), *Journal of the Royal Anthropological Institute*, LXVIII (1938), pp. 263–281.

1947 *Manuel d'ethnographie* (stenotyped lectures, edited by Denise Paulme). Paris, Payot, 1947, Pb. 1967.

1950 *Sociologie et anthropologie*. With an Introduction by Claude Lévi-Strauss, "Introduction à l'œuvre de Marcel Mauss", Paris, P. U. F. 1966[3], 1968[4]. (Contains six studies previously published by Mauss).

1968–1969 *Œuvres*. Edited by Victor Karady. Vol. 1: *Les fonctions sociales du sacré*, 1968; Vol. 2: *Représentations collectives et diversité des civilisations*, 1969; Vol. 3: *Cohésion sociale et divisions de la Sociologie*, 1969. Paris, Editions de Minuit.

CHRISTOPHER MEINERS

1. Biography and Bibliography

Ihle, A., *Christopher Meiners und die Völkerkunde*. Göttingen, 1931. Bibliography, pp. 148–152.
Wenzel, H., *Christoph Meiners als Religionshistoriker*. Frankfurt a. Oder, 1917.

2. Main Publications

1772 *Revision der Philosophie*. Göttingen–Gotha.
1775–1776 *Vermischte Philosophische Schriften*, 3 vols. Leipzig.
1775 "Abhandlung über den Thierdienst der Egyptier, und die wahscheinlichen Ursachen seiner Entstehung und Erweiterung," in: *Vermischte Philosophische Schriften*, I, pp. 192–250. Leipzig.

1775 "Einige Bemerkungen aus der Geschichte der Insel-Bewohner der Süd-
see," in: *Vermischte Philosophische Schriften*, I, pp. 251–273. Leipzig.
1776 "Über die Mysterien der Alten, besonders über die Eleusinischen Geheim-
nisse," in: *Vermischte Philosophische Schriften*, III, pp. 164–342. Leipzig.
1775 *Versuch über die Religionsgeschichte der ältesten Völker, besonders der
Egyptier*. Göttingen.
1781–1782 *Geschichte des Ursprungs, Fortgangs und Verfalls der Wissenschaften
in Griechenland und Rom*. Lemgo.
1785 *Grundriss der Geschichte aller Religionen*. Lemgo.
1785 *Grundriss der Geschichte der Menschheit*. Lemgo.
1806–1807 *Allgemeine kritische Geschichte der Religionen*, 2 vols. Hannover.
1811–1815 *Untersuchungen über die Verschiedenheiten der Menschennaturen(die
verschiedenen Menschenarten) in Asien und den Südländern, in den Ost-
indischen und Südseeinseln, nebst einer historischen Vergleichung der vor-
mahligen und gegenwärtigen Bewohner dieser Continente und Englande*,
3 vols. Tübingen.

THEODOR MOMMSEN

1. Bibliography

Zangmeister, C. F., *Theodor Mommsen als Schriftsteller; ein Verzeichnis seiner
Schriften, Bücher und Abhandlungen*. 1887; Bearbeitet und fortgesetzt
von Emil Jacobs. 1905.
Zeitschrift für Numismatik. (Berlin), XXIV (1904), pp. 372–376.

2. Biography and Appreciation

Mommsen und Wilamowitz. Briefwechsel, 1872–1903. Ed. by Baron J. F. W·
R. A. and Baroness Dorothea Maria Hiller von Gaertringen. Berlin, 1935·
Bardt, G., *Theodor Mommsen*, 1903.
Buonamici, F., *Dopo la Morte di Teodoro Mommsen*. Commemorazione etc.
(Annali della Università Toscane, Vol. 25). 1905.
Harnack, C. G. A., *Rede bei der Begräbnisfeier Theodor Mommsen*. 1903.
Hartmann, Luco M., *Theodor Mommsen. Eine biographische Skizze*. Mit einem
Anhange: Ausgewählte politische Aufsätze Mommsens. 1908.
Mommsen, A., *Theodor Mommsen im Kreise der Seinen*. Berlin, 1936.
Wilamowitz-Moellendorf, M. von, *Theodor Mommsen: Ansprache* etc. Berlin,
Weidmann, 1918.
Zangmeister, K. F. and Jacobs, Emil, *Theodor Mommsen als Schriftsteller*.
Heidelberg, Winter, 1887; Berlin, Weidmann, 1905².

3. Main Publications

1854–1856 *Römische Geschichte*, 3 vols. Leipzig, Weidmannsche Buchhandlung.
Berlin, 1856–1857²; 1888–1894⁸ (5 vols.).

English translation with additions by W. P. Dickson: *The History of Rome*, 4 vols. Preface by L. Schmitz. London, Bentley, 1862–1876; 1868–1886[2]; A new revised edition, 5 vols. London, Bentley, 1894; A reissue, London, Macmillan, 1908[2]; With an introduction by E. A. Freeman, 4 vols. 1911; 1913[2].

1871 *Römischer Staatsrecht*, 3 vols. (J. Marquardt and T. Mommsen, *Handbuch der Römischen Altertümer*). 1887[3] (2 vols.).

1899 *Römisches Strafrecht*. (Alsoni : *Systematisches Handbuch der deutschen Rechtswissenschaft* by C. Binding, Abt. 1, Tl. 4, 1883).

1905 *Reden und Aufsätze von Theodor Mommsen*. Ed. by H. O. Hirschfeld. Berlin.

1905–1913 *Gesammelte Schriften*. With a preface by O. H. Hirschfeld, 8 vols. Berlin.

GEORGE FOOT MOORE

1. Bibliography

The published writings of George Foot Moore. 1920 (Pamphlet).

2. Biography

Fenn, W. W., "George Foot Moore. A memoir," *Proceedings of the Massachusetts Historical Society*, Vol. 64 (February 1932).

3. Main Publications

1911 "The Covenanters of Damascus; a hitherto unknown Jewish sect," *Harvard Theological Review*, IV (July 1911), pp. 330–377.

1912 "Zoroastrianism," *Harvard Theological Review*, V (April 1912), pp. 180–226.

1913 *The Literature of the Old Testament*. New York, H. Holt and Company. London, Oxford University Press, 1948[2] (Revised by L. H. Brockington); (Home University Library of Modern Knowledge, 84).

1913–1919 *History of Religions*, 2 vols. (The International Theological Library). New York, Scribner. Edinburgh, Clark, 1914–1920; 1919–1921[2]. Reprinted New York, Scribner, 1941, 1947[2] (revised).

1914 *Metempsychosis*. (The Ingersoll Lectures, 1914). Cambridge, Mass., Harvard University Press. 1925[2].

1923 *The Birth and Growth of Religion*. (Being the Morse Lectures of 1922). Edinburgh, Clark; New York, Scribner. 1934[3].

1927–1930 *Judaism in the First Centuries of the Christian Era. The Age of Tannaim*, 3 vols. Cambridge, Mass., Harvard University Press. Reprinted 1946–1948[2]; 1962[3].

LEWIS HENRY MORGAN

1. Bibliography, Biography and Appreciation

Engels, Friedrich, *Der Ursprung der Familie, des Privateigenthums und des Staats. Im Anschluss an L. H. Morgans Forschungen.* Zürich, Hottingen, 1884.
English translation by Ernest Untermann: *The Origin of the Family, Private Property and the State.* Chicago, 1902.
Later *English* translation by Alick West, revised by Dona Torr: *The Origin of the Family, Private Property and the State. In the Light of the Researches of L. H. Morgan.* London, Lawrence and Wishart, 1940, 1943² (In Marxist–Leninist Library).
Hart, C. H., *Memoir of Lewis H. Morgan.* Rochester (N. Y.)–Philadelphia, 1883.
Lowie, Robert, H., "Lewis H. Morgan in historical perspective," in: *Essays in Anthropology Presented to Alfred Louis Kroeber.* Berkeley, University of California Press, 1936, pp. 169–181. Reprinted in: H. Lowie, *Selected Papers on Anthropology,* Berkeley–Los Angeles, University of California Press, 1960, pp. 372–390.
The Morgan Centennial Celebration at Wells College, Aurora. New York, State Archaeological Association, Lewis H. Morgan Chapter. Rochester, N. Y., 1919.
Stern, Bernhard J., *Lewis Henry Morgan, Social Evolutionist.* Chicago, University of Chicago Press, 1931. With bibliography.
White, Leslie A., ed., *Pioneers in American Anthropology. The Bandelier-Morgan Letters, 1873–1883.,* 2 vols. Albuquerque, University of New Mexico Press, 1940.
White, Leslie A., ed., *Extracts from the European Travel Journal of Lewis H. Morgan.* (Publication Fund Series, Vol. 16, Part 2) Rochester, N. Y., Rochester Historical Society, 1937.

2. Main Publications

1851 *League of the Ho-de-no-sau-nee, or Iroquois.* Rochester, N. Y.
1871 *Systems of Consanguinity and Affinity of the Human Family.* (Smithsonian Contributions to Knowledge, Vol. 17). Columbia, Smithsonian Institution.
1877 *Ancient Society, or Reseraches in the Lines of Human Progress from Savagery to Civilization.* New York–London.
1881 *Houses and House-Life of the American Aborigines.* (Contributions to North American Ethnology, Vol. 4). Washington, Geographical and Geological Survey of the Rocky Mountain Region.

CARL OTFRIED MÜLLER

1. Biography and Appreciation

Lebensbild in Briefen an seine Eltern mit dem Tagebuch seiner italienisch–griechischen Reise. Hrsg. von Otto und Else Kern. Berlin, 1908.
Briefe aus einem Gelehrtenleben 1797–1840. Hrsg. und erl. von Siegfried Reiter. Berlin, 1950.

2. Main Publications

1825 *Prolegomena zu einer wissenschaftlichen Mythologie.* Göttingen, Vandenhoeck & Ruprecht, 1825.
1848 *Handbuch der Archäologie der Kunst.* Breslau, 1848.

FRIEDRICH MAX MÜLLER*

1. Bibliography

W[internitz], M., *Catalog of Principal Works, Published by Professor F. Max Müller.* Iussed on the 50th Anniversary of Müller's receiving the Doctor's Degree in the University of Leipzig. Oxford, H. Hart (Printer), n. d. (1893), 20 p.
"Bibliographie des ouvrages de M. F. Max Müller," in: M. J. de Goeje, *Notice sur la vie et les travaux de M. Max Müller.* Paris, 1902.

2. Biography and Appreciation

Achelis, Th., *Max Müller und die vergleichende Religionswissenschaft.* Hamburg, 1893.
Berkenkopf, P., *Die Voraussetzungen der Religionsphilosophie Fr. M. Müllers.* Phil. Diss. Münster, 1914.
Brown F. S. A., Robert, *Semitic Influences in Hellenic Mythology.* With special reference to the recent mythological works of the Rt. Hon. F. Max Müller and A. Lang. London, 1898.
Dasgupta, R. K., "Max Müller as an Indologist," *Max Müller Bhavan Publications. Year Book 1962.* New Delhi, 1962, pp. 10 ff.
Gaidoz, H., "Comme quoi M. Max Müller n'a jamais existé: étude de mythologie comparée," *Mélusine,* II (1884), pp. 73–90.
Goeje, M. J. de, *Notice sur la vie et les travaux de M. Max Müller.* Lue dans la scéance du 25 avril 1902. Institut de France, Académie des Inscriptions et Belles Lettres. Paris, Imprimerie de l'Institut de France, 1902.
Jackson, A. V. Williams, "Max Müller and his work," *The Forum* (New York), XXX (Sept. 1900–Febr. 1901), pp. 620–629.

Kielhorn, Franz, "Max Müller," *Nachrichten von der Königlichen Gesellschaf der Wissenschaften zu Göttingen. Gesellschaftliche Mitteilungen*, Heft I (1901), pp. 35—39.

Mozoomdar, Pratap Chunder, "Professor Max Müller's relations to India," *East and West*, I, 1 (1901), pp. 91–96.

Müller, F. Max, *Auld Lang Syne* (Recollections), 2 vols. London, 1898–99.
Authorized *German* translation by H. Groschke: *Alte Zeiten–Alte Freunde. Lebenserinnerungen von F. Max Müller*, Professor der vergleichenden Sprachwissenschaft zu Oxford. Gotha, Perthes, 1901.

—, *My Autobiography. A Fragment.* Edited by W. G. Max Müller. London, 1901.
Authorized *German* translation by H. Groschke: *Aus meinem Leben. Fragmente zu einer Selbstbiographie.* With 'Vorwort' by W. G. Max Müller. Gotha, Perthes, 1902.

—, *The Life and Letters of the Rt. Hon. Friedrich Max Müller.* Edited by his wife Georgina, 2 vols. London, 1902.

—, *Thoughts on Life and Religion. An Aftermath from the Writings of the Rt. Hon. Friedrich Max Müller.* Edited by his wife. London, Constable, 1906.

Noiré, L., *Max Müller and the Philosophy of Language.* London, 1879.

Prat, F., "La science de la religion et la science du langage d'après M. Müller," *Revue des Questions Scientifiques*, XLIX (1901), pp. 508 ff.; L (1902), pp. 563 ff.

Regnaud, "Max Müller et les origines de la mythologie," *Revue d'Histoire des Religions*, XVII, pp. 46 ff.

Rovers, M. A. N., "Friedrich Max Müller," in: J. Kalff Jr., ed., *Mannen van Betekenis*, VIII, 2. Haarlem, 1877.

Schmidt, E. von, *Die Philosophie der Mythologie und Max Müller.* 1880.

Tiele, C. P., *M. Müller und Fr. Schultze, über ein Problem der Religionswissenschaft*, Leipzig, 1871.

Voigt, Johannes H., "Max Müller's political thought," *Max Müller Bhavan Publications. Year Book 1965.* New Delhi, 1965, pp. 65 ff.

—, "Die Auseinandersetzung zwischen Theodor Mommsen und Max Müller über den Burenkrieg," *Geschichte in Wissenschaft und Unterricht*, February 1966.

—, "Friedrich Max Müller und die Schleswig-Holstein-Frage in den deutsch-englischen Beziehungen," *Zeitschrift der Gesellschaft für Schleswig-Holsteinische Geschichte*, 1966.

—, "Max Müller's ideas on science and religion," *Transition*, Nr. 3 (Oct.–Dec. 1966), pp. 9–16.

—, *Max Müller. The Man and his Ideas.* Calcutta, Mukhopadhyay, 1967.

Windisch, Ernst, "F. Max Müller," in: Ernst Windisch, *Geschichte der Sanskrit-Philologie und indischen Altertumskunde*, Vol. II (In: *Grundriss der Indo-Arischen Philologie und Altertumskunde*, hrsg. von H. Lüders und J. Wackernagel; I. Band, 1. Heft B, II. Teil). Berlin–Leipzig, W. de Gruyter, 1920, pp. 270–304.

3. Main Publications

1844 *Hitopadesa*. Eine alte indische Fabelsammlung aus dem Sanskrit zum ersten Mal ins Deutsche übersetzt. Leipzig. (English translation, see under 1866).

1847 *Meghadûta*. Der Wolkenbote, dem Kâlidâsa nachgedichtet. Königsberg.
1847 "On the relation of the Bengali to the Aryan and aboriginal languages of India," *Transactions of the British Association for 1847*.
1849–1873 *Rig-Veda Samhitâ*. The Sacred Hyms of the Brâhmans, together with the Commentary of Sâyanâkârya. Edited and translated with commentary, 6 vols. London. New edition critically revised, 4 vols., London, 1890–1892.
1855 *The Languages of the Seat of War in the East*. With a Survey of the three Families of Language, Semitic, Aryan and Turanian. 2nd edition, with an Appendix on the Missionary Alphabet and an Ethnological Map by A. Petermann. London.
1856 "Comparative Mythology," in: *Oxford Essays*. London.
   French translation: *Essai de mythologie comparée*. Preface by E. Renan. Paris, Durand; London, Norgates, 1859.
1856–1869 *Rig-Veda Prâtisâkhya*. Das älteste Lehrbuch der Vedischen Phonetik. Sanskrit Text mit Überzetzung und Anmerkungen, 2 vols. Leipzig.
1857 *Deutsche Liebe. Aus den Papieren eines Fremdlings*. Leipzig. 1889[9], 1898[13].
1857 "Buddism and Buddhist-Pilgrims. A review of Stan. Julien's 'Voyages des pélerins bouddhistes'." Reprinted with additions from the *Times*.
1858 *The German Classics from the Fourth to the Nineteenth Century*. London. New edition by F. Lichtenstein, 2 vols. Oxford, 1886.
1859 *A History of the Ancient Sanskrit Literature*. so far as it illustrates the primitive religion of the Brahmans. London. 1860[2].
1861–1864 *Lectures on the Science of Language*. Delivered at the Royal Institution of Great Britain, 2 vols. London. 1871[6], 1886[14]. Revised edition under the title *The Science of Language*. London, 1891 etc.
   German translation by C. Böttger: *Vorlesungen über die Wissenschaft der Sprache*, 2 vols. Leipzig, 1861–1866, 1866[2]–1870[2].
1863 "Zendstudien," *Sitzungsberichte der phil.-hist. Classe der Kaiserlichen Akademie der Wissenschaften*, XL (December 1862), pp. 635 ff. Also separately printed, Vienna, 1863.
1866 "The hymns of the Gaupâyanas and the legend of King Asamâti," *Journal of the Royal Asiatic Society*.
1866 *Hitopadesa*. Sanskrit Text, with interlinear Translation, Grammatical Analysis and English Translation. London.
1866 *A Sanskrit Grammar for Beginners*. In Devanâgarî and Roman letters throughout. London. 1870[2]. New edition abridged by Ant. Macdonell, 1886.
1867–1875 *Chips from a German Workshop*, 4 vols. London. Contains for a part previously published essays and papers:
   1. Essays on the Science of Religion, 1867, 1868[2].
   2. Essays on Mythology, Tradition and Custom, 1867, 1868[2].
   3. Essays on Literature, Biography and Antiquities, 1870.
   4. Essays chiefly on the Science of Language, 1875.
   Dutch translation: *Voorlezingen over de wetenschap van den godsdienst*. 's Hertogenbosch, 1871.
   French translation by G. Perrot. Paris.
   German authorized translation by Hermann Brunnhofer, Buchheim, Julius Eggeling and G. Oppert: *Essays*, 4 vols. Leipzig, Liebknecht-Fritzsche, 1869–1876. Based on the 2nd English edition.
1868 Wilhelm Müller, *Gedichte*. Edited with introduction and annotations by F. Max Müller. Leipzig.

1868 *On the Stratification of Language* (Lecture). London.
French translation by L. Havet: *La stratification du langage.* Paris, 1872.

1869 *Rig-Veda Samhitâ.* The Sacred Hymns of the Brâhmans, translated and explained. Vol. 1: Hymns to the Maruts. London. Extended version under the title "Vedic Hymns" in: *Sacred Books of the East,* Vol. 32. London, 1891.

1869 *Über den Buddhistischen Nihilismus* (Vortrag). Kiel.
English translation: *Lecture on Buddhist Nihilism.* London, 1869.

1870 *Buddhaghosha's Parables.* Translated from Burmese by Captain T. Rogers, with an Introduction containing Buddha's Dhammapada, translated from Pâli by F. Max Müller. London. Republished in: *Sacred Books of the East,* Vol. 10, 1898².

1872 *Über die Resultate der Sprachwissenschaft* (Address). Straszburg.
Dutch translation by G. Penon, with an introduction by H. E. Moltzer: *De uitkomsten van de wetenschap der taalkunde.* Groningen, 1872.

1873 *The Hymns of the Rig-Veda in the Samhitâ and Pada Texts.* Reprint of the editio princeps, 2 vols. London.

1873 *On Missions. A Lecture delivered in Westminster Abbey.* With an Introductory Sermon by A. P. Stanley. London.
German translation: *Eine Missionsrede in der Westminsterabtei am 3. Dec. 1873 gehalten.* Mit einer einleitenden Predigt von A. P. Stanley. Straszburg, 1874.

1873 *Introduction to the science of Religion.* Four lectures delivered at the Royal Institution, with two essays on false analogies, and the philosophy of mythology. London. 1880².
French translation by H. Dietz: *La science de la religion.* Paris, 1893.
German translation: *Einleitung in die vergleichende Religionswissenschaft.* Vier Vorlesungen, nebst zwei Essays 'Uber falsche Analogien' und 'Über Philosophie der Mythologie'. Straszburg. 1876².
Swedish translation: Inledning till den jämfürande religionsvetenskapen. Stockholm, 1874.

1878 *Lectures on the Origin and Growth on Religion, as illustrated by the Religions of India* (Hibbert Lectures, London, 1878). London.
Dutch translation by A. H. Raaber: *De oorsprong en ontwikkeling van den godsdienst, nagegaan in de godsdiensten van Indië.*
German translation: *Vorlesungen über den Ursprung und die Entwicklung der Religion, mit besonderer Rücksicht auf die Religionen des alten Indiens.* Straszburg, 1880.

1879– Müller, F. Max, ed., *Sacred Books of the East.* Translated by various Oriental scholars. Oxford, Clarendon Press; London, Henry Frowde.

1879–1884 *The Upanishads Translated.* In: *Sacred Books of the East,* Vols. 1 and 15. London.

1881 *Selected Essays on Language, Mythology and Religion,* 2 vols. London. (Previously published as part of *Chips from a German Workshop,* 1867–1875).

1881 *Emmanuel Kant's Critique of Pure Reason.* In Commemoration of the Centenary of its first publication. Translated by Max Müller, with an Introduction by L. Noiré. London.

1881 *The Dhammapada.* Translated from Pâli. In: *Sacred Books of the East,* Vol. 10, Part 1. London.

1881 *Buddhist Texts from Japan*. Edited in the 'Aryan Series' of the *Anecdota Oxoniensia*, I, 1.
   French translation by L. de Milloué: "Textes sanscrits découverts au Japon," *Annales du Musée Guimet* (Lyon), II, 1.
1883 *Sukhâvatîvyûha*. Description of Sukhâvatî, the Lands of Bliss. Edited by F. Max Müller and Bunyiu Nanjio. In: *Anecdota Oxoniensia*, I, 2.
1883 *India, what can it teach us?* London. 1892², 1910³.
   German authorized translation by C. Capeller: *Indien in seiner weltgeschichtlichen Bedeutung*. Leipzig, 1884.
1884 *Biographical Essays*. London.
1884 *The Ancient Palm-Leaves*. Containing the Pragñâ-Pâramitâ-Hridaya-Sûtra and the Ushnîsha-Vigaya-Dhâranî. Edited by F. Max Müller and Bunyiu Nanjio, with an Appendix by G. Bühler. In: *Anecdota Oxoniensia*, I, 3.
1887 *The Science of Thought*. London.
   German translation by E. Schneider: *Das Denken im Lichte der Sprache*. Leipzig, 1888.
1888 *Biographies of Words and the Home of the Aryas*. London.
1888 *Three Introductory Lectures on the Science of Thought*. Delivered at the Royal Institution. London–Chicago.
1889 *Three Lectures on the Science of Language and its Place in General Education*. London. New edition, with a supplement 'My Predecessors', London, 1891.
1889 *Natural Religion* (Gifford Lectures, 1888). London.
   German translation by E. Schneider: *Natürliche Religion*. Leipzig, 1890.
1891 *Physical Religion* (Gifford Lectures, 1890). London.
   German translation by R. Otto Franke: *Physische Religion*. Leipzig, 1892.
1892 *Anthropological Religion* (Gifford Lectures, 1891). London.
   German translation by M. Winternitz: *Anthropologische Religion*. Leipzig, 1894.
1892 *Address*. Delivered at the Opening of the 9th Int. Congress of Orientalists, London, 5 September 1892. With the replies of G. Bühler and Count Ang. de Gubernatis. Oxford.
1893 *Theosophy or Psychological Religion* (Gifford Lectures, 1892). London.
   German translation by M. Winternitz: *Theosophie oder psychologische Religion*. Leipzig, 1895.
1894 *Three Lectures on the Vedanta Philosophy*. Delivered at the Royal Institution, March 1894. London.
   French translation by Léo Sorg: *Introduction à la philosophie Védanta*. Paris, 1899.
1895– Müller, F. Max, ed., *Sacred Books of the Buddhists*. Translated by various Oriental scholars under the auspices of the Pali Text Society. London, Luzac and Oxford University Press; Henry Frowde.
1897 *Contributions to the Science of Mythology*, 2 vols. London.
   German translation: *Beiträge zur Wissenschaft der Mythologie*. Leipzig, 1897.
1898 *Râmakrishna, his Life and Sayings*. London.
1899 *The Six Systems on Indian Philosophy*. London.
   German translation: *Sechs Systeme indischer Philosophie*. Leipzig, 1899.
.... *Âpastamba-Yagña-Paribhâshâ-Sûtras*. Translated. In: *Sacred Books of the East*, Vol. 30: The Grihya-Sutras, Rules of Vedic Domestic Ceremonies.

N

ERICH NEUMANN

Main Publications

1949 *Die Ursprungsgeschichte des Bewusstseins.* Zürich, Rascher.
English translation by R. F. C. Hull: *The Origins and History of Conscious-
ness.* (Bollingen Series, 42). London, Routledge & Kegan Paul; New
York, Pantheon Books, 1954; 1964².

1949 *Tiefenpsychologie und neue Ethik.* Zürich.
English translation by E. Rolfe: *Depth Psychology and a New Ethic.*
London, Hodder & Staughton, 1969.

1952 *Apuleius Madaurensis: Amor und Psyche.* Mit einem Kommentar. Ein
Beitrag zur seelischen Entwicklung des Weiblichen. Zürich, Rascher.
English translation from the German by Ralph Mannheim: *Apuleius
Madaurensis: Amor and Psyche. The Psychic Development of the Feminine.*
A commentary on the tale by Apuleius. (Bollingen Series, 54). New York,
Pantheon Books, 1956.

1953 *Umkreisung der Mitte.* Aufsätze zur Tiefenpsychologie der Kultur. Vol. I.:
Kulturentwicklung und Religion: Vol. II.: *Zur Psychologie des Weiblichen.*
Zürich, Rascher.

1955 *The Great Mother. An Analysis of the Archetype.* Translation from the
German manuscript by Ralph Mannheim. (Bollingen Series, 47). London,
Routledge & Kegan Paul; New York, Pantheon Books, 1955; 1963².
German edition: Zürich, Rhein Verlag, 1956.

1959 *The Archetypal World of Henry Moore.* New York.

1959 *Der schöpferische Mensch.* Zürich, Rhein Verlag.
English translation by Ralph Mannheim: *Art and the Creative Unconscious.*
4 Essays. (Bollingen Series, 61). New York, Pantheon Books, 1959.

1963 *Das Kind. Struktur und Dynamik der werdenden Persönlichkeit.* Herausg.
von Julie Neumann. Zürich, Rhein Verlag.

H. RICHARD NIEBUHR

1. Biography and Bibliography

Godsey, J. D., *The Promise of H. Richard Niebuhr*. Philadelphia, 1970. With bibliography.
Hoedemaker, L. A., *Faith in Total Life. Style and Direction of H. Richard Niebuhr's Theology*. Groningen, Drukkerij V. R. B., 1966.
Ramsey, P., ed., *Faith and Ethics. The Theology of H. Richard Niebuhr*. New York, Harper, 1957. Bibliography compiled by R. P. Morris, pp. 291–301.

2. Main Publications

1924 *Ernst Troeltsch's Philosophy of Religion*. Unpubl. doctoral dissertation. Yale University.
1929 *The Social Sources of Denominationalism*. New York. New York, Mer. World Publ., 1958².
1937 *The Kingdom of God in America*. New York. New Brunswick, N. J., Loestring Press, 1956²; New York, Harper Torchbook, 1959³.
1951 *Christ and Culture*. New York. London, 1952; New York, Harper Torch-Book, 1956².
1958 *Pious and Secular America*. New York, Scribner.
1960 *Radical Monotheism and Western Culture*. With supplementary essays. New York. London, 1961; New York, Harper Torchbook.
1963 *The Responsible Self. An Essay in Christian Moral Philosophy*. With an introduction by James M. Gustafson. New York, Harper & Row.

ANTON W. NIEUWENHUIS

1. Biography and Appreciation

Bertling, C. Tj., "In memoriam A. W. Nieuwenhuis," *Tijdschrift van het Koninklijk Aardrijkskundig Genootschap*, Second Series, Vol. LXX (1953), pp. 421–422.

2. Main Publications

1904–1907 *Quer durch Borneo; Ergebnisse seiner Reisen in den Jahren: 1894 1896–'97, und 1898–1900*. Leiden.
1917 *Die Wurzeln des Animismus*. Eine Studie über die Anfänge der naiven Religion, nach den unter primitiven Malaien beobachteten Erscheinungen. (Internationales Archiv für Ethnographie. Band 24, Supplement). Leiden.
1918 *Die Veranlagung der Malaiischen Völker des Ost. Ind. Archipel*. Leiden. 1921².
1920 *De mensch in de werkelijkheid. Zijn Kenleer in den heidenschen Godsdienst* (Address). Leiden.

1924 *Die Grundbegriffe der Magie und ihre psychologische Bedeutung.* The Hague.
1926 *Das höchste Wesen im Heidentum.* Leiden.
1926 *Der primitive Mensch und seine Umwelt.* Leipzig.
1930 *Die Entstehung der Polynesier und ihrer Kultur.* Leiden.
1931 *Der Sexualtotemismus als Basis der dualistischen Kulturen und derer Exogamie in Ozeanien.* (Internationales Archiv für Ethnographie. Band 31, Supplement). Leiden.
1933 *Die dualistische Kultur in Amerika.* (Internationales Archiv für Ethnographie. Band 32, Supplement). Leiden.
1935 *Die Entstehung des Sexualwortgenus Männlich-Weiblich als Kulturelement des Sexualtotemismus und seiner Formen in den Ausstrahlungsgebieten in Amerika, Australien und Ozeanien.* Leiden, Brill.

MARTIN P. NILSSON*

1. Bibliography

Knudtzon, Erik J., "Beiträge zu einer Bibliographie Martin P. Nilsson, 1897–1939," *Dragma.* Festschrift Martin P. Nilsson. Lund, 1939, pp. 571–656. Reprinted in: *Scripta Minora Regiae Societatis Humaniorum Litterarum Lundensis,* 1967–1968 (1), pp. 29–116.
Callmer, Christian, "The published writings of professor Martin P. Nilsson 1939–1967," *Scripta Minora Regiae Societatis Humaniorum Litterarum Lundensis,* 1967–1968 (1), pp. 117–139.

2. Biography and Appreciation

Edsman, Carl-Martin, "Martin P. Nilsson 1874–1967," *Temenos,* Vol. 3 (1968), pp. 173–176.
Gjerstadt, Einar, "Martin P. Nilsson in memoriam," *Scripta Minora Regiae Societatis Humaniorum Litterarum Lundensis,* 1967–1968 (1), pp. 5–16 (Swedish), pp. 17–28 (English translation).
—, "Martin P. Nilsson," *Gnomon,* XL (1968), pp. 100–103.
Nilsson, M. P., "Emeritus med nya upplagor" (Interview), *Dagens nyheter,* 12 August 1962.
—, "Magister Sven Nilssonsskola," *Västra Göinge hembygdsförenings skriftserie,* XII (1964), pp. 48–49.

3. Main Publications

1900 *Studia de Dionysiis atticis.* Lund.
1901 *Das Ei im Totenkultus der Griechen.* Lund. Reprinted in: *Från Filologiska Föreningen i Lund. Språkliga uppsatser,* II, Lund, 1902.
"Dödsklagan och tragedi," in: *Commentationes philologae in honorem Johannis Paulson.* Göteborg, pp. 7–24.

German abstract "Totenklage und Tragödie," *Archiv für Religionswissenschaft*, IX (1906), pp. 286–287.

1906 *Griechische Feste von religiöser Bedeutung mit Ausschluss der attischen.* Leipzig. Darmstadt, 1957.

1906 *Zur Geschichte des Bühnenspiels in der römischen Kaiserzeit* (Acta universitatis Lundensis, Bd. 40 (1904). Afd. 1, Nr. 3). Lund.

1908 "Das Ei im Totenkult der Alten," *Archiv für Religionswissenschaft*, XI (1908), pp. 530–546.

1909 *Studien zur Geschichte des alten Epeiros* (Acta universitatis Lundensis. N. F. Afd. 1. Bd. 6 (1910), Nr. 4). Lund, 1909.

1909 *Timbres amphoriques de Lindos. Publiés avec une étude sur les timbres amphoriques rhodiens.* København.

1911 "Apollon, sjudagarsveckan och Orienten," in *Skrifter tillägnade Pehr Gustaf Eklund.* Lund, pp. 559–568.
German translation: "Die älteste griechische Zeitrechnung, Apollo und der Orient," *Archiv für Religionswissenschaft*, XIV (1911), pp. 423–448.

1911 "Der Ursprung der Tragödie," *Neue Jahrbücher für das klassische Altertum, Geschichte und deutsche Literatur und für Pädagogik*, vol. XXVII (1911) [= *Neue Jahrbücher für das klassische Altertum, Geschichte und deutsche Literatur*, vol. XIV (1911)], pp. 609–642 and 673–696.

1911 *Primitiv religion.* Stockholm. Revised and enlarged 1923[2], revised and enlarged 1934[3].
Danish translation by Fr. Birket-Smith. København—Kristiania, 1912.
German translation: *Primitive Religion*, Tübingen, 1911.

1912 "Den stora folkvandringen i andra årtusendet f. Kr.", *Ymer*, XXXII (1912), pp. 188–232, 308–333, 435–478.

1912 "Die Grundlagen des spartanischen Lebens," *Klio*, XII (1912), pp. 308–340.

1913 "Grekisk religion och mytologi," *Kristendomen och vår tid*, VIII (1913), pp. 13–20, 97–107.

1913 *Stichwörterverzeichnis für ein Lexikon der griechisch-römischen Religion.* Leipzig.

1914 *Die volkstümlichen Feste des Jahres.* Tübingen.
Danish translation by Fr. Birket-Smith: *Aarets folkelige Fester.* København—Kristiania, 1914.
Enlarged *Swedish* edition: *Årets folkliga fester.* Stockholm, 1915, 1936[2] (revised and enlarged).

1914 "Uppfostran och undervisning iden klassiska forntiden," in: Sven Lundqvist and N. H. Nyman, ed. *Urkunder till uppfostrans historia*, I *Antiken.* Stockholm, pp. 1–34 (with translated texts).

1915 "Die Anthesterien und die Aiora," *Eranos*, XV (1915), pp. 181–200.

1916 "Die Prozessionstypen im griechischen Kult. Mit einem Anhang über die dionysischen Prozessionen in Athen," *Jahrbuch des kaiserlich deutschen archäologischen Instituts*, XXXI (1916), pp. 309–339.

1917 Ed. with Hans Larsson and Claes Lindskog, *Athena. Bilder ur den hellenska kulturvärlden.* Stockholm, (esp. pp. 3–92).

1917 "Studien zur Vorgeschichte des Weihnachtsfestes," *Archiv für Religionswissenschaft*, XIX (1916–19), pp. 50–150.

1918 *Daimon. Gudemagter og psykologi hos Homer.* Translated into Danish by Edv. Lehmann. (Studier fra Sprog- og Oldtidsforskning udgivne af det filologisk-historiske Samfund. Bd. 28 (1918), Nr. 111). København.

1918 "Das Rosenfest," *Beiträge zur Religionswissenschaft herausgegeben von der religionswissenschaftlichen Gesellschaft in Stockholm*, II (1918), pp. 133–154.

1918 *Die Entstehung und religiöse Bedeutung des griechischen Kalenders*. (Acta universitatis Lundensis, N. F. Afd. 1. Bd 14 : 2, Nr. 21). Lund–Leipzig. Lund, 1962² (rev. and enl.).

1918–1919 *Olympen. En framställning av den klassiska mytologien*, 2 vols. Stockholm. Also in one volume, Stockholm, 1919, 1964².
    Danish translation by H. P. Hoff-Hansen, 2 vols. København, 1922 and 1923. Also in one volume, København, 1923, 1966² (Ed. by Henrik Hertig).

1920 *Den kristne Kirke og det antike Samfund*. Translated into Danish by Holger Mosbech. (Ny theologisk Forenings Smaaskrifter, Aarg. II, H. 5). København.

1920 *Primitive time-reckoning. A Study in the Origins and First Development of the Art of Counting Time Among the Primitive and Early Culture Peoples*. Lund, Gleerup. 1960².

1921 *Den grekiska religionens historia*. (Olaus Petri föreläsningar hållna vie Uppsala universitet). Stockholm.
    English translation by F. J. Fielden: *A History of Greek Religion*. With a Preface by James G. Frazer. Oxford.
    Spanish translation by Atilio Gamerro: *Historia de la religión griega*. Buenos Aires, 1961.

1921 *Den romerska kejsartiden*, 2 vols. Stockholm.
    English translation: Oxford, Clarendon Press, 1925, 1949². Pb. New York, Norton, 1964.
    G. C. Richards: *Imperial Rome*. 1: *Man and Events;* 2: *The Empire and Its Inhabitants*. London–New York, 1926. Pb. New York, Schocken Books, 1962.

1921 *Die Anfänge der Göttin Athene* (Historisk-filologiske Meddelelser utgivne af det kgl. danske Videnskabernes Selskab. Bd. 4: 7). København.

1921 "The race problem of the Roman empire," *Hereditas*, II (1921), pp. 370–390.

1922 "Gesichtspunkte und Probleme (griechische Religion, römische Religion)," in: Sam Wide, *Griechische und römische Religion*. Durchgesehen und erweitert von Martin P. Nilsson. Vol. II, Leipzig–Berlin, 1922³, pp. 273–284 and pp. 315–316.

1923 "Der mykenische Ursprung der griechischen Mythologie," in: *Antidoron. Festschrift Jacob Wackernagel*. Göttingen, pp. 137–142.

1924 "Den grekiska och remerska religionen," in: Edv. Lehmann, ed.: *Illustrerad Religionshistoria*. Stockholm, 1924 (= *Illustreret Religionshistorie*. København, 1924), pp. 391–478.

1924 "Götter und Psychologie bei Homer," *Archiv für Religionswissenschaft*, XXII (1923–24), pp. 363–390.

1925 "Die Griechen," in: Alfred Bertholet and Edvard Lehmann, *Lehrbuch der Religionsgeschichte*. Begründet von Chantepie de la Saussaye, Vol. II. Tübingen, 1925⁴, pp. 280–417.

1925 *Festdagar och vardagar. Uppsatser om folkseder och kalender*. Stockholm.

1926 "La computation du temps chez les peuples primitifs et l'origine du calendrier," *Scientia*, XXXIX (1926), pp. 393–400.

1926 *Orientens forntid. Egypten, Babylonien, den kretisk-mykenska kulturkretsen o. s. v.* Stockholm. Revised by Krister Hanell, 1952².

1927 "Das homerische Königtum," *Sitzungsberichte der preussischen Akademie der Wissenschaften. Philos.-hist. Klasse*, pp. 23–40.

1927 *Die Religion der Griechen* (Religionsgeschichtliches Lesebuch, ed. Alfred Bertholet). Tübingen.

1927 "Kindchen Jesus. Ett bidrag till julklappenshistoria," in: *Religionshistoriska studier tillägnade Edvard Lehmann den 19 augusti 1927.* Lund, pp. 165–177.

1927 "Staat und Religion im alten Griechenland," *Scientia*, XLI (1927), pp. 413–422.
     French translation, *idem*, Suppl. pp. 176–184.

1927 *The Minoan-Mycenaean Religion and Its Survival in Greek Religion.* Lund. Revised 1950².

1928 *Hellas' arv. Sex radioföredrag.* Stockholm.

1928 *Hellas och de hellenistika rikena.* (Norstedts Världshistoria, ed. by Sven Tunberg and S. E. Bring, Vol. 2). Stockholm.

1929 *Rom och det romerska riket.* (Norstedts Världshistoria, ed. by Sven Tunberg and S. E. Bring, Vol. 3). Stockholm.

1930 "Existiert ein primitiver Seelenbegriff?", *Actes du Vᵉ congrès international d'histoire des religions à Lund, 27–29 août 1929.* Lund, pp. 90–99.
     French translation: "Existe-t-il une conception primitive de l'âme?", *Revue d'Histoire et de Philosophie Religieuses*, X (1930), pp. 115–125.

1930 *Solkalender og Solreligion.* Translated into Danish by E. Spang-Hansen (Studier fra Sprog- og Oldtidsforskning. Bd. 39, Aarg. 1929, Nr. 154). København – Oslo.
     German translation: "Sonnenkalender und Sonnenreligion," *Archiv für Religionswissenschaft*, XXX (1930), pp. 141–173.

1930 "Ueber die Glaubwürdigkeit der Volksüberlieferung mit besonderem Bezug auf die alte Geschichte," *Scientia*, XLVIII (1930), pp. 319–328.
     French translation: "Sur le degré de confiance que l'on peut avoir dans les traditions populaires en considérant particulièrement l'histoire ancienne," *idem*, Suppl. pp. 114–121.

1932 "Die Götter des Symposions," *Symbolae philologicae O. A. Danielsson octogenario dicatae.* Uppsala, pp. 218–230.

1932 "Moderne mythologische Forschung," *Scientia*, LI (1932), pp. 289–298.
     French translation: "Etat actuel des études sur la mythologie grecque," *idem*, Suppl. pp. 144–152.

1932 *The Mycenaean Origin of Greek Mythology.* Cambridge and Berkeley. New York, W. W. Norton, 1963.

1933 *De arkeologiska upptäckterna i den klassiska södern och den forna orienten.* Stockholm.

1933 *Homer and Mycenae.* London, Methuen. New York, Cooper Square Publ., 1968.

1933 "Wesensverschiedenheiten der römischen und der griechischen Religion," *Mitteilungen des Deutschen archaeologischen Instituts, Röm. Abt.*, XLVIII (1933), pp. 245–260.

1935 "Altgriechische Religion," *Revue Internationale des Etudes Balkaniques*, I, 2 (1935), pp. 408–423 (70–75).

1935 "Early orphism and kindred religious movements," *Harvard Theological Review*, XXVIII (1935), 181 pp. ff.

1935 *Homeros. Den grekiska epikens ursprung och utveckling.* Stockholm.

1936 *Forntidens historia.* Stockholm. 1937². Revised by Krister Hanell, 1958³

M.P. Nilsson 195

1936 "L'origine religieuse d'une évolution morale dans la Grèce antique". *Revue d'Histoire et de Philosophie Religieuses*, 1936, pp. 131–140.

1936 "Reflexe von dem Durchbruch des Individualismus in der griechischen Religion um die Wende des 5. und 4. Jhts. v. Chr.," *Mélanges Franz Cumont. Annuaire de l'Institut de philologie et d'histoire orientales et slaves*, IV 1, (1936), pp. 365–372.

1936 *The Age of the Early Greek Tyrants* (Lecture). Belfast.

1937 *Straff och sällhet i den andra världen i förkristen religion*. Stockholm. New edition with main title *Helvetets förhistoria*, 1963.

1938 "Der homerische Dichter in der homerischen Welt," *Die Antike*, XIV (1938), pp. 22–35.

1938 M. P. Nilsson, ed., *Årets högtider*. (Nordisk kultur, 22). Oslo—København. (See esp. article "Julen", written by Nilsson, pp. 14–63).

1938 "Vater Zeus," *Archiv für Religionswissenschaft*, XXXV (1938), pp. 156–171.

1939 "Folkfester och julseder," in: Ewer Wrangel, ed., *Svenska folket genom tiderna*. Vol. VIII, Malmö, pp. 379–400, 405.

1939 "Über Genetik und Geschichte," *Hereditas*, XXV (1939), pp. 211–223.

1940 *Greek Popular Religion*. New York, Columbia University Press. 1947². Reissued under the title of *Greek Folk Religion*, with a Foreword by Arthur Darby Nock. Pb. New York, Harper Torchbook, 1961. *French* translation by Frans Durif: *La religion populaire dans la Grèce antique*. Paris, 1954. *Greek* translation, Athens, 1953.

1941 *The Historical Hellenistic Background of the New Testament*. Cambridge (Mass.), Harvard University Press.

1941–1950 *Geschichte der griechischen Religion*. München. I: *Die Religion Griechenlands bis zur griechischen Weltherrschaft*, 1941. Rev. and exp. 1955². rev. and exp. 1967³. II: *Die hellenistische und römische Zeit*, 1950. Rev. and enlarged 1960².

1942 "Die eleusinische Religion," *Die Antike*, XVIII (1942), pp. 210–231.

1943 *The Rise of Astrology in the Hellenistic Age*. (Meddelande från Lunds astronomiska observatorium. Ser. 2, Nr. 111. Historical notes and papers, 18). Lund.

1943 "Problems of the history of Greek religion in the Hellenistic and Roman age," *The Harvard Theological Review*, XXXVI (1943), pp. 251–275.

1944 "Die eleusinischen Kulte der attischen Demen und das neue Sakralgesetz aus Paiania," *Eranos*, XLII (1944), pp. 70–76.

1944 "La Grèce — La mythologie," in: *Histoire générale des religions*, II: *Grèce-Rome*. Paris, pp. 151–289.

1945 "Pagan divine service in late antiquity," *The Harvard Theological Review*, XXXVIII (1945), pp. 63–69.

1946 *Det nye Verdensbillede i den graeske Religion*. Translated into Danish by E. Spang-Hanssen. (Studier fra Sprog- og Oldtidsforskning, 200). København.

1946 *Grekisk religiositetet*. Stockholm. 1960². *English* translation by Herbert Jennings: *Greek Piety*. Oxford, Clarendon Press, 1948, 1951². *French* translation by Matila Ghyka: *Les croyances religieuses de la Grèce antique*. Paris, Payot, 1955. *German* translation by Benedict Christ: *Griechischer Glaube*. Bern, 1950; München, 1959.

Italian translation by Carlo Diano: *Religiosità greca*. Firenze, 1949.
Spanish translation by Martín Sánches Ruipérez: *Historia de la religiosidad griega*. Madrid, 1953.
1946 "Den sengrekiska religionens psykologiska bakgrund," *Svensk Teologisk Kvartalskrift*, XXII (1946), pp. 21–31.
English translation: "The psychological background of late Greek paganism," *The Review of Religion*, XI (1946–47), pp. 115–125.
1946 "The new conception of the universe in late Greek paganism," *Eranos*, XLIV (1946, *Eranos Rudbergianos*), pp. 20–27.
1947 "Greek mysteries in the Confession of St. Cyprian," *The Harvard Theological Review*, XL (1947), pp. 167–176.
1948 "Den grekiska och romerska religionen," in: Johs. Pedersen, ed., *Illustreret Religionshistorie*. København, pp. 335–431.
1948 "Die klassische Altertumswissenschaft in Schweden seit dem Jahre 1940," *Würzburger Jahrbücher*, III (1948), pp. 321–324.
1948 "Die Religion in den griechischen Zauberpapyri," *Kungl. Humanistiska vetenskapssamfundet i Lund. Årsberättelse*, 1947–48, pp. 59–93.
1949 "Letter to Professor Arthur D. Nock on some fundamental concepts in the science of religion," *The Harvard Theological Review*, XLII (1949), pp. 71–107.
Italian translation with introduction by Giorgio Pasquale: *Fondamenti di scienza delle religioni*. Firenze, 1950.
1949 "Symbolisme astronomique et mystique dans certains cultes publics grecs," in: *Hommages à Joseph Bidez et à Franz Cumont*. Bruxelles, pp. 217–225.
1950 "Om Homeros," *Nordisk Tidskrift*, N. S. XXVI (1950), pp. 1–9.
Greek translation by I. A. Thomopoulos in *Nea Hestia*, L (1951), pp. 1225–1229.
1951 *Cults, Myths, Oracles, and Politics in Ancient Greece*. With two appendices: The Ionian phylae, The phratries. Lund, C. W. K. Gleerup.
1951–1960 *Opuscula Selecta Linguis Anglica, Francogallica, Germanica Conscripta*, 3 vols. Lund, 1951, 1952, 1960.
1951 "Second letter to Professor Nock on the positive gains in the science of Greek religion," *The Harvard Theological Review*, XLIV (1951), pp. 143–151.
1951 "Universell religion," *Svensk Teologisk Kvartalskrift*, XXVII (1951), pp. 188–192.
English translation: "Universal religion," *The Review of Religion*, XVII (1952), pp. 5–10.
1952 "Det hellenistiska konungsidealet," in *Arkeologiska forskningar och fynd. Studier utg. med anledning av H. M. Konung Gustaf VI Adolfs sjuttioårsdag*. Stockholm, 1952, pp. 9–16.
1952 "Dionysos Liknites," *Kungl. humanistiska vetenskapssamfundet i Lund. Årsberättelse*, 1951–52, pp. 1–18.
1953 "Grekisk religionshistorisk forskning," *Lychnos*, 1953, pp. 75–91.
1953 "The Bacchic mysteries of the Hellenistic and Roman age," *The Harvard Theological Review*, XLVI (1953), pp. 175–202.
1953 "The prehistoric migrations of the Greeks," *Opuscula atheniensia* (Skrifter utg. av Svenska institutet i Athen, 4e, 2), I (1953), pp. 1–8.
1954 *Den grekiska skolan*. (Humanistisk kultur, 4). Stockholm.
1954 "Die astrale Unsterblichkeit und die kosmische Mystik," *Numen*, 1 (1954), pp. 106–119.

1954 "Religion as man's protest against the meaninglessness of events," *Kungl·
Humanistiska vetenskapssamfundet i Lund. Årsberättelse*, 1953–54, pp·
25–92. Also published separately: Lund, Gleerup, 1954.
1955 *Die hellenistische Schule*. München.
1955 "Das frühe Griechenland, von innen gesehen," *Historia*, III (1955), pp.
257–282.
1955 "New evidence for the Dionysiac mysteries," *Eranos*, LIII (1955), pp.
28–40.
1957 *The Dionysiac Mysteries of the Hellenistic and Roman Age:* (Skrifter utg.
av Svenska institutet i Athen, 8ᵉ, 5). Lund, C. W. K. Gleerup.
1957 "Die Griechengötter und die Gerechtigkeit," *The Harvard Theological
Review*, L (1957), pp. 193–210.
1958 "Das delphische Orakel in der neuesten Literatur," *Historia*, VII (1958),
pp. 237–250.
1962 "Beiträge zur spätantiken Religionsgeschichte (1. Der bakchische Kult
in der Spätantike. 2. Die religiöse Begründung des Herrscherkultes),"
Vetenskaps-societeiten i Lund. Årbok, 1962, pp. 115–126.
1963 "The high god and the mediator," *The Harvard Theological Review*, LVI
(1963), pp. 101–120.

ARTHUR D. NOCK

1. Bibliography

Stewart, Zeph, "Bibliography of the published writings of Arthur Darby Nock,"
in: Arthur Darby Nock, *Essays on Religion and the Ancient World*. Selected
and edited, with an Introduction, Bibliography of Nock's writings, and
Indexes, by Zeph Stewart, Vol. II. Oxford, Clarendon Press, 1972, pp.
966–986.

2. Biography and Appreciation

Chadwick, H., and Dodds, E. R., "Obituary A. D. Nock," *The Journal of Roman
Studies*, Vol. 53 (1963), pp. 168–169.
Nilsson, M. P., "Arthur Darby Nock," *Gnomon*, Vol. 35 (1963), pp. 318–319.
Stewart, Zeph, "Introduction," to Arthur Darby Nock, *Essays on Religion and
the Ancient World*, Vol. I. Oxford, Clarendon Press, 1972, pp. 1–5
"Faculty Minute on the later Arthur Darby Nock," see issue of *Harvard University Gazette*, 22 February 1964. Reprinted in: *Harvard Studies in Classical Philology*, 1964, and in: *Harvard Theological Review*, Vol. 68 (1964,)
14 XI–XIV.

3. Main Publications

1926 *Sallustius: Concerning the Gods and the Universe*. Edited with prolegomena
and translation. Cambridge, University Press.

1933 *Conversion: The Old and New in Religion from Alexander the Great to Augustine of Hippo*. Oxford, Clarendon Press. London, Oxford University Press, 1952; 1961².

1934 "Religious Developments from the Close of the Republic to the Death of Nero," Part 10 in: *The Cambridge Ancient History*. Edited by J. B. Bury a.o. Cambridge, University Press.

1938 *St. Paul*. (The Home University Library of Modern Knowledge). London, Butterworth. 1948²; 1960³.

1945 *Corpus Hermeticum*. Texte établi par A. D. Nock et traduit par A. J. Festugière. (Collection des Universités de France). Paris (Greek and French text).

1962 *Early Gentile Christianity and its Hellenistic Background*. With an introduction by the author, 1962 (pp. 321–359) and two additional essays, "A Note on the Resurrection" and "Hellenistic Mysteries and Christian Sacraments". New York, Harper Torchbook 111, 1964.

1972 *Essays on Religion and the Ancient World*. Selected and edited, with an Introduction, Bibliography of Nock's Writings, and Indexes, by Zeph Stewart, 2 vols. Oxford, Clarendon Press, XVII + XVII + 1029p.

HERMANN OLDENBERG

Main Publications

1881 *Buddha. Sein Leben, seine Lehre, seine Gemeinde.* Berlin, Wilhelm Hertz, 1881. Hrsg. von Helmuth von Glasenapp: Stuttgart, 1921[9]; 1959[13]. *English* translation by W. Hoey: *Buddha, his Life, his Doctrine, his Order.* London, 1882.
1894 *Die Religion des Veda.* Berlin. 1923[2]; Darmstadt, 1970.
1903 *Die Literatur des alten Indien.* Stuttgart. 1923[2].
1905 *Veda-forschung.* Stuttgart.
1906 *Indien und die Religionswissenschaft.* Stuttgart–Berlin.
1909 *Rgveda.* Berlin.
1915 *Die Lehre der Upanishaden und die Anfänge des Buddhismus.* Göttingen.
1919 *Vorwissenschaftliche Wissenschaft. Die Weltanschauung der Brâhmana-Texte.* Göttingen.
1922 *Buddha: Reden. Lehre, Verse, Erzählungen.* Translated and introduced. München, Kurt Wolff.
1922 *Das Mahâbhârata. Seine Entstehung, sein Inhalt, seine Form.* Göttingen.
1967 *Kleine Schriften*, 2 vols. Hrsg. von Klaus Ludwig Janert. Wiesbaden.

TRAUGOTT KONSTANTIN ÖSTERREICH

Main Publications

1906 *Kant und die Metaphysik.* Berlin.
1910 *Phänomenologie des Ich.* Leipzig.
1915 *Die religiöse Erfahrung als philosophisches Problem.* Berlin.
1917 *Einführung in die Religionspsychologie.* Berlin.
1921 *Der Okkultismus im modernen Weltbild.* Dresden.
   English translation from the second German edition: *Occultism and modern science.* London, Methuen, 1923.
1920 *Das Weltbild der Gegenwart.* Berlin.

1921 *Die Besessenheit.* Langensalza.
    English authorized translation by D. Ibberson: *Possession, Demonical
    and Other, among Primitive Races, in Antiquity, the Middle Ages, and
    Modern Times.* London, Kegan Paul, 1930.
1923–1026 Neubearbeitung von Friedrich Ueberwegs: *Grundriss der Geschichte
    der Philosophie,* vols.:
    IV: *Die Deutsche Philosophie des 19. Jahrhunderts und der Gegenwart.*
    Völlig neu bearbeitet. Berlin, E. S. Mittler & Sohn, 1923¹², 734 p.
    V: *Die Philosophie des Auslandes vom Beginn des 19. Jahrhunderts bis auf
    die Gegenwart.* In grossenteils völlig neuer Bearbeitung. Berlin, E. S. Mittler
    & Sohn, 1926¹², 431 p.

RUDOLF OTTO*

1. Bibliography

"Veröffentlichungen Rudolf Ottos", in: Hans-Walter Schütte, *Religion und
    Christentum in der Theologie Rudolf Ottos.* Berlin, Walter de Gruyter & Co
    1969, pp. 143–150.

2. Biography and Appreciation

Baetke, Walter, *Das Heilige im Germanischen.* Tübingen, 1942.
Benz, Ernst, "Rudolf Otto in seiner Bedeutung für die Erforschung der Kir-
    chengeschichte," *Zeitschrift für Kirchengeschichte,* LVI (1937), pp.
    375–398.
—, ed., *Rudolf Otto's Bedeutung für die Religionswissenschaft und die Theologie
    heute. Zur Hundertjahrfeier seinesGeburtstags 25. September 1969.* (Beihefte
    der Zeitschrift für Religions- und Geistesgeschichte, 14). Leiden, E. J.
    Brill, 1971.
—, "Rudolf Otto als Theologe und Persönlichkeit," in: E. Benz, ed., *Rudolf
    Otto's Bedeutung...* (1971), pp. 30–48.
Boeke, Rudolf, *Divinatie, met name bij Rudolf Otto.* Diss. Leiden; Leeuwarden,
    1957.
—, "Rudolf Otto, Leben und Werk," *Numen,* XIV (1967), pp. 130–143.
Bornhausen, Karl, "Das religiöse Apriori bei Ernst Troeltsch und Rudolf Otto,"
    Zeitschrift für Philosophie und philosophische Kritik, CXXXIX (1910),
    pp. 193–206.
—, "Wider den Neofriesianismus in der Theologie," *Zeitschrift für Theologie
    und Kirche,* XX (1910), pp. 341–405.
Bousset, Wilhelm, "Kantisch-Friessche Religionsphilosophie und ihre Anwen-
    dung auf die Theologie," *Theologische Rundschau,* XII (1909), pp. 419–436,
    471–488.
Brunner, Peter, "Der Begriff der Religion bei William James und Rudolf Otto,"
    Theologische Blätter, 1928, pp. 97–104.
Claussen, Willy, *Rudolf Ottos Religionsphilosophie in ihrem ideengeschichtlichen
    Zusammenhang.* Phil. Diss. Erlangen, 1924.

Davidson, R. F., *Rudolf Otto's Interpretation of Religion*. Princeton, Princeton University Press, 1947.
Delekat, Fr., "Rudolf Otto und das Methodenproblem in der heutigen systematischen Theologie," *Die Christliche Welt*, 1930, pp. 4–11, 113–119.
Feigel, Friedrich Karl, "*Das Heilige.*" *Kritische Abhandlung über Rudolf Ottos gleichnamiges Buch*. Haarlem, 1929; Tübingen, 1948².
Forell, H. Frick, and F. Heiler, *Religionswissenschaft in neuer Sicht*. Drei Reden über Rudolf Ottos Persönlichkeit und Wert anläszlich der feierlichen Übergabe des Marburger Schlosses an die Universität, 1950. Marburg, 1951.
Frick, Heinrich, *Rudolf Otto und das Heilige* (Marburger Theologische Studien, Heft 3). Gotha, 1931.
—, "Rudolf Otto," *Mitteilungen, Universitätsbund Marburg*, Heft 2 (1937), pp. 36–39.
—, *Rudolf Otto. Zum Gedächtnis. Trauerfeier und Gedächtnisrede*. Leipzig, 1937.
—, "Zum Gedächtnis von Rudolf Otto," *Die Furche*, XXIII (1937), pp. 180 ff.
—, "Gedächtnisrede auf Rudolf Otto gehalten am 20. Juni 1937 in der Aula der Philipps-Universität," *Mitteilungen, Universitätsbund Marburg*, Heft 3 (1937), pp. 54–63.
—, "Gedächtnisrede," *Rudolf-Otto-Gedächtnisfeier der Theologischen Fakultät der Phillipps-Universität Marburg*. Berlin, 1938, pp. 11–25.
—, "Rudolf Otto innerhalb der theologischen Situation," *Zeitschrift für Theologie und Kirche*, 1938, pp. 3–15.
—, "Zur Diskussion um 'Das Heilige' nach Rudolf Otto," *Theologische Literaturzeitung*, 1944, pp. 1–10.
See also under: Forell, H. Frick, and F. Heiler.
Gaede, Erich, *Die Lehre von dem Heiligen und der Divination bei Rudolf Otto*. Oschersleben, 1932.
Geiselmann, Josef Ruprecht, "Das Irrationale Ottos im Lichte der katholischen Glaubensbegriff," *Theologische Quartalschrift*, CIV (1923), pp. 51–75.
Geyser, Joseph, *Intellekt oder Gemüt? Eine philosophische Studie über Rudolf Ottos Buch 'Das Heilige'*. Freiburg, 1922.
Gibbons, Alan, *Religion und Sprache. Eine Untersuchung über Rudolf Ottos Buch*. Bern–Münster, Francke Verlag, 1970, 112 pp.
Graf, L. Gerhard, *Die Auffassung von der Entwicklung der Religion bei Wilhelm Wundt und Rudolf Otto*. Phil. Diss., Bonn, 1953.
Häring, Bernhard, *Das Heilige und das Gute. Religion und Sittlichkeit in ihrem gegenseitigen Bezug*. Krailing vor München, 1950.
—, " 'Das Heilige' Rudolf Ottos in der neueren Kritik," *Geist und Leben, Zeitschrift für Aszese und Mystik*, XXIV (1951), pp. 66–71.
Harnack, Adolf von, "Rudolf Otto, *Das Heilige*," (review), *Deutsche Literaturzeitung*, 1924, pp. 993 ff.
Harvey, John W., "Translator's Preface" to the second edition of *The Idea of the Holy*, 1949.
Haubold, Wilhelm, *Die Bedeutung der Religionsgeschichte für die Theologie Rudolf Ottos*. Leipzig, 1940.
Heiler, Friedrich, "Ein evangelischer Theologe. Rudolf Ottos Lebenswerk," *Münchener Neueste Nachrichten*, LXXIX (12. Oktober, 1926), p. 7.
—, "Vom Wesen der Religion. Rudolf Ottos Lebenswerk," *Kultur der Gegenwart* (Kulturbeilage Nr. 17 der *Kölnischen Zeitung* vom 24. April 1937).
—, "Protestantischer Universalismus. Rudolf Ottos Lebenswerk, Eine heilige Kirche," *Hochkirche*, XIX (1937), pp. 133–141.

Heiler, "Erfahrung des Heiligen. Theologischer Universalismus. Zum 20. Todestag Rudolf Ottos (6. März)," *Geist und Leben, Blätter für Wissenschaft, Kunst und Kultur* (1957), p. 7.
See also under Forell, H. Frick, and F. Heiler.

Heim, Karl, "Ottos Kategorien des Heiligen und der Absolutheitsanspruch des Christentums," *Zeitschrift für Theologie und Kirche*, 1920, pp. 14–41.

Hølm, Søren, "Apriori und Urphänomen bei Rudolf Otto," in: E. Benz, ed., *Rudolf Otto's Bedeutung...* (1971), pp. 70–83.

Kattenbusch, Ferdinand, "Das Heilige," *Die Christliche Welt*, 1917, pp. 656, 665–670, 682–687, 697–700.

Küssner, Karl, *Verantwortliche Lebensgestaltung. Gespräche mit Rudolf Otto über Fragen der Ethik.* Stuttgart, 1941; 3rd edition Lüneburg, n. d.

Lemaître, Auguste-Antoine, *La pensée religieuse de Rudolf Otto et le mystère du Divin.* Lausanne, 1924.

Leeuw, Gerardus van der, "Rudolf Otto und die Religionsgeschichte," *Zeitschrift für Theologie und Kirche*, N. F., XIX (1938), pp. 71–81.

Mensching, Gustav, "Rudolf Ottos religionsgeschichtliche Arbeit," *Zeitschrift für Theologie und Kirche*, N. F., XIX (1938), pp. 118–128.

—, "Rudolf Otto und die Religionsgeschichte," in: E. Benz, ed., *Rudolf Otto's Bedeutung...* (1971), pp. 49–69.

Moore, John Morrison, "The a priori in Rudolf Otto's Theory of Religious Experience," *Review of Religion*, II (1938).

—, *Theories of Religious Experience. With Special Reference to James, Otto and Bergson.* New York, 1938, pp. 75–112.

Müller, Friedrich, *Erkenntnistheoretischer Idealismus und Realismus in der Religionsphilosophie (unter Berücksichtigung Natorps, Ottos und Külpes).* Gieszen, 1924.

Mulert, Hermann, "Ottos ökumenisches Interesse," *Zeitschrift für Theologie und Kirche*, 1938, pp. 155–160.

Nygren, Gotthard, "Die Religionsphilosophie Rudolf Otto's," in: E. Benz, ed., *Rudolf Otto's Bedeutung...* (1971), pp. 84–96.

Rudolf-Otto-Gedächtnisfeier der Theologischen Fakultät der Philipps-Universität. Ansprachen und Gruszworte. Edited by the Theologische Fakultät Marburg, Berlin, 1938.

Paus, Ansgar, *Religiöser Erkenntnisgrund. Herkunft und Wesen der Aprioritheorie Rudolf Ottos.* Leiden, E. J. Brill, 1966.

Schaeder, Hans-Heinrich, "Rudolf Otto und die Religionsgeschichte," *Die Christliche Welt*, Vol. 54, Nr. 10 (18 May 1940), pp. 223–227.

Schilling, Werner, "Das Phänomen des Heiligen. Zu Baetkes Kritik an Rudolf Otto," *Zeitschrift für Religions- und Geistesgeschichte*, II (1949–50), pp. 206–222.

—, "Rudolf Otto. Entwurf einer Biographie," in: E. Benz, ed., *Rudolf Otto's Bedeutung...* (1971), pp. 1–29.

Schinzer, Reinhard, *Werturteil und Seinsurteil in den nachgelassenen dogmatischen Vorlesungen Rudolf Ottos.* Theol. Diss., Marburg, 1967.

Schulz, Walther, "Das Numinose als metaphysisches Problem. Bemerkungen zu Rudolf Ottos Schrift 'Das Heilige'," *Theologische Studien und Kritiken*, 1922, pp. 230–252.

Schütte, Hans–Walter, *Religion und Christentum in der Theologie Rudolf Ottos.* (Theologische Bibliothek Töpelmann, 15). Berlin, De Gruyter, 1969.

Seifert, Paul, *Die Religionsphilosophie bei Rudolf Otto. Eine Untersuchung über ihre Entwicklung.* Düsseldorf, 1936.

Siegfried, Theodor, *Grundfragen der Theologie bei Rudolf Otto.* (Marburger Theologische Studien, Heft 7). Gotha, 1931.

—, "Theologie als Religionswissenschaft bei Rudolf Otto," *Zeitschrift für Theologie und Kirche*, 1938, pp. 16–45.

Sommer, J. W. Ernst, *Der heilige Gott und der Gott der Gnade bei Rudolf Otto.* Frankfurt a. M., 1950.

Strauss, Leo, "Rudolf Otto, Das Heilige," (review), *Der Jude. Eine Monatszeitschrift*, VII (1923), pp. 240 ff.

Tillich, Paul, "Die Kategorie des 'Heiligen' bei Rudolf Otto," *Theologische Blätter*, 1923, pp. 11–12.

—, "Denker der Zeit. Der Religionsphilosoph Rudolf Otto," *Vossische Zeitung*, Nr. 308 (2. Juli 1925).

Troeltsch, Ernst, "Zur Religionsphilosophie. Aus Anlasz des Buches von Rudolf Otto über das Heilige," *Kant-Studien*, 1919, pp. 65–76.

Wach, Joachim, "Rudolf Otto und der Begriff des Heiligen," in: A. Bergsträsser, ed., *Deutsche Beiträge zur geistigen Überlieferung*, II (1953), pp. 200–217.

Weinel, Heinrich, "Das Erfühlen des Überweltlichen. Zu Rudolf Ottos religionsphilosophischer Arbeit," *Die freie Volkskirche*, XXI (1933), pp. 198–203.

Windelband, Wilhelm, "Das Heilige. Skizze zur Religionsphilosophie," *Präludien. Aufsätze und Reden zur Einleitung in die Philosophie*, Vol. II, Tübingen, 1924[9], pp. 295–332.

Zeitschrift für Theologie und Kirche, N. F., XIX, 1–2 (1938): "Rudolf Otto. Gedenkheft zum Jahrestag seines Todes am 6. März. With contributions of H. Frick, G. v. d. Leeuw, G. Mensching, and Th. Siegfried.

3. Main Publications

1898 *Geist und Wort nach Luther.* Theol. Diss., Göttingen.

1898 *Die Anschauung vom Heiligen Geiste bei Luther. Eine historisch-dogmatische Untersuchung.* Göttingen.

1901 *Die historisch-kritische Auffassung vom Leben und Wirken Jesu.* Göttingen. 1905[4].

1903 "Die mechanistische Lebenstheorie und die Theologie," *Zeitschrift für Theologie und Kirche* (1903), pp. 179–213.

1904 "Die Überwindung der mechanistischen Lehre vom Leben in der heutigen Naturwissenschaft," *Zeitschrift für Theologie und Kirche* (1904), pp. 234–272.

1904 *Naturalistische und religiöse Weltansicht.* Tübingen. 1929[3].
    English translation by J. Arthur Thomson and Margaret R. Thomson: *Naturalism and Religion.* Edited with an introduction by W. D. Morrison. London, Williams and Norgate; New York, G. P. Putnam's Sons, 1907.

1909 "Jakob Friedrich Fries' Religionsphilosophie," *Zeitschrift für Theologie und Kirche*, (1909), pp. 31–108.

1909 "Jakob Friedrich Fries' praktische Philosophie," *Ibidem*, pp. 204–245.

1909 *Kantisch–Fries'sche Religionsphilosophie und ihre Anwendung auf die Theologie. Zur Einleitung in die Glaubenslehre für Studenten der Theologie.* Tübingen. 1921.

English translation by E. B. Dicker, with a Foreword by W. Tudor Jones: *The Philosophy of Religion, based on Kant and Fries.* London, Williams and Norgate, 1931.

1909 "Darwinismus und Religion," *Abhandlungen der Fries'schen Schule,* N.F., III (1909), pp. 14–40. Revised edition in: *Sünde und Urschuld und andere Aufsätze zur Theologie.* München, 1932, pp. 190–225.

1910 "Mythus und Religion in Wundts Völkerspsychologie," *Theologische Rundschau* (1910), pp. 251–275 and 293–305. Also as "Mythus und Religion nach W. Wundt," in: *Deutsche Literaturzeitung* (1910), pp. 2373 ff. Revised edition in: *Das Gefühl des Überweltlichen (Sensus Numinis).* München, 1932, pp. 11–57.

1916 *Dīpikā des Nivasa. Eine indische Heilslehre.* Aus dem Sanskrit. Tübingen.

1916 "Artha pancaka oder Die fünf Artikel," übersetzt und erläutert, *Theologische Studien und Kritiken* (1916), pp. 253–282.

1916 "Von indischer Frömmigkeit," *Die Christliche Welt* (1916), pp. 255 f., 348–350, 423–425, 528–530, 571–572, 727–729, 755.

1916 "Aller Meister Lehren," aus dem Sanskrit, *Zeitschrift für Missionskunde und Religionswissenschaft,* XXXI (1916), pp. 73 ff., 97 ff.

1917 *Das Heilige. Über das Irrationale in der Idee des göttlichen und sein Verhältnis zum Rationalen.* Breslau, München, 1963[31–35].
Dutch translation by J. W. Dippel: *Het heilige. Over het irrationeele in de idee van het goddelijke en de verhouding ervan tot het rationeele.* Preface by G. van der Leeuw. Amsterdam, Seyffardt, 1928.
English translation from the ninth German edition by John W. Harvey: *The Idea of the Holy. An Inquiry into the Non-Rational Factor in the Idea of the Divine and its Relation to the Rational.* London and New York, Oxford University Press H. Milford, 1923, 1926[4] (revised with additions), 1929 (revised), 1946, 1950[2]. Pb. New York, Oxford University Press, Galaxy Book 14, 1958.
French authorized translation by A. Jundi from the 18th German edition: *Le sacré, l'élément non-rationnel dans l'idée du divin et sa relation avec le rationnel* (Bibliothèque Scientifique). Paris, Payot, 1929; 1949[3]. Pb. 1969.
Italian translation by E. Buonaiuto: *Il Sacro.* Bologna, N. Zanichelli 1926. Pb. 1966.
Japanese translation: *Seisho-naru mono.* Tokyo, 1927.
Spanish translation by Fernando Vela: *Lo Santo* . . . Madrid, Revista de Occidente, 1925.
Swedish translation by Ernst Logren: *Det Heliga* . . . Stockholm, 1924.

1917 *Vischnu-Nārāyana,* (Texte zur indischen Gottesmystik, I). Jena. Tübingen, 1923[2].

1917 *Siddhānta des Rāmānuja. Ein Text zur indischen Gottesmystik,* (Texte zur indischen Gottesmystik, II). Jena. Tübingen, 1923[2].

1917 "Bhakti-Hundertvers (Bhakti-Satakam) von Rāma-Sandra," übertragen, *Zeitschrift für Missionskunde* . . ., (XXXII) (1917), pp. 65 ff.

1919 "Die Missionspflicht der Kirche gegenüber der religionslosen Gesellschaft," in: F. Thimme and E. Rolffs, ed., *Revolution und Kirche.* Berlin, pp. 273–300.

1923 *Aufsätze das Numinöse betreffend.* Stuttgart—Gotha, Perthes.

1923 "Prophetische Gotteserfahrung," *Die Christliche Welt,* (1923), pp. 437–447. Revised edition in: *Sünde und Urschuld und andere Aufsätze zur Theologie,* München, 1932, pp. 61–78.

1924 "Östliche und westliche Mystik," *Logos*, XIII (1924), pp. 1–30.
1925 "Meister Eckehart's Mystik im Unterschiede von östlicher Mystik," *Zeitschrift für Theologie und Kirche* (1925), pp. 325–350, 418–436.
1925 "Indischer Theismus," *Zeitschrift für Missionskunde* . . ., XL (1925), pp. 289–307.
1926 *West-Östliche Mystik. Vergleich und Unterscheidung zur Wesensdeutung.* Gotha. 1929². Dritte Auflage überarbeitet von Gustav Mensching. München, C. H. Beck, 1971³.
    English translation by Bertha L. Bracey and Richenda C. Payne: *Mysticism East and West. A comparative Analysis of the Nature of Mysticism.* New York, Macmillan, 1932.
    French translation and preface by Jean Houillard: *Mystique d'Orient et mystique d'Occident, distinction et unité.* (Bibliothèque Scientifique). Paris, Payot, 1051.
1929 "Ein Stück indischer Theologie," *Zeitschrift für Theologie und Kirche* (1929), pp. 241–293.
1929 "Bewusztseins-Phänomenologie des personalen Vedānta," *Logos*, XVIII (1929), pp. 151–184.
1930 *Die Gnadenreligion Indiens und das Christentum. Vergleich und Unterscheidung.* München.
    English translation by Frank Hugh Foster: *India's Religion of Grace and Christianity Compared and Contrasted.* London, SCM Press; New York, Macmillan, 1930.
1931 *Religious Essays. A Supplement to 'The Idea of the Holy'.* London, Oxford University Press Humphrey Milford. (A selection of previously published essays and papers, translated by Brian Lunn).
1932 *Das Gefühl des Überweltlichen (Sensus Numinis).* München. (Contains some previously published essays and papers, sometimes in a changed form). See also 1910.
1932 *Sünde und Urschuld und andere Aufsätze zur Theologie.* München. (Contains some previously published essays and papers, sometimes in a changed form).
1932 *Gottheit und Gottheiten der Arier.* Gieszen.
1934 *Reich Gottes und Menschensohn. Ein religionsgeschichtlicher Versuch.* München. 1954³.
    English translation from the revised German edition and edited by Floyd V. Filson and Bertram Lee Woolf: *The Kingdom of God and the Son of Man, a Study in the History of Religion.* London, Lutterworth Press; Grand Rapids (Mich.), Zondervan, 1938. New and revised edition: London, Lutterworth Press, 1951.
1934 *Die Urgestalt der Bhagavad-Gita.* (Sammlung gemeinverständlicher Vorträge und Schriften aus dem Gebiet der Theologie und Religionsgeschichte, 176). Tübingen.
1935 *Die Lehr-Traktate der Bhagavad-Gita.* (Sammlung gemeinverständlicher Vorträge und Schriften, . . . 179). Tübingen.
1935 *Der Sang des Hehr-Erhabenen. Die Bhagavad-Gita übertragen und erläutert.* Stuttgart.
1935 "Krishna's Lied," *Zeitschrift für Missionskunde* . . ., L (1935), pp. 1–12.
1936 *Die Katha-Upanishad. Übertragen und erläutert.* Berlin.
1936 "Die Katha-Upanishad in ihrer Urgestalt," *Zeitschrift für Missionskunde...,* LI (1936), pp. 33–40.

1936 „Vom Naturgott zur Brautmystik," *Zeitschrift für Missionskunde...*, LI (1936), pp. 1–16.
1940 *Freiheit und Notwendigkeit.* Mit Nachwort herausgegeben von Th. Siegfried. Tübingen.
1948 *Varuna-Hymen des Rig-Veda.* (Religionsgeschichtliche Texte, Heft 1). Edited by G. Mensching. Bonn.

WALTER F. OTTO*

1. Bibliography

Fritz, Kurt von, "Bibliographie der Schriften Walter F. Ottos," in: Walter F. Otto, *Das Wort der Antike.* Edited by Kurt von Fritz. Darmstadt, Wissenschaftliche Buchgesellschaft, 1962, pp. 383–386.

2. Biography and Appreciation

Fritz, Kurt von, "Vorwort," in: Walter F. Otto, *Das Wort der Antike.* Edited by Kurt von Fritz. Darmstadt, Wissenschaftliche Buchgesellschaft, 1962. pp. 5–8.
Kerényi, Karl, "Walter F. Otto. Eine Widmung von Karl Kerényi," *Paideuma. Mitteilungen zur Kulturkunde,* III, 6/7 (June, 1949), pp. 199–206·
—, "Walter F. Otto zum 80. Geburtstage," *Paideuma,* VI (1954), pp. 1–5.
—, "Walter Friedrich Otto. Erinnerung und Rechenschaft," in: Walter F. Otto, *Die Wirklichkeit der Götter. Von der Unzerstörbarkeit griechischer Weltsicht.* Hamburg, Rowohlt Verlag (RoRoRo pb. 170), 1963, pp. 144–154. First published in *Paideuma,* VII (June 1959).
Theiler, Willy, "Walter F. Otto," *Gnomon,* XXXII (1960), pp. 87–90.

3. Main Publications

1905 "Iuno," *Philologus,* LXIV (1905), pp· 161 ff.
1908 "Mania und Lares," *Archiv für lateinische Lexikographie und Grammatik,* XV (1908), pp. 113 ff.
1909 "Römische 'Sondergötter'," *Rheinisches Museum für Philologie,* LXIV (1909), pp. 449 ff.
1909–1911 "Religio und Superstitio," *Archiv für Religionswissenschaft,* XII (1909), pp. 533 ff.; XIV (1911), pp. 406 ff.
1912–1913 "Römische Sagen," *Wiener Studien,* XXXIV (1912), pp. 318 ff.; XXXV (1913), pp. 62 ff.
1913 "Die Luperci und die Feier der Lupercalien," *Philologus,* LXXII (1913), pp. 161 ff.
1916 "Lustrum," *Rheinisches Museum für Philologie,* LXXI (1916), pp. 17 ff.
1920–1921 "Das Weltgefühl des Klassischen Heidentums," *Die Tat. Monatschrift für die Zukunft deutscher Kultur,* XII, 2 (1920–21), pp. 123 ff.
1923 *Der Geist der Antike und die christliche Welt.* Bonn.

1923 *Die Manen, oder von den Urformen des Totenglaubens. Eine Untersuchung zur Religion der Griechen, Römer und Semiten und zum Volksglauben überhaupt.* Bonn. Darmstadt, 1958².

1925 "Apollon und Artemis," *Die Antike,* I (1925), pp. 338 ff.

1926 *Die altgriechische Gottesidee* (Address). Berlin. Reprinted in: *Die Gestalt und das Sein.* Düsseldorf–Köln, 1955; Darmstadt, 1955², pp. 115 ff.

1926 "Zeit und Antike. Eine Ansprache," *Der Frankfurter Gelehrten Reden und Abhandlungen,* VIII, (1926), pp. 7 ff.

1929 "Vom Wesensgehalt des altgriechischen Götterglaubens," *Forschungen und Fortschritte,* V (1929), 365 ff.

1929 *Die Götter Griechenlands. Das Bild des Göttlichen im Spiegel des griechischen Geistes.* Bonn. Frankfurt am Main, G. Schulte–Bulmke, 1934², 1947³, 1956⁴, 1970⁶.
English translation by Moses Hadas: *The Homeric Gods: The Spiritual Significance of Greek Religion.* New York, Pantheon, 1954.
Italian translation: *Gli dei della Grecia.* Firenze, 1941.

1931 *Vergil.* (Schriften der Straszburger Wissenschaftlichen Gesellschaft an der Universität Frankfurt am Main, 13). Berlin. Reprinted in: *Die Gestalt und das Sein,* 1955, pp. 339 ff.

1931 *Der europäische Geist und die Weisheit des Ostens. Gedanken über das Erbe Homers.* Frankfurt am Main. Reprinted in: *Die Gestalt und das Sein,* 1955, 91 ff.

1933 *Dionysos. Mythos und Kultus.* Frankfurt am Main. 1939²; Darmstadt, 1960³.
English translation by Robert Palmer: *Dionysos, Myth and Cult.* Indiana, Southern Illinois Press.
French translation by Patrick Lévy: *Dionysos, le mythe et le culte.* Paris, Mercure de France, 1969.

1934 "Die griechische Göttergestalt und ihre Bedeutung für die griechische Kultur," *Geistige Arbeit,* I, 16 (1934), p. 5.

1934 "Der Durchbruch zum antiken Mythos im 19. Jahrhundert," in: *Vom Schicksal des deutschen Geistes.* Berlin. pp. 35 ff. Reprinted in: *Die Gestalt und das Sein,* 1955, pp. 211 ff.

1937 "Der griechische Mensch und die Nachwelt," *Europäische Revue,* XIII (1937), pp. 635 ff. Reprinted in: *Die Gestalt und das Sein,* 1955, pp. 159 ff.

1939 "Der Sinn der Eleusinischen Mysterien," *Eranos Jahrbuch,* VII (1939), pp. 83 ff. Reprinted in: *Die Gestalt und das Sein,* 1955, 313 ff.

1939 *Der griechische Göttermythos bei Goethe und Hölderlin.* Berlin. Reprinted in: *Die Gestalt und das Sein,* 1955, pp. 181 ff.

1940 "Die Frage der geistigen Überlieferung. Zwei Briefe: Ernesto Grassi an Walter F. Otto, Walter F. Otto an Ernesto Grassi," *Geistige Überlieferung,* I (1940), pp. 7 ff.

1940 "Der Ursprung von Mythos und Kultus. Zu Hölderlins Empedokles," *Geistige Überlieferung,* I (1940), pp. 85 ff. Reprinted in: *Die Gestalt und das Sein,* 1955, pp. 227 ff.

1942 "Zwei Briefe: Ernesto Grassi, 'Über das Problem des Wortes und des individuellen Lebens'. An Walter F. Otto; Walter F. Otto, 'Erwiderung'. An Ernesto Grassi," *Geistige Überlieferung,* II (1942), pp. 7 ff.

1942 *Der Dichter und die alten Götter.* Frankfurt am Main.

1943 "Die Berufung des Dichters," in: *Hölderlin. Gedenkschrift zu seinem 100. Todestag.* Tübingen, pp. 203 ff. Reprinted in: *Die Gestalt und das Sein,* 1955, pp. 285 ff.

1943 "Das lächelnde Götterkind," in: *Neue Beiträge deutscher Forschung.* *Wilhelm Worringer zum 60. Geburtstag.* Königsberg, pp. 191 ff.

1948–1949 "Hölderlin und die Griechen," *Hölderlin–Jahrbuch,* pp. 48 ff.

1949 "Apollon," *Neues Abendland,* IV 3 (1949), pp. 80 ff.

1949 *Das Vorbild der Griechen.* Tübingen–Stuttgart. Reprinted in: *Die Gestalt und das Sein,* 1955, pp. 137 ff.

1950 "Ein griechischer Kultmythos vom Ursprung der Pflugkultur," *Paideuma.* *Mitteilungen zur Kulturkunde,* IV (1950), pp. 111 ff.

1950 "Die Zeit und das Sein," in: *Anteile. Festschrift für Martin Heidegger.* pp. 1 ff. Reprinted in: *Die Gestalt und das Sein,* 1955, pp. 1 ff.

1951 *Gesetz, Urbild und Mythos.* Stuttgart. Reprinted in: *Die Gestalt und das Sein,* 1955, pp. 25 ff.

1954 *Die Musen und der göttliche Ursprung des Singens und Sagens.* Düsseldorf. Darmstadt, 1956².

1955 "Der Mythos," *Studium Generale,* VIII (1955), pp. 263 ff.

1955 *Die Gestalt und das Sein. Gesammelte Abhandlungen über den Mythos und seine Bedeutung für die Menschheit.* Düsseldorf–Köln, E. Diederichs. Darmstadt, Wissenschaftliche Buchgesellschaft, 1955².

1956 *Menschengestalt und Tanz.* München. Also published in: *Die Gestalt und das Sein,* 1955, pp. 399 ff.

1956 *Theophania. Der Geist der altgriechischen Religion,* (RoRoRo pb. 15). Hamburg, Rowohlt Verlag.

1956 "Der ursprüngliche Mythos im Lichte der Sympathie von Mensch und Welt," *Eranos Jahrbuch,* XXIV (1956), pp. 303 ff.

1956–1957 "Hölderlin und das Göttliche," *Das Neue Forum,* VI (1956–57), pp. 217 ff.

1959 "Apollon," *Paideuma. Mitteilungen zur Kulturkunde,* VII (1959), pp. 19 ff.

1959 "Sprache als Mythos," *Gestalt und Gedanke,* V (1959), pp. 171 ff. Reprinted in: *Die Sprache.* Edited by the Bayerische Akademie der schönen Künste. Darmstadt, 1959.

1962 *Das Wort der Antike (Nachgelassene Schriften I).* Edited by Kurt von Fritz. Darmstadt, Wissenschaftliche Buchgesellschaft.

1962 *Mythos und Welt (Nachgelassene Schriften II).* Edited by Kurt von Fritz, in collaboration with Egidius Schmalzriedt. Stuttgart, E. Klett.

RAFFAELE PETTAZZONI*

1. Bibliography

Gandini, Mario, "Nota bibliografica degli scritti di Raffaele Pettazzoni," *Studi e Materiali di Storia delle Religioni*, XXXI (1960), pp. 3–21.
—, "Il contributo di Raffaele Pettazzoni agli studi storico-religiosi: appunti per una bibliografia," in: E. de Martino, A. Donini and M. Gandini, *Raffaele Pettazzoni e gli studi storico-religiosi in Italia.* (Biblioteca Comunale "G. C. Croce", San Giovanni in Persiceto). Bologna, Forni Editore, 1969, pp. 1–48 (See esp. pp. 4–22). [First published in *Strada Maestra* (Bologna), II (1969)].

2. Biography and Appreciation

Antonietta, E. "Raffaele Pettazzoni," *Nordeste* (Resistencia), 1961, pp. 221–223.
Bianchi, Ugo, "Il metodo comparativo e la categoria 'religione' in R. Pettazzoni," in: *Storia delle religioni*, under the direction of Giuseppe Castellani, 6th ed. Torino, U.T.E.T., 1970, pp. 166–168.
Bleeker, C. J., "In memoriam Raffaele Pettazzoni," *Numen*, VI, 2 (December 1959), pp. 76a–76b.
—, "In memoriam Raffaele Pettazzoni," in: *X. Internationaler Kongress für Religionsgeschichte (1960).* Marburg, 1961, pp. 47–48.
Brelich, A., "In memoriam Raffaele Pettazzoni," *Numen*, VI, 2 (December 1959), pp. 76b–76c.
—, "Gli ultimi appunti di Raffaele Pettazzoni," *Studi e Materiali di Storia delle Religioni*, XXXI (1960), pp. 23–55.
—, "Discorso 26 marzo 1960. Commemorazione di Raffaele Pettazzoni," *Studi e Materiali . . .*, XXXI (1960), pp. 191–202.
Bulek, V. van, "Raffaele Pettazzoni (3.2.1883–19.12.1959)," *Anthropos*, LV (1960), pp. 870–874.
Cantimori, D., "Raffaele Pettazzoni," *Nuova Rivista Storica*, XLIV (1960), pp. 179–187.
Cirese, A. M., "Impegno civile di Pettazzoni," *Paese sera-Libri* (Roma) and *L'Ora-Libri* (Palermo), 6 October 1967, pp. 7–8.

De Martino, Ernesto, "Commemorazione di Raffaele Pettazzoni," in: E. de Martino, A. Donini and M. Gandini, *Raffaele Pettazzoni e gli studi storico-religiosi in Italia*. Bologna, Forni editore, 1969, pp. 81–92.

Donini, Ambrogio, "Raffaele Pettazzoni e gli studi storico-religiosi in Italia," in: E. de Martino, A. Donini and M. Gandini, *Raffaele Pettazzoni e gli studi storico-religiosi in Italia*. Bologna, Forni editore, 1969, pp. 54–70.

Dupront, A., "D'une histoire 'existencielle' des religions: la quête de Raffaele Pettazzoni," *La Table Ronde* (Paris), nr. 154 (October 1960), pp. 129–133.

Falconi, C., "La religione di un laico," *L'Espresso* (Roma), V, 51 (20 December 1959), p. 8.

Franci, G. R., "Raffaele Pettazzoni," *Quaderni dell' Istituto di glottologia dell' Università di Bologna*, IV (1959), pp. 117–119.

Gabrieli, F., "Ricordo di Pettazzoni," *Il Mondo* (Roma), XI, 51 (22 December 1959), p. 8. Reprinted in: F. Gabrieli, *Tra Mimnermo e Solone*. Roma, 1968, pp. 43–46.

Gandini, Mario, "La vita e le opere di Raffaele Pettazzoni," in: Comune di San Giovanni in Persiceto . . ., *In memoria di Raffaele Pettazzoni*. Modena, 1960, pp. 13–29. Partly reprinted in: *Lares* (Firenze), XXVI (1960), pp. 81–89.

—, "Il contributo di Raffaele Pettazzoni agli studi storico-religiosi: appunti per una bibliografia," in: E. de Martino, A. Donini and M. Gandini, *Raffaele Pettazzoni e gli studi storico-religiosi in Italia*. Bologna, Forni Editore, 1969, pp. 1–48.

—, *Presenza di Pettazzoni*. Bologna, Forni Editore, 1970. [First published in *Strada Maestra*, (Bologna), III (1970)].

Gentile, Carlo, "Intervista con Raffaele Pettazzoni," *L'Italia Illustrata* (Napoli), XIII, 6–7 (1959), p. 5.

James, E. O., "Professor Raffaele Pettazzoni," *Folk-Lore*, LXXI (1960), pp. 132–133.

Lameere, W., "A' Raffaele Pettazzoni," in: *The Sacral Kingship*. Contribution to the central theme of the VIIIth International Congress for the History of Religions (Rome, April 1955). Leiden, E. J. Brill, 1959, pp. V–IX.

—, "Per il 75 compleanno di Raffaele Pettazzoni," *Studi e Materiali di Storia delle Religioni*, XXX (1959), pp. 131–135.

Lanternari, Vittorio, "Raffaele Pettazzoni," *Rivista di Antropologia* (Roma), XLVI (1959), pp. 283–286.

—, "Scienza delle religioni e storicismo," *Annali della facoltà di lettere e filosofia dell'Università di Bari*, VI (1960), pp. 51–65.

Laurenzi, L., "In memoria di Raffaele Pettazzoni," *Mem. dell'Acc. sc. di Bologna cl. sc. mor.*, V, 8 (1960), pp. 285–290.

Leeuw, G. van der, "Sündenbekenntnis. Das Lebenswerk Raffaele Pettazzonis,' *Theologische Rundschau*, N. F., X (1938), pp. 201 ff.

Margul, T., "Raffaele Pettazzoni i badania historyczno-religijne we Wloszech," *Euhemer. Przeglad Religioznawczy* (Warszawa), III (1959), pp. 243–252.

Marót, K., "In memoriam Raffaele Pettazzoni" (English text), *Acta Ethnografica* (Budapest), IX (1959), pp. 305–306. Hungarian text: *Studia antiqua* (Budapest), VII (1960), pp. 83–84.

Nowaczyk, M., "Historyzm R. Pettazzoniego w swietle 'Ostatnich notatek'," *Euhemer. Przeglad Religioznawczy* (Warszawa), IX, 4 (1965), pp. 39–47.

—, "Etapy rozwoju swiadomosci metodologicznej Raffaele Pettazzoniego," *Euhemer. Przeglad Religioznawczy* (Warszawa), XV, 2 (1971), pp. 80 ff.

Picard, Ch., "Raffaele Pettazzoni," *Revue de l'Histoire des Religions*, LXXIX, Nr. 157 (1960), pp. 260–266.

Pincherle, A., "Hommage à la mémoire de R. Pettazzoni," *La nouvelle Clio* (Bruxelles), X, pp. 167–172.

—, "R. Pettazzoni," *Annuario dell Università di Roma*, 1960–61, pp. 975–978.

Poniatowski, Z., "Raffaele Pettazzoni," in: R. Pettazzoni, *Wszechwiedza bogów*. Warszawa, 1967, pp. XI–XXIV.

Rousseau, H. "Le problème du monothéisme et l'œuvre de R. Pettazzoni," *Critique* (Paris), XIV, 18 (1962), pp. 432–450.

Sabbatucci, D., "Raffaele Pettazzoni," *Numen*, X (1963), pp. 1–41.

Salvatorelli, L., "L'opera storico-religiosa di R. Pettazzoni," in: Accademia nazionale dei Lincei, *Rendic. cl. sc. mor. st. e filol.*, VIII, 15 (1960), pp. 157–164. Reissued in: *Rivista Storica Italiana*, LXXII (1960), pp. 480–488.

—, "La personalità morale di Raffaele Pettazzoni," in: U. Bianchi, C. J. Bleeker and A. Bausani, eds., *Problems and Methods of the History of Religions*. Leiden, E. J. Brill, 1971, pp. 11 ff.

Simon, M., "In memoriam: R. Pettazzoni," *Bulletin de la Faculté des Lettres de Strasbourg*, XXXVIII (1959–60), pp. 233–234.

Toschi, P., "Raffaele Pettazzoni," *Emilia* (Bologna), XXIV (February 1954), pp. 49–50. Reissued in: *"Fabri" del folklore*. Roma, 1958, pp. 160-164.

Tucci, Giovanni, "Raffaele Pettazzoni," *Rivista di Etnografia* (Napoli), XIII (1959), pp. 3–14.

Wagenvoort, H., "Herdenking van Raffaele Pettazzoni," *Jaarboek der Koninklijke Nederlandse Akademie van Wetenschappen*, 1959–60, pp. 387–390.

Widengren, Geo, "Raffaele Pettazzoni septuagénaire," *Numen*, I (1954), pp. I–II.

—, "In memoriam Raffaele Pettazzoni," *Numen*, VI (1959), pp. 76c–76d.

3. Method and Theory

1912 "Lo studio delle religioni in Italia," *Nuova Antologia*, XXXXVII (11 maggio 1912), pp. 107–110.

1913 "La scienza delle religioni e il suo metodo," *Scientia* (Bologna), VII (1913), pp. 239–247.
    French translation: "La science des religions et sa méthode," *Scientia* (French), XIII (1913), pp. 128–136 (Supplement).

1914 "Storia del cristianesimo e storia delle religioni," *Scientia* (Bologna), VIII (1914), pp. 88–100.

1924 *Svolgimento e carattere della storia delle religioni*. Bari.
    Polish translation: "Rozwój i charakter historji religji," *Przeglad Współczesny* (Kraków), r. V, t. 17 (1926), pp. 3–22.

1936 "La storia delle religioni," *Enciclopedia Italiana*, XXIX, pp. 29–33. Roma, 1936.

1937 "A functional view of religions," *The Review of Religions*, I (1936–37), pp. 225–237.
    Polish translation: "Funkcjonalna rola religii," *Przeglad Klasyczny*, V (1939), pp. 283–295.

1937 "L'etnologia come scienza storica," *Rivista di Antropologia*, XXXI (1935–37), pp. 455–457.

1941 "La Scuola di studi storico-religiosi della R. Università di Roma," *Annali della Universite d'Italia*, III (1941–42), pp. 125–130.

1954 "Aperçu introductif," *Numen*, I, 1 (1954), pp. 1–7. Partly reprinted as "Histoire et phénoménologie dans la science des religions," *La Table Ronde* (Paris), Nr. 154 (1960), pp. 136–138.
Partly translated into *English* under the title of "History and phenomenology in the science of religion," in: R. Pettazzoni, *Essays on the History of Religions*. Leiden, E. J. Brill, 1954, 1967[2], pp. 215–219.
1959 "Il metodo comparativo," *Numen*, VI, 1 (1959), pp. 1–14. Reprinted in: R. Pettazzoni, *Religione e Società*, 1966, pp. 99–114.
1960 "Gli ultimi appunti di Raffaele Pettazzoni," (ed. by A. Brelich), *Studi e Materiali di Storia delle Religioni*, XXXI (1960), pp. 23–55. Reprinted in: *Religione e Società*, 1966, pp. 115–136.

4. Main Publications

1912 *La religione primitiva in Sardegna*. Piacenza. Reprint of pp. 3–36 in: G. Dessí, ed., *Scoperta della Sardegna*. Antologia di testi di autori italiani e stranieri a cura e con introduzione di G. Dessí. Milano, 1965, Vol. I, pp. 63–80.
1912 "Mythologie australienne du rhombe," *Revue de l'Histoire des Religions*, XXXIII (1912), pp. 149–170.
1914 "Le origini dell'idea di Dio," *Atti Soc. It. Progr. Sc.* (7a riun., Siena, 1913). Roma, 1914, pp. 647–674.
1914 "L'idea di Dio," *Liberi Pensieri* (Roma), 1914, pp. 61–71.
1916 "Bollettino di scienza delle religioni," *Rivista di scienza delle religioni*, I (1916), pp. 57–79.
1920 *La religione di Zarathustra nella storia religiosa dell'Iran*. Bologna.
1921 *La religione nella Grecia antica fino ad Alessandro*. Bologna. New revised edition, Torino, 1953, 1954[2].
French translation: *La religion dans la Grèce antique des origines à Alexandre le Grand*. Paris, 1953.
1922 *Dio: formazione e sviluppo del monoteismo nella storia delle religioni*. Vol. I: *L'essere celeste nelle credenze dei popoli primitivi*. Roma, Anthenaeum.
1923 "La formation du monothéisme," *Revue de l'Histoire des Religions*, XXXXIV (1923), pp. 193–229.
1924 *I misteri: saggio di una teoria storico-religiosa*. Bologna.
1925 "Le problème du monothéisme," *Actes du Congrès International d'Histoire des Religions* (Paris, 1923), Vol. I, Paris, pp. 70–82.
1925 "Ahura-Mazda, the Knowing Lord," in: *Indo-Iranian Studies in honour of D. D. P. Sanjana*. London–Leipzig, pp. 149–161.
1927 "Studi recenti in rapporto con la teoria degli esseri celesti e del monoteismo," *Studi e Materiali . . .*, III (1927), pp. 97–113.
1927 "Busswesen, I: religionsgeschichtlich," in: *Religion in Geschichte und Gegenwart*, 2nd ed., I, Tübingen, 1927[2], 1388–1393.
1929–1936 *La confessione dei peccati*. Bologna, Zanichelli. Parte prima, 1929; Parte seconda, 2 vols., 1935–1936. Reprint of the whole work 1968[2].
French translation by R. Monnot of the first part: *La confession des péchés: première partie*, 2 vols. Paris, Ernest Leroux, 1931 and 1932.
1930 "Monolatrie," in: *Religion in Geschichte und Gegenwart*, 2nd ed., IV, Tübingen, 1930[2], pp. 183–184.

1930 "Monotheismus und Polytheismus, I: religionsgeschichtlich," in: *Religion in Geschichte und Gegenwart*, 2nd ed., IV, Tübingen, 1930[2], pp. 185–191.

1931 "Les Mages et les origines du zoroastrisme," *Revue de l'Histoire des Religions*, LII (1931), pp. 144–150.

1931 "Allwissende höchste Wesen bei primitivsten Völkern," *Archiv für Religionswissenschaft*, XXIX (1931), pp. 108–129, 209–243.

1932 "Persian mysteries," *Journal of the Cama Oriental Institute* (Bombay), nr. 20 (1932), pp. 151–206.

1934 "Syncrétisme et Conversion," *Revue d'Histoire et de Philosophie Religieuses*, XIV (1934), pp. 126–129.

1936 "La confession des péchés dans l'histoire des religions," in: *Mélanges F. Cumont*, Vol. 2. Bruxelles, 1936, pp. 893–901.

1937 "La confessione dei peccati: metodo e risultati," *Scientia*, XXXI (1937), pp. 226–232.

1941 "Le ciel chez les primitifs et les anciens: les dieux du ciel," in: *Le Ciel dans l'histoire et dans la science*, Paris, 1941, pp. 13–28.

1946 *Saggi di storia delle religioni e di mitologia*. Roma.

1946 "Monoteismo e 'Urmonotheismus'," *Studi e Materiali . . .*, XIX–XX (1943–46), pp. 170–177.

1946 "The pagan origins of three-headed representation of the Christian Trinity," *Journal of the Warburg and Court Institute*, IX (1946), pp. 135–151.

1948 "Per la storia religiosa d'Italia," *Ricerche religiose*, XIX (1948), pp. 29–41.

1948–1963 *Miti e Leggende* (ed.). I: Africa–Australia, 1948, 1963[2]; II: Oceania (by V. Lanternari), 1963; III: America settentrionale, 1953, 1966[2]; IV: America centrale e meridionale (in coll. with T. Tentori), 1959. 4 vols. Torino, 1948–63.

1948 "Verità del mito," *Studi e Materiali . . .*, XXI (1947–48), pp. 104–116. Reprinted in: *Religione e Società*, 1966, pp. 5–18.
English translation: "The truth of myth," in: *Essays on the History of Religions*. 1954, 1967[2], pp. 11–23.
Partly *French* translation: "Vérité du mythe," *La Table Ronde*, Nr. 154 (October 1960), pp. 133–136.
German Translation: "Die Wahrheit des Mythos," *Paideuma*, IV (1950), pp. 1–10. Reprinted in: Karl Kerényi, ed., *Die Eröffnung des Zugangs zum Mythos. Ein Lesebuch*. (Wege der Forschung, 20). Darmstadt, Wissenschaftliche Buchgesellschaft, 1967, pp. 253–261.

1949 "La formazione del monoteismo," in: *Il problema di Dio*. Roma, pp. 195–203.
English translation: "The formation of monotheism," in: *Essays on the History of Religions*, 1954, 1967[2], pp. 1–10.
French translation: "La formation du monothéisme," *Revue de l'Université Libre de Bruxelles*, II (1949–50), pp. 209–219.

1950–51 *Mitologia e monoteismo*. Edited by some students (A cura di alcuni studenti). Roma.

1951 "Der babylonische Ritus des Akitu und das Gedicht der Weltschöpfung," *Eranos Jahrbuch*, XIX (1950), pp. 403–430.

1951 "Mythes des origines et mythes de la création," *Proceedings of the 7th Congress of the History of Religions* (Amsterdam 1950). Amsterdam, pp. 67–78.

English translation: "Myths of beginning and creation-myths," in: *Essays on the History of Religions*, 1954, 1967², pp. 24–36.

1952 "Italia religiosa — Religione dello Stato e religione dell'uomo," in: R. Pettazzoni, ed., *Italia religiosa*. Bari, pp. 7–28. This had been published in 1947 and 1948 under other titles, and was reprinted in: *Religione e Società*, 1966, pp. 141–154.

English translation (revised): "State religion and individual religion in the religious history of Italy," in: *Essays on the History of Religions*, 1954, 1967², pp. 202–214.

French translation: "Religion de l'Etat et religion de l'Homme," *La Revue de Culture Européenne*, III, 5 (1953), pp. 45–55.

1952 "Introduzione alla storia della religione greca," *Studi e Materiali . . .*, XXIII (1951–52), pp. 20–33. Reprinted in: *Religione e Società*, 1966, pp. 19–31.

English translation: "Introduction to the history of Greek religion", in: *Essays on the History of Religion*, 1954, 1967², pp. 68–80.

1953 "La confession des péchés: essai d'interprétation générale," *Journal de Psychologie Normale et Pathologique*, XLVI (1953), pp. 257–268.

English translation: "Confession of sins: an attempted general interpretation," in: *Studies on the History of Religions*, 1954, 1967², pp. 43–54.

1954 *Essays on the History of Religions*. (English translation of nineteen previously published essays and papers). Leiden, E. J. Brill. 1967².

1954 "Les mystères grecs et les religions à mystère de l'Antiquité: recherches récentes et problèmes nouveaux," *Cahiers d'Histoire Mondiale*, II (1954), pp. 303–312.

1954 "Bibliographie des religions à mystère dans l'Antiquité," *Cahiers d'Histoire Mondiale*, II (1954), pp. 661–667.

1955 "On the attributes of God," *Numen*, II, 1 (1955), pp. 1–27.

1955 "La condition humaine," in: C. J. Bleeker, ed., *Anthropologie religieuse*. Leiden, E. J. Brill, pp. 1–3.

1955 "L'esprit du paganisme," *Diogène*, IX (January, 1955), pp. 3–10.

Italian text: "Lo spirito del paganesimo," reprinted in: *Religione e Società*, 1966, pp. 91–98.

1955 *L'onniscienza di Dio*. Torino, Einaudi.

English translation: *The All-Knowing God: Researches into Early Religion and Culture*. London, Methuen & Co., 1956.

Polish translation by B. Sieroszewska: *Wsechwiedza bogów*. Warszawa, 1967. Preface by Zygmunt Poniatowski, pp. XI—XXIV.

1956 "Das Ende des Urmonotheismus?," *Numen*, III (1956), pp. 156–159.

1957 *L'essere supremo nelle religioni primitive (L'onniscienza di Dio)*. Torino, Einaudi. 1965².

German authorized translation by E. Adalbert Voretzsch: *Der allwissende Gott: zur Geschichte der Gottesidee*. Pb. Frankfurt–Hamburg, Fischer Bücherei, 1960.

1958 "Das Ende des Urmonotheismus," *Numen*, V (1958), pp. 161–163.

1959 "Per la libertà religiosa in Italia," in: R. Pettazzoni and A. C. Jemolo, *Per la libertà religiosa in Italia*. Roma, Associazione per la libertà religiosa in Italia, pp. 5–10. Reprinted in: *Religione e Società*, 1966, pp. 205–212.

1959 "The supreme being: phenomenological structure and historical developments," in: M. Eliade and J. M. Kitagawa, ed., *The History of Religions: Essays in Methodology*. Chicago, University of Chicago Press.

German translation of the article: "Das höchste Wesen: phänomenologische Struktur und historische Entwicklung," in: *Grundfragen der Religionswissenschaft. Acht Studien.* Salzburg, 1963, pp. 136–146.
1959 "Forma e verità del mito," *Nuovi Argumenti* (Roma), Nr. 37 (March–April 1959), pp. 49–53.
1959 *Letture religiose* (ed.). Firenze.
1959 "Oriente e Occidente: tradizioni antiche e prospettive nuove," *Rend. Acc. Lincei, Adun. sol.* (Roma), VI (1959), pp. 75–80. Reprinted in: *Religione e Società,* 1966, pp. 213–221.
1960 "Gudebilete med fleire hovud," *Norveg* (Oslo), VII, pp. 1–12.
1960 "Sur un prétendu monothéisme japonais," *Proceedings of the 9th Int. Congress of the History of Religions* (Tokyo and Kyoto, 1958). Tokyo, pp. 393–397.
1960 "Some parallels in the historical development of religion, Western and Japanese," *Proceedings of the 9th Int. Congress of the History of Religions* (Tokyo and Kyoto, 1958). Tokyo, pp. 773–776.
1966 *Religione e Società.* (Fifteen previously published essays and papers). Preface by V. Lanternari. Bologna, Ponte Nuovo.

OTTO PFLEIDERER

1. Biography and Appreciation

Dickson, W. P., *The Methods of the 'Higher Criticism', illustrated in an Examination of Dr. Pfleiderer's Theory as to the Resurrection* [in his work: *Das Urchristentum,* 1887]. Glasgow, James Maclehose, 1890.

2. Main Publications

1866 *Theorie des Aberglaubens.* (Sammlung gem. wissens. Vorträge, Heft 167). Berlin.
1869 *Die Religion, ihr Wesen und ihre Geschichte,* 2 vols. Leipzig.
1871 *Moral und Religion nach ihrem gegenseitigen Verhältnis geschichtlich und philosophisch erörtert.* Haarlem, Teylers Godgeleerd Genootschap (Nieuwe Serie, 2).
1873 *Der Paulinismus. Ein Beitrag zur Geschichte der urchristlichen Theologie.* Leipzig, Fues.
   English translation by E. Peters: *Paulinism. A Contribution to the History of primitive Christian Theology.* 2 vols. (Theological Translation Fund Library). London.
1878 *Religionsphilosophie auf geschichtlicher Grundlage.* Vol. I: *Geschichte der Religionsphilosophie von Spinoza bis auf die Gegenwart;* Vol. II: *Genetisch-spekulative Religionsphilosophie.* Berlin. 1883² (expanded edition).
   English translation of the 2nd edition by A. Stewart and A. Menzies: *The Philosophy of Religion on the Basis of its History,* 4 vols. (Theological Translation Fund Library, Vols. 34–37). London, 1886–1888.

1885 *Lectures on the Influence of the Apostle Paul on the Development of Christianity.* Delivered in London and Oxford in April and May 1885. (The
Hibbert Lectures). Translated by J. F. Smith. London, Williams & Norgate.

1891 *Die Entwicklung der protestantischen Theologie in Deutschland seit Kant
und in Grossbrittanien seit 1825.* Freiburg i. Br.
English translation by J. F. Smith: *The Development of Theology in Germany since Kant, and its Progress in Great Brittain since 1825.* (Library
of Philosophy: The Muirhead Library of Philosophy). London, Sonnenschein, 1891.

1894 *Philosophy and Development of Religion.* Being the Gifford Lectures
delivered before the University of Edinburgh, 2 vols. London–Edinburgh,
Blackwood, 1894.
English translation by A. Huebsch: *Religion and Historic Faiths.* London.
Fisher Unwin; New York, B. W. Huebsch. 1907.

1887 *Das Urchristentum, seine Schriften und Lehren in geschichtlichem Zusammenhang.* Berlin, 1887, 1902² (revised and expanded).
English translation by W. Montgomery and edited by W.D.Morrison. *Primitive Christianity, its writings and teachings in their historical connections,*
4 vols. (Theological Translation Fund Library, Vols. 22, 26, 27, 31).
London, 1906–1911.

1903 *Das Christusbild des urchristlichen Glaubens in religionsgeschichtlicher
Beleuchtung.* Vortrag. Berlin.
English translation: *The Early Christian Conception of Christ: its signi-
ficance and value in the history of Religion.* Expanded from a lecture
delivered at Amsterdam, September 1903. (Crown Theological Library,
Vol. 10). London, 1910.

1904 *Vorbereitung des Christentums in der griechischen Philosophie.* Halle a. S.

1905 *Entstehung des Christentums.* München.
English translation by D. A. Huebsch: *Christian Origins.* London, Fisher
Unwin, 1906.

1906 *Religion und Religionen.* München.

1907 *Entwicklung des Christentums.* München.
English translation by D. A. Huebsch: *The Development of Christianity.*
London, Fisher Unwin; New York, B. W. Huebsch, 1910.

1910 *Evolution and Theology and other Essays.* Edited by O. Cone. London,
Black, 1910.

JAMES BISSETT PRATT

Main Publications

1907 *The Psychology of Religious Belief.* New York, Macmillan.

1909 *What is Pragmatism?* (Lectures). New York, Macmillan.

1916 *India and its Faiths. A Traveller's Record.* Boston–New York, Houghton
Mifflin Co.; London, Constable.

1920 *The Religious Consciousness, a psychological Study.* New York, Macmillan.
1951².

1922 *Matter and Spirit. A Study of Mind and Body in their relation to the spiritual Life.* New York, Macmillan; London, Allen & Unwin, 1923, 1926².
1928 *The Pilgrimage of Buddhism and a Buddhist Pilgrimage.* New York–London, Macmillan.
1931 *Adventures in Philosophy and Religion.* New York, Macmillan.
1937 *Personal Realism.* New York, Macmillan.
1939 *Naturalism* (Powell Lectures on Philosophy at Indiana University. Ser. 3). New Haven, Yale University Press; London, Milford and Oxford University Press.
1940 *Why Religions die?* Berkeley–Los Angeles, University of California Press.
1941 *Can we keep the Faith?* New Haven, Yale University Press; London, Milford and Oxford University Press.
1949 *Reason in the Art of Living.* A textbook of ethics. New York, Macmillan.
1950 *Eternal Values in Religion.* Essays. New York, Macmillan.

KONRAD THEODOR PREUSZ

1. Biography and Appreciation

Lehmann, F. Rudolf, "K. Th. Preusz," *Zeitschrift für Ethnologie*, Jrg. 71 (1939), pp. 145–150.

2. Main Publications

1894 *Die Begräbnisarten der Amerikaner und Nordasiaten.* Inaugural-Dissertation. Königsberg.
1904 *Religionen der Naturvölker.* (Sonderabdruck aus *Archiv für Religionswissenschaft*, Bd. VII). Leipzig.
1904–1905 "Der Ursprung von Religion und Kunst," *Globus*, LXXXVI (1904), pp. 321ff., and LXXXVII (1905), pp. 333ff.
1912 *Die Nayarit-Expedition.* Textaufnahmen und Beobachtungen unter mexikanischen Indianern. Unternommen und herausgegeben im Auftrage und mit Mitteln des Königlichen Preusz. Kultus Ministeriums von Konrad Theodor Preusz. Leipzig, Teubner, 1912.
1914 *Die Geistige Kultur der Naturvölker.* Leipzig–Berlin, Teubner, 1923².
1914 "Religionen der Naturvölker," *Archiv für Religionswissenschaft*, XVII (1914), pp. 544–546.
1921 *Religion und Mythologie der Nitito.* Textaufnahmen und Beobachtungen bei einem Indianerstamm in Kolombien, Südamerika. (Quellen der Religionsgeschichte, Band 10/11). Göttingen–Leipzig.
1922 "Die höchste Gottheit bei den kulturarmen Völkern," *Psychologische Forschung*, II (1922), pp. 161–208.
1926 *Die Eingeborenen Amerikas.* (Religionsgeschichtliches Lesebuch, 2). Tübingen, Mohr, 1926².
1926 *Glauben und Mystik im Schatten des höchsten Wesens.* Leipzig, Hirschfeld.
1926 *Forschungsreise zu den Kägaba.* Beobachtungen, Textaufnahmen und sprachliche Studien bei einem Indianerstamme in Kolombien, Süd-Amerika. Wien.

1930 *Der Unterbau des Dramas.* Vorträge 1927–1928. (Kulturwissenschattliche Bibliothek Warburg). Hamburg.
1933 *Der religiöse Gehalt der Mythen.* Tübingen, Mohr, 1933.
1937 *Die Amerikanische Bilderhandschrift Historia Tolteca-Chichimeca.* Übersetzt und erläutert von K. Th. Preusz und E. Mengin. 1937, Baesler-Archiv.
1939 *Lehrbuch der Völkerkunde.* In erster Auflage herausgegeben von K. Th. Preusz. Unter Mitwirkung von Fachgenossen in zweiter Teilweise veränderter Auflage, herausgegeben von R. Thurnwald. Stuttgart.

JEAN PRZYLUSKI

1. Biography and Appreciation

Charles Picard, "Jean Przyluski," *Revue Archéologique,* Vol. 56, Nr. 35 (janvier 1950), pp. 101–102. See also: *Isis,* Vol. 41, Nr. 3–4 (1950), p. 302

2. Main Publications

1914 "Le nord-ouest de l'Inde dans le Vinaya des Mūla-Sarvāstivādin et les textes apparentés," *Journal Asiatique,* nov.–dec. 1914. (Translation of selections of the Chinese Tripitaka).
1923 *La légende de l'Empereur Açoka (Açoka-Avadāna) dans les textes indiens et chinois.* Thèse, Paris.
   English translation with additional notes and comments by Dilip Kumar Biswas: *The Legend of Emperor Asoka in Indian and Chinese texts.* Calcutta, Firme K. L. Mukhopadhyay, 1967.
1923 *A-Yu-Tchouan; Chronique des premiers Siècles du Bouddhisme.* Traduite du chinois et annotée. Thèse complémentaire. Paris, Geuthner.
1926 *Le concile de Rājagṛha.* Introduction à l'histoire des canons et des sectes bouddhiques. Paris.
1932 *Le Bouddhisme.* Paris, Rieder.
1936 "Y a-t-il une Science des Religions?," *Revue de l'Histoire des Religions,* 114 (1936), pp. 52–68.
1939 I. *Ursprünge und Entwicklung des Kultes der Mutter-Göttin.*
   II. *Die Mutter-Göttin als Verbindung zwischen den Lokal-Göttern und dem Universal-Gott.* Zürich, Rhein Verlag.
   French translation: *La grande Déesse. Introduction à l'étude comparative des Religions.* With a Preface by Charles Picard. Paris, 1950.
1940 *La participation.* Paris.
1942 *L'évolution humaine.* Paris, Presses Universitaires de France.
1943 *Créer.* Paris, Presses Universitaires de France.

ALFRED R. RADCLIFFE-BROWN*

1. Bibliography

Brown, Ina Corinne, "Bibliography of A. R. Radcliffe-Brown," in: Fred Eggan, ed., *Social Anthropology of North American Tribes. Essays in Social Organization, Law and Religion.* Presented to Professor A. R. Radcliffe-Brown upon the occasion of his accepting of the chair of social anthropology at Oxford University. Chicago, University of Chicago Press, 1937, pp. XV–XVII.

Pardee, Ruth, "Bibliography of Professor A. R. Radcliffe-Brown," in: Meyer Fortes, ed., *Social Structure.* Studies presented to A. R. Radcliffe-Brown. Oxford, Clarendon Press, pp. 226–228.

2. Biography and Appreciation

"Alfred Reginald Radcliffe-Brown. Obituary," *Africa*, XXVI (1956), p. 1.

Eggan, Fred and Warner, W. Lloyd, "Alfred Reginald Radcliffe-Brown. 1881–1955," *American Anthropologist*, LVIII, 3 (June 1956), pp. 544–547.

Elkin, A. P., "A. R. Radcliffe-Brown, 1880 [1881]–1955," *Oceania*, XXVI, 4 (June 1956), pp. 239–251.

Firth, R., "Alfred Reginald Radcliffe-Brown, 1881–1955," *Proceedings of the British Academy*, XLII (1957).

Fortes, Meyer, "Radcliffe-Brown's contributions to the study of social organization," *The British Journal of Sociology*, VI, 1 (March 1955).

—, "Alfred Reginald Radcliffe-Brown, 1881–1955. A memoir," *Man*, LVI (November 1956), pp. 149–153.

Homans, G. C., "Anxiety and ritual: the theories of Malinowski and Radcliffe–Brown," *American Anthropologist*, XLIII (1941), pp. 164–172.

Josselin de Jong, J. P. B. de, "Herdenking van Alfred Reginald Radcliffe-Brown (17 Januari 1881–24 Oktober 1955)," *Jaarboek der Koninklijke Nederlandse Akademie van Wetenschappen*, 1955–1956, pp. 1–8.

Redfield, Robert, "Introduction" in: Fred Eggan, ed., *Social Anthropology of North American Tribes. Essays in Social Organization, Law, and Religion.* Chicago, University of Chicago Press, 1937, 1955^2.

Srinivas, M. N., "Introduction," in: M. N. Srinivas, ed., *Method in Social Anthropology. Selected Essays by A. R. Radcliffe-Brown.* Chicago, University of Chicago Press, 1958, pp. IX–XX.

3. Method and Theory

1914 "The definition of totemism," *Anthropos*, IX (1914), pp. 622–630.

1923 "The methods of ethnology and social anthropology," *The South African Journal of Science*, XX (1923), pp. 124–147. Reprinted in: *Method in Social Anthropology*, 1958, pp. 3–38.

1930 "Historical and functional interpretations of culture in relation to the practical application of anthropology to native peoples," *Proceedings of the Fourth Pacific Science Congress* (Java, 1929), Vol. III. Batavia-Bandoeng. Reprinted in: *Method in Social Anthropology*, 1958, pp. 39–41.

1930 "The sociological theory of totemism," *Proceedings of the Fourth Pacific Science Congress* (Java, 1929), Vol. III. pp. 295–309; Vol. VIII, pp. 537–538. Batavia–Bandoeng. Reprinted in: *Structure and Function in Primitive Society*, 1952, pp. 117–132.

1931 "The present position of anthropological studies," Presidential address Section H, *British Association for the Advancement of Science*, Centenary Meeting in London. Reprinted in: *Method in Social Anthropology*, 1958, pp. 42–95.

1935 "On the concept of function in the social sciences," *American Anthropologist*, N. S., XXXVII (1935), pp. 394–402. Reprinted in: *Structure and Function in Primitive Society*, 1952, pp. 178–187.

1940 "On social structure," *Journal of the Royal Anthropological Institute*, LXX (1940), pp. 1–12. Reprinted in: *Structure and Function in Primitive Society*, 1952, pp. 188–204.

1944 "The meaning and scope of social anthropology," *Nature*, No. 3904 (August 26, 1944), pp. 257–260. Reprinted in: *Method in Social Anthropology*, 1958, pp. 96–107.

1945 "Religion and society" (The Henry Myers Lecture, 1945), *Journal of the Royal Anthropological Institute*, LXXV (1945), pp. 33–43. Reprinted in: *Structure and Function in Primitive Society*, 1952, pp. 153–177.

1946 "A note on functional anthropology," *Man*, XLVI, 30 (1946), pp. 38–41.

1952 "The comparative method in social anthropology," *Journal of the Royal Anthropological Institute*, LXXXI (1951), pp. 15–22. Reprinted in: *Method in Social Anthropology*, 1958, pp. 108–129.

1952 "Introduction," in *Structure and Function in Primitive Society*. London, Cohen & West 1968[7] (also in pb.), pp. 1–14.

1958 *Method in Social Anthropology. Selected Essays.* Edited by M. N. Srinivas. Preface by Fred Eggan. (Mostly previously published). Chicago, University of Chicago Press.

4. Main Publications*

1909 "The religion of the Andaman Islanders," *Folk-Lore*, XX, 3 (1909), pp. 257–271. Comp. pp. 492–497.

* Until 1922 published under the name of: A. R. Brown.

1910 "Puluga: a reply to Father Schmidt," *Man*, X, 17 (1910).
1910 "Marriage and descent, North Australia," *Man*, X, 32 (1910), pp. 55–59.
1912 "Marriage and descent in North and Central Australia," *Man*, XII, 64 (1912), pp. 123–124.
1912 "Beliefs concerning childbirth in some Australian tribes," *Man*, XII, 96 (1912), pp. 180–182.
1913 "Three tribes of Western Australia," *Journal of the Royal Anthropological Institute*, XLIII (1913).
1914 "Relationship system of the Dieri tribe," *Man*, XIV, 33 (1914), pp. 53–56.
1916 "Australian rafts," *Man*, XVI, 4 (1916).
1918–1923 "Notes on the social organization of Australian tribes," *Journal of the Royal Anthropological Institute*, XLVIII (1918), pp. 222–253 and LIII (1923), pp. 424–447.
1922 *The Andaman Islanders*. Cambridge, Cambridge University Press. Enlarged 1933².
1924 "The mother's brother in South Africa," *The South African Journal of Science*, XXI (1924), pp. 542–555. Reprinted in *Structure and Function in Primitive Society*, 1952, pp. 15–31.
1925 "Culture areas of Africa," *American Anthropologist*, N. S., XXVII (1925).
1925 "Native dolls in the Transvaal Museum," *Annals of the Transvaal Museum*, XI, 2 (1925).
1926 "Father, mother, and child," *Man*, XXVI, 103 (1926), pp. 159–161.
1926 "Arrangement of stones in Australia," *Man*, XXVI, 133 (1926), pp. 204–205.
1926 "The Rainbow-Serpent myth of Australia," *Journal of the Royal Anthropological Institute*, LVI (1926), pp. 19–25.
1927 "The regulation of marriage in Ambryn," *Journal of the Royal Anthropological Institute*, LVII (1927).
1929 "Age organization terminology," *Man*, XXIX, 13 (1929).
1929 "A further note on Ambryn," *Man*, XXIX, 35 (1929), pp. 50–53.
1929 "Bride price, earnest or indemnity," *Man*, XXIX, 96 (1929).
1929 "Bilateral descent," *Man*, XXIX, 157 (1929).
1929 "Notes on totemism in Eastern Australia," *Journal of the Royal Anthropological Institute*, LIX (1929), pp. 399–415.
1930 "Editorial," *Oceania*, I, 1 (1930).
1930 "Former numbers and distribution of the Australian aborigines," *Official Yearbook of the Commonwealth of Australia*, No. 23 (1930), pp. 687–696.
1930 "The Rainbow-Serpent myth in South-East Australia," *Oceania*, I, 3 (1930), pp. 342–347.
1930 "A system for notation of relationships," *Man*, XXX, 93. (1930).
1931 *The Social Organization of Australian Tribes*. First published in *Oceania*, I, 1–4 (1930–31). (Oceania Monographs, 1), Melbourne.
1933 "Social Sanctions," *Encyclopaedia of the Social Sciences*, Vol. XIII. New York. Reprinted in: *Structure and Function in Primitive Society*, 1952, pp. 205–211.
1935 "Anthropology and Indian administration," *American Indian Life*, No. 26 (1935).
1935 "Kinship terminologies in California," *American Anthropologist*, N. S., XXXVII (1935).

1935 "Patrilineal and matrilineal succession," *Iowa Law Review*, XX, 2 (1935), pp. 286–303. Reprinted in: *Structure and Function in Primitive Society*, 1952, pp. 32–48.
1935 "Primitive Law," *Man*, XXXV, 48 (1935).
1937 "Australian social organization," *Man*, XXXVII, 201 (1937).
1938 "Motherhood in Australia," *Man*, XXXVIII, 14 (1938), pp. 15–16.
1939 *Taboo*. (The Frazer Lecture, 1939). Cambridge, Cambridge University Press. Reprinted in: *Structure and Function in Primitive Society*, 1952, pp. 133–152.
1940 "On joking relationships," *Africa*, XIII, 3 (1940) pp. 195–210. Reprinted in: *Structure and Function in Primitive Society*, 1952, pp. 90–104.
1941 "The study of kinship systems," *Journal of the Royal Anthropological Institute*, LXXI (1941), pp. 1–18. Reprinted in: *Structure and Function in Primitive Society*, 1952, pp. 49–89.
1947 "Evolution. Social or cultural?," *American Anthropologist*, N. S., XLIX (1947), pp. 78–83.
1947 "Australian social organization," *American Anthropologist*, N. S., XLIX (1947), pp. 151–154.
1949 "A further note on joking relationships," *Africa*, XIX (1949), pp. 133–140. Reprinted in: *Structure and Function in Primitive Society*, 1952, pp. 105–116.
1950 A. R. Radcliffe-Brown and Daryll Forde, *African Systems of Kinship and Marriage*. London.
1951 "Murngin social organization," *American Anthropologist*, LIII (1951), pp. 37–55.
1952 *Structure and Function in Primitive Society*. Essays and addresses [previously published]. With a foreword by E. E. Evans-Pritchard and Fred Eggan. London, Cohen & West 1968[7].
1956 "On Australian local organization," *American Anthropologist*, LVIII (1956), pp. 363–367.
1957 *A Natural Science of Society*. With a foreword by Fred Eggan. Glencoe (Ill.), The Free Press.
1958 *Method in Social Anthropology. Selected Essays*. Edited by M. N. Srinivas. Chicago, University of Chicago Press.

PAUL RADIN*

1. Bibliography

Werbner, Richard, "A bibliography of writings by Paul Radin," in: Stanley Diamond, ed., *Culture in History*. . . . (1960), pp. 1001–1010.

2. Biography and Appreciation

Bidney, David, "Paul Radin and the problem of primitive monotheism," in: Stanley Diamond, ed, *Culture in History*. . . . (1960,) pp. 363–379.
Diamond, Stanley, ed., *Culture in History. Essays in Honor of Paul Radin*. Published for Brandeis University by Columbia University Press, New York.

Du Bois, Cora, "Paul Radin: An Appreciation," in: Stanley Diamond, ed.,
Culture in History, . . . (1960), IX–XVI.
Hoijer, Harry, "Paul Radin, 1883–1959," *American Anthropologist*, LXI
(October, 1959), pp. 839–843.

3. Method and Theory

1918 "Ethnology and history," *University of California Chronicle*, XX,
2 (1918), pp. 16–21.
1929 "A history of ethnological theories," *American Anthropologist*, N. S.,
XXXI (1929), pp. 9–33.
1933 *The Method and Theory of Ethnology. An Essay in Criticism*. New York-
London, McGraw-Hill, 1933.
1934 "The method and theory of ethnology. A reply to R. R. Marett's review,"
American Anthropologist, N. S., XXXVI (1934), pp. 315–316.

4. Main Publications

1909 "Winnebago tales," *Journal of American Folklore*, XXII (1909), pp. 288–
313.
1911 "The ritual and significance of the Winnebago medicine dance," *Journal
of American Folklore*, XXIV, No. 92 (1911), pp. 148–208.
1913 "Personal reminiscences of a Winnebago Indian," *Journal of American
Folklore*, XXVI, No. 102 (1913), pp. 293–318.
1914 *Some Myths and Tales of the Ojibwa of South-Eastern Ontario*. (Anthropology Series of the Canada Geological Survey, Memoir 48, No. 2). Ottawa.
1914 "Religion of the North American Indians," *Journal of American Folklore*,
XXVII, No. 106 (1914), pp. 335–373.
1915 *The Social Organization of the Winnebago Indians. An Interpretation*.
(Anthropology Series of the Canada Geological Survey, No. 5. Museum
Bulletin No. 10). Ottawa.
1915 *Literary Aspects of North American Mythology*. (Anthropology Series of the
Canada Geological Survey, No. 6. Museum Bulletin No. 16). Ottawa.
1915 "The Hare Cycle of the Winnebago Indians," in: *Studies in North
American Mythology*. Vol. 1, Part 1. Santa Fe (New Mexico).
1915 "Religion of the North American Indians," in: Franz Boas *et alii*, *Anthropology in North America*. New York, G. E. Stechert, pp. 259–305.
1915 "The Winnebago myth of the Twins," in: *Papers of the Southwestern
Anthropological Society*, I (1915), pp. 1–56.
1915 Editor, with Aurelio M. Espinosa: "Folk-tales from Oaxaca," *Journal
of American Folklore*, XXVIII, No. 110 (1915), pp. 370–408.
1917 Editor, with Aurelio M. Espinoza; *El Folk-Lore de Oaxaca*. New York,
G. E. Stechert.
1920 "The autobiography of a Winnebago Indian," *University of California
Publications in American Archaeology and Ethnology*, XVI (1920), pp.
381–473. Reissued: Dover Books, 1963.
1920 "The sources and authenticity of the history of the ancient Mexicans,"
*University of California Publications in American Archaeology and Ethno-
logy*, XVII (1920), pp. 1–150.

1923 "The Winnebago Tribe," in: *Thirty-seventh Annual Report of the United States Bureau of American Ethnology*. Washington, D. C., pp. 35–550.

1924 *Monotheism among Primitive Peoples*. (The Arthur Davis Memorial Lecture before the Jewish Historical Society). Foreword by Israel Zangwill. London, G. Allen and Unwin. Reissued as "Special Publication of Bollingen Foundation. No. 4", Basel, Ethnographical Museum, 1954.

1924 "Ojibwa ethnological chit-chat," *American Anthropologist*, N. S., XXVI (1924), pp. 491–530.

1924 "Wappo Texts, First Series," *University of California Publications in American Archaeology and Ethnology*, XIX (1924), pp. 1–147.

1926 "Literary aspects of Winnebago mythology," *Journal of American Folklore*, XXXIX (1926), pp. 18–52.

1926 "Winnebago myth cycles," *Primitive Culture*, I (1926), pp. 8–86.

1926 Editor: Crashing Thunder, *The Autobiography of an American Indian*. New York–London, Appleton.

1927 *Primitive Man as Philosopher*. Foreword by John Dewey. New York, Appleton. Enlarged edition: New York, Dover Publications, 1957.

1927 *The Story of the American Indian*. New York, Boni and Liveright. Revised edition: New York, Liveright, 1934.
      French translation by Eva Métraux: *Histoire de la civilisation indienne*. Paris, Payot, 1936.

1928 In collaboration with A. B. Reagan: "Ojibwa myths and tales," *Journal of American Folklore*, XLI (1928), pp. 61–146.

1932 *Social Anthropology*. New York–London, McGraw-Hill.

1934 *The Racial Myth*. New York, Whittlesey House, 1934.

1935 *An Historical Legend of the Zapotecs*. (Ibero–Americana Series). Berkeley, University of California Press.

1937 *Primitive Religion: Its Nature and Origin*. New York, Viking Press. Enlarged edition: New York, Dover Publications, 1937.
      French translation by Alfred Métraux: *La religion primitive. Sa nature et son origine*. Paris, Gallimard, 1937.

1937 "Economic factors in primitive religion," *Science and Society*, I, 3 (1937).

1942 *Indians of South America*. (American Museum of Natural History Science Series, Vol. 8). Garden City (N. Y.), Doubleday.

1943–1944 "Cuentos y Leyendas de los Zapotecos," *Tlalocan*, I (1943/44), pp. 3–30, 134–154, and 194–226.

1944 "The nature and problems of Mexican Indian mythology," *Journal of American Folklore*, LVII (1944), pp. 26–36.

1945 *The Plot of Life and Death. A Ritual Drama of the American Indians*. (Bollingen Series, No. 5). Foreword by Mark van Doren. New York, Pantheon Books.

1948 *Winnebago Hero Cycles; A Study in Aboriginal Literature*. (Indiana University Publications in Anthropology and Linguistics, Memoir 1). Bloomington (Ind.). Also Memoir 1 as Supplement to *International Journal of American Linguistics*, XIV, 3.

1949 *Winnebago Culture as Described by Themselves*. (Special Publication of the Bollingen Foundation, No. 1). Supplement to *International Journal of American Linguistics*, XV, 1.

1949 "The basic myth of the American Indians," *Eranos Jahrbuch*, XVII (1948), pp. 359–419.

1950 *The Origin Myth of the Medicine Rite; Three Versions. The Historical Origin of the Medicine Rite.* (Special Publication of the Bollingen Foundation, No. 2). Supplement to *International Journal of American Linguistics*, XVI, 1.

1950 "The religious experiences of an American Indian," *Eranos Jahrbuch*, XVIII (1949), pp. 250–290.

1951 *Die religiöse Erfahrung der Naturvölker.* Zürich, Rhein Verlag.

1951 "The esoteric rituals of the North American Indians," *Eranos Jahrbuch*, XIX (1950), pp. 282–349.

1951 "Primitive literature," in: C. G. E. Laird, ed. *The World through Literature.* New York, Appleton.

1952 *African Folktales and Sculpture.* (Bollingen Series, 32). New York, Pantheon Books. London, 1964².

1953 *The World of Primitive Man.* (Life of Science Library). New York, Schuman.
  German translation by Margherita von Wyss: *Gott und Mensch in der Primitiven Welt* (revised and enlarged). Zürich, Rhein Verlag, 1953.

1954–1956 *The Evolution of an American Indian Prose Epic; A Study in Comparative Literature*, 2 vols. (Special Publication of the Bollingen Foundation No's 3 and 5). Basel, Ethnographical Museum.

1955 "The dreams of an American Indian: their meaning and function," in: *Studien zur Analytischen Psychologie C. G. Jungs.* Zürich, Rascher Verlag, Vol. II, pp. 146–170.

1955 "The literature of primitive peoples," *Diogenes*, XII (1955), pp. 1–28.

1956 *The Trickster; A Study in American Indian Mythology.* With commentaries by Karl Kerényi and C. G. Jung. London, L. Routledge; New York, Philosophical Library.
  French translation by Arthur Reiss: *Le fripon divin. Un mythe indien.* Genève, Georg, 1958.
  German translation by Ilse Kramer: *Der göttliche Schelm. Ein indianischer Mythenzyklus.* Zürich, Rhein-Verlag, 1954.

FRIEDRICH RATZEL

1. Bibliography

Hantzsch, V., "Bibliographie," in: Friedrich Ratzel, *Kleine Schriften*... München–Berlin, 1906.

2. Main Publications

1876 *Die chinesische Auswanderung. Ein Beitrag zur Kultur- und Handelsgeographie.* Breslau.

1878 *Aus Mexico. Reiseskizzen aus den Jahren 1874–75.* Breslau, J. U. Kern.

1885–1888 *Völkerkunde*, 3 Volumes.
  English translation by A. J. Butler: *The History of Mankind.* With an Introduction by E. B. Taylor, 3 vols. London, Macmillan 1896–1898.

1895 *Anthropogeographische Beiträge*. Leipzig, Duncker & Humblot.
1899 *Anthropo-Geographie oder Grundzüge der Anwendung der Erdkunde auf die Geschichte*, 2nd edition. Stuttgart, J. Engelhorn, 1921–22.
1906 *Kleine Schriften*. Ausgewählt und herausgegeben durch H. Helmolt, mit einer Bibliographie von V. Hantzsch, 2 vols. München–Berlin.

SALOMON REINACH

1. Bibliography

Bibliographie de Salomon Reinach, 1874–1922. Avec supplément. Saint-Germain, Musée de Saint-Germain, 1922–1927.
Ricci, Seymour de, "Bibliographie des Traveaux de S. Reinach relatifs au Judaisme," *Revue d'Etudes Juives*, XCIV (1933), pp. 11–28.

2. Biography and Appreciation

Batiffol, P., *Orpheus et l'Evangile*. Paris, 1910.
    English translation by G. C. H. Pollen: *The Credibility of the Gospel*. London, Longmans, 1912.
Lagrange, M. J., *Quelques remarques sur 'l'Orpheus' de M. Salomon Reinach*. Paris, J. Gabala, 1910.
    English translation by C. C. Martindale: *Notes on the 'Orpheus' of M. S. Reinach*. Oxford, Blackwell; London, Simpking Marshall, 1910.
Réal, J., *La Science des religions et le problème religieus au XXe siècle. A Propos de' l'Orpheus' de M. Salomon Reinach*. Paris, 1909.
Ricci, Seymour de, "Salomon Reinach (1858–1932)," *Revue d'Etudes Juives*, XCIV (1933), pp. 1–10.
Simon, A., and Toutain, J., *Compléments et corrections aux 'Ephémérides d'Alesia' de M. S. Reinach*. Paris, 1926.

3. Main Publications

1904 *Apollo. Histoire générale des arts plastiques*. Paris, Hachette. 1919².
    English translation by F. Simmonds: *The Story of Art throughout the Ages*. London, Heinemann, 1904. 1907² (revised and expanded).
1905–1906 *Cultes, Mythes et Religions*, 3 vols. Paris. 1922³ (expanded).
    English translation by E. Frost: *Cults, Myths and Religions*. Selected Chapters. London, Nutt, 1912.
1909 *Orpheus. Histoire générale des religions*. Paris, Picard.
    English authorized translation by F. Simmonds: *Orpheus. A General History of Religions*. London, Heinemann; New York, Putnam, 1909. London, Routledge, 1931 (revised), New York, Liveright, 1942.
1925 *Ephémérides d'Alesia. Histoire, Fouilles, Controverses*. Revue Archéologique. (Série 5, Vol. 21). Paris.
1928–1930 *Ephémérides de Glozel*, 2 vols. Paris.
1930 *Amalthée. Mélanges d'archéologie et d'histoire*, 2 vols. Paris, Leroux.

RICHARD REITZENSTEIN

1. Bibliography

R. Reitzenstein (Berlin), "Richard Reitzensteins Schriften," in: *Festschrift Richard Reitzenstein*, zum 2. April 1931 dargebracht von Ed. Fraenkel and others. Leipzig–Berlin, Teubner, 1931, pp. 160–168.

2. Main Publications

1904 *Poimandres*. Studien zur griechisch–ägyptischen und frühchristlichen Literatur. Leipzig, Teubner.

1906 *Hellenistische Wundererzählungen*. Leipzig, Teubner. 1922².

1907 *Werden und Wesen der Humanität im Altertum*. Kaisergeburtstagrede. Strassburg, Heitz.

1910 *Die hellenistischen Mysterienreligionen*. Ihre Grundgedanken und Wirkungen. Vortrag gehalten in dem wiss. Prediger-Verein für Elsass-Lotharingen den 11. XI. 1909. Leipzig–Berlin, Teubner. 1920²; 1927³ (enlarged).

1912 *Das Märchen von Amor und Psyche bei Apuleius*. Antrittsrede Freiburg 1911. Leipzig–Berlin, Teubner.

1912 "Religionsgeschichte und Eschatologie," *Zeitschrift für neutestamentliche Wissenschaft*, 13 (1912), pp. 1–28.

1912 "Die Areopagrede des Paulus," *Neue Jahrbücher für das klassisches Altertum*, 31 (1913), pp. 193–422.

1916 *Historia Monachorum und Historia Lausiaca*. Eine Studie zur Geschichte des Mönchtums und der frühchristlischen Begriffe Gnostiker und Pneumatiker. (Forschungen zur Religion und Literatur des Alten und Neuen Testament, N. F., Heft 7). Göttingen, Vandenhoeck & Ruprecht.

1916 "Die Formel 'Glaube, Liebe, Hoffnung' bei Paulus," *Nachrichten der Gesellschaft der Wissenschaften zu Göttingen. Phil.-hist. Kla.*, 1916, pp. 367–416.

1917 "Die Formel 'Glaube, Liebe, Hoffnung' bei Paulus. Ein Nachwort," *Nachrichten der Gesellschaft Wissenschaften zu Göttingen. Phil.-Kl.*, 1917, pp. 130–151.

1919 *Das mandäische Buch des Herrn der Grösse und die Evangelienüberlieferung*, (Sitzungsberichte d. K. Preuss. Akad. d. Wiss. Berlin, Heidelberg, Winter 1919. Vol. 12).

1921 *Das iranische Erlösungsmysterium*. Religionsgeschichtliche Untersuchungen. Bonn, Marcus & Weber.

1922 "Augustin als antiker und als mittelalterlicher Mensch," *Vorträge der Bibliothek Warburg*, II (1922/23), I. Teil, pp. 28–65.

1922 "Vorchristliche Erlösungslehren," *Kyrkohistorisk Årsskrift*, 22 (1922), pp. 94–128.

1922 "Gedanken zur Entwicklung des Erlöserglaubens," *Historische Zeitschrift*, 126 (1922), pp. 1–57.

1922 "Weltuntergangsvorstellungen. Eine Studie zur vergleichenden Religionsgeschichte," *Kyrkohistorisk Årsskrift*, 24 (124), pp. 1–22.

1926 *Studien zum antiken Synkretismus aus Iran und Griechenland*. By R. Reitzenstein and H. H. Schaeder. (Studien der Bibliothek Warburg, 7) Leipzig & Berlin, Teubner.

1929 *Die Vorgeschichte der christlichen Taufe.* Mit Beiträgen von L. Troje.
  Leipzig & Berlin, Teubner.
1929 "Zwei Arten religionsgeschichtlicher Forschung," *Archiv für Religionswissenschaft*, 27 (1929), pp. 241–277.
1930 "Noch einmal Eros und Psyche," *Archiv für Religionswissenschaft*, 28
  (1930), pp. 42–87.

ERNEST RENAN*

1. Bibliography

Girard, Henri et Moncel, Henri, *Bibliographie des œuvres de Ernest Renan*
  (Publications de la Société Ernest Renan. Histoire religieuse, Vol. 1).
  Paris, Presses Universitaires de France, 1923.

2. Biography

Alexander, William, *M. Renan on the Kingdom of God.* Exeter Hall Lectures,
  1864–65. Oxford, 1865.
Alfarice, Prosper, *Les manuscrits de la "Vie de Jésus" d'Ernest Renan.* Avec
  introduction, notes, concordances. Paris, Les Belles-Lettres, 1939.
Allier, Raoul, La philosophie d'Ernest Renan. Paris, 1895.
Auzies, Célestine, *Les origines de la Bible et M. Ernest Renan.* Paris, Letouzey
  & Aué, 1889.
Barrès, Maurice, *Huit jours chez M. Renan. Trois stations de psychothérapie. Toute
  licence sauf contre l'amour.* Paris, E. Paul frères, 1913[8]. Reprinted: Paris,
  Pauvert, 1965.
  —, *Ernest Renan.* Discours prononcé à la Sorbonne au nom de l'Académie
  Française le 28 février 1923. Abbeville, F. Paillart, 1923.
Barry, William F., *Ernest Renan.* London, Hodder and Stoughton; New York,
  C. Scribner's Sons, 1905.
Bauer, Bruno, *Philo, Strauss und Renan und das Urchristenthum.* Berlin, G.
  Hempel, 1874.
Blinkenberg, Andreas, *Ernest Renan. Bidrag til belysning af hans filosofisk-
  religiose ungdomskrise.* København, Engelsen & Schroder, 1923.
Boulanger, Jacques, *Renan et ses critiques.* Paris, 1925.
Brauer, H. G. A., "The philosophy of Ernest Renan," *Bulletin of the University
  of Wisconsin*, No. 55. *Philology and literature series*, II, 3 (1903), pp.
  205–379. Also published separately: Madison, Wis., 1903 (Ph. D. diss.).
Chadbourne, Richard McClaim, *Ernest Renan as an Essayist.* Cornell University
  Press, 1957.
  —, *Ernest Renan.* New York, Twayne Publications, 1968.
Chaix-Ruy, Jules, *"L' Averroès" d'Ernest Renan.* Alger, 1950.
  —, *Ernesto Renan.* Brescia, Morcellina, 1954.
  French translation: *Ernest Renan.* Paris, Vitte, 1956.
Cresson, André, *Ernest Renan. Sa vie, son œuvre, avec un exposé de sa philosophie.*
  ("Philosophes"). Paris, P. U. F., 1949.

Delaporte, Victor, "L' 'Apothéose' de Renan,", *Etudes*, novembre 1892. Also published separately: Paris, V. Retaux et fils, 1893.

Desportes, Henri, *Ernest Renan, sa vie et son œuvre*. Préface J. de Biez. Paris, Tobra, 1893.

Dubreuil, Léon, *Rosmapamon. La vieillesse bretonne de Renan*. Paris, Ariane, 1946.

Duclaux, Agnes M. F. (Robinson) [Madame J. Darmesteter], *La vie de Ernest Renan*. Paris, Calmann Lévy, 1898[2].
　English translation: *The Life of Ernest Renan*, by Madame James Darmesteter (A. Mary F. Robinson). London, Methuen & Co, 1898[2]; Boston, Houghton & Mifflin, 1899.

Dussaud, René, *L'œuvre scientifique d'Ernest Renan*. Paris, P. Geuthner, 1951.

Espinasse, Francis, *Life of Ernest Renan*. London, W. Scott Ltd, 1895.

Ferla, Giuseppe la, *Renan, politico*. Torino, F. de Silva, 1953.

Galand, René M., *L'âme celtique de Renan*. Institut d'Etudes Françaises de Yale University. New Haven, Yale University Press, 1959.

Grant Duff, Sir Mountstuart Elphinstone, *Ernest Renan. In Memoriam*. London, Macmillan and Co, 1893.

Guilloux, Pierre, *L'esprit de Renan*. Paris, J. de Gigord, 1920.

Hello, Ernest, *M. Renan, l'Allemagne et l'athéisme au XIX*[e] *siècle*. Paris, C. Doumiol, 1859.

Huré, Anne, *Entretiens avec Monsieur Renan*. Paris, R. Julliard, 1962.

Jaspar, Marcel Henri, *Ernest Renan et sa république*. Paris, Albert, 1934.

—, *Le génie libéral de la France: essai sur Renan*. New York, Ed. Moretus, 1942.

Küchler, Walther, *Ernest Renan. Der Dichter und der Künstler*. Gotha, 1921.

Lasserre, Henri, *L'évangile selon Renan*. Paris, V. Palmé, 1863[5].

Lasserre, Pierre, *Renan et nous*. Paris, B. Grasset, 1923.

—, *La jeunesse d'Ernest Renan. Histoire de la crise religieuse au XIX*[e] *siècle*, 3 vols. Paris, Garnier, 1925–1932.

Lefranc, Abel, *Ernest Renan en Italie. Sa mission scientifique et littéraire, juillet 1849–juillet 1850, d'après sa correspondance, et vingt lettres inédites*. Paris, N. R. C., 1938.

Le Nordez, Albert, *M. Renan d'après lui-même, ou étude critique et psychologique à l'occasion de son dernier ouvrage: La réforme intellectuelle et morale de la France*. Contances, Librairie Daireau, 1872.

Le libre d'or de Renan. Paris, A. Joanin et Cie, 1903.

Marriot, Maurice, *La vie de Renan suite à la vie de Jésus*. Toulouse, Delboy, 1863[4].

Massis, Henri, *Jugements* (le série). *Renan–France–Barrès*. Paris, Plon-Nourrit et Cie, 1923.

—, *Portrait de Monsieur Renan*. Paris, Cayla, 1949.

Millepierres, François, *La vie d'Ernest Renan, sage d'Occident*. Paris, 1961.

Milsaud, Philibert, *Bibliographie des publications relatives au livre de M. Renan. Vie de Jésus, de juillet 1863 à juin 1864*. Paris, Denter, 1864.

Molt, L. F., *Ernest Renan*. New York, D. Appleton and Co, 1921.

Monod, G. J. J., *Les maîtres de l'histoire: Renan, Taine, Michelet*. Paris, 1895 (pp. 1–49).

Parigot, Hippolyte, *Renan, l'égoïsme intellectuel*. Paris, n. d. (1909).

—, *La jeunesse cléricale d'Ernest Renan–Saint Sulpice*. (Publications de la Faculté des Lettres de l'Université de Strasbourg, fasc. 55). Paris, 1933.

Peyre, Henri, *Sagesse de Renan*. Paris, P. U. F., 1968.
—, *Ernest Renan*. Paris, P. U. F., 1969.
Platzhoff, Ed., *Ernest Renan. Seine Entwicklung und Weltanschauung* (Inaug. Diss. Bern). Dresden, 1900.
Pommier, Jean, *Renan, d'après des documents inédits*. Paris, 1923.
—, "Comment fut composée la 'Prière sur l'Acropole'," Revue de Paris, 15 septembre 1923.
—, *La pensée religieuse de Renan*. Paris, 1925.
—, *Renan et Strasbourg*. Paris, 1926.
Psichari, Henriette, *Renan d'après lui-même*. Paris, Plon, 1937.
—, *Renan et la guerre de 70*. Paris, 1947.
—, *La prière sur l'Acropole et ses mystères*. Paris, 1956.
Psichari, Jean, *Ernest Renan, jugements et souvenirs*. Paris, Les éditions du monde moderne, 1925.
Renan, Ernest, *Henriette Renan. Souvenir pour ceux qui l'ont connue*. Paris, Claye, 1862. Reprinted under the title of *Ma sœur Henriette*. Paris, C. Lévy, 1895; also 1896 together with *Lettres intimes*. New edition 1923: *Henriette Renan. Souvenir pour ceux qui l'ont connue*. Paris, Ferroud, 1923. Reissued under the title of *Ma sœur Henriette*, with a preface by Henriette Psichari. Paris, Imprimerie Steff, 1964.
  English translation by Lady M. Lloyd: *Brother and sister . . . A Memoir and the Letters of Ernest and Henriette Renan*. London, W. Heinemann, 1896.
—, *Souvenirs d'enfance et de jeunesse* . . . Paris, C. Lévy, 1883, 1897[23], 1922[68].
  Parts had appeared earlier in *Revue des Deux-Mondes*, 3e période, T. 14, 15 mars 1876, pp. 241–261; 3e période, T. 18, 1 décembre 1876, pp. 481–507; 3e période, T. 42, 1 novembre 1880, pp. 68–94; 3e période, T. 54, 1–15 novembre 1882, pp. 5–26.
  Another edition appeared in the series "Les Maîtres du Livre": Paris, G. Crès, n. d. Also in "Collection Nelson": Paris (Edinburgh), T. Nelson, 1912. It appeared with Introduction and Notes by Irving Babitt in "Heath's Modern Languages Series", Boston, 1902. The book was reissued under the title of: *Souvenirs d'enfance et de jeunesse*. Texte et documents inédits présentés par Gilbert Guisan. Lausanne, éd. Rencontre, 1961. Pb. Paris, Le livre de poche, 1967.
  Czech translation by Ad. Gottwald: *Vzpominky z mládi*. V. Praze, 1913.
  English translation by C. B. Pitman and revised by Mme Renan: *Recollections of my youth* . . . New York and London, Chapman and Hall, 1883, 1892[2].
  There is also an edition *Recollections and Letters*, translated by Isabel F. Hapgood: New York, 1892.
  Finnish translation by Eino Kaila: *Lapsuuden ja nuoruuden muistelmia* Helsinki, 1921.
  German authorized translation by Stephan Born: *Erinnerungen aus meiner Kindheit und Jugendzeit*. Basel, Bernheim, 1883.
  Swedish translation by Walborg Hedberg: *Barndoms- och ungdomsminnen*. Stockholm, 1915.
—, *Feuilles détachées, faisant suite aux "Souvenirs d'enfance et de jeunesse . . .".* Paris, C. Lévy, 1892, 1902[6], 1922[17]
—, *Lettres intimes (1842–1845) d'Ernest Renan et Henriette Renan*. Précédées de *Ma sœur Henriette*. Paris, C. Lévy, 1896, 1896[4], 1922[9], 1925[11]. (These letters had been published previously by Ary Renan under the title of

"Correspondance intime (1842–1845)" in *Revue de Paris*, August and September 1895).

—, *Nouvelles lettres intimes (1846–1850)*. (Correspondance between Ernest Renan and Henriette Renan, 1846–1850). Paris, 1923[3].

—, *Lettres du Séminaire (1838–1846)*. Publiées par Mme Jean Psichari, née Noémi Renan. Paris, C. Lévy, 1902, 1902[3], 1923[4]. (These letters had been published previously in *Revue de Paris*, 1901 and 1902).

—, *Cahiers de jeunesse (1845–1846)*. Publiés par Mme Noémi Renan. Paris, C. Lévy, 1906, 1906[2]. (Previously published in *Revue des Revues*, April–May 1906, and in *Revue Politique et Littéraire (Revue Bleue)*, April 1906.

—, *Nouveaux cahiers de jeunesse*. Paris, C. Lévy, 1907. (Previously published in *Revue Politique et Littéraire (Revue Bleue)*, January, May and June 1907).

—, *Fragments intimes et romancsques*. Paris, Calmann–Lévy, 1914.

—, "Compositions scolaires d'E. Renan au Petit Séminaire St-Nicolas du Chardonnet (1838–1841)," publiées par Jean Pommier. *Grande Revue*, XXIV, 8 (août 1920), pp. 229–251.

—, *Correspondance, 1846–1871, 1872–1892*. Publiée par Mme Noémi Renan, 2 vols. Paris, C. Lévy, 1926–1928.

—, *Souvenirs d'enfance et de jeunesse, suivis des Lettres d'Italie (1849–1850)*. Paris, C. Lévy, 1923, 1956. New edition: Paris, 1959 (Texte établi et présenté par Jean Pommier).

—, *Voyages (Italie 1849, Norvège 1870)*. Paris, n. d. (1928?).

—, *Travaux de jeunesse, 1843–1844*. Edited by Jean Pommier (Publications de la Faculté des Lettres de l'Université de Strasbourg, Fasc. 54). Paris, 1931.

—, *Ernest Renan et l'Allemagne. Textes recueillis et commentés*. Par Emile Buré. New York, Brentano's, 1945.

Renan, E., et Berthelot, M., *Correspondance 1847–1892*. Edited by M. Berthelot. Paris, C. Lévy, 1898, 1910[3]. (Major part previously published in *Revue de Paris*, 1897 and 1898).

Renan, Henriette, *Souvenirs et impressions. Pologne, Rome, Allemagne, Voyage en Syrie*. Publié avec des notes par Henri Moncel. Introduction Mary Duclaux. Paris, la Renaissance du livre, 1930.

Renard, Edmond, *Renan. Les étapes de sa pensée*. Paris, Bloud et Gay, 1929.

Robertson, J. M., *Ernest Renan*. London, 1924.

Séailles, Gabriel, *E. Renan. Essai de biographie psychologique*. Paris, 1894.

Soman, Mariette, *La formation philosophique d'Ernest Renan jusqu'à l'Avenir de la science* (d'après des documents inédits). Paris, F. Alcan, 1914.

Sorel, *Le système historique de Renan*, 2 vols. Paris, 1905–1906.

Strauss, Gaston, *La politique de Renan*. Paris, n. d. (1909).

Tieghem, Philippe van, *Renan*. Paris, 1948.

Tielrooy, Johannes, *Ernest Renan. Een groot humanist. Zijn leven en werken*. Amsterdam, E. Querido, 1948.
    French translation by Louis Laurent: *Ernest Renan. Sa vie et ses œuvres*. Paris, 1958.

Tronchon, Henri, *Ernest Renan et l'étranger* (Publications de la Faculté des Lettres de Strasbourg, 2e série, fasc. 4). Paris, 1928.

Wardman, H. W., *Ernest Renan. A critical Biography*. London, 1964.

Weiler, Maurice, *La pensée de Renan*. Grenoble, 1945.

3. *Main Publications*

1848 "Le libéralisme clérical," *La Liberté de Penser*, I (mai 1848), pp. 510–531. Reprinted in *Questions contemporaines*, 1868, pp. 419–460.

1848 "De l'origine du langage," *La Liberté de Penser*, II (sept. 1848), pp. 368–380; III (déc. 1848), pp. 64–83. Also published separately as *De l'origine du langage*. Paris, Joubert, 1848; Paris, M. Lévy frères, 1858[2] (considerably enlarged), 1859[3], 1864[4], 1922[9], 1925[10]. Russian translation, Voronej, 1866.

1849 "Les historiens critiques de la Vie de Jésus," *La Liberté de Penser*, III (15 mars 1849), pp. 365–384, and III (15 avril 1849), pp. 437–470. Reprinted in *Etudes d'histoire religieuse*. Paris, 1857, pp. 133–215.
Dutch translation: *De historische Kritiek en het leven van Jezus . . .*, 's Hertogenbosch, 1868.

1850 "Mission en Italie, confiée a MM. Daremberg et Renan. Premier rapport à M. le Ministre de l'instruction publique et des cultes," *Archives des Missions Scientifiques et Littéraires*, I (mai 1850), pp. 241–292 and 429–444.

1850 "Rapport adressé à M. le Ministre de l'instruction publique et des cultes, par M. Ernest Renan, chargé d'une mission scientifique et littéraire en Italie, conjointement avec M. le docteur Daremberg," *Archives des Missions Scientifiques et Littéraires*, I (juillet-août 1850), pp. 365–409.

1851 "Mahomet et les origines de l'Islamisme," *Revue des Deux-Mondes*. Nouvelle période, T. XII (15 déc. 1851), pp. 1063–1101. Also published separately: Paris, Impr. de Gordes, n. d. Reprinted in *Etudes d'histoire religieuse*, 1857, pp. 217–299.

1852 *Averroès et l'Averroïsme. Essai historique* (Diss.). Paris, A. Durand. 1861[2], 1866[3]. Paris, C. Lévy, 1922[7]. (*Œuvres complètes*, Vol. III).
Russian translation, Kiev, B. K. Fuchs, 1902.
Spanish translation by Edmundo Gonzalez-Blanco: *Averrœs y el Averroïsmo* (*Ensayo històrico*) 2 vols. Valencia, F. Sempere, n. d.

1852 *De Philosophia peripatetica apud Syros commentationem historicam scripsit E. Renan* Diss. Paris, A. Durand.

1853 "Des religions de l'antiquité et de leurs derniers historiens," *Revue des Deux-Mondes*. Nouvelle période, 2me série. T. II (15 mai 1853), pp. 821–848. Also published separately: Paris, Impr. de J. Claye, 1853. Reprinted in *Etudes d'histoire religieuse*. Paris, 1857, pp. 1–72.
Russian translation in 1864.

1853 "Fragment du livre gnostique intitulé: *Apocalypse d'Adam*, ou *Pénitence d'Adam*, ou *Testament d'Adam*, publiés d'après deux versions syriaques . .", *Journal Asiatique*, V[e] série, T. II (déc. 1853), pp. 427–471. Published separately: Paris, Franck, 1854.

1854 "De la poésie des races celtiques," *Revue des Deux-Mondes*. Nouvelle période, 2e série, T. V (1er février 1854), pp. 473–506. Reprinted in *Essais de morale et de critique*, 1859, pp. 375–456.
English translation, also of other essays, with introduction and notes by W. G. Hutchison: *The Pœtry of the Celtic Races, and other Studies*. London, W. Scott, 1896.

1855 *Histoire générale et système comparé des langues sémitiques . . .* I: *Histoire générale des langues sémitiques*. Paris, Impr. impériale. 1858[2], 1863[3], 1863[4]. (*Œuvres complètes*, Vol. VIII).

1857 *Etudes d'histoire religieuse.* Paris, M. Lévy frères. 1857², 1858³, 1864⁷ (rev.), 1907⁹. (*Œuvres complètes*, Vol. VII).
English translations:
a) authorized translation by O. B. Frothingham: *Studies of Religious History and Criticism.* With a biographical introduction. New York, Carleton, 1864.
b) by Henry F. Gibbons: *Studies of Religious History.* London, W. Heinemann, 1893.
c) some essays by W. M. Thomson in: *Studies in Religious History. History of the People of Israel and Religions of Antiquity* (London, Mathieson, 1895), and in: *Leaders of Christian and Anti-Christian thought* (London, Mathieson, 1895).
Russian translations, St. Petersburg, 1901, 1904³; and St. Petersburg, 1908 (under different titles).
Spanish translation by Cristobal Litran: *Estudios de historia religiosa.* Valencia, El Pueblo, n. d.

1858 "L'école libérale, ses principes et ses tendances," *Revue des Deux-Mondes,* 2ᵉ période, T. XVI (1ᵉʳ août 1858), pp. 662–685. Reprinted in *Essais de morale et de critique,* 1859, pp. 1–50.

1858 "Les traductions de la Bible," *Journal des Débats,* 8 déc. 1858. Reprinted in *Nouvelles Etudes d'Histoire Religieuse,* 1884, pp. 167–183.

1858 *Le livre de Job, traduit de l'hébreu. Etude sur l'âge et le caractère du poème.* ("Biblia Gallica"). Paris, M. Lévy frères. 1859², 1865³, 1922⁷. (*Œuvres complètes*, Vol. VII).
English translation by H. F. G. (Henry Frederick Gibbons) and W. M. T. (William Moy Thomas): *The Book of Job, translated from the Hebrew, with a study upon the age and character of the poem.* London, W. M. Thomson, 1889.

1858 "Mémoire sur l'origine et le caractère véritable de l'histoire phénicienne qui porte le nom de Sanchoniathon," *Académie des Inscriptions et Belles-Lettres, Mémoires,* XXIII (1858), pp. 241–334.

1859 "Nouvelles considérations sur le caractère général des peuples sémitiques et en particulier sur leur tendance au monothéisme," *Journal Asiatique,* Vᵉ série, T. XIII (février-mars 1859), pp. 214–282 and 417–450. Also published separately: Paris, Impr. impériale, 1859.

1859 *Essais de morale et de critique.* Paris, M. Lévy frères. 1859², 1867³, 1922⁸. (*Œuvres complètes*, Vol. II).
Russian translation, Kiev, 1902.

1860 "De la métaphysique et de son avenir," *Revue des Deux-Mondes,* 2ᵉ période, XXV (15 janvier 1860), pp. 365–392. Reprinted in *Dialogues et fragments philosophiques,* 1876, pp. 257–334.

1860 "Mémoire sur l'âge du livre intitulé *Agriculture nabatéenne*," *Mémoires de l'Académie des Inscriptions et Belles-Lettres,* XXIV (1861), pp. 139–190. Also published separately: Paris, Impr. nationale, 1860. Reprinted under the title of "Sur des débris de l'ancienne littérature babylonienne conservés dans les traductions arabes," *Revue Germanique,* X (avril 1860), pp. 136–166.
English translation by S. Symonds, afterwards Dunn: *An Essay on the Age and Antiquity of the Book of Nabathaean Agriculture, to which is added an inaugural lecture on the Position of the Semitic Nations in the History of Civilization.* London, 1862.

1860 *Le Cantique des Cantiques, traduit de l'hébreu, avec une étude sur le plan, l'âge et le caractère du poème* ("Biblia Gallica"). Paris, M. Lévy frères. 1870[3], 1891[7], 1922[11]. Other edition: Paris, Hachette,   1886. *(Œuvres complètes*, Vol. VII).
English translation by William M. Thomson: *The Song of Songs. Translated from the Hebrew, with a study of the plan, the age, and the character of the poem.* London, W. M. Thomson, 1895.

1860 "De l'avenir religieux des sociétés modernes," *Revue des Deux-Mondes*, 2e période, XXIX (15 oct. 1860), pp. 761–797. Reprinted in *Questions contemporaines*, 1868, pp. 337–418.

1861–62 "Rapports sur la mission scientifique de M. Ernest Renan en Orient," *Académie des Inscriptions et Belles-Lettres. Comptes rendus*, V (1861), pp. 35–43, 74, 150–157, 176–177; VI (1862), pp. 22–31. Comp. also *Moniteur Universel*, 25 et 27 février 1861, 8 et 11 juillet 1861; 21, 22 et 26 février 1862.

1862 *De la part des peuples sémitiques dans l'histoire de la civilisation.* Discours d'ouverture des cours de langues hébraïque, chaldaïque et syriaque au Collège de France. Paris, M. Lévy frères, 1862 (1e–5e éd.). Reprinted in *Mélanges d'histoire et de voyages*, 1878, pp. 1–25.
Dutch translation: *Over het aandeel der semietische volken in de geschiedenis der beschaving.* Amersfoort, 1862.
English translation by S. Symonds, afterwards Dunn, in: *An Essay on the Age and Antiquity of the Book of Nabathaean Agriculture, to which is added an inaugural lecture on the Position of the Semitic Nations in the History of Civilization.* London, 1862.
Italian translation: *Della parte dei popoli semitici nella storia della civiltà: prolusione.* Firenze, Le Monnier, 1862.
Russian translation, Moscow, V. N. Marakonev, 1888.

1862 "L'art du Moyen Age et les causes de sa décadence," *Revue des Deux-Mondes*, 2e période, XL (1er juillet 1862), pp. 203–228. Reprinted in *Mélanges d'histoire et de voyages*, 1878, pp. 209–252.
Dutch translation by J. H. Leliman: "De kunst der Middeleeuwen en de oorzaken van haar verval," *Bouwkundige Bijdragen*, XV, 2 (1865).

1862 *Henriette Renan*, Reprinted as *Ma Sœur Henriette*, 1895. See under 2. *Biography and Appreciation*.

1862–1893 Contributions to the *Histoire Littéraire de la France* (Paris, Firmin-Didot et Impr. nationale) in: XXIV (1862), XXV (1869), XXVI (1877), XXVII (1877), XXVIII (1881), XXIX (1885), XXX (1888), XXXI (1893).

1863 *Vie de Jésus.* Paris, M. Lévy frères, 1863 (1e–10e éd.), 1864[11,12]; 1864[13] (revised), 1921[61]. Other edition, with illustrations by Godefroy Durand: Paris, Michel Lévy frères, 1870. Popular edition, abridged: Paris, Michel Lévy frères, 1864 (1e–15e éd.), 1880[32], 1921[130]. Other French editions, which appeared abroad: Berlin, J. Springer, 1863; Naumburg, Pätz, 1863, 1863–1864 (2e–12e éd.). Reissued: Paris, Calmann-Lévy, 1960; pb. Paris, Le livre de poche, 1965; Paris, Le Club français du Livre, 1967. *(Œuvres complètes*, Vol. IV).
Czech translation by V. B. [Bambas]: *Život Ježišův.* Prague, Steinhauser, 1864. Several other Czech translations and editions appeared later.
Dutch translation: *Het leven van Jezus.* Haarlem, 1866.
Danish translation by I. Hjerrild: *Jesu Levnet.* København, Fr. Woldike, 1864; København, V. Pio, 1872[2].

English translations: *The Life of Jesus*. London, Trübner, 1863 etc. Translation by C. E. Wilbour: New York, Carleton, 1864 etc. Several other English translations were published, also in an abridged popular edition. The book appeared under the title of *Life of Christ* as Volume I in the translation edition: *History of the Origins of Christianity*. London, Mathieson, 1896.

Esperanto translation of the 78th French edition, by Emilo Gasse: *Vivo de Jesuo*. Le Havre, Gasse, 1907.

German translations: Authorized edition: *Das Leben Jesu*. Leipzig, G. Wigand, 1863; Leipzig, Brockhaus, 1865², 1870³ (enlarged), 1880⁴ (revised and enlarged), 1893⁵. In Leipzig, Brockhaus, appeared also in 1870: *Supplement (zu früheren Ausgaben)*. Neue Vorreden des Verfassers und einen Anhang über das 4. Evangelium enthaltend. Besides this Leipzig edition, numerous other German translations were published, also in (sometimes abridged) popular editions. The book appeared as Volume I in the translation edition: *Geschichte der Anfänge des Christentums* (translation by Ludwig Eichler). Berlin, Schlingmann, 1864.

Greek translation by A. Pharmakopulu: βιος τοῦ 'Ιησοῦ . Athens, 1892. Another Greek translation was made of the 13th French edition by Aristu Kampanè: 'ο βίος τοῦ 'Ιησοῦ. Athens, 1915.

Hungarian translation: *Jézus élete*. Wien, Beck, 1864. Another translation by Sarosi Kornel appeared later: *Jézus élete*. Budapest, 1893.

Italian translation by Filippo de Boni: *Vita di Gesù*. Milano G. Daelli, 1863. Comp. the translation and refutation by Carlo Passaglia: *La Vita di Gesù scritta da E. Renan, discussa e confutata da Carlo Passaglia, colla traduzione del testo*, 2 parts. Torino, tip. del "Mediatore", 1864–1865. Other Italian editions of the book appeared in Florence, Rome and Milan.

Portuguese translation by F. F. da Silva Vieira: *Vida de Jesus*. Lisboa, tip. do "Futuro", 1864. Another translation was made by J. A. X. de Magalhães. Lisboa, tip. de Salles, 1864. In 1894 an edition appeared: Porto, Lello e Irmão.

Russian translation, Dresden, Wienecke, 1864, 1865². Several other Russian translations and editions appeared later.

Spanish translation by Federico de La Vega: *Vida de Jesus*. Paris, A. Ledoux, 1864; Bogotá, 1865. Another Spanish translation by F. Adelantado appeared in the edition "Historia de los origenes del cristianismo": *Vida de Jesus*. Madrid, Impr. de Rivadeneira, 1869.

Swedish translation by Thor Brunius: *Jesu lefverne*. Norrköping, 1863. Another Swedish translation was made of the 93rd French edition by Algot Ruhe: *Jesu lefnad*. Stockholm, "Ljus", 1907.

1863–1883 *Histoire des origines du christianisme*, 7 vols. plus index *(Œuvres complètes*, Vols. IV, V):

I. Vie de Jésus, 1863	V. Les Evangiles, 1877
II. Les apôtres, 1866	VI. L'Église chrétienne, 1879
III. Saint Paul, 1869	VII. Marc-Aurèle, 1882
IV. L'antéchrist, 1873	VIII. Index, 1883

See under the respective years.

Complete *English* translation: *History of the Origins of Christianity*, 7 vols. London, Mathieson, 1888–1890.

Complete *Russian* translation, St. Petersburg, n. d., 7 vols.

1864 "De l'instruction supérieure en France, son histoire et son avenir," *Revue des Deux-Mondes*, 2ᵉ période, LI (1ᵉʳ mai 1864), pp. 73–95. Reprinted in *Questions contemporaines*. Paris, 1868, pp. 69–115.

1864–1874 *Mission de Phénicie*, 7 vols. Paris, Imprimerie impériale.

1865 "Les antiquités égyptiennes et les fouilles de M. Mariette. Souvenirs d'un voyage en Egypte. Sur le Nil, d'Assouan au Caire, décembre 1864," *Revue des Deux-Mondes*, 2ᵉ période, LVI (1ᵉʳ avril 1865), pp. 660–689. Reprinted in *Mélanges d'histoire et de voyages*, 1878, pp. 27–75.

   Dutch translation: E. Renan and W. Wattenbach, *Egypte, Ninivé en Babylon*. 's Hertogenbosch, 1869.

   Russian translation in 1865.

1865 "L'exégèse religieuse et l'esprit français," *Revue des Deux-Mondes*, 2ᵉ période, LX (1ᵉ November 1865), pp. 235–245.

1866 *Les Apôtres* (Histoire des origines du christianisme, II). Paris, M. Lévy frères, 1866, 1921²⁴.

   Czech translation by V. B. (Bambas): *Apoštolové*. V Praze, 1866. Other Czech translations by Fr. Vl. Lorenc (V Praze, Neubert, 1891) and by Boř. Vajgrt (V Praze, 1897).

   Danish translation of 8th French edition by A. Wolff: *Apostlene*. Köbenhavn, A. Giese, 1883.

   Dutch translation by A. A. Deenik: *De apostelen*. Haarlem, 1866.

   English translation: *The Apostles*. New York, Carleton, 1866; London, N. Trübner, 1869, 1889. Another English translation by William G. Hutchison: *The Apostles*. London, Watts, 1905.

   German authorized edition: *Die Apostel*. Leipzig, Brockhaus, 1866. German translation by Ludw. Eichler: *Die Apostel* (Geschichte der Anfänge des Christenthums, II). Berlin, Hasselbergsche Verlagshaus, 1866–1867 (4 parts in one volume). Another German translation by David Haek: *Die Apostel*. Leipzig, P. Reclam, 1894.

   Greek translation by Mpampè Anninu: Οἱ Ἀπόστολοι. Athens, n. d.

   Italian translation by Eugenio Torelli-Violler: *Gli apostoli*. Milano, Sonzogno, 1866.

   Portuguese translation by F. Ferreira da Silva Vieira: *Os apostolos*. Lisboa, tip. do "Futuro", 1866. Another Potuguese translation was made by Eduardo Augusto Salgado: *Os apostolos*. Porto, Impr. moderna, 1904.

   Russian translation, St. Petersburg, M. V. Piropskov, 1907.

   Spanish translation by Enrique L. de Verneuil: *Los apostoles*. Barcelona, 1868.

1868 *Questions contemporaines*. Paris, M. Lévy frères. 1868², 1922⁶ (*Œuvres complètes*, Vol. I).

1869 "Les services que la science rend au peuple," *Grande Revue*, XVII (1 mai 1901), pp. 261–272. Reprinted in *Mélanges religieux et historiques*. Paris, 1904, pp. 131–151.

1869 *Saint Paul* (Histoire des origines du christianisme, III). Avec une carte des voyages de Saint Paul par M. Kiepert. Paris, M. Lévy, 1920²⁴.

   Czech translation by Ad. Gottwald: *Svatý Pavel*. V Praze, 1914.

   English translation by Lockwood: *Saint Paul*. New York, Carleton, 1869; London, Temple Company, 1887 (2 vol.).

   German authorized translation: *Paulus*. Leipzig, Brockhaus, 1869.

   Portuguese translation by Campos Lima: *S. Paulo*. Porto, Lello e Irmao, 1908.

Russian translation, St. Petersburg, O. Glagolev, 1907.
Spanish translation by Juan de la Cuesta: *San Pablo*. Barcelona, 1869.
1871 *La réforme intellectuelle et morale*. Paris, M. Lévy frères 1872[3], 1922[9] Reissued: Paris, Union générale d'édition, 1967. (*Œuvres complètes* Vol. I.).
Russian translation, Kiev, B.K. Fuchs, 1902.
1873 *L'Antéchrist*. (Histoire des origines du christianisme, IV) Paris, M. Lévy frères. 1920[16].
Czech translation by Fr. P. Soukup: *Antikrist*. V Praze, Dělnícka Kníhtískárna, 1887.
English translation and edition by Joseph Henry Allen: *Antichrist*. London, 1897. Another English translation was made, with an introduction, by William G. Hutchison: *Antichrist*. London, W. Scott, 1899.
German authorized translation: *Der Antichrist*. Leipzig, Brockhaus, 1873.
Greek translation by Elia Oikonomopulu: ʿΟ 'Αντιχρίδτος. Athens, 1910.
Portuguese translation by João de Campos Lima: *O Anti-Christo*. Porto, Lello e Irmão, 1909.
Russian translation, St. Petersburg, V. Kaufman, 1906. Another Russian edition appeared in St. Petersburg, M. V. Piropskov, 1907.
Spanish translation by E. Heras: *El Anticristo*. Valencia, Impr. de El Pueblo, 2 vols., n. d.
1874 "La crise religieuse en Europe," *Revue des Deux-Mondes*, 3e période, I (15 février 1874), pp. 752—779. Reprinted in *Mélanges religieux et historiques*, 1904, pp. 1–66.
1875 "L'apocalypse de l'an 97. Le dernier prophète des Juifs," *Revue des Deux-Mondes*, 3e période, VIII (1 mars 1875), pp. 127—144. Partly reprinted in *Les Evangiles*, 1877, pp. 348–373.
1876 "Prière sur L'Acropole. Le Bonhomme système et la petite Noémi" (Souvenirs d'enfance et de jeunesse, II), *Revue des Deux-Mondes*, 3e période, XVIII (1 décembre 1876), pp. 481–507. Also separate publication: *La prière sur l'Acropole*. Paris, E. Pelletan, 1899. Reprinted in *Cahiers de la quinzaine*, 5e série, no 3. Another separate publication: Paris, Librairie des amateurs, 1920. Reissued: Paris, Les Bibliophiles comtois, 1969.
Russian translation, Moscow, Marakonev, 1886.
1876 *Dialogues et fragments philosophiques*. Paris, C. Lévy. 1922[9] (*Œuvres complètes*, Vol. I).
English translation by Râs Bihâri Mukharjî: *Philosophical Dialogues and Fragments*. London, Trübner, 1883.
German authorized translation by Konrad von Zdekauer: *Philosphische Dialoge und Fragmente*. Leipzig, E. Koschny, 1877. Another German edition appeared under the same title: Heidelberg, Weiss, 1877.
Spanish translation by V. Ballester Soto: *Dialogos filosóficos*. Valencia, F. Sempere, n.d.
1877 *Spinoza*. Discours prononcé à La Haye le 21 février 1877, a l'occasion du 200e anniversaire de sa mort. La Haye, M. Nijhoff, 1877. Another edition under the title of: *Spinoza*. Conférence tenue à La Haye . . . etc. Paris, C. Lévy, 1877. Reprinted in *Nouvelles études d'histoire religieuse*, 1884, pp. 499—533.
English translation by Mrs. William Smith in: Professor Knight, ed., *Spinoza: 1677 and 1877*. Four essays by Land, K. Fischer, J. van Vloten and E. Renan. London, Williams and Norgate, 1882.
German authorized translation by C. Scharschmidt: *Spinoza*. Rede am

21. Februar 1877 bei dessen 200jährigen Todesfeier gehalten im Haag. Heidelberg, Weiss Leipzig, Koschny, 1877. Another German translation by Richard Lesser: *Spinoza*. Festrede zu seiner 200jährigen Todesfeier am 21. Februar 1877, gehalten im Haag. Wien, Hartleben, 1877.

1877 *Les Evangiles et la seconde génération chrétienne* (Histoire des origines du christianisme, V). Paris, C. Lévy. 1922[12].
Portuguese translation by Eduardo Pimenta: *Os Evangelhos e a segunda geração christã*. Porto, Lello e Irmão, 1911.
Russian translation, St. Petersburg, N. Glagolev, 1907.
Spanish translation by Carmen de Burgos Segni: *Los Evangelios y la segunda generacion cristiana*, 2 vols. Valencia, Impr. de El Pueblo, n.d.

1877 "Les rabbins français du commencement du XIVe siècle," *Histoire Littéraire de la France*, XXVII. Paris, Impr. nationale, 1877, pp. 431–753. Also published separately: Paris, Impr. nationale, 1877.

1878 *Caliban*. Suite de la "Tempête", drame philosphique. Paris, C. Lévy. Reissued and edited by Colin Smith, Manchester, Manchester University Press, 1954.
Danish translation by Tyge Möller: *Caliban*. Jyderup, K. Petersen, 1895.
English translation with introduction by E. G. Vickery: *Caliban*. A philosophical drama continuing "The Tempest" of William Shakespeare (Publications of the Shakespeare Society of New York, Vol. 9). New York, Shakespeare Press; London, Kegan Paul, 1896.
Swedish translation by Edvard Alkman: *Caliban*. Drama i fem akter. Stockholm, 1896.

1878 *Mélanges d'histoire et de voyages*. Paris, C. Lévy. 1916[5] *(Œuvres complètes*, vol. II).

1879 *L'Eglise chrétienne* (Histoire des origines du christianisme, VI). Paris, C. Lévy, 1922[12].
Portuguese translation by Eduardo Pimenta: *A Igregja christã*. Porto, Lello e Irmão, n.d.
Russian translation, St. Petersburg, N. Glagolev, 1908.

1880 *Conférences d'Angleterre. Rome et le Christianisme. Marc Aurèle*. Hibbert Lectures: Rome et le Christianisme. Paris, C. Lévy, 1880, 1896[5] *(Œuvres complètes*, Vol. VII).
English translation by C. Beard: *Lectures on the Influence of the Institutions, Thought and Culture of Rome on Christianity and the Development of the Catholic Church*. The Hibbert Lectures, 1880. London, Williams and Norgate, 1880, 1885.
German edition by Gottfried Hessel: *Vorträge* [gehalten in London April 1880]. Leipzig, O. Wigand, 1880.
Swedish translation by A. F. Åkerberg: *Rom och Kristendomen*. Föreläsningar hållna i London i April 1880. Stockholm, 1880.

1881 *L'eau de Jouvence*. Suite de "Caliban". Paris, C. Lévy.
Russian translation by G. Spasski, Moscow, 1909.

1882 *Qu'est-ce qu'une nation?* Conférence faite en Sorbonne, le 11 mars 1882. Paris, C. Lévy, 1882[2]. Reprinted in *Discours et conférences*. Paris, 1887.
Swedish translation: *Hvad är en nation?* Helsingfors, 1882.
Russian translation, St. Petersburg, V. Berman and S. Voitinskii, 1885.
New Dutch translation by J. Tielrooy, with an introduction by H. R. Roetink. Amsterdam, 1945.

1882 *L'Ecclésiaste.* Traduit de l'hébreu, avec une étude sur l'âge et le caractère du livre. Paris, C. Lévy, 1882, 1922⁶.
English translation in: *Cohelet. Priest of Nemi. L'abbesse de Jouarre.* London, Temple Company, 1895.

1882 *Marc-Aurèle et la fin du monde antique* (Histoire des origines du christianisme, VII). Paris, C. Lévy, 1882, 1922¹⁹.
English translation: *History of Origins of Christianity. Book VII: Marcus Aurelius.* London, Mathieson, 1899. Another English edition of the same book, translated, with introduction, by William G. Hutchison: *Marcus Aurelius.* London, W. Scott, 1904.
Russian translation, St. Petersburg, 1907.

1883 *Souvenirs d'enfance et de jeunesse.* See under "Biography . . . ," p. 230.

1883 *Le Judaïsme comme race et comme religion.* Conférence. Paris, C. Lévy, 1883, 1883². Reprinted in *Discours et conférences,* 1887, pp. 341–374.
German translation: *Das Judenthum vom Gesichtspunkt der Rasse und der Religion.* Vortrag. Basel, Bernheim, 1883.
Rumanian translation by E. S. [Schwarzfeld]: *Judaïsmul ca rasă si ca religie.* Bucuresti, tip. S. Mihalescu, 1883.
Russian translation in 1883.

1883 *L'Islamisme et la science.* Conférence. Paris, C. Lévy, 1883. Reprinted in *Journal des Débats,* 30 mars 1883. Also reprinted in *Discours et conférences.* Paris, 1887, pp. 375–401.
German translation: *Der Islam und die Wissenschaft.* Vortrag gehalten in der Sorbonne am 29. März 1883. Kritik dieses Vortrags vom Afghanen Scheik Djemmal Eddin und E. Renan's Erwiderung. Basel, Bernheim, 1883.
Russian translation, Moscow, 1888.

1883 *Le Judaïsme et le christianisme. Identité originelle et séparation graduelle.* Conférence. Paris, C. Lévy, 1883. Reprinted in *Revue Politique et Littéraire (Revue Bleue),* IIIᵉ série, V (2 juin 1883), pp. 687–693. Also reprinted in *Annuaire de la Société des Etudes Juives,* 3ᵉ année (1884), pp. 73–95. From this published separately: Versailles, Cerf et fils, 1884.
German translation: *Judenthum und Christenthum, ihre ursprüngliche Identität und allmähliche Scheidung.* Basel, Bernheim, 1883. Reprinted in *Discours et conférences,* 1887, pp. 311–340.

1884 *Nouvelles études d'histoire religieuse.* Paris, C. Lévy. 1907⁴ *(Œuvres complètes,* vol. VII).
English authorized edition: *Studies in Religious History.* Second series. London, R. Bentley and son, 1886. Some essays have been translated by W. M. Thomson and published in: *Studies in Religious History. History of the People of Israel and Religions of Antiquity* (London, Mathieson, 1895), and in: *Leaders of Christian and Anti-Christian thought* (London, Mathieson, 1895).

1885 *Le prêtre de Nemi.* Drame philosophique, Paris, C. Lévy. 1886². Reprinted in *Drames philosophiques,* 1888, pp. 251–400.
Czech translation: „Kněz z Nemi. Le prêtre de Nemi," *Pokrok,* 1885.
English translation in: *Cohelet. Priest of Nemi. L'abbesse de Jouarre.* London, Temple Company, 1895.

1885 "Raymond Lulle. Biographie et critique générale," *Histoire Littéraire de France,* XIX (1885), pp. 1–67.

1886 "L'année 1886. Prologue au Ciel," *Journal des Débats,* 1ᵉʳ janvier 1886. Reprinted in *Drames philosophiques,* 1888, pp. 545–566.

1886 "Les origines de la Bible. Histoire et légende," *Revue des Deux-Mondes,* 3ᵉ période, LXXIV (1–15 mars 1886), pp. 5–27 and 241–266. Mostly reprinted in *Histoire du peuple d'Israël,* 5 vols., 1887–1893.

1886 *L'abbesse de Jouarre.* Paris, C. Lévy, 1886 etc.
English translation in: *Cohelet. Priest of Nemi. L'abbesse de Jouarre.* London, Temple Company, 1895.
Italian translation by Enrico Panzacchi: *L'abbadessa di Jouarre: dramma.* Milano, Treves, 1887.

1886 "Les origines de la Bible. La Loi," *Revue des Deux-Mondes,* 3ᵉ période, LXXVIII (1ᵉʳ et 15 déc. 1886), pp. 522—550 and 799—822. Reprinted in *Histoire du peuple d'Israël,* 5 vols., 1887–1893.

1887–1893 *Histoire du peuple d'Israël,* 5 vols. Paris, C. Lévy (with reprints of each volume). (*Œuvres complètes,* Vol. VI).
English translation by C. B. Pitman and D. V. Bingham: *History of the People of Israel,* 3 vols. London, Chapman and Hall, 1888–1891.
German authorized translation by E. Schaelsky: *Geschichte des Volkes Israel,* 5 vols. Berlin, S. Cronbach, 1894.
Russian translation of Vols. I–IV, St. Petersburg, 1907. Russian translation of parts of Vols. I–V, St. Petersburg, 1907.

1887 *Discours et conférences.* Paris, C. Lévy. 1919⁶ (*Œuvres complètes,* Vol. I).
Russian translation, Kiev, B. K. Fuchs, 1902.

1888 "La question de l'amour," (Lettre écrite a Rosmapamon, le 4 août 1888), *Figaro,* Supplément littéraire, 11 août 1888. Reprinted in *Feuilles détachées,* 1892, pp. 64–72.

1888 *Drames philosophiques.* Paris, C. Lévy. (*Œuvres complètes,* Vol. III).
Czech translation: *Filosoficka dramata.* V Praze, K. St. Sokol, 1902.
Russian translation by V. N. Mikhailov: Kiev, B. K. Fuchs, 1902.

1888 "Le livre des secrets aux philosophes ou Dialogue de Placide et Timeo. Le coeur des secrets de philosophie," *Histoire Littéraire de la France,* XXX (Paris, Impr. nationale, 1888), pp. 567–595. Also published separately.

1889 "Examen de conscience philosophique," *Revue des Deux-Mondes,* 3e période, XCIV (15 août 1889), pp. 721–737. Reprinted in *Temps,* 16 août 1889. Also reprinted in Feuilles détachées, 1892, pp. 401–443.

1890 "Emma Kosilis," *Figaro,* supplément littéraire, 29 mars 1890. Reprinted in *Feuilles détachées,* 1892, pp. 1–39.
Russian translation in 1893.

1890 *L'avenir de la science.* Pensées de 1848. Paris, C. Lévy, 1890, 1890³, 1922¹⁸ (*Œuvres complètes,* Vol. III).
English translation by A. D. Vandam and C. B. Pitman: *The Future of Science.* Ideas of 1848. London, Chapman and Hall, 1891.
Russian translation, 2 vols. Kiev, B. K. Fuchs, 1902.
Spanish translation by Roberto Robert (fils): *El porvenir de la ciencia* (Pensamiento de 1848), 2 vols. Valencia, Impr. de El Pueblo, n.d.

1890 *Pages choisies, à l'usage des lycées et des écoles.* Paris, C. Lévy. 1922⁴³.

1892 *Feuilles détachées.* Faisant suite aux "Souvenirs d'enfance et de jeunesse..", Paris, C. Lévy. 1902⁶, 1922¹⁷. (*Œuvres complètes,* Vol. II).

1893 "Les écrivains juifs français du XIVe siècle [Additions et corrections]," *Histoire Littéraire de la France* (Paris), XXXI, pp. 351–789 and 796–802. Also published separately: Paris, Impr. Nationale, 1893.

1899 *Etudes sur la politique religieuse du règne de Philippe le Bel.* Edited by

Mme Jean Psichari, born Noémi Renan, in coll. with P. Caron. Three essays previously published in *Histoire Littéraire de France*. Paris, C. Lévy.

1901 *Le broyeur de lin*. Paris, L. Corteret. Reissued: Paris, G. Servant, 1922. Critical edition by Colin Duckworth: London–Toronto–Wellington, G. G. Harrap and Co., 1963.

1904 *Mélanges religieux et historiques*. Collection of previously published essays and papers. Paris, C. Lévy. 1904². *(Œuvres complètes*. Vol. VIII).

1908 "Patrice, fragment de roman," edited by Mme Noémi Renan, *Revue des Deux-Mondes*, 5ᵉ période, XLV (15 mai 1908), pp. 241–284. Also published separately: Paris, C. Lévy, 1908.

1914 *Fragments intimes et romanesques*. Paris, c. Lévy. *(Œuvres complètes* Vol. IX).

1920 "Essai psychologique sur Jésus-Christ (1845)," published by Jean Pommier: *Revue de Paris*, 27ᵉ année, V (15 sept. 1920), pp. 224–261. Also published separately: Paris, Ed. de "La Connaissance", 1921.

1921 *Pages françaises*. Edited by Mme Noémi Renan. Previously published essays and papers. Paris, C. Lévy. 1922⁹.

1926 *Sur Corneille, Racine et Bossuet*. (Les Cahiers de Paris, 2ᵉ série, Cahier V). Paris.

1947–1961 *Œuvres complètes*. Edited by Henriette Psichari, 10 vols. Paris, Calmann-Lévy.

ALBERT RÉVILLE

1. Bibliography, Biography and Appreciation

Albert Réville. In Memoriam. Angers, 1907, 59 p.

Harlez, C. de, *La Religion en Chine. A Propos du dernier livre de* M. A. Réville. 1889.

Marty, J., *Albert Réville, sa Vie, son Oeuvre*. Cahors & Alençons, Coueslant. 1912. With bibliography, pp. 163–198.

2. Main Publications

1860 *Essais de critique religieuse*. Paris.

1864 *La Vie de Jésus de M. Renan devant les Orthodoxies et devant la Critique*. Paris, Cherbuliez, 1864².

1869 *Histoire du Dogme de la Divinité de Jésus Christ*. Paris. 1904³ (revised). *English* translation by Ann Swaine: *History of the Doctrine of the Deity of Jesus Christ*. London, 1870; 1878². Revised translation by Ann Swaine from the third French edition of 1904: *History of the Dogma of the Deity of Jesus Christ*. London, Philip Green, 1905.

1870 *Histoire du Diable. Ses Origines, sa Grandeur et sa Décadence*. Strassbourg. *English* translation, with prefatory Notes, by H. A.: *The Devil, his Greatness and Decadence*. London, Williams & Norgate, 1871.

1881 *Prolégomènes de l'Histoire des Religions*. Paris.
   English translation by A. S. Squire: *Prolegomena of the History of Religions;*
   With an Introduction by F. M. Müller. London, Williams & Norgate, 1884.
1883–1889 *Histoire des Religions*. Vol. I: *Les Religions des peuples non-civilisés;*
   Vol. II: *Les Religions du Mexique, de l'Amérique Centrale et du Pérou,*
   Vol. III: *La Religion chinoise.* Paris.
1884 *Lectures on the Origin and Growth of Religion, as illustrated by the native
   Religions of Mexico and Peru.* Translated by Philip H. Wicksteed. (The
   Hibbert Lectures, 1884). London, Williams & Norgate, 1884.
1897 *Jésus de Nazareth. Étude critiques sur les antécédents de l'Histoire évangélique
   et la Vie de Jésus,* 2 Vols. Paris. 1906².
1909 *Les Phases successives de l'Histoire des Religions.* Paris.

WILLIAM H. RIVERS

1. Biography and Bibliography

Haddon, C., Barlett, F. C., and Fegan, E. S., "Obitu ary," *Man*, 22 (1922)
   pp. 97–104. With bibliography by E. S. Fegan.

2. Main Publications

1901–1912 Parts of *Report of the Cambridge Anthropological Expedition to Torre
   Straits*. Vols. II (1901), V (1904), VI (1908), IV (1912).
1906 *The Todas.* London, Macmillan.
1907 "On the origin of the classificatory system of relationships," in: *Anthropological Essays presented to E. B. Tylor.* Oxford, 1907, pp. 309–323.
1909 "Totemism in Polynesia and Melanesia," *Journal of the Royal Anthropological Institute*, XXXIX (1909), pp. 156–180.
1912 "The sociological significance of myth," *Folk-Lore*, XXIII (1912), pp.
   307–331.
1913 W. H. Rivers, A. E. Jenks and S. G. Morely: *Reports upon the present
   Condition and future Needs of the Science of Anthropology.* Washington,
   Gibson.
1913 "Suncult and Megaliths in Oceania," (Royal Institute Lectures), *Report
   of the meeting of the British Association for the Advancement of Science*,
   London, 1913, p. 634, and *American Anthropologist*, N. S., XVII (1913),
   pp. 431–445.
1914 *The History of Melanesian Society.* Percy Sladen Trust Expedition to
   Melanesia, 2 vols. Cambridge, University Press.
1914 *Kinship and Social Organisation.* (Studies in Economic and Political
   Science, 36). London, Constable.
1916–1917 "Medicine, Magic and Religion," (Fitzpatrick Lectures, 1915),
   Lancet, XCIV (1916), pp. 59–65, 117–123; XCV (1917), pp. 919–923,
   959–964. Published separately:
   London, Kegan Paul, Trench, Trubner, 1924, 1927²; New York, Harcourt
   & Brace, 1924.

1917 *Dreams and Primitive Culture. Extract from Bulletin of the John Rylands Library* (IV, 5) (1917–1918), pp. 387–410). London, Longmans & Green, 1918.
1920 *Instinct and the Unconscious. A Contribution to a Biological Theory of the Psycho-Neuroses.* Cambridge, University Press, 1920. 1922²; 1924³.
1920 "The Concept of Soul-Substance in New Guinea and Melanesia," *Folk-Lore*, XXXI (1920), pp. 48–69.
1922 "The Symbolism of Rebirth," *Folk-Lore*, XXXIII (1922), pp. 14–33.
1923 *Conflict and Dream.* (International Library of Psychology, Philosophy and Scientific Method). London.

ERWIN ROHDE

1. Biography and Appreciation

Crusius, O., *E. Rohde. Ein biographischer Versuch.* Mit einer Auswahl von Aphorismen und Tagebuchblättern Rhode's Ergänzungsheft zu Erwin Rhode's *Kleine Schriften.* Leipzig, 1902.
Nietzsche, F. W., *Friedrich Nietzsche: Briefwechsel mit E. Rohde.* 1923.

2. Main Publications

1869 *Über Lucians Schrift Λουκιος ἡ 'Ονος und ihr Verhältniss zu Lucius von Patrae und den Metamorphosen des Apulejus. Eine literarhistorische Untersuchung.* Leipzig, 1869.
1872 *Afterphilologie. Zur Beleuchtung des von dem Dr. Phil. U. von Wilamowitz-Moellendorff herausgegeben Pamphlets: 'Zukunftsphilologie!'. Sendschreiben eines Philologen an Richard Wagner.* Leipzig.
1876 *Der griechische Roman und seine Vorläufer.* Leipzig, 1900² (Zweite durch Zusätze aus dem Handexemplar des Verfassers und durch den Vortrag über griechische Novellistik vermehrte Auflage. Ed. by F. Schöll); 1914³ (Dritte durch einen zweiten Anhang vermehrte Auflage).
1890–1894 *Psyche. Seelencult und Unsterblichkeitsglaube der Griechen,* 2 vols. Freiburg i. B., 1896²; Tübingen–Leipzig, 1903³ (ed. by F. Schöll); 1907⁴. *English* translation from the eighth edition by W. B. Hillis: *Psyche. The Cult of Souls and Belief in Immortality among the Greeks.* (International Library of Psychology). London, Kegan Paul, 1925.
1901 *Kleine Schriften.* Mit Zusätzen aus den Handexemplaren des Verfassers. Vol. I: *Beiträge zur Chronologie, Quellenkunde und Geschichte der griechischen Litteratur;* Vol. II: *Beiträge zur Geschichte des Romans und der Novelle, zur Sagen-, Märchen- und Alterthumskunde.* Tübingen–Leipzig.

S

EDWARD SAPIR

1. Bibliography

Spier, L., "Edward Sapir – Bibliography," *American Anthropologist*, 41 (1939), pp. 469–477.

2. Biography and Appreciation

Benedict, R., *An Anthropologist at Work*. London, 1959.
—, "Edward Sapir," *American Anthropologist*, 41 (1939), pp. 465–468.

3. Main Publications

1907 "Religious ideas of the Takelma Indians of Southwestern Oregon," *Journal of American Folk-lore*, 20 (1907), pp. 33–49.

1916 "Time perspective in aboriginal American culture. A study in method," in: *Geological Survey of Canada* (Ottawa) (Memoir 70, Anthropological Series, 13), pp. 1–87.

1924 "Culture, Genuine and Spurious," *American Journal of Sociology*, 29 (1924), pp. 401–429.

1927 "Anthropology and Sociology," in: *The Social Sciences and their Inter-relations*. Ed. by W. F. Ogburn and A. Goldenweiser. Boston. Chapter 9, pp. 97–113.

1928 "The Meaning of Religion," *The American Mercury*, 15 (1928), pp. 72–79.

1929 "Religions and Religious Phenomena," in: *Religious Life*, Vol. 11, pp. 1–33, in *Man and his World*. Ed. by Baker Brownell. New York.

1932 "Cultural Anthropology and Psychiatry," *Journal of Abnormal and Social Psychology*, 27 (1932), pp. 229–242.

1934 "Symbolism," in: *Encyclopaedia of the Social Sciences*. New York, Vol. 14, pp. 492–495.

1937 "The Contribution of Psychiatry to an Understanding of Behavior in Society," *American Journal of Sociology*, 42 (1937), pp. 862–870.

1949 *Selected Writings in Language, Culture and Personality*. Ed. by David G. Mandelbaum. Berkeley–Los Angeles, University of California.

HANS HEINRICH SCHAEDER

1. Bibliography

Eilers, W., "Bibliography," *Kratylos*. Kritisches Berichts- und Rezensions-
organ für indogermanische und allgemeine Sprachwissenschaft (Wiesbaden, Otto Harrassowitz) III (1958), pp. 84–93.

2. Biography and Appreciation

Eilers, W., "Nekrolog H. H. Schaeder," *Kratylos*, III (1958), pp. 82–84.
Protsak, Omeljan, "Hans Heinrich Schaeder. 31. Jan 1896 – 13. März 1957.
Ein Nekrolog," *Zeitschrift der Deutschen Morgenländischen Gesellschaft*,
CVIII (1958), pp. 21–40.

3. Main Publications

1925 "Die islamische Lehre vom vollkommenen Menschen, ihre Herkunft und
ihre dichterische Gestaltung," *Zeitschrift der Deutschen Morgenländischen
Gesellschaft*, 79 (1925), pp. 192–268.
1926 *Studien zum antiken Synkretismus.* By R. Reitzenstein and H. H. Schaeder.
Vol. II, pp. 199–355: "Iranische Lehren". Leipzig, Teubner.
1929 "Das Individuum im Islam," in: *Biologie der Person.* Ein Handbuch
der Konstitutionslehre. Hrsg. Th. Brugsch und F. H. Lewy. Berlin–Wien,
Urban & Schwarzenberg. Vol. 4, pp. 913–955.
1930 *Esra der Schreiber.* Tübingen, Mohr.
1930 *Iranische Beiträge I.* (Schriften der Königsberger Gelehrten Ges., Geistes-
wiss. Kl., 6. Jg., H. 5). Halle, Niemeyer.
1931 "Historische Theologie und Religionsgeschichte," *Zeitschrift für Systematische Theologie*, IX (Festschrift für Erich Schaeder), pp. 567–579.
1934 *Iranica* (Abhandlungen der Gesellschaft der Wissenschaften zu Göttingen.
Phil.-hist. Klasse. Folge 3, 10). Berlin.
1936 "Die Orientforschung und das abendländische Geschichtsbild," *Welt als
Geschichte* (Stuttgart) II, 5 (1936), pp. 377–396.
1937 "Der Vordere Orient," in: *Handbuch der Kulturgeschichte.* Hrsg. von H.
Kindermann: "Kultur der orientalischen Völker," pp. 161–250. Potsdam,
Akademische Verlagsanstalt.
1938 *Goethes Erlebnis des Ostens.* Leipzig, Hinrichs.
1960 *Der Mensch in Orient und Okzident.* Grundzüge einer eurasiatischen
Geschichte. Hrsg. von Grete Schaeder unter Mitarbeit von Kurt Heinrich
Hansen mit einer Einleitung von Ernst Schulin. München, Piper.
1968 *Studien zur orientalischen Religionsgeschichte.* Hrsg. und mit einem Nachwort von Carsten Colpe. Darmstadt, Wissenschaftliche Buchgesellschaft.

MAX SCHELER*

1. Bibliography

Hartmann, Wilfried, *Max Scheler. Bibliographie.* Stuttgart, F. Frommann Verlag (G. Holzboog), 1963.

Noble, Bernard, "Bibliography of Scheler's published works," in: Max Scheler, *On the Eternal in Man.* Translated by Bernard Noble. London, SCM Press, 1960; New York, Harper, 1961.

Ranley, Ernest W., "Bibliography of primary sources," in: Ernest W. Ranley, *Scheler's Phenomenology of Community.* The Hague, Martinus Nijhoff, 1966, pp. 104–124.

2. Biography and Appreciation

Besgen, Achim, *Religion und Philosophie bei Max Scheler.* Diss., Bonn, 1949.

Blessing, Eugen, *Die erkenntnistheoretischen Grundlagen der Religionsphilosophie Max Schelers.* Diss. Bonn, 1946.

—, "Das Ewige im Menschen. Die Grundkonzeption der Religionsphilosophie Max Schelers," *Theological Quarterly*, 133 (1953), pp. 1–29, 176–209, 294–325, 446–487.

Bobbio, N., "La fenomenologia secondo Max Scheler," *Rivista di Filosofia* (Milano), 27 (1936), pp. 227–249.

—, "La personalita di Max Scheler," *Rivista di Filosofia* (Milano), 29 (1938), pp. 97–126.

Clark, M. E., "A phenomenological system of ethics," *Philosophy*, VII (1932) and VIII (1933).

—, "The contribution of Max Scheler to the Philosophy of Religion," *The Philosophical Review* (New York), XLIII (1934), pp. 577–597.

Dupuy, Maurice, *La philosophie de Max Scheler. Son évolution et son unité.* I: *La critique de l'homme moderne et la philosophie théorique.* II: *De l'éthique à la dernière philosophie. Epiméthés. Essais philosophiques.* Paris, P. U. F., 1959.

—, *La philosophie de la religion chez Max Scheler.* Paris, P. U. F., 1959.

Eschweiler, Karl, "Religion und Metaphysik. Zu Max Schelers 'Vom Ewigen im Menschen'," *Hochland*, XIX, 1 (1921/22).

Fries, Heinrich, *Die katholische Religionsphilosophie der Gegenwart. Der Einflusz Max Schelers auf ihre Formen und Gestalten. Eine problemgeschichtliche Studie.* Heidelberg, 1949.

Frings, Manfred S., *Max Scheler. A concise Introduction into the World of a Great Thinker.* Pittsburgh (Pa.), Duquesne University Press; Louvain, E. Nauwelaerts, 1965.

—, "Der Ordo Amoris bei Max Scheler in seinen Beziehungen zu Materialer Wertethik und Ressentiment," *Zeitschrift für Philosophische Forschung*, XIX, 4 (1965).

Getzeni, Heinrich, "Um die Religionsphilosophie Max Schelers," *Hochland*, XXI, 1 (1923/24).

Geyser, Josef, "Augustin und die phänomenologische Religionsphilosophie der Gegenwart, mit besonderer Berücksichtigung M. Schelers," *Veröffentlichungen des katholischen Instituts für Philosophie.* Köln, 1923.

—, *Max Schelers Phänomenologie der Religion nach ihren wesentlichen Lehren allgemeinverständlich dargestellt und beurteilt*. Freiburg i. Br., Herder, 1924.

Haecker, Theodor, "Geist und Leben. Zum Problem Max Scheler," *Hochland*, XXIV, 2 (1926/27).

Hafkesbrink, Hanna, *Das Problem des religiösen Gegenstandes bei Max Scheler*. Gütersloh, 1930.

—, "The meaning of objectivism and realism in Max Scheler's Philosophy of Religion. A contribution to the understanding of Max Scheler's catholic period," *Philosophy and Phenomenological Research*, II (1942).

Hartmann, Wilfried, *Die Philosophie Max Schelers in ihren Beziehungen zu Eduard von Hartmann*. Düsseldorf, 1956.

Heber, Johannes, *Das Problem der Gotteserkenntnis in der Religionsphilosophie Max Schelers*. Diss. Leipzig, 1931.

Herzfeld, Hans, *Begriff und Theorie vom Geist bei Max Scheler*. Diss. Leipzig, 1930.

Hessen, Johannes, *Max Scheler*. Essen, 1948.

Hildebrand, Dietrich von, "Max Scheler als Ethiker," *Hochland*, XXI, 1 (1923/24).

—, "Max Schelers Stellung zur Katholischen Gedankenwelt," *Der katholische Gedanke*, I (1928).

—, "Max Scheler als Persönlichkeit," *Hochland*, XXVI (1928/29).

Hollenback, J. M. (S. J.), "Urleidenschaft und natürliche Gotteserkenntnis. Zu Max Schelers Fundierung des religiösen Bewusstseins," in: *Der beständige Aufbruch*, Nürnberg, Glock und Lutz, 1959, pp. 40–47.

I Lambias de Azevedo, Juan, "La filosofia de la religion de Max Scheler," *Ciencia y Fe* (Buenos Aires), I (1944), pp. 9–40, 60–63.

Kanthack, Katharina, *Max Scheler*. Berlin–Hannover, 1948.

Kraenzlin, Gerhard, *Max Schelers Phänomenologische Systematik*. Leipzig, 1934.

Kreppel, Friedrich, *Die Religionsphilosophie Max Schelers*. Diss. München, 1926.

—, "Max Scheler und das Philosophieren," *Zeitschrift für Religions- und Geistesgeschichte*, XI (1959), pp. 383–386.

Kuhn, Helmut, "Max Scheler im Rückblick," *Hochland*, LI, 4 (1959), pp. 324–338.

Landsberg, P. L., "L'acte philosophique de Max Scheler," *Recherches Philosophiques* (Paris), VI (1936–37), pp. 299–312.

Lorscheid, Bernhard, *Max Schelers Phänomenologie des Psychischen*. Bern, 1957.

Lützeler, Heinrich, "Zu Max Schelers Persönlichkeit," *Hochland*, XXVI (1928/29).

—, *Der Philosoph Max Scheler*. Bonn, 1947.

Mandrioni, Hector D., "La esencia de la filosofia según Max Scheler," *Revista de Filosofia* (La Plata), IX (1960), pp. 40–56.

Martin-Izquierdo, Honorio, *Das religiöse Apriori bei Max Scheler*. Bonn, C. Weyler, 1964.

Mazzantani, Carlo, "L'irrazionalismo nella Filosofia della Religione, con particulare riuardo a Max Scheler e Rudolph Otto," in: *Problema dell'Esperienza Religiosa*. Brescia, Morcelliana, 1961, pp. 294–301.

Molitor, Jacob, *Max Schelers Kritik am Pragmatismus*. Frankfurt am Main, 1961.

Montcheuil, G. de, "Le 'ressentiment' dans la vie morale et religieuse, d'après Max Scheler," *Recherches de Science Religieuse* (Paris), XXVII (1937), pp. 129–164, 309–325.

Muller, Philippe, *De la psychologie à l'anthropologie, à travers l'œuvre de Max Scheler*. Neuchâtel, Baconnière, 1946.

Newe, H., "Max Schelers Auffassung von der religiösen Gotteserkenntnis und ihrem Verhältnis zur metaphysischen," *Abhandlungen zur Philosophie und Psychologie*, Heft 16/17, Würzburg, 1928.

Nystedt, Hans, *Max Schelers Religionsfilosofi. Med särstkild hansyn till dess utveckling och dess plats i hans totalôskôdning*. Stockholm, Svenska Kyrkans Diakonistyrelses Förlag, 1947.

Oesterreicher, John M., "Max Scheler and the Faith," *Thomist*, XIII (1950).

Passweg, Salcia, *Phänomenologie und Ontologie, Husserl–Scheler–Heidegger*. Zürich, Hertz, 1939.

Pellegrino, Ubaldo, "Religione e Metafisica i Max Scheler," in: *Studi di Filosofia e di Storia della Filosofia*. Milano, Vita e Pensiero, 1962, pp. 389–403.

Pöll, W., *Wesen und Wesenserkenntnis. Untersuchungen mit besonderer Berücksichtigung der Phänomenologie Husserls und Schelers*. München, Reinhardt, 1936.

Przywara, Erich, *Religionsbegründung, Max Scheler – J. H. Newman*. Freiburg, 1923.

—, "Zu Max Schelers Religionsauffassung," *Zeitschrift für Katholische Theologie*, 1923.

Quiles, Ismael, "Observationes a la Filosofia de la Religion de Scheler," *Ciencia y Fe* (Buenos Aires), I (1944), pp. 41–59, 64–76.

Ranley, Ernest W., *Scheler's Phenomenology of Community*. The Hague, Martinus Nijhoff, 1966, pp. 104–124.

Schilpp, Paul A., "Max Scheler 1874–1928," *Philosophical Review*, XLVIII (1929).

Schindler, Johann F. A., *Gott und Mensch in ihrer gegenseitigen Zuordnung in der philosophischen Konzeption Max Schelers*. Augsburg, 1968.

Staude, John R., *Max Scheler, 1874–1928. An Intellectual Portrait*. New York etc., 1967.

Temuralp, T., *Über die Grenzen der Erkennbarkeit bei Husserl und Scheler*. Berlin, Verlag für Staatswissenschaft und Geschichte, 1937.

Trautner, Werner, *Der Apriorismus der Wissenschaften. Eine Studie zur Wissenssoziologie Max Schelers*. München, 1969.

Vandenbussche, Frans, "De verhouding tussen godsdienst en metaphysica volgens Max Scheler," *Bijdragen*, XX (1959), pp. 411–425. (Zusammenfassung: "Das Verhältnis zwischen Religion und Metaphysik nach Max Scheler", pp. 425–7).

—, "Max Schelers Godsdienstfilosofie," *Bijdragen*, XXI (1960), pp. 53–68.

Vanni-Rovighi, S., "Filosofia e religione nel pensiero di Max Scheler," *Rivista di Filosofia Neo-Scolastica* (Milano), XXVIII (Suppl.), 1936, pp. 157–169.

Vos, Harmen de, *Het godsdienstig kennen volgens Max Scheler*. Assen, 1927.

Welch, E. Parl, *Max Scheler's Philosophy of Religion*. Ph. D., University of Southern California, 1934.

Wohlgemuth, Josef, *Grundgedanken der Religionsphilosophie Max Schelers in jüdischer Beleuchtung*. Berlin, 1931.

3. Main Publications

1899 *Beiträge zur Feststellung der Beziehung zwischen den logischen und ethischen Prinzipien.* Jena, Vopelius.

1900 *Die transzendentale und die psychologische Methode. Eine grundsätzliche Erörterung zur philosophischen Methodik.* Jena, Dürr; Leipzig, Meiner 1922².

1901 "Kultur und Religion," in: *Der Wahrheitsgehalt der Religion.* Leipzig, Veit & Co. Reprinted in: *Allgemeine Zeitung* (München), Beilage Nr. 30 (1903), pp. 233–236.

1912 "Über Ressentiment und moralisches Werturteil. Ein Beitrag zur Pathologie der Kultur," *Zeitschrift für Pathopsychologie* I, 2–3 (1912), pp. 268–368. Enlarged and reissued under the title of "Das Ressentiment im Aufbau der Moralen," *Abhandlungen und Aufsätze* (1915) and its second edition *Vom Umsturz der Werte*, 1919², 1923³, 1955⁴, pp. 33–147.
English translation by William A. Holdheim, edited with an Introduction by Lewis A. Coser: *Ressentiment.* New York, The Free Press of Glencoe, 1961.
French translation by J.–P. de Menasce: *L'homme du ressentiment.* Paris, Gallimard, 1958.

1913 *Zur Phänomenologie und Theorie der Sympathiegefühle und von Liebe und Hass. Mit einem Anhang über den Grund zur Annahme der Existenz des fremden Ich.* Halle, Niemeyer. Second, enlarged edition under the title of *Wesen und Formen der Sympathie.* Bonn, Cohen, 1923, 1926³; Frankfurt am Main, Schulte-Bulmke, 1931⁴, 1948⁵.
English translation of the fifth edition by Peter Heath: *The Nature of Sympathy.* With a general introduction to Scheler's work by W. Stark. London, Routledge and Kegan Paul, and New Haven, Yale University Press, 1954.
French translation by M. Lefebvre: *Nature et formes de la sympathie. Contribution à l'étude des lois de la vie affective.* Paris, Payot, pb. 1971.

1913–1916 "Der Formalismus in der Ethik und die materiale Wertethik. Mit besonderer Berücksichtigung der Ethik I. Kants," *Jahrbuch für Philosophie und phänomenologische Forschung*, I (1913), pp. 405–565; II (1916), pp. 21–478. Also published separately: Halle, Niemeyer, 1916. Second edition with the subtitle "Neuer Versuch der Grundlegung eines ethischen Personalismus," Halle, Niemeyer, 1921², 1927³. Fourth edition in *Gesammelte Werke*, Vol. II. Bern, Francke, 1954⁴.
French translation by Maurice de Gandillac: *Le formalisme en éthique et l'éthique matérial des valeurs. Essai nouveau pour fonder un personnalisme éthique.* Paris, Gallimard, 1955.

1913–1914 "Der Bourgeois und die religiösen Mächte," *Die Weissen Blätter* (Leipzig), I (1913–14), pp. 1171–1191. Reprinted in: *Abhandlungen und Aufsätze* (1915) and its second edition: *Vom Umsturz der Werte*, 1919², 1923³, 1955⁴, pp. 341–395.

1915 *Abhandlungen und Aufsätze*, 2 vols. Leipzig, Verlag der Weissen Bücher. Second edition under the title of *Vom Umsturz der Werte*, 2 vols. Leipzig, Neue Geist-Verlag, 1919²; Leipzig, Reinhold, 1923³. Fourth edition in *Gesammelte Werke*, Vol. III. Bern, Francke, 1955.

1915 "Liebe und Erkenntnis," *Die Weissen Blätter* (Leipzig), II (1915), pp. 991–1016. Reprinted in: *Krieg und Aufbau*, 1916, and in: *Schriften zur Soziologie und Weltanschauungslehre*, part I: *Moralia*, Leipzig, 1923;

reissued in: *Gesammelte Werke*, Vol. VI, Bern, Francke, 1963, pp· 77–98.

1916 *Krieg und Aufbau* (Essays). Leipzig, Verlag der Weissen Bücher.

1921 *Vom Ewigen im Menschen. Religiöse Erneuerung.* Leipzig, Neue Geist-Verlag. 1923[2] (in two volumes); Berlin, Neue Geist-Verlag, 1933 (abridged edition). Fourth edition: in *Gesammelte Werke*, Vol. V. Bern, Francke, 1954.
English translation by Bernard Noble: *On the Eternal in Man.* With a Foreword by August Brunner, a Note on the Author by I. M. Bochenski, and a Bibliography of Scheler's published works. London, SCM Press, 1960; New York, Harper, 1961.

1923 *Wesen und Formen der Sympathie.* See above, under 1913.

1923–1924 *Schriften zur Soziologie und Weltanschauungslehre.* In four parts. Leipzig, Der Neue Geist-Verlag. Second edition in: *Gesammelte Werke*, Vol. VI. Bern, Francke, 1963.

1924 "Probleme einer Soziologie des Wissens," in: Max Scheler, ed., *Versuche zu einer Soziologie des Wissens.* München, Duncker & Humblot, pp. 1–146. Enlarged and reprinted: in *Die Wissensformen und die Gesellschaft*, Leipzig, Neue Geist-Verlag, 1926; Bern, Francke, 1960[2], pp. 15–190.

1926 *Die Wissensformen und die Gesellschaft.* Leipzig, Neue Geist-Verlag. Second edition in: *Gesammelte Werke*, Vol. VIII. Bern, Francke, 1960.

1927 "Die Sonderstellung des Menschen," *Der Leuchter* (Darmstadt), VIII (1927), pp. 161–254. Published separately under the title of *Die Stellung des Menschen im Kosmos.* Darmstadt, Reichl, 1928, 1929[2], 1930[3]; München, Nymphenburger Verlagsanstalt, 1947[4], 1949[5]; Bern, Francke, 1962[6].
English translation with an Introduction by Hans Meyerhoff: *Man's Place in Nature.* Boston, Beacon Press, 1961; pb. The Noonday Press, 1962.
French translation with preface by M. Dupuy: *La situation de l'homme dans le monde.* Paris, Aubier, 1951.

1929 *Philosophische Weltanschauung.* Bonn, Cohen; Bern, Francke, 1954[2].
English translation by Oscar A. Haac: *Philosophical Perspectives.* Boston, Beacon Press, 1958.
French translation of a part by M. Dupuy: *L'homme et l'histoire.* Suivi par *Les formes du savoir et la culture.* Paris, Aubier, 1955.

1933 *Schriften aus dem Nachlass.* I *Zur Ethik und Erkenntnislehre.* Edited by Maria Scheler. Berlin, Neue Geist-Verlag. Second enlarged edition in: *Gesammelte Werke*, Vol. X. Bern, Francke, 1957.

1944 *Le Saint, le génie, le héros.* Traduction et présentation par Emile Marmy. Fribourg en Suisse, Egloff; Lyon, E. Vitte, 1958.

1952 *Mort et Survie.* Suivi par *Le phénomène du tragique.* Traduit et préfacé par M. Dupuy. Paris, Aubier.

1952 *La Pudeur.* Traduit par M. Dupuy. Paris, Aubier.

1953 *L'Idée de paix et le pacifisme.* Traduit par R. Tandonnet. Paris, Aubier.

1954–1963 *Gesammelte Werke*, 10 vols. Edited by Maria Scheler. Bern–München, A. Francke.

FRIEDRICH W. J. VON SCHELLING

1. Bibliography

Schneeberger, G., *F. W. J. von Schelling. Eine Bibliographie*. Bern, 1954.

2. Main Publications

1856–1858 *Sämtliche Werke*, 14 vols. Stuttgart–Augsburg, Cotta.
1856 *Einleitung in die Philosophie der Mythologie*. Stuttgart.
1857 *Philosophie der Mythologie*. Stuttgart.
1858 *Philosophie der Offenbarung*. Stuttgart.
1927–1943 *Werke*. Nach der Orginalausgabe in neuer Anordnung hrsg. von Manfred, 5 vols. München & Oldenburg.

WILHELM SCHMIDT*

1. Bibliography

Bornemann, Fritz, "Verzeichnis der Schriften von P. W. Schmidt S. V. D. (1868–1954)," *Anthropos*, XXXXIX (1954), pp. 385–432.

2. Biography and Appreciation

Baumann, Hermann, "P. Wilhelm Schmidt und das Mutterrecht," *Anthropos*, LIII (1958), 212–228.
Bornemann, Fritz, "P. W. Schmidts Aufsätze und Vorträge," *Anthropos*, XXXXIX (1954), pp. 663–668.
—, "P. W. Schmidts Vorlesungen über den Entwicklungsgedanken in der ältesten Religion," *Anthropos*, XXXXIX (1954), pp. 669–682.
—, "P. W. Schmidt's Bedeutung für die Theologie," *Schw. K. Z.*, 15 August 1954.
—, "J. M. Garmans Materialien über die Negrito der Philippinen und P. W. Schmidts Notizen dazu," *Anthropos*, L (1955), pp. 899–930.
—, "P. W. Schmidts Vorarbeiten für eine Neuauflage von 'Völker und Kulturen'," *Anthropos*, LI (1956), pp. 291–308.
—, "P. W. Schmidts Studien über den Totemismus in Asien und Ozeanien," *Anthropos*, LI (1956), pp. 595–734.
—, "P. W. Schmidts Studien über den Totemismus in Afrika," *Anthropos*, LIII (1958), pp. 945–1003.
Bulek, G. van, "W. Schmidt 16.2.1868–10.2.1954. Un demi-siècle d'ethnologie," *Zaïre*, VIII (1954), pp. 1029–1042.
Burgmann, Arnold, "W. Schmidt als Linguist," *Anthropos*, XXXXIX (1954), pp. 627–658.
Fahrenfort, J. J., *Het hoogste wezen der primitieven*. Groningen 1927.
—, *Wie der Urmonotheismus am Leben erhalten wird*. Groningen, 1930.

Gusinde, Martin, "Gedenkfeier der japanischen Ethnologen und Anthropologen für W. Schmidt," *Anthropos*, L (1955), pp. 935–937.

Haekel, Josef, "Wilhelm Schmidt (1868–1954)," *Tribus*, N. F. 4/5 (1954–1955), pp. 412–414.

—, "Prof. Wilhelm Schmidts Bedeutung für die Religionsgeschichte des vorkolumbischen Amerika," *Saeculum*, VII (1956), pp. 1–39.

—, "Zum heutigen Forschungsstand der historischen Ethnologie," in: *Die Wiener Schule der Völkerkunde Festschrift*. Wien, 1956, pp. 17–90.

—, "Zur gegenwärtigen Forschungssituation der Wiener Schule der Ethnologie," in *Beiträge Österreichs zur Erforschung der Vergangenheit und Kulturgeschichte der Menschheit*. Wien, 1959, pp. 127–147.

Henninger, Joseph, "P. Wilhelm Schmidt (1868–1954). Eine biographische Skizze," *Anthropos*, LI (1956), pp. 19–60.

—, "Einleitung," in: Wilhelm Schmidt, *Wege der Kulturen. Gesammelte Aufsätze*. Herausgegeben vom Anthropos-Institut (Studia Instituti Anthropos, Vol. 20), St. Augustin, 1964, pp. XI–XXVIII.

Koppers, Wilhelm, "Professor Pater Wilhelm Schmidt. Eine Würdigung seines wissenschaftlichen Lebenswerkes," *Mitteilungen der Anthropologischen Gesellschaft in Wien*, LXXXIII (1954), pp. 87–96. Also in *Zeitschrift für Ethnologie*, LXXIX (1954), pp. 243–253.

—, "Professor Pater Wilhelm Schmidt. Eine Würdigung seines Lebenswerkes," *Anthropos*, LI (1956), pp. 61–80.

Kühn, H., *Das Problem des Urmonotheismus*. Wiesbaden, 1950.

Pinard, H., "La méthode historico-culturelle dans l'étude des religions," *Recherches de Science Religieuse*, 1921, pp. 273–305.

Schebesta, Paul, "Wilhelm Schmidt: 1868–1954," *Man*, LIV (1954), No. 128, pp. 89–90.

Walk, L., "Der Kausalitätsbegriff bei Schmidt-Koppers und Othmar Spann," in: W. Koppers, ed., *Festschrift W. Schmidt*. Vienna, 1928, pp. 969–977.

3. Method and Theory

1902 "Die Fr. Müller'sche Theorie über die Melanesier," *Mitteilungen der anthropologischen Gesellschaft in Wien*, XXXII (1902), pp. 149–160.

1903 "W. Wundts 'Völkerpsychologie'. Erster Band: Die Sprache," *Mitteilungen der anthropologischen Gesellschaft in Wien*, XXXIII (1903), pp. 361–389.

1906 "Die moderne Ethnologie. L'Ethnologie moderne," *Anthropos*, I (1906), pp. 134–163, 318–387, 593–643, 950–997.

1908 "Die ethnologischen Grundlagen der Soziologie," in: *Fünf Vorträge vor der Limburger Versammlung der Görresgesellschaft* (3. Vereinsschrift der Görres-Gesellschaft für 1908), Köln, 1908, pp. 7–24.

1909 "Abgrenzung und Begriffsbestimmung der Ethnologie," *Anthropos*, IV (1909), pp. 254–255, 527–528.

1911 "Is Ethnological Information Coming from Missionaries Sufficiently Reliable?," *Anthropos*, VI (1911), pp. 430–431.

1911 "Die kulturhistorische Methode in der Ethnologie," *Anthropos*, VI (1911), pp. 1010–1036.
    French translation: "La méthode de l'ethnologie," *Revue des Sciences Philosophiques et Théologiques* (Le Saulchoir, Kain), VII, 1913, pp. 218–244.

1911 "Voies nouvelles en Science comparée des religions et en sociologie comparée," *Revue des Sciences Philosophiques et Théologiques*, V (1911), pp.
46–74.
German translation: "Neue Wege der vergleichenden Religions- und Gesell-
schaftswissenschaften," *Die Kultur* (Vienna), XII (1911), pp. 3–25.
1912 "Die kultur-historische Methode in der Ethnologie," *Anthropos*, VII (1912),
pp. 253–254.
1912 "La Semaine d'Ethnologie religieuse. Cours d'introduction à la Science
comparée des Religions, tenu à Louvain du 27 août à 4 septembre 1912,"
Anthropos, VII (1912), pp. 1049–1055.
1912 "Kulturhistorischer Zusammenhang oder Elementargedanke," *Anthropos*,
VII (1912), pp. 1060–1062.
1913 "La méthode de l'ethnologie," *Revue des Sciences Philosophiques et Théologiques* (Le Saulchoir, Kain), VII (1913), pp. 218–244.
1913 "'The Conception of the Causal Relation in Sociological Science' von
Gerald Camden Wheeler," *Anthropos*, VIII (1913), pp. 252–254.
1913 "A la recherche d'une définition de la Magie," *Anthropos*, VIII (1913), pp.
883–885.
1913 "Religion et Magie," *Anthropos*, VIII (1913), pp. 1144–1147.
1914 "Das Problem des Totemismus. Eine Diskussion über die Natur des
Totemismus und die Methode seiner Erforschung, 1. Einführung," *Anthropos*, IX (1914), pp. 287–289.
1917 "Über die Anwendung der kulturhistorischen Methode auf Amerika,"
Anthropos, XII/XIII (1917/1918), pp. 1120–1127.
1920 "La Semaine d'Ethnologie religieuse. Cours d'Introduction à la Science
comparée des Religions," *Anthropos*, XIV/XV (1919/1920), pp. 492–495.
1920 "Die kulturhistorische Methode und die nordamerikanische Ethnologie,"
Anthropos, XIV/XV (1919/1920), pp. 546–563.
1922 "Die Abwendung vom Evolutionismus und die Hinwendung zum Histori-
zismus in der Amerikanistik," *Anthropos*, XVI/XVII (1921/1922), pp.
487–519.
1922 "Ethnologische Bemerkungen zu theologischen Opfertheorien," *Jahrbücher
des Missionshauses St. Gabriel* (Wien-Mödling), I (1922), pp. 1–68.
1923 "Mission und Wissenschaft," *Jahrbücher des akademischen Missionsbundes
der Universität Freiburg, Schweiz*, IV (1923), pp. 9–22.
1923 "Recul de l'Evolutionnisme dans la sociologie et dans l'histoire des religions
au cours des dix dernières années," *Recherches de Science Religieuse*
(Paris), XIII (1923), pp. 385–396.
1924 "Werden und Wirken der Völkerkunde," in: W. Schmidt und W. Koppers,
Gesellschaft und Wirtschaft der Völker (Der Mensch aller Zeiten, Natur und
Kultur der Völker der Erde, Band III: *Völker und Kulturen*). Regensburg, pp. 1–130. Newly printed within another publication: Wilhelm
Schmidt, *Werden und Wirken der Völkerkunde. Geschichte und Grundfragen der Gesellschaftslehre. Familie und Staat auf der Urstufe*. Regensburg, 1937, pp. 1–130.
Japanese translation by Shunichi Ōno: *Minzokugaku no Rekishi to Hōhō*.
Tokio, 1944.
1926 "Critères pour établir la position ethnologique des cercles culturels les
plus anciens," *Semaine Internationale d'Ethnologie Religieuse, IV*e *Session,
Milan, 17–25 septembre 1925*, Paris, pp. 126–142.
1926 "Distinction et répartition des cercles culturels," *Ibidem*, pp. 341–353.

1928 "Ein Versuch zur Rettung des Evolutionismus," *Internationales Archiv für Ethnographie*, XXIX (1928), pp. 1–28.

1929 "Eine wissenschaftliche Abrechnung mit der Psychoanalyse," *Das Neue Reich* (Vienna–Innsbruck–München), XI (1928–29), pp. 266–267.

1929 "Prof. Dr. Freuds psychologische (psycho-analytische) Theorie zum Ursprung der Familie und der Religion," *Schönere Zukunft* (Vienna–Regensburg), IV (1928–29), pp. 263–265, 287–289, 308–310.

1930 *Handbuch der vergleichenden Religionsgeschichte zum Gebrauch für Vorlesungen an Universitäten, Seminarien usw. und zum Selbststudium. Ursprung und Werden der Religion. Theorien und Tatsachen*. Münster i. W.

   Chinese translation by Herm. Köster, Ch'en Hsiang-Ch'un, and Su Shih-i: *Pi-chiao tsung-chiao shih*. Peking, 1948.

   English translation by H. J. Rose: *The Origin and Growth of Religion. Facts and Theories*. London, Methuen, 1931.

   French translation by A. Lemonnyer: *Origine et évolution de la religion. Les théories et les faits* (Collection "La vie Chrétienne"). Paris, 1931.

   Italian translation by Giuseppe Bugatto: *Manuale di Storia comparata delle Religioni. Ad uso degli insegnanti di università, seminari e per los studio privato. Origine e Sviluppo della Religione. Teorie et Fatti* (Collezione Fides, 7). Brescia, 1934, 1938[2] (revised and enlarged), 1943[3], 1949[4] (enlarged).

   Spanish translation by Emilio Huidobro and Edith Tech de Huidobro. *Manual de Historia comparada de las Religiones. Origen y formaciòn de la religiòn. Teorías y hechos*. Bilbao–Madrid–Barcelona, 1932, 1941[2] (enlarged).

1931 "Methodologisches und Inhaltliches zum Zweigeschlechterwesen," *Anthropos*, XXVI (1931), pp. 55–98.

1933 "Um die rechte katholische Wissenschaft," *Schönere Zukunft* (Vienna–Regensburg), VIII. (1932–33), pp. 1204–1206.

1934 "Was vermag der Katholizismus der Wissenschaft zu bieten? Katholischer Universitätsgedanke und gegenwärtige Zeitlage," *Schönere Zukunft* (Vienna–Regensburg), IX (1933–34), pp. 793–794, 811–812.

1935 "Fritz Graebner," *Anthropos*, XXX (1935), pp. 203–214.

1937 *Handbuch der Methode der kulturhistorischen Ethnologie*. Mit Beiträgen von Wilhelm Koppers. Münster i. W.

   English translation by S. A. Sieber: *The Culture Historical Method of Ethnology. A Scientific Approach to the Racial Question*. Preface by Clyde Kluckhohn. Notes by Wilhelm Koppers. New York, Fortuny's 1939.

   Italian translation by Luigi Vannicelli: Schmidt Guglielmo e Koppers Guglielmo, *Manuale di metodologia etnologica*. Milano, 1949.

1939 "Der Gang der Entwicklung in Religion und Kultur," in: *Festschrift St. Gabriel zum 50-jährigen Jubiläum*. Wien–Mödling, St. Gabriel-Verlag, pp. 553–570. Reprinted in: Wilhelm Schmidt, *Wege der Kulturen. Gesammelte Aufsätze herausgegeben vom Anthropos-Institut* (Studia Instituti Anthropos, Vol. 20). St. Augustin, 1964, pp. 287–299.

1941 "Untersuchungen zur Methode der Ethnologie I: W. Mühlmanns Funktionalismus," *Anthropos*, XXXV–XXXVI (1940–41), pp. 379–380.

1951 "In der Wissenschaft nur Wissenschaft," *Anthropos*, XXXXVI (1951) pp. 611–614.

1954 *Die Völker in der Heilsgeschichte der Menschheit* (Schriftenreihe der Katholischen Glaubensberatung). Steyl.

1964 "Die Entfaltung der Gottesidee in der Geschichte der Menschheit," *Wege der Kulturen*. St. Augustin, pp. 301–304.

4. Publications: The Origin of the Idea of God

1910 *L'origine de l'idée de Dieu. Etude historico-critique et positive.* I: *Historico-critique.* French translation by J. Pietsch. Vienne. Earlier published in *Anthropos,* III. (1908), pp. 125–162; 336–368; 559–611; 801–836; 1081–1120. IV (1909), pp. 207–250; 505–524; 1075–1091. V (1910), pp. 231–246 (Compare V (1911), p. 1041). VII (1912), pp. 796–797.

1912–1955 *Der Ursprung der Gottesidee. Eine historisch-kritische und positive Studie,* 12 vols. Münster i. W.

I: *Historisch-kritischer Teil.* 1912 (German text of the foregoing study), 1926² (enlarged).

II: *Die Religionen der Urvölker,* I: Die Religionen der Urvölker Amerikas. 1929.

III: *Die Religionen der Urvölker,* II: Die Religionen der Urvölker Asiens und Australiens. 1931.

IV: *Die Religionen der Urvölker,* III: Die Religionen der Urvölker Afrikas. 1933.

V: *Die Religionen der Urvölker,* IV: Nachträge zu den Religionen der Urvölker Amerikas, Asiens und Australiens. 1934.

VI: *Die Religionen der Urvölker,* V: Endsynthese der Religionen der Urvölker Amerikas, Asiens, Australiens, Afrikas. 1935.

VII: *Die Religionen der Hirtenvölker,* I: Die afrikanischen Hirtenvölker: Hamiten und Hamitoiden. 1940.

VIII: *Die Religionen der Hirtenvölker,* II: Die afrikanischen Hirtenvölker: Niloten und Synthese mit Hamiten und Hamitoiden. 1949.

IX: *Die Religionen der Hirtenvölker,* III: Die asiatischen Hirtenvölker: Die primären Hirtenvölker der Alt-Türken, der Altai- und der Abakan-Tartaren. 1949.

X: *Die Religionen der Hirtenvölker,* IV: Die asiatischen Hirtenvölker. Die sekundären Hirtenvölker der Mongolen, der Burjaten, der Yuguren, sowie der Tungusen und der Yukagiren. 1952.

XI: *Die Religionen der Hirtenvölker,* V: Die asiatischen Hirtenvölker der Jakuten und der Sojoten-Karagassen sowie der Jenisseier und die Synthese der benachbarten Nicht-Hirtenvölker. 1954.

XII: *Die Religionen der Hirtenvölker,* VI: Endsynthese der Religionen der asiatischen und afrikanischen Hirtenvölker. Mit einem Vorwort von F. Borneman. 1955.

1911 "L'origine de l'idée de Dieu," *Anthropos,* VI (1911), p. 1041.

1911 "Die Uroffenbarung als Anfang der Offenbarungen Gottes," in: Gerhard Esser and Joseph Mausbach, eds., *Religion, Christentum, Kirche,* Vol. I. Kempten-München, pp. 479–632. 1913, 1920, 1921, 1923. Also separately published in 1913, 1920, 1921.

English translation by Joseph J. Baierl: *Primitive Revelation.* London, St. Louis, 1939.

French translation by A. Lemonnyer: *La révélation primitive et les données actuelles de la science d'après l'ouvrage allemand du R. P. G. Schmidt.* Paris, 1914.

1922 "Der Ursprung der Gottesidee. Eine weiterführende Uberschau," *Anthropos,* XVI/XVII (1921/22), pp. 1006–1051

1926 "La formation du monothéisme," *Anthropos,* XXI (1926), pp. 269–272.

1928 "Historische Tatsächlichkeiten des Zustandenkommens meines 'Der Ursprung der Gottesidee'," *Anthropos*, XXIII (1928), pp. 471–474.
1930 "Der Monotheismus der Primitiven," *Anthropos*, XXV (1930), pp. 703–709.

5. Other Publications

1909 "Die soziologische und religiös-ethische Gruppierung der australischen Stämme," *Zeitschrift für Ethnologie* (Berlin), XXXXI (1909), pp. 328–377.
1910 *Grundlinien einer Vergleichung der Religionen und Mythologien der austronesischen Völker* (Denkschriften der Kaiserlichen Akademie der Wissenschaften in Wien, Phil.-hist. Klasse, Band 53, Abhandlung 3). Vienna.
1910 *Die Stellung der Pygmäenvölker in der Entwicklungsgeschichte des Menschen* (Studien und Forschungen zur Menschen- und Völkerkunde, VI/VII). Stuttgart.
1913 "Kulturkreise und Kulturschichten in Südamerika," *Zeitschrift für Ethnologie*, XXXXV (1913), pp. 1014–1124.
   Portuguese translation by Sérgio Buarque de Hollanda: *Ethnologia Sulamericana. Círculos culturaes e estratos culturaes na América do Sul* (Bibliotheca Pedagógica Brasileira. Série 5a: Brasiliana. Vol. 218). São Paulo - Rio de Janeiro, 1942.
1914 "Une soi-disant critique des 'Grundlinien einer Vergleichung der Religionen und Mythologien der austronesischen Völker' du P. W. Schmidt," *Anthropos*, IX (1914), pp. 330–331.
1914 "Das religiöse Innenleben des Individuums," *Anthropos*, IX (1914), pp. 1023–1025.
1923 *Die geheime Jugendweihe eines australischen Urstammes. Mit einem Abrisz der soziologischen und religionsgeschichtlichen Entwicklung der südostaustralischen Stämme.* (Dokumente der Religion, Band III). Paderborn.
1923 *Menschheitswege zum Gotterkennen, rationale, irrationale, superrationale. Eine religionsgeschichtliche und religionspsychologische Untersuchung.* München–Kempten.
1924 "Die menschliche Gesellschaft," in: W. Schmidt und W. Koppers, *Gesellschaft und Wirtschaft der Völker* ("Der Mensch aller Zeiten, Natur und Kultur der Völker der Erde", Band III: *Völker und Kulturen*). Regensburg, pp. 131–374.
1926 *Zwei Mythen kalifornischer Indianen.* (Religiöse Quellenschriften, Heft 25). Düsseldorf.
1927 *Rasse und Volk. Eine Untersuchung zur Bestimmung ihrer Grenzen und zur Erfassung ihrer Beziehungen.* München. Appeared also in *Hochland* (München–Kempten), XXIV (1926–27), pp. 407–425, 558–580. Second edition: *Rasse und Volk. Ihre allgemeine Bedeutung. Ihre Geltung im deutschen Raum.* Salzburg–Leipzig, 1935. Third edition: *Die Rassen des Abendlandes.* Luzern, 1946.
1930 "Der Ödipus-Komplex der Freudschen Psychoanalyse und die Ehegestaltung des Bolschewismus. Eine kritischen Prüfung ihrer ethnologischen Grundlagen," *Nationalwirtschaft* (Berlin), II (1929), pp. 401–436.
1931 *L'anima dei primitivi* (Collezione Missionaria. Saggi e Studi, 1). Rome.
1932 "Die Errichtung des 'Anthropos-Institutes'," *Anthropos*, XXVII (1932), pp. 275–277.

1933 *High Gods in North America.* (Upton Lectures in Religion, Manchester College, Oxford 1932). Oxford, Clarendon Press.

1934 *The Religion of Earliest Man.* (Studies in Comparative Religion, 2, 102). London. 1948², (rev.), 1952³.

1934 *The Religion of Later Primitive Peoples.* (Studies in Comparative Religion, 3, 103). London. 1948, 1952.

1935 "The Position of Women with Regard to Property in Primitive Society," *American Anthropologist*, XXXVII, 2 (1935), pp. 244–256.

1935 "Primitive Man. A brief critical examination of the subject and a systematic statement based on demonstrated facts," in: Eyre Edward, ed., *European Civilisation. Its Origin and Development.* Vol. I: *Prehistoric Man and Earliest Known Societies.* Oxford, pp. 1–82.

1935 *Neue Wege zur Erforschung der ethnologischen Stellung Japans.* With Japanese translation by Masao Oka, and with an address by Prof. Dr. W. Schmidt. Tokyo, 1935.

1936 *Religionen hos urkulturens folk.* (Olaus-Petri-föreläsningar vid Uppsala Universitet). Translated by Erik Gren. Stockholm.

1937–1942 *Das Eigentum auf den ältesten Stufen der Menschheit.* Munster i. W. Vol. I: *Das Eigentum in den Urkulturen*, 1937. Vol. II: *Das Eigentum im Primärkulturkreis der Herdenviehzüchter Asiens*, 1940. Vol. III: *Das Eigentum im Primärkulturkreis der Herdenviehzüchter Afrikas*, 1942.

1939 "Ursprung und Entwicklung des Eigentums," *Scientia* (Milan), Ser. IV, Nr. 33 (1939), pp. 47–58.
    French translation: "Origine et évolution de la propriété," *Ibidem*, pp. 27–36.

1946–1949 *Rassen und Völker in Vorgeschichte und Geschichte des Abendlandes.* Luzern. Vol. I: *Die Rassen des Abendlandes* (3rd edition of *Rasse und Volk*, 1927), 1946. Vol. II: *Die Völker des Abendlandes*. 1946. Vol. III: *Gegenwart und Zukunft des Abendlandes*, 1949 (Sammlung Stocker, Bd. 1, 2, 3)

1949 "Geist und Ethos des Menschen der Urkultur," *Wissenschaft und Weltbild* (Vienna), II, (1949), pp. 212–221. This appeared separately with the title: *Das Menschenbild der Urkultur.* Vienna, 1949.

1949 "Die Herkunft der Indogermanen und ihr erstes Auftreten in Europa," *Kosmos* (Stuttgart), XXXXV, 3 (1949), pp. 116–118; XXXV, 4 (1949), pp. 159–160.

1951 "Vorwort," in: Franz König, ed., *Christus und die Religionen der Erde. Handbuch der Religionsgeschichte.* Vol. I, Vienna, pp. VII–XIII.

1953 "Die Mythologien und Religionen der Mikronesier," *Archiv für Völkerkunde* (Vienna), VIII (1953), pp. 172–227.

1953 "Sexualismus, Mythologie und Religion in Nord-Australien," *Anthropos*, XXXXVIII (1953), pp. 898–924.

1954 *Aufsätze und Vorträge.* (Micro-Bibliotheca Anthropos, 17). Posieux-Freiburg (Sw.).

1954 *Der Entwicklungsgedanke in der ältesten Religion.* (Micro-Bibliotheca Anthropos, 18). Posieux-Freiburg (Sw.).

1954 *Gebräuche des Gatten bei Schwangerschaft und Geburt. Mit Richtigstellung des Begriffs der Couvade.* Mit einem Vorwort von W. Koppers (Wiener Beiträge zur Kulturgeschichte und Linguistik, 10). Vienna.

1954 *Das Mutterrecht.* Mit einem Vorwort von F. Bornemann (Studia Instituti Anthropos, 10). Mödling-Vienna.

1955 *Totemismus in Asien und Ozeanien.* (Micro-Bibliotheca Anthropos, 15). Posieux-Freiburg (Sw.).

1955 *Totemismus in Afrika.* (Micro-Biblio theca Anthropos, 16). Posieux
    Freiburg (Sw.).
.... *Religion und Religionen, ihre Formen, ihre Entwicklung.* (Text belonging
    to *Gloria-Bildband*). Vienna, no date (before 1938, III + 29 p.).

LEOPOLD VON SCHRÖDER

1. Biography

Leopold von Schröder, *Lebenserinnerungen.* Hrsg. von Felix von Schröder.
Leipzig, 1921.

2. Main Publications

1884 *Pythagoras und die Inder. Eine Untersuchung über die Herkunft und
    Abstammung der pythagoreischen Lehren.* Leipzig.
1887 *Indiens Literatur und Kultur in historischer Entwicklung.* Ein Zyklus
    von fünfzig Vorlesungen, zugleich als Handbuch der indischen Literatur-
    geschichte, nebst zahlreichen in deutscher Übersetzung mitgeteilten
    Proben aus indischen Schriftwerken. Leipzig, Haessel.
1887 *Griechische Götter und Heroen.* Eine Untersuchung ihres ursprünglichen
    Wesens mit Hilfe der vergleichenden Mythologie. Heft I. (Aphrodite,
    Eros und Hephästos). Berlin, Weidmannsche Buchhandlung.
1895 *Über die Entwicklung der Indologie in Europa und ihre Beziehungen zur
    allgemeinen Völkerkunde.* Antrittsvorlesung an der Universität Innsbruck.
    (Separat-Abdruck aus den *Mitteilungen der Anthropol. Ges. in Wien).*
    Wien.
1899 *Indiens geistige Bedeutung für Europa.* Antrittsvorlesung, gehalten am
    6. Mai 1899 an der K. K. Universität Wien.
1905 *Wesen und Ursprung der Religion, ihre Wurzeln und deren Entfaltung,*
    (in: Beiträge zur Weiterentwicklung der Christlischen Religion). München,
    Lehmanns Verlag.
1908 *Mysterium und Mimus im Rigveda.* Leipzig, Haessel.
1910 *Die Wurzeln der Sage vom heiligen Gral.* (Sitz.-Ber. der Kais. Ak. der
    Wiss. in Wien, Phil.-hist. Kl., Bd. 166, 2. Abhdl.). Wien.
1911 *Die Vollendung des arischen Mysteriums in Bayreuth.* München, Leh-
    manns Verlag.
1912 *Bhagavadgîta. Des Erhabenen Sang.* Übertragen und eingeleitet von L.
    von Schroeder, Jena, Verlag Eugen Diederichs. 1915[2].
1914 *Herakles und India. Eine mythenvergleichende Untersuchung.* (Denkschrif·
    ten der Kais. Ak. der Wiss. in Wien, Phil.-hist. Kl., Bd. 58, 3. Abhdl.).
    Wien.
1914–1916 *Arische Religion.* Vol. I: *Einleitung. Der altarische Himmelsgott.
    Das höchste gute Wesen;* Vol. II: *Naturverehrung und Lebensfeste.* Leipzig,
    Haessel Verlag.
1913 *Reden und Aufsätze, vornehmlich über Indiens Literatur und Kultur.*
    Leipzig, Haessel Verlag.

HEINRICH SCHURTZ

1. Biography and Appreciation

Ratzel, Friedrich, "Heinrich Schurtz, geboren am 11. Dez. 1863, gestorben am 2. Mai 1903," *Deutsche Demographische Blätter*, XXVI (1903), pp. 51–63. Reprinted in: Friedrich Ratzel, *Kleine Schriften*, Vol. I, München, 1906, pp. 522–530.

2. Main Publications

1894 "Der Begriff 'Religion' vom Standpunkte der Völkerkunde," in: *P. J. Veth – Feestbundel ter gelegenheid van zijn 80ste Geboortedag*. Leiden.
1898 *Grundriss einer Entstehungsgeschichte des Geldes*. Weimar.
1898 "Über Wertvernichtung durch den Totenkult," in: *Zeitschrift für Sozialwissenschaft*, pp. 41–52.
1900 *Urgeschichte der Kultur*. Leipzig–Wien.
1902 *Altersklassen und Männerbünde*. Eine Darstellung der Grundformen der Gesellschaft. Mit einer Verbreitungskarte. Berlin, Georg Reimer.

WILHELM SCHWARTZ

Main Publications

1870 *Die ethische Bedeutung der Sage für das Volksleben im Alterthum und in der Neuzeit*. Berlin.
1884 *Prähistorisch-anthropologische Studien. Mythologisches und Kulturhistorisches*. Berlin.
1885 *Indogermanischer Volksglaube. Ein Beitrag zur Religionsgeschichte der Urzeit*. Berlin.
1894 *Nachklänge prähistorischen Volksglaubens in Homer. Mit einem Anhang über eine Hexenfahrt der Hera und die sogenannte Hexensalbe*. Berlin.

ALBERT SCHWEITZER*

1. Bibliography

Robert Amadou, *Albert Schweitzer: éléments de biographie et de bibliographie*. Paris, 1952.

2. Biography and Appreciation

Amadou, R., ed., *Albert Schweitzer. Etudes et témoignages*. Paris, 1952.

Babel, H. A., *La pensée d'Albert Schweitzer: sa signification pour la théologie et la philosophie contemporaines*. Neuchâtel, 1954.

Bähr, H. W., ed., *Albert Schweitzer. Sein Denken und sein Weg*. Tübingen, 1962.

Bremi, W., and others, *Albert Schweitzer. Mensch und Werk*. Bern, 1959.

Buri, F., *Christentum und Kultur bei Albert Schweitzer. Eine Einführung in sein Denken als Weg zu einer christlichen Weltanschauung*. Bern, 1941.

—, "Der existentielle Charakter des konsequent-eschatologischen Jesus-Verständnisses Albert Schweitzers im Zusammenhang mit der heutigen Debatte zwischen Bultmann, Barth und Jaspers," in: F. Buri, ed., *Ehrfurcht vor dem Leben. Albert Schweitzer. Eine Freundesgabe zu seinem 80. Geburtstag*. Bern, 1954.

Clark, H. B., *The Ethical Mysticism of Albert Schweitzer. A Study of the Sources and Significance of Schweitzer's Philosophy of Civilization*. With two Essays by Albert Schweitzer. Boston, 1962. New edition with the title: *The Philosophy of Albert Schweitzer*. With two Essays by Albert Schweitzer. London, 1964.

Feschotte, J., *Albert Schweitzer*. Avec des textes inédits. Paris, Editions Universitaires, 1952, 1955³. 1958⁴.

> *English* translation by J. Russell: *Albert Schweitzer: an Introduction*. With two unpublished addresses by Albert Schweitzer. London, 1954.

"Friends of Albert Schweitzer," *A Selection of Writings of and about Albert Schweitzer*. Boston, 1958.

Grabs, R., *Albert Schweitzer. Gehorsam und Wagnis*. Hamburg, 1949. New edition (revised): Frankfurt/M, Büchergilde Gutenberg, 1957.

—, ed., *Albert Schweitzer. Denken und Tat*. Hamburg, 1952.

—, *Die Weltreligionen im Blickpunkt Albert Schweitzers*. Berlin, Evangelischer Verlag, 1953.

—, *Albert Schweitzer als religiöser Charakter und als religionswissenschaftlicher Denker*, Diss. Leipzig, 1954.

Hygen, J., *Albert Schweitzers tankar om Kulturen*. Stockholm, 1954.

Kossen, H. B., *Op zoek naar de historische Jezus. Een studie over Albert Schweitzers visie op Jezus' Leven* (Diss. Amsterdam). Assen, 1960.

Kraus, O., *Albert Schweitzer. Sein Werk und seine Weltanschauung*, Berlin, 1929² (exp.).

> *English* translation: *Albert Schweitzer: his Work and his Philosophy*. London, 1944.

Langfeldt, G., *Albert Schweitzer. En personlighetsstudie. Med et forsøk på belysning av hans syn på religion og moral*. Oslo, 1958.

> *English* translation by M. Michael: *Albert Schweitzer: a Study of his Philosophy of Life*. London, 1960.

Lind, E., *Albert Schweitzer. Aus seinem Leben und Werk*. Bern, 1948.

Linton, O., "Albert Schweitzer's Interpretation of St. Paul's Theology," in: A. A. Robach, ed., *The Albert Schweitzer Jubilee Book*. Cambridge (Mass.), 1946, pp. 441 ff.

Lönnebo, M., *Albert Schweitzers etisk-religiösa ideal*. Stockholm, 1964.

Mozley, E. N., *The Theology of Albert Schweitzer for Christian Inquirers*. With an Epilogue by Albert Schweitzer. London, A. and C. Black, 1950.

Neuenschwander, Ulrich, "Introduction," in: Albert Schweitzer, *The Kingdom of God and Primitive Christianity*. London, 1968.

Picht, W. R. V., *Albert Schweitzer. Wesen und Bedeutung*. Hamburg, 1960. *English* translation by E. Fitzgerald: *Albert Schweitzer: the Man and his Work*. London, A. and C. Black, 1964.

Pierkal, J., *Albert Schweitzer. The Life of a Great Man*. London, 1957.

Raab, K., *Albert Schweitzer. Persönlichkeit und Denken*. Düsseldorf, 1937.

Ratter, M. C., *Albert Schweitzer*. London, 1949.

Regester, J. *Albert Schweitzer. The Man and his Work*. New York, 1931.

Roback, A. A., ed., *The Albert Schweitzer Jubilee Book*. Edited by A. A. Roback with the co-operation of J. S. Bixler and G. Sarton. Cambridge, (Mass), 1946.

Scholder, K., "Albert Schweitzer and Ferdinand Christian Baur," in: H. W. Bähr, ed., *Albert Schweitzer*. Tübingen, 1962, pp. 184 ff.

Schweitzer, Albert, *Aus meiner Kindheit und Jugendzeit*, 1924.
English translation by C. T. Campion: *Memoirs of Childhood and Youth*. New York, Macmillan, 1925.
French translation: *Souvenirs de mon enfance*. Paris, Istra, 1950.

—, *Aus meinem Leben und Denken*, 1931.
English translation by C. T. Campion: *My Life and Thought. An Autobiography*. London, G. Allen & Unwin, 1933. New edition under the title of *Out of my Life and Thought. An Autobiography*. Postscript by Everett Skillings. New York, H. Holt, 1949.
French translation: *Ma vie et ma pensée*. Paris, A. Michel, 1959. New edition: Paris, Club des éditeurs, 1960.

—, *Albert Schweitzer's Leben und Denken*. Selections chosen from the autobiographical writings of the author and edited by Kurt Bergel. New York, H. Holt, 1951.

—, *Selbstzeugnisse: Aus meiner Kindheit und Jugendzeit, Zwischen Wasser und Urwald, Briefe aus Lambarene* (Previously published essays). München, C. H. Beck, 1959, 1963.[2]

Seaver, G., *Albert Schweitzer. The Man and his Mind*. London, 1947.

Skinitz, B., *Albert Schweitzer. Leben, Werk, Botschaft*. Wien, 1959[2].

3. Main Publications

1899 *Die Religionsphilosophie Kants von der Kritik der reinen Vernunft bis zur Religion innerhalb der Grenzen der bloszen Vernunft*. Diss., Freiburg.

1901 *Das Messianitäts- und Leidensgeheimnis. Eine Skizze des Lebens Jesu*. Tübingen. 1929[2].
English translation with introduction by Walter Lowrie: *The Mystery of the Kingdom of God. The Secret of Jesus' Messiahship and Passion*. London, A. and C. Black, 1950.
French translation by Annie Anex-Heimbrod: *Le secret historique de la vie de Jésus*. Preface by Henry Babel. Paris, A. Michel, 1961.

1901 *Das Abendmahlsproblem auf Grund der wissenschaftlichen Forschung des 19. Jahrhunderts und der historischen Berichte*. Tübingen. 1929[2].

1906 *Von Reimarus zu Wrede. Eine Geschichte der Leben-Jesu-Forschung*. Tübingen, 1906. New edition, revised and enlarged, under the title *Geschichte der Leben-Jesu-Forschung*, Tübingen, 1913[2] etc.

English translation by W. Montgomery: *The Quest of the Historical Jesus, a Critical Study of its Progress from Reimarus to Wrede.* Preface by F. C. Burkitt. London, A. and C. Black, 1910, 1911[2] etc.; New York, 1948 etc.

1911 *Geschichte der paulinischen Forschung von der Reformation bis auf die Gegenwart.* Tübingen.
English translation: *Paul and his Interpreters, a Critical History.* London, A. and C. Black, 1912, etc.

1913 *Die psychiatrische Beurteilung Jesu* (Diss.). Straszburg. Reprint, Tübingen, 1933[2].

1923 *Kulturphilosophie*, 2 vols. I: *Verfall und Wiederaufbau der Kultur ;* II: *Kultur und Ethik.* München und Bern, 1923; München, Beck, 1951[8]. *English* translation of both volumes by C. T. Campion, resp.: *Civilisation and Ethics*, 1949[3] (revised by Charles E. B. Russell), and: *The Decay and the Restoration of Civilisation*, 1950[2]. Both volumes published by A. and C. Black, London.

1923 *Das Christentum und die Weltreligionen.* München und Bern.
English translation by Johanna Powers: *Christianity and the Religions of the World.* With a Foreword by Nathaniel Micklem. New York, G. H. Doran Co., 1923. Reprinted New York, Macmillan, 1951.

1929 "Selbstdarstellung," in: *Die Philosophie der Gegenwart in Selbstdarstellung,* vol. VII. Leipzig. Also published separately.

1930 *Die Mystik des Apostels Paulus.* Tübingen, 1954[2].
English translation by William Montgomery: *The Mysticism of Paul the Apostle.* Preface by F. C. Burkitt. London, A. and C. Black, 1931. *French* translation by Marcelle Guéritot: *La mystique de l'apôtre Paul.* Introduction by Georges Marchal. Paris, A. Michel, 1962.

1934 "Religion in modern civilization," in: G. Seaver, *Albert Schweitzer. The Man and his Mind.* London, 1947, pp. 335 ff.

1935 *Die Weltanschauung der indischen Denker: "Mystik und Ethik",* München–Bern.
English translation by Mrs. Charles E. B. Russell: *Indian Thought and its Development.* New York, H. Holt and Co., 1936.
French translation: *Les grands penseurs de l'Inde. Etude de philosophie comparée.* Paris, Payot, 1952, 1956; pb. 1962.

1936 "The ethics of reverence for life," in: H. Clark, *The Ethical Mysticism of Albert Schweitzer.* Boston, 1962 etc., pp. 180 ff.

1947 "The state of civilization," *The Christian Register,* CXXVI, 8 (September 1947), pp. 320 ff.

1947 *Albert Schweitzer: an Anthology.* Edited by Charles R. Joy. Boston, Beacon Press. 1965[2] (enlarged).
French translation: *Albert Schweitzer. Une anthologie.* Paris, Payot, 1950.

1950 "The conception of the Kingdom of God in the transformation of eschatology," in: E. N. Mosley, *The Theology of Albert Schweitzer for Christian Inquirers.* London, A. and C. Black, pp. 80 ff.

1967 *Reich Gottes und Christentum.* Edited with a Preface by Ulrich Neuenschwander. Tübingen, Mohr.
English translation by L. A. Garrard: *The Kingdom of God and Primitive Christianity.* Introduction by Ulrich Neuenschwander. London, Black, 1968.

ERNST SIECKE

Main Publications

1892 *Liebesgeschichte des Himmels.* Orpheus and Eurydice, Weisse und Schwarze Braut, Schwanensage, Freyr, Freyja, Gerdha, Iduna, Skodi, Der Zahl Neun, Fiölsvid. Strassburg, 1892.
1896 *Über die Bedeutung der Grimmschen Märchen für unser Volksthum.* (Sammlung gem. wissens. Vorträge, 253). Hamburg.
1901 *Mythologische Briefe.* Vol. I: *Grundsätze der Sagenforschung;* Vol. II: *Uhland's Behandlung der Thorsagen.* Berlin.
1907 *Drachenkämpfe. Indogermanische Sagenkunde.* (Gesellschaft für vergleichende Mythenforschung. Mythologische Bibliothek. Band 1, Heft 1). Leipzig.
1908 *Hermes der Mondgott.* (Mythologische Bibliothek. Band 2, Heft 1). Leipzig.
1909 *Götterattribute und sogenannte Symbole.* Jena.
1914 *Der Vegetationsgott.* (Mythologische Bibliothek. Band 6, Heft 10). Leipzig.
1926 *Die Religiosität griechischer Denker und Dichter.* Leipzig.
1916 "Über einige mythologisch wichtige Tiere," in: *Vier Abhandlungen.* By E. Siecke, Carl Fries and Hugo Kunike. Leipzig.
1914 *Pûshan.* Studien zur Idee des Hirtengottes im Anschluss an die Studien über "Hermes den Mondgott". Pûshan im Rig-Veda. (Mythologische Bibliothek. Band 7, Hefte 1, 2). Leipzig.

HERBERT SILBERER

Main Publications

1914 *Probleme der Mystik und ihrer Symbolik.* Wien.
1915 *Durch Tod zum Leben.* (Beiträge zur Geschichte der neueren Mystik und Magie, Heft 4). Leipzig, Wilhelm Heims.
1919 *Der Traum. Einführung in die Traumpsychologie.* Stuttgart.
1921 *Der Zufall und die Koboldstreiche des Unbewussten.* Bern–Leipzig, Bircher.

GEORG SIMMEL

1. Bibliography

Buch des Dankes an Georg Simmel. Briefe, Erinnerungen. Bibliographie zu seinem 100. Geburtstag. Berlin, 1958.
Brücke und Tür. Stuttgart, 1957. Bibliography, pp. 274–279.
Rosenthal, Erich, and Oberlaender, Kurt, "Books, papers and essays by Georg Simmel," *The American Journal of Sociology,* LI (1945/46), pp. 238-247.

2. Biography and Appreciation

Adler, Max, *Georg Simmels Bedeutung für die Geistesgeschichte*. Wien, 1919.
Beerling, R. F., *De sociologie van Georg Simmel*. Amsterdam, De Bussy, 1969.
Knevels, Wilhelm, *Simmels Religionstheorie. Ein Beitrag zum religiösen Problem der Gegenwart*. Leipzig, Hinrichs, 1920.
Loose, Gerhard, *Die Religionssoziologie G. Simmels*. Dissertation, Leipzig, 1933.
Séguy, Jean, "Aux enfances de la sociologie des religions: Georg Simmel," *Archives de Sociologie des Religions*, 9e Année, No 17 (janvier–juin 1964), pp. 5–11.
Spykman, Nicholas J., *The Social Theory of Georg Simmel*. Chicago, University of Chicago Press, 1925.
Tjalsma, Pieter Douwes, "De religie zonder God van Georg Simmel," *Vox Theologica*, XVII (1946/47), pp. 54–62.
Wolff, Kurt H., "Introduction," to *Sociology of Georg Simmel*, tr. by Kurt H. Wolff. Glencoe, Ill., Free Press, 1950.

3. Main Publications

1890 *Über soziale Differenzierung. Soziologische und psychologische Untersuchungen*. (Staats- und sozialwissentschaftlische Forschungen 10, 1). Leipzig, Duncker & Humblot. 1910³.
1892 *Die Probleme der Geschichtsphilosophie. Eine erkenntnistheoretische Studie*. Leipzig, Duncker & Humblot. 1923⁵.
1892–1893 *Einleitung in die Moralwissenschaft. Eine Kritik der ethischen Grundbegriffe*, 2 vols. Berlin, Hertz. 1911³.
1905 "A contribution to the sociology of religion," *American Journal of Sociology* Vol. 11, Nr. 3 (1905), pp. 360–368.
1906 *Die Religion*. (Die Gesellschaft, 2) Frankfurt a. Main, Rütten & Loening. 1922³.
1908 *Soziologie. Untersuchungen über die Formen der Vergesellschaftung*. Leipzig, Duncker & Humblot. 1958⁴.
1910 *Hauptprobleme der Philosophie*. Leipzig, Göschen. (Sammlung Göschen, 500); Berlin, De Gruyter, 1950⁷.
1911 *Philosophische Kultur. Gesammelte Essays*. (Philosophisch-Soziologische Bücherei, 27). Leipzig, Klinkhardt. 1923³.
1917 *Grundfragen der Soziologie. Individuum und Gesellschaft*. Berlin–Leipzig, Göschen (Sammlung Göschen, 101); Berlin–Leipzig, Vereinigung Wissenschaftliche Verleger, 1920².
1918 *Vom Wesen des historischen Verstehens*. (Geschichtliche Abende im Zentralinstitut für Erziehung und Unterricht, 5). Berlin, Mittler. See also *Brücke und Tür*, 1957, pp. 59–85.
1923 *Fragmente und Aufsätze aus dem Nachlass und Veröffentlichungen der letzten Jahre*. Herausg. und mit einem Vorwort von Gertrud Kantonowicz. München, Drei Masken-Verlag.
1950 *Sociology of Georg Simmel*. Translated and introduced by Kurt H. Wolff. Glencoe, Ill., Free Press.
1957 *Brücke und Tür. Essays des Philosophen zur Geschichte, Religion, Kunst und Gesellschaft*. Im Verein mit M. Susman, hrsg. von M. Landmann. Stuttgart, Koehler.

1959 *Sociology of Religion*. Translated by C. Rosenthal. New York, Philosophical Library.
1964 "Problèmes de la sociologie des reli℃.ons," *Archives de Sociologie des Religions*, 9e Année, No 17 (janvier–juin 1964), pp. 12–44.

WILLIAM ROBERTSON SMITH*

1. Bibliography

"Bibliography," in: John Sutherlánd Black and George Chrystal, *The Life of William Robertson Smith*. London, A. and C. Black, 1912, pp· 617–628.

2. Biography and Appreciation

Black, John Sutherland, and Chrystal, George, *The Life of William Robertson Smith*. London, A. and C. Black, 1912.
Frazer, J. G., "William Robertson Smith," *The Fortnightly Review* (London), N.S. LV (June 1894), pp. 800–807. Reprinted in J. G. Frazer, *Sir Roger de Coverley*, 1920, pp. 194–209; and in J. G. Frazer, *The Gorgon's Head*, 1927, pp. 278–290.
University of Aberdeen, *Centenary of the Birth on 8th November 1846 of the Reverend Professor W. Robertson Smith*. (Aberdeen University Studies, 128). Aberdeen, 1951.
White, J. F., *In memoriam William Robertson Smith*. (Aurora Borealia Academica). Aberdeen, 1899.

3. Method and Theory

1876 "The progress of Old Testament studies," *British and Foreign Evangelical Review*, July 1876.
1876 "Remarks on a Memorandum of the Sub-Committee on the article 'Bible'," November 8, 1876. Reprinted in *Report of College Committee*.
1877 "On the study of the Old Testament in 1876," *British and Foreign Evangelical Review*, July 1877.
1878 *Answer to the Form of Libel now before the Free Church Presbytery of Aberdeen*. Laid before Presbytery on February 12, 1878.
1878 *Additional Answer to the Libel, with some Account of the Evidence that Parts of the Pentateuchal Law are later than the Time of Moses*. April 16, 1878.
1879 *Answer to the Amended Libel: with an Appendix containing Plea in Law*. Laid before Presbytery on July 1, 1879.
1885 "Preface," in: Julius Wellhausen, *Prolegomena to the History of Israel*. With a reprint of the article 'Israel' from the 'Encyclopaedia Britannica'. Translated by Mr. Black. Edinburgh, A. and C. Black, 1885.
1884 "The attitude of Christians to the Old Testament," *The Expositor*, 2nd series, VII, pp. 241–251.

4. Main Publications

1874 "St. Augustine and his English translators," *Daily Review*, November 1874.

1875 "Old Testament exegesis" (Review of works), *British and Foreign Evangelical Review*, January 1875.

1875 "Bible," in *Encyclopaedia Britannica*, 9th edition, Vol. III.

1876 "On the name Jehovah and the doctrine of Ex. III. 14," *British and Foreign Evangelical Review*, January 1876.

1881 *The Old Testament in the Jewish Church. A Course of Lectures on Biblical Criticism*. London, A. and C. Black. 1892² (revised and enlarged).

1882 *The Prophets of Israel and their Place in History to the Close of the Eighth Century B.C.* London, A. and C. Black. 1895².

1885 *Kinship and Marriage in Early Arabia*. London, A. and C. Black. 1903² (enl.).

1889 *Lectures on the Religion of the Semites. First Series: The Fundamental Institutions*. (Burnett Lectures 1888–89). London, A. and C. Black. 1894² (revised); 1927³ with Introduction and Notes by Stanley A. Cook. Comp. "Letter on Professor Sayce's critique of *The Religion of the Semites*," in the *Academy*, December 2, 1889.
German translation by R. Stube: *Die Religion der Semiten*. Preface Prof. Kautzsch, 1899.

1912 *Lectures and Essays of William Robertson Smith*. Edited by J. S. Black and G. Chrystal. London.

NATHAN SÖDERBLOM*

1. Bibliography

Ågren, S., "Bibliographie över N. Söderbloms tryckta skrifter," in: Nils Karlström, ed., *Nathan Söderblom in memoriam*. Stockholm, Svenske Kyrkans diakonistyrelses bokförlag, 1931, pp. 391–451 and 458–459. Comp. S. Dahlquist's supplement in *Svensk teologisk kvartalskrift*, VIII (1932), p. 171 ff.

Holmström, Folke, "Bidrag till Nathan Söderbloms bibliografi," *Svensk teologisk kvartalskrift*, XIII (1937), p. 251 ff. Also published separately, Lund, 1937.

Katz, Peter, "Nathan Söderbloms schriftstellerisches Werk. Versuch eines Überblicks," *Die Eiche* (Berlin), XXI (1933) pp. 49–56. Also published separately, Berlin, 1933.

"Schriften in deutscher Sprache," *Eine Heilige Kirche*, XVIII (1936), pp. 193–196.

2. Biography and Appreciation

Adams, Charles J., *Nathan Söderblom as an Historian of Religions*. Ph. D. Dissertation, Divinity School, The University of Chicago, 1955.

Andrae, Tor, "Nathan Söderblom som religionshistoriker," in: Nils Karlström, ed., *Nathan Söderblom in memoriam*. Stockholm, Svenske Kyrkans diakonistyrelses bokförlag, 1931, pp. 25–62.

—, *Nathan Söderblom*. Uppsala, 1931, 1932[5].
Dutch translation: *Nathan Söderblom*. With an introduction by W. A. Visser 't Hooft. Zutphen, Ruys' Uitgeversmaatschappij, 1935.
German translation: *Nathan Söderblom*. Berlin 1938, 1957[2].

—, *Minne av Nathan Söderblom, inträdestal i Svenska Akademien den 20 December 1932*. Stockholm, 1933.

Aulén, Gustaf, "Nathan Söderblom och nutida svensk teologi," *Svensk teologisk kvartalskrift*, I (1926), pp. 3–19.

—, "Den teologiska gärningen," in: Nils Karlström, ed., *Nathan Söderblom in memoriam*. Stockholm, Svenske Kyrkans diakonistyrelses bokförlag, 1931, pp. 63–104.

—, "Nathan Söderblom och Einar Billing — kontraster i samverkan," *Svensk teologisk kvartalskrift*, XXXVIII (1962), pp. 205–223.

Berggrav, E., "Nathan Söderblom, geni og karakter," *Kirke og Kultur* (Oslo), XXXVIII (1931), pp. 321–359. Also published separately, Oslo, 1931.

Biezais, H., "Nathan Söderblom och den religionshistoriska forskningens genombrott," *Religion och Kultur*, Vol. 42, Nr. 2 (June 1971).

Brilioth, Yngve, "Biographical Introduction," in: Nathan Söderblom, *The Living God ; Basal Forms of Personal Religion*. London, H. Milford and Oxford University Press, 1933, pp. XI–XXIX.

Carlson, Edgar M., "Introduction," in: Nathan Söderblom, *The Nature o Revelation*. Edited and with an Introduction by Edgar M. Carlson. Translated by Frederic E. Pamp. London, Oxford University Press, 1932. Seminar Edition pb, Philadelphia, Fortress Press, 1966, pp. 1–33.

Dorr, Hanna, "Söderbloms Beitrag zur Offenbarungsfrage. 1. Religionsgeschichte als Funktion der Kirche. 2. Seine Auseinandersetzung mit der natürlichen Theologie," *Zeitschrift für Theologie und Kirche*, N. F., XVII (1936), pp. 82–91, 169–190.

—, *Der lebendige Gott. Nathan Söderbloms Beitrag zur Offenbarungsfrage*. Emsdetten, 1938.

Edsman, Carl-Martin, "Nathan Söderblom in Leipzig," *Forschungen und Fortschritte*, Vol. 40, Nr. 11 (1966), pp. 342–346.

—, "Ur Nathan Söderbloms arbetsverkstad," *Religion och Bibel* (Nathan Söderblom-Sällskapets Årsbok), XXV (1966), pp. 18–44.

—, "Nathan Söderblom och det helige," *Svenska Dagbladet*, 15 Jan. 1966, p. 4.

Ehnmark, Erland, *Religionsproblemet hos Nathan Söderblom*. Lund, 1949.

Estborn, Sigfrid, *Under Guds grepp. En studie i Nathan Söderbloms förkunnelse*. Stockholm, 1944.

Gloede, Günter, "Nathan Söderblom, Erzbischof und schwedischer Initiator der Ökumene," *Ökumenische Profile, Brückenbauer der Einen Kirche*. Berlin, n.d.; Stuttgart, 1961.

Hedin, Sven, "Gedächtnis-Ansprache," *Die Eiche* (Berlin), XX, 1–2 (1932), pp. 58–62.

Heiler, Friedrich, "Gelehrter, Bischof und Heiliger. Erzbischof Söderbloms Leben und Wirken," *Die Hochkirche*, XIII (1931), pp. 302–314.
Italian translation: "Scienziato, vescovo e santo. La vita e l'opera dell'Arcivescovo Söderblom," *Ricerche Religiose* (Roma), VII (1931), pp. 481–496.

—, "En härold för de heligas samfund," *Hågkomster och Livsintryck*, XIV: "Till minnet av Nathan Söderblom." Uppsala, Lindblads Förlag, 1933, pp. 209–232.

  German translation: "Erinnerungen an Erzbischof Söderblom," *Eine Heilige Kirche*, XVIII (1936), pp. 169–184.

—, "Offenbarungsreligion und Mystik bei Nathan Söderblom," *Eine Heilige Kirche*, XX (1938), pp. 343–347.

—, "Vorwort des Herausgebers," in: Nathan Söderblom, *Der lebendige Gott im Zeugnis der Religionsgeschichte*. Nachgelassene Gifford-Vorlesungen. In Verbindung mit Dr. Christel Matthias Schröder und Dr. Rudolf Hafner deutsch herausgegeben von Friedrich Heiler. München, Ernst Reinhardt, 1942, pp. I–XII.

—, "Nathan Söderblom als Religionshistoriker," *Theologische Literaturzeitung*, 1950, Nr. 4/5, pp. 313–320.

—, "Ein Lebensbild von Nathan Söderblom," in: Nathan Söderblom, *Der lebendige Gott im Zeugnis der Religionsgeschichte*. Nachgelassene Gifford-Vorlesungen von L. O. J. N. Söderblom. Herausgegeben von Friedrich Heiler. Second edition. München, Ernst Reinhardt, 1966², pp. XI–LI.

Herklots, Hugh G. C., *Nathan Söderblom. Apostle of Christian Unity*. London, SCM Press, 1948.

Hoffmann, Jean G. H., *Nathan Soederblom. Prophète de l'œcuménisme*. Avec une Préface de Marc Boegner. Genève, 1948.

Holmström, Folke, *Uppenbarelsereligion och mystik — en undersökning av Nathan Söderblom's teologi*. Stockholm, Svenska Kyrkans diakonistyrelses bokförlag, 1937.

Karlström, Nils, *Kristna samförståndssträvanden under världskriget 1914–1918, med särskild hänsyn till Nathan Söderbloms insats*. Stockholm, 1947.

Katz, Peter, *Nathan Söderblom. Ein Führer zu kirchlicher Einheit*. Halle/Saale, 1925.

—, *Nathan Söderblom. A Prophet of Christian Unity*. (Selections from memorial writings.) London, G. Clarke, 1949.

Leeuw, G. van der, "Söderblom's wetenschappelijke beteekenis," *Stemmen des Tijds*, XX, 2 (1931), pp. 136–144.

Neander, Herman, *Med Nathan Söderblom*. Stockholm, 1932.

Nystedt, Olle, *Nathan Söderblom*. Stockholm, 1931.

  German translation: *Nathan Söderblom. Ein Lebensbild*. Berlin, 1932.

Runestam, S., "Anteckningar om Nathan Söderbloms handskriftssammling," *Religion och Bibel* (Nathan Söderblom-Sällskapets Årsbok), Vol. 23/24 (1964–65), pp. 59–80.

Schwede, Alfred Otto, *Nathan Söderblom. Ein Lebensbild*. Berlin, Evangelische Verlags Anstalt, n. d.

Sharpe, E. J., "Nathan Söderblom and the study of religion," *Religious Studies*, Vol. 4 (1969), pp. 259–274.

Siegmund-Schultze, D. F., *Nathan Söderblom. Briefe und Botschaften an einen deutschen Mitarbeiter*. Gedächtnisschrift zum hundertsten Geburtstag des schwedischen Erzbischofs. Marburg/Lahn, Oekumenischer Verlag Dr. R. F. Edel, 1966.

Söderblom, Anna, *En Amerikabok*, Stockholm, 1925.

—, *På livets trottoir. Några minnesanteckningar*. Lund, 1948.

—, *På livets trottoir. Efterlämnade minnesanteckningar*. Lund, 1956.

Söderblom, Nathan, *Herdabref till prästerskapet och församlingarna i Uppsala ärkestift*. Uppsala, 1914 (esp. p. 77ff.).
—, "Hemma i Hälsingland," *Svensk Turistfören. Årsskrift*. Stockholm, 1923, pp. 1–12.
—, "Warum ich Lutheraner bin," *Christentum und Wissenschaft*, I, pp. 193–203.
—, "Nathan Söderbloms självbiografiska uttalanden om ungdomsårens avgörande kriser." Edited by Folke Holmström. *Svensk teologisk kvartalskrift*, XI (1935), pp. 328–339.
Sundkler, Bengt, *Nathan Söderblom. His Life and Work*. Lund, Gleerup, 1968.
Veen, J. M. van, *Nathan Söderblom. Leven en denken van een godsdiensthistoricus*. Amsterdam, H. J. Paris, 1940.
Visser 't Hooft, W. A., "Nathan Söderblom," in: *Heel de Kerk voor heel de Wereld. Belang van de Oecumene*. Utrecht–Baarn, Ambo – Bosch & Keuning 1968, pp. 186–199.
Westman, Knut B., *Minnestal över Nathan Söderblom*. Stockholm, 1934.

3. Collective Contributions

1931 *Nathan Söderblom in memoriam* (Swedish). Edited by Nils Karlström. With contributions by G. Aulén, Y. Brilioth, M. Björquist, and others. With a bibliography of N. Söderblom's printed work, by S. Ågren. Uppsala–Stockholm, Svenske Kyrkans diakonityrelses bokförlag.
1931 *Minnesnummer över Ärkebiskop Nathan Söderblom. Gedächtnisheft von Kristen Gemenskap*. Edited by Nils Karlström. Uppsala–Stockholm.
1931 *Till minnet av Ärkebiskop Nathan Söderblom, 15.1.1866–12.7.1931.* Stockholm, Ahlen & Akerlunds Förlag, 37 pp. (double paged).
1931 *His Grace the Most Reverend Nathan Söderblom, Archbishop of Upsala, 1866–1931.* A memorial to the first President of the Universal Christian Council for Life and Work, known as the "Stockholm Movement". With contributions by V. Ammundsen, J. Jézéquel, W. A. Brown, Archbishop Germanos, and others. Geneva.
1931 *Erzbischof Nathan Söderblom*. Edited by Friedrich Heiler. Special issue of *Die Hochkirche* (München), XIII (September–October, 1931).
1931–1934 *Hågkomster och livsintryck av svenska män och kvinner*. Three volumes contain personal memoirs of Nathan Söderblom. 12:e samlingen: *Till minnet av Erik Axel Karlfeldt och Nathan Söderblom* ; 14:e samlingen: *Till minnet av Nathan Söderblom av 70 utländska författare* ; 15:e samlingen: *Till minnet av Nathan Söderblom av 42 författare*. Uppsala, J. A. Lindblads förlag.
1932 *Mgr. Nathan Söderblom, sa personne, son œuvre, sa pensée*, par J. Viénot, H. Monnier, W. Monod. Paris.
1936 *Erinnerungen an Erzbischof Söderblom zu seinem 5. Todestage, 12. Juli 1931/36*. Edited by Friedrich Heiler. With contributions by Yngve Brilioth, Nikolai Glubokowski, Hermann Hoffmann. Special issue of *Eine Heilige Kirche* (München), XVIII (May–June, 1936).

4. Main Publications

1893 *Den lutherska reformationens grundtankar.* Upsala.

1898 "Religionen och den sociala utvecklingen" (address), in: S.A. Fries, ed., *Religionsvetenskapliga kongressen i Stockholm 1897.* Stockholm. Also published separately.
German translation: *Die Religion und die soziale Entwicklung.* Freiburg i. Br., 1898.

1899 *Les Fravashis. Etude sur les traces dans le Mazdéisme d'une ancienne conception sur la survivance des morts.* Paris.

1900 "Frestelseberättelsena om Gotama Buddha, Zarathustra och Jesus Kristus," *Relig. och kyrkl. frågor*, XXXV (1900), pp. 12–50.

1901 *La vie future d'après le Mazdéisme à la lumière des croyances parallèles dans les autres religions. Etude d'eschatologie comparée* (Annales du Musée Guimet, Bibliothèque d'études, Vol. IX). Paris.

1901 *Den allmänna religionshistorien och den kyrkliga teologien.* (Inaugural lecture). Uppsala.

1903 *Tiele's Kompendium der Religionsgeschichte.* Translated from the Dutch by F. W. T. Weber; edited, revised and expanded by Nathan Söderblom. Breslau, 1903³; Berlin, Theophil Biller's Verlag, 1912⁴; Berlin–Schöneberg, 1920⁵, 1931⁶.
French translation by W. Corswant: *Manuel d'histoire des religions.* Paris, 1925.

1903 *Treenighet.* Upsala.

1903 "Uppenbarelsereligion. Några synpunkter i anledning af Babel-Bibeldiskussionen," *Skrifter i teologiska och kyrkliga ämnen tillägnade C. A. Thorén.* Uppsala, pp. 199–253. Also published separately, Uppsala, 1903. Revised edition published together with two other essays as *Uppenbarelsereligion.* Stockholm, 1930².
English translation by Frederic E. Pamp: *The Nature of Revelation*, edited with Introduction by Edgar M. Carlson. Oxford–London, Oxford University Press, 1932. Pb. Philadelphia, Fortress Press, 1966.

1904 *Kristendomen och religionerna. En öfverblick.* Stockholm. 1912².
Danish translation by K. Heiberg: *Kristendommen og Religionerne. En Oversigt.* København, 1905.
Finnish translation by L. Hendell: *Maailman uskonnet.* Helsingissä, 1907.
French translation: *Les religions. Coup d'œil historique.* Saint Blaise, 1911.
German translation: *Die Religionen der Erde.* Halle, 1905; Tübingen, 1919².
Italian translation by Aschenbrödel, with three appendices added: *Le religione del mondo.* Roma, 1908.

1906 "Hemliga regler och traditioner hos ett stenåldersfolk," *Nordisk Tidskrift*, (1906), pp. 159–180.

1906 "Mysterieceremonier och deras ursprung," *Ymer*, XXVI (1906), pp. 193–209 and 251–272. Reissued under the title of "Mysterier hos ett stenåldersfolk" in: N. Söderblom, *Ur religionens historia.* Stockholm, 1915, pp. 99–162.

1907 "Die Allväter der Primitiven. Zur Frage nach den Anfängen des Gottesgedankens," *Religion und Geisteskultur*, I (1907), pp. 315–322.

1907–1908 N. Söderblom, in collaboration with K. F. Johansson, K. V. Zetterstéen, E. Heuman and others: *Främmande religionsurkunder i urval och öfversättning*, 3 vols. Stockholm, 1907–1908.

1908 *Studiet av religionen.* Stockholm.
1908 "The place of the Christian Trinity and the Buddhist Triratna amongst Holy Triads," *Transactions of the 3rd International Congress for the History of Religions.* Vol. II, Oxford, pp. 391–410.
    German translation and expanded edition: *Vater, Sohn und Geist unter den heiligen Dreiheiten und vor der religiösen Denkweise der Gegenwart.* Tübingen, 1909.
1910 *Religionsproblemet inom katolicism och protestantism.* Stockholm.
1911 *Ett bidrag till den kristna uppenbarelsetrons tolkning.* Inbjudn. till teol. doktorspromotion. Upsala. Reprinted in: N. Söderblom, *Uppenbarelse-religion.* Stockholm, 1930².
1911 "Does God continue to reveal himself to mankind?," *Report of the Conference of the World Student Christian Federation, Constantinopel 1911.* London, p. 59 ff.
1912 *Översikt av allmänna religionshistorien.* Stockholm. 1914² (revised), 1919³ (revised), 1935⁴.
    Danish authorized translation by H. Haar: *Almindelig Religionshistorie.* København, 1918.
    German translation: *Einführung in die Religionsgeschichte.* Leipzig, 1920, 1928² (enlarged).
1912 "Gedanken über Religion und Mystik. Zu Baron Friedrich von Hügels Werk: The mystical element of religion," *Religion und Geisteskultur,* VI (1912) p. 298 ff.
1913 "Holiness (General and primitive)," *Encyclopaedia of Religion and Ethics,* Vol. VI, pp. 731–741.
1913 *Natürliche Theologie und allgemeine Religionsgeschichte.* Stockholm–Leipzig.
    Enlarged *Swedish* translation: *Naturlig religion och religionshistoria. En historik och ett program.* Stockholm, 1914.
1914 *Gudstrons uppkomst. Studier.* Stockholm. 1941².
    Danish translation by H. Haar: *Gudstroens Oprindelse. Studier.* København, 1921.
    German translation, edited and revised by R. Stübe: *Das Werden des Gottesglaubens. Untersuchungen über die Anfänge der Religion.* Leipzig, 1916, 1926² (revised).
1914 "Wissenschaftliche Erforschung und religiöse Beurteilung des primitiven Heidentums," *Deutsch-Evangelisch,* V (1914), pp. 193–206.
1914 "Über den Zusammenhang höherer Gottesideen mit primitiven Vorstellungen," *Archiv für Religionswissenschaft,* XVII (1914), pp. 1–16.
1915 *Ur religionens historia.* Stockholm.
1919 "Evangelisk Katolicitet," in: E. Lehmann, N. Söderblom, K. B. Westman, *Enig Kristendom.* Stockholm.
1919 *Humor och melankoli och andra Lutherstudier.* (Sveriges kristliga studentrörelse skrift serie). Stockholm–Uppsala.
1919 *Liten lärobok i religionshistoria för skolan.* Stockholm. 1925².
1922 *Tre livsformer: mystik (Sundar Singh), förtröstan, vetenskap.* Stockholm, Hugo Gerbers Förlag.
1924 *Från Upsala till Rock Island.* Stockholm.
1925 *Der evangelische Begriff eines Heiligen* (Lecture). Greifswald.
1926 *Kristenhetens möte i Stockholm augusti 1925.* Stockholm, Svenske Kyrkans Diakonistyrelses Bokförlag.

1927 "Evangelische Katholizität," in: *Festgabe für Adolf Deismann zum 60. Geburtstag 7. Nov. 1926.* Tübingen, pp. 327–334.
1927 "Randanmärkningar till Lausanne," *Svensk teologisk kvartalskrift,* III (1927), pp. 336–381.
   German abstract: "Randbemerkungen zu Lausanne," *Zeitschrift für systematische Theologie,* VI (1929), pp. 538 ff.
1932 *Den levende Guden. Grundformer av personlig religion.* Published posthumously by Jon Olof Söderblom, in collaboration with Tor Andrae and W. P. Paterson. Stockholm, Svenske Kyrkans Diakonistyrelses Bokförlag.
   The more complete original *English* text was published in 1933: *The Living God. Basal Forms of Personal Religion.* The Gifford Lectures, delivered in the University of Edinburgh in the year 1931. With a Biographical Introduction by Dr. Yngve Brilioth. London, Oxford University Press, 1933; Pb. Boston, Beacon Press, 1962.
   French translation with introduction by J. de Coussange: *Dieu vivant dans l'histoire.* Paris, 1937.
   German translation of the collated English and Swedish texts by Friedrich Heiler, ed., in collaboration with Christel Matthias Schröder and Rudolf Hafner: *Der lebendige Gott im Zeugnis der Religionsgeschichte.* München, Ernst Reinhardt, 1942, 1966². The second edition contains "Ein Lebensbild von Nathan Söderblom" by Friedrich Heiler (pp. XI–LI).
1933–1941 *Svenskars fromhet.* Edited by Anna Söderblom, 2 vols. Stockholm.
1941 *Sommarminnen.* Edited by Anna Söderblom, 2 vols. Stockholm.

HERBERT SPENCER*

1. Bibliography

Duncan, David, "List of Herbert Spencer's writings," in: David Duncan, *The Life and Letters of Herbert Spencer.* London, Methuen; New York, Appleton 1908, pp. 577–587.
Rumney, Judah, "Herbert Spencer Bibliography," in: Judah Rumney, *Herbert Spencer's Sociology.* A study in the history of social theory, to which is appended a bibliography of Spencer and his work. London, Williams and Norgate Ltd, 1934, pp. 311–351 (Contains also literature on Spencer). Reprinted New York, Atheling Book, 1966.

2. Biography and Appreciation

Absi, Marcelle, *La théorie de la religion chez Spencer et ses sources.* Diss. Paris. Beyrouth, 1952.
Alviella, Comte Goblet d', *Harrison contre Spencer sur la valeur religieuse de l'Inconnaissable.* Paris, 1885.
Ardigò, Roberto, *La dottrina Spenceriana dell'inconoscibile.* Roma, Capaccini, 1899.

Arfridsson, Henrik Daniel, *Religion och Vetenskap i deras ömsesidiga förhållande med särskild hänsyn till Herbert Spencer uppfattning af frågon.* Akademisk afhandling, etc. Lund, H. Ohlsson, 1894.

Bager-Sjögren, Johan, *Herbert Spencer och utvecklingsfilosofien; en studie.* Akademisk afhandling, etc. Lund, Collin & Zickerman, 1893.

Baker, Misses [an.], *Home Life with Herbert Spencer by Two.* Bristol, Arrowsmith, 1906.

Barnes, E. H., "Herbert Spencer and the evolutionary defense of individualism," in: E. H. Barnes, ed., *An Introduction to the History of Sociology.* Chicago, 1948, pp. 110–137.

Boutroux, Emile, "La religion selon Herbert Spencer. Conférence faite à l'Institut Général Psychologique. Paris, le 6 juin 1905," *Bulletin de l'Institut Général Psychologique*, V, 4 (1905).
English translation by A. S. Morries: "Religion according to Herbert Spencer. A lecture delivered at l'Institut Général Psychologique. Paris, 6 June, 1905." Edinburgh, etc., 1907.

Chávez, Ezequiel A., *Resumen sintético de los Principios de moral de Herbert Spencer.* Mexico and Paris, C. Bouret, 1898, 1910.

Collins, F. Howard, *An Epitome of the Synthetic Philosophy.* Preface by Herbert Spencer. London, 1889, 1897, 1901.
French translation by Henry de Varigny: *Résumé de la philosophie de Herbert Spencer.* Paris, F. Alcan, 1891.

Crespi, A., *La religione nella filosofia di Eberto Spencer.* 1904.

Dewey, John, "The philosophical work of Herbert Spencer," *The Philosophical Review*, XIII (1904), pp. 159–175.

Diaconide, Elias, *Etude critique sur la sociologie de Herbert Spencer.* (Diss. Amsterdam). Paris, R. Pichon et R. Durand-Auzias, 1938.

Drey, S., *Herbert Spencer's Theory of Religion.* London, 1887.

Duncan, David, *The Life and Letters of Herbert Spencer.* London, Methuen & Co; New York, D. Appleton and Co., 1908.

Elliott, Hugh S. R., *Herbert Spencer.* London, Constable 1917.

Ethical Review, "Herbert Spencer Memorial Number," *Ethical Review* No. 4 (Dec. 1906).

Gaupp, Otto, *Herbert Spencer.* Stuttgart, F. Frommann, 1897, 1900^2 (enlarged), 1923^5.

Gounelle, Elie, *L'agnosticisme de M. Herbert Spencer.* Montauban, 1889.

Greef, Guillaume, de, *Abrégé de psychologie d'après Herbert Spencer.* Avec préface. Bruxelles, 1882.

Grosse, Ernst, *Herbert Spencer's Lehre von dem Unerkennbaren.* Leipzig, Veit & Co, 1890.

Ground, William David, *An Examination of the structural principles of Spencer's philosophy.* Intended as a proof that Theism is the only theory of the universe that can satisfy reason. Oxford – London, Parker Co, 1883.

Guthmann, Johannes, *Entwicklung und Selbstentfaltung bei Herbert Spencer.* (Diss. Würzburg). Ochsenfurt am Main, Fritz & Rappert, 1930.

Guthrie, Malcolm, *On Mr. Spencer's Formula of Evolution as an exhaustive Statement of the Changes of the Universe.* Followed by a resumé of the most important criticisms of Spencer's "First principles". London, Trübner & Co, 1879.

—, *On Mr. Spencer's Unification of Knowledge.* London, Trübner & Co, 1882.

—, *On Mr. Spencer's Data of Ethics.* London, The Modern Press, 1884.

Harrison, Frederic, and Spencer, Herbert, *The Nature and Reality of Religion. A controversy between Frederic Harrison and Herbert Spencer*. With an introduction, notes and an appendix on the religious value of the unknowable by Count D'Alviella. With a preface by E. L. Y[ouman]. New York, Appleton, 1885. Reissued as: *The Insuppressible Book. A controversy between Herbert Spencer and Frederick Harrison*. From the *Nineteenth Century* and *Pall Mall Gazette*, with comments by Gail Hamilton (pseud. for Mary Abagail Dodge). Boston, 1885.
　　British edition: *Religion. A retrospect and prospect. The Nature and Reality of Religion*. With an introduction, notes and an appendix on the religious value of the Unknowable by Count d'Alviella. With a preface by E. L. Y[ouman]. London, 1885.

Harrison, Frederic, *Herbert Spencer*, The Herbert Spencer Lecture, delivered at Oxford, March 9, 1905. Oxford, Clarendon Press, 1905.

Heidt, Albert, *Philosophische Beiträge aus Herbert Spencers Autobiographie*. Inaug. Diss., Göttingen, 1908.

Hudson, William Henry, *An Introduction to the Philosophy of Herbert Spencer, with a Biographical Sketch*. New York, D. Appleton & Co, 1894. London, 1897.

—, *Henry Spencer*. New York – London, Constable, 1908.

Laurens, C., *L'évolution et M. Herbert Spencer*. Paris, 1889.

Lacy, William M., *An Examination of the Philosophy of the Unknowable as expounded by Herbert Spencer*. Philadelphia, B. F. Lacy, 1883.

Lucas, George J., *Agnosticism and Religion*. Being an examination of Spencer's Religion of the Unknowable, preceded by a History of Agnosticism Baltimore, J. Murphy & Co, 1895.

Macpherson, Hector Cersewell, *Spencer and Spencerism*. New York, Doubleday, Page & Co, 1900.

—, *Herbert Spencer. The man and his work*. London, 1900.

Mariupolsky, L., *Die philosophische Begründung der Evolutionstheorie Herbert Spencers*, 1904.

Nardi, Pietro de, *L'assoluto inconoscibile di Herbert Spencer. Esposizione, Storia e Critica*. Forli, Tip. Sociale, 1904.

Parisot, Edmond, *Herbert Spencer*. Choix de textes et étude du système philosophique. Paris, 1912.

Royce, Josiah, *Herbert Spencer, an estimate and review*. Together with a chapter of personal reminiscences by James Collier. New York, Fox, Duffield & Co, 1904.

Rumney, Judah, *Herbert Spencer's Sociology*. A study in the history of social theory, to which is appended a bibliography of Spencer and his work. With a preface by Morris Ginsberg. London, Williams & Norgate 1934.

Sacerdote, Salvatore, *La vita di Herbert Spencer ed "I primi principii."* Torino, S. Lattes & Co, 1907.

Salvadori, G., *Herbert Spencer e l'opera sua*. 1900.

Santayana, George, *The Unknowable*. (The Herbert Spencer Lecture, 1923). Oxford, 1923.

Schwarze, C., *Herbert Spencer*. London, 1902.

Spencer, Herbert, *An Autobiography*. Edited by A. Herbert, H. C. Bastian and D. Duncan, 2 vols. London, Watts & Co.; New York, D. Appleton & Co., 1904, 1926.

French translation by Henri de Varigny: *Une autobiographie*. Paris, F. Alcan, 1907.

German authorized translation by Ludwig and Helene Stein: *Eine Auto-biographie*. Nebst einer Einführung in die Philosophie und Soziologie Herbert Spencers von Ludwig Stein, 2 vols. Stuttgart, R. Lutz, 1905.

—, *Life and Letters of Herbert Spencer*. By David Duncan, 2 vols. London-New York, D. Appleton & Co., 1908.

Spicker, Gideon, *Spencer's Ansicht über das Verhältnis der Religion zur Wissenschaft*. Münster, Coppenrath, 1889.

Taylor, Alfred Edward, *Herbert Spencer*. New York, 1928.

Thomson, John Arthur, *Herbert Spencer*. London, J. M. Dent & Co.; New York, E. P. Dutton & Co., 1906.

Thouverez, Émile, *Herbert Spencer*. Paris, Blond et Cie, 1905, 1913.

Tillett, Alfred William, *Spencer's Synthetic Philosophy: What it is all about*. An Introduction to *Justice*, 'the most important part'. London, 1914.

—, *Militancy versus civilization. An introduction to, and epitome of, the teaching of Herbert Spencer*. London, 1915.

-, *Herbert Spencer betrayed*. With some account of the repudiation of the Descriptive Sociology by his Trustees. London, P. S. King 1939.

—, *The Theology of the Future*. Westminster, P. S. King 1941.

"Two," *Home Life with Herbert Spencer*. By Two. See under: Baker, Misses.

Varrenkamp, A., *Het agnosticisme van Herbert Spencer*. Groningen, 1897.

Waite, C. B., *Herbert Spencer and his critics*. London, 1900.

Wiese und Kaiserswalden, Leopold von, *Herbert Spencers Einführung in die Soziologie*. Köln, Westdeutscher Verlag, 1960.

Zuccante, Guiseppi, *Herbert Spencer*. Vicenza, 1904.

Main Publications (only the French, German, Italian and Spanish translations are indicated).

a) *A System of Synthetic Philosophy*. London, Williams & Norgate, 1910.

I *First Principles*, 1862, 1900⁶ (revised). Reprinted 1904, 1910, 1928, 1937 (Watts & Co.). Reissued with an introduction by T. W. Hill (The Thinker's Library, No. 62). London, 1946.

French translation by M. E. Cazelles: *Les premiers principes*. Paris, G. Baillière, 1871, 1883³ etc. The first part of the book was reissued under the title of: *Les premiers principes. L'inconnaissable*. Paris, F. Alcan, 1935.

German translation by B. Vetter: *Grundlagen der Philosophie*. Stuttgart, 1875.

Italian translation by Guglielmo Salvadori: *I primi principii*. Torino, fr. Bocca, 1901².

Spanish translation by J. Andrés Irueste: *Los primeros principios*. Paris, 1879.

II *The Principles of Biology*. Vol. I: 1864, 1898² (revised and enlarged). Vol. II: 1867, 1899² (revised and enlarged).

French translation by M. E. Cazelles: *Principes de biologie*, 2 vols. Paris, G. Baillière, 1877–78, 1893–94⁴.

German translation by B. Vetter: *Die Principien der Biologie*, 2 vols. Stuttgart, 1876–77.

Italian translation by Guglielmo Salvadori in 2 vols.: *Le basi della vita* and *L'evoluzione della vita*. Torino, Fr. Bocca, 1905 and 1906. Partial *Spanish* translation: *La especie human ; la creación y la evolución*. Madrid, 1885. Comp. *Creación y evolución*, translation by A. Gómez Pinilla (essays). Valencia, 1904.

III *The Principles of Psychology*, 1 vol. 1855; 2 vols. 1870–72², 1899⁴. *French* translation by Th. Ribot and A. Espinas: *Principes de psychologie*, 2 vols. Paris, 1874–75, 1898².

German translation by B. Vetter: *Die Principien der Psychologie*, 2 vols. Stuttgart, 1882–86.

Italian translation by Guglielmo Salvadori in 2 vols.: *Le basi del pensiero* and *L'evoluzione del pensiero*. Torino, fr. Bocca, 1907 and 1909.

For a *Spanish* translation, comp. *Filosofia experimental. Extracto de las doctrinas psicologicas de Herbert Spencer*, por Ignacio V. Espinosa. Bogota, Bruce, 1910².

IV *The Principles of Sociology*. Vol. I (1. *The data of sociology ; 2. The inductions of sociology ; 3. Domestic institutions)*, 1876, 1877², 1885³ (enlarged). Vol. II (4. *Ceremonial institutions; 5. Political institutions*, resp. 1879 and 1882), 1882. [Vols. I and II also published at New York, D. Appleton & Co., 1882–83]. Vol. III (6. *Ecclesiastical institutions*, 1885; 7. *Professional institutions* and *Industrial institutions*, 1896), 1896. Comp. the abridged edition *Principles of Sociology*, edited by Stanislav Andreski. London, 1969.

French translation by M. E. Cazelles: *Principes de sociologie*, 4 vols. (Parts 1–6). Paris, G. Baillière, 1878–1887. Parts 7 and 8 were translated by Henry de Varigny: *Les institutions professionnelles et industrielles. Fin des Principes de Sociologie*. Paris, Guillaumin, 1898.

German translation by B. Vetter: *Die Principien der Sociologie*, 4 vols. Stuttgart, 1877–1897.

Italian translation of a part of Part 6: *Scienza e religione*. Milano, 1884.

Spanish translation of Parts 1–5 by E. Cazorla: *Principios de sociología*, 2 vols. Madrid, 1883–84. Translation of Part 4: *Instituciones sociales*. Madrid, 1894. Translation of Part 6: *Las instituciones ecclesiásticas*. Madrid, 1894. Comp. *De la leyes en general*, translated by Miguel de Unamuno. Madrid, 1895; *El origen de las profesiones*, translated with notes by Francisco Caravaca. Barcelona, Iberia, 1933. Comp. *The Evolution of Society. Selections from Herbert Spencer's Principles of Sociology*. Edited with an introduction by Robert L. Carneiro. Un. of Chicago Press, 1967.

V *The Principles of Ethics*. Vol. I (1. *The data of ethics*, 1879; 2. *Ethics of different people*, and 3. *Personal ethics)*, 1892, 1900². Vol. II (4. *Justice*, 1891; 5. *Positive beneficence*, and 6. *Negative beneficence)*, 1893, 1904².

French translation: *Principes de la morale*. Paris, 1879–1896. Translation of Part 1: *Les bases de la morale évolutionniste*. Paris, G. Baillière, 1880, 1881²; F. Alcan, 1905⁸. Translation of the same Part 1 by Desclos-Auricoste: *Qu'est-ce que la morale?* Paris, Schleicher, 1909. Translation of Parts 2 and 3 by E. Castelot and E. Martin Saint-Léon: *La morale des différents peuples et la morale personnelle*.

Paris, 1896. Translation of Part 4 by E. Castelot: *Justice*. Paris, Guillaumin, 1893, 1903³. Translation of Parts 5 and 6 by E. Castelot and E. Martin Saint-Léon: *Le rôle moral de la bienfaisance*. Paris, Guillaumin, 1895. Comp. *Problèmes de morale et de sociologie*, traduction et avant-propos de Henry de Varigny. Paris, 1894.

German translation by B. Vetter and J. V. Carus: *Die Principien der Ethik*, 2 vols. Stuttgart, 1879 and 1895. Comp. *Von der Freiheit zur Gebundenheit*, translated by W. Bode, Berlin, L. Simion, 1891.

Italian translation by Guglielmo Salvadori in 2 vols.: *Le basi della morale*. With an introduction by G. Sergi (Milano, 1881; Piacenza, 1881, 1904², 1920³; Torino, fr. Bocca, 1881 etc.). Also *L'evoluzione morale*. Torino, fr. Bocca, 1909. Translation of Part 4 by S. Fortini Santarelli: *La Giustizia*. Con un studio sul sistema etico-giuridico di H. Spencer del Prof. I. Vanni. Città di Castello, 1893. Translation of Parts 5 and 6 by S. Fortini-Santarelli: *Beneficenza negativa e positiva*. Introduction prof. Felice di Tocco. Citta di Castello, 1894.

Spanish translation of Part 4: *La jiustizia*. Madrid, 1893, 1897². Comp. *Etica de las prisiones* (and other essays), translated by Miguel de Unamuno. Madrid, 1895. *Exceso de la legislacion* (and other essays), translated by Miguel de Unamuno. Madrid, 1895.

On *A System of Synthetic Philosophy*, comp. F. Howard Collins, *An Epitome of the Synthetic Philosophy*. Preface by Herbert Spencer. London, 1889, 1897, 1901.

b) *Other Main Publications*

1851 *Social Statics. Or the conditions essential to human happiness specified, and the first of them developed*. London, J. Chapman. Stereotyped edition London, 1868. Reissued London, Watts & Co., 1910. Abridged and revised edition, together with *The Man versus the State:* London, Williams and Norgate, 1892. New edition New York, Robert Schalkenbach Foundation, 1854; New York, 1969.

1852 *A Theory of Population, deduced from the general law of animal fertility*. London, J. Chapman. Reissued under the title of *A New Theory of Population*, London, 1857.

1855 *Principles of Psychology*. London, Longman, Brown, Green and Longmans. (Later editions are part of „A System of Synthetic Philosophy," see under a).

1857–1874 *Essays: Scientific, Political, and Speculative*. London. First series, 1857; Second Series, 1863; Third Series, 1874. 3 vols. London, Williams & Norgate, 1868–1874, 1891² (revised).

French translation by A. Burdeau: *Essais de morale, de science et d'esthétique*, 3 vols. Paris, 1877–79, 1885–86², 1891³, 1898⁴.

Italian translation of a part of the *Essays* by Guglielmo Salvadori: *Il progresso umano*. Torino, Fr. Bocca, 1908.

Spanish translation of a part of the *Essays* by José González Llana: *Ensayos científicos*. Madrid, 1908.

1861 *Education. Intellectual, Moral, and Physical*. London. 1905⁴, 1929 (Watts & Co.). New York, D. Appleton & Co., 1864 etc. Reissued with a preface by Charles T. Smith (The Thinker's Library, Nr. 2). London, 1949². Comp. *Essays on Education and kindred subjects*. Introd. Charles W. Eliot, London, J. M. Dent, 1911, 1914. Comp. *Herbert Spencer on Education*.

Edited with an introduction by F. A. Cavenagh. Cambridge, Cambridge University Press, 1932. Also *Herbert Spencer on Education.* Edited, with an introduction and notes, by Andreas M. Kazamias. New York, Teachers College Press, Columbia University, 1966.

French translation: *De l'éducation intellectuelle, morale et physique.* Paris, G. Baillière, 1878, 1921[15]. Abridged edition: *De l'éducation,* idem, 1880, 1898[8]. Traduction nouvelle avec une introduction, des sommaires et des notes, par Alexis Bertrand. Paris, Belin, 1887.

German translation by Fritz Schultze: *Herbert Spencer's Erziehungslehre. Die Erziehung in geistiger, sittlicher und leiblicher Hinsicht.* Jena, 1874, 1905[2], 1927[3].

Spanish translation with notes by S. García del Mazo: *De la educación intelectual, moral e física.* Madrid, 1879, 1884[2] (enlarged). Another translation of the same book was made by Narciso Sevillano: *Educación intelectual, moral e física.* Valencia, 1906.

1864 *The Classification of the Sciences.* To which are added reasons for dissenting from the philosophy of M. Comte. London. 1869[2], 1871[3]. New edition of the second part: London, Williams & Norgate, 1884.

French translation by F. Réthoré: *Classification des sciences.* Paris, G. Baillière, 1871, 1881[3]; F. Alcan, 1888[4], 1923[10].

1871 *Recent Discussions in Science, Philosophy, and Morals.* New York, D. Appleton & Co.

1873 *The Study of Sociology.* London, Williams & Norgate, 1880[8]. New edition with an introduction by Talcott Parsons: Ann Arbor, University of Michigan Press, 1961, pb. 1969.

French translation: Introduction à la science sociale. Paris, G. Baillière, 1874, 1894[11].

German translation by Heinrich Marquardsen: *Einleitung in das Studium der Sociologie,* 2 vols. Leipzig, 1875.

Italian translation: *Introduzione alle scienza sociale.* Torino, fr. Bocca, 1904[3].

1880 *Philosophy of style.* New York, D. Appleton & Co.

1884 *The Man versus the State* (Four previously published essays and papers). London. 1886[2], etc.; New York, D. Appleton & Co., 1884 etc. Edition together with an abridged and revised version of *Social Statics:* London, 1892. New edition London, Watts & Co., 1940, 1950[2]. New edition with an introduction by Albert Jay Nock: Caldwell, Idaho, Caxton Printers, 1940, 1960[2]. Pb. Boston, Beacon Press, 1950.

French translation by J. Gerschel: *L'individu contre l'Etat.* Paris, F. Alcan, 1892, 1895[4]. Comp. *Le droit d'ignorer l'Etat,* translated by Manuel Devaldès (Brochure mensuelle, no. 10, oct. 1923). Paris, Groupe de propagande par la brochure, 1923.

Italian translation by S. Fortini-Santarelli: *L'individuo e lo Stato.* Preface by G. Barzelotti. Città di Castello, 1886. Comp. *Il diritto d'ignorare lo Stato,* con saggio biografico-critico di Manuel Devaldès. Roma, Edizioni di "Fede", n.d. (1921 ?).

Spanish translation by A. Gómez-Pinilla: *El individo contra el Estado.* Valencia, 1904.

1885 Herbert Spencer and Frederic Harrison, *The Nature and Reality of Religion. A controversy between Frederic Harrison and Herbert Spencer.* With an introduction, notes and an appendix on the religious value of the unknowable by Count D'Alviella. With a preface by E. L. Y.[ouman]. New York, D. Appleton & Co. Reissued under the title of *The Insuppressible Book. A controversy between Herbert Spencer and Frederic Harrison.* From the *Nineteenth Century* and *Pall Mall Gazette*, with comments by Gail Hamilton [pseud. for Mary Abagail Dodge]. Boston, 1885. *British* edition: *Religion. A retrospect and prospect.* London, 1885.

1887 *The Factors of Organic Evolution.* London, Williams & Norgate.

1893 *Inadequacy of Natural Selection.* London.

1894 *Aphorisms from the writings of Herbert Spencer.* Selected and arranged by J. R. Gingell. London, Chapman & Hall.

1897 *Various Fragments.* London, Williams and Norgate. 1900² (enlarged).

1902 *Facts and Comments.* London.
> *French* translation by Auguste Dietrich: *Faits et commentaires.* Paris, Hachette, 1903, 1904².
> *Italian* translation by Guglielmo Salvadori: *Fatti e commenti.* Torino, Fr. Bocca, 1903.
> *Spanish* translation by S. García del Mazo: *Hechos y explicaciones.* Madrid, 1903.

1912 *Choix de textes et étude du système philosophique.* Translation by E. Parisot. Paris.

1951 *Literary Style and Music.* Including two short essays on gracefulness and beauty. New York, Phil. Library.

EDWIN DILLER STARBUCK

Main Publications

1897 "Some Aspects of Religious Growth," *The American Journal of Psychology,* IX, 1 (1897), pp. 70–124.

1899 *The Psychology of Religion. An empirical Study of the Growth of religious Consciousness.* With a Preface by William James. (The Contemporary Science Series). New York, Scribner. 1891, 1901², 1913³; London, Scott, 1899, 1901, 1908, 1914.

1930 *Familiar Haunts.* Fairy Tales selected by E. D. Starbuch. New York, Macmillan.

1930 *Enchanted Paths.* Fairy Tales selected by E. D. Starbuck and Frank K. Shuttleworth. New York, Macmillan.

1930 *Far Horizons.* Fairy Tales selected by E. D. Starbuck and Frank K. Shuttleworth. New York, Macmillan.

HEYMANN STEINTHAL

1. Biography and Appreciation

Achelis, T., *Heymann Steinthal.* (Sammlung gem. wissens. Vorträge, N. F., Heft 296). 1898.

Glogau, G., *Steinthal's psychologische Formeln zusammenhängend entwickelt*. 1876.
Glogau, M., "Briefwechsel Glogau–Steinthal," in: *Gustav Glogau. Sein Leben*. 1906.

2. Main Publications

1850 *Die Classification der Sprachen dargestellt als die Entwicklung der Sprach-idee*. Berlin. 2nd revised edition, see under 1860; 3rd revised edition, see under 1871.

1851 *Der Ursprung der Sprache, im Zusammenhange mit den letzten Fragen alles Wissens. Eine Darstellung der Ansicht W. von Humboldts, verglichen mit denen Herders und Hamanns*. Berlin. 1858[2] (revised and enlarged); 1877[3] (revised and enlarged); 1888[4] (enlarged).

1860 *Charakteristik der hauptsächlisten Typen des Sprachbaues*. Berlin. See also 1871.

1863 *Geschichte der Sprachwissenschaft bei den Griechen und Römern, mit besonderer Rücksicht auf die Logik*. Berlin. 1890–1891[2], 2 vols. (enlarged).

1866 *Mythos und Religion* (Sammlung gem. wissens. Vorträge, Heft 97).

1871–1881 *Einleitung in die Psychologie und Sprachwissenschaft*. Vol. I: Abriss *der Sprachwissenschaft*, Part 1: *Die Sprache im Allgemeinen. Mit Zusätzen*; Part 2: *Charakteristik*... (Revised by Mistelli, 1893).

1877 *Two Essays*. I: *The original form of the legend of Prometheus*; II: *The legend of Samson*. In: I. Goldziher, *Mythology among the Hebrews*. London, 1877.

1880 *Gesammelte kleine Schriften*. Berlin.

1890 *Zu Bibel und Religionsphilosophie*. Vorträge und Abhandlungen. Berlin. 1895[2] *Neue Folge*, in 2 Parts.

1900 "Allgemeine Einleitung in die Mythologie," *Archiv für Religionswissenschaft*, III (1900), pp. 249–273, 297–323.

1906 *Über Juden und Judentum*. Vorträge und Aufsätze. Herausg. von G. Karpeles. Berlin, Gesellschaft für Förderung der Wissenschaft des Judentums, 1906.

DAVID FRIEDRICH STRAUSS

1. Biography, Appreciation and Bibliography

Bachaus, Gunther, *Kerygma und Mythos bei D. F. Strauss und Rudolf Bultmann*. Hamburg–Bergstedt, 1956.

Barth, Karl, *D. F. Strauss als Theologe. 1839–1939*. Zürich, Zollikon, 1939.

Lévy, Albert, *D. F. Strauss: Vie et Œuvre*. Paris, 1910.

Nober, P., "D. F. Strauss (1808–1873)," *E. C.*, XI (1954), pp. 107–153.

Rapp, Adolf, *Briefwechsel zwischen Strauss und Vischer*. Stuttgart, Ernst Klett Verlag, 1953. Bibliography, pp. 340–347.

2. Main Publications

1835–1836 *Das Leben Jesu, kritisch bearbeitet,* 2 vols. Tübingen, Osiander. 1837² (2nd improved edition); 1838³; 1840⁴, etc.
    English translations: *The Life of Jesus, or, a critical Examination of his History,* 3 vols. Translated by Marian Evans, afterwards Cross. London, Sonnenschein, 1846; 1892².
    The Life of Jesus. Translated from the fourth German Edition by George Eliot. With an Introduction by O. Pfleiderer. London, Sonnenschein, 1898.
1840–1841 *Die christlische Glaubenslehre in ihrer geschichtlichen Entwicklung und im Kampfe mit der modernen Wissenschaft,* 2 vols. Tübingen–Stuttgart.
1862 *Kleine Schriften biographischen, literatur- und kunstgeschichtlichen Inhalts.* Leipzig, Brockhaus.
1866 *Kleine Schriften, Neue Folge.* Leipzig, Brockhaus.
1872 *Der alte und der neue Glaube. Ein Bekenntnis.* Leipzig, Hirzel. Bonn, Strauss, 1873.
    English translations: *The Old Faith and the New.* Authorized translation from the sixth edition by M. Blind. London, 1873². Third English edition. Translated (with final preface) and an original memoir of the Author, by M. Blind. London, 1874.
    The Old Faith and the New. American edition, 2 vols. The translation was revised and partly rewritten and preceded by an American version of the author's "Prefatory Postscript" (by J. Fitzgerald). New York, 1873.
1876–1878 *Gesammelte Schriften.* Eingeleitet und mit erklärenden Nachweisungen versehen von Eduard Zeller, 12 vols. Bonn, Strauss.

T

CORNELIS PETRUS TIELE*

1. Bibliography

Ridder, J. H. de, "Lijst van geschriften van Dr. C. P. Tiele," in: J. Kalff Jr., ed., *Mannen en vrouwen van beteekenis in onze dagen. Levensschetsen en portretten.* Haarlem, Tjeenk Willink, 1900, pp. 358–364.

2. Biography and Appreciation

Beijerman, J. A., "Prof. C. P. Tiele," *Remonstrantsche Broederschap*, XIII (1902), pp. 129 ff.

Chantepie de la Saussaye, P. D., "Cornelis Petrus Tiele, 16 December 1830–11 Januari 1902," *Jaarboek van de Koninklijke Akademie van Wetenschappen*, 1902, pp. 125–154. Reprinted in: P. D. Chantepie de la Saussaye, *Portretten en Kritieken.* Haarlem, Bohn, 1909, pp. 82–120.

Hanne, J. R., "C. P. Tiele," *Protestantische Monatschrift*, VI (1902), pp. 114 ff.

Jastrow, M., "C. P. Tiele. In commemoration of his 70th birthday," *The Open Court*, XIV, 12 (December 1900), pp. 728–733.

Kristensen, W. Brede, "Religionshistorikeren C. P. Tiele," *Ringeren* (Kristiania), I, 16 (16 April 1898), pp. 3–7.

—, "Professor C. P. Tiele," *Woord en Beeld* (Haarlem), October 1899, pp. 348–354.

Manen, W. C. van, "In memoriam C. P. Tiele," *Theologisch Tijdschrift*, XXXVI (1902), pp. 190 ff.

Réville, A., "C. P. Tiele," *Revue d'Histoire des Religions*, XLV (1902), pp. 70 ff.

Ridder, J. H. de, "Cornelis Petrus Tiele," in: J. Kalff Jr., ed., *Mannen en vrouwen van beteekenis in onze dagen. Levensschetsen en portretten.* Haarlem, Tjeenk Willink, 1900, pp. 321–364.

Schlegel, G., "C. P. Tiele," *T'oung Pao*, 1902, pp. 39 ff.

3. Method and Theory

1860 "Het onderwijs in de godsdienstgeschiedenis aan de Leidsche Hoogeschool," *De Gids*, XXIV (June 1860), pp. 815–830.

1865 "De oorsprong der mythologie," *De Gids*, XXIX (April 1863), pp. 1–27.
1865 "De verwantschap van mythologie en taalwetenschap," *Handelingen van het VIIIe Ned. Taal- en Letterkundig Congres* (Rotterdam, 11–13 September 1865), 1865, pp. 3–7.
1866 "Theologie en Godsdienstwetenschap," *De Gids*, XXX (May 1866), pp. 205–244.
1867 "Godsdienstwetenschap en Theologie. Nadere toelichting van het artikel 'Theologie en Godsdienstwetenschap' in De Gids van Mei 1866,"*Theologisch Tijdschrift*, I (1867), pp. 38–52.
1869 "Godsdienstwetenschap en Wijsbegeerte in het jongste Ontwerp van Wet op het Hooger Onderwijs," *De Gids*, XXXIII (July 1869), pp. 121–138.
1870 "De oorsprong van mythologie en godsdienst. Naar aanleiding der theorieën van de Quatrefages en Brinton," *Theologisch Tijdschrift*, IV (1870), pp. 1–27.
1871 "Een probleem der godsdienstwetenschap," *De Gids*, XXXV (January 1871), pp. 98–128.
       German translation: *Max Müller und Fritz Schultze über ein Problem der Religionswissenschaft*. Leipzig, 1871 (enlarged).
1871 "De oorsprong van mythologie en godsdienst," *Theologisch Tijdschrift*, V (1871), pp. 373–406.
1871 "Het wezen en de oorsprong van den godsdienst," *Theologisch Tijdschrift*, V (1871), pp. 373–406.
1873 *De plaats van de godsdiensten der natuurvolken in de godsdienstgeschiedenis* (Inaugural lecture). Amsterdam.
1873 "Over de geschiedenis der oude godsdiensten, haar methode, geest en belang," *Theologisch Tijdschrift*, VII (1873), pp. 573–589.
1874 "De ontwikkelingsgeschiedenis van den godsdienst en de hypotheze waarvan zij uitgaat," *De Gids*, XXXVIII (June 1874), pp. 421–450.
1874 "Over de wetten der ontwikkeling van den godsdienst," *Theologisch Tijdschrift*, VIII (1874), pp. 225–262.
1875 "Over den aanvang en de ontwikkeling van den godsdienst. Een verweerschrift," *Theologisch Tijdschrift*, IX (1875), pp. 170–192.
1876 "Eene ontleding van het godsdienstig geloof," *Theologisch Tijdschrift*, X (1876), pp. 583–604.
1885 "Le mythe de Kronos. A propos d'une nouvelle méthode en mythologie comparée," *Revue d'Histoire des Religions*, XII (1885).
1887 "Tweeërlei godsdienstgeschiedenis," *Theologisch Tijdschrift*, XXI (1887), pp. 253–271.
1892 "Eenige woorden ter inleiding van den nieuwen cursus over de Wijsbegeerte van den Godsdienst," *Theologisch Tijdschrift*, XXVI (1892), pp. 1—9.

4. Main Publications

1855 *Het Evangelie van Joannes beschouwd als bron voor het leven van Jezus*. Amsterdam.
1862 "De oorsprong van het monotheïsme bij de Israëlieten," *De Gids*, XXVI (February 1862), pp. 161–205.
1864 *De Godsdienst van Zarathustra, van haar ontstaan in Baktrië tot den val van het Oud-Perzische Rijk*. Haarlem, A. C. Kruseman, 1864. (Appeared

under the title of *De Godsdienst van Zarathustra bij de oud-Perzische volken* in the series "De voornaamste Godsdiensten", Vol. II. Haarlem, 1864.

1866 "De Hindusche godsdiensten in den Oost-Indischen Archipel," *De Vaderlandsche Letteroefeningen*, N. S. 1866 ("Wetenschap en Belletrie", No. XII), pp. 819–846.

1869–1872 *Vergelijkende Geschiedenis der Oude Godsdiensten*. Vol. I *De Egyptische en Mesopotamische Godsdiensten*. Edition of Book 1: *Geschiedenis van den Egyptischen Godsdienst*. Amsterdam, P. N. van Kampen, 1869.

English translation of this first book, with the cooperation of the author, by James Ballingal: [*Comparative History of the Egyptian and Mesopotamian Religions*, Vol. I] *History of the Egyptian Religion*. Boston–New York, 1882; London, 1882, 1884[2].

Edition of Books 1 and 2: *Vergelijkende geschiedenis van de Egyptische en Mesopotamische Godsdiensten: Egypte, Babel-Assur, Yemen, 'Harran, Fenicië, Israel*. Amsterdam, P. N. van Kampen, 1872.

French translation by G. Collins: *Histoire comparée des anciennes religions de l'Egypte et des peuples sémitiques*. With a preface by A. Réville. Paris, 1882.

1870 "Eene proeve van vergelijkende godsdienstwetenschap," *Theologisch Tijdschrift*, IV (1870), pp. 158–168.

1876 *Geschiedenis van den Godsdienst tot aan de heerschappij der Wereldgodsdiensten*. Amsterdam, 1876, ...[2] (enlarged). A completely revised and enlarged edition of this book appeared in 1893–1901 under the title of *Geschiedenis van den Godsdienst in de Oudheid tot op Alexander den Groote* (see below under 1893–1901).

Danish authorized translation by F. Buhl: *Kortfattet Religionshistorie, efter C. P. Tiele's "Geschiedenis van den godsdienst"*. Kjøbenhavn, 1884.

English translation by J. Estlin Carpenter: *Outlines of the History of Religion, to the Spread of the Universal Religions*. London, Trübner & Co., 1877, 1880[2], 1892[5].

French translation of the second Dutch edition by M. L. Vernes: *Manuel de l'histoire des Religions. Esquisse d'une histoire de la Religion jusqu'au triomphe des religions universalistes*. Paris, 1880.

German translation and edition by F. W. T. Weber: *Kompendium der Religionsgeschichte. Ein Handbuch zur Orientierung und zum Selbststudium*. Berlin, 1880; Prenzlau, 1887[2]. The following editions were revised and enlarged by N. Söderblom: Breslau, 1903[3], 1912[4], 1920[5], 1931[6].

Swedish authorized translation by P. E. M. Fischier: *Allmän Religionshistoria*. Stockholm, 1887.

1877 *De vrucht der Assyriologie voor de vergelijkende geschiedenis der godsdiensten* (Inaugural lecture). Amsterdam.

German translation by K. Friederici: *Die Assyriologie und ihre Ergebnisse für die vergleichende Religionsgeschichte*. Leipzig, 1878.

1877 "Christus en Kṛṣna," *Theologisch Tijdschrift*, XI (1877), pp. 63–82.

1880 "Over de ontwikkeling der Indische godsdiensten," *De Indische Gids*, September 1880, pp. 1–16.

1880 "Esquisse du développement religieux en Grèce," *Revue d'Histoire des Religions*, I (1880).

1880 "Comment distinguer les éléments exotiques de la mythologie grecque," *Revue d'Histoire des Religions*, II (1880).

1881 "La religion des Phéniciens d'après les plus récents travaux," *Revue d'Histoire des Religions*, III (1881).

1882 "Is Šumer en Akkâd hetzelfde als Makan en Mêlucha?," *Jaarboek Koninklijke Akademie van Wetenschappen*, 1882, pp. 199–208.

1884 "La déesse Ištar, surtout dans le mythe babylonien," *Travaux de la 6e session du Congrès international des Orientalistes à Leiden*, Vol. II. Leiden, 1884. Also published separately, Leiden, 1884.

1884 "Religions," *Encyclopaedia Britannica*, 9th edition.

1884 "De jongste Nederlandsche werken over Godsdienstgeschiedenis," *De Gids*, XLVIII (May 1884), pp. 331–361.

1886 "De hoofdtempel van Babel en die van Borsippa (Naar de opschriften van Nebukadrezar)," *Jaarboek Koninklijke Akademie van Wetenschappen*, 1886, pp. 103–132.

1886–1888 *Babylonisch-Assyrische Geschichte bis zur Eroberung Babels durch Cyrus*. Vol. I: *Von den ältesten Zeiten bis zum Tode Sargons II*. Vol. II: *Von der Thronbesteigung Sinacheribs bis zur Eroberung Babels durch Cyrus* ("Handbücher der alten Geschichte". Ser. I, Abt. 4), 2 vols. Gotha, F. A. Perthes.

1887 "Bemerkungen über Ê-sagila in Babel und Ê-zida in Borsippa zur Zeit Nebukadrezars II," *Zeitschrift für Assyriologie*, I (1887), pp. 179–190.

1887 "De beteekenis van Êa en zijn verhouding tot Maruduk en Nabû (Naar aanleiding van een nieuw ontdekt heiligdom van Êa in den hoofdtempel te Babel)," *Jaarboek Koninklijke Akademie van Wetenschappen*, 1887, pp. 67–81.

1889 "Over de spijkerschrift-tafels onlangs te Tell-el-Amarna gevonden," *Jaarboek Koninklijke Akademie van Wetenschappen*, 1889, pp. 140–149.

1893 *West-Azië in het licht der jongste ontdekking* (Rectorial address). Leiden, E. J. Brill.
English translation by Elizabeth J. Taylor: *Western Asia, according to the most recent discoveries* [the Tell el-Amarna Tablets]. London. 1894[2].

1893–1901 *Geschiedenis van den Godsdienst in de Oudheid tot op Alexander den Groote* (This is a completely revised and enlarged edition of *De geschiedenis van den Godsdienst tot aan de heerschappij der wereldgodsdiensten*). Vol. I: *Egypte, Babylonië-Assyrië, Voor-Aziaten inclusief Israël*. Vol. II, Book 1: *Zarathustrische Godsdienst*. 2 vols. Amsterdam.
English translation of a part of Vol. II by G. K. Narriman in: *The Religion of the Iranian Peoples*. Bombay, Parsi Publication Comp., 1912.
German authorized translation by G. Gehrich: *Geschichte der Religion bis auf Alexander den Grossen*, 2 vols. Gotha, 1896–1903.

1894 "Une nouvelle hypothèse sur l'antiquité de l'Avesta," *Revue d'Histoire des Religions*, XXIX (1894).

1897–1899 *Elements of the Science of Religion*. Part I: *Morphological*. Part II: *Ontological*. Gifford Lectures delivered before the University of Edinburgh in 1896 and 1898, 2 vols. Edinburgh and London, W. Blackwood and Sons; New York, Scribner's and Son.
Dutch text: *Inleiding tot de godsdienstwetenschap*, 2 vols. Amsterdam, 1897–1899, 1900[2].
German authorized translation by G. Gehrich: *Einleitung in die Religionswissenschaft*, 2 vols. Gotha, 1899–1901.
Swedish authorized translation by Jan H. Ahlstedt: *Inledning till religionsvetenskapen*. With a foreword by N. Söderblom. Stockholm, Fahlcrantz 1903.

1898 "Zur Frage nach dem Alter der Avesta," *Archiv für Religionswissenschaft*,
I (1898).
1901 *Hoofdtrekken der godsdienstwetenschap.* Amsterdam, P. N. van Kampen.
German authorized edition by G. Gehrich: *Grundzüge der Religionswissen-*
schaft. Eine kurzgefasste Einführung in das Studium der Religion und ihrer
Geschichte. Tübingen and Leipzig, 1904.

ERNST TROELTSCH

1. Bibliography

Gesammelte Schriften, Vol. IV, 1925, pp. 863–872.
Adams, J. L., *Troeltsch Bibliography.* Widener Library, Harvard University,
Cambridge, Mass. (mimeo.).

2. Biography and Appreciation

Adams, J. L., "Ernst Troeltsch as an analyst of religion," *Journal of the*
Scientific Study of Religion, I, 1 (1961), pp. 98–109.
Antoni, Carlo, *Dallo storicismo alla sociologia.* Firenze, Sansoni, 1940, 1951[2].
English translation by H. V. White: *From History to Sociology.* The
transition in German historical thinking (in the Works of Dilthey,
Troeltsch, Meinecke, Weber, Huizinga and Wölfflin). London, Merlin
Press, 1962.
Bainton, R. H., "Ernst Troeltsch: Thirty years later," *Theology Today*, VIII,
1 (1951), pp. 70–96.
Bodenstein, Walter, *Neige des Historismus. Ernst Troeltsch Entwicklungsgang.*
Gütersloh, Ernst Mohn, 1959.
Bosse, Hans, *Marx, Weber, Troeltsch. Religionssoziologie und marxistische*
Ideologiekritik. München, Kaiser Verlag; Mainz, Grünewald Verlag, 1970.
Brachmann, Wilhelm, *Ernst Troeltschs historische Weltanschauung.* Halle (Saale),
Niemeyer, 1940.
Dermidoff, F., *Religione e storia nel pensiero de E. Troeltsch.* Diss. Genova, 1966.
Drescher, Hans Georg, *Glaube und Vernunft bei E. Troeltsch.* Eine kritische Deu-
tung seiner religionsphilosophischen Grundlegung. Theol. Diss. Marburg,
1957.
Kasch, Wilhelm F., *Die Sozialphilosophie von Ernst Troeltsch.* Tübingen, Mohr,
1963.
Koehler, Walter Erich, *Ernst Troeltsch.* Tübingen, Mohr, 1941.
Lessing, Eckhard, *Die Geschichtsphilosophie von Ernst Troeltsch.* (Theologische
Forschung, 39). Hamburg–Bergstedt, 1965.
Ogletree, Thomas W., *Christian Faith and History. A Critical Comparison of*
Ernst Troeltsch and Karl Barth. New York– Nashville, Abingdon Press,
1965.
Pauck, Wilhelm, *Harnack and Troeltsch: Two Historical Theologians.* New
York, Oxford University Press, 1968.
Reist, Benjamin, A., *Toward a Theology of Involvement. The Thought of Ernst*
Troeltsch. Philadelphia, Westminster Press, 1966.

Schlippe, Gunnar von, *Die Absolutheit des Christentums bei Ernst Troeltsch auf dem Hintergrund der Denkfelder des 19. Jahrhunderts*. Theol. Diss. Marburg, 1966, 131 pp.

Séguy, Jean, "Ernst Troeltsch et ses *Soziallehren*," *Archives de Sociologie des Religions*, 6e Année, No 11 (janvier–juin 1961), pp. 7–14.

—, "Ernst Troeltsch, ou de l'essence de la religion à la typologie des christianismes," *Archives de Sociologie des Religions*, 13e Année, No 25 (janvier–juin 1968), pp. 3–11.

Tillich, Paul, "Ernst Troeltsch. Versuch einer geistesgeschichtlichen Würdigung," *Kantstudien*, XXIX (1924), pp. 351–358.

Wickelhaus, Manfred, *Kirchengeschichtsschreibung und Soziologie im neunzehnten Jahrhundert und bei Ernst Troeltsch*. Heidelberg, 1965.

3. Main Publications

1912–1925 *Gesammelte Schriften*. Tübingen, Mohr.
1. *Die Soziallehren der christlichen Kirchen und Gruppen* (1912);
2. *Zur religiösen Lage. Religionsphilosophie und Ethik* (1913, 1922²);
3. *Der Historismus und seine Probleme. I: Das logische Problem der Geschichtsphilosophie* (1922);
4. *Aufsätze zur Geistesgeschichte und Religionssoziologie*. Herausgegeben von Dr. Hans Baron (1925).

1924 *Der Historismus und seine Überwindung*. Fünf Vorträge. Eingeleitet von Friedrich von Hügel–Kensington. Berlin, Heise.

4. English Translations

1912 *Protestantism and Progress*. A historical study of the relation of protestantism to the modern world. Translated by W. Montgomery. New York, Putnam; London, Williams & Norgate. Boston, Beacon Press, 1958².

1923 *Christian Thought, its History and Application*. Translation [of *Der Historismus und seine Überwindung*] made by various hands and edited with an introduction and index by Baron F. von Hügel. Lectures written for delivery in England during March 1923. London, University of London Press. New York, Meridian Books: Living Age Books, 1957².

1949 *The Social Teaching of the Christian Churches*. Translation [of *Die Soziallehren der christlichen Kirchen und Gruppen*] made by O. Wyon. With an introductory note by C. Gore. (Halley Stewart Publications, 1). London–New York, 2 vols. Macmillan. New York, Harper Row, 1960².

1971 *The Absoluteness of Christianity and the History of Religions*. Introduction by James Luther Adams. Translated by David Reid. Richmond, Virg., John Know Press, 1971.

1974 *Collected Essays (?)*. Introduction by James Luther Adams and Walter F. Bense. Translations made by several scholars. Publication expected in 1974.

Microfilm of typewritten copy of *Historism and its Problems. I: The Logical Problem of the Philosophy of History* [Translation of *Der Historismus und seine Probleme. I: Das logische Problem der Geschichtsphilosophie*]. Available in the Widener Library, Harvard University, Cambridge, Mass.

EDWARD BURNETT TYLOR*

1. Bibliography

Barbara W. Freire-Marreco, "A Bibliography of Edward Burnett Tylor from
1861 to 1907," in: H. Balfour, ed., *Anthropological Essays presented to
Edward Burnett Tylor, in honour of his 75th birthday Oct. 2, 1907*. Oxford,
Clarendon Press, 1907, pp. 375–409.

2. Biography and Appreciation

Bohannan, Paul, "Introduction," in Edward B. Tylor, *Researches. . .*, 1964.
Bros, A., "L'animisme de Tylor et de Spencer," in: *Semaine d'ethnologie r eli-
gieuse, Session I*, Louvain, 27 août–4 septembre 1912. Paris et Bruxelles,
1913, pp. 93–98.
Hervé, G., "E. B. Tylor," *Revue Anthropologique*, XXVII (1917), pp. 91–94.
Hodgen, M. T., *Doctrine of Survivals*. A Chapter in the History of Scientific
Method in the Study of Man. London, 1936.
Kardiner, A. and Preble, E., "Mr. Tylor's Science," in: A. Kardiner and E.
Preble, *They Studied Man*. New York, 1963, pp. 50–68.
Lang, Andrew, "Edward Burnett Tylor," in: H. Balfour, ed. and abr., *Anthro-
pological Essays presented to Edward Burnett Tylor . . . .* Oxford, Clarendon
Press, 1907, pp. 1–15.
Lowie, Robert H., "Edward B. Tylor," *American Anthropologist*, XIX (1917),
pp. 262–268. Reprinted in C. du Bois, ed., *Lowie's Selected Papers in
Anthropology.* Berkeley – Los Angeles, University of California Press,
1960, pp. 365–371.
—, "Edward B. Tylor (1832–1917)," in: Robert H. Lowie, *The History of
Ethnological Theory*. London, 1937, pp. 68–85.
Marett, Robert Ranulph, *Sir Edward Burnett Tylor*. (Modern Sociologists
Series). London, Chapman Hall; New York, 1936.
Pascher, Josef, *Der Seelenbegriff im Animismus Edward Burnett Tylors ; ein
Beitrag zur Religionswissenschaft* (Abhandlungen zur Philosophie und
Psychologie der Religion, Heft 23). Würzburg, Becker, 1929.
Radin, Paul, "Introduction to the Torchbook Edition," in: Sir Edward Burnett
Tylor, *Religion in Primitive Culture* (Part II of "Primitive Culture").
Harper Torchbook TB 34, New York, 1958, pp. IX–XVII.
Read, C. H., "Sir Edward Burnett Tylor. Born October 2nd, 1832, died January
2nd, 1917," *Man*, XVII, 25 (February 1917), pp. 16–17.
Smith, G. Eliott, *The Diffusion of Culture*. London, Watts & Co., 1933.
Tylor, Edward B. and Wallace, Alfred Russ., *Letters*. Edited by K. Rob. v.
Wikman (Acta Academiae Aboensis. Humaniora XIII 7). Åbo, 1940.
Wallis, W. D., "Anthropology in England early in the present century,"
American Anthropologist, LI (October 1957), pp. 781–790.
White, Leslie A., "Foreword," in Leslie A. White, ed. and abr.: Edward Bur-
nett Tylor, *Anthropology*. Ann Arbor, University of Michigan Press, 1960.

3. Method and Theory

1866 "The Religion of Savages," *Fortnightly Review*, Nr. 6 (August 1866), pp. 71–86.
1875 "Anthropology," *Encyclopaedia Britannica*, 9th Edition, Vol. II, pp. 107–123.
1877 "Mr Spencer's 'Principles of Sociology'," (Review of Herbert Spencer, *The Principles of Sociology*, Vol. I, 1876) in: *Mind*, II, 2 (April 1877), pp. 141–156.
1877 "Letters to Mr Spencer," *Academy*, XI, pp. 392 and 462, and *Mind*, II, pp. 419–423 and 429.
1880 "Anniversary Address," *Journal of the Anthropological Institute*, IX (1880), pp. 443–458. [Comp. also the following "Anniversary Addresses"].
1882 "The Study of Customs," *Macmillan's Magazine*, XXXXVI (May 1882), pp. 73–86.
1898 "Remarks on Totemism, with special reference to some Modern Theories respecting it," *Journal of the Anthropological Institute*, XXVIII (1898), pp. 138–148.

4. Main Publications

1861 *Anahuac: or Mexico and the Mexicans, Ancient and Modern.* London: Longman.
1865 *Researches into the Early History of Mankind and the Development of Civilization.* London, Murray. 1870², 1878³ (revised: London, Murray New York, Henry Holt & Co.).
German translation by H. Müller: *Forschungen über die Urgeschichte der Menschheit und die Entwicklung der Civilisation.* Leipzig, Abel, n. d. (1866).
1866 "The Science of Language" (Review article), *Quarterly Review*, Nr. 119 (April 1866), pp. 394–435.
1869 "The Condition of Prehistoric Races, as inferred from observation of Modern Tribes," *Transactions of the International Congress of Prehistoric Archeology*, (London), pp. 11–25.
1870 "The Philosophy of Religion among the Lower Races of Mankind," *Transactions of the Ethnological Society*, N. S., II, pp. 369–379.
1871 *Primitive Culture: Researches into the Development of Mythology, Philosophy, Religion, Art, and Custom*, 2 vols. London, Murray. 1873², 1874; (American edition based on the 2nd English edition: New York, Henry Holt & Co.), 1891³ (revised), 1903⁴ (revised).
French translation by Mme Pauline Brunet, based on the 2nd English edition: *La Civilisation Primitive*, 2 vols. Paris, Reinwald, 1876.
German translation by J. W. Spengel and Fr. Poske, with the collaboration of the author: *Die Anfänge der Cultur: Untersuchungen über die Entwicklung der Mythologie, Philosophie, Religion, Kunst und Sitte*, 2 vols. Leipzig, Winter, 1873.
Polish translation by Z. A. Kowerska (Madame Rzad), based on the 3rd English edition; with preface, biographical sketch, and notes by Jan Karlowicz: *Cywilizacja Pierwotna. Badania rozwoju mitologji, filo-*

zofji, wiary, mowy, sztuki i zwyczajów, 2 vols. Warsaw, The "Glos": F. Czernak, 1896 and 1898.

Russian translation by D. A. Koropčevski: *Pervobytnaya Kultura: izslêdovaniya razvitya mythologii, philosophii, religii, iskusstva i obyčayev* 2 vol. St. Petersburg, Office of the Znanie, 1872.

1873 "Primitive Society," *Contemporary Review*, Nrs. 21 (April 1873), pp. 701–718, and 22 (June 1873), pp. 53–72. Also in *Eclectic Magazine*, N. S. Nr. 17, pp. 641–652, and Nr. 19, pp. 722–740.
Russian translation, St. Petersburg, Office of the Znanie, 1873.

1881 *Anthropology: An Introduction to the Study of Man and Civilization*. London, Macmillan; New York, Appleton. 1889² (with corr.), 1892³ (with corr.), 1895⁴.
German translation by G. Siebert, authorized by the author: *Einleitung in das Studium der Anthropologie und Civilisation*. Brunswick, Vieweg, 1883.
Polish translation by Aleksandra Bakowska: *Antropologia. Wstep do Badania Czlowieka i Cywilizacyi*. Warsaw, Naklad tygodnika "Prawda", 1889; Warsaw, Stefan Demby, 1902².
Russian translation by E. C. Evena: *Anthropologiya: vvedenie k isyčeniio čelovka i tsivilizatsii*. St. Petersburg, 1882.
Spanish translation by Don Antonio Machada y Álvarez: *Antropología: Introducción al Estudio del Hombre y de la Civilización*. Madrid, Falcón, 1887.

1883 "Magic", *Encyclopaedia Britannica*, 9th edition, vol. XV, pp. 199–206.

5   Recent pocket editions

1958 *The Origins of Culture*. 2 vols. New York, Harper Torchbooks.
1960 *Anthropology*. Abridged and with a Foreword by Leslie A. White. Ann Arbor, University of Michigan Press.
1964 *Researches into the Early History of Mankind and the Development of Civilization*. Edited and abridged with an Introduction by Paul Bohannan from the 3rd (revised) edition, Chicago, University of Chicago Press.

EVELYN UNDERHILL

1. Bibliography

In: Underhill, E., *Collected Papers*. New York, 1946, p. 37.

2. Biography and Appreciation

Underhill, E., *Letters*. Ed. and intr. by Charles Williams. London, 1947.

3. Main Publications

1911 *Mysticism*. A study in the Nature and Development of Man's spiritual consciousness. London, Methuen. 1945[15]; New York, Dutton, 1930 (revised ed.); Pb. New York, Dutton. 1961.
1913 *The Mystic Way*. A psychological study in Christian origins. London–Toronto, Dent and Sons; New York, Dutton.
1915 *Ruysbroeck*. London.
1920 *The Essentials of Mysticism*. London; New York, Dutton, Pb., 1960.
1925 *The Mystics of the Church*. London, Clarke; New York, Doran, 1926.
1927 *Man and the Supernatural*. London, Methuen; New York, Dutton, 1928.
1936 *Worship*. London, Nisbet; New York, Harper Torchbooks, 1957.
1946 *Collected Papers*. New York.

HERMANN USENER

1. Bibliography

Biographisches Jahrbuch für die Alterthumskunde, XXXI (1908), p. 53.

2. Biography and Appreciation

Usener und Wilamowitz. Ein Briefwechsel 1870–1905. Ed. by Hermann
    Dietrich and Friedrich Hiller von Gaertringen. Leipzig–Berlin, 1934.
"Hermann Usener in Memorian," Archiv für Religionswissenschaft, VIII
    (1905) pp. I–XI. Signed: A. D. (= Albrecht Dietrich).
Compare "Beiheft gewidmet an H. Usener zum 70. Geburtstag," together with
    Archiv für Religionswissenschaft, Vol. VIII (1905).

3. Main Publications

1879 Legenden der Pelagia. Bonn.
1889 Das Weihnachtsfest. Bonn.
1889–1899 Religionsgeschichtliche Untersuchungen, 3 vols. Bonn.
1896 Götternamen; Versuch einer Lehre von der religiösen Begriffsbildung. Bonn.
1899 Die Sintfluthsagen. Bonn.
1907 Sonderbare Heilige. Texte und Untersuchungen. Leipzig.
1907 Vorträge und Aufsätze. Leipzig.
1912–1913 Kleine Schriften. 4 vols. Ed. by L. Radermacher. Leipzig–Berlin.

V

JAN P. M. L. DE VRIES

1. Bibliography

Kijlstra, Andries, "Bibliographie," in: Jan de Vries, *Kleine Schriften*. Herausg. von Klaas Heeroma und Andries Kijlstra. Berlin, 1965.

2. Biography and Appreciation

Bolle K. W., "Jan de Vries (1890–1964)," *History of Religions*, V (1965), pp. 173–177.
Heeroma, Klaas, "Vorwort," in: Jan de Vries, *Kleine Schriften*. Herausg. von Klaas Heeroma und Andries Kijlstra. Berlin, 1965, pp. V–VII.

3. Main Publications

1931 *Contributions to the Study of Othin, especially in his Relation to agricultural Practices in modern popular Lore*. Helsinki.
1933 *The Problem of Loki*. Helsinki.
1934 *Die Welt der Germanen*. Leipzig.
1935–1937 *Altgermanische Religionsgeschichte*, 2 vols. Berlin, De Gruyter, 1956–57², 2 vols. (completely revised).
1941–1942 *Altnordische Literaturgeschichte*, 2 vols. Berlin. 1964–65², 2 vols. (completely revised).
1943 *Die geistige Welt der Germanen*. Halle (Saale). 1945²; Darmstadt, Wissenschaftliche Buchgesellschaft, 1964³.
1954 *Betrachtungen zum Märchen besonders in seinem Verhältnis zu Heldensage und Mythos*. Helsinki.
1957 *Untersuchung über das Hüpfspiel, Kinderspiel, Kulttanz*. Helsinki.
1959 *Heldenlied en Heldensage*. Utrecht–Antwerpen, Het Spectrum (Aula 25,), 1959.
English translation by B. J. Timmer: *Heroic Song and heroic Legend*. London, 1963.
1960 *Kelten und Germanen*. (Bibliotheca Germanica, 9). Berlin.

1961 *Forschungsgeschichte der Mythologie*. Freiburg–München, Karl Alber.
1961 *Keltische Religion*. (Die Religionen der Menschheit, Band 18). Stuttgart, Kohlhammer.
1961 *Godsdienstgeschiedenis in vogelvlucht*. Utrecht–Antwerpen, Het Spectrum (Aula 56), 1961.
English translation by Kees W. Bolle: *The Study of Religion. A historical Approach*. New York Chicago–San Francisco–Atlanta, Harcourt, Brace & World, 1967.
1965 *Kleine Schriften*. Herausg. von Klaas Heeroma und Andries Kijlstra. Berlin.

W

JOACHIM WACH*

1. Bibliography

Kitagawa, Joseph M., Heiler, Friedrich, and Neumann, Käthe, "Bibliographie Joachim Wachs," in: Joseph M. Kitagawa, *Gibt es ein Verstehen fremder Religionen?* ("Joachim Wach-Vorlesungen der Theologischen Fakultät der Philipps-Universität Marburg/Lahn", Vol. I). Leiden, E. J. Brill, 1963, pp. 32–36.
"Bibliography of Joachim Wach (1922–55)," in: Joseph M. Kitagawa, ed., *Understanding and Believing. Essays by Joachim Wach* (Harper Torchbooks). New York and Evanston, Harper & Row, 1968, pp. 188–196.
Bibliography in: *Archives de Sociologie des Religions*, I, 1 (janvier–juin 1956), pp. 64–69.

2. Biography and Appreciation

Benz, E., "Bericht über das Werk von Joachim Wach: 'Types of Religious Experience, Christian and non-Christian', London 1951," *Zeitschrift für Religions- und Geistesgeschichte*, IX (1957), pp. 371–374.
Bolle, Kees W., "Wach's legacy: reflexions on a new book," *History of Religions*, X, 1 (August 1970), pp. 80–90.
Desroche, H., "Sociologie et théologie dans la typologie religieuse de Joachim Wach," *Archives de Sociologie des Religions*, I, 1 (janvier–juin 1956), pp. 41–63.
Heiler, Friedrich, "Joachim Wach" (Memorial Address), *The Divinity School News* (University of Chicago), XXII, 4 (November 1955), pp. 28–32.
French translation: "Souvenirs sur Joachim Wach," *Archives de Sociologie des Religions*, I, 1 (janvier–juin 1956), pp. 21–24.
Kitagawa, Joseph M., "A glimpse of Professor Wach," *The Chicago Theological Seminary Register*, XLV, 4 (November 1955).
—, "Joachim Wach" (Memorial Address), *The Divinity School News* (University of Chicago), XXII, 4 (November 1955). Reprinted in: Joseph M. Kitagawa, ed., *Understanding and Believing. Essays by Joachim Wach.* (Harper Torchbooks). New York and Evanston, Harper & Row, 1968. pp. 197–201.

—, "Joachim Wach and Sociology of Religion," *The Journal of Religion*, XL, 3 (July 1957).
French translation: "Joachim Wach et la sociologie de la religion," *Archives de Sociologie des Religions*, I, 1 (janvier–juin 1956). pp. 25—40.

—, "The life and thought of Joachim Wach," in: Joachim Wach, *The Comparative Study of Religions*. New York, Columbia University Press, 1958, pp. XIII–XLVIII.
A *Dutch* translation "Het leven en denken van Joachim Wach" appeared in the Dutch edition of the book: Joachim Wach, *Vergelijkende godsdienstwetenschap* (Aula 218). Utrecht–Antwerpen, Het Spectrum, 1965, pp. 9–41.
A *German* translation of this introduction appeared in the German edition of this book: Joachim Wach, *Vergleichende Religionsforschung*. (Urbanbücher, 52). Stuttgart, Kohlhammer, 1962, pp. 10–34.

—, "Joachim Wach, Leben, Forschung und Lehre," in: Joseph M. Kitagawa, *Gibt es ein Verstehen fremder Religionen?* Leiden, Brill, 1963, pp. 1–31.

—, "Gibt es ein Verständnis fremder Religionen? Zur Religionspsychologie und Religionssoziologie von Joachim Wach," in: Joseph M. Kitagawa, *Gibt es ein Verstehen fremder Religionen?* Leiden, Brill, 1963, pp. 37–66.

—, "Introduction" in: Joseph M. Kitagawa, ed., *Understanding and Believing. Essays by Joachim Wach.* ("Harper Torchbooks"). Evanston and New York, Harper & Row, 1968, pp. VII–XVIII.

—, *Verstehen* and *Erlösung*: some remarks on Joachim Wach's Work," *History of Religions*, XI, 1 (August 1971), pp. 31–53.

Klimkeit, Hans-Joachim, "Das Prinzip des Verstehens bei Joachim Wach," *Numen*, Vol. XIX, Fasc. 2–3 (July–December, 1972), pp. 216–228.

Poniatowski, Zygmunt, „Joachim Wach," *Euhemer. Przeglad Religioznaw.zy*, 1958, Nr. 2, pp. 39—45.

—, "Joachim Wach jako socjolog religii," in: J. Wach, *Socjologia religii*. Warszawa, Wstęp, 1960, pp. IX—XXIX.

Rudolph, Kurt, "Joachim Wach (1898–1955)," in: *Bedeutende Gelehrte in Leipzig*. Leipzig, 1965, pp. 229–237.

Séguy, Jean, "Joachim Wach, sociologue des religions," *Archives de Sociologi des Religions*, 7e Année, No 14 (juillet–décembre 1962), pp. 27–34.

Werblowsky, R. J. Zwi, "The Comparative Study of Religions – a Review Essay," *Judaism*, Vol. 8, No. 4 (Fall 1959), pp. 1–9.

Scheimann, Richard, W., *Wach's Theory of the Science of Religion*. Ph. D. Diss. University of Chicago, 1963.

Schoeps, Hans-Joachim, "Joachim Wachs wissenschaftliche Bedeutung," *Zeitschrift für Religions- und Geistesgeschichte*, IX (1957), pp. 368–371.

3. *Method and Theory*

1923 "Bemerkungen zum Problem der 'extremen' Würdigung der Religion," *Zeitschrift für Missionskunde und Religionswissenschaft* (Berlin), XXXVIII (1923), pp. 161–183.

1923 "Zur Methodologie der allgemeinen Religionswissenschaft," *Zeitschrift für Missionskunde ...*, XXXVIII (1923).

1924 *Religionswissenschaft: Prolegomena zu ihrer wissenschaftstheoretischen Grundlegung*. Leipzig, J. C. Hinrichs.

1924 " 'Nur'. Gedanken über den Psychologismus," *Zeitschrift für Missions-kunde* . . ., XXXIX (1924), pp. 209–215.

1925 "Wilhelm Dilthey über 'Das Problem der Religion'," *Zeitschrift für Missionskunde* . . ., XXXX (1925), pp. 66–81.

1926–1933 *Das Verstehen: Grundzüge einer Geschichte der hermeneutischen Theorie im 19. Jahrhundert*, 3 vols. Tübingen, Mohr.

1927 "Jakob Burckhardt und die Religionsgeschichte," in: *Die Religion in Geschichte und Gegenwart*, 2nd edition, Vol. I, 1927, pp. 1270–1271.

1929 "Die Geschichtsphilosophie des 19. Jahrhunderts und die Theologie der Geschichte", *Historische Zeitschrift*, Nr. 142 (1929), pp. 1–15.

1929 "Und die Religionsgeschichte?," *Zeitschrift für Systematische Theologie* (Gütersloh), VI (1929), pp. 484–497.

1929 "Idee und Realität in der Religionsgeschichte," *Zeitschrift für Theologie und Kirche* (Tübingen), (1927?), pp. 334–364.

1930 "Religionsphilosophie", "Religionssoziologie", "Religionswissenschaft," in: *Religion in Geschichte und Gegenwart*, 2nd edition, Vol. IV, 1930.

1930 "Zur Hermeneutik heiliger Schriften," *Theologische Studien und Kritiken* (Stuttgart and Gotha), CII (1930), pp. 280–290.

1931 "Verstehen," in: *Die Religion in Geschichte und Gegenwart*, 2nd edition, Vol. V, 1931, pp. 1570–1573.

1931 "Religionssoziologie," in: A. Vierkandt, ed., *Handwörterbuch der Soziologie*. 1931, pp. 479–494.

1931 "Das religiöse Gefühl," in: *Das Problem der Kultur und die ärztliche Psychologie*. Vorträge des Instituts der Medizin an der Universität Leipzig, Nr. 4, Leipzig, Thieme, 1931, pp. 9–33 *(idem, 1932)*.

1934 "Religiöse Existenz," *Zeitschrift für Missionskunde* . . ., XXXIX (1934), pp. 193–201.

1935 "Sinn und Aufgabe der Religionswissenschaft," *Zeitschrift für Missionskunde* . . ., Band L, Heft 5 (1935), pp. 133–147.
English translation: "The Meaning and Task of the History of Religions (Religionswissenschaft)" in: J. M. Kitagawa, ed., with the coll. of Mircea Eliade and Charles H. Long, *The History of Religions: Essays on the Problem of Understanding*. Chicago, University of Chicago Press, 1967, pp. 1–17. Reprinted in: *Understanding and Believing*. (Harper Torchbooks). New York, Harper & Row, 1968, pp. 125–145.

1937 "Der Begriff des Klassischen in der Religionswissenschaft," in: *Quantula-cunque. Studies presented to Kirsopp Lake*. London, Christophers, 1937, pp. 87–97.
English translation "The concept of the 'classical' in the study of religions," in: Joachim Wach, *Types of Religious Experience. Christian and non-Christian*. Chicago, Un. of Chicago Press, 1951, pp. 48–57.

1939 "Religionssoziologie," in: S. R. Steinmetz, ed., *Gesammelte kleine Schriften zur Ethnologie und Soziologie*, pp. 479–494.

1945 "Sociology of Religion," in: Georges Gurvitch, *Twentieth Century Sociology*. New York, Philosophical Library, pp. 405–437.

1946 "On Understanding," in: A. A. Roback, ed., *The Albert Schweitzer Jubilee Book*. Cambridge (Mass.), SCI-ART Publishers, pp. 131–146.

1947 "The Place of the History of Religions in the Study of Theology," *Journal of Religion*, XXVII, 3 (July 1947), pp. 157ff. Reprinted in: *Types of Religious Experience, Christian and non-Christian*. Chicago, University of Chicago Press, 1951.

1950 "On Teaching History of Religions," in: *Pro Regno pro Sanctuario*
     [*Festschrift*, G. van der Leeuw]. Nijkerk (Holland), Callenbach.
1952 "Radhakrishnan and the comparative study of religion," in: Paul A.
     Schilpp, ed., *The Philosophy of Sarvepalli Radhakrishnan*. New York,
     Tudor Publishing Co., pp. 443–458.
1953 "Rudolph Otto und der Begriff des Heiligen," in: Arnold Bergsser, ed.,
     Deutsche Beiträge. Chicago, Henry Regnery Co., pp. 200–217.
1954 "General Revelation and the Religions of the World," *Journal of Bible
     and Religion*, XXII, 2 (April 1954), pp. 83 ff.

4. Main Publications

1922 *Der Erlösungsgedanke und seine Deutung.* (Veröffentlichungen des For-
     schungsinstituts für vergleichende Religionsgeschichte an der Univer-
     sität Leipzig, 8). Leipzig, J. C. Hinrichs.
1925 *Mahayana, besonders im Hinblick auf das Saddharma-Pundarika-Sutra:
     eine Untersuchung über die religionsgeschichtliche Bedeutung eines heiligen
     Textes der Buddhisten.* München–Neubiberg, Schloss.
1925 *Meister und Jünger: zwei religionsgeschichtliche Betrachtungen.* Tübingen,
     J. C. B. Mohr.
1931 *Einführung in die Religionssoziologie.* Tübingen, J. C. B. Mohr.
1932 *Typen religiöser Anthropologie: ein Vergleich der Lehre vom Menschen
     im religionsphilosophischen Denken von Orient und Okzident.* Tübingen,
     J. C. B. Mohr.
1934 *Das Problem des Todes in der Philosophie unserer Zeit.* Tübingen, J. C. B.
     Mohr.
1935 "Eine neue katholische Philosophie der Religionsgeschichte," *Zeitschrift
     für Missionskunde* . . ., L (1935), pp. 375–385.
1935 J. Wach, ed., *Religion und Geschichte.* Heft I, Stuttgart, Kohlhammer.
1944 *Sociology of Religion.* Chicago, University of Chicago Press. Also London,
     Kegan Paul, 1947.
     French translation by M. Lefevere: *Sociologie de la religion.* Paris, Payot,
     1954.
     German translation: *Religionssoziologie*, by Helmut Schoek, based on
     the 4th edition. Tübingen, J. C. B. Mohr, 1951.
     Polish translation with introduction by Zygmunt Poniatowski: *Socjologia
     religii.* Warszawa, Wstęp, 1960.
1951 *Types of religious experience, Christian and non-Christian.* Chicago, Uni-
     versity of Chicago Press. Collection of papers. For 'Method and Theory'
     see especially "Universals in the History of Religion" and "The concept
     of the 'classical' in the Study of Religions." Fifth impression, pb., 1972.
1958 *The Comparative Study of Religions.* Edited with Introduction by Joseph
     M. Kitagawa. New York, Columbia University Press.
     German translation: *Vergleichende Religionsforschung.* (Urban Bücher).
     Stuttgart, W. Kohlhammer Verlag, 1962.
     Spanish translation: *El Estudio Comparado de las Religiones.* Buenos
     Aires, Editorial Paidos, 1967.
1968 Kitagawa, Joseph M., ed., *Understanding and Believing. Essays by Joachim
     Wach* (Collection of 17 papers with Bibliography and In Memoriam).
     New York–Evanston, Harper.

CLEMENT C. J. WEBB

1. Bibliography

Religious Experience. A public Lecture delivered on 19 May 1944 by C. C. J. Webb. Printed together with a bibliography of his published writtings [by L. W. Grensted], and presented to him by some of his Friends and Pupils on the Occasion of his 80th Birthday. London, Oxford University Press, 1945, pp. 49–70.

2. Main Publications

1908 *The Notion of Revelation.* (Pan-Anglican Papers S. B. 5). London, Society for Promoting Christian Knowledge.

1912 *Natural and Comparative Religion.* An inaugural Lecture. Oxford, Clarendon Press.

1915 *Studies in the History of Natural Theology.* Oxford, Clarendon Press.

1916 *Group Theories of Religion and the Individual.* London, Allen & Unwin; New York, Macmillan.

1933 *Religion and Theism.* The Forwood Lectures delivered at Liverpool University. Together with a chapter on the psychological Accounts of the Origin of Belief in God. London, Allen & Unwin, Oxford University Press.

1935 *The historical Elements in Religion.* (Lewis Fry Lectures 1934). London, Allen & Unwin.

MAX WEBER*

1. Bibliography

Weber, Marianne, "Bibliographie," in: Marianne Weber, *Max Weber. Ein Lebensbild.* Tübingen, Mohr, 1926, pp. 715–719.

Prades, J. A., "Liste chronologique des travaux de Max Weber," in: J. A. Prades, *La sociologie de la religion chez Max Weber.* Louvain — Paris, Nauwelaerts et Béatrice-Nauwelaerts, 1969², pp. 259–271.

2. Biography and appreciation

Adams, L. J., "'The Protestant Ethic' with fewer tears," in: *In the Name of Life.* Essays in Honor of Erich Fromm. New York, Holt, Rinehart and Winston, 1971, pp. 174–190.

Aron, R., "Introduction," in: Max Weber, *Le savant et le politique.* Paris, Plon, 1959, pp. 34–57.

—, *Les grandes doctrines de sociologie historique.* Vol. II: *Emile Durkheim, Vilfredo Pareto, Max Weber.* Paris, C. D. U., 1962.

Baumgarten, Edward, "Einleitung," in: J. Winckelmann, ed., Max Weber, *Soziologie, Weltgeschichtliche Analysen, Politik.* Stuttgart, Kröner Verlag. 1960², pp. XI–XXVI.

    Max Weber. Werk und Person. Dokumente ausgewählt und kommentiert. Tübingen, Mohr, 1964.

Bendix, Reinhard, *Max Weber. An Intellectual Portrait*, New York, Doubleday, 1960.

    German translation by Renate Rausch: *Max Weber. Das Werk. Darstellung. Analyse. Ergebnisse.* Preface René König. München, Piper, 1964.

Bendix, Reinhard, and Roth, Guenther, *Scholarship and Partisanship. Essays on Max Weber.* Berkeley–Los Angeles–London, University of California Press, 1970.

Birnbaum, N., "Conflicting interpretations of the rise of capitalism: Marx and Weber," *British Journal of Sociology*, IV (1953), pp. 125–141.

Bosse, Hans, *Marx, Weber, Troeltsch. Religionssoziologie und marxistische Ideologie Kritik.* München, Kaiser Verlag; Mainz, Grünewald Verlag, 1970.

Bourdieu, P., "Une interprétation de la théorie de la religion selon Max Weber," *Archives Européennes de Sociologie*, XII, 1 (1971), pp. 3–21.

Brann, H. W., "Max Weber and the United States," *Southwestern Social Science Quarterly* (June, 1944), pp. 18–30.

Dux, G., "Religion, Geschichte und sozialer Wandel in Max Webers Religionssoziologie," *Internationales Jahrbuch für Religionssoziologie*, Vol. 7. Köln–Opladen, 1971, pp. 60–94.

Eisenstadt, S. N., "The Protestant Ethic thesis in an analytical and comparative framework," in S. N. Eisenstadt, ed., *The Protestant Ethic and Modernization.* New York, Basic Books, 1968.

Fechner, E., "Der Begriff des kapitalistischen Geistes bei Sombart und Max Weber," *Weltwirtschaftliches Archiv* (1929), pp. 194–211.

Fischler, K. H., "Kritische Beiträge zu Prof. M. Webers Abhandlungen: Die protestantische Ethik," *Archiv für Sozialwissenschaft und Sozialpolitik*, XXV, 1 (1907), pp. 232–242.

Fischoff, Ephraim, "The Protestant Ethic and the Spirit of Capitalism: the history of a controversy," *Social Research*, II (February, 1944), pp. 53–77. Reprinted in: Robert W. Green, ed. *Protestantism and Capitalism: the Weber Thesis* (Problems in European Civilization). Boston, Heath, 1959, pp. 107–114.

Freund, J. and Luthy, H., "Controverse sur Max Weber," *Preuves*, 163 (1964), pp. 85–92.

Freund, Julien, "L'éthique économique et les religions mondiales selon Max Weber," *Archives de Sociologie des Religions*, 13e Année, No 26 (juillet–décembre 1968), pp. 3–25.

    , *Max Weber* ("Philosophes"). Paris, P. U. F., 1969.

Gerth, H. H. and Gerth, H. I., "Bibliography on Max Weber," *Social Research*, XVI (1949), pp. 70–98.

Gerth, H. H. and Mills, C. Wright, "Introduction: the man and his work," in: H. H. Gerth and C. Wright Mills, *From Max Weber: Essays in Sociology.* Translated, edited and with an Introduction. New York, Oxford University Press, 1946, pb. 1958, pp. 1–74.

Goldschmidt, D., "Bericht über die Verhandlungen zum Rahmenthema: Die Aktualität Max Webers in der modernen Religionssoziologie," in: O. Stammer, ed., *Max Weber und die Soziologie heute. Verhandlungen des 15. deutschen Soziologentages*. Tübingen, Mohr, 1965, pp. 221–246.

Gordon–Walker, P. C., "Capitalism and the Reformation," *Economic History Review*, VIII, 1 (1937), pp. 1–19.

Gouldner, Alvin W., "On Weber's analysis of bureaucratic rules," in: R. K. Merton, ed., *Reader in Bureaucracy*. Glencoe (Ill.), Free Press, 1952.

Green, Robert W., ed., *Protestantism and Capitalism: The Weber Thesis and its Critics*. (Problems in European Civilization). Boston, Heath, 1959.

Halbwachs, Maurice, "Economistes et historiens: Max Weber, un homme une œuvre," *Annales d'Histoire Economique et Sociale*, No 1 (janvier 1929).

Henrich, D., *Die Einheit der Wissenschaftslehre Max Webers*. Tübingen, Mohr, 1952.

Honingsheim, P., "Max Weber. His religious and ethical background and development," *Church History*, XIX, 4 (Dec. 1950).

Jaspers, Karl, *Gedenkrede* (Max Weber), Heidelberg, 17. Juli 1920. In print 1921.

—, *Max Weber. Deutsches Wesen im politischen Denken, im Forschen und Philosophieren*, 1932. New revised edition under the title of *Max Weber. Politiker, Forscher, Philosoph*. München, Piper Verlag, 1946, 1948, 1958.

Kolko, G., "Max Weber on America," *History and Theory* (The Hague). I, 3 (1961), pp. 243–260.

König, René, and Winckelmann, Johannes, eds., *Max Weber zum Gedächtnis. Materialien und Dokumente zur Bewertung von Werk und Persönlichkeit* (Kölner Zeitschrift für Soziologie und Sozialpsychologie, Sonderheft 7). Köln–Opladen, 1963.

Kosa, J., and Rachiele, L. D., "The spirit of capitalism, traditionalism and religiousness: A re-examination of Weber's concepts," *Sociological Quarterly*, IV, 3 (1963), pp. 243–260.

Lennert, R., *Die Religionstheorie Max Webers*. Diss. Leipzig, 1931; in print 1935.

Lopes, J. R., "Max Weber," *Sociologica*, XVIII, 1 (1956), pp. 51–69.

Löwith, Karl, "Max Weber und Karl Marx," *Archiv für Sozialwissenschaft und Sozialpolitik*, LXVII, 1 (1932), pp. 53–99 and 175–214.

Mitzman, Arthur, *The Iron Cage. An Historical Interpretation of Max Weber*. New York, Knopf, 1970.

Mommsen, Wolfgang, *Max Weber und die deutsche Politik 1890–1920*. Tübingen, Mohr, 1959.

Moth, G. and Bendix, R., "Max Webers Einfluss auf die amerikanische Soziologie," *Kölner Zeitschrift für Soziologie und Sozialpsychologie*, XI (1959), pp. 38–53.

Oppenheimer, H., *Die Logik der soziologischen Begriffsbildung mit besonderer Berücksichtigung von Max Weber*. Tübingen, Mohr, 1925.

Palyi, Melchior, and Schulze-Gaevernitz, Gerhart von, and others, *Erinnerungsgabe für Max Weber*, 2 vols. München, 1923.

Parsons, Talcott, "The author and his career," in: Max Weber, *The Theory of Social and Economic Organization*. Glencoe (Ill.), Free Press, 1947, pp. 1–5.

—, "Translator's Preface," in: Max Weber, *The Protestant Ethic and the Spirit of Capitalism*. Translated by Talcott Parsons. London, 1930. Pb. New York, Charles Scribner's Sons, 1958, pp. IX–XI.

—, "Preface to New Edition," in: Max Weber, *The Protestant Ethic and the Spirit of Capitalism*. Translated by Talcott Parsons. Pb. New York, Charles Scribner's Sons, 1958, pp. XIII–XVII.

—, "Introduction," in: Max Weber, *The Sociology of Religion*. Translated by Ephraim Fischoff. Boston, Beacon Press, pb. 1964, pp. XIX–LXVII.

—, "Wortgebundenheit und Objektivität in den Sozialwissenschaften. Eine Interpretation der Beiträge Max Webers," in: P. Stammer, ed., *Max Weber und die Soziologie heute. Verhandlungen des 15. deutschen Soziologentages*. Tübingen, Mohr, 1965, pp. 39–64.

Paul, R. S., "Weber and Calvinism: the effects of a 'calling'," *Canadian Journal of Theology*, XI, 1 (1965), pp. 25–41.

Prades, J. A., *La sociologie de la religion chez Max Weber*. Louvain — Paris, Nauwelaerts et Béatrice-Nauwelaerts, 1969².

Rheinstein, Max, *Max Weber on Law in Economy and Society*. Cambridge, Harvard University Press.

Robertson, H. M., *Aspects of the Rise of Economic Individualism. A Criticism of Max Weber and his School*. New York, Kelley and Millman, 1933, 1959².

Salman, D. H., "Psychology and sociology in Weber's theories," *Social Compass*, X, 6 (1963), pp. 536–539.

Salmon, J. H. M., "Religion and economic motivation: some French insights on an old controversy," *Journal of Religious History*, II, 2 (1963), pp. 181–203.

Samuelsson, Kurt, *Ekonomi och religion*. 1957.
    English translation by E. Geoffrey French: *Religion and Economic Action. A Critique of Max Weber*. New York, Harper Torchbooks, 1964.
    French translation: *Économie et religion. Une critique de Max Weber*. Introduction par D. C. Coleman. (L'Œuvre sociologique, 2). Paris–The Hague, Mouton, 1971.

Schaaf, J. J., *Geschichte und Begriff. Eine kritische Studie zur Geschichtsmethodologie von E. Troeltsch und M. Weber*. 1946.

Schelting, Alexander von, *Die Wissenschaftslehre Max Webers*. Tübingen, 1934.

Schill, B., *Die Rezeption von M. Webers Lehre des sozialen Handelns durch Talcott Parsons*. Diss. München, 1964.

Schnipper, L., "Max Weber on the sociological basis of the Jewish Religion," *Jewish Journal of Sociology*, I, 2 (1959), pp. 250–260.

Shils, Edward A., "Foreword" in: Edward A. Shils and Henry A. Finch, tr. and ed., Max Weber, *On the Methodology of the Social Sciences*. Glencoe (Ill.), Free Press, 1949.

Sprenkel, O. B. van der, "Max Weber on China," *History and Theory* (The Hague), III, 3 (1964), pp. 348–370.

Stammer, O., ed., *Max Weber und die Soziologie heute*. Verhandlungen des 15. deutschen Soziologentages. Tübingen, Mohr, 1965.

Stark, W., "Capitalism, calvinism and the rise of modern science," *Sociological Review*, XLIII, 5 (1951), pp. 95–104.

—, "Max Weber's sociology of religious belief," *Sociological Analysis*, XXV, 1 (1964), pp. 41–49.

Steeman, T. M., "Max Weber's sociology of religion," *Sociological Analysis*, XXV, 1 (1964), pp. 50–58.

Strötgen, J., *Zur Literatur über M. Webers Aufsatz "Die protestantische Ethik und der Geist des Kapitalismus,"* Un. Köln, Soziologisches Seminar, 1960–1961.

Tawney, R. H., "Foreword" in: Max Weber, *The Protestant Ethic and the Spirit of Capitalism*. Translated by Talcott Parsons. London, 1930. Pb. New York, Charles Scribner's Sons, 1958, pp. 1 (a)–1 (e)–11.

Tellegen, E., *De sociologie in het werk van Max Weber*. Meppel, Boom Pers, 1968.

Tenbruck, F., "Die Genesis der Methodologie Max Webers," *Kölner Zeitschrift für Soziologie und Sozialpsychologie*, XI (1959), pp. 573–630.

Thorner, I., "Ascetic protestantism and the development of science and technology," *American Journal of Sociology*, LVIII, 1 (1952), pp. 25–33.

Turksma, L., "Protestant ethic and rational capitalism: a contribution to a never ending discussion," *Social Compass*, IX, 5–6 (1962), pp. 445–473.

Weber, Marianne, *Max Weber. Ein Lebensbild*. Tübingen, Mohr, 1926; Heidelberg, 1950².

—, *Lebenserinnerungen*. Bremen, Storm, 1948.

Weber, Max, "Politische Briefe", in: *Gesammelte Politische Schriften*. München, Drei Masken, 1921, pp. 451–488.

—, *Jugendbriefe 1876–1893*. Edited by Marianne Weber. Tübingen, Mohr, n. d. (1936).

Weinrich, M., *Max Weber, l'homme et le savant*. Paris, Vrin, 1938.

Winckelmann, Johannes, *Legitimität und Legalität in Max Webers Herrschaftssoziologie*. Mit einem Anhang: Max Weber, "Die drei Typen der legitimen Herrschaft." Tübingen, Mohr, 1952.

3. Method and Theory

1904 "Die Objektivität sozialwissenschaftlicher und sozialpolitischer Erkenntnis," *Archiv für Sozialwissenschaft und Sozialpolitik*, XIX (1904), pp. 22–87. Reprinted in *Gesammelte Aufsätze zur Wissenschaftslehre*, Tübingen, Mohr, 1924, pp. 146–201.
Spanish translation: "La objetividad del conocimiento propio de las ciencias sociales y de la política social," *Revista de Economía Política*, VII/2–3 (1956), pp. 423–490.

1906 "Kritische Studien auf dem Gebiet der kulturwissenschaftlichen Logik. I: Zur Auseinandersetzung mit Eduard Meyer. II: Objektive Möglichkeit und adäquate Verursachung in der historischen Kausalbetrachtung," *Archiv für Sozialwissenschaft und Sozialpolitik*, XXII (1906), pp. 143–207, Reprinted in *Gesammelte Aufsätze zur Wissenschaftslehre*, Tübingen Mohr, 1924, pp. 215–290.

1909 "Energetische Kulturtheorien," *Archiv für Sozialwissenschaft und Sozialpolitik*, XXIX (1909), pp. 575–598. Reprinted in *Gesammelte Aufsätze zur Wissenschaftslehre*, Tübingen, Mohr, 1924, pp. 376–402.

1913 "Über einige Kategorien der verstehenden Soziologie," *Logos*, IV (1913), pp. 253–294. Reprinted in *Gesammelte Aufsätze zur Wissenschaftslehre*, Tübingen, Mohr, 1924, pp. 403–450.

1917 "Der Sinn der Wertfreiheit der soziologischen und ökonomischen Wissenschaften," *Logos*, VII (1917), pp. 40–88. Reprinted in *Gesammelte Aufsätze zur Wissenschaftslehre*, Tübingen, Mohr, 1924, pp. 451–502.

1924 *Gesammelte Aufsätze zur Wissenschaftslehre* (Collected essays). Edited by Marianne Weber. Tübingen, Mohr. 1951² (expanded; edited by J. Winckelmann).
Partial *English* translation by Edward A. Shils and Henry A. Finch, with a Foreword by Edward A. Shils: *Max Weber, On the Methodology of the Social Sciences*. Glencoe (Ill.), Free Press, 1949.

French translation of part of the book with introduction by Julien Freund: *Essais sur la théorie de la science*. Paris, Plon, 1965.
Partial *Italian* translation by P. Rossi: *Il metodo delle scienze storico-soziali*. Torino, Einaudi, 1958.
1960 *Soziologische Grundbegriffe*. Tübingen, Mohr.
English translation: *Basic Concepts in Sociology*. New York, The Philosophical Library, 1962.
1968 *Methodologische Schriften*. Studienausgabe. Edited with an introduction by Johannes Winckelmann. Frankfurt am Main.

4. Main Publications

1889 *Zur Geschichte der Handelsgesellschaften im Mittelalter*. Nach südeuropäischen Quellen. Stuttgart. Amsterdam, 1964.
1891 *Die römische Agrargeschichte in ihrer Bedeutung für das Staats- und Privatrecht*. Stuttgart. Amsterdam, 1962.
Italian translation: *La storia agraria romana*. Milano, Società Editrice Libraria, 1907.
1892 *Die Verhältnisse der Landarbeiter im ostelbischen Deutschland, dargestellt auf Grund der vom Verein für Sozialpolitik veranstalteten Erhebungen*. Leipzig.
1895 *Der Nationalstaat und die Volkswirtschaftspolitik* (Inaugural Address). Freiburg i. Br. Reprinted in *Gesammelte Politische Schriften*, München, Drei Masken, 1921, pp. 7–30.
1896 "Die sozialen Gründe des Untergangs der antiken Kultur," *Die Wahrheit*, VI (1896), pp. 57–77. Reprinted in *Gesammelte Aufsätze zur Sozial- und Wirtschaftsgeschichte*. Tübingen, Mohr, 1924, pp. 289–311.
English translation by C. Mackauer: "The social causes of the decay of ancient civilization," *The Journal of General Education* (Chicago), V (1950), pp. 75–88.
Spanish translation: "La decadencia de la cultura antigua," *Revista de Occidente*, XIII (1926), pp. 25–59.
1905 *Die protestantische Ethik und der Geist des Kapitalismus*. First published in *Archiv für Sozialwissenschaft und Sozialpolitik*, XX (1905), pp. 1–54, and XXI (1905), pp. 1–110. Then published separately. Reprinted in *Gesammelte Aufsätze zur Religionssoziologie*, Vol. I. Tübingen, Mohr, 1920, pp. 1–236.
Reprinted many times. New edition: *Die protestantische Ethik*. Edited by Johannes Winckelmann, Vol. I: *Eine Aufsatzsammlung*. Vol. II: *Kritiken und Antikritiken*. München–Hamburg, Siebenstern-Taschenbuch, 2 vols. 1965–1968.
English translation by Talcott Parsons: *The Protestant Ethic and the Spirit of Capitalism*. With a foreword by R. H. Tawney. London and New York, 1930, 1948, 1950. Pb. New York, Scribner, 1958.
French translation by Jacques Chavy: *L'éthique protestante et l'esprit du capitalisme*. Suivi d'unun autre essai. Paris, Plon, 1964.
Italian translation by P. Burresi: *Etica protestante e lo spirito del capitalismo*. Roma, Leonardo, 1945.
Spanish translation: *La ética protestante y el espíritu del capitalismo*. Madrid, Editorial Revista Derecho Privado, 1955.

1906 "Die protestantischen Sekten und der Geist des Kapitalismus," *Frankfurter Zeitung* (13 und 14 April 1906). Reprinted in *Gesammelte Aufsätze zur Religionssoziologie*, Vol. I. Tübingen, Mohr, 1920.

1908 "Kritische Bemerkungen zu H. K. Fischers Aufsatz, "Kritische Beiträge zu Max Webers Abhandlung 'Die protestantische Ethik und der Geist des Kapitalismus' "," *Archiv für Sozialwissenschaft und Sozialpolitik*, XXV (1908), pp. 243–249.

1908 "Bemerkungen zu der 'Replik' von H. K. Fischers Protestantische Ethik und Geist des Kapitalismus," *Archiv für Sozialwissenschaft und Sozialpolitik*, XXVI (1908), pp. 275–283.

1908–1909 "Zur Psychophysik der industriellen Arbeit," *Archiv für Sozialwissenschaft und Sozialpolitik*, XXVII (1908), pp. 730–770; XXVIII (1909), pp. 219–277, 719–761; XXIX (1909), pp. 513–542. Reprinted in *Gesammelte Aufsätze zur Soziologie und Sozialpolitik*. Tübingen, Mohr, 1914, pp. 61–255.

1910 "Antikritisches zum 'Geist' des Kapitalismus," *Archiv für Sozialwissenschaft und Sozialpolitik*, XXX (1910), pp. 176–202.

1910 "Antikritisches Schlusswort zum 'Geist' des Kapitalismus," *Archiv für Sozialwissenschaft und Sozialpolitik*, XXXI (1910), pp. 554–599.

1914 *Gesammelte Aufsätze zur Soziologie und Sozialpolitik* (Collected essays). Tübingen, Mohr.

1916–1919 "Die Wirtschaftsethik der Weltreligionen. Einleitung. I: Konfuzianismus und Taoismus. Zwischenbetrachtung: Theorie der Stufen und Richtungen religiöser Weltablehnung. II: Hinduismus und Buddhismus. III: Das antike Judentum," *Archiv für Sozialwissenschaft und Sozialpolitik*, XLI (1916), pp. 1–87; 335–421; 613–744; XLII (1916/17) pp. 345–461; 687–814; XLIV (1917), pp. 52–138; 349–443; 601–626; XLVI (1919), pp. 40–113; 311–366; 541–604. Reprinted in *Gesammelte Aufsätze zur Religionssoziologie*. Tübingen, Mohr, 1920, Vol. I, pp. 237–573, Vol. II, Vol. III, pp. 1–400. For the English translations, see under 1920–1921.

1917 "Die Pharisäer" (manuscript), in *Gesammelte Aufsätze zur Religionssoziologie*, Tübingen, Mohr, 1920, Vol. III, pp. 401–442.

1919 *Wissenschaft als Beruf*. München, Duncker und Humblot. Reprinted in *Gesammelte Aufsätze zur Wissenschaftslehre*. Tübingen, Mohr, 1922, pp. 524–555.
     English translation: "Science as a vocation" in *From Max Weber: Essays in Sociology* (1946, pb. 1958, 1964), pp. 129–156.
     French translation by Julien Freund in: Max Weber, *Le savant et le politique*. Introduction by Raymond Aron. Paris, Plon, 1959; Paris, Union générale d'éditions, 1963.
     Italian translation: *Il lavoro intellettuale come professione*. Torino, Einaudi, 1948.

1919 *Politik als Beruf*. München, Duncker und Humblot. Reprinted in *Gesammelte politische Schriften*. München, Drei Masken, 1921, pp. 396–450; Berlin, 1964[4].
     English translation: "Politics as a vocation" in: *From Max Weber: Essays in Sociology* (1946, pb. 1958, 1964), pp. 129–156.
     French translation by Julien Freund in: Max Weber, *Le savant et le politique*. Introduction by Raymond Aron. Paris, Plon, 1959; Paris, Union générale d'éditions, 1963.

1920–1921 *Gesammelte Aufsätze zur Religionssoziologie*, 3 vols. Tübingen, Mohr.
Vol. I: "Die protestantische Ethik und der Geist des Kapitalismus",
"Die protestantischen Sekten und der Geist des Kapitalismus", "Die
Wirtschaftsethik der Weltreligionen I: Einleitung, Konfuzianismus und
Taoismus, Zwischenbetrachtung (Theorie der Stufen und Richtungen
religiöser Weltablehnung)" (1947[4], 1963[5]). Vol. II: "Die Wirtschaftsethik
der Weltreligionen II: Hinduismus und Buddhismus" (1963[3], 1966[4]).
Vol. III: "Die Wirtschaftsethik der Weltreligionen III: Das antike Juden-
tum, Nachtrag (Die Pharisäer)." (1963[3], 1966[4]).
English translations:
Volume I was partly translated by Talcott Parsons in *The Protestant
Ethic and the Spirit of Capitalism* (see above, under 1905). Part of it was
translated by Hans H. Gerth and C. Wright Mills in *From Max Weber:
Essays in Sociology* (1946, pb. 1958, 1964), pp. 267–359. The third part of
Volume One was translated separately by Hans H. Gerth: *The Religion
of China: Confucianism and Taoism*. Pb. Glencoe, Ill., Free Press, 1951.
A fragment of this can be found in *From Max Weber: Essays in Sociology*
(1946, pb. 1958, 1964), pp. 416–444.
Volume II was translated by Hans H. Gerth and Don Martindale: "The
Hindu social system," *The University of Minnesota Sociology Club Bulletin*,
Nr. 1, 1950. It was reissued under the title of *The Religion of India.
The Sociology of Hinduism and Buddhism*. New York, The Free Press;
London, Collier-Macmillan, 1958, pb. 1967. A fragment of this can be
found in *From Max Weber: Essays in Sociology* (1946, pb. 1958, 1964),
pp. 396–415.
Volume III was translated by Hans H. Gerth and Don Martindale:
Ancient Judaism. Pb. Glencoe (Ill.), Free Press, 1952.
French translation: *Etudes de sociologie de la religion*. Vol. I, Part I:
L'éthique protestante et l' esprit du capitalisme. Translated by Jacques
Chavy. Paris, Plon, 1964.

1921 "Die Stadt. Eine soziologische Untersuchung," *Archiv für Sozialwissenschaft und Sozialpolitik*, XLVII (92), pp. 62 –772. Reprinted in *Gesammelte Aufsätze zur Sozial- und Wirtschaftsgeschichte*. Tübingen, Mohr,
1924, pp. 54 – 60.
English translation by Don Martindale and Gertrude Neuwirth: *The City*.
Glencoe (Ill.), Free Press, 1958. Pb. New York – London, Free Press, 1966.
Italian translation: *La città*. Milano, Bompiani, 1950.

1921 *Die rationalen und soziologischen Grundlagen der Musik*. Published with
an introduction by Theodor Kroyer. München, 1924[2]. Reprinted in
Wirtschaft und Gesellschaft. Tübingen, Mohr, 1922, pp. 818–869.
English translation by Don Martindale, Johannes Riedel and Gertrude
Neuwirth: *The Rational and Social Foundations of Music*. Southern
Illinois University Press, 1958.

1921 *Gesammelte politische Schriften*. Tübingen, Mohr. New edition by Johannes
Winckelmann, with a preface by Theodor Heuss, 1958[2].

1922 "Die drei Typen der legitimen Herrschaft," *Preussische Jahrbücher*, 187
(1922), pp. 1–12. Reprinted in Johannes Winckelmann, *Legitimität und
Legalität in Max Webers Herrschaftssoziologie*. Tübingen, Mohr, 1952.
English translation by H. H. Gerth: "The three types of legitimate rule,"
Berkeley Publications in Society and Institutions, IV, 1 (1958).
Italian translation: *Carismatica e i tipi del podere*. Torino, Unione, 1934.

1922 *Wirtschaft und Gesellschaft. Grundriss der verstehenden Soziologie.* Tübingen, Mohr, 1922, 1925², 1947³. A new revised edition, edited by Johannes Winckelmann, appeared in 2 vols., Tübingen, Mohr, 1956. A study edition appeared in Köln–Berlin, 1964 (2 vols.). This study contains "Religionssoziologie", which was also published separately: Tübingen, Mohr, 1922.

The following books contain *English* translations of parts of *Wirtschaft und Gesellschaft:*

1946 *From Max Weber: Essays in Sociology.* Translated and edited by Hans H. Gerth and C. Wright Mills. New York, Oxford University Press, 1946; pb. 1958; London, 1948, 1952, 1967. (pp. 159–266).

1947 *The Theory of Social and Economic Organization.* Translated by A. M. Henderson and Talcott Parsons, with an Introduction and Annotations by T. Parsons. London–New York, Oxford University Press, 1947, 1950. Pb. Glencoe (Ill.), Free Press, 1957.

1954 *On Law and Economy in Society.* Translated by Edward Shils and Max Rheinstein. Edited with Introduction and Notes by Max Rheinstein (20th Century Legal Philosophy Series, 6). Cambridge (Mass.), Harvard University Press, 1954.

1958 *The Rational and Social Foundations of Music.* Translated and edited by Don Martindale, Johannes Riedel and Gertrude Neuwirth. Southern Illinois University Press, 1958.

1961 *Theories of Society.* Edited by Talcott Parsons, Edward Shils, Kaspar D. Naegele, Jesse R. Pitts, 2 vols. Glencoe (Ill.), Free Press, 1961.

1963 *The Sociology of Religion.* Translated by Ephraim Fischoff, with an Introduction by Talcott Parsons. Boston, Beacon Press, 1963, pb. 1964; London, Social Science Paperbacks, 1966.

1968 *On Charisma and Institution Building. Selected Papers.* Edited with an Introduction by S. N. Eisenstadt. Chicago–London, University of Chicago Press, 1968. Phoenix pb. 1968.

Italian translation: *Economia e società.* Milano, Communita, 1962.

Spanish translation by J. M. Echavarría and others: *Economía y sociedad.* 4 vols. México, Fondo de cultura económica, 1944.

1922 *Gesammelte Aufsätze zur Wissenschaftslehre.* See above, under '3. Method and Theory'.

1923 *Wirtschaftsgeschichte. Abriss der universalen Sozial- und Wirtschaftsgeschichte.* Edited by S. Hellmann and M. Palyi. München, Mohr. 1924², 1958³ (expanded and edited by Johannes Winckelmann).

English translation by Frank H. Knight: *General Economic History.* New York–London, George Allen and Unwin, 1927; Glencoe (Ill.), Free Press, 1950.

Spanish translation by Manuel Sánchez Sarto: *Historia económica general.* México, Fondo de cultura económica, 1942, 1956².

1924 *Gesammelte Aufsätze zur Sozial- und Wirtschaftsgeschichte.* Edited by Marianne Weber. Tübingen, Mohr.

1924 *Gesammelte Aufsätze zur Soziologie und Sozialpolitik.* Edited by Marianne Weber. Tübingen, Mohr.

1956 *Soziologie, Weltgeschichtliche Analysen,* **Politik.** Edited and annotated by Johannes Winckelmann. Introduction by Eduard Baumgarten. Stuttgart, Kröner.

1956 *Staatssoziologie. Soziologie des rationalen Staates und der modernen politischen Parteien und Parlamente.* Edited with Introduction by Johannes Winckelmann. Tübingen, Mohr.
1960 *Rechtssoziologie.* Edited from the manuscript, with Introduction, by Johannes Winckelmann (Soziologische Texte, 2). Neuwied, H. Luchterhand, 1960; Berlin, 1966².

FRIEDRICH G. WELCKER

Main Publications

1844–1867 *Kleine Schriften*, 5 vols. Bonn, Weber.
1857–1862 *Griechische Götterlehre*, 3 vols. Göttingen, Dietrich.

JULIUS WELLHAUSEN*

1. Bibliography

Alfred Rahlfs, "Verzeichnis der Schriften Julius Wellhausens," (Studien zur semitischen Philologie und Religionsgeschichte Julius Wellhausen zum siebzigsten Geburtstag am 17. Mai 1914 gewidmet von Freunden und Schülern und in ihrem Auftrag herausgegeben von Karl Marti), *Beihefte zur Zeitschrift für die Alttestamentliche Wissenschaft*, XXVII (1914), pp. 351–368.

2. Biography and Appreciation

Baumgartner, W., "Wellhausen und der heutige Stand der alttestamentlichen Wissenschaft," *Der Theologische Rundschau*, N. F. II (1930), pp. 287–307.
Baxter, W. L., Sanctuary and Sacrifice. A Reply to Wellhausen. London, Eyre, 1896.
Becker, C. H., "Julius Wellhausen," *Der Islam*, IX (1918), pp. 95–99. Reprinted in: C. H. Becker, *Islamstudien. Vom Werden und Wesen der islamischen Welt*, Vol. II. Berlin, 1932, pp. 474–480.
Boschwitz, Fr., Julius Wellhausen. *Motive und Maszstäbe seiner Geschichtsschreibung.* Diss. Phil., Marburg, 1938.
Cohen, H., "*Julius Wellhausen. Ein Abschiedsgrusz,*" *Jüdische Schriften*, Vol. II. Berlin, 1924, pp. 463–468.
Greszmann, H., "Julius Wellhausen," *Protestantenblatt*, 1918, Nr. 6.
Jepsen, A. "Wellhausen in Greifswald," *Festschrift zur 500-Jahrfeier der Universität Greifswald*, Vol. II, 1956, pp. 47–56.
Perlitt, Lothar, *Vatke und Wellhausen. Geschichtsphilosophische Voraussetzungen und historiographische Motive für die Darstellung der Religion und Geschichte*

Israels durch Wilhelm Vatke und Julius Wellhausen. Berlin, A. Töpelmann, 1965.

Schwartz, Eduard, "Julius Wellhausen," *Nachrichten von der Königlichen Gesellschaft der Wissenschaften zu Göttingen. Geschäftliche Mitteilungen aus dem Jahre 1918*, (Berlin) 1918, pp. 43–70. Reprinted in: Eduard Schwartz, *Gesammelte Schriften*, Vol. I. Berlin, 1938, pp. 326–361.

Wellhausen, Julius, "Wellhausens Briefe aus seiner Greifswalder Zeit (1872–1879) an den anderen Heinrich Ewald-Schüler Dillmann," edited by E. Barnikol. *Wissenschaftliche Zeitschrift der Universität Halle*, Ges. Sprachw., VI, 5 (1957), pp. 701–712. Reprinted in: *Gottes ist der Orient. Festschrift für Otto Eissfeldt*. Berlin, 1959, pp. 28–39.

3. Main Publications

1870, *De gentibus et familiis Judaeis quae 1. Chr. 2.4 enumerantur* (Theol. Liz.– Diss.). Göttingen.

1871 *Der Text der Bücher Samuelis untersucht*. Göttingen, Vandenhoeck & Ruprecht.

1874 *Die Pharisäer und die Sadducäer. Eine Untersuchung zur inneren jüdischen Geschichte*. Greifswald. Reprinted Hannover, Lafaire, 1924.

1876–1877 "Die Composition des Hexateuchs," *Jahrbücher für Deutsche Theologie*: 1876, pp. 392–450 and 531–602; 1877, pp. 407–479. Reprinted as *Skizzen und Vorarbeiten II. Die Composition des Hexateuchs*. Berlin, Reimer, 1885. Reprinted in *Die Composition des Hexateuchs und der historischen Bücher des Alten Testaments*, Berlin, Reimer, 1889², 1899³. Reprinted Berlin, Walter de Gruyter & Co, 1963⁴.

1878 *Geschichte Israels*. Vol. I. Berlin, Reimer, 1878. The following editions appeared under the title of *Prolegomena zur Geschichte Israels*. Berlin, Reimer, 1883², 1886³, 1895⁴, 1899⁵, 1905⁶; Reprinted Berlin–Leipzig, 1927⁶.
English translation by J. S. Black and Allan Menzies: *Prolegomena to the History of Israel, with a Reprint of the Article "Israel" from the "Encyclopaedia Britannica."* With a Preface by W. Robertson Smith. Edinburgh, A. & C. Black, 1885. Pb. New York, Meridian Books, 1957.

1880 *Geschichte Israels*. Printed as a manuscript in about twenty copies. Greifswald, Christmas 1880. A revised and enlarged edition appeared under the title "Abriss der Geschichte Israels und Juda's" in *Skizzen und Vorarbeiten*, Vol. I. Berlin, Reimer, 1884.
English translation, considerably enlarged, as article "Israel" in *Encyclopaedia Britannica*, 9th edition, Vol. XIII, pp. 396–431. This article was published separately under the title *Sketch of the History of Israel and Judah*. London, A. & C. Black, 1891³. It was also reprinted as an appendix to *Prolegomena to the History of Israel*. Edinburgh, A. & C. Black, 1885; New York, 1957.
The "Abriss der Geschichte Israels und Juda's" is a German expanded translation of the article "Israel" in the *Encyclopaedia Britannica*.

1882 *Muhammed in Medina. Das ist Vakidi's Kitab al Maghazi in verkürzter deutscher Wiedergabe herausgegeben*. Berlin, Reimer, 1882.

1883 "Mohammedanism. Part I: Mohammed and the first four caliphs," *Encyclopaedia Britannica*, 9th edition, Vol. XVI, pp. 545–565.

1884–1899 *Skizzen und Vorarbeiten.* 6 vols. Berlin, Reimer.
I: *1. Abriss der Geschichte Israels und Juda's. 2. Lieder der Hudhailiten, arabisch und deutsch.* 1884.
II: *Die Composition des Hexateuchs.* 1885.
III: *Reste arabischen Heidentums.* 1887. Second edition under the title of *Reste arabischen Heidentums gesammelt und erläutert.* 1897[2]. Reprinted Berlin, de Gruyter, 1961[3].
IV: *1. Medina vor dem Islam. 2. Muhammads Gemeindeordnung von Medina. 3. Seine Schreiben, und die Gesandtschaften an ihn.* 1889.
V: *Die kleinen Propheten übersetzt, mit Noten.* 1892, 1893[2], 1898[3]. Reprinted Berlin, Walter de Gruyter & Co, 1963[4].
VI: *1. Prolegomena zur ältesten Geschichte des Islams. 2. Verschiedenes.* 1899.

1885 "Pentateuch and Joshua," *Encyclopaedia Britannica*, 9th edition, Vol. XVIII (1885), pp. 505–514. Reprinted as "Hexateuch," *Encyclopaedia Biblica*, Vol. II (1901), pp. 2045–2056.

1885 "Scholien zum Diwan Hudail No. 139–280. Herausgegeben von Julius Wellhausen," *Zeitschrift der Deutschen Morgenländischen Gesellschaft*, 1885, pp. 411–480.

1886 "Septuagint," *Encyclopaedia Britannica*, 9th edition, Vol. XXI (1886), pp. 667–670.

1893 "Die Ehe bei den Arabern," *Nachrichten von der Königlichen Gesellschaft der Wissenschaften zu Göttingen*, 1893, pp. 431–481.

1893 "The Babylonian exile," *The New World*, II (1893), pp. 601–611.

1894 *Israelitische und jüdische Geschichte.* Berlin, Reimer. 1895[2], 1897[3], 1901[4], 1904[5], 1907[6], 1914[7]. Reprinted Berlin, 1958[9].

1895 *The Book of Psalms.* (Part 14 of "The Sacred Books of the Old Testament, A critical edition of the Hebrew text printed in colors, with notes", under the editorial direction of Paul Haupt). Translation of the notes by J. D. Prince. Leipzig, Hinrichs; Baltimore, The Johns Hopkins Press; London, David Nutt, 1895.

1895 "Der syrische Evangelienpalimpsest vom Sinai," *Nachrichten von der Königlichen Gesellschaft der Wissenschaften zu Göttingen, Phil.-Historische Klasse*, pp. 1–12.

1895 "Die Rückkehr der Juden aus dem babylonischen Exil," *Nachrichten von der Königlichen Gesellschaft der Wissenschaften zu Göttingen, Phil.-Historische Klasse*, pp. 166–186.

1898 *The Book of Psalms. A new translation. With explanatory notes and an Appendix on the Music of the Ancient Hebrews* (Part 14 of "The Sacred Books of the Old and New Testaments. A new English translation with explanatory notes and pictorial illustrations," edited with the assistance of H. H. Furness by P. Haupt). Translation of the psalms by H. H. Furness; translation of the notes by J. Taylor; translation of the appendix by J. A. Paterson. London, James Clarke; New York, Dodd, Mead, and Co. Reprinted Leipzig, Hinrichs, 1904.

1901 *Die religiös-politischen Oppositionsparteien im alten Islam* ("Abhandlungen der Königlichen Gesellschaft der Wissenschaften zu Göttingen," Phil.-Historische Klasse, Neue Folge, Band V, Nr. 2). Berlin, Weidmann.

1901 "Die Kämpfe der Araber mit den Romäern in der Zeit der Umajjaden," *Nachrichten von der Königlichen Gesellschaft der Wissenschaften zu Göttingen, Phil.-Historische Klasse*, pp. 414–447.

1902 *Das arabische Reich und sein Sturz.* Berlin, Reimer. Reprinted Berlin, Walter de Gruyter & Co, 1960².
English translation by Margaret Graham Weir: *The Arab Kingdom and Its Fall.* Calcutta, University of Calcutta, 1927 (with Index).

1903 *Das Evangelium Marci übersetzt und erklärt.* Berlin, Reimer. 1909².

1904 *Das Evangelium Matthaei übersetzt und erklärt.* Berlin, Reimer.

1904 *Das Evangelium Lucae übersetzt und erklärt.* Berlin, Reimer.

1905 *Einleitung in die drei ersten Evangelien.* Berlin, Reimer, 1911².

1905 "Israelitisch-jüdische Religion," in: P. Hinneberg, ed., *Die Kultur der Gegenwart* (Teil I, Abt. IV: "Die christliche Religion mit Einschlusz der israelitisch-jüdischen Religion"). Berlin–Leipzig, Teubner, 1905, pp. 1–40; 1909², pp. 1–41.

1905 "Über den geschichtlichen Wert des zweiten Makkabäerbuchs," *Nachrichten von der Königlichen Gesellschaft der Wissenschaften zu Göttingen, Phil.-Historische Klasse*, pp. 117–168.

1907 *Erweiterungen und Änderungen im vierten Evangelium.* Berlin, Reimer.

1907 „Noten zur Apostelgeschichte," *Nachrichten von der Königlichen Gesellschaft der Wissenschaften zu Göttingen, Phil.-Historische Klasse*, pp. 1—21

1907 *Analyse der Offenbarung Johannis* („Abhandlungen der Königlichen Gesellschaft der Wissenschaften zu Göttingen," Phil.-Historische Klasse, Neue Folge, Band IX, Nr. 4). Berlin, Weidmann.

1908 *Das Evangelium Johannis.* Berlin, Reimer.

1914 *Kritische Analyse der Apostelgeschichte* ("Abhandlungen der Königlichen Gesellschaft der Wissenschaften zu Göttingen," Phil.-Historische Klasse, Neue Folge, Band XV, Nr. 2). Berlin, Weidmann.

1965 *Grundrisse zum Alten Testament.* Edited by Rudolf Smend. München

ARENT JAN WENSINCK

1. Bibliography

In: A. J. Wensinck, *Semietische Studiën* . . ., 1941, pp. 9–12.

2. Biography and Appreciation

Huizinga J., "Levensbericht van Arent Jan Wensinck (7 augustus 1882–19 september 1939)," *Jaarboek der Koninklijke Nederlandsche Akademie van Wetenschappen* (1939–1940), pp. 215–224.

Massignon, L., "A. J. Wensinck," *Journal Asiatique*, CCXXXIII (1941–1942) pp. 213–215.

Pedersen, J., "Arent Jan Wensinck," *Acta Orientalia*, XVIII (1940), pp. 161–163.

3. Main Publications

1908 *Mohammed en de Joden te Medina.* Dissertation. Leiden, Brill.

1911–1913 *Legends of Eastern Saints, chiefly from Syriac sources, edited and partly translated*. Vol. I: *The story of Archelides;* Vol. II: *The Legend of Hilaria.* Leiden, Brill.

1916 *The ideas of the Western Semites concerning the navel of the earth.* (Verhandelingen Koninklijke Akademie van Wetenschappen, afd. Letterkunde. N. R. XVII, no. 1). Amsterdam, J. Müller.

1919 *Bar Hebraeus's Book of the Dove, together with some Chapters from his Ethikon.* With an introduction, notes and registers. Leiden, Brill.

1921 *Tree and bird as cosmological symbols in western Asia.* (Verhandelingen Koninklijke Akademie van Wetenschappen, afd. Letterkunde). Amsterdam.

1922 "The Semitic New Year and the Origin of Eschatology," *Acta Orientalia,* I (1922), pp. 158–199.

1923 *Mystic treatises by Isaac of Niniveh, translated from Bedjan's Syriac text with an introduction and registers.* (Verhandelingen Koninklijke Akademie van Wetenschappen, afd. Letterkunde. N. R. XXIII, no. 1). Amsterdam.

1924 "Mohammed und die Propheten," *Acta Orientalia,* II (1924), pp. 168–198.

1925 *The Second Commandment.* (Mededeelingen Koninklijke Akademie van Wetenschappen, afd. Letterkunde, deel 59, serie A, no. 6). Amsterdam.

1927 *A Handbook of Early Muhammedan Tradition, alphabetically arranged.* Leiden, Brill. Reprinted 1971.

1932 *The Muslim Creed, its Genesis and Historical Development.* Cambridge, University Press. Reprinted London, Frank Cass & Co., 1965.

1933 *On the relation between Ghazali's Cosmology and his Mysticism.* (Mededeelingen Koninklijke Akademie van Wetenschappen, afd. Letterkunde, deel 75, serie A, no. 7). Amsterdam, Noord-Hollandse Uitgevers-Maatschappij.

1936 *Les preuves de l'existence de Dieu dans la théologie musulmane.* (Mededeelingen Koninklijke Akademie van Wetenschappen, afd. Letterkunde, deel 81, serie A, no. 2). Amsterdam, Noord-Hollandse Uitgevers-Maatschappij.

1936–1971 *Concordance et Indices de la tradition musulmane...* Par A. J. Wensinck, avec le concours de nombreux orientalistes, 6 vols. Leiden, Brill.

1940 *La pensée de Ghazzālī.* Paris, Adrien-Maisonneuve.

1941 *Semietische studiën uit de nalatenschap van Prof. Dr. A. J. Wensinck (7 augustus 1882–19 september 1939).* Leiden, Sijthoff.

EDVARD A. WESTERMARCK

1. Biography and Appreciation

Ginsberg, Morris, "The life and work of Edward Westermarck," in: Morris Ginsberg, *Reason and Unreason in Society (Essays in Sociology and Social Philosophy,* Vol. Two). London, Heinemann, 1947 (repr. 1956, 1960, 1965), pp. 61–83.

Hirn, Yrjö, "Edvard Westermarck and his English Friends," *Transactions of the Westermarck Society* (Gothenburg), I (1947), pp. 39–51.

Lagerborg, Rolf, *Edvard Westermarck och verken från hans verkstad 1902–1939*. (Skrifter utgivna av Svenska Litteratursällskapet i Finlands natur og folk. Heft 97, No. 1). Helsingfors–København, 1951.
Tenkku, Jussi, *Westermarcks Definition of the Concept of the World*. Copenhagen, 1962.

2. Main Publications

1891 *The History of Human Marriage*, 3 vols. London, Macmillan. 1894²; 1901³; 1921⁵.
1906–1908 *Origin and Development of the Moral Ideas*, 2 vols. London, Macmillan. 1912².
1914 *Marriage Ceremonies in Morocco*. London, Macmillan.
1926 *Ritual and Belief in Morocco*, 2 vols. London, Macmillan.
1927 *Minnen ur mitt liv*. Helsingsfors, Schilat.
　　English translation from the Swedish by Anna Barwell: *Memories of My Life*. London, Allen & Unwin, 1929.

ULRICH VON WILAMOWITZ-MOELLENDORF

1. Bibliography

Wilamowitz-Bibliographie, 1868 bis 1929. Hrsg. von F. H. von Gaertringen und G. Klaffenbach. Berlin, Weidemannsche Buchhandlung, 1929.

2. Biography and Appreciation

Mommsen und Wilamowitz. Briefwechsel, 1872–1903. Ed. by Baron J. F. W. R. A. and Baroness Dorothea M. H. von Gaertringen. Berlin, 1935.
Ulrich von Wilamowitz–Moellendorf, *Erinnerungen 1848–1914*. Leipzig, Koehler, 1928.
Ulrich von Wilamowitz–Moellendorf. Dem Meister der Altertumswissenschaft zum 80. Geburtstage gewidmet. Berlin–Leipzig, 1929.
Usener und Wilamowitz. Ein Briefwechsel, 1870–1905. Ed. by Hermann Dietrich and Friedrich Hiller von Gaertringen. Leipzig–Berlin, 1934.

3. Main Publications

1901 *Reden und Vorträge*. 1902², 1913³ (expanded), 1925–1926⁴ (revised and expanded, 2 vols.).
1921 *Geschichte der Philologie*. Einleitung in die Altertumswissenschaft. Leipzig.
1935 *Kleine Schriften*. Besorgt von Paul Maas, Edw. Schwartz, Ludolf Malten. Berlin. (Only Volumes 1 and 5 appeared).

RICHARD WILHELM

Main Publications

1910 *Kungfutse – Gespräche.* (Translation). Jena. 1923[2].
1910 *Laotse – Das Buch des Alten vom Sinn und Leben.* (Translation). Jena.
     1923[2].
1914 *Chinesische Volksmärchen.* Jena.
     English translation by Frederick H. Martens: *The Chinese Fairy Book.*
     Selected from Chinesische Volksmärchen. London, Fisher Unwin, 1922.
1923–1924 *I Ging: Das Buch der Wandlungen,* 2 vols. (Translation). Jena.
1925 *Die Seele Chinas.* Berlin, Hobbing.
     English translation: *The Soul of China.* Text transl. by John Holroyd
     Reece, Poems by Arthur Waley. London, Jonathan Cape; New York,
     Harcourt, Brace and Co., 1928.
1925 *Konfuzius.*
     English translation by George H. Danton and Annina Periam Danton:
     Confucius and Confucianism. New York, Harcourt, Brace and Co., 1931.
1925 *Laotse und der Taoismus.* (Frommanns Klassiker der Philosophie, Bd. 26).
     Stuttgart.
1925 *Kung-Tse. Leben und Werk.* (Frommanns Klassiker der Philosophie, Bd.
     25). Stuttgart.
1928 *Geschichte der chinesischen Kultur.* München, 1928.
     English translation by Joan Joshua: *A Short History of Chinese Civilisation.*
     Introduction by Lionel Giles. London, G. G. Harrap and Co.; New York,
     The Viking Press, 1929.
1931 *Der Mensch und das Sein.* (Vorträge und Aufsätze). Hrsg. von S. Wilhelm.
     Jena. 1939[2].
1956 *Wandlung und Dauer. Die Weisheit des I. Ging.* First published in: *Der
     Mensch und das Sein,* 1931. Düsseldorf.

GEORGE A. WILKEN

1. Bibliography

Kinderen, T. H. der, "Lijst der in druk verschenen geschriften van Dr. G. A.
     Wilken," *Bijdragen tot de Taal-, Land- en Volkenkunde van Nederlandsch
     Indië,* Series V, Part 7 (1892), pp. 154–156.
Wilken, G. A., *Verspreide Geschriften,* 1912, Vol. I, pp. 18–24.
—, *Opstellen over Adatrecht,* 1926, pp. XXVII–XXX.

2. Biography and Appreciation

Goeje, M. J. de, "Levensbericht van G. A. Wilken," in: *Jaarboek van de Konink-
     lijke Akademie van Wetenschappen,* 1892.
Kinderen, T. H. der, "Levensbericht van Dr. G. A. Wilken," *Bijdragen tot
     de Taal-, Land en Volkenkunde van Nederlandsch Indië.* Series V, Part 7

(1892), pp. 139–154. Reprinted in *Verspreide Geschriften*, 1912, Vol. I, pp. 3–17.
Veth, P. J., "De ethnologische studiën van G. A. Wilken," *Internationales Archiv für Ethnographie*, IV (1891), pp. 282–284.

3. Main Publications

1885 *Het Animisme bij de Volken van den Indischen Archipel.* Amsterdam, De Bussy. First published in *Indische Gids*, VI and VII, 1884 and 1885.
1886–1887 "Über das Haaropfer und einige andere Trauergebräuche bei den Völkern Indonesiens," *Revue Coloniale Internationale*, II (1886), pp. 225–279; and III (1887), pp. 345–426.
1893 *Handleiding voor de vergelijkende Volkenkunde van Nederlands Indië.* Ed. by C. M. Pleyte. Leiden.
1912 *Verspreide Geschriften*, 4 vols. Ed. by Mr. F. D. E. van Ossenbruggen. Semarang–Soerabaja–The Hague, Van Dorp and Co.
1926 *Opstellen over Adatrecht.* Ed. by Mr. F. D. E. van Ossenbruggen. Semarang–Soerabaja–Bandoeng–The Hague, Van Dorp and Co.

HUGO WINCKLER

1. Bibliography

"Winckler-Bibliographie" by O. Schroeder, in: *Mitteilungen der Vorderasiatischen Gesellschaft*, XX. 1 (1916), pp. 25–48.

2. Main Publications

1897–1905 *Altorientalische Forschungen*, 3 vols. Leipzig.
1900 *Geschichte Israels, Die Legende* (Völker und Staaten des alten Orients, II; Die Geschichte Israels in Einzeldarstellungen). Leipzig, Pfeiffer.
1901 "Die altbabylonische Weltanschauung," *Preussische Jahrbücher*.
1901 *Himmels- und Weltbild der Babylonier als Grundlage der Weltanschauung und Mythologie alter Völker.* Leipzig. 1903².
1901 Arabisch–semitisch-orientalisch. Kulturgeschichtlich–mythologische Untersuchung," in: *Mitteilungen Vorderasiatische Gesellschaft*. Jahrg. 6. Berlin.
1903 *Abraham als Babylonier, Joseph als Egypter. Der weltgeschichtliche Hintergrund der biblischen Vätergeschichten auf Grund der Keilschriften dargestellt.* Leipzig.
1904 *Die Weltanschauung des alten Orients.* Leipzig.
1905 *Zur babylonisch-assyrischen Geschichte.* Leipzig.
English authorized translation and ed. by James Alexander Craig: *The History of Babylonia and Assyria.* London, Hodder & Stoughton, 1907.
1906 *Altorientalische Geschichtsauffassung.* Leipzig.
1907 *Die jüngsten Kämpfer wider den Panbabylonismus.* Leipzig.
1913 *Vorderasien im 2. Jahrtausend.* Leipzig.

GEORG WISSOWA

1. Bibliography

Kern, Otto, "Schriften von G. Wissowa," *Jahresbericht über die Fortschritte der Klassischen Altertumswissenschaft.* CCXLV (1934), 4. Abt., pp. 120–145.

2. Main Publications

1885 *Religion und Kultus der Römer.* (Handbuch der Klassischen Altertumswissenschaft. Bd. 5, Abt. 4). München, 1912².
1893 *Pauly's Real-Encyclopädie der classischen Altertumswissenschaft.* Herausg. von G. Wissowa.
1904 *Gesammelte Abhandlungen zur römischen Religions- und Stadtgeschichte.* Ergänzungsband zu des Verfassers *Religion und Kultus der Römer.* München.

GEORG WOBBERMIN

1. Bibliography

In: *Luther, Kant, Schleiermacher in ihrer Bedeutung für den Protestantismus.* Georg Wobbermin zum 70. Geburtstag (27. 10. 1939), dargebracht von Kollegen, Schülern und Freunden. Berlin, 1939, pp. 578–588.

2. Main Publications

1896 *Religionsgeschichtliche Studien zur Frage der Beeinflussung des Urchristentums durch das antike Mysterienwesen.* Berlin, Ebering.
1902 *Der christliche Gottesglaube in seinem Verhältnis zur heutigen Philosophie und Naturwissenschaft.* Berlin, Alexander Duncker. Leipzig, Hinrichs, 1911³.
    English translation from the third German edition by Daniel Sommer Robinson: *Christian Belief in God.* New Haven, Yale University Press, 1918.
    Japanish edition, Fukuoka, 1920.
1910 "Der gegenwärtige Stand der Religionspsychologie," *Zeitschrift für angewandte Psychologie,* III (1910), pp. 488–540.
1910 *Aufgabe und Bedeutung der Religionspsychologie.* Sonderausgabe aus dem Protokoll des 5. Weltkongresses für Freies Christentum und Religiösen Fortschrift. Berlin–Schöneberg, Protestantischer Schriftenvertrieb.
1911 *Geschichte und Historie in der Religionswissenschaft.* Über die Notwendigkeit, in der Religionswissenschaft zwischen Geschichte und Historie strenger zu unterscheiden, als gewöhnlich geschieht. Adolf Harnack zu seinem sechzigsten Geburtstage. Tübingen, Mohr.

1911 *Monismus und Monotheismus.* Vorträge und Abhandlungen zum Kampf um die monistische Weltanschauung. Tübingen, Mohr.
1913 *Zum Streit um die Religionspsychologie.* Berlin–Schöneberg, Protestantischer Schriftenvertrieb.
1915 "Die Frage nach den Anfängen der Religion in religionspsychologischer Bedeutung," *Zeitschrift für Angewandte Psychologie,* IX (1915), pp. 333–390.
1913–1921 *Systematische Theologie nach religionspsychologischer Methode.* Leipzig, Hinrichs.
    1. *Die religionspsychologische Methode in Religionswissenschaft und Theologie.* 1925[2] with title: *Einleitung in die systematische Theologie. Prinzipien und Methoden-Lehre in Hinblick auf ihre Geschichte seit Schleiermacher.*
    2. *Das Wesen der Religion.* 1925[2].
    English translation by Theophil Menzel and Prof. Dr. Daniel S. Robinson: *The Nature of Religion.* With an Introduction by Prof. Douglas Clyde Macintosh, Yale University. New York, Thomas Y. Crowell Company, 1933.
    Japanese edition: Fukuoka, 1937.
    3. *Wesen und Wahrheit des Christentums.* 1925[2]; 1926[3].
1921 *Religion. Die Methoden der religionspsychologischen Arbeit.* Berlin, Urban Schwarzenberg. (Später in dem Sammelwerk von Emil Abderhalden: *Handbuch der biologischen Arbeitsmethoden,* Abt. VI, Teil C. Berlin, Urban & Schwarzenberg, 1928.)

WILHELM WUNDT

1. Bibliography

Wilhelm Wundts Werke. Ein Verzeichnis seiner sämtlichen Schriften. Ed. by E. Wundt. München, 1927.

2. Biography and Appreciation

Hess, S., *Das religiöse Bedürfnis. Eine kritische Studie anhand der Religionstheorie W. Wundts.* St. Gallen, 1935.
Hoffmann, Arthur, *Wilhelm Wundt. Eine Würdigung* (by several writers). Herausg. von A. Hoffmann. (Beiträge zur Philosophie des deutschen Idealismus, Bd. 2. Schlussheft). Erfurt, 1922.
Petersen, P., *Wilhelm Wundt und seine Zeit.* (Frommanns Klassiker der Philosophie, Bd. 13). Stuttgart, 1925.
Sganzini, C., *Die Fortschritte der Völkerpsychologie von Lazarus bis Wundt.* (Neue Berner Abhandlungen zur Philosophie und ihrer Geschichte, Heft 2). Bern, 1913.
Trebitsch, Rudolf, *Wilhelm Wundt's "Elemente der Völkerpsychologie" und die moderne Ethnologie.* Leipzig, 1914.

3. Main Publications

1873–1874 *Grundzüge der physiologischen Psychologie.* Leipzig, 1880[2] (revised edition, 2 vols.); 1902[4] (completely revised with index made by W. Wirth, 3 vols.); 1908–11[6] (revised edition, 3 vols.).
English translation from the fifth German edition, 1902, by E. B. Titchener: *Principles of Psychological Psychology.* London, Swan Sonnenschein, 1904.

1880–1883 *Logik, eine Untersuchung der Principien der Erkenntniss und der Methoden wissenschaftlicher Forschung,* 2 vols. Stuttgart. 1893–95[2]; 1906–1908[3]; 1919–21[4].

1885 *Essays.* Leipzig. 1906[2] *(mit Zusätzen und Anmerkungen).*

1896 *Grundriss der Psychologie.* Leipzig. 1905[7]; 1911[10].
English translation with the cooperation of the author by C. H. Judd: *Outlines of Psychology.* Leipzig, Engelmann, 1897. 1902[2] (revised English edition from the fourth revised German edition).

1900–1920 *Völkerpsychologie. Eine Untersuchung der Entwicklungsgesetze von Sprache, Mythus und Sitte,* 10 vols., Leipzig. See especially Vols. IV–VI: *Mythus und Religion.*

1910–1921 *Kleine Schriften,* 3 vols. Leipzig.

1911 *Probleme der Völkerpsychologie.* Leipzig.

1912 *Elemente der Völkerpsychologie. Grundlinien einer psychologischen Entwicklungsgeschichte der Menschheit.* Leipzig.
English authorized translation by E. L. Schaub: *Elements of Folk Psychology.* London, Allen & Unwin; New York, Macmillan, 1916.

1913 *Reden und Aufsätze.* Leipzig.

1914 *Sinnliche und Übersinnliche Welt.* Leipzig.

1920 *Erlebtes und Erkanntes.* Stuttgart.

Z

HEINRICH R. ZIMMER

Main Publications

1930 *Ewiges Indien*. Leitmotive indischen Daseins. Potsdam–Zürich.
1935 *Indische Sphären*. Der indische Mythos – Der Brauch der Fische – **Yoga** und Maya – Buddha. München.
1935 *Integrating the Evil. A celtic Myth and a christian Legend*. (Guild Lecture, No. 39). London, Guild of Pastoral Psychology.
1936 *Maya. Der Indische Mythos*. Stuttgart–Berlin.
1947 *Myths and Symbols in Indian Art and Civilisation*. Ed. by Joseph Campbell, New York, Pantheon Books.
1948 *The King and the Corpse. Tales of the Soul's Conquest of Evil*. New York.
1948 *Hindu Medicine*. Ed. by L. Edelstein. Baltimore, Johns Hopkins Press.
1951 *Philosophy and India*. Ed. by Joseph Campbell. London, Routledge & Kegan Paul; New York, 1951. New York Meridan Books, 1956.
1955 *The Art of Indian Asia; its Mythology and Transformations*, 2 vols. (Bollingen Series, No. 39.) New York, Pantheon Books.

Contents
Volume One: Introduction and Anthology

PART 3. *Religion as a Special Subject of Research*

PART 5. *Perspectives of a Phenomenological Study of Religion*

Contents
Volume Two: Bibliography

*The names indicated in the Bibliography with an asterisk are those of scholars represented in the Anthology in Volume One.

*The names indicated in the Bibliography with an asterisk are those of
scholars represented in the Anthology in Volume One.

*The names indicated in the Bibliography with an asterisk are those of
scholars represented in the Anthology in Volume One.

*The names indicated in the Bibliography with an asterisk are those of scholars represented in the Anthology in Volume One.

*The names indicated in the Bibliography with an asterisk are those of scholars represented in the Anthology in Volume One.

*The names indicated in the Bibliography with an asterisk are those of scholars represented in the Anthology in Volume One.